# My Boyfriend is a VAMPiRE

## Book 7 & 8

**Yu-Rang Han**

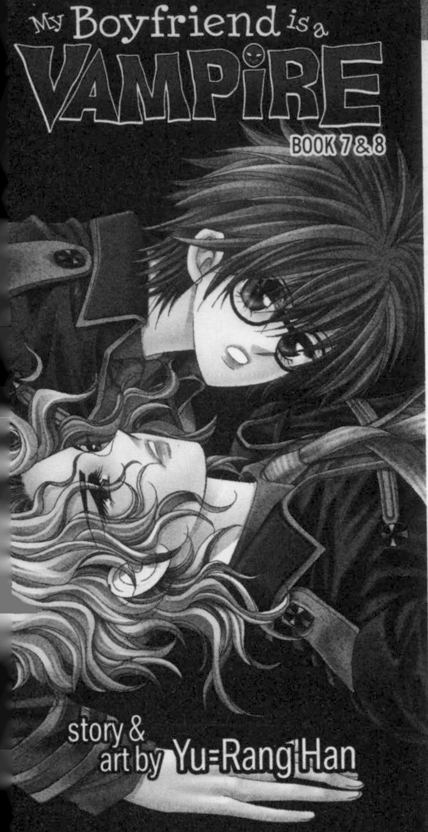
My Boyfriend is a
VAMPIRE
BOOK 7 & 8
story &
art by Yu-Rang Han

## STAFF CREDITS

translation ChanHee Grace Sung
adaptation Bambi Eloriaga-Amago
lettering Roland Amago
layout Mheeya Wok
cover design Nicky Lim
copy editor Shanti Whitesides
editor Adam Arnold

publisher Jason DeAngelis
Seven Seas Entertainment

MY BOYFRIEND IS A VAMPIRE BOOK 7 & 8

First published in Korea in 2010 by Samyang Publishing Co., Ltd.
English translation rights arranged by Samyang Publishing Co., Ltd. through TOPAZ Agency Inc.



ISBN: 978-1-937867-27-0

Printed in Canada

First Printing: April 2013

10 9 8 7 6 5 4 3 2 1



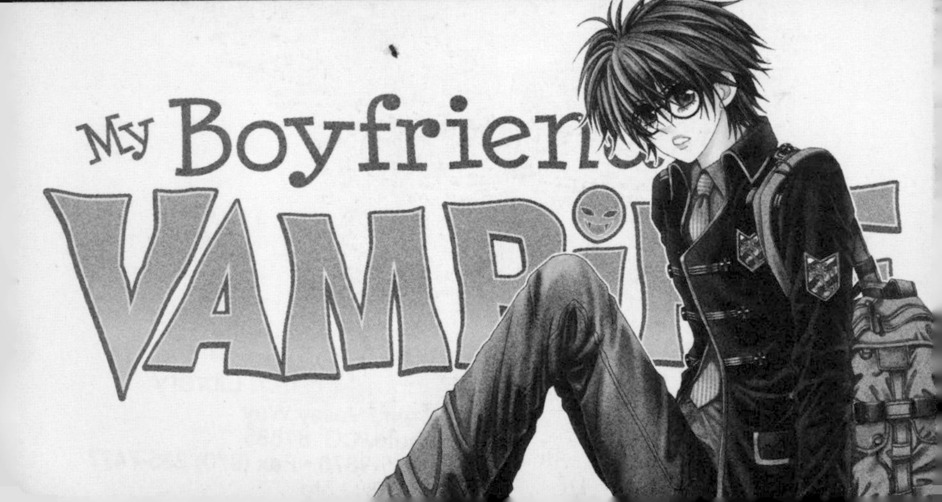
My Boyfrien
VAMP

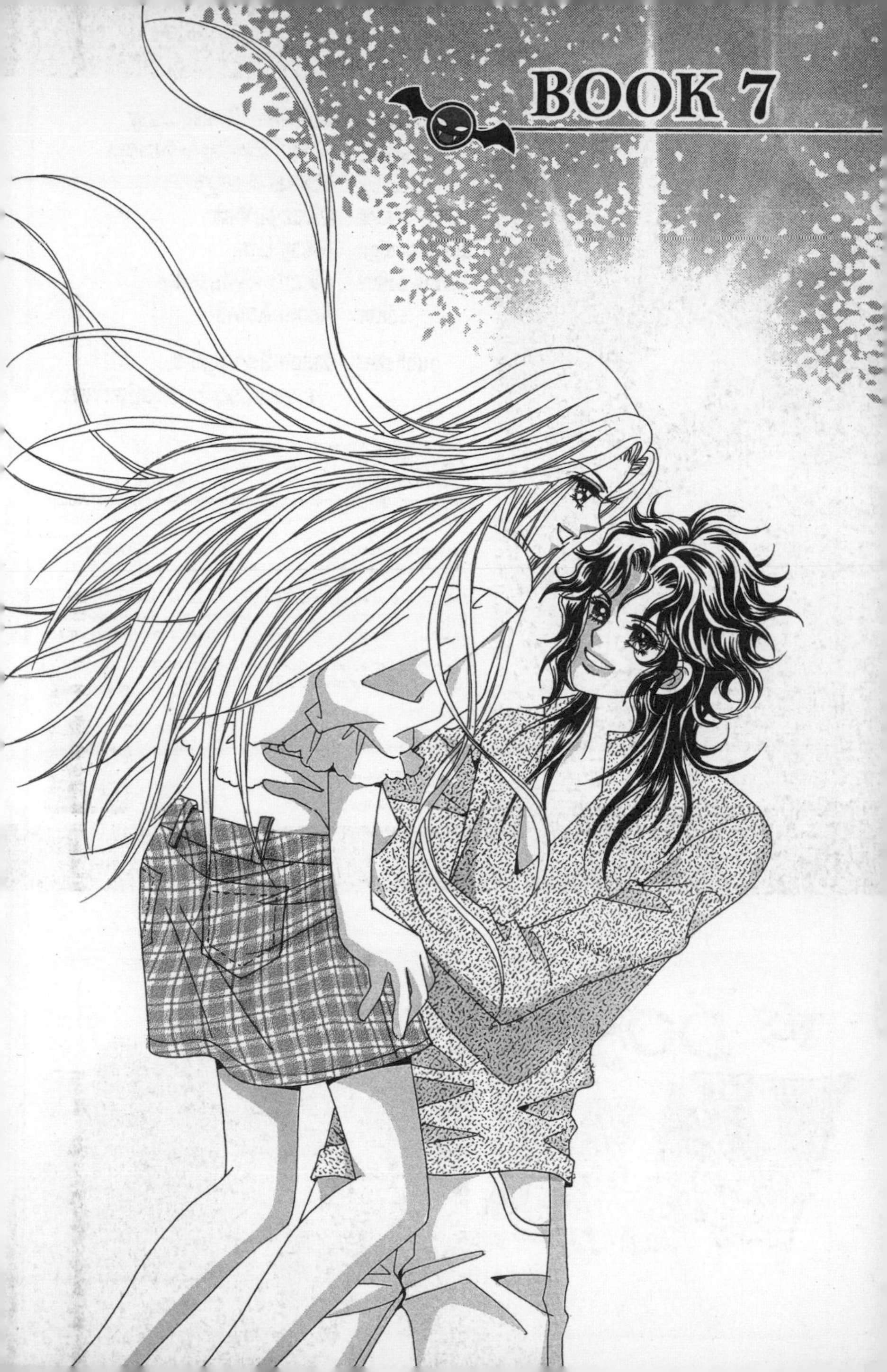
BOOK 7

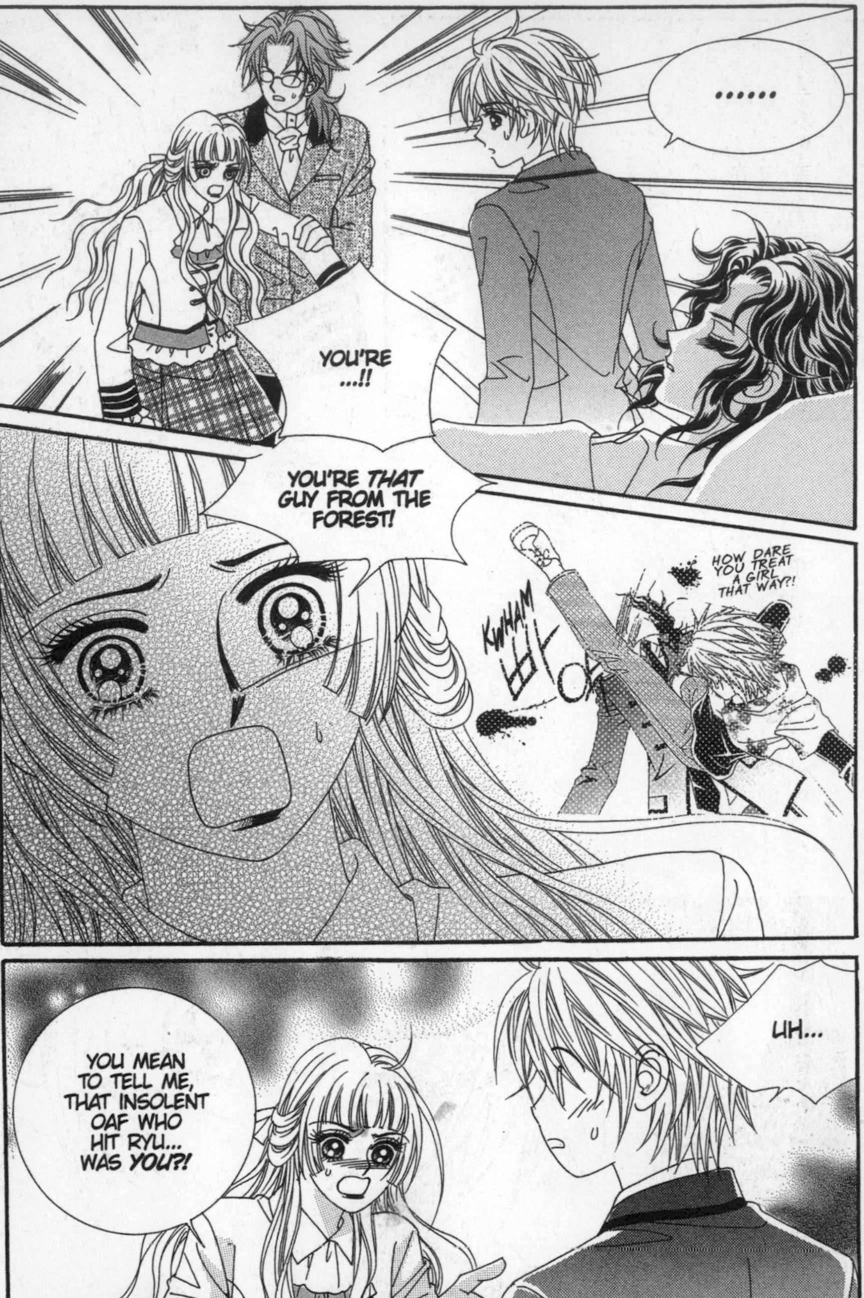
......
YOU'RE ...!!
YOU'RE *THAT* GUY FROM THE FOREST!
HOW DARE YOU TREAT A GIRL THAT WAY?!
KWHAM
YOU MEAN TO TELL ME, THAT INSOLENT OAF WHO HIT RYU... WAS ***YOU***?!
UH...

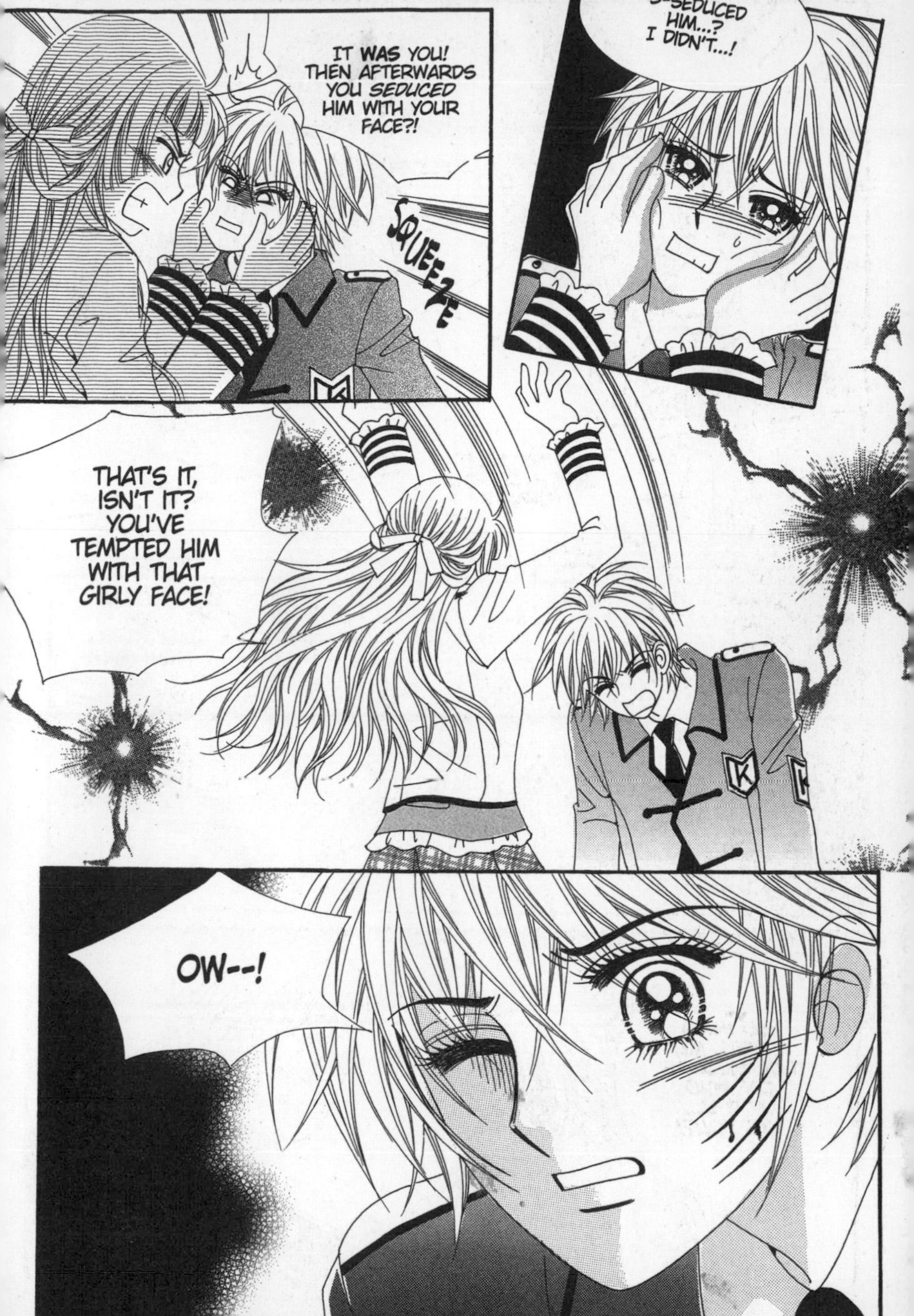
IT WAS YOU! THEN AFTERWARDS YOU SEDUCED HIM WITH YOUR FACE?!
SQUEEZE
S-SEDUCED HIM...? I DIDN'T...!
THAT'S IT, ISN'T IT? YOU'VE TEMPTED HIM WITH THAT GIRLY FACE!
OW--!

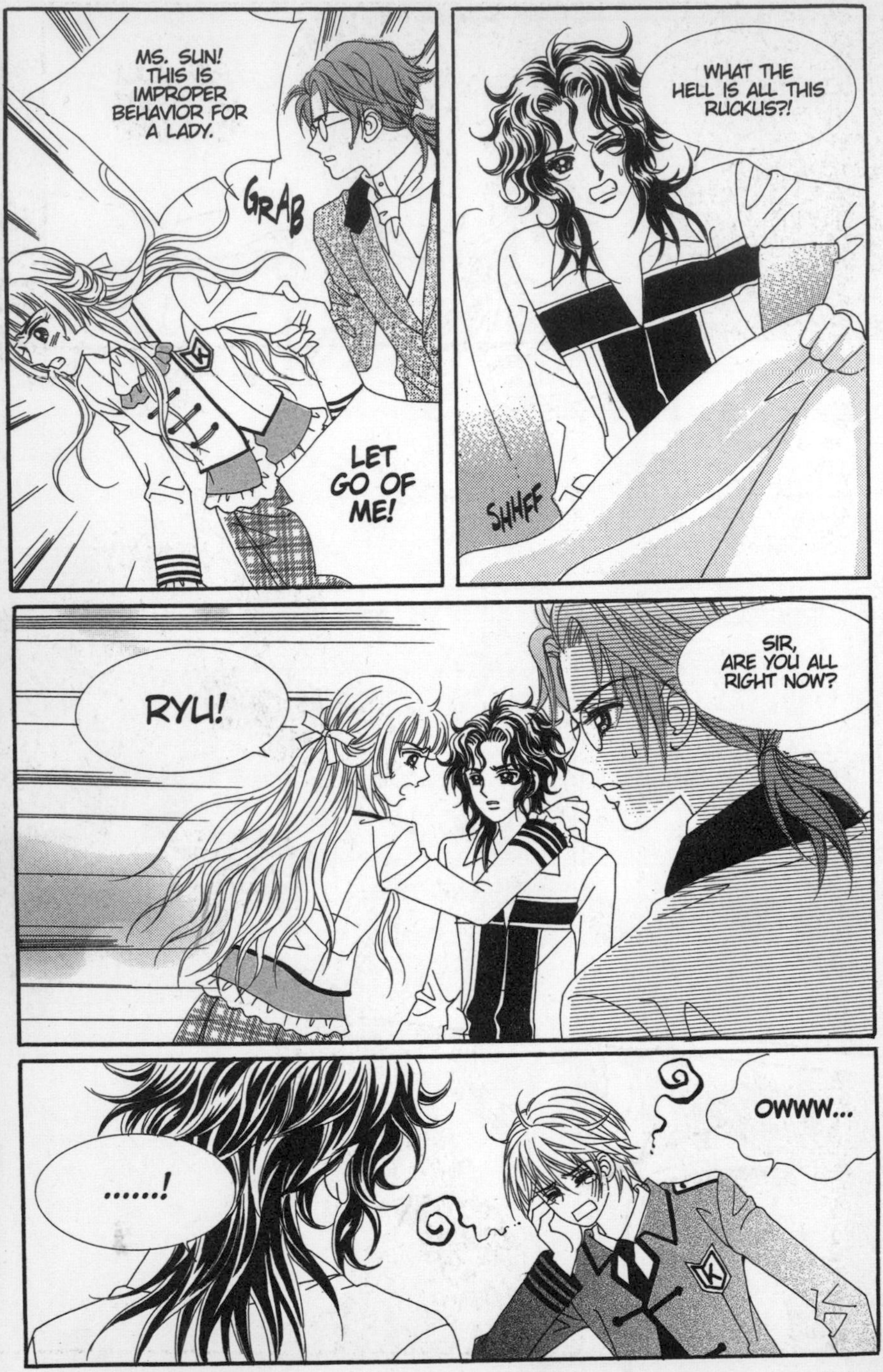
MS. SUN! THIS IS IMPROPER BEHAVIOR FOR A LADY.
GRAB
LET GO OF ME!
WHAT THE HELL IS ALL THIS RUCKUS?!
SHHFF
RYU!
SIR, ARE YOU ALL RIGHT NOW?
......!
OWWW...

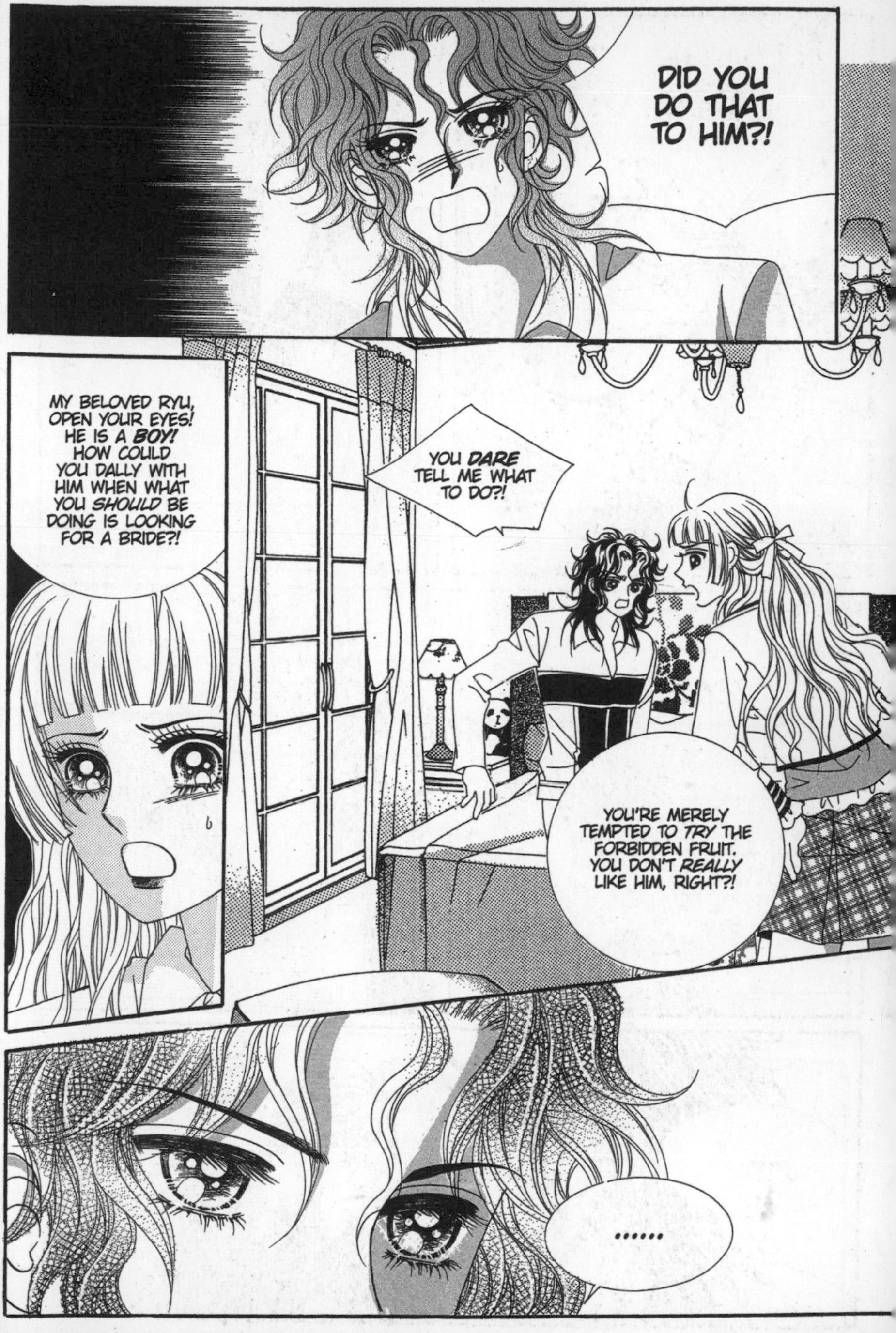
DID YOU DO THAT TO HIM?!
MY BELOVED RYU, OPEN YOUR EYES! HE IS A *BOY!* HOW COULD YOU DALLY WITH HIM WHEN WHAT YOU *SHOULD* BE DOING IS LOOKING FOR A BRIDE?!
YOU *DARE* TELL ME WHAT TO DO?!
YOU'RE MERELY TEMPTED TO *TRY* THE FORBIDDEN FRUIT. YOU DON'T *REALLY* LIKE HIM, RIGHT?!
......

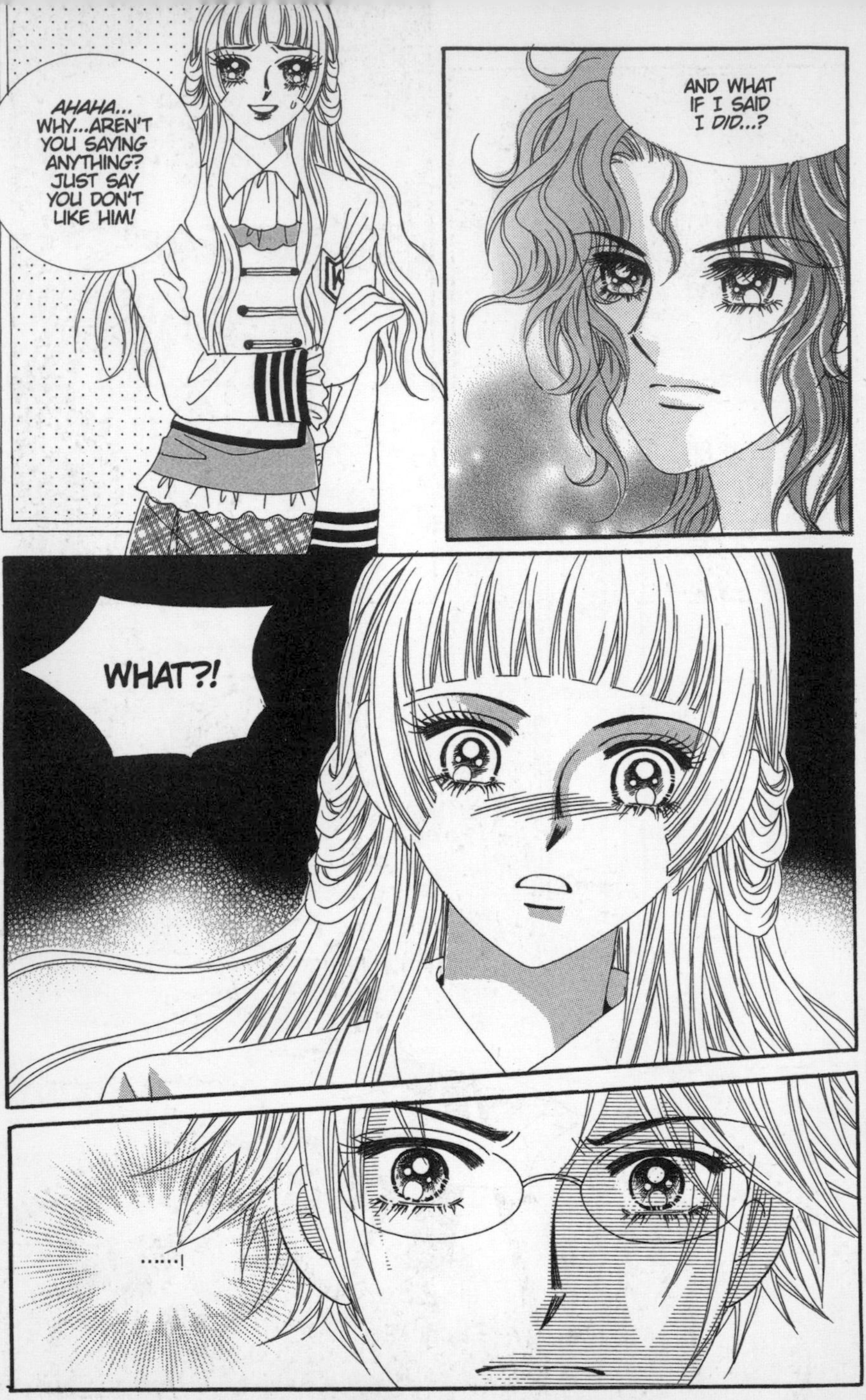
AHAHA... WHY...AREN'T YOU SAYING ANYTHING? JUST SAY YOU DON'T LIKE HIM!
AND WHAT IF I SAID I DID...?
WHAT?!
......!

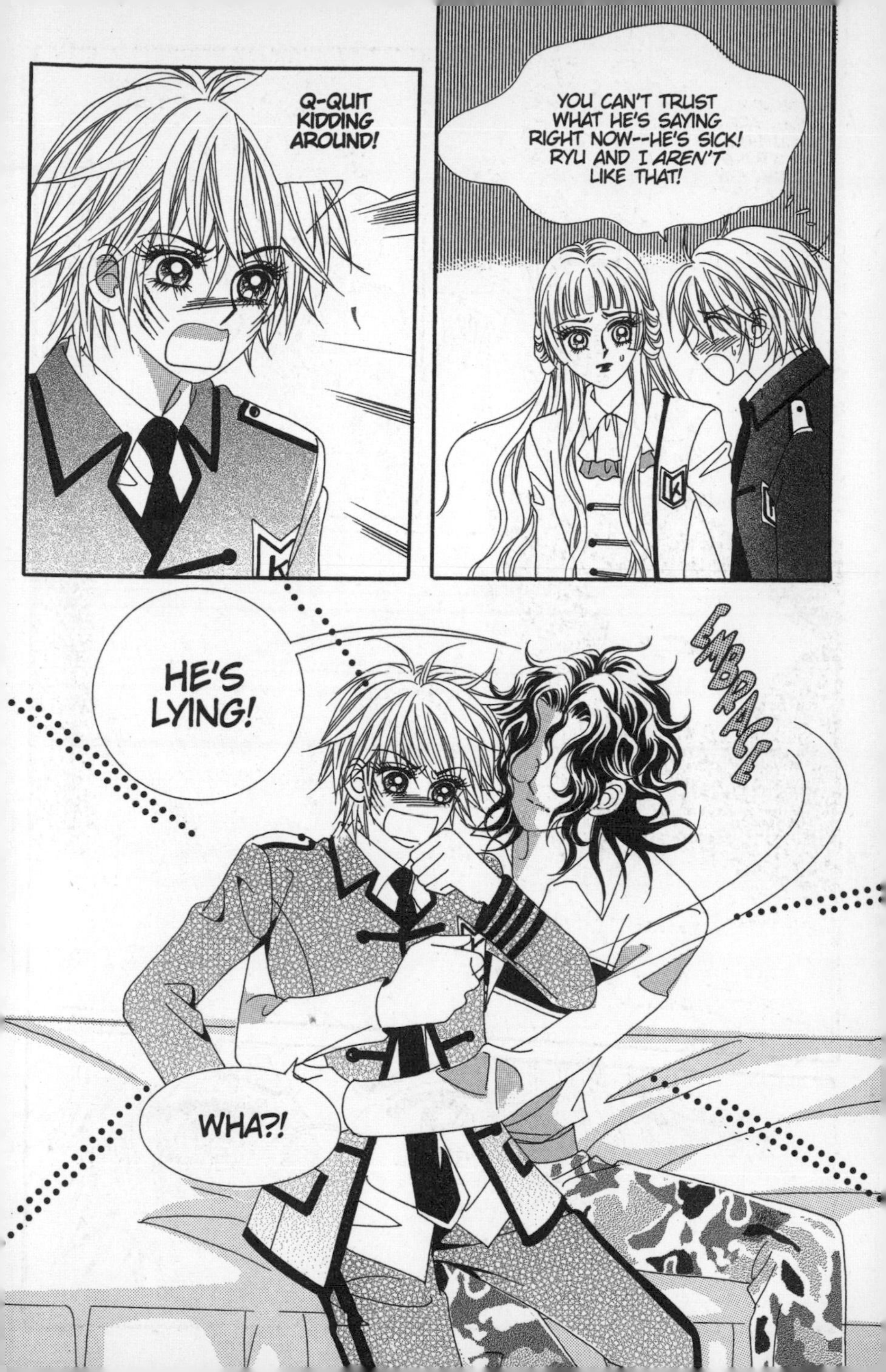
Q-QUIT KIDDING AROUND!
YOU CAN'T TRUST WHAT HE'S SAYING RIGHT NOW--HE'S SICK! RYU AND I *AREN'T* LIKE THAT!
HE'S LYING!
EMBRACE
WHA?!

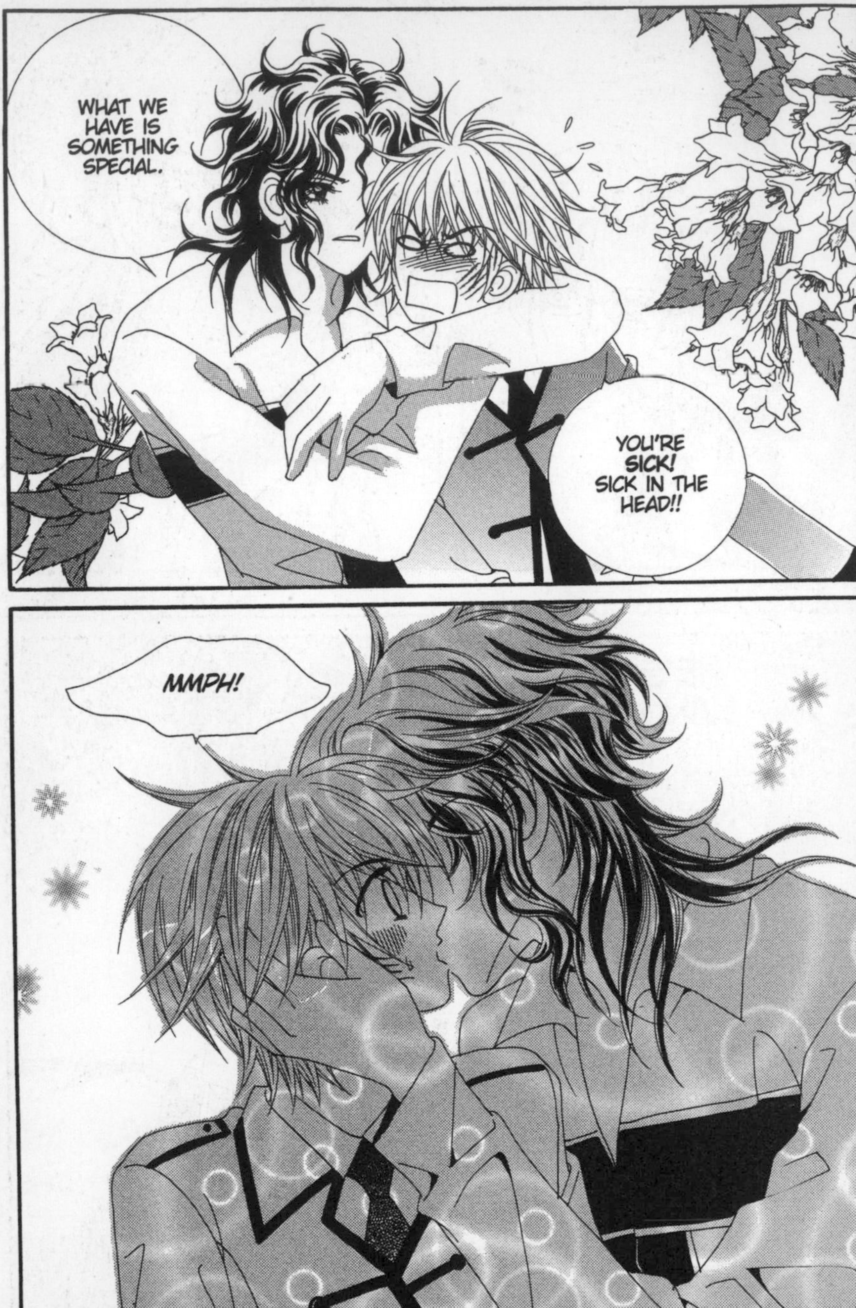
WHAT WE HAVE IS SOMETHING SPECIAL.
YOU'RE SICK! SICK IN THE HEAD!!
MMPH!

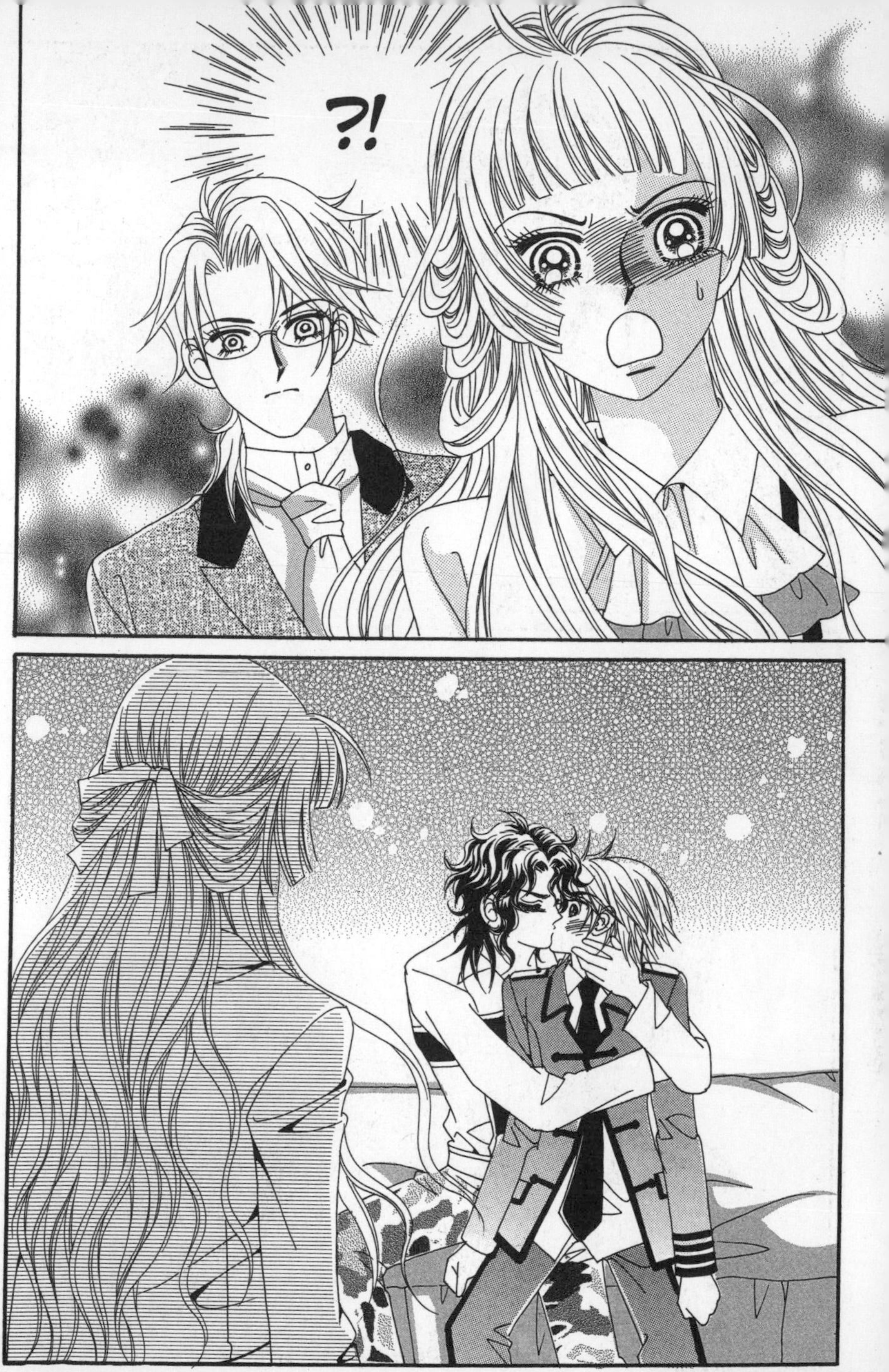
?!

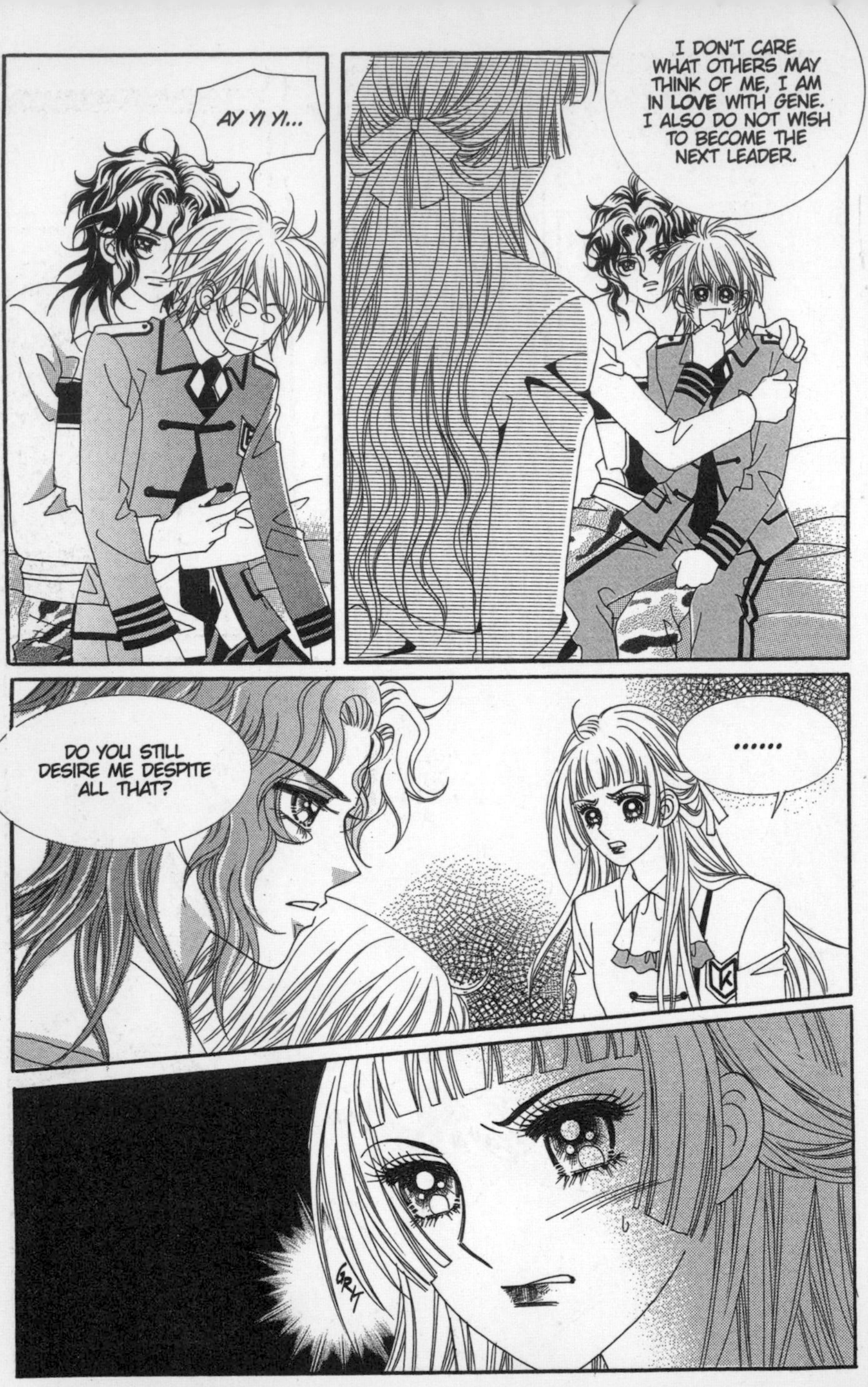
AY YI YI...
I DON'T CARE WHAT OTHERS MAY THINK OF ME, I AM IN LOVE WITH GENE. I ALSO DO NOT WISH TO BECOME THE NEXT LEADER.
DO YOU STILL DESIRE ME DESPITE ALL THAT?
......
GR-K

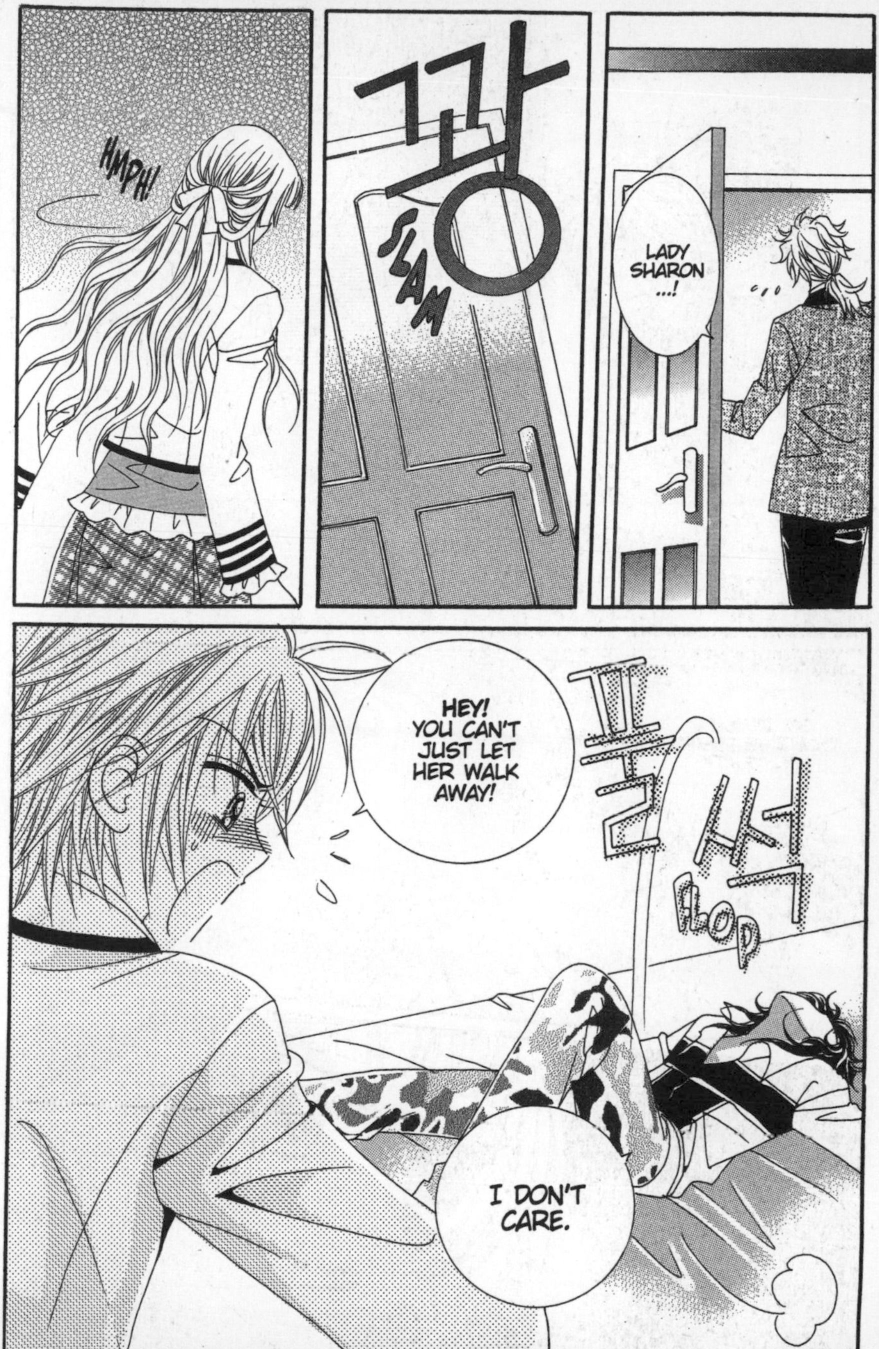
HMPH!
쾅
SLAM
LADY SHARON ...!
HEY! YOU CAN'T JUST LET HER WALK AWAY!
풀썩
FLOP
I DON'T CARE.

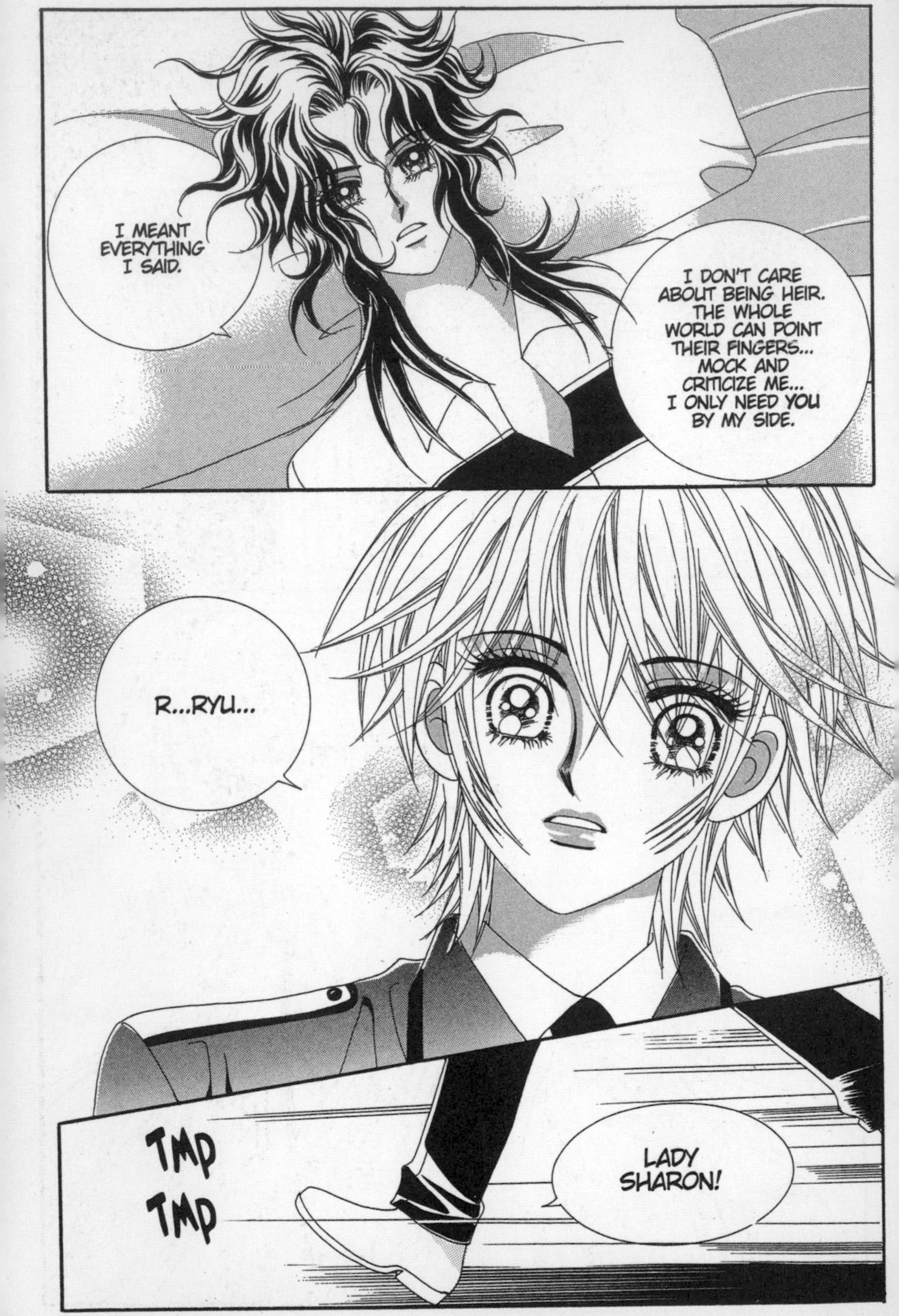
I MEANT EVERYTHING I SAID.
I DON'T CARE ABOUT BEING HEIR. THE WHOLE WORLD CAN POINT THEIR FINGERS... MOCK AND CRITICIZE ME... I ONLY NEED YOU BY MY SIDE.
R...RYU...
TMP TMP
LADY SHARON!

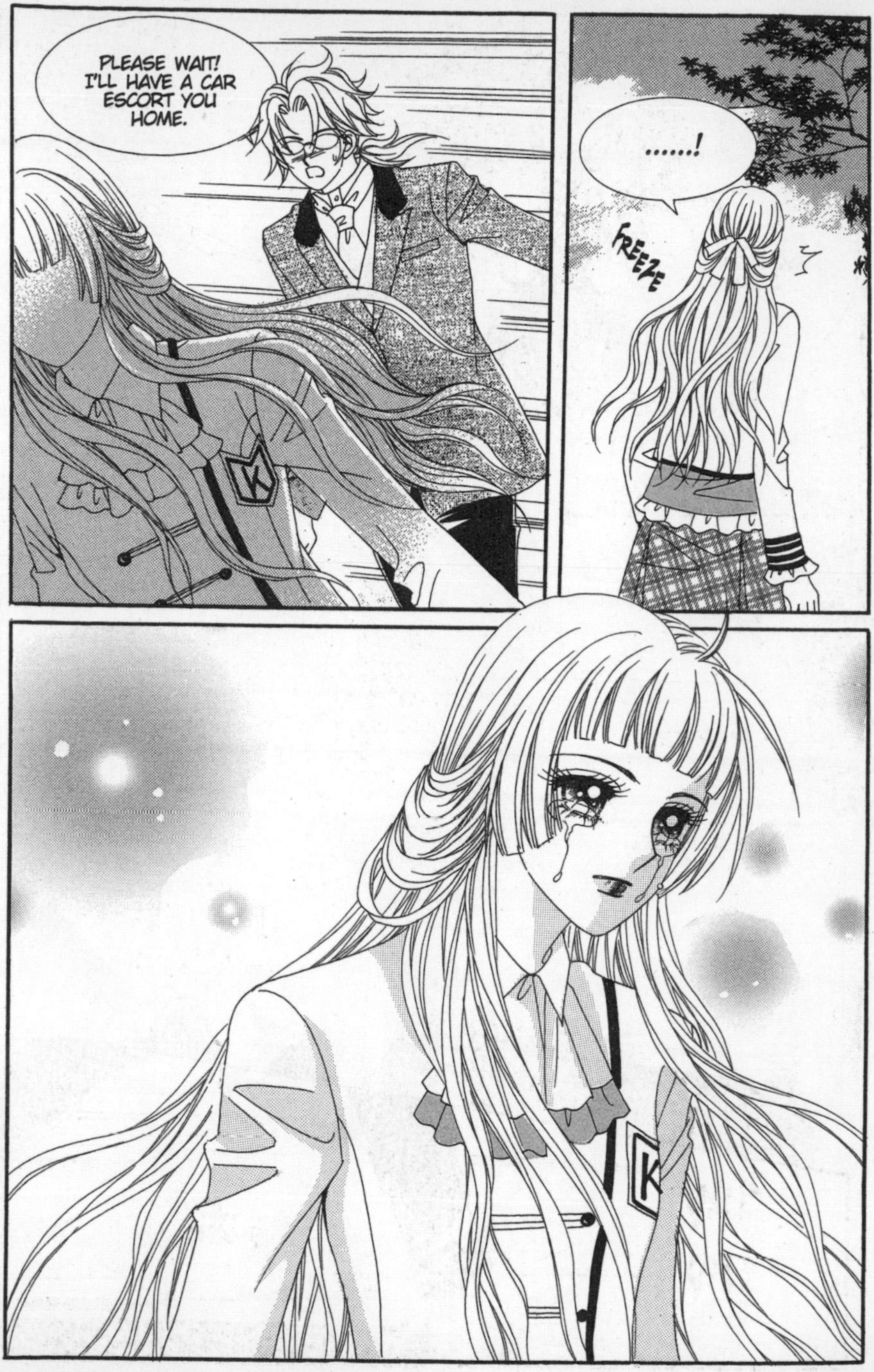
PLEASE WAIT! I'LL HAVE A CAR ESCORT YOU HOME.
......!
FREEZE

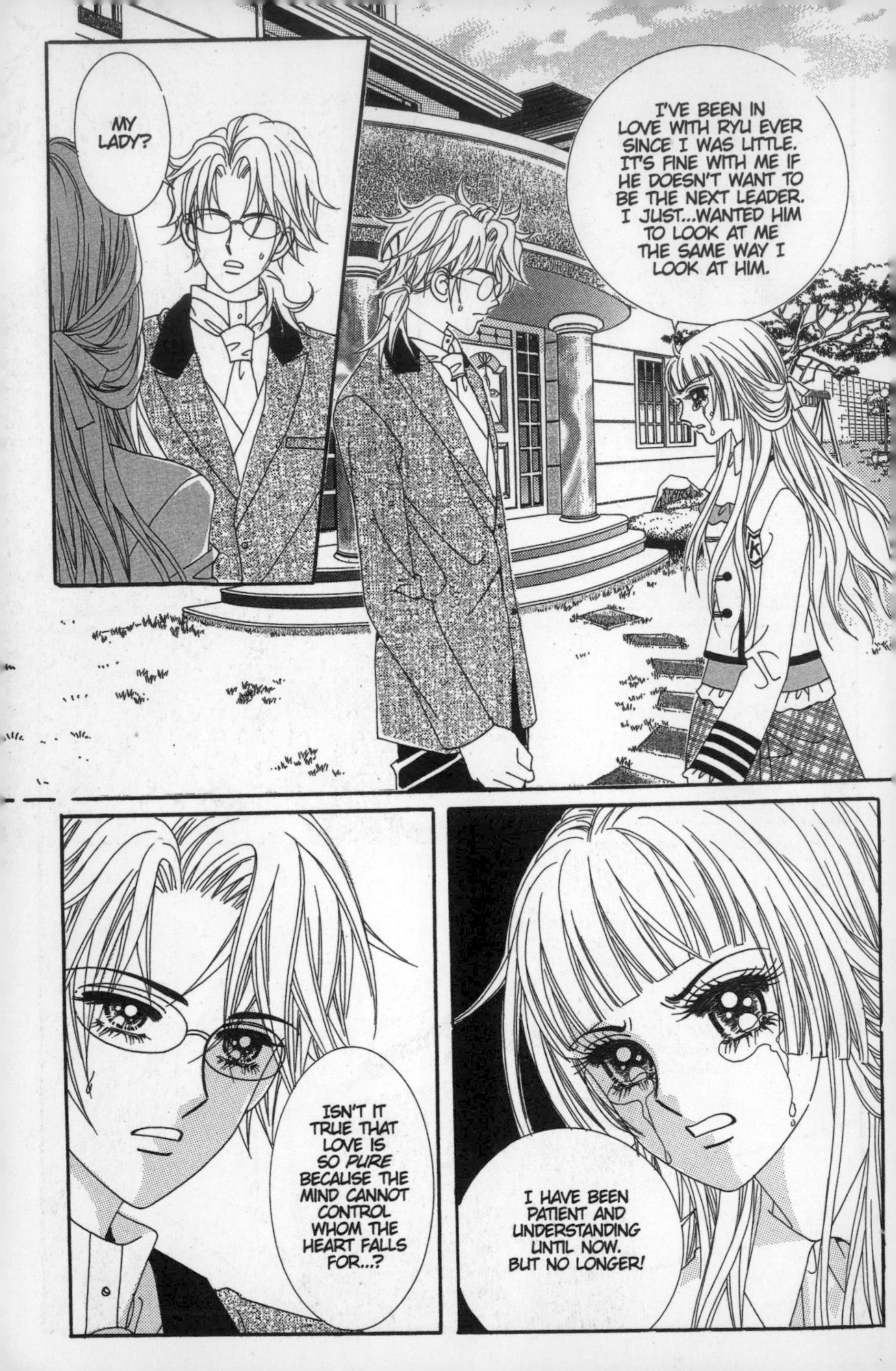
MY LADY?
I'VE BEEN IN LOVE WITH RYU EVER SINCE I WAS LITTLE. IT'S FINE WITH ME IF HE DOESN'T WANT TO BE THE NEXT LEADER. I JUST...WANTED HIM TO LOOK AT ME THE SAME WAY I LOOK AT HIM.
ISN'T IT TRUE THAT LOVE IS SO *PURE* BECAUSE THE MIND CANNOT CONTROL WHOM THE HEART FALLS FOR...?
I HAVE BEEN PATIENT AND UNDERSTANDING UNTIL NOW. BUT NO LONGER!

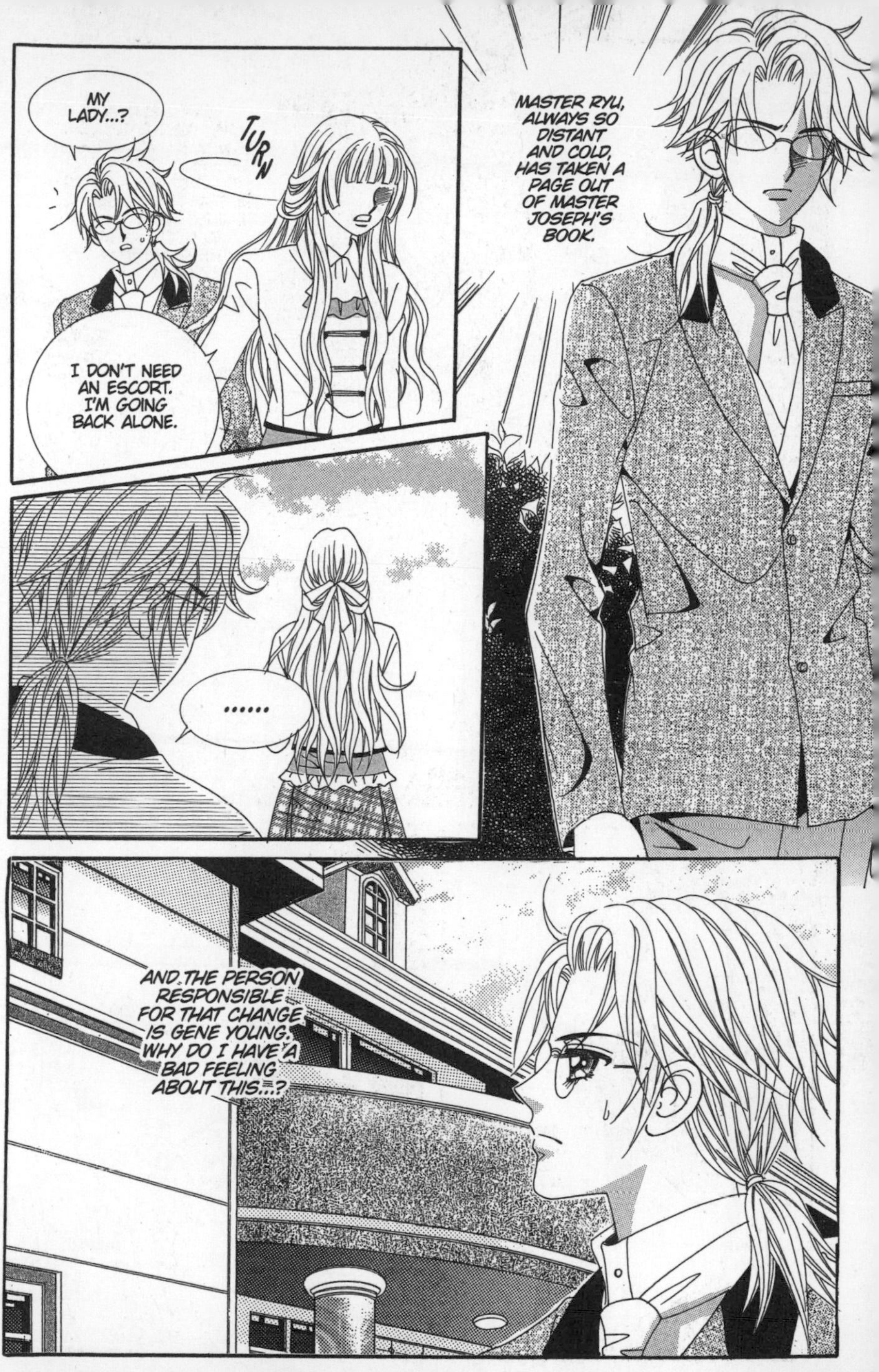
MY LADY...?
TURN
I DON'T NEED AN ESCORT. I'M GOING BACK ALONE.
......
MASTER RYU, ALWAYS SO DISTANT AND COLD, HAS TAKEN A PAGE OUT OF MASTER JOSEPH'S BOOK.
AND THE PERSON RESPONSIBLE FOR THAT CHANGE IS GENE YOUNG. WHY DO I HAVE A BAD FEELING ABOUT THIS...?

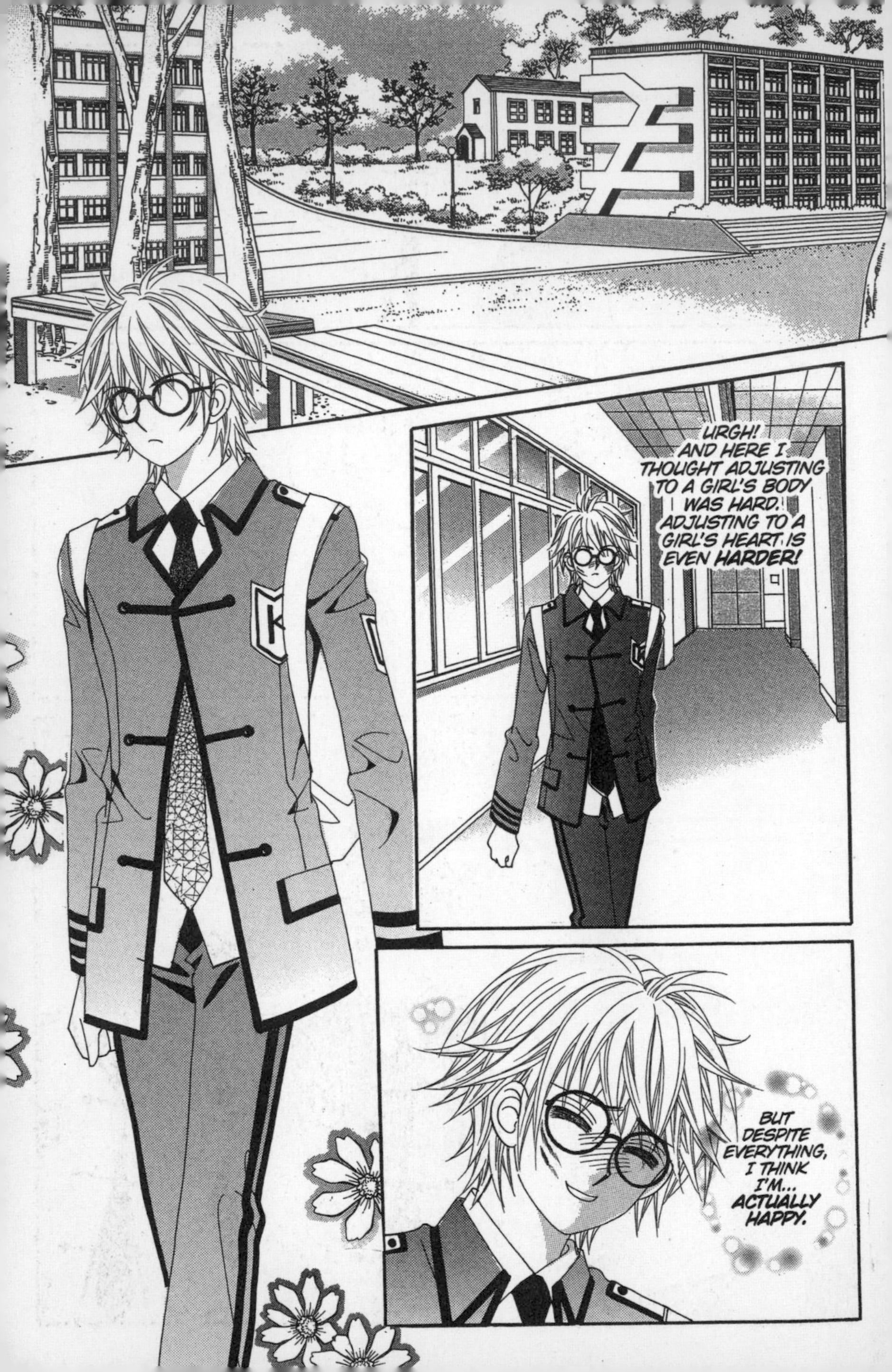
URGH! AND HERE I THOUGHT ADJUSTING TO A GIRL'S BODY WAS HARD. ADJUSTING TO A GIRL'S HEART IS EVEN **HARDER!**
BUT DESPITE EVERYTHING, I THINK I'M... **ACTUALLY HAPPY.**

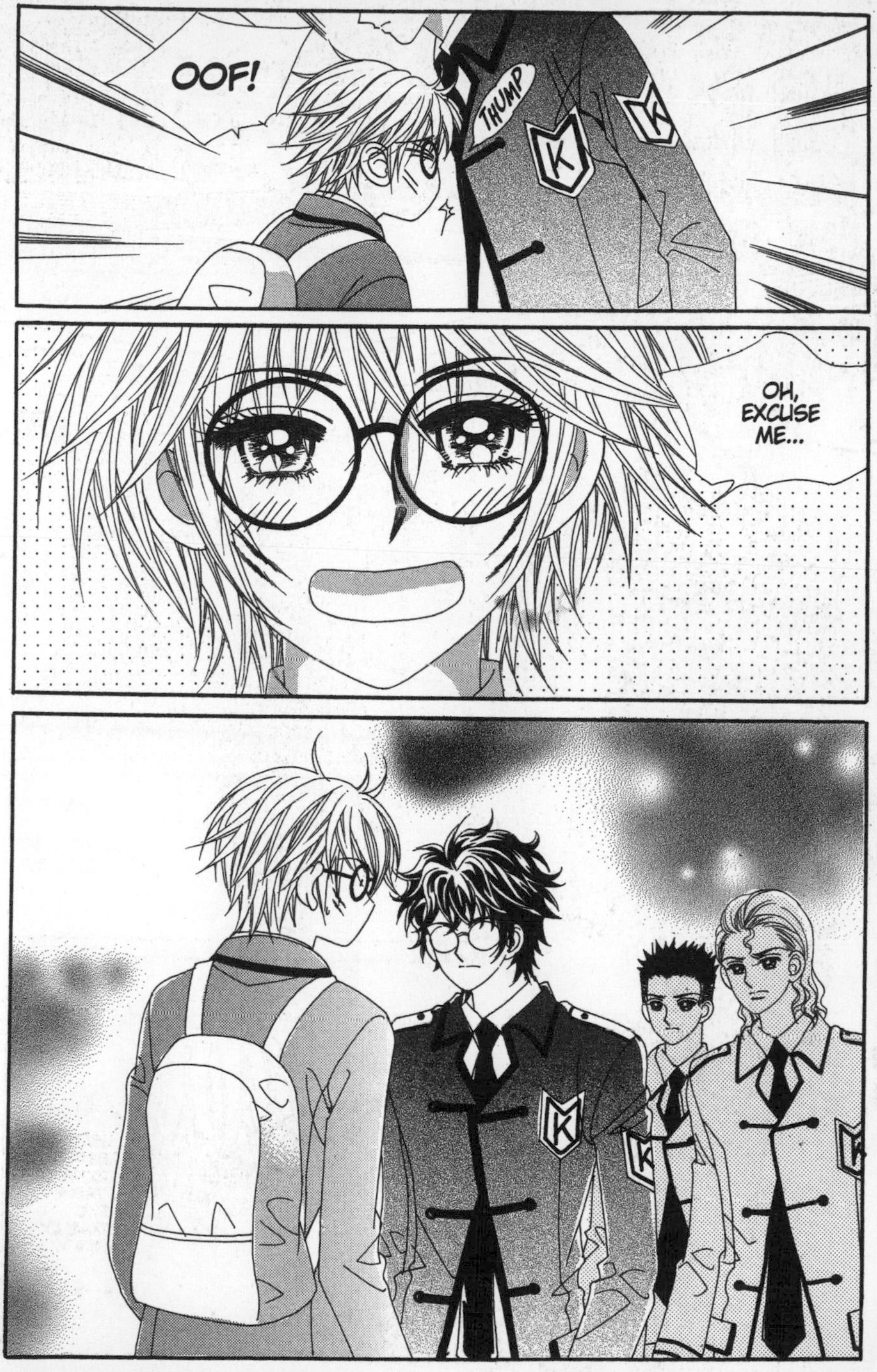
OOF!
THUMP
OH, EXCUSE ME...

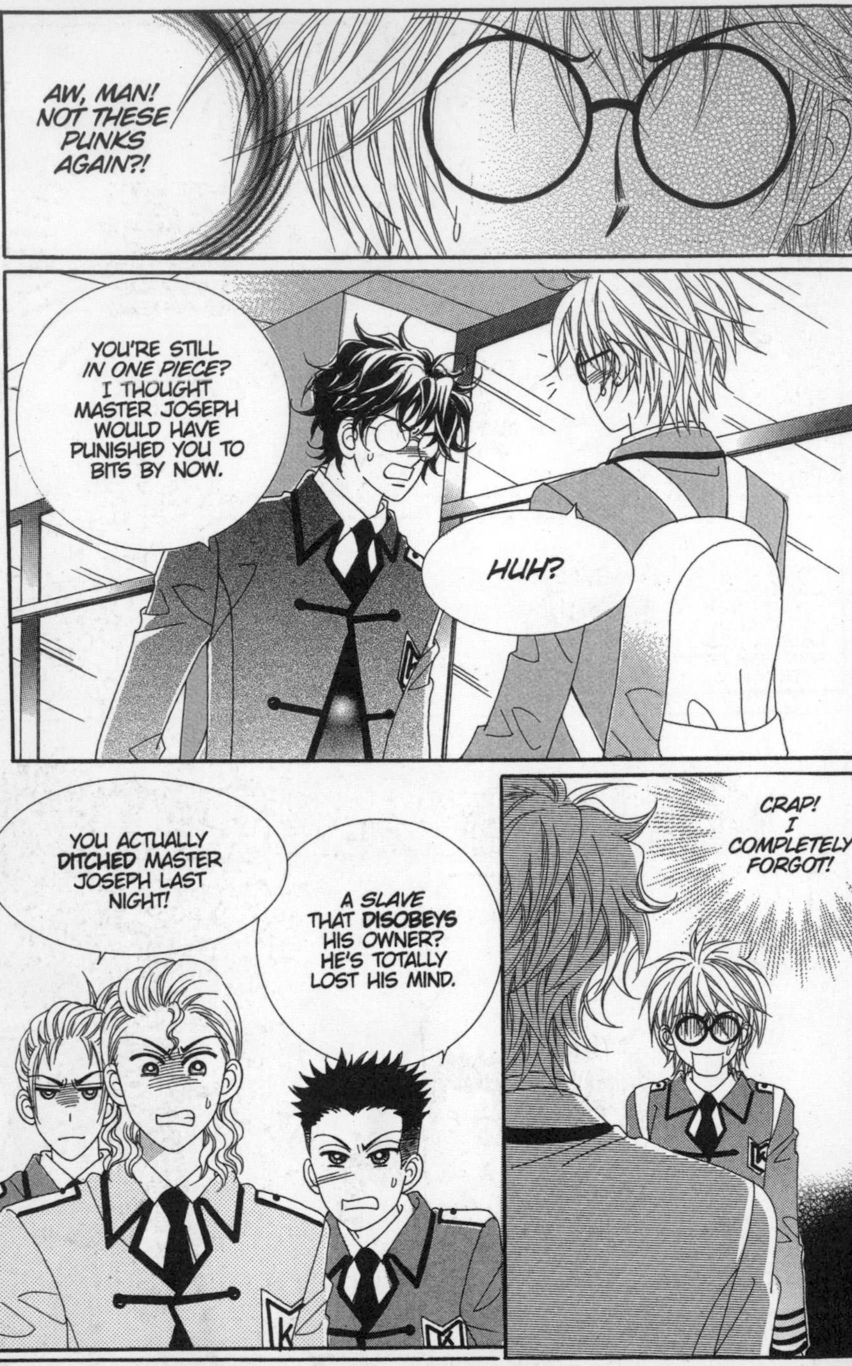
AW, MAN! NOT THESE PUNKS AGAIN?!
YOU'RE STILL IN ONE PIECE? I THOUGHT MASTER JOSEPH WOULD HAVE PUNISHED YOU TO BITS BY NOW.
HUH?
YOU ACTUALLY DITCHED MASTER JOSEPH LAST NIGHT!
A SLAVE THAT DISOBEYS HIS OWNER? HE'S TOTALLY LOST HIS MIND.
CRAP! I COMPLETELY FORGOT!

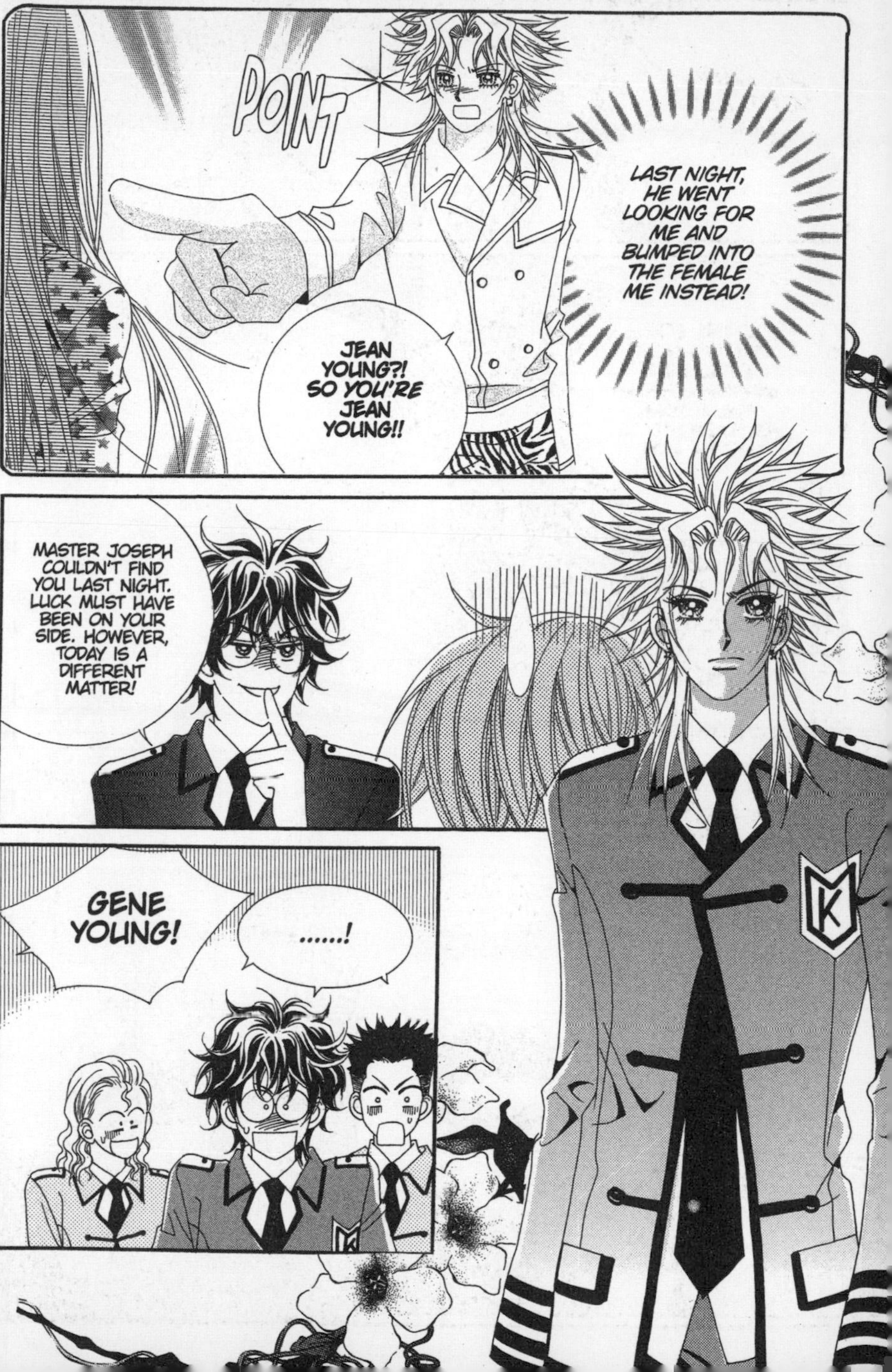
POINT
LAST NIGHT, HE WENT LOOKING FOR ME AND BUMPED INTO THE FEMALE ME INSTEAD!
JEAN YOUNG?! SO YOU'RE JEAN YOUNG!!
MASTER JOSEPH COULDN'T FIND YOU LAST NIGHT. LUCK MUST HAVE BEEN ON YOUR SIDE. HOWEVER, TODAY IS A DIFFERENT MATTER!
GENE YOUNG!
......!

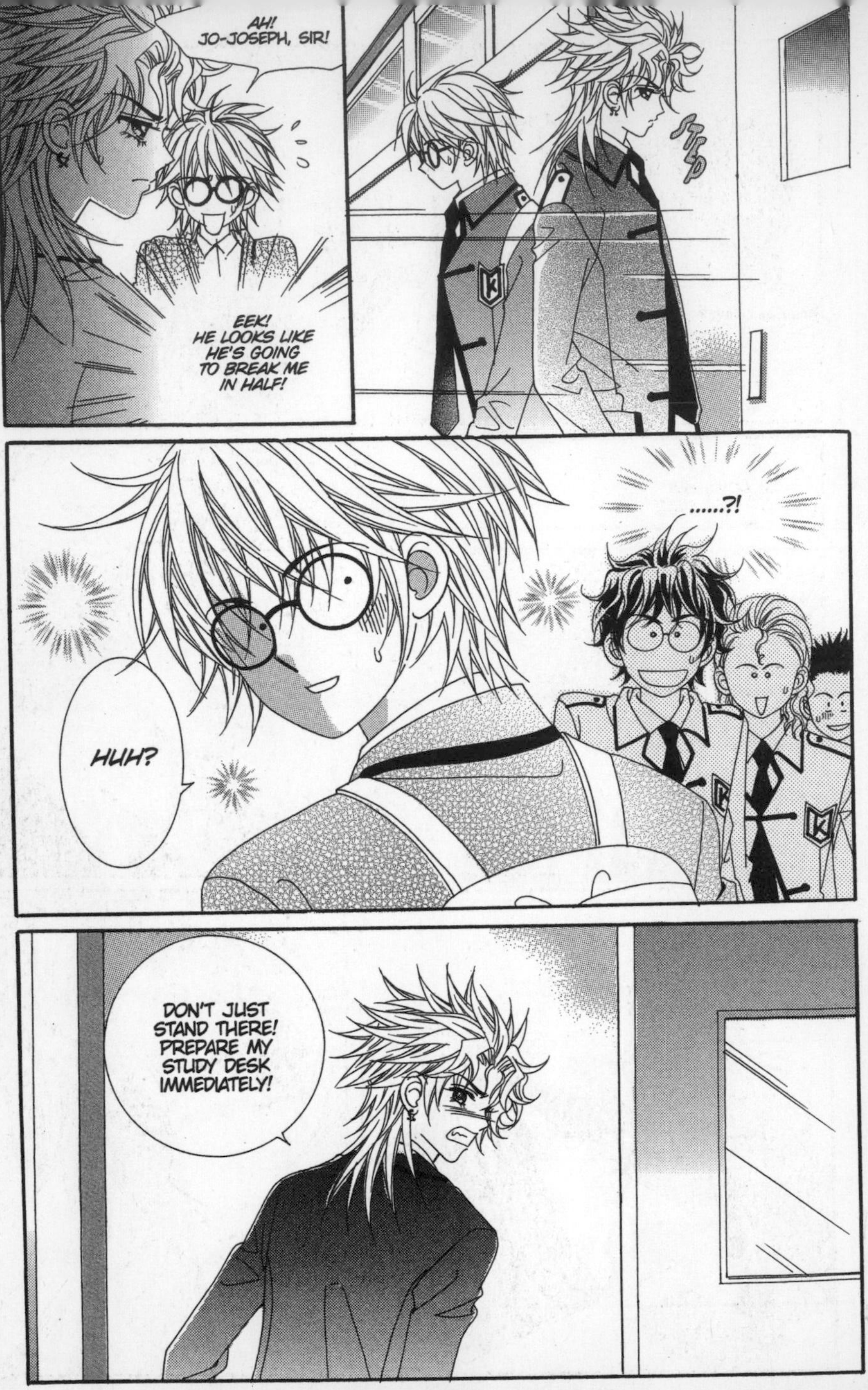
AH! JO-JOSEPH, SIR!
EEK! HE LOOKS LIKE HE'S GOING TO BREAK ME IN HALF!
......?!
HUH?
DON'T JUST STAND THERE! PREPARE MY STUDY DESK IMMEDIATELY!

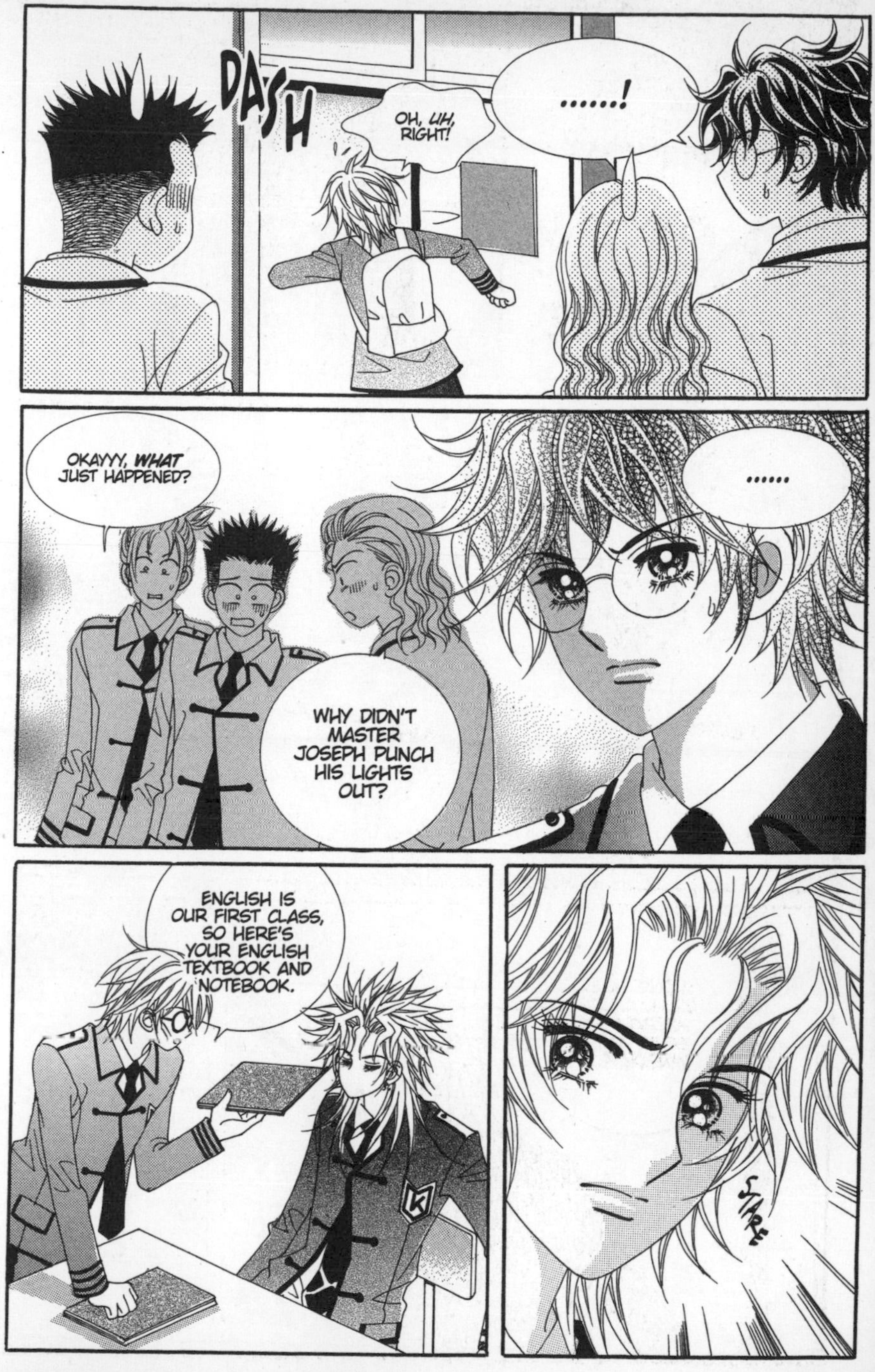
DASH
OH, UH, RIGHT!
......!
OKAYYY, WHAT JUST HAPPENED?
......
WHY DIDN'T MASTER JOSEPH PUNCH HIS LIGHTS OUT?
ENGLISH IS OUR FIRST CLASS, SO HERE'S YOUR ENGLISH TEXTBOOK AND NOTEBOOK.
STARE

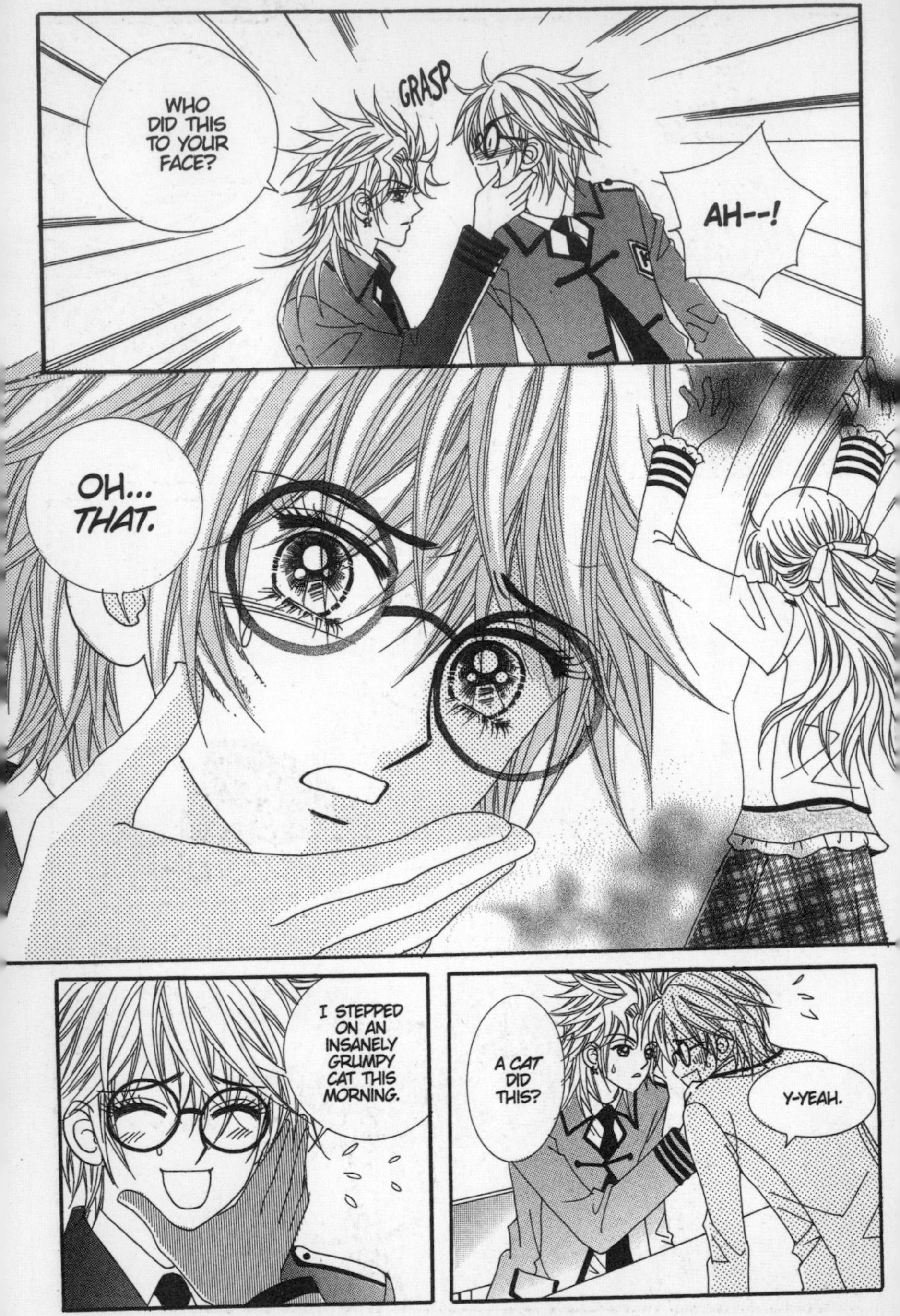
WHO DID THIS TO YOUR FACE?
GRASP
AH--!
OH... THAT.
I STEPPED ON AN INSANELY GRUMPY CAT THIS MORNING.
A CAT DID THIS?
Y-YEAH.

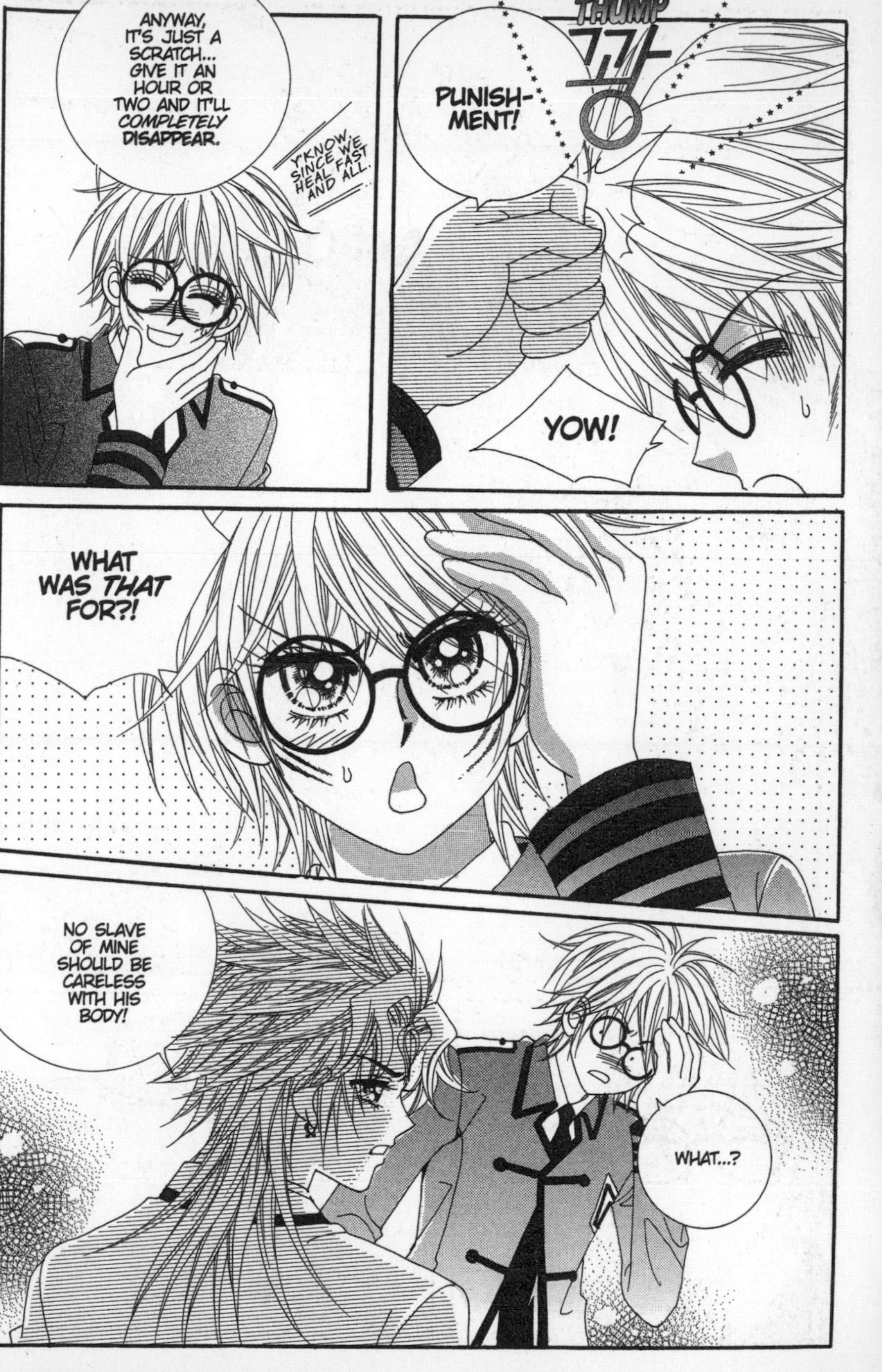
ANYWAY, IT'S JUST A SCRATCH... GIVE IT AN HOUR OR TWO AND IT'LL COMPLETELY DISAPPEAR.
Y'KNOW, SINCE WE HEAL FAST AND ALL.
THUMP
PUNISH-MENT!
YOW!
WHAT WAS THAT FOR?!
NO SLAVE OF MINE SHOULD BE CARELESS WITH HIS BODY!
WHAT...?

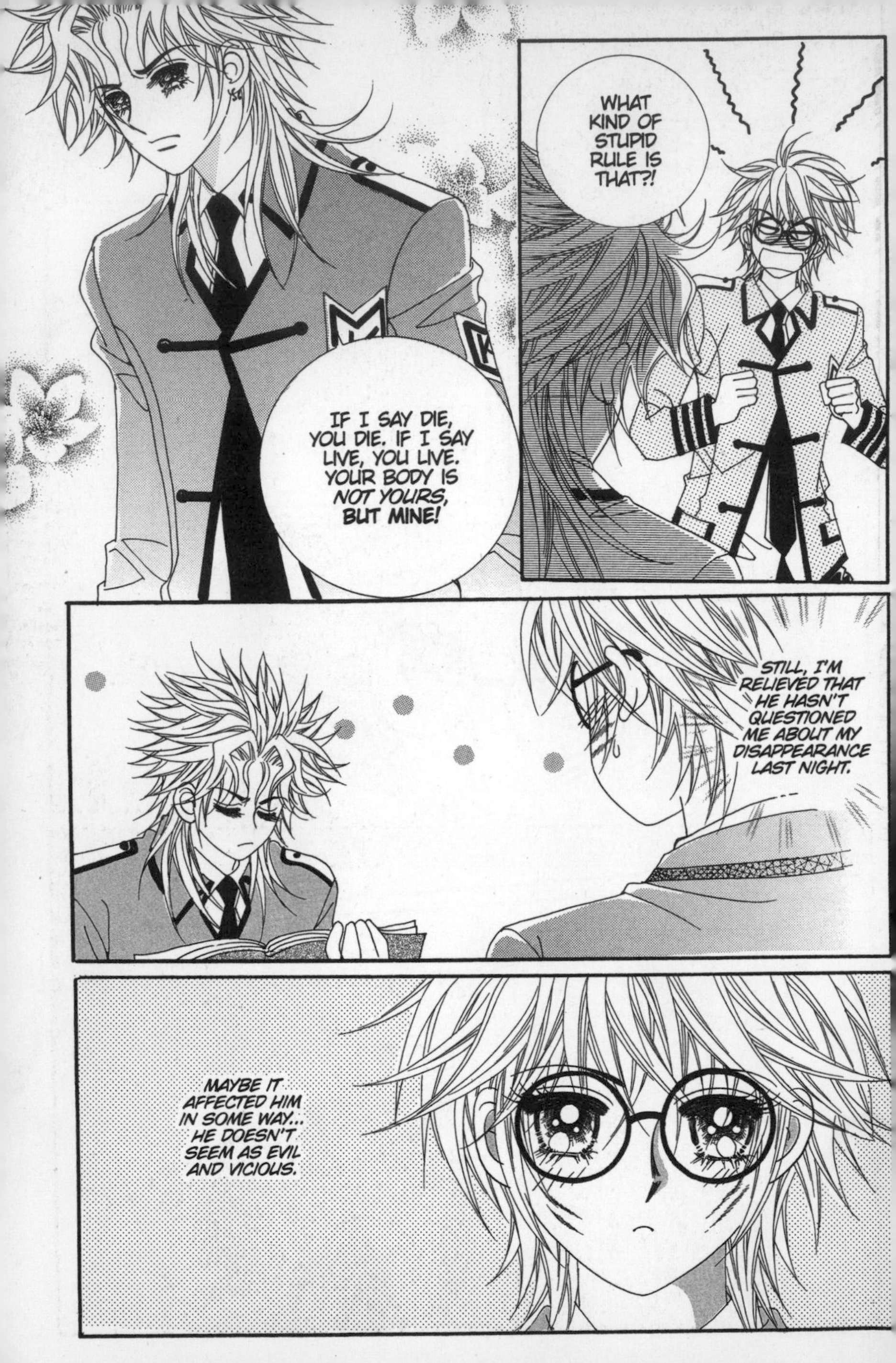
IF I SAY DIE, YOU DIE. IF I SAY LIVE, YOU LIVE. YOUR BODY IS *NOT YOURS*, BUT MINE!
WHAT KIND OF STUPID RULE IS THAT?!
STILL, I'M RELIEVED THAT HE HASN'T QUESTIONED ME ABOUT MY DISAPPEARANCE LAST NIGHT.
MAYBE IT AFFECTED HIM IN SOME WAY... HE DOESN'T SEEM AS EVIL AND VICIOUS.

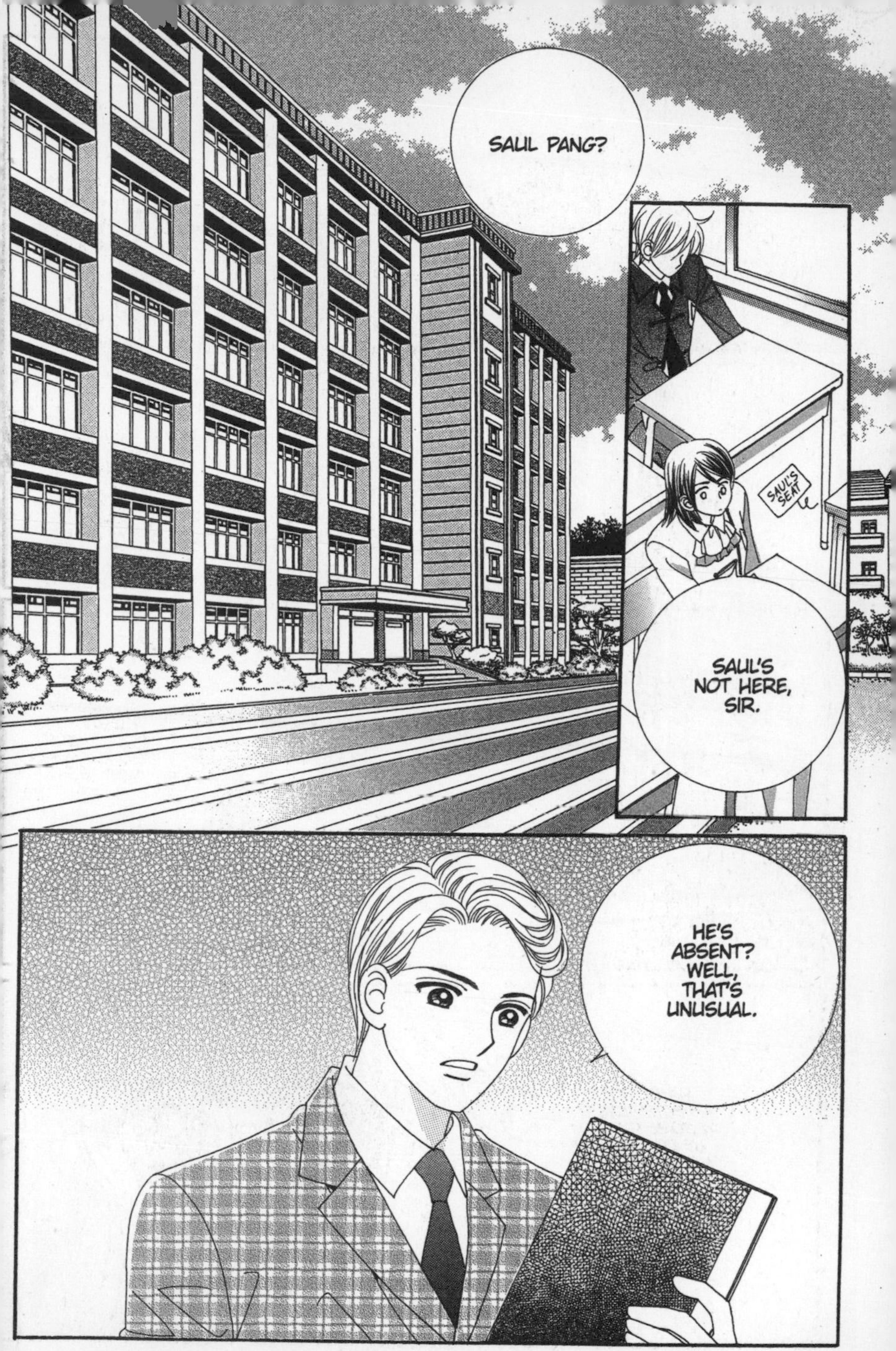
SAUL PANG?
SAUL'S SEAT
SAUL'S NOT HERE, SIR.
HE'S ABSENT? WELL, THAT'S UNUSUAL.

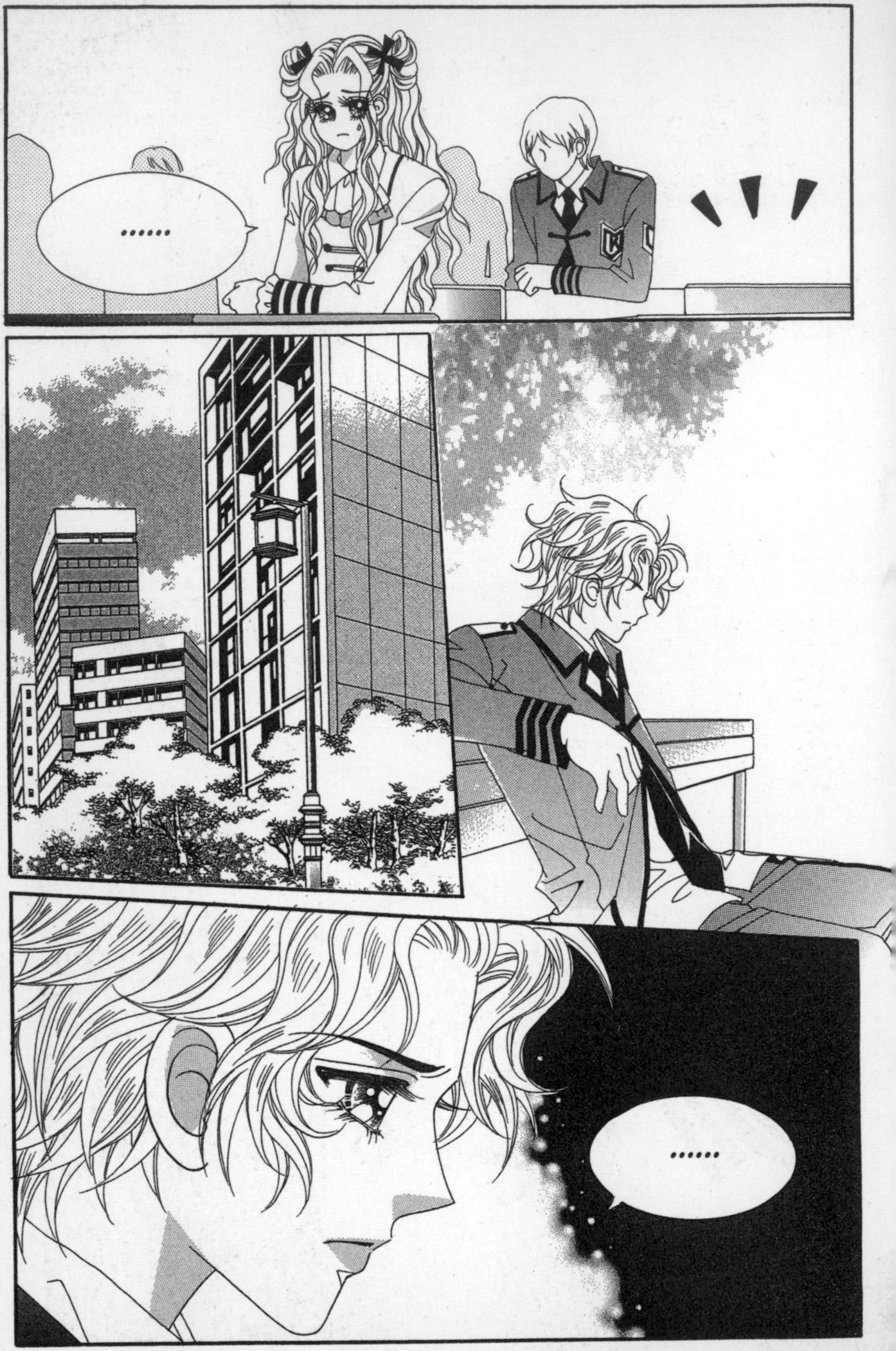
......
......

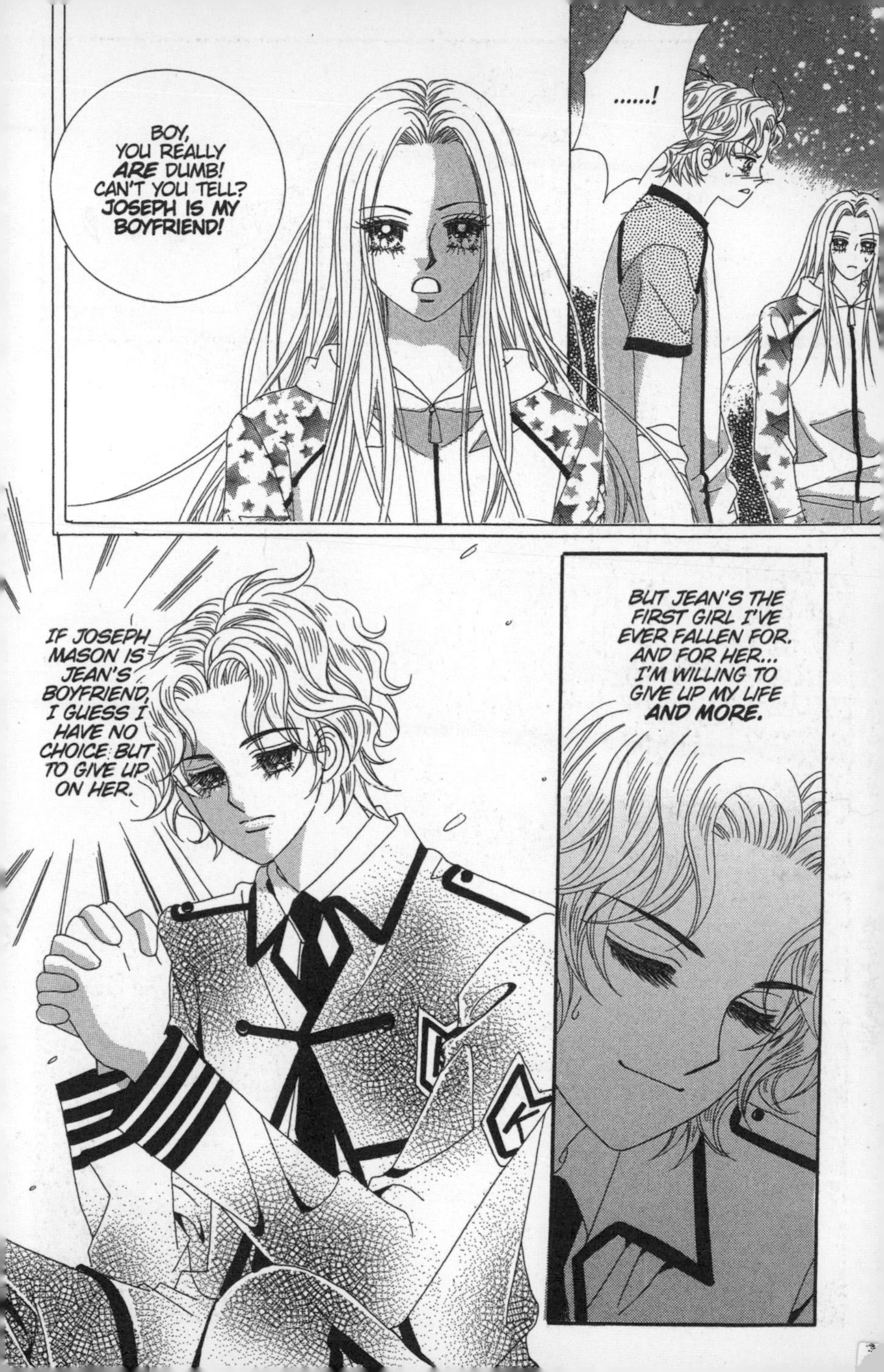
BOY, YOU REALLY ARE DUMB! CAN'T YOU TELL? JOSEPH IS MY BOYFRIEND!
......!
IF JOSEPH MASON IS JEAN'S BOYFRIEND, I GUESS I HAVE NO CHOICE BUT TO GIVE UP ON HER.
BUT JEAN'S THE FIRST GIRL I'VE EVER FALLEN FOR. AND FOR HER... I'M WILLING TO GIVE UP MY LIFE AND MORE.

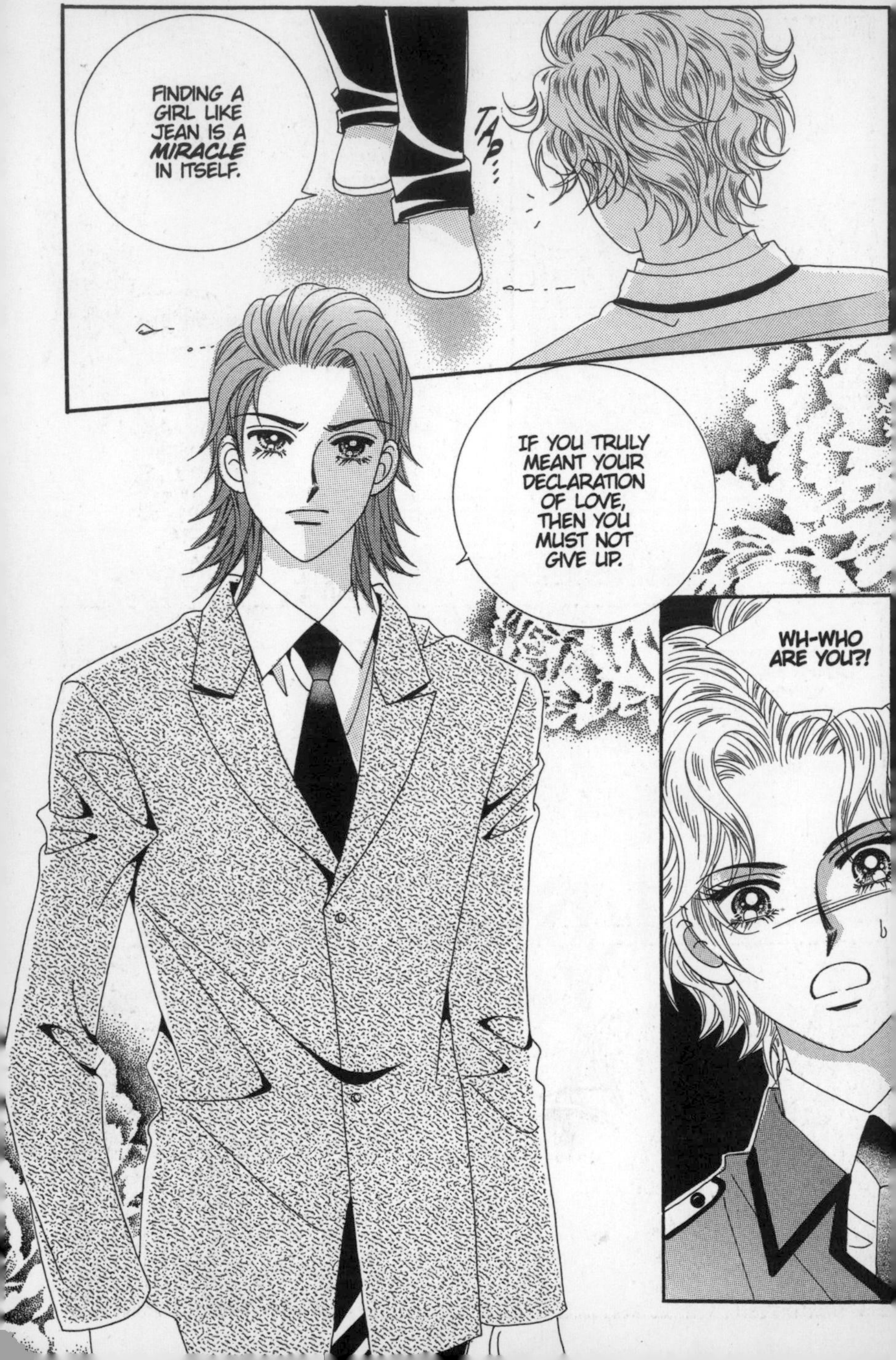
FINDING A GIRL LIKE JEAN IS A *MIRACLE* IN ITSELF.
TAP...
IF YOU TRULY MEANT YOUR DECLARATION OF LOVE, THEN YOU MUST NOT GIVE UP.
WH-WHO ARE YOU?!

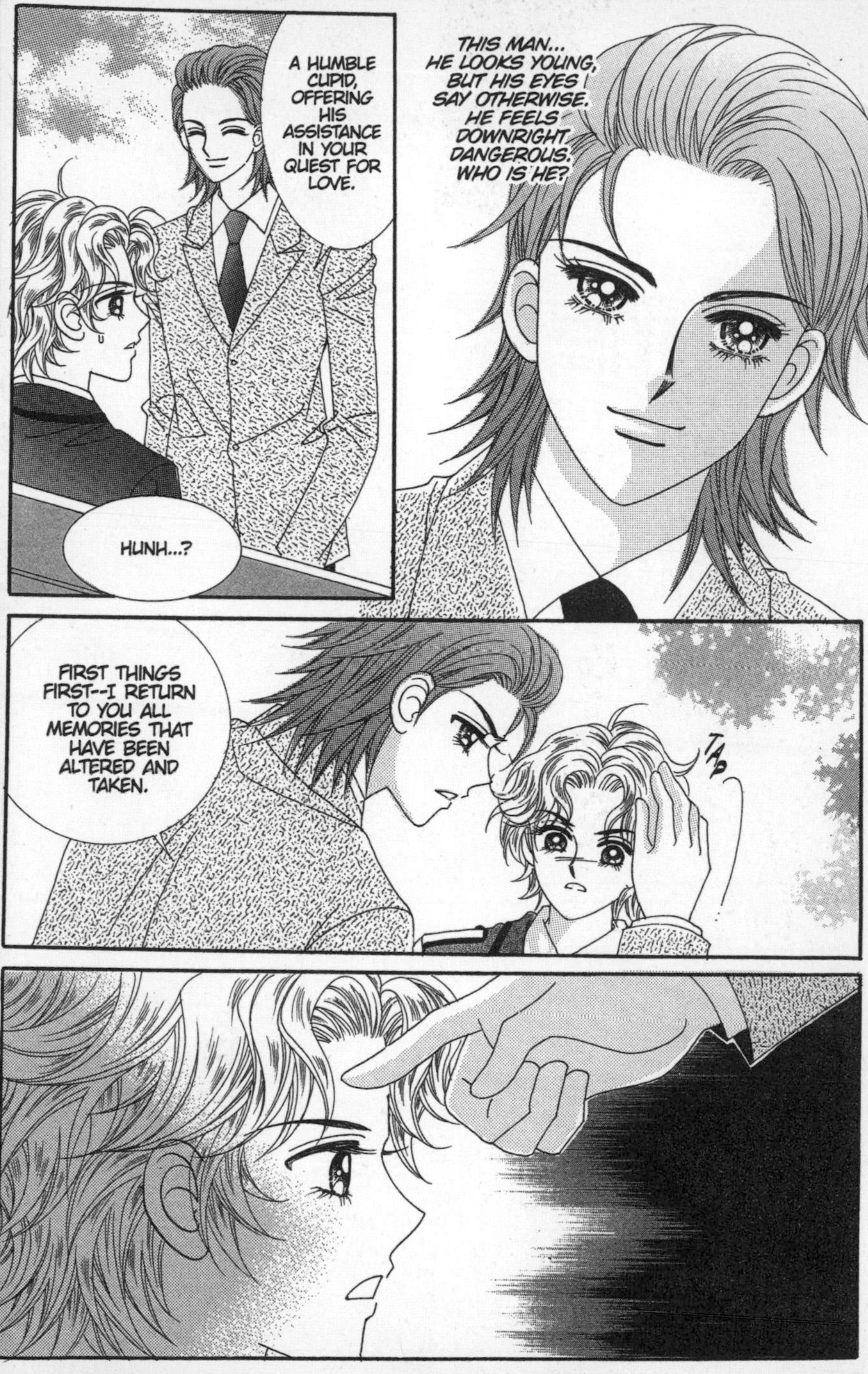
A HUMBLE CUPID, OFFERING HIS ASSISTANCE IN YOUR QUEST FOR LOVE.
HUNH...?
THIS MAN... HE LOOKS YOUNG, BUT HIS EYES SAY OTHERWISE. HE FEELS DOWNRIGHT DANGEROUS. WHO IS HE?
FIRST THINGS FIRST--I RETURN TO YOU ALL MEMORIES THAT HAVE BEEN ALTERED AND TAKEN.
TAP

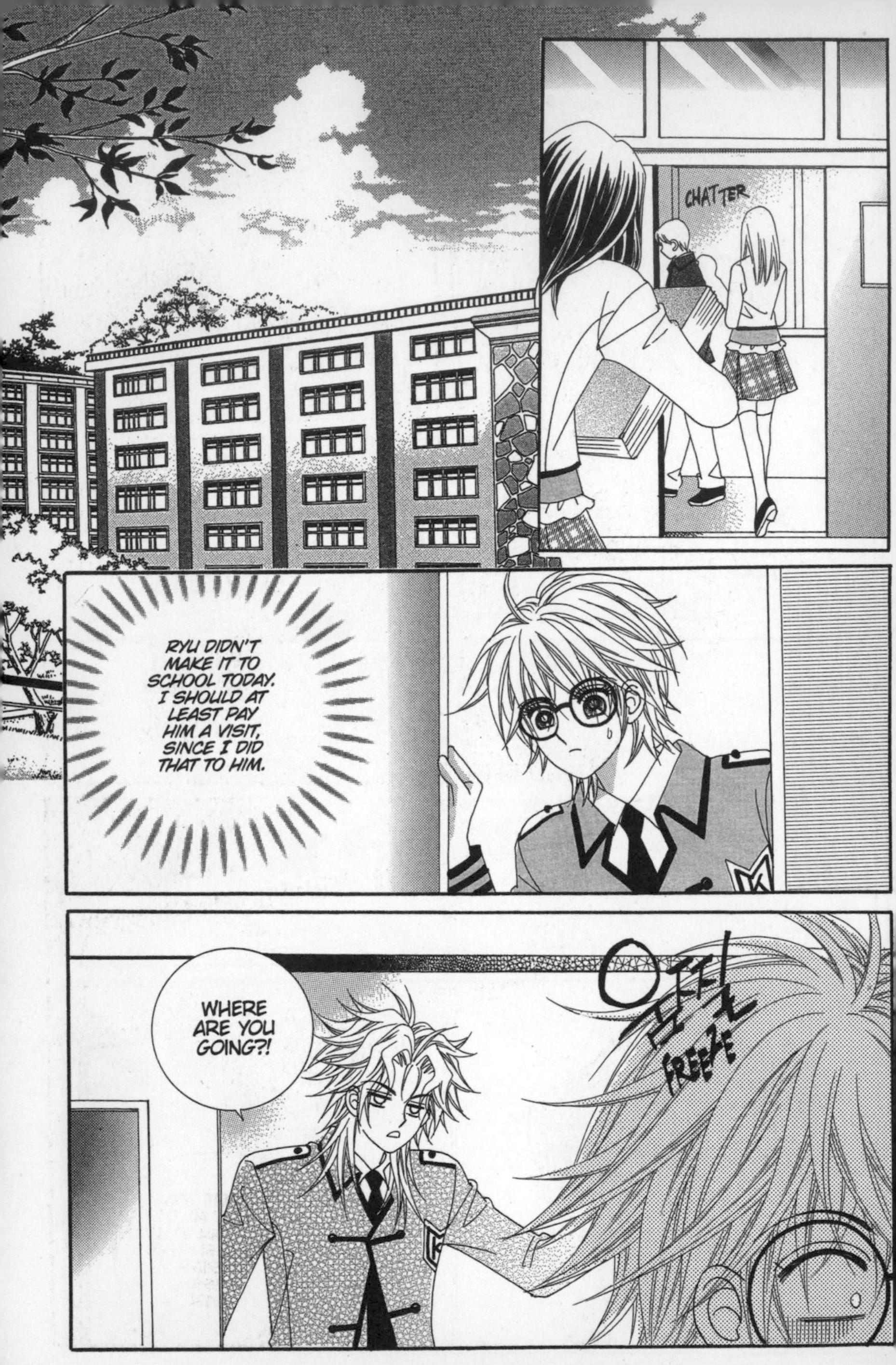
CHATTER
RYU DIDN'T MAKE IT TO SCHOOL TODAY. I SHOULD AT LEAST PAY HIM A VISIT, SINCE I DID THAT TO HIM.
WHERE ARE YOU GOING?!
FREEZE

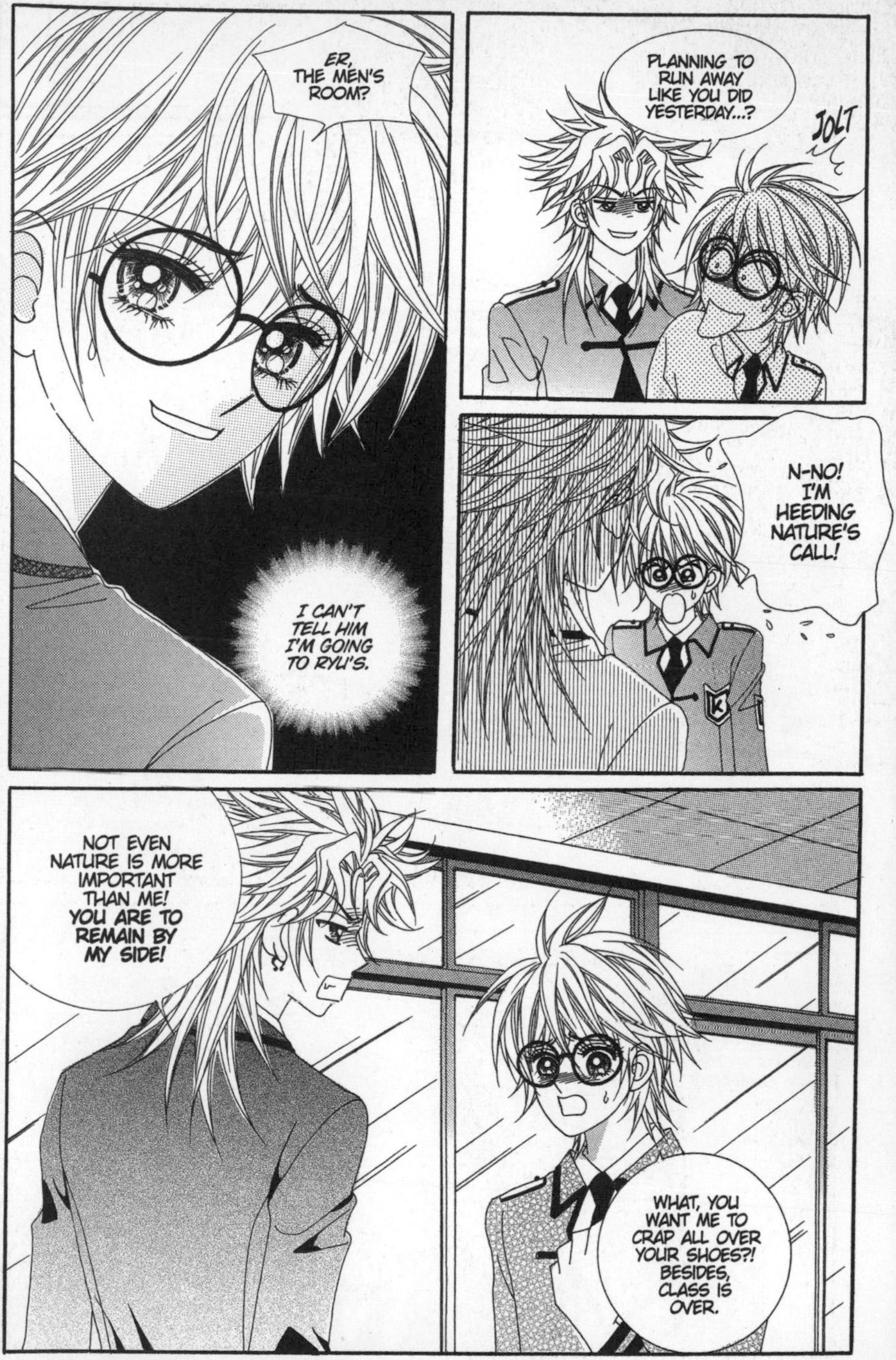
ER, THE MEN'S ROOM?
I CAN'T TELL HIM I'M GOING TO RYU'S.
PLANNING TO RUN AWAY LIKE YOU DID YESTERDAY...?
JOLT
N-NO! I'M HEEDING NATURE'S CALL!
NOT EVEN NATURE IS MORE IMPORTANT THAN ME! YOU ARE TO REMAIN BY MY SIDE!
WHAT, YOU WANT ME TO CRAP ALL OVER YOUR SHOES?! BESIDES, CLASS IS OVER.

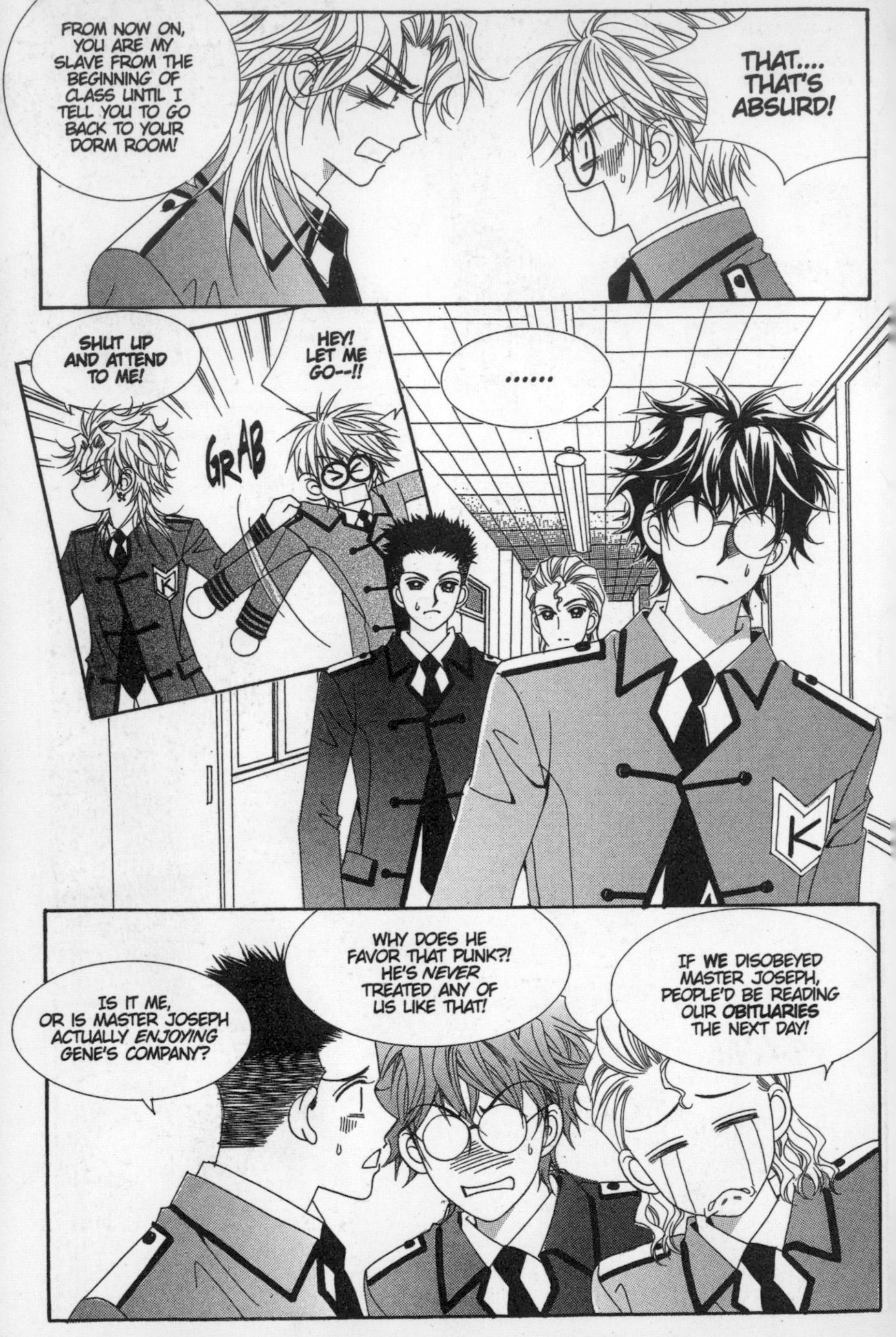
FROM NOW ON, YOU ARE MY SLAVE FROM THE BEGINNING OF CLASS UNTIL I TELL YOU TO GO BACK TO YOUR DORM ROOM!
THAT.... THAT'S ABSURD!
SHUT UP AND ATTEND TO ME!
GRAB
HEY! LET ME GO--!!
......
IS IT ME, OR IS MASTER JOSEPH ACTUALLY ENJOYING GENE'S COMPANY?
WHY DOES HE FAVOR THAT PUNK?! HE'S NEVER TREATED ANY OF US LIKE THAT!
IF WE DISOBEYED MASTER JOSEPH, PEOPLE'D BE READING OUR OBITUARIES THE NEXT DAY!

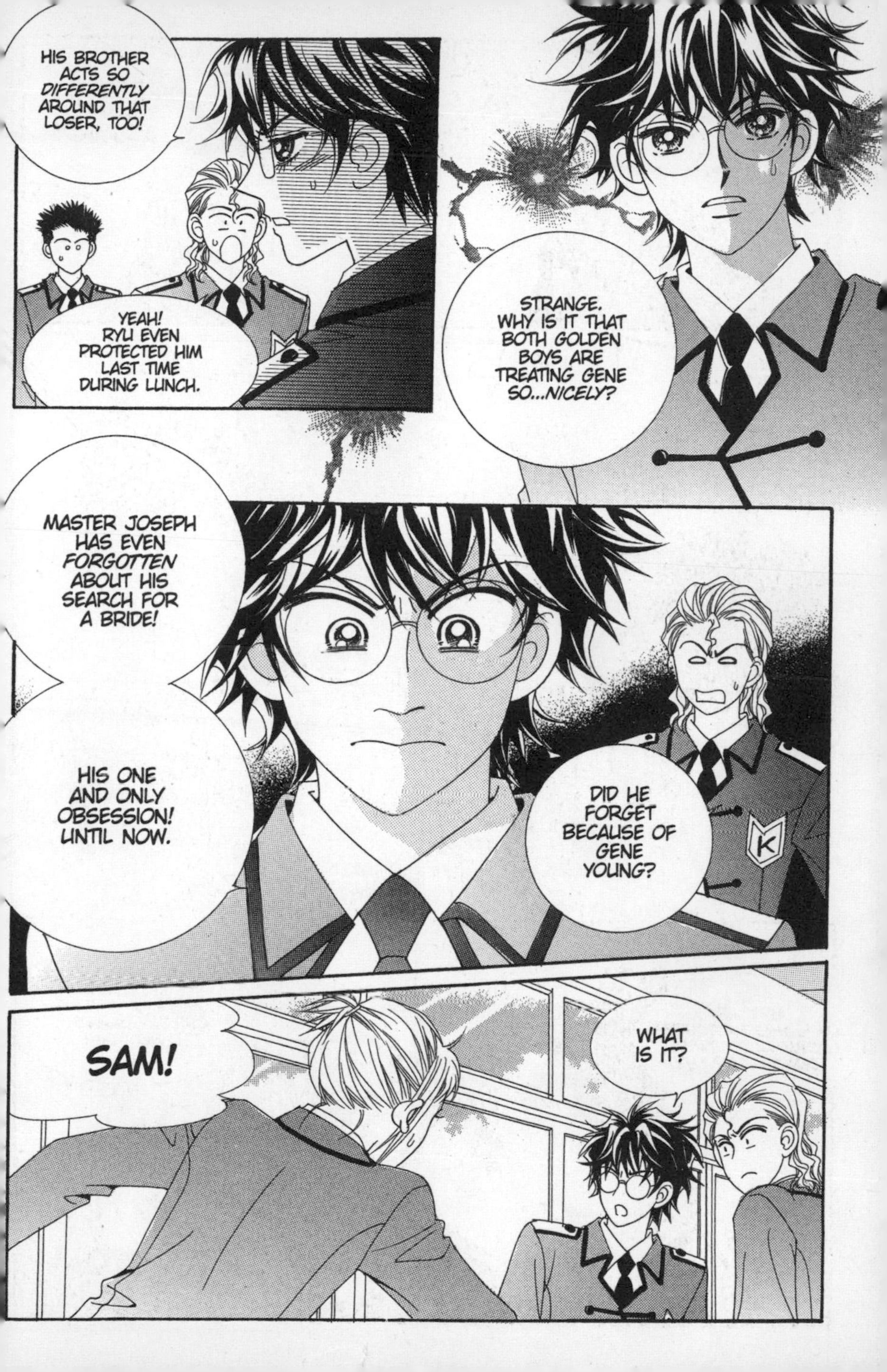
HIS BROTHER ACTS SO *DIFFERENTLY* AROUND THAT LOSER, TOO!
YEAH! RYU EVEN PROTECTED HIM LAST TIME DURING LUNCH.
STRANGE. WHY IS IT THAT BOTH GOLDEN BOYS ARE TREATING GENE SO...*NICELY*?
MASTER JOSEPH HAS EVEN *FORGOTTEN* ABOUT HIS SEARCH FOR A BRIDE!
HIS ONE AND ONLY OBSESSION! UNTIL NOW.
DID HE FORGET BECAUSE OF GENE YOUNG?
SAM!
WHAT IS IT?

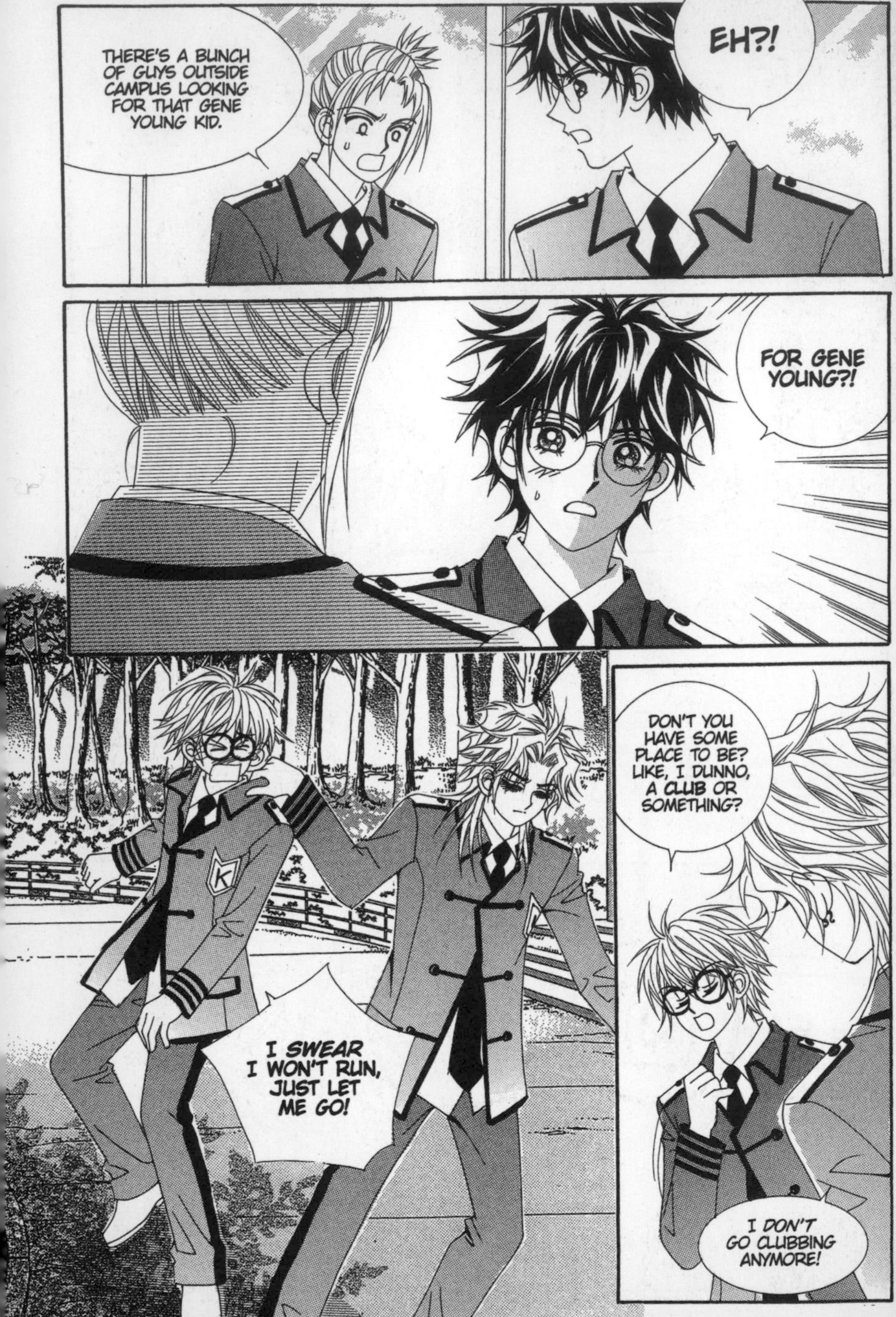
THERE'S A BUNCH OF GUYS OUTSIDE CAMPUS LOOKING FOR THAT GENE YOUNG KID.
EH?!
FOR GENE YOUNG?!
I SWEAR I WON'T RUN, JUST LET ME GO!
DON'T YOU HAVE SOME PLACE TO BE? LIKE, I DUNNO, A CLUB OR SOMETHING?
I DON'T GO CLUBBING ANYMORE!

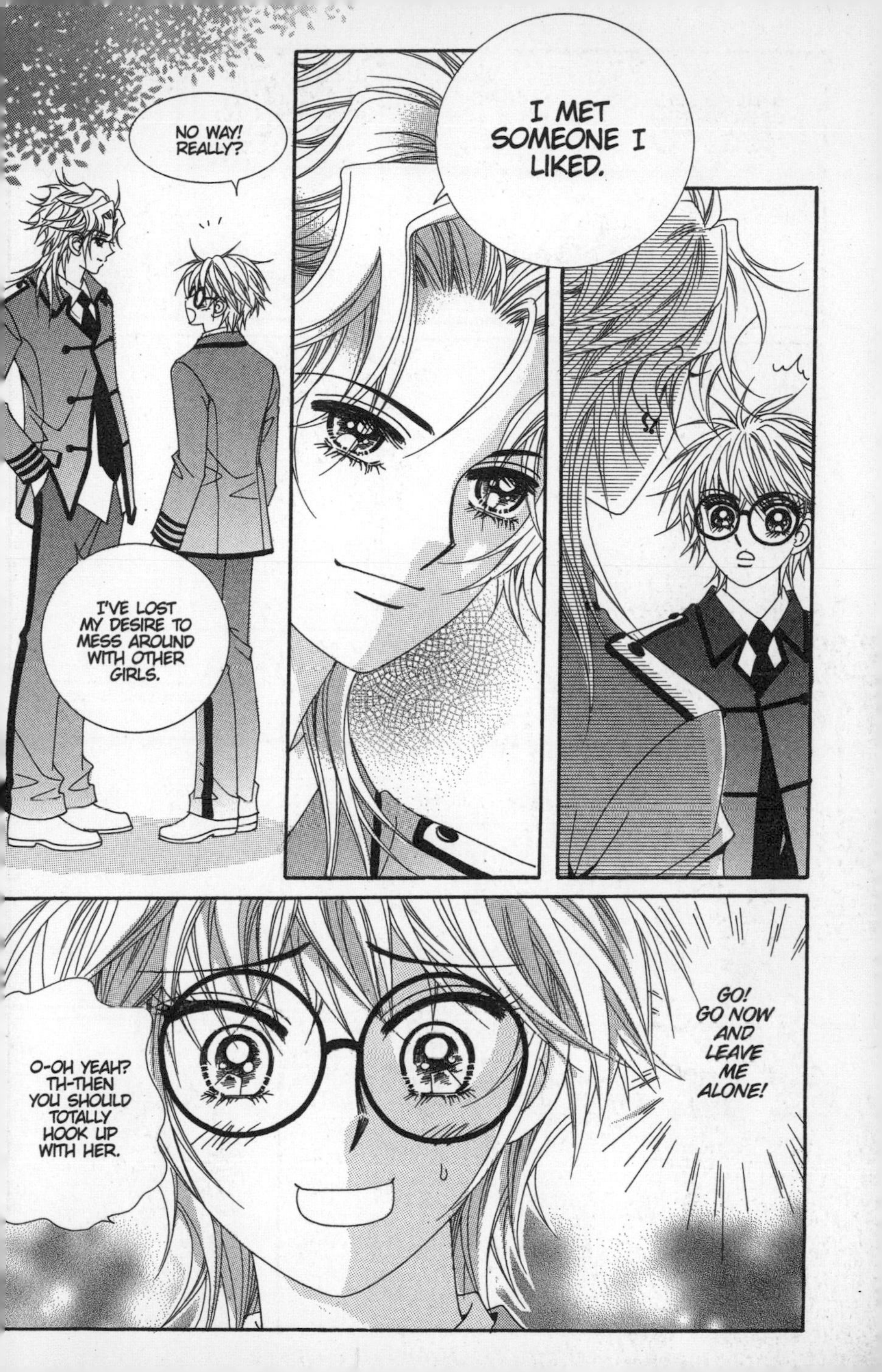
NO WAY! REALLY?
I'VE LOST MY DESIRE TO MESS AROUND WITH OTHER GIRLS.
I MET SOMEONE I LIKED.
O-OH YEAH? TH-THEN YOU SHOULD TOTALLY HOOK UP WITH HER.
GO! GO NOW AND LEAVE ME ALONE!

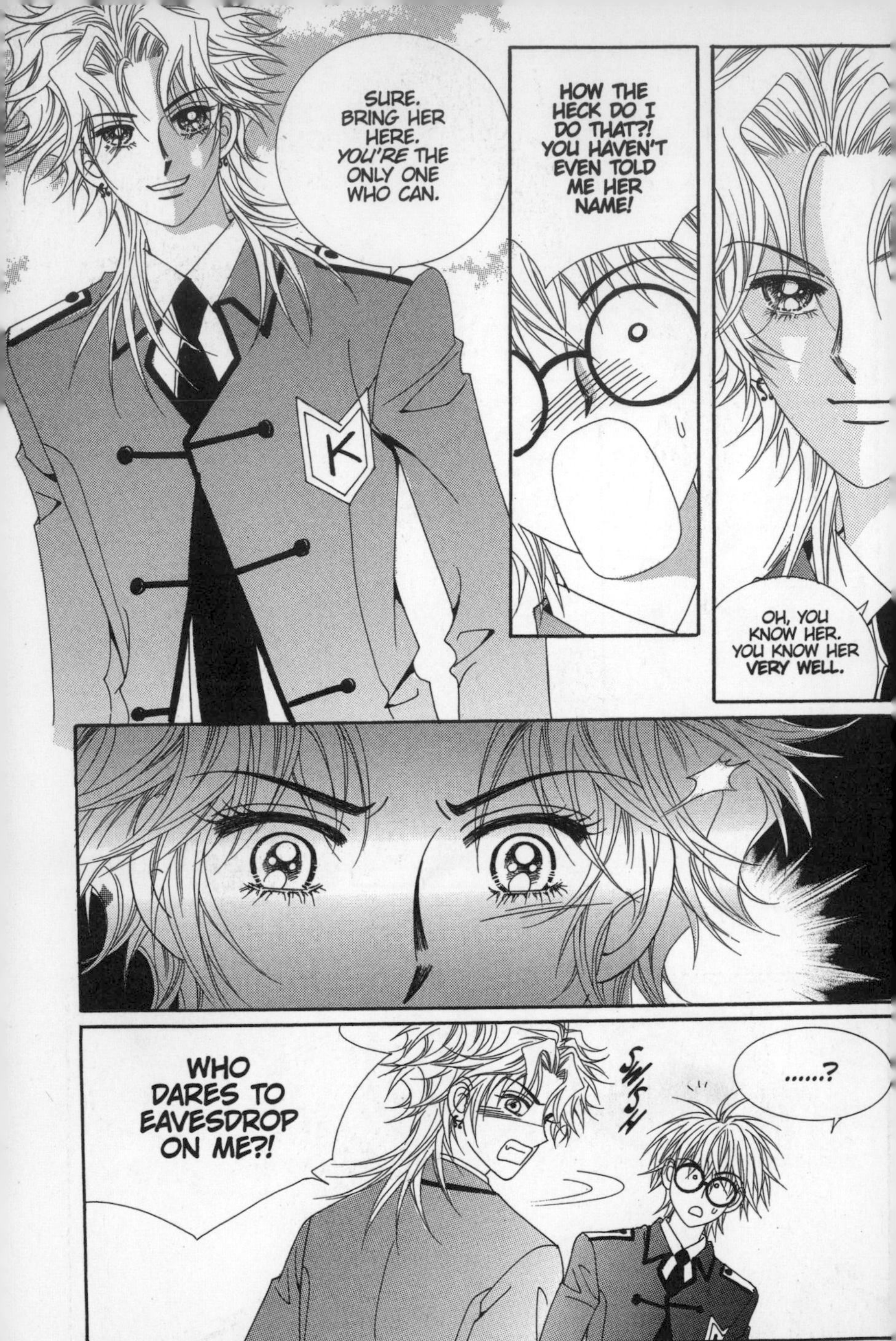
SURE. BRING HER HERE. YOU'RE THE ONLY ONE WHO CAN.
HOW THE HECK DO I DO THAT?! YOU HAVEN'T EVEN TOLD ME HER NAME!
OH, YOU KNOW HER. YOU KNOW HER VERY WELL.
WHO DARES TO EAVESDROP ON ME?!
SWISH
......?

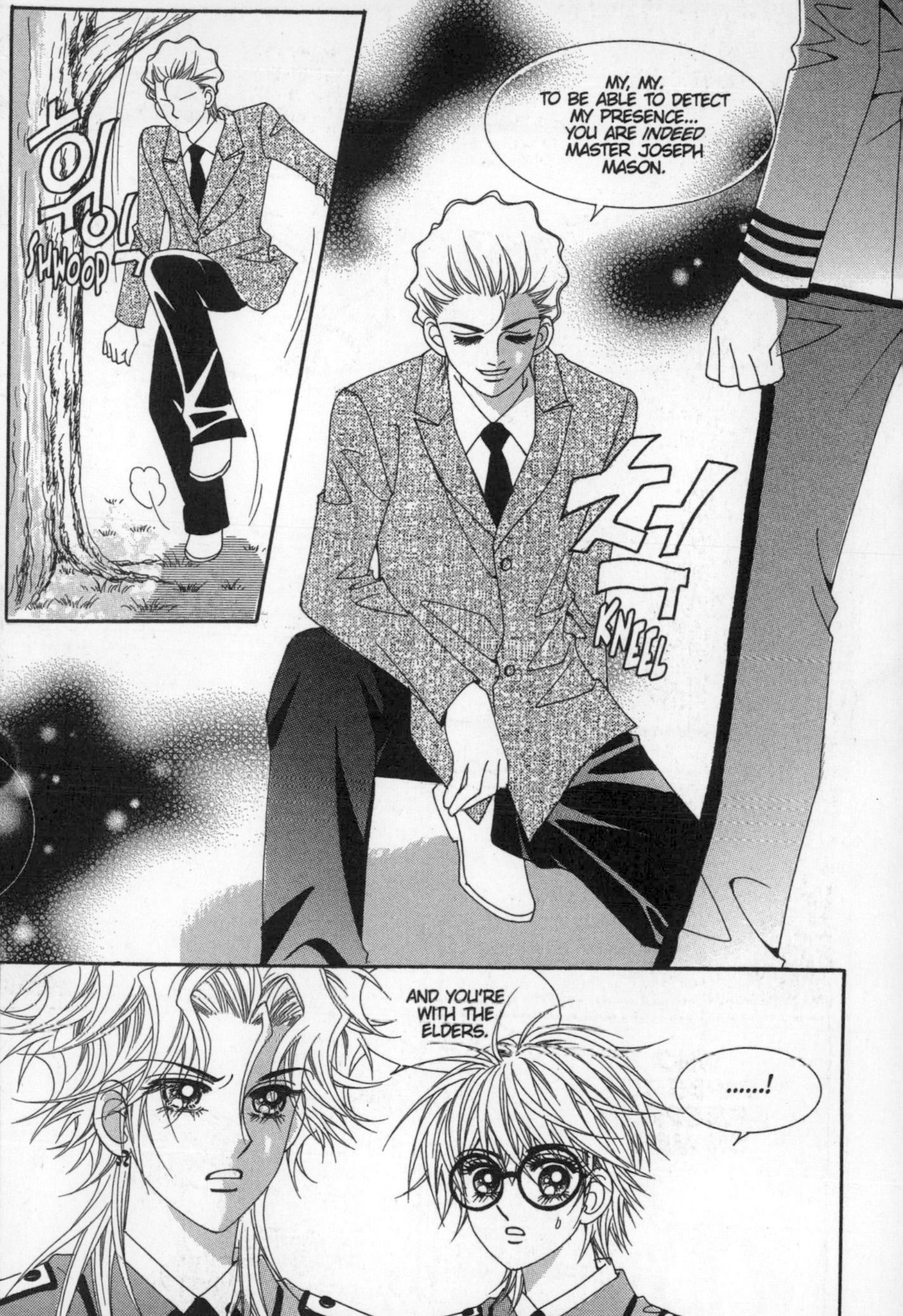
SHWOOP
MY, MY. TO BE ABLE TO DETECT MY PRESENCE... YOU ARE *INDEED* MASTER JOSEPH MASON.
KNEEL
AND YOU'RE WITH THE ELDERS.
......!

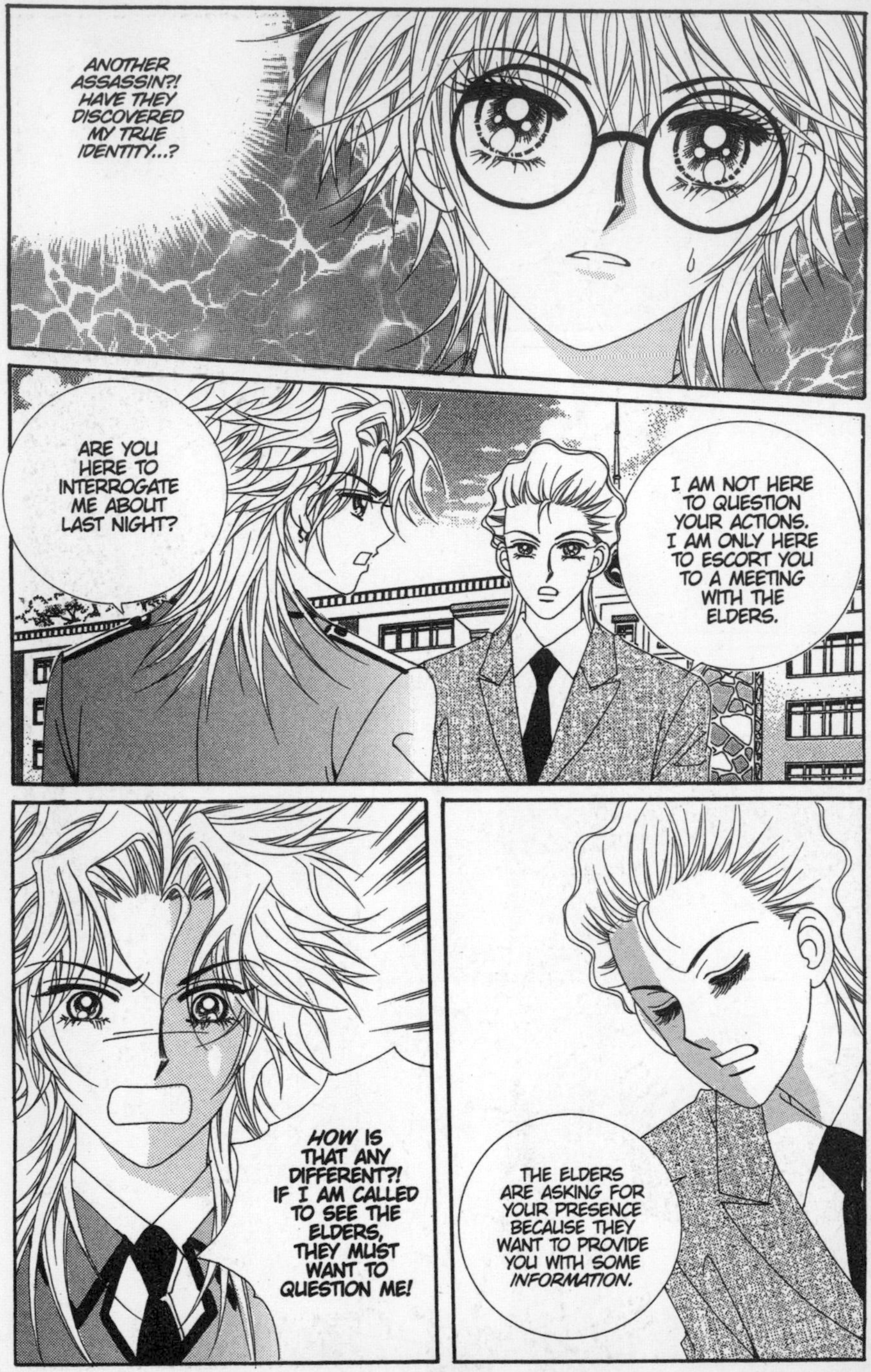
ANOTHER ASSASSIN?! HAVE THEY DISCOVERED MY TRUE IDENTITY...?
ARE YOU HERE TO INTERROGATE ME ABOUT LAST NIGHT?
I AM NOT HERE TO QUESTION YOUR ACTIONS. I AM ONLY HERE TO ESCORT YOU TO A MEETING WITH THE ELDERS.
*HOW* IS THAT ANY DIFFERENT?! IF I AM CALLED TO SEE THE ELDERS, THEY MUST WANT TO QUESTION ME!
THE ELDERS ARE ASKING FOR YOUR PRESENCE BECAUSE THEY WANT TO PROVIDE YOU WITH SOME *INFORMATION*.

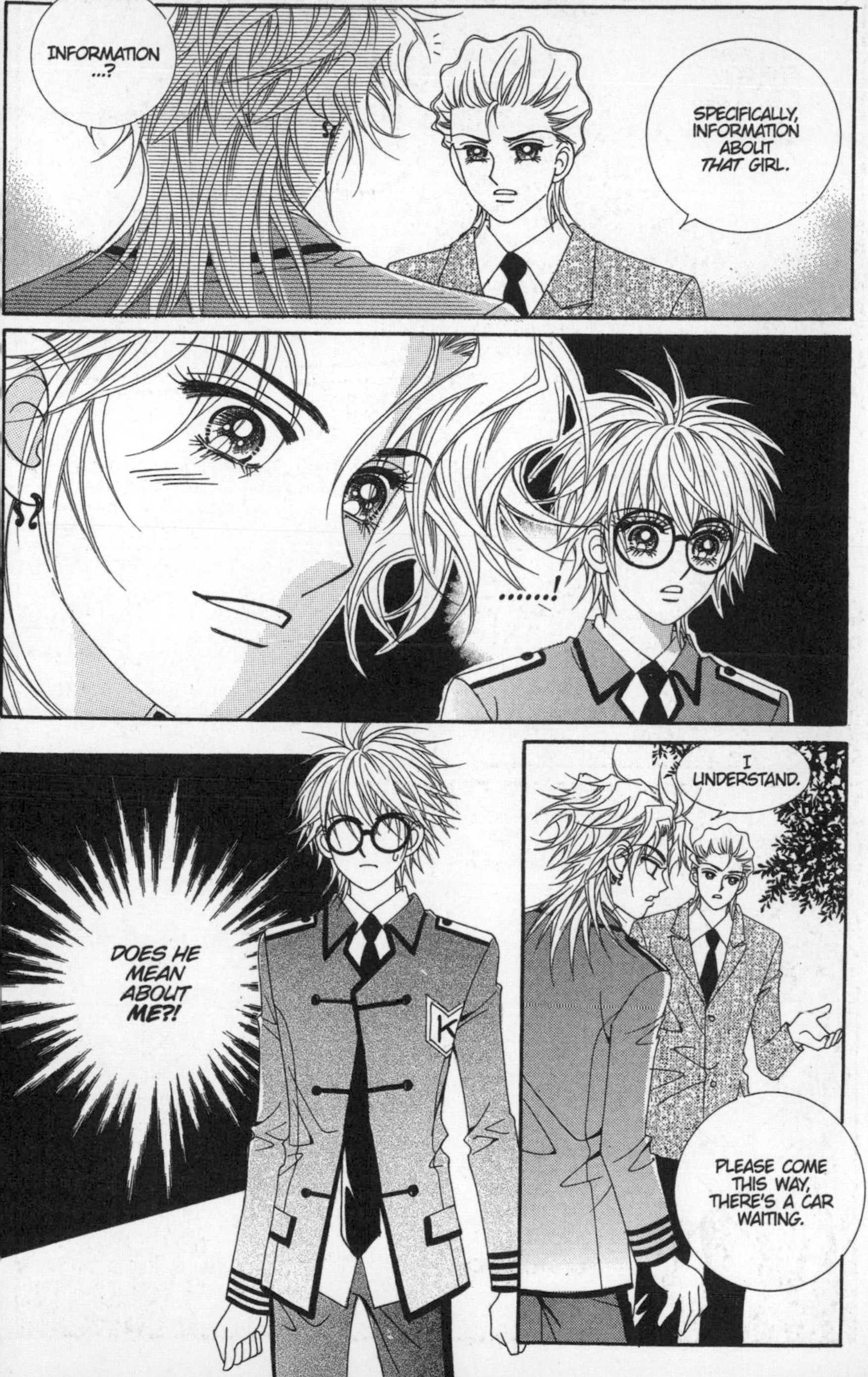
INFORMATION ...?
SPECIFICALLY, INFORMATION ABOUT *THAT* GIRL.
......!
DOES HE MEAN ABOUT ME?!
I UNDERSTAND.
PLEASE COME THIS WAY, THERE'S A CAR WAITING.

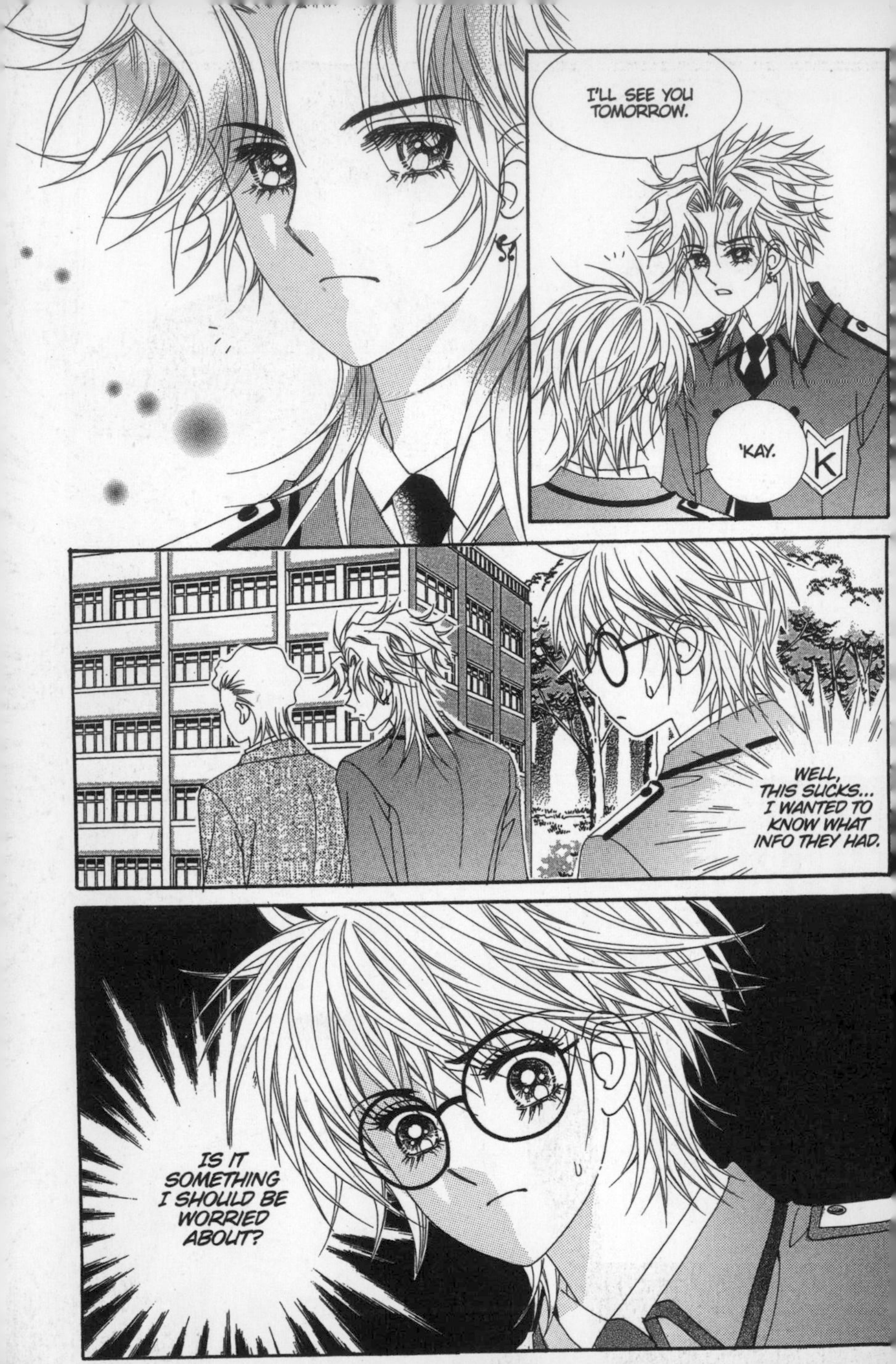
I'LL SEE YOU TOMORROW.
'KAY.
K
WELL, THIS SUCKS... I WANTED TO KNOW WHAT INFO THEY HAD.
IS IT SOMETHING I SHOULD BE WORRIED ABOUT?

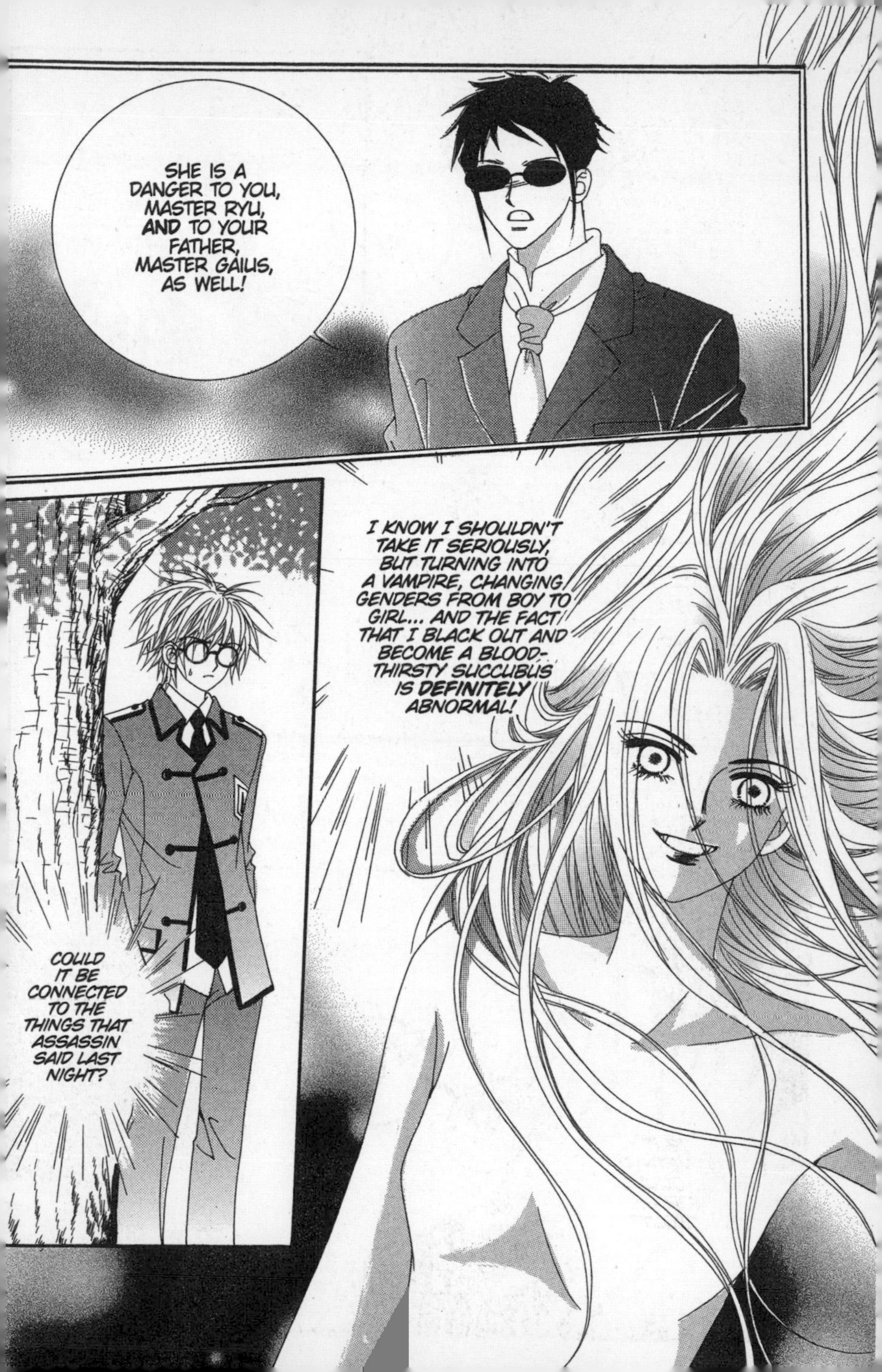
SHE IS A DANGER TO YOU, MASTER RYU, AND TO YOUR FATHER, MASTER GAIUS, AS WELL!
COULD IT BE CONNECTED TO THE THINGS THAT ASSASSIN SAID LAST NIGHT?
I KNOW I SHOULDN'T TAKE IT SERIOUSLY, BUT TURNING INTO A VAMPIRE, CHANGING GENDERS FROM BOY TO GIRL... AND THE FACT THAT I BLACK OUT AND BECOME A BLOOD-THIRSTY SUCCUBUS IS DEFINITELY ABNORMAL!

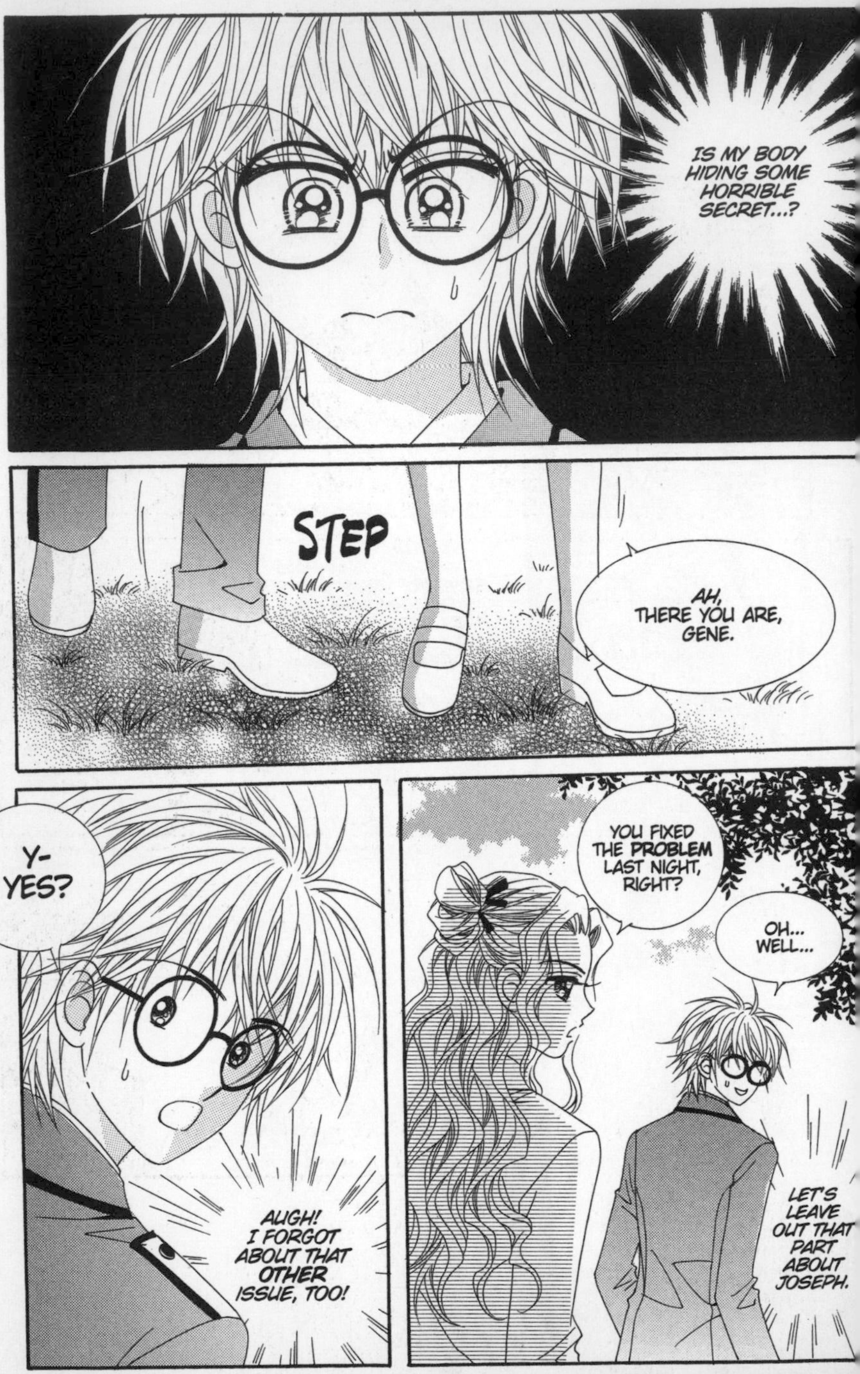
IS MY BODY HIDING SOME HORRIBLE SECRET...?
STEP
AH, THERE YOU ARE, GENE.
Y-YES?
AUGH! I FORGOT ABOUT THAT OTHER ISSUE, TOO!
YOU FIXED THE PROBLEM LAST NIGHT, RIGHT?
OH... WELL...
LET'S LEAVE OUT THAT PART ABOUT JOSEPH.

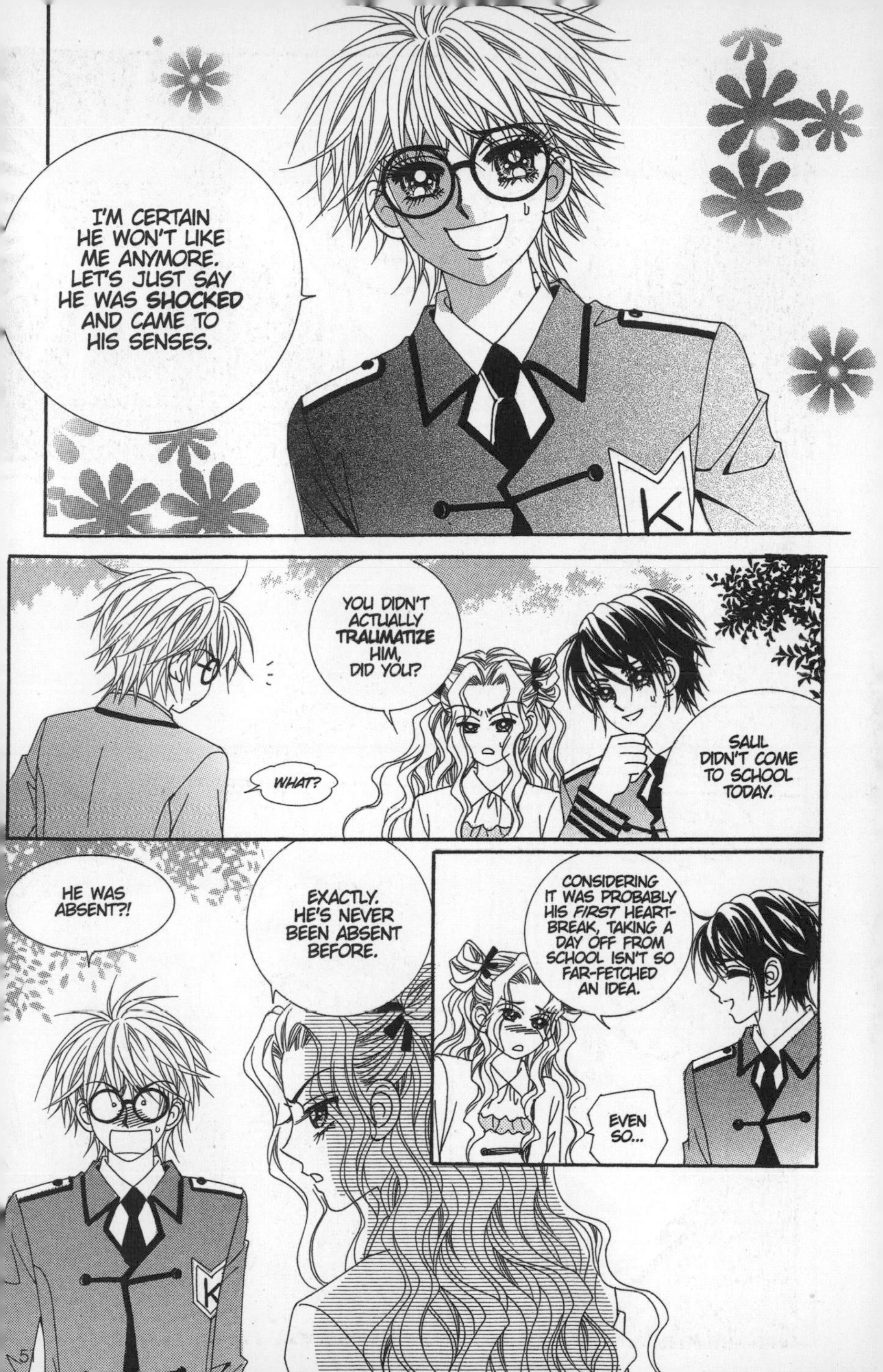
I'M CERTAIN HE WON'T LIKE ME ANYMORE. LET'S JUST SAY HE WAS SHOCKED AND CAME TO HIS SENSES.
YOU DIDN'T ACTUALLY TRAUMATIZE HIM, DID YOU?
WHAT?
SAUL DIDN'T COME TO SCHOOL TODAY.
HE WAS ABSENT?!
EXACTLY. HE'S NEVER BEEN ABSENT BEFORE.
CONSIDERING IT WAS PROBABLY HIS *FIRST* HEART-BREAK, TAKING A DAY OFF FROM SCHOOL ISN'T SO FAR-FETCHED AN IDEA.
EVEN SO...

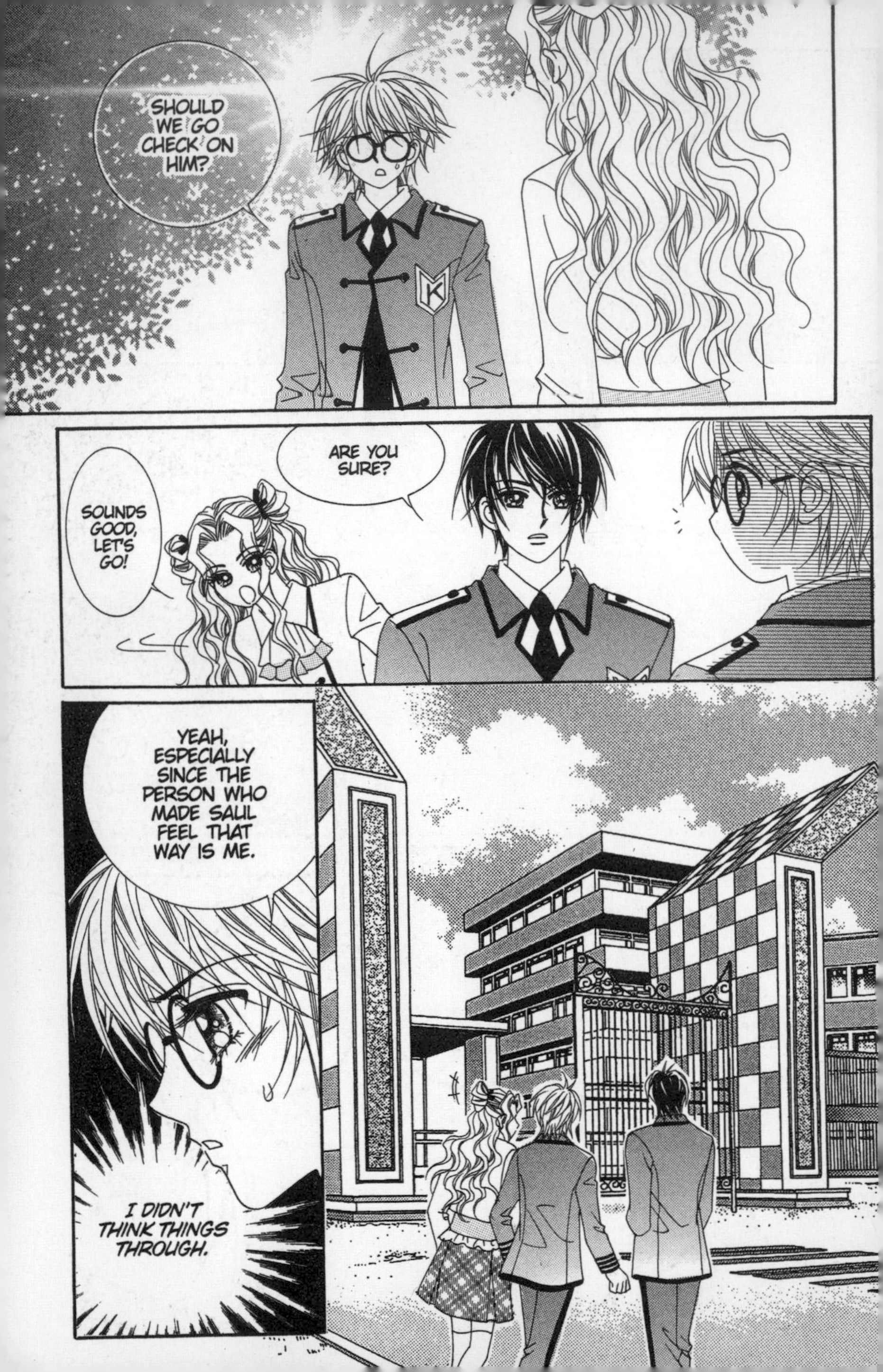
SHOULD WE GO CHECK ON HIM?
SOUNDS GOOD, LET'S GO!
ARE YOU SURE?
YEAH, ESPECIALLY SINCE THE PERSON WHO MADE SAUL FEEL THAT WAY IS ME.
I DIDN'T THINK THINGS THROUGH.

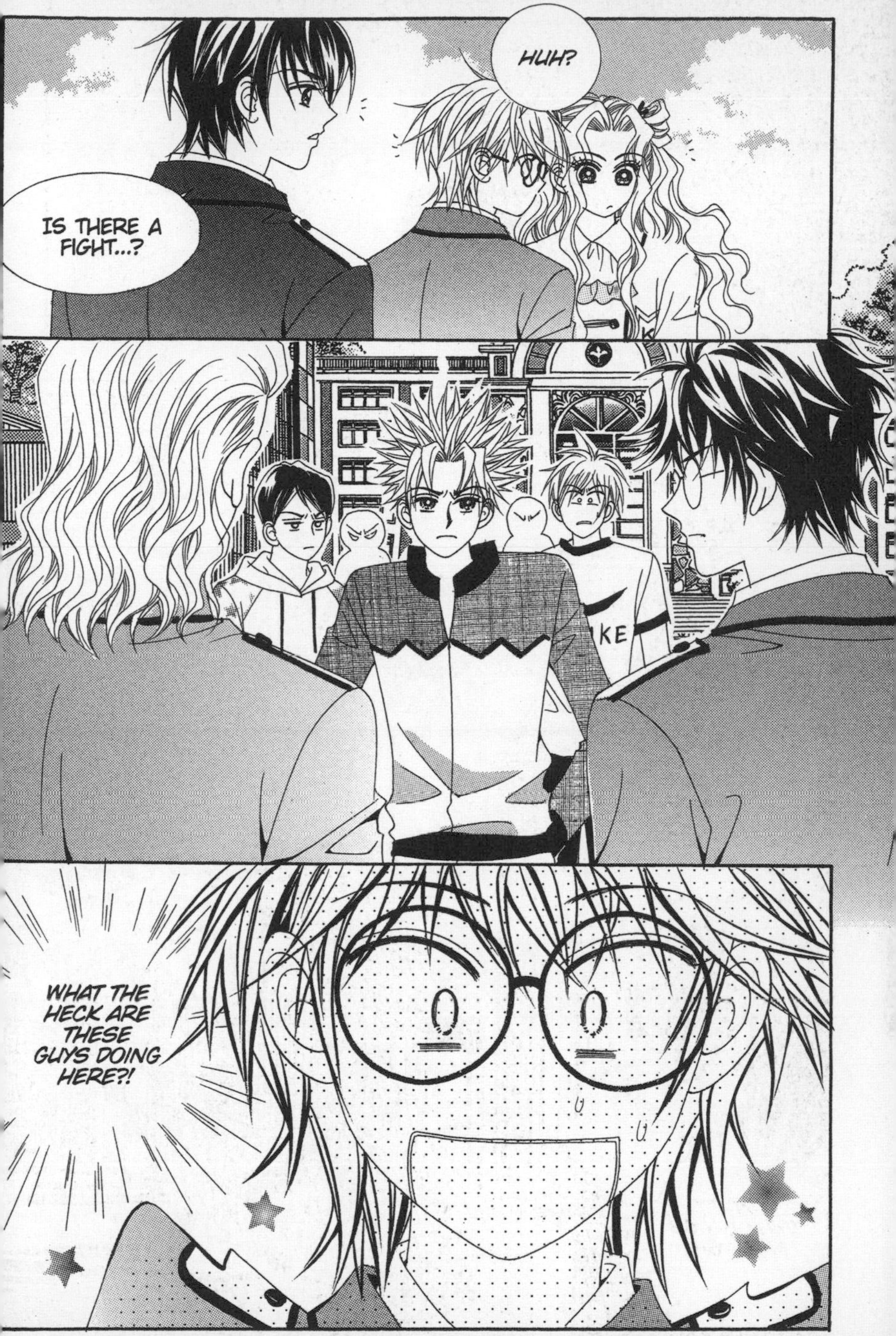
IS THERE A FIGHT...?
HUH?
WHAT THE HECK ARE THESE GUYS DOING HERE?!

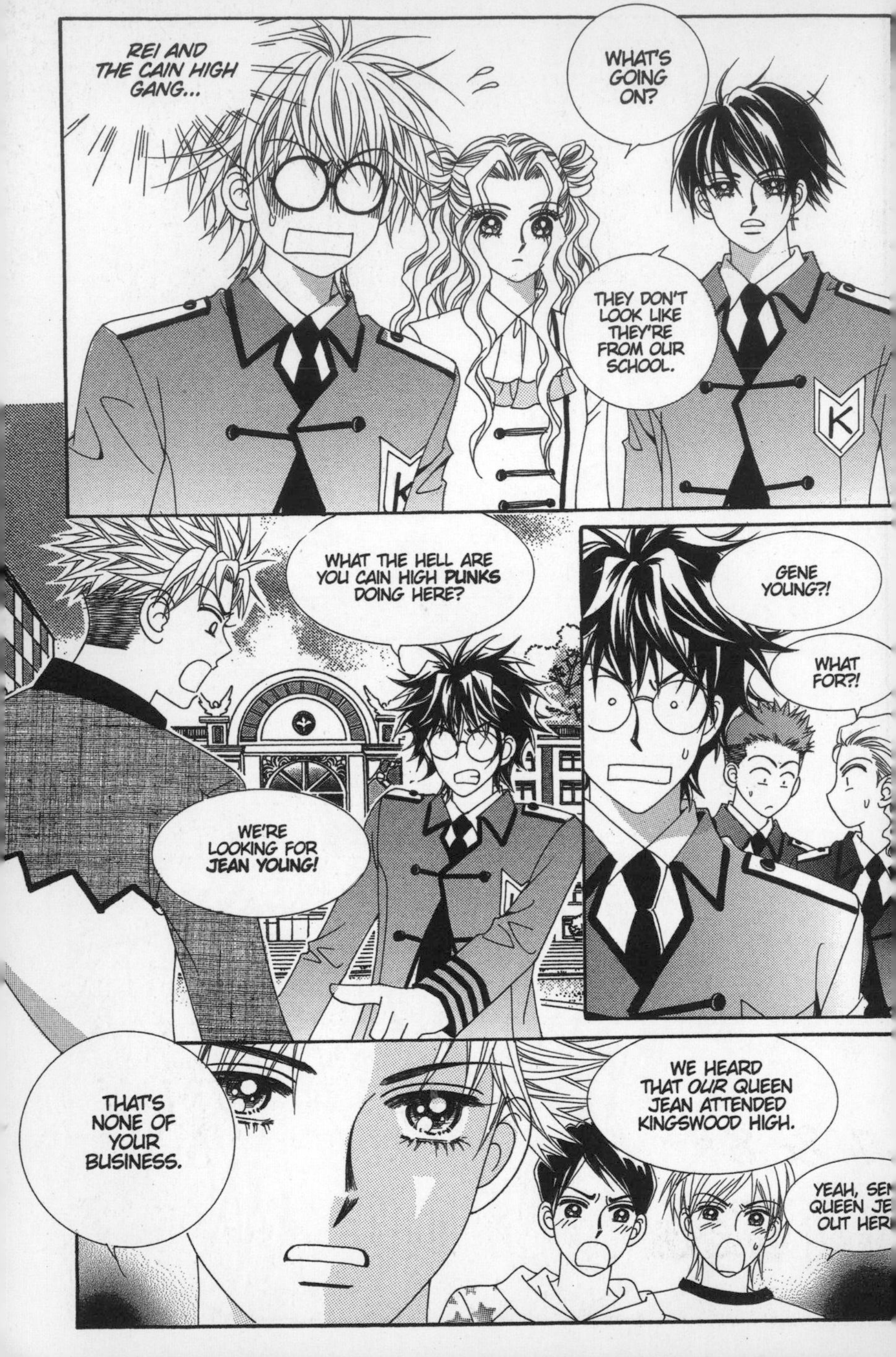

REI AND THE CAIN HIGH GANG...
WHAT'S GOING ON?
THEY DON'T LOOK LIKE THEY'RE FROM OUR SCHOOL.
WHAT THE HELL ARE YOU CAIN HIGH PUNKS DOING HERE?
WE'RE LOOKING FOR JEAN YOUNG!
GENE YOUNG?!
WHAT FOR?!
THAT'S NONE OF YOUR BUSINESS.
WE HEARD THAT *OUR* QUEEN JEAN ATTENDED KINGSWOOD HIGH.
YEAH, SE QUEEN JE OUT HER

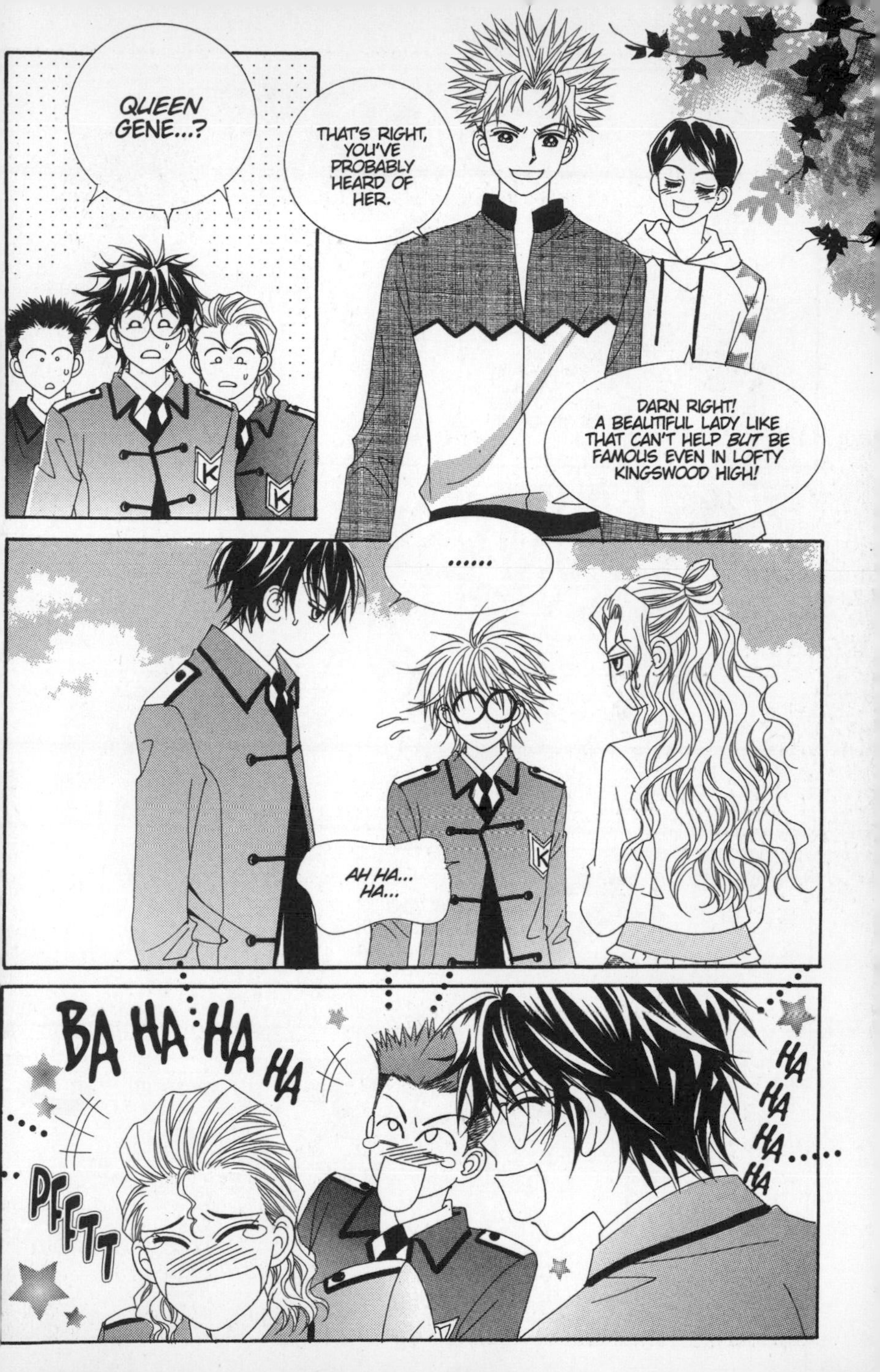
QUEEN GENE...?
THAT'S RIGHT, YOU'VE PROBABLY HEARD OF HER.
DARN RIGHT! A BEAUTIFUL LADY LIKE THAT CAN'T HELP *BUT* BE FAMOUS EVEN IN LOFTY KINGSWOOD HIGH!
......
AH HA... HA...
BA HA HA HA HA
PFFFTT
HA HA HA HA HA

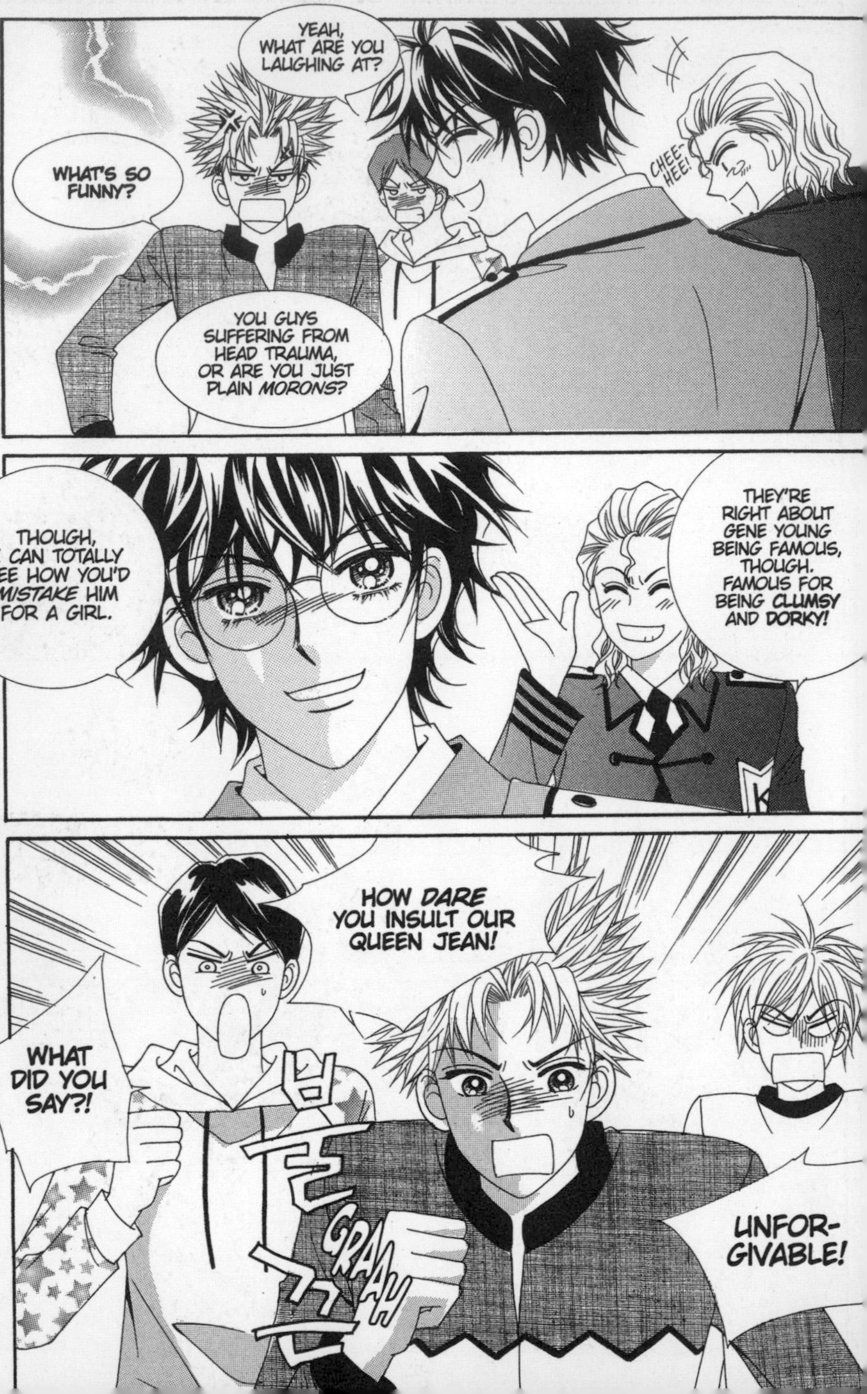
WHAT'S SO FUNNY?
YEAH, WHAT ARE YOU LAUGHING AT?
CHEE-HEE!
YOU GUYS SUFFERING FROM HEAD TRAUMA, OR ARE YOU JUST PLAIN *MORONS?*
THOUGH, I CAN TOTALLY SEE HOW YOU'D *MISTAKE* HIM FOR A GIRL.
THEY'RE RIGHT ABOUT GENE YOUNG BEING FAMOUS, THOUGH. FAMOUS FOR BEING **CLUMSY** AND **DORKY**!
WHAT DID YOU SAY?!
HOW *DARE* YOU INSULT OUR QUEEN JEAN!
GRAAH
UNFORGIVABLE!

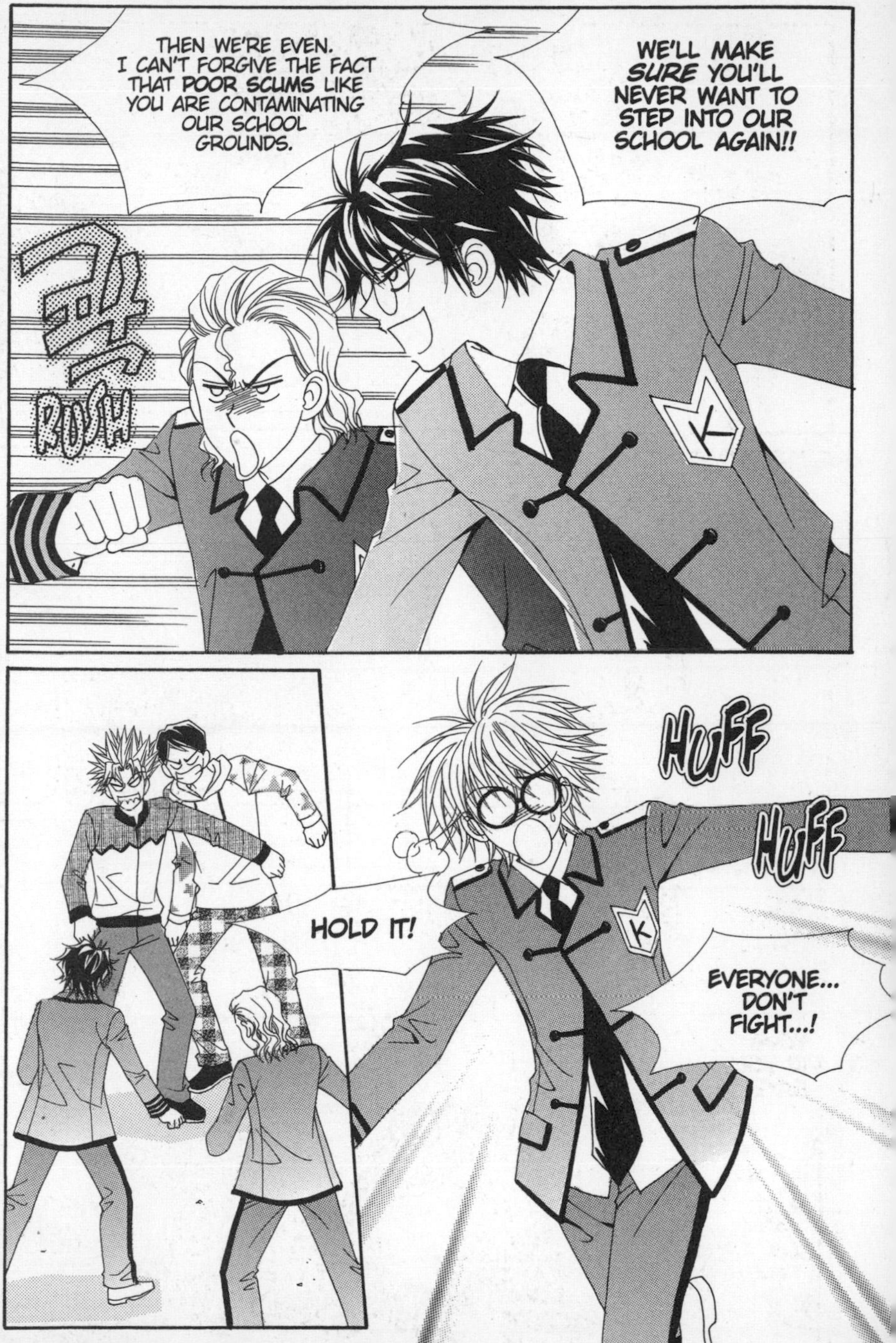
THEN WE'RE EVEN. I CAN'T FORGIVE THE FACT THAT POOR SCUMS LIKE YOU ARE CONTAMINATING OUR SCHOOL GROUNDS.
WE'LL MAKE SURE YOU'LL NEVER WANT TO STEP INTO OUR SCHOOL AGAIN!!
RUSH
HUFF
HUFF
HOLD IT!
EVERYONE... DON'T FIGHT...!

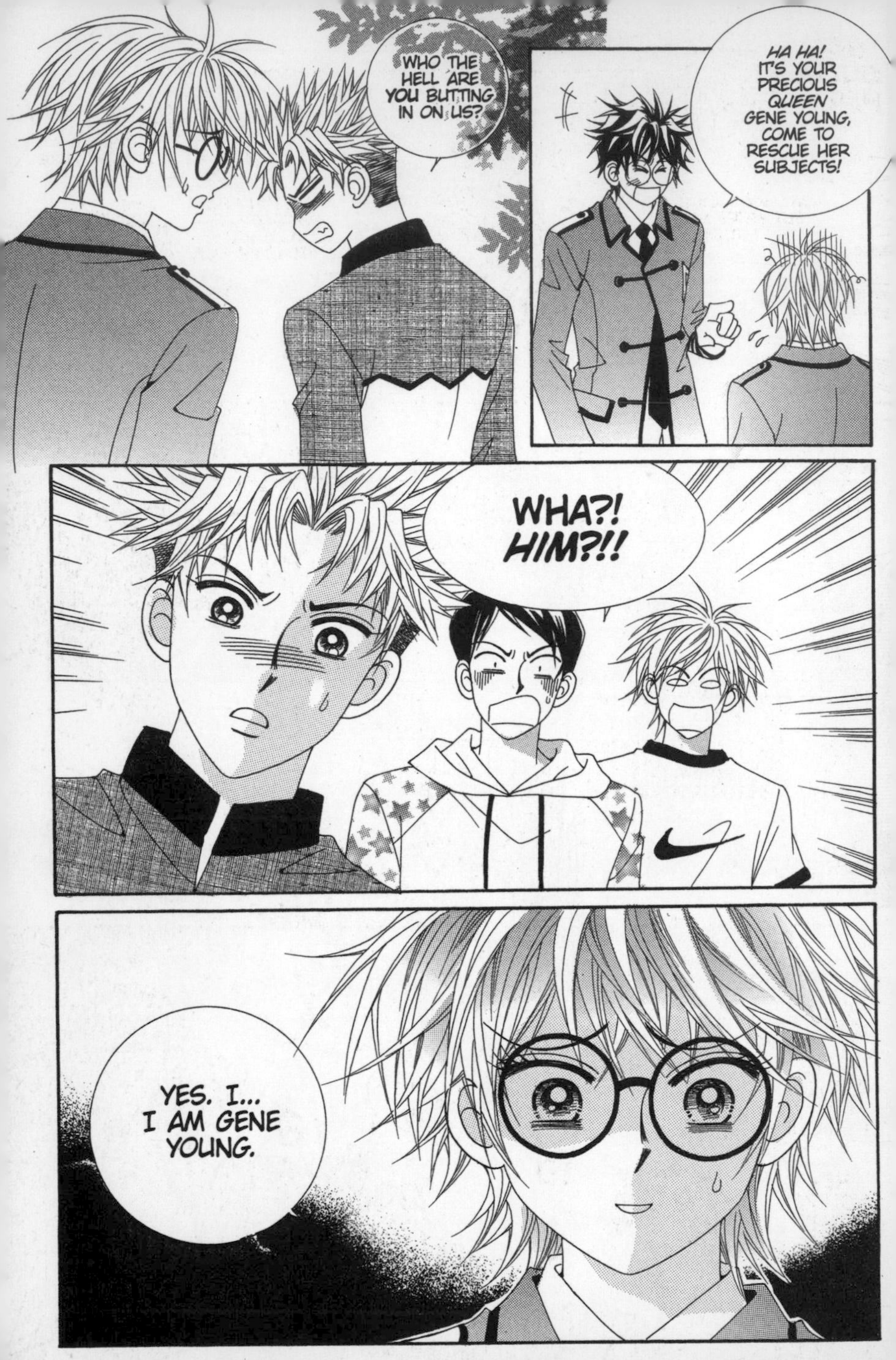
WHO THE HELL ARE YOU BUTTING IN ON US?
HA HA! IT'S YOUR PRECIOUS QUEEN GENE YOUNG, COME TO RESCUE HER SUBJECTS!
WHA?! HIM?!!
YES. I... I AM GENE YOUNG.

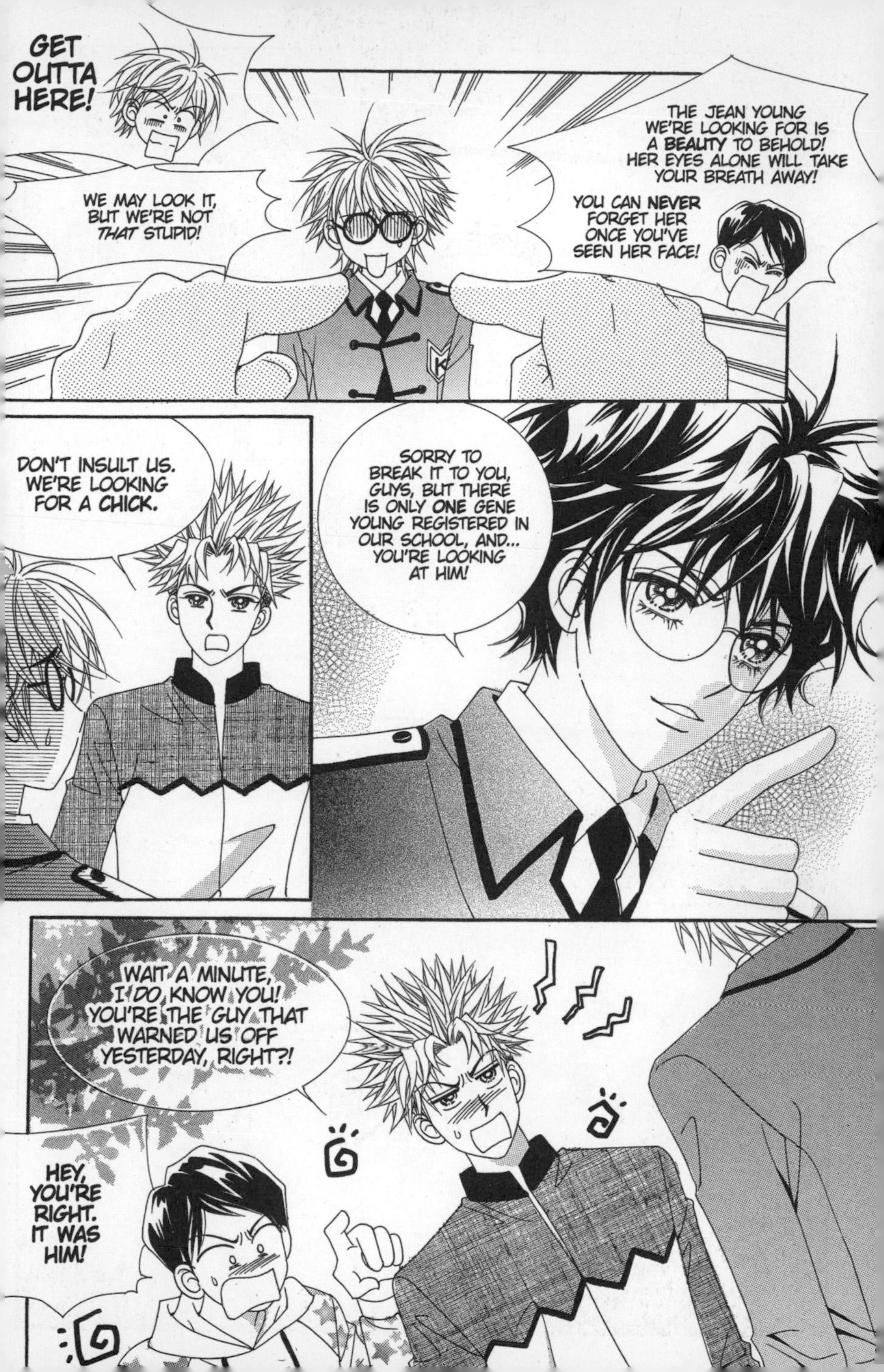
GET OUTTA HERE!
WE MAY LOOK IT, BUT WE'RE NOT *THAT* STUPID!
THE JEAN YOUNG WE'RE LOOKING FOR IS A **BEAUTY** TO BEHOLD! HER EYES ALONE WILL TAKE YOUR BREATH AWAY!
YOU CAN **NEVER** FORGET HER ONCE YOU'VE SEEN HER FACE!
DON'T INSULT US. WE'RE LOOKING FOR A **CHICK**.
SORRY TO BREAK IT TO YOU, GUYS, BUT THERE IS ONLY **ONE** GENE YOUNG REGISTERED IN OUR SCHOOL, AND... YOU'RE LOOKING AT HIM!
WAIT A MINUTE, I *DO* KNOW YOU! YOU'RE THE GUY THAT WARNED US OFF YESTERDAY, RIGHT?!
HEY, YOU'RE RIGHT. IT WAS HIM!

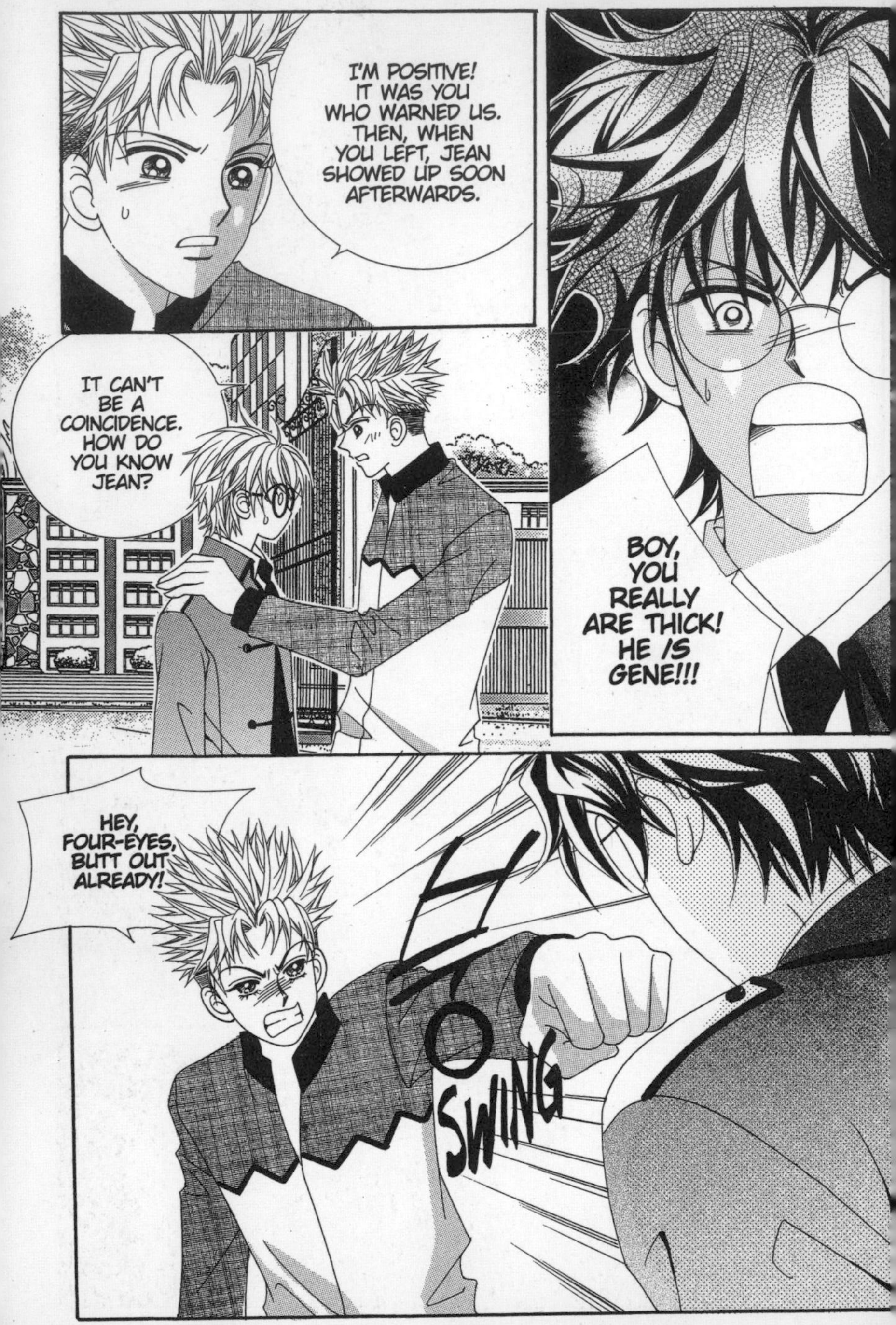
I'M POSITIVE! IT WAS YOU WHO WARNED US. THEN, WHEN YOU LEFT, JEAN SHOWED UP SOON AFTERWARDS.
IT CAN'T BE A COINCIDENCE. HOW DO YOU KNOW JEAN?
BOY, YOU REALLY ARE THICK! HE IS GENE!!!
HEY, FOUR-EYES, BUTT OUT ALREADY!
SWING

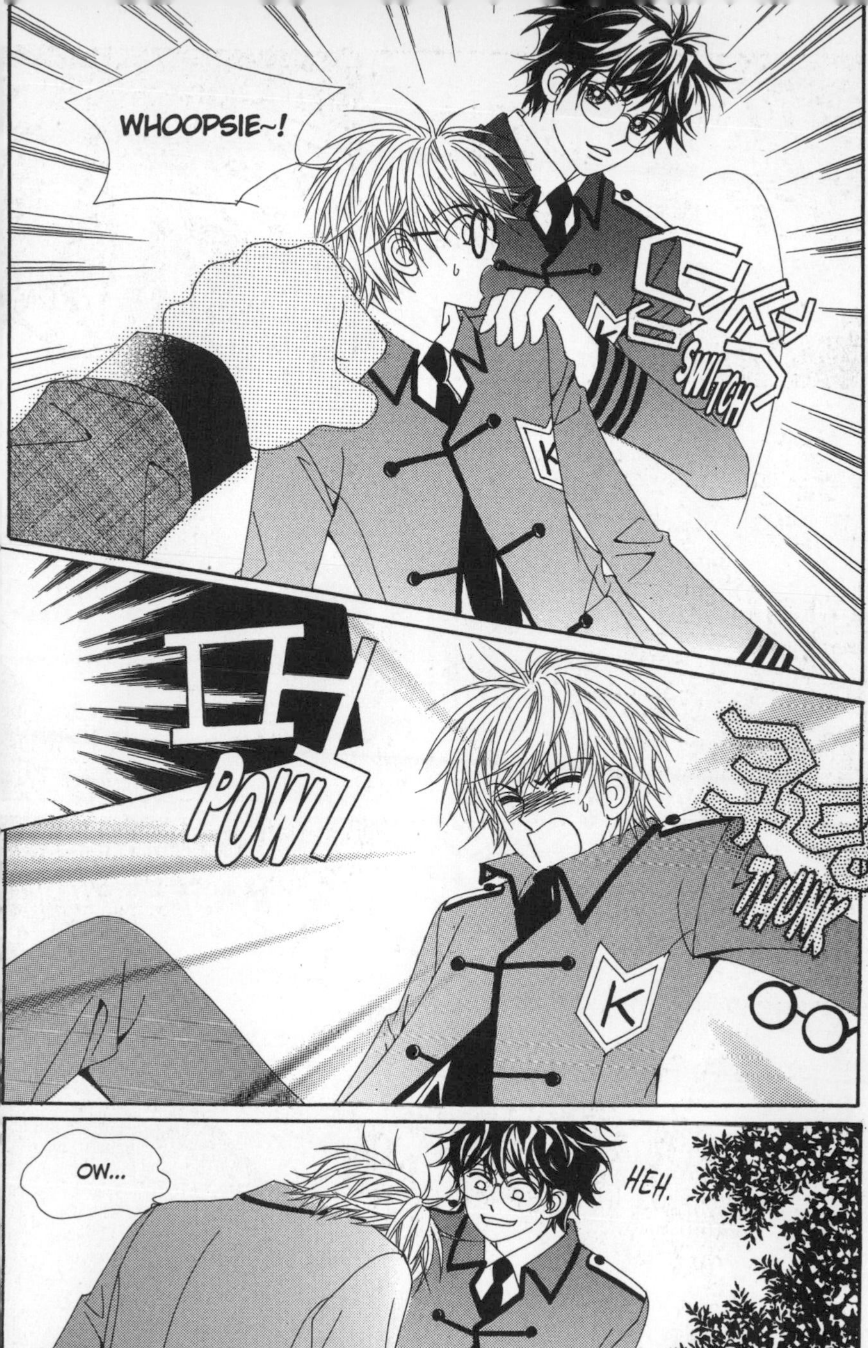
WHOOPSIE~!
SWITCH
POW
THUNK
OW...
HEH.

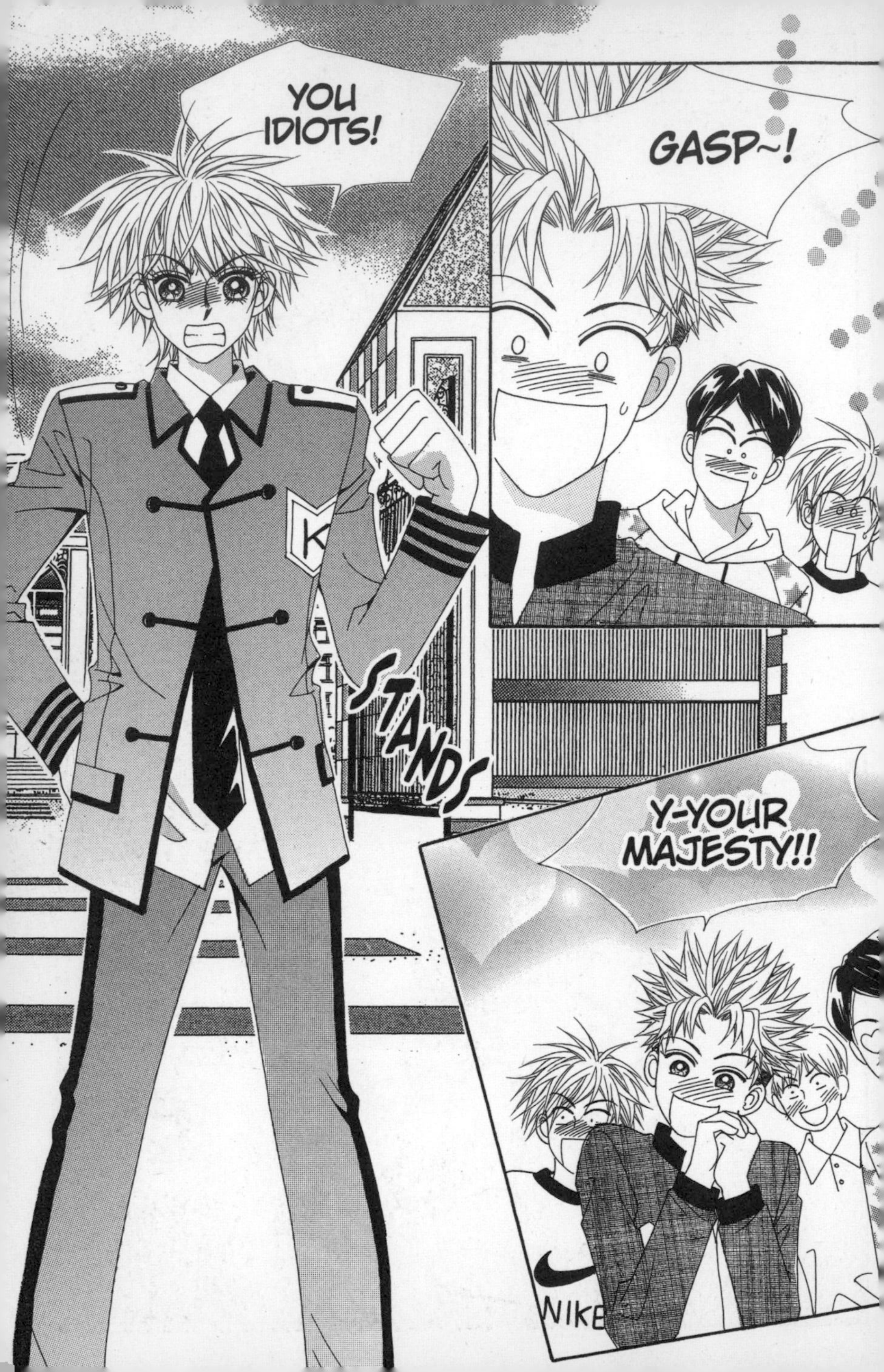
YOU IDIOTS!
STANDS
GASP~!
Y-YOUR MAJESTY!!
NIKE

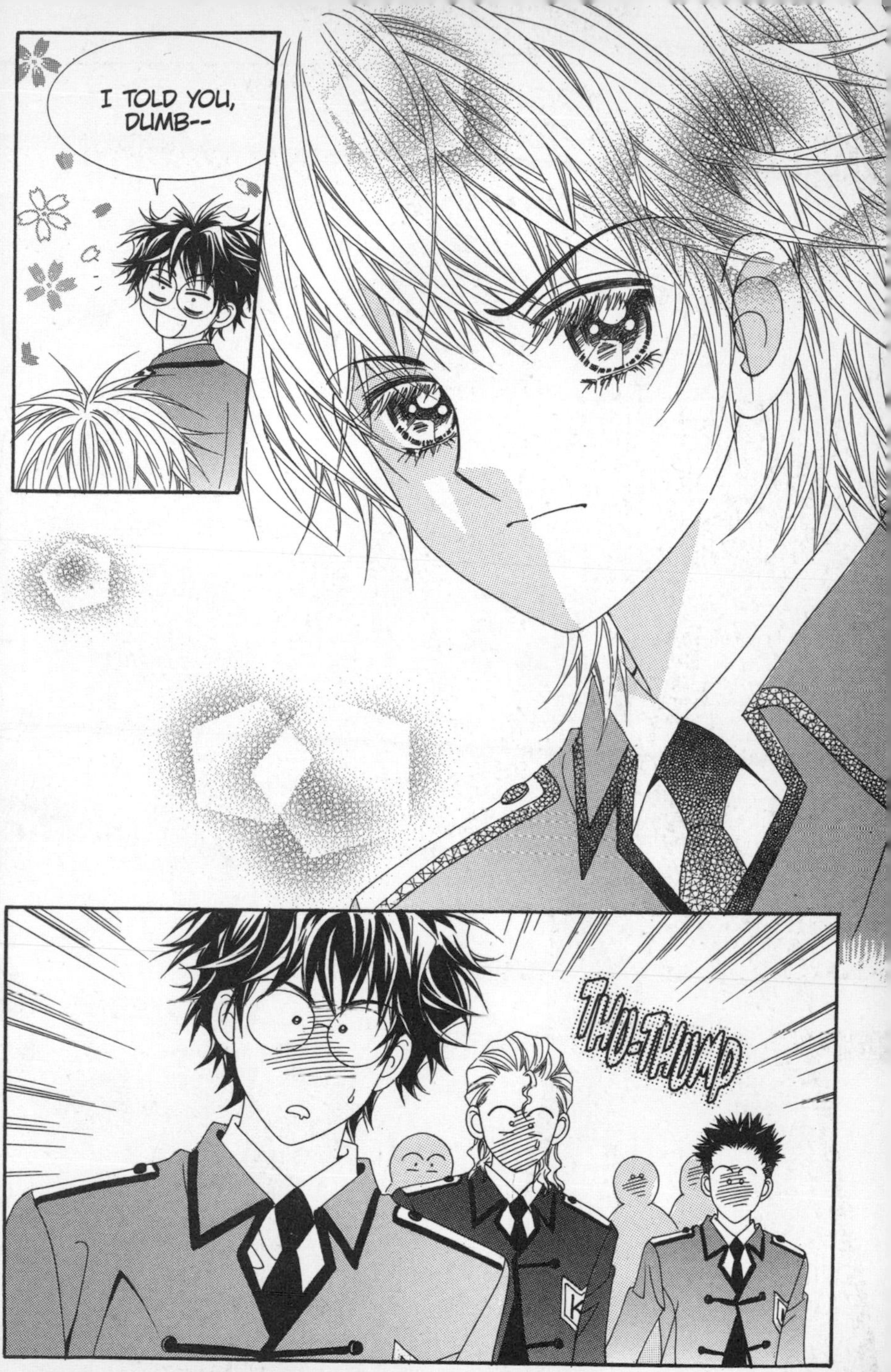

I TOLD YOU, DUMB--
THU-THUMP

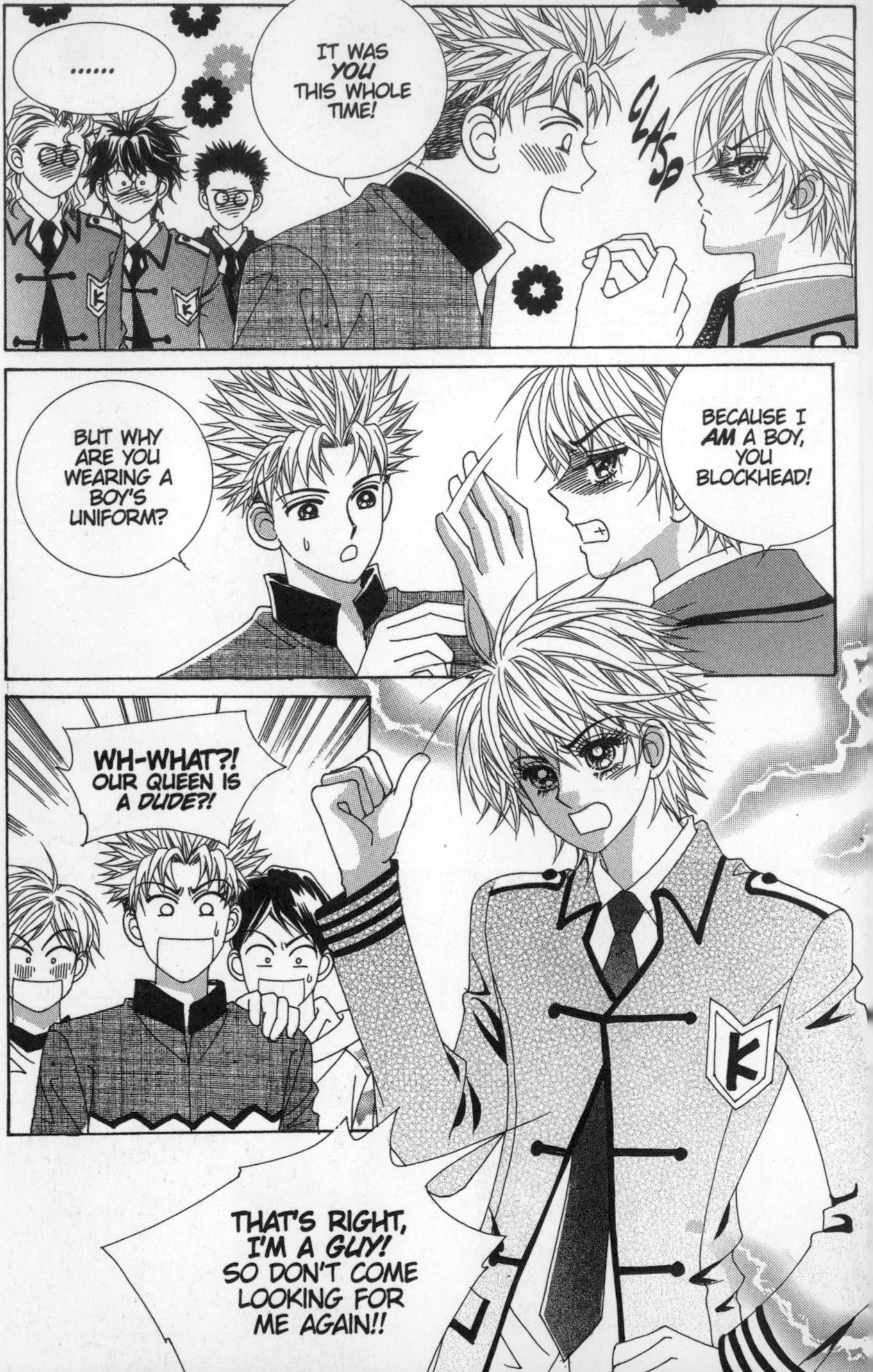
......
IT WAS YOU THIS WHOLE TIME!
CLASP
BUT WHY ARE YOU WEARING A BOY'S UNIFORM?
BECAUSE I AM A BOY, YOU BLOCKHEAD!
WH-WHAT?! OUR QUEEN IS A DUDE?!
THAT'S RIGHT, I'M A GUY! SO DON'T COME LOOKING FOR ME AGAIN!!

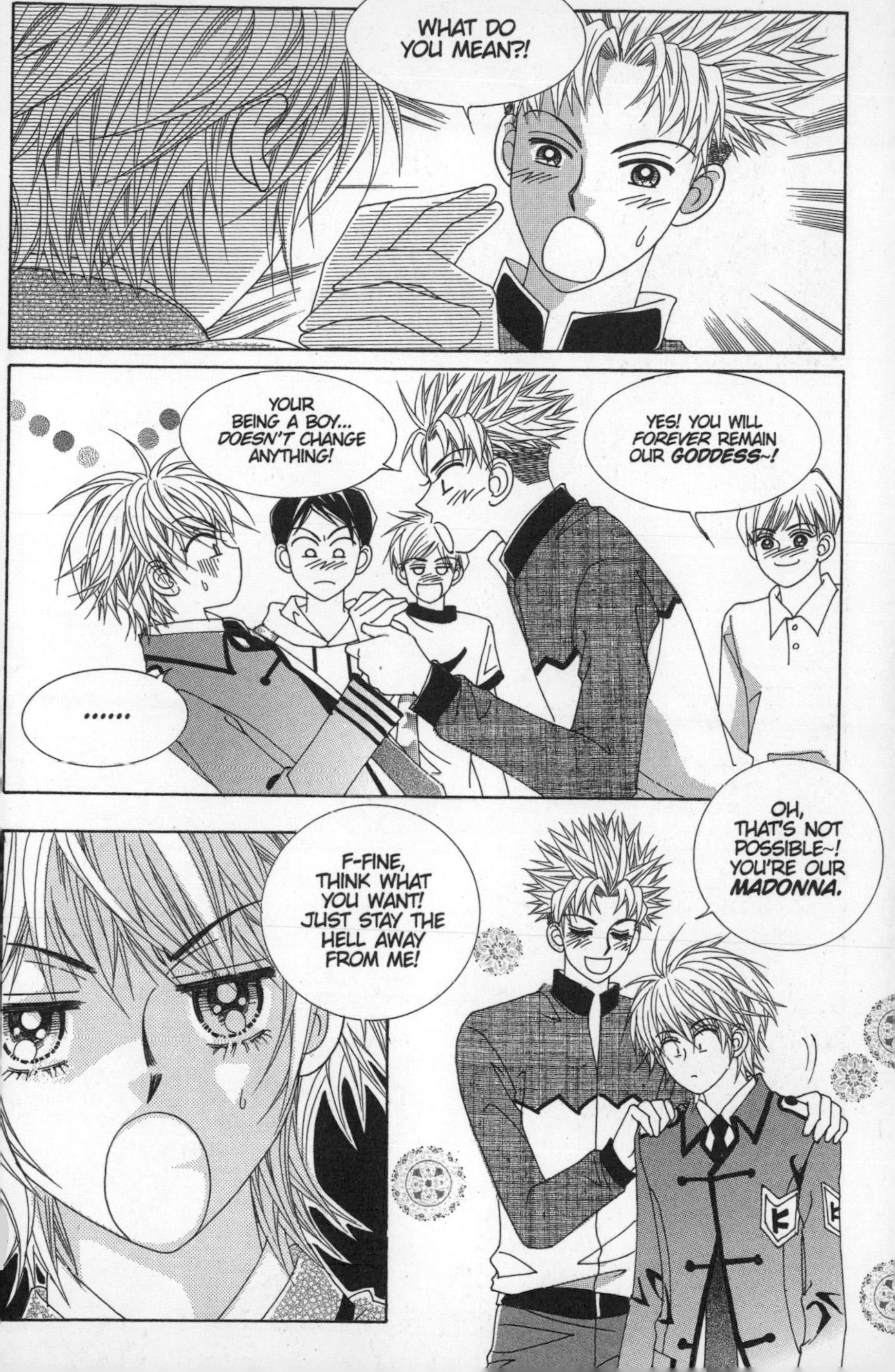
WHAT DO YOU MEAN?!
YOUR BEING A BOY... DOESN'T CHANGE ANYTHING!
YES! YOU WILL FOREVER REMAIN OUR GODDESS~!
......
F-FINE, THINK WHAT YOU WANT! JUST STAY THE HELL AWAY FROM ME!
OH, THAT'S NOT POSSIBLE~! YOU'RE OUR MADONNA.

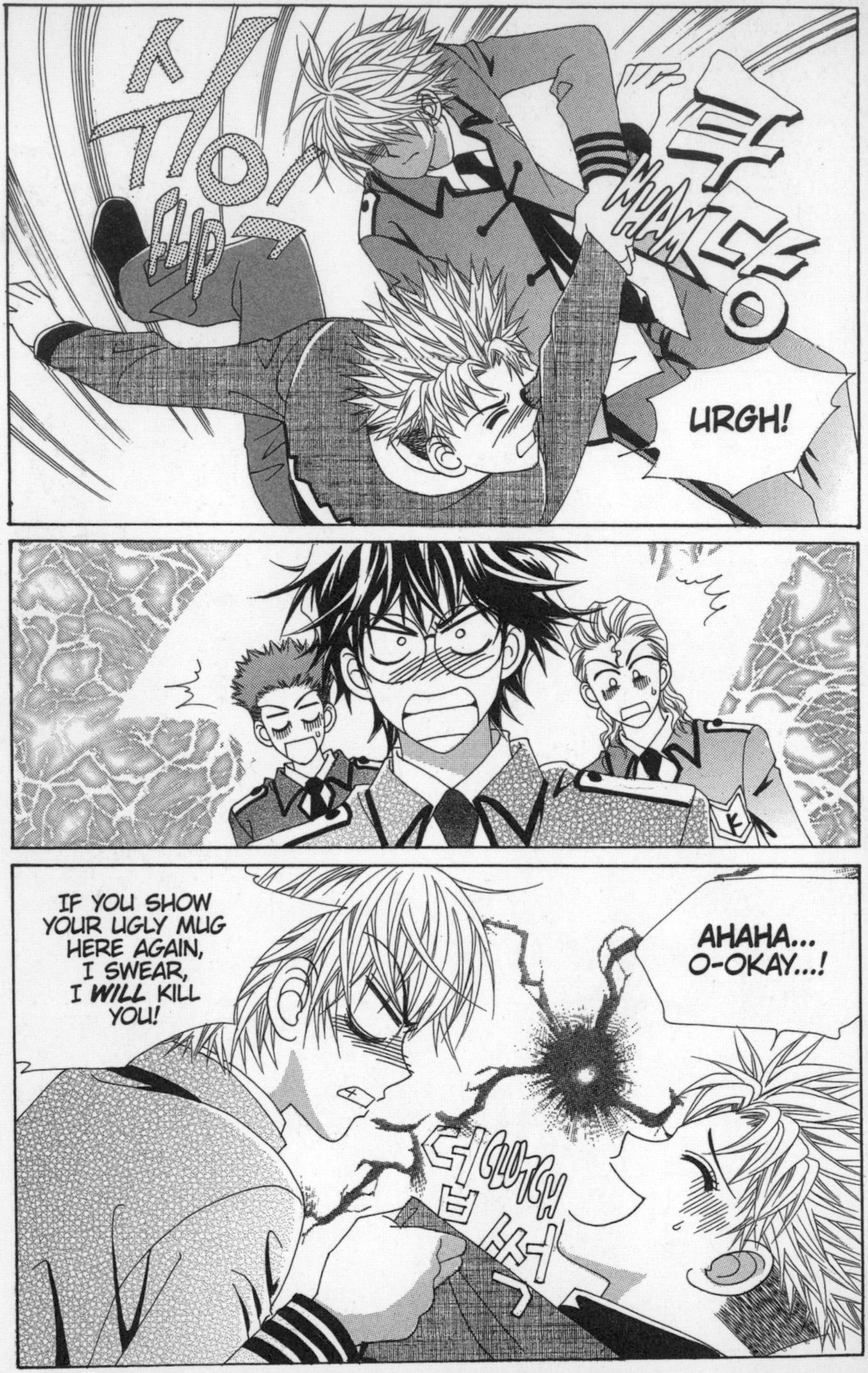
FLIP
WHAM
URGH!
IF YOU SHOW YOUR UGLY MUG HERE AGAIN, I SWEAR, I *WILL* KILL YOU!
AHAHA... O-OKAY...!
CLUTCH

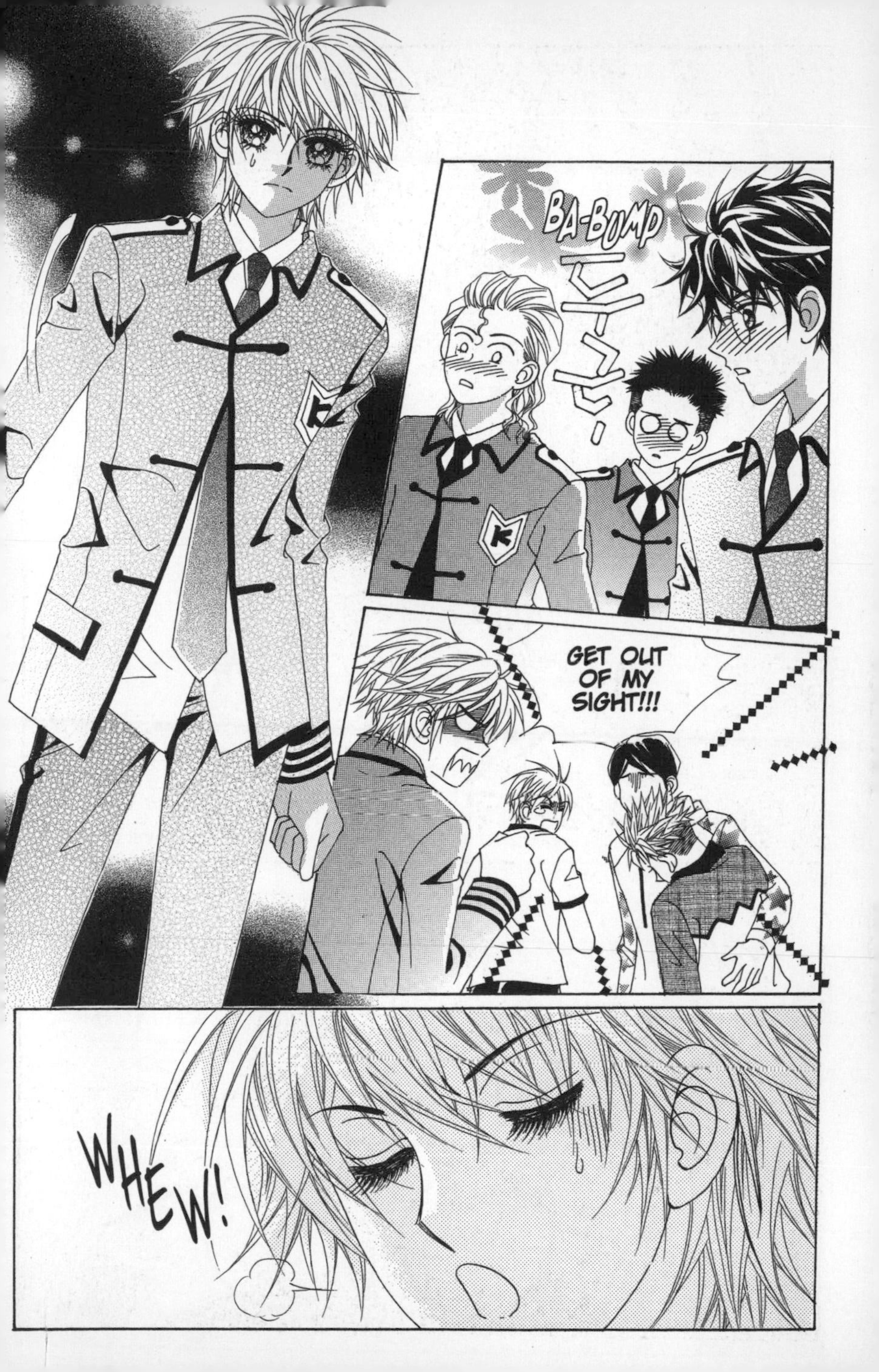
BA-BUMP
GET OUT OF MY SIGHT!!!
WHEW!

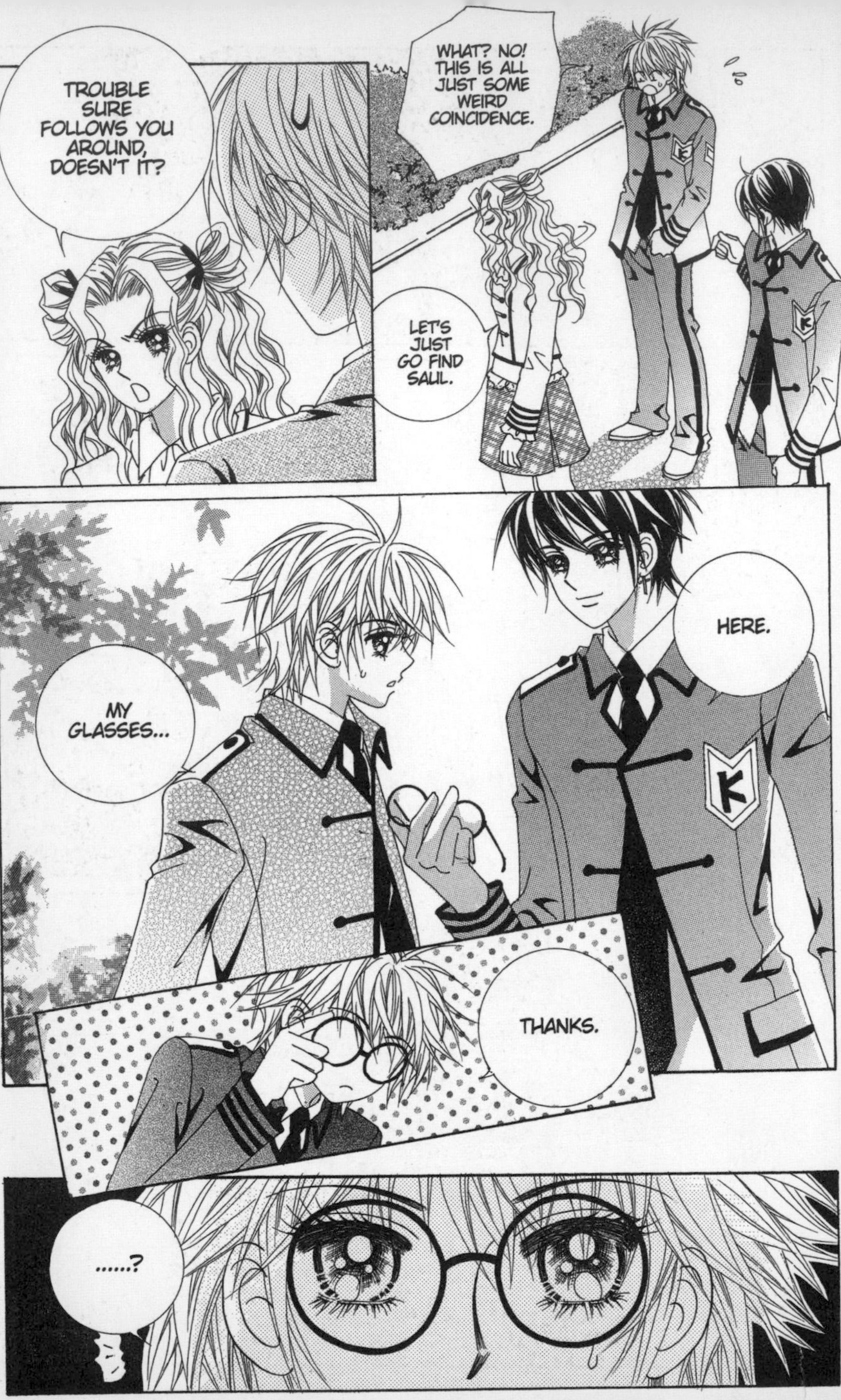
TROUBLE SURE FOLLOWS YOU AROUND, DOESN'T IT?
WHAT? NO! THIS IS ALL JUST SOME WEIRD COINCIDENCE.
LET'S JUST GO FIND SAUL.
MY GLASSES...
HERE.
THANKS.
......?

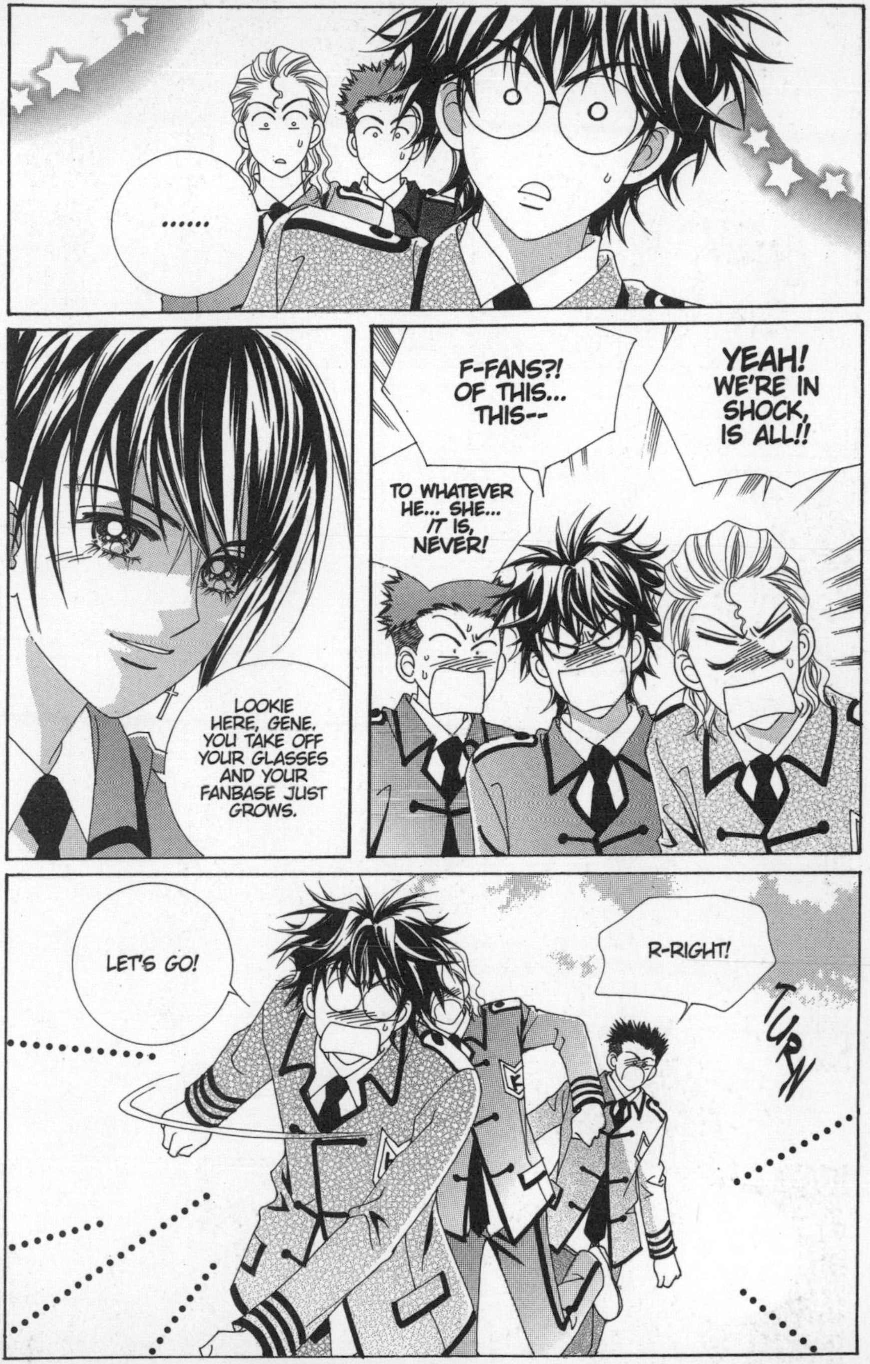
......
LOOKIE HERE, GENE. YOU TAKE OFF YOUR GLASSES AND YOUR FANBASE JUST GROWS.
F-FANS?! OF THIS... THIS--
YEAH! WE'RE IN SHOCK, IS ALL!!
TO WHATEVER HE... SHE... *IT* IS, NEVER!
LET'S GO!
R-RIGHT!
TURN

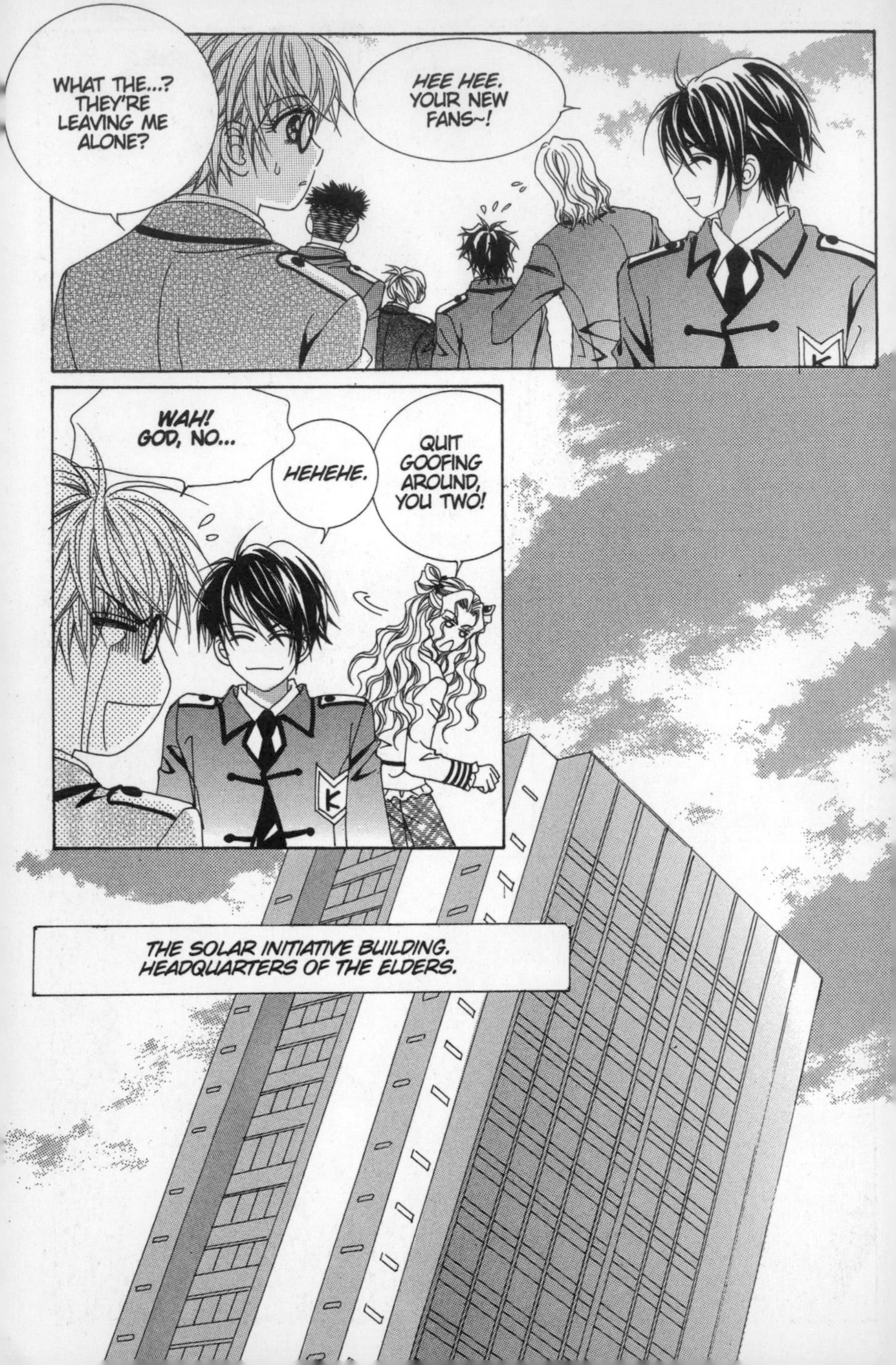
WHAT THE...? THEY'RE LEAVING ME ALONE?
HEE HEE. YOUR NEW FANS~!
WAH! GOD, NO...
HEHEHE.
QUIT GOOFING AROUND, YOU TWO!
THE SOLAR INITIATIVE BUILDING. HEADQUARTERS OF THE ELDERS.

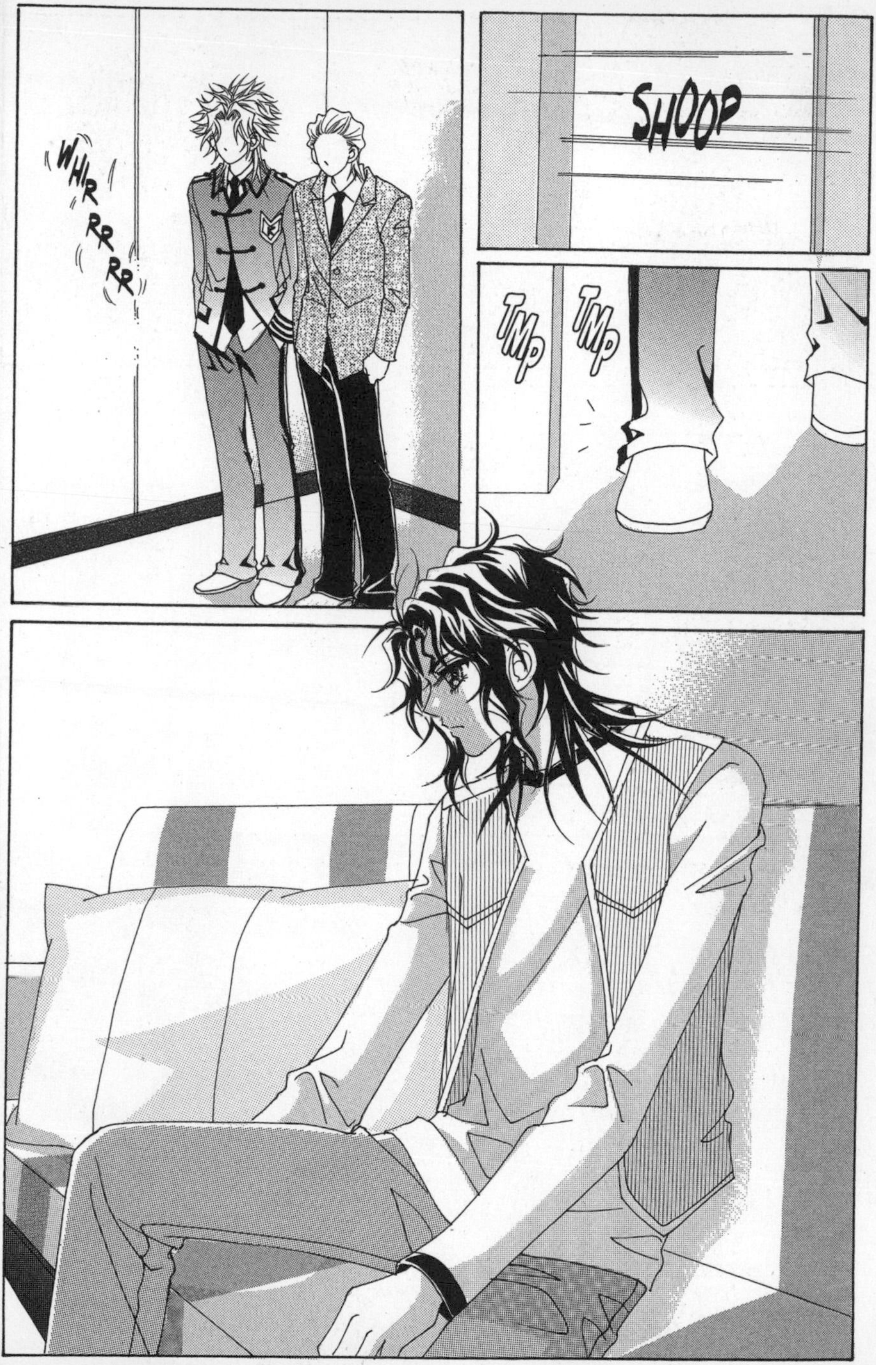
WHIRRRRRR
SHOOP
TMP TMP

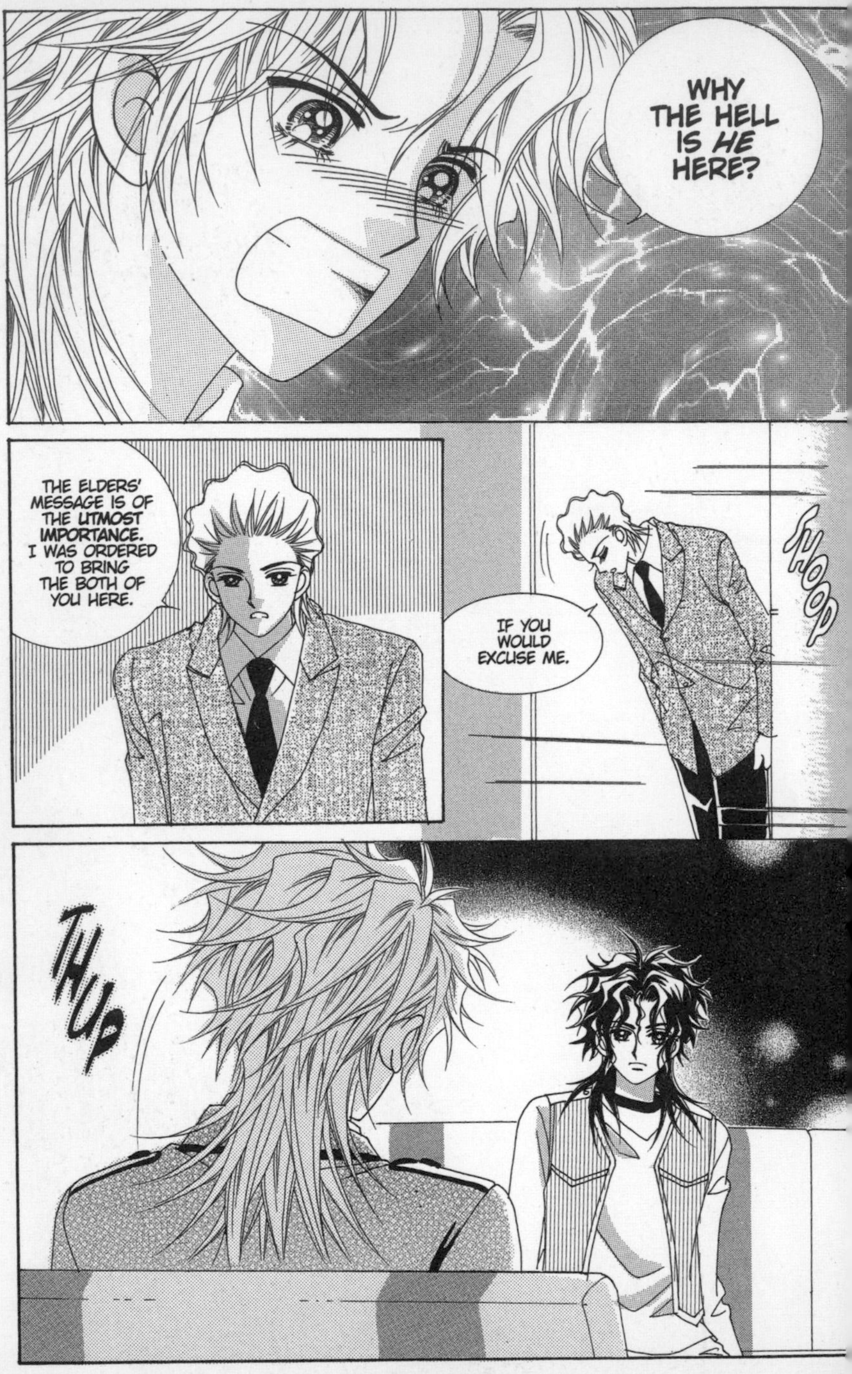
WHY THE HELL IS *HE* HERE?
THE ELDERS' MESSAGE IS OF THE UTMOST IMPORTANCE. I WAS ORDERED TO BRING THE BOTH OF YOU HERE.
IF YOU WOULD EXCUSE ME.
SHOOP
THUP

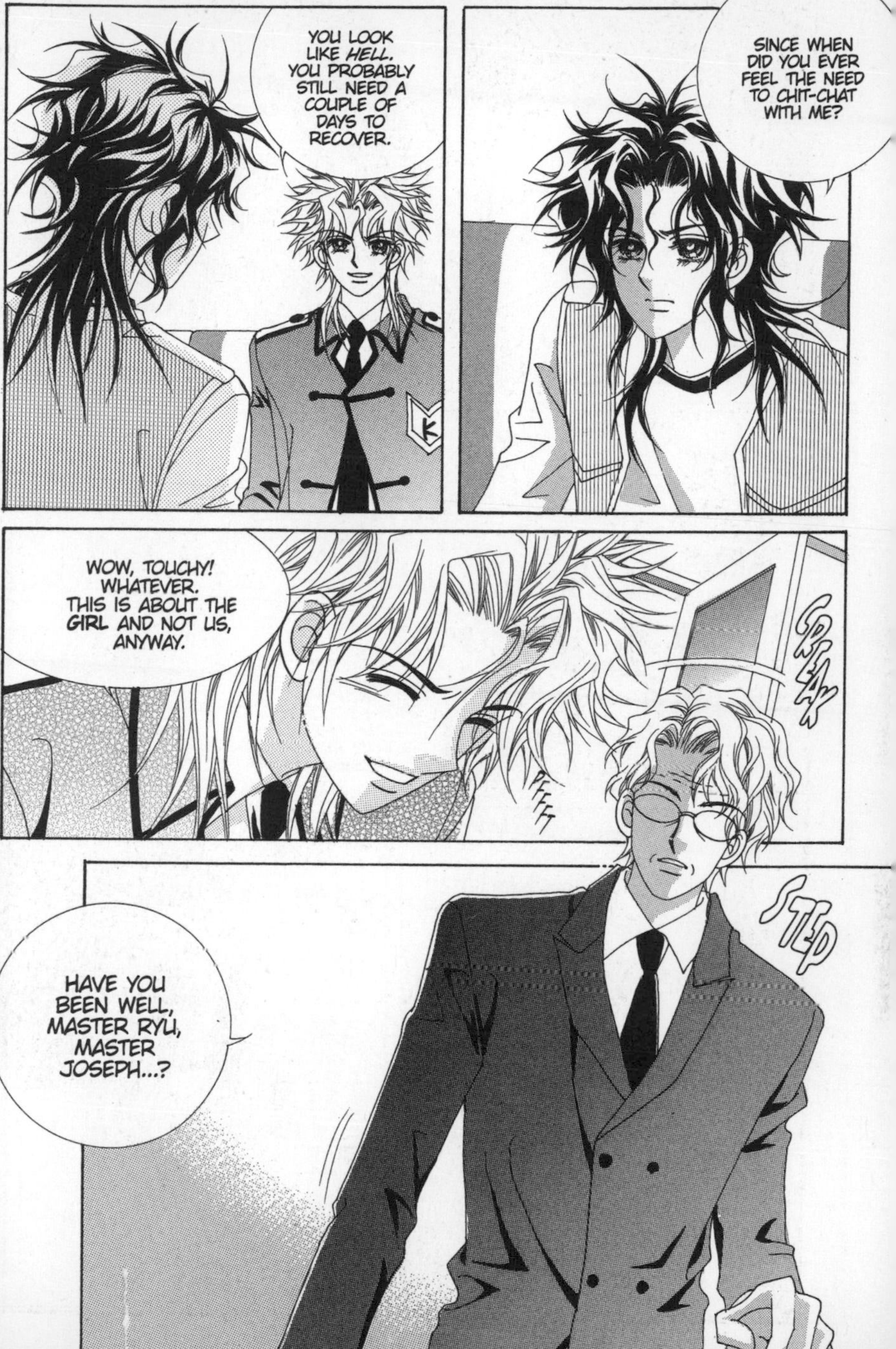
YOU LOOK LIKE *HELL*. YOU PROBABLY STILL NEED A COUPLE OF DAYS TO RECOVER.
SINCE WHEN DID YOU EVER FEEL THE NEED TO CHIT-CHAT WITH ME?
WOW, TOUCHY! WHATEVER. THIS IS ABOUT THE GIRL AND NOT US, ANYWAY.
PFFFT
CREAK
STEP
HAVE YOU BEEN WELL, MASTER RYU, MASTER JOSEPH...?

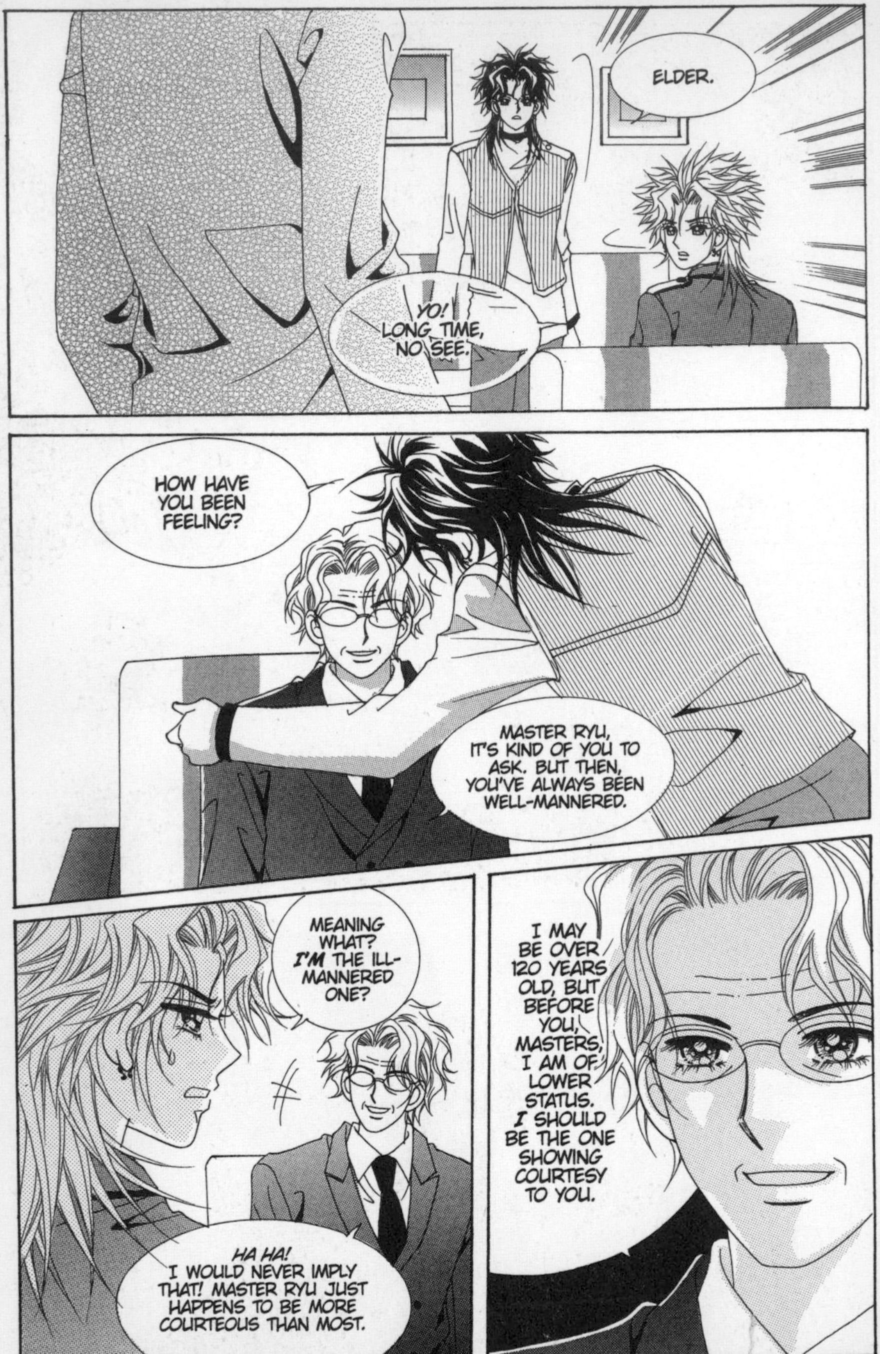
ELDER.
YO! LONG TIME, NO SEE.
HOW HAVE YOU BEEN FEELING?
MASTER RYU, IT'S KIND OF YOU TO ASK. BUT THEN, YOU'VE ALWAYS BEEN WELL-MANNERED.
MEANING WHAT? I'M THE ILL-MANNERED ONE?
HA HA! I WOULD NEVER IMPLY THAT! MASTER RYU JUST HAPPENS TO BE MORE COURTEOUS THAN MOST.
I MAY BE OVER 120 YEARS OLD, BUT BEFORE YOU, MASTERS, I AM OF LOWER STATUS. I SHOULD BE THE ONE SHOWING COURTESY TO YOU.

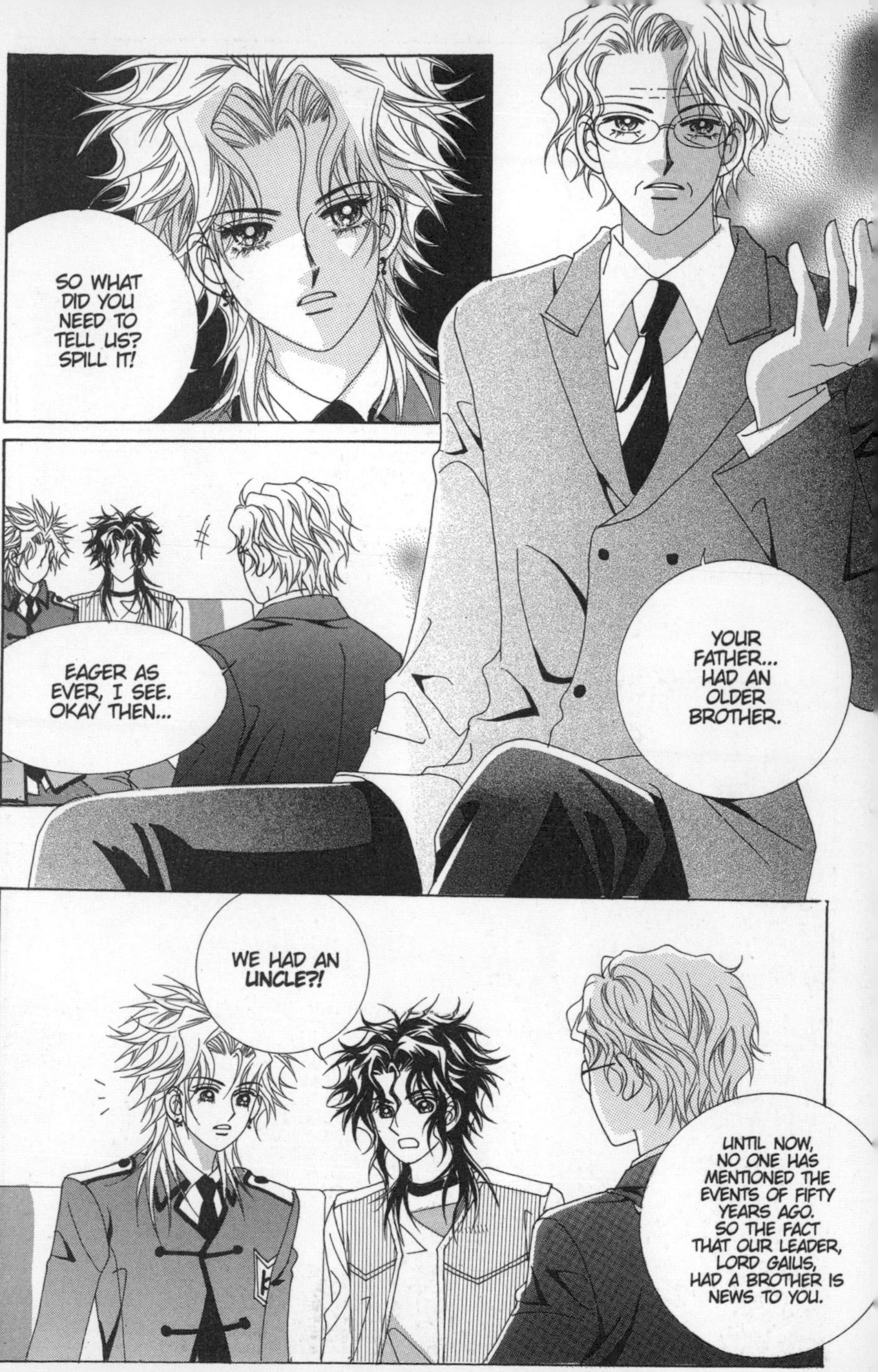
SO WHAT DID YOU NEED TO TELL US? SPILL IT!
EAGER AS EVER, I SEE. OKAY THEN...
YOUR FATHER... HAD AN OLDER BROTHER.
WE HAD AN UNCLE?!
UNTIL NOW, NO ONE HAS MENTIONED THE EVENTS OF FIFTY YEARS AGO. SO THE FACT THAT OUR LEADER, LORD GAIUS, HAD A BROTHER IS NEWS TO YOU.

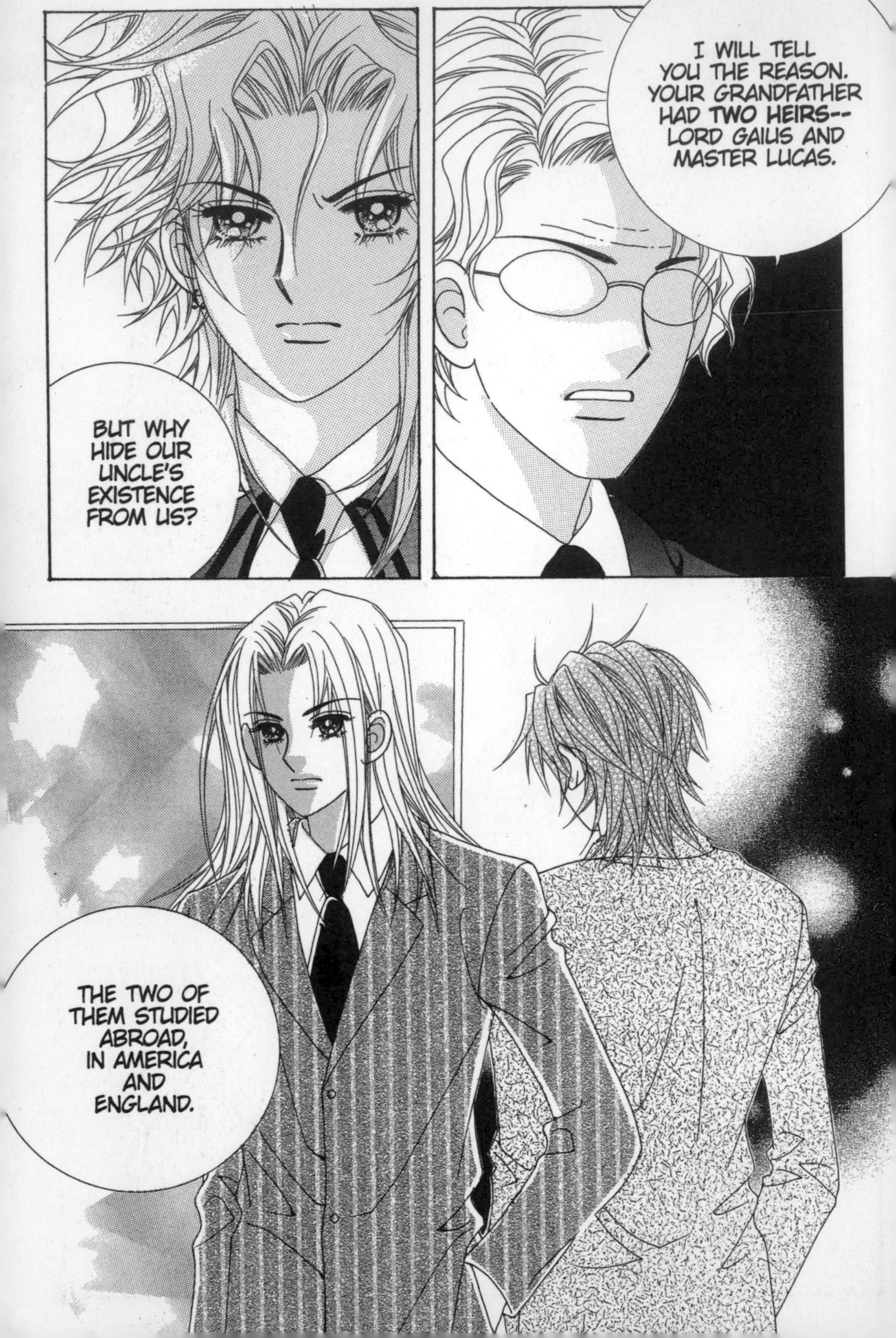
BUT WHY HIDE OUR UNCLE'S EXISTENCE FROM US?
I WILL TELL YOU THE REASON. YOUR GRANDFATHER HAD TWO HEIRS-- LORD GAIUS AND MASTER LUCAS.
THE TWO OF THEM STUDIED ABROAD, IN AMERICA AND ENGLAND.

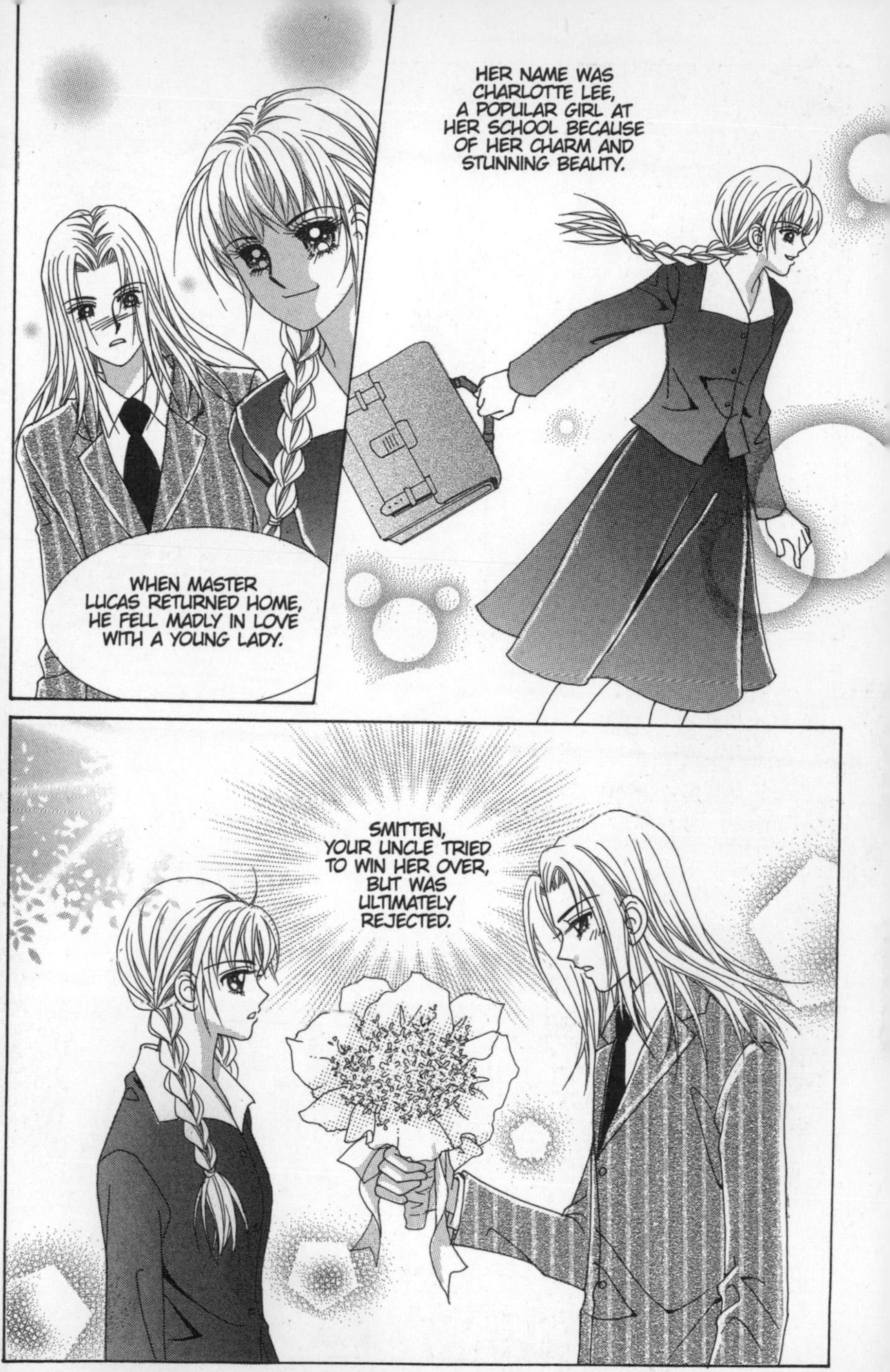
WHEN MASTER LUCAS RETURNED HOME, HE FELL MADLY IN LOVE WITH A YOUNG LADY.
HER NAME WAS CHARLOTTE LEE, A POPULAR GIRL AT HER SCHOOL BECAUSE OF HER CHARM AND STUNNING BEAUTY.
SMITTEN, YOUR UNCLE TRIED TO WIN HER OVER, BUT WAS ULTIMATELY REJECTED.

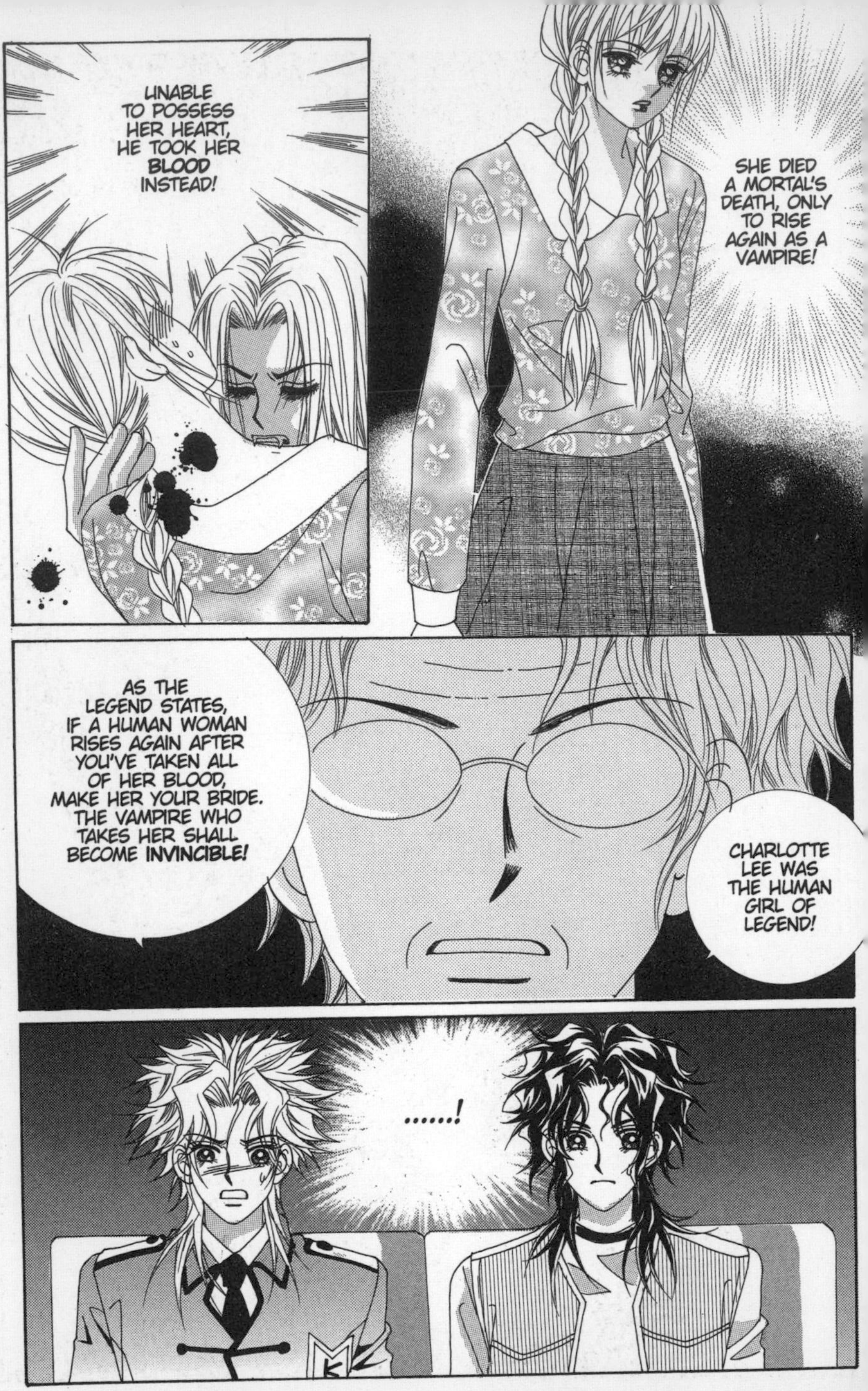
UNABLE TO POSSESS HER HEART, HE TOOK HER BLOOD INSTEAD!
SHE DIED A MORTAL'S DEATH, ONLY TO RISE AGAIN AS A VAMPIRE!
AS THE LEGEND STATES, IF A HUMAN WOMAN RISES AGAIN AFTER YOU'VE TAKEN ALL OF HER BLOOD, MAKE HER YOUR BRIDE. THE VAMPIRE WHO TAKES HER SHALL BECOME INVINCIBLE!
CHARLOTTE LEE WAS THE HUMAN GIRL OF LEGEND!
......!

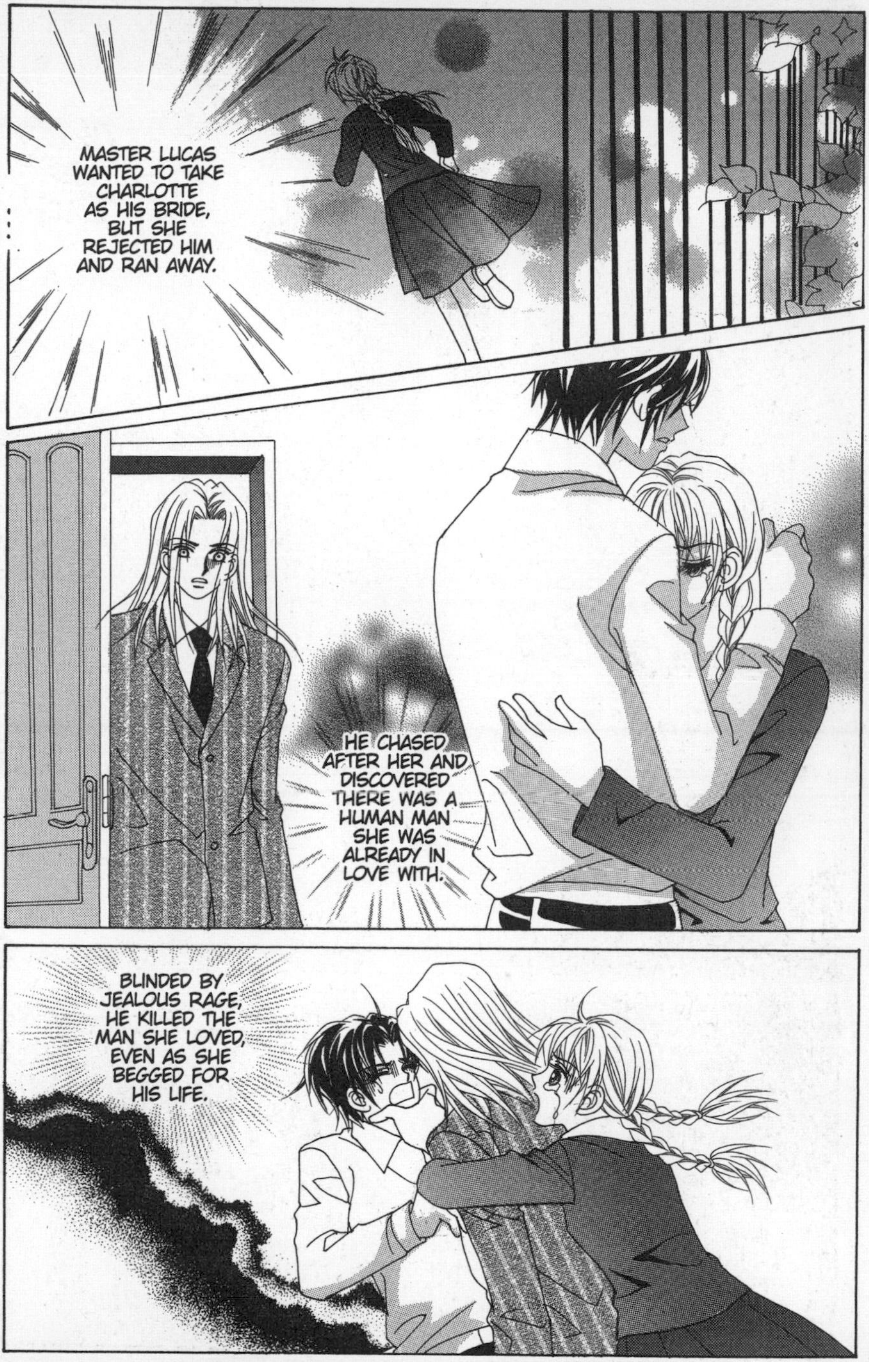
...
MASTER LUCAS WANTED TO TAKE CHARLOTTE AS HIS BRIDE, BUT SHE REJECTED HIM AND RAN AWAY.
HE CHASED AFTER HER AND DISCOVERED THERE WAS A HUMAN MAN SHE WAS ALREADY IN LOVE WITH.
BLINDED BY JEALOUS RAGE, HE KILLED THE MAN SHE LOVED, EVEN AS SHE BEGGED FOR HIS LIFE.

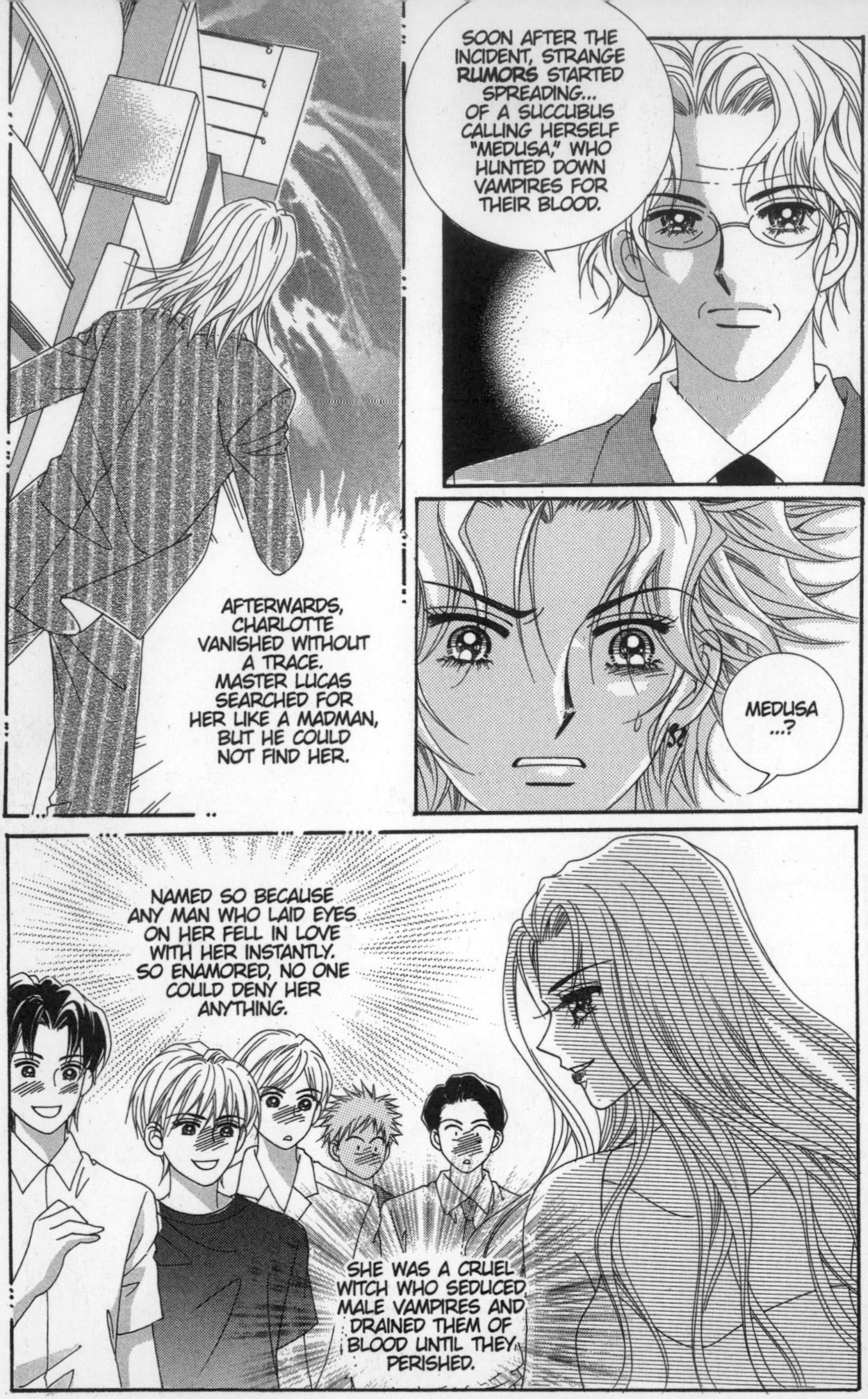
AFTERWARDS, CHARLOTTE VANISHED WITHOUT A TRACE. MASTER LUCAS SEARCHED FOR HER LIKE A MADMAN, BUT HE COULD NOT FIND HER.
SOON AFTER THE INCIDENT, STRANGE RUMORS STARTED SPREADING... OF A SUCCUBUS CALLING HERSELF "MEDUSA," WHO HUNTED DOWN VAMPIRES FOR THEIR BLOOD.
MEDUSA ...?
NAMED SO BECAUSE ANY MAN WHO LAID EYES ON HER FELL IN LOVE WITH HER INSTANTLY. SO ENAMORED, NO ONE COULD DENY HER ANYTHING.
SHE WAS A CRUEL WITCH WHO SEDUCED MALE VAMPIRES AND DRAINED THEM OF BLOOD UNTIL THEY PERISHED.

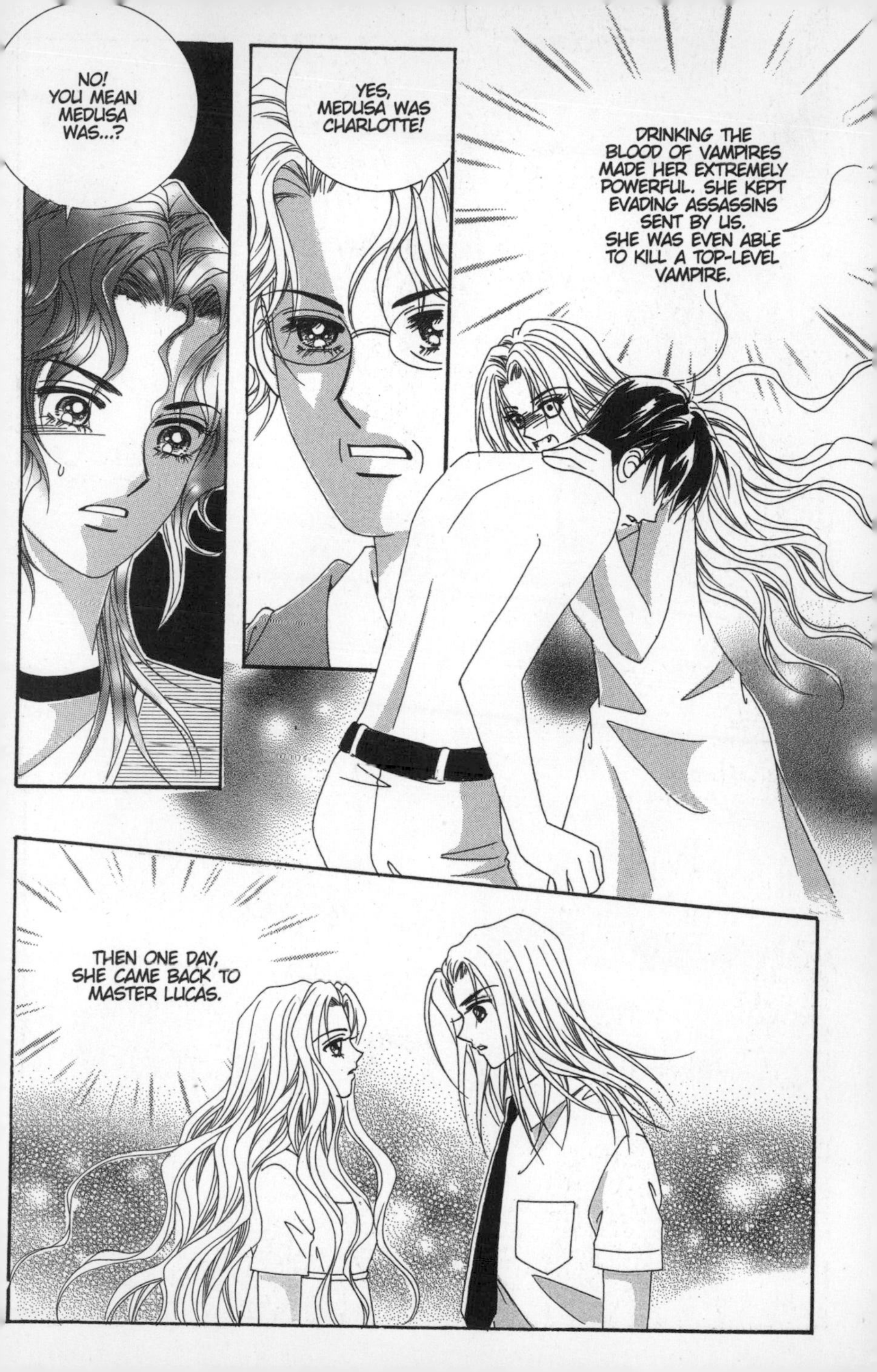
NO! YOU MEAN MEDUSA WAS...?
YES, MEDUSA WAS CHARLOTTE!
DRINKING THE BLOOD OF VAMPIRES MADE HER EXTREMELY POWERFUL. SHE KEPT EVADING ASSASSINS SENT BY US. SHE WAS EVEN ABLE TO KILL A TOP-LEVEL VAMPIRE.
THEN ONE DAY, SHE CAME BACK TO MASTER LUCAS.

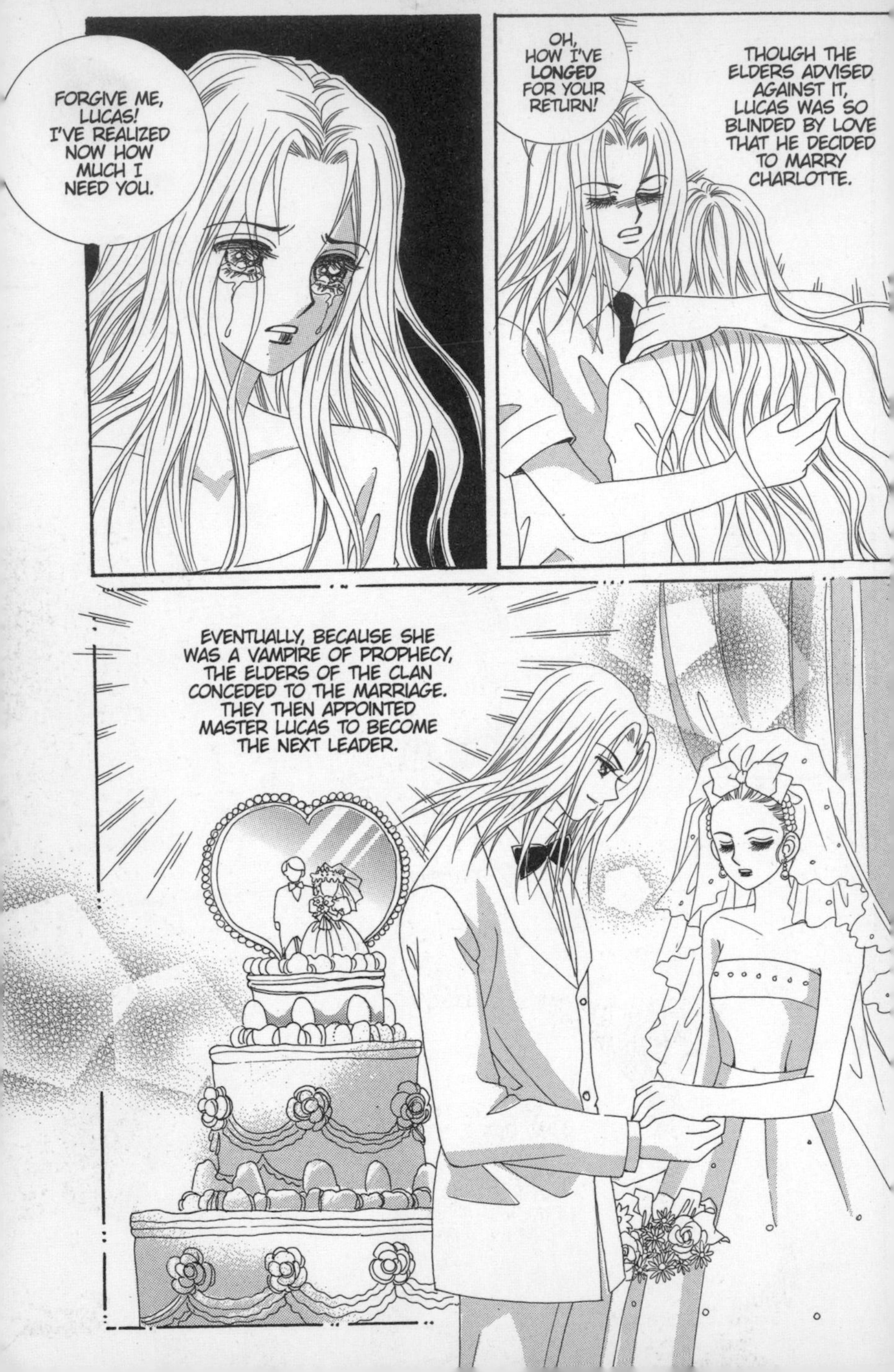
FORGIVE ME, LUCAS! I'VE REALIZED NOW HOW MUCH I NEED YOU.
OH, HOW I'VE LONGED FOR YOUR RETURN!
THOUGH THE ELDERS ADVISED AGAINST IT, LUCAS WAS SO BLINDED BY LOVE THAT HE DECIDED TO MARRY CHARLOTTE.
EVENTUALLY, BECAUSE SHE WAS A VAMPIRE OF PROPHECY, THE ELDERS OF THE CLAN CONCEDED TO THE MARRIAGE. THEY THEN APPOINTED MASTER LUCAS TO BECOME THE NEXT LEADER.

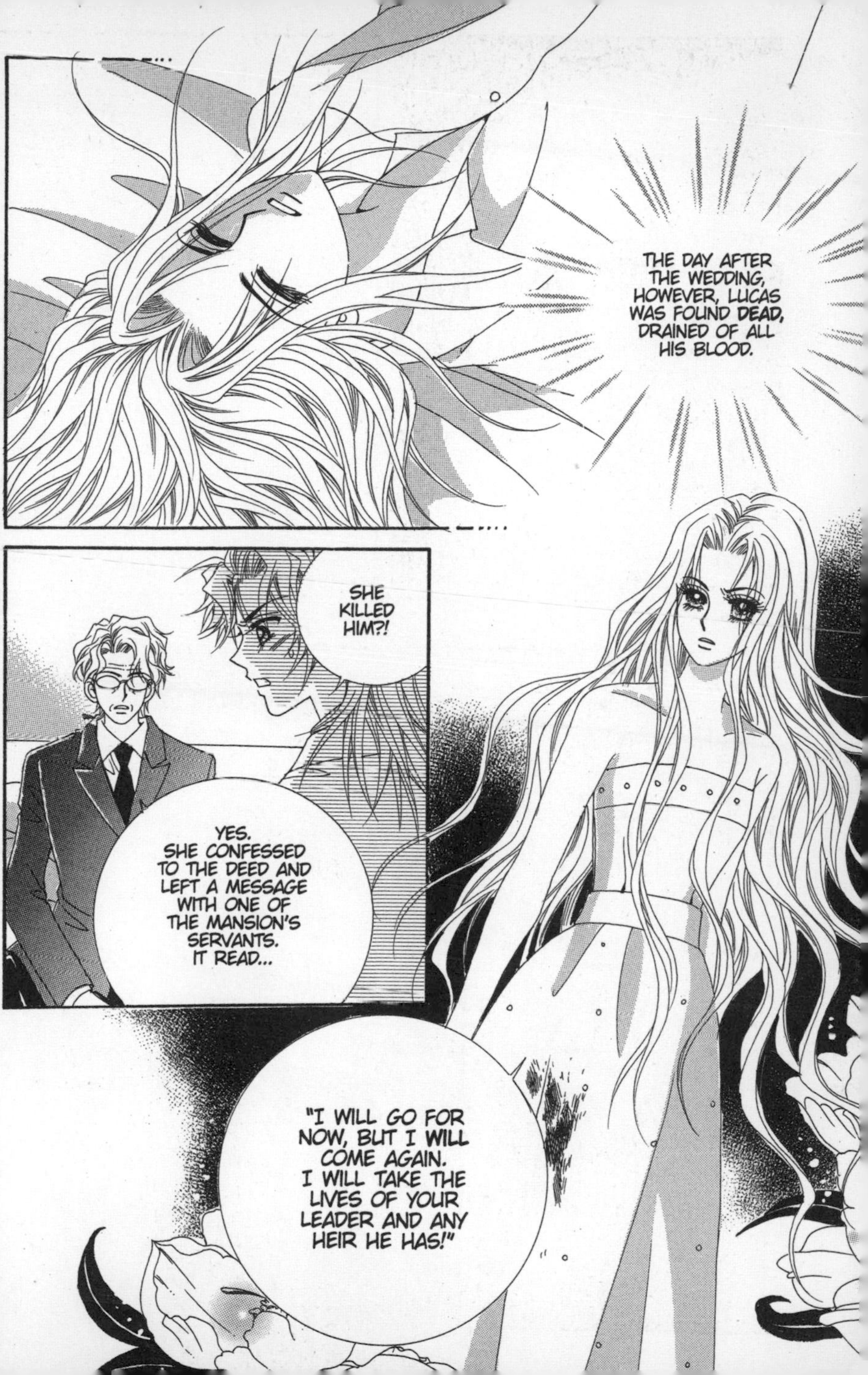
THE DAY AFTER THE WEDDING, HOWEVER, LUCAS WAS FOUND DEAD, DRAINED OF ALL HIS BLOOD.
SHE KILLED HIM?!
YES. SHE CONFESSED TO THE DEED AND LEFT A MESSAGE WITH ONE OF THE MANSION'S SERVANTS. IT READ...
"I WILL GO FOR NOW, BUT I WILL COME AGAIN. I WILL TAKE THE LIVES OF YOUR LEADER AND ANY HEIR HE HAS!"

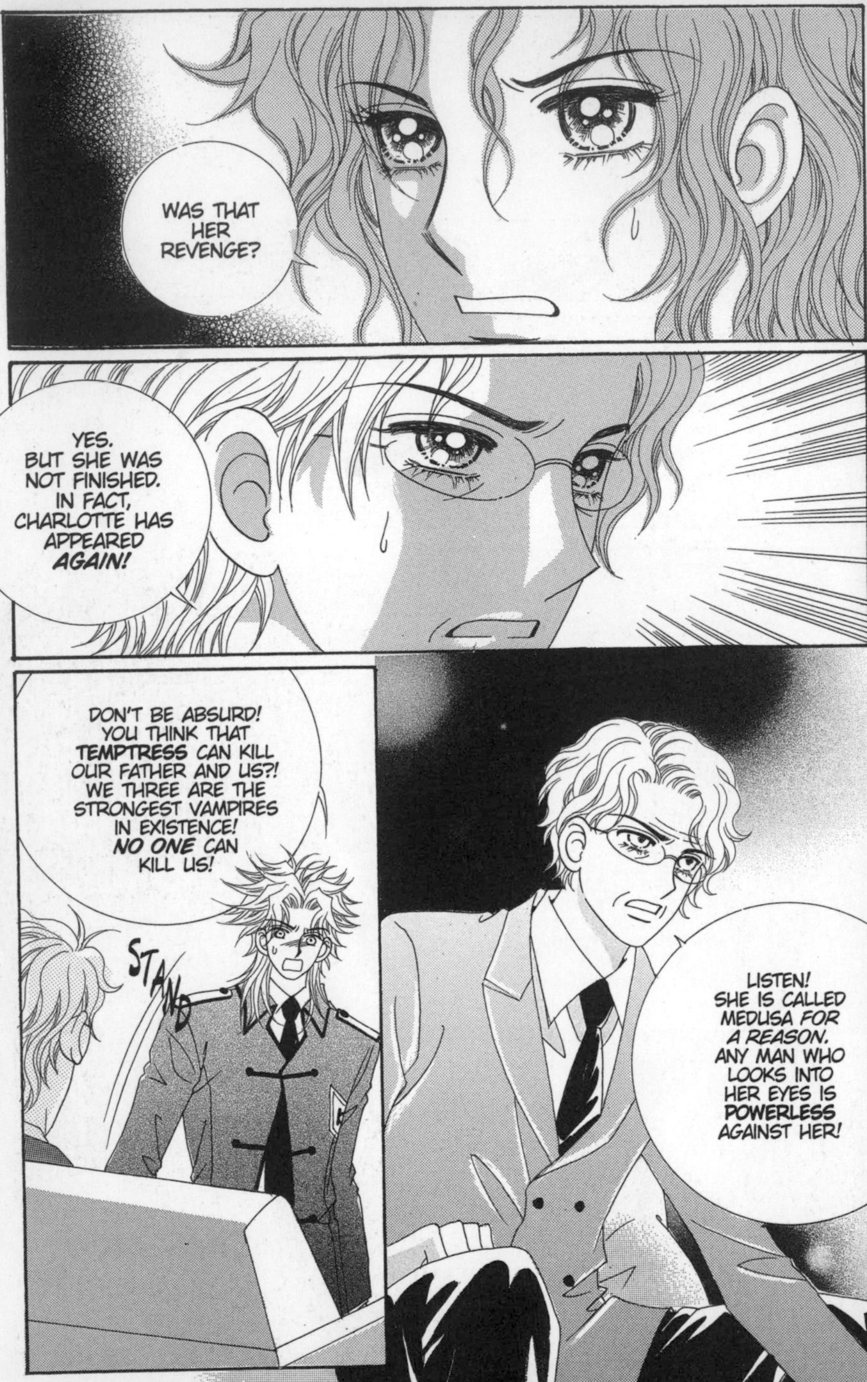
WAS THAT HER REVENGE?
YES. BUT SHE WAS NOT FINISHED. IN FACT, CHARLOTTE HAS APPEARED **AGAIN!**
DON'T BE ABSURD! YOU THINK THAT **TEMPTRESS** CAN KILL OUR FATHER AND US?! WE THREE ARE THE STRONGEST VAMPIRES IN EXISTENCE! ***NO ONE*** CAN KILL US!
STAND
LISTEN! SHE IS CALLED MEDUSA *FOR A REASON*. ANY MAN WHO LOOKS INTO HER EYES IS **POWERLESS** AGAINST HER!

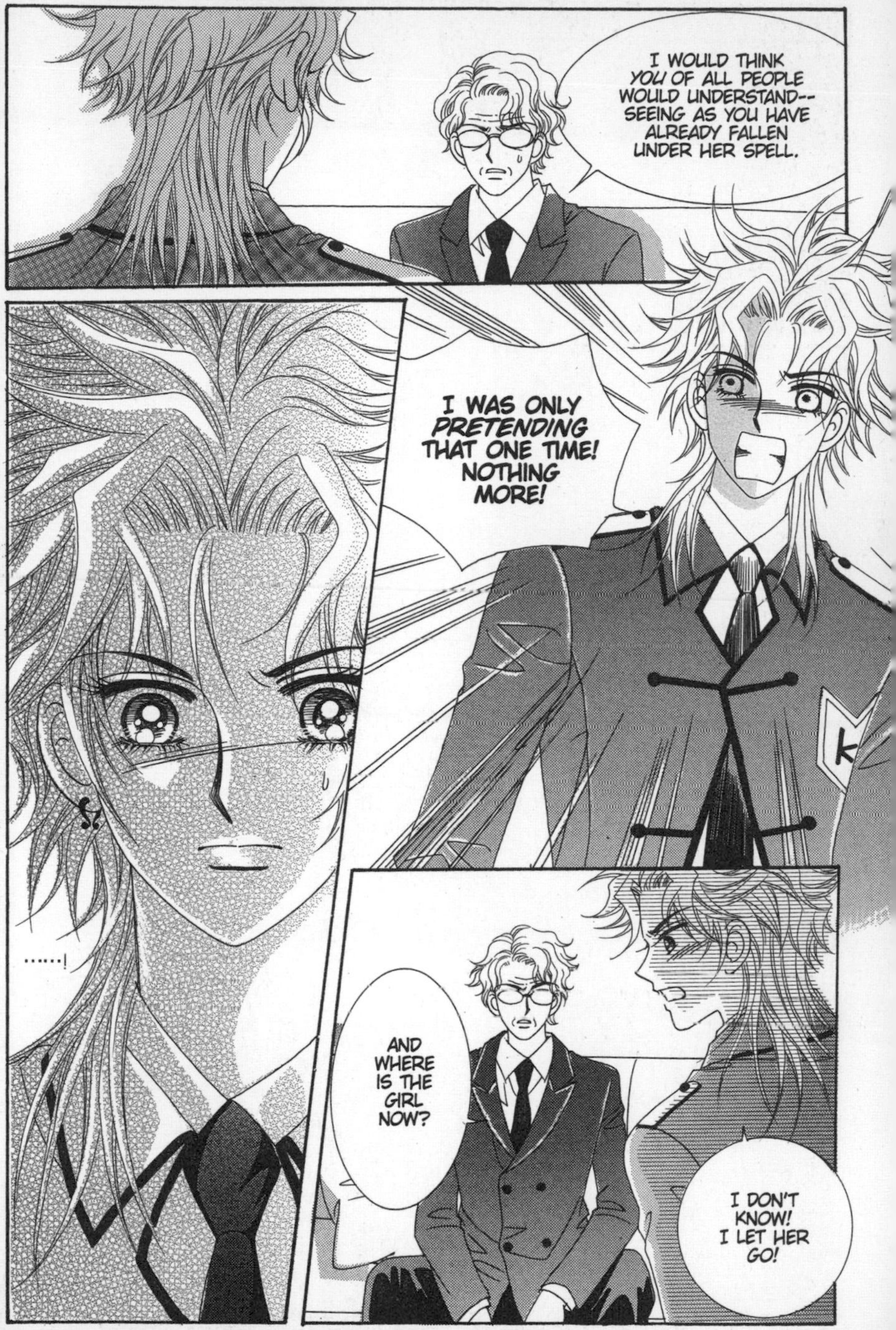
I WOULD THINK YOU OF ALL PEOPLE WOULD UNDERSTAND-- SEEING AS YOU HAVE ALREADY FALLEN UNDER HER SPELL.
......!
I WAS ONLY PRETENDING THAT ONE TIME! NOTHING MORE!
AND WHERE IS THE GIRL NOW?
I DON'T KNOW! I LET HER GO!

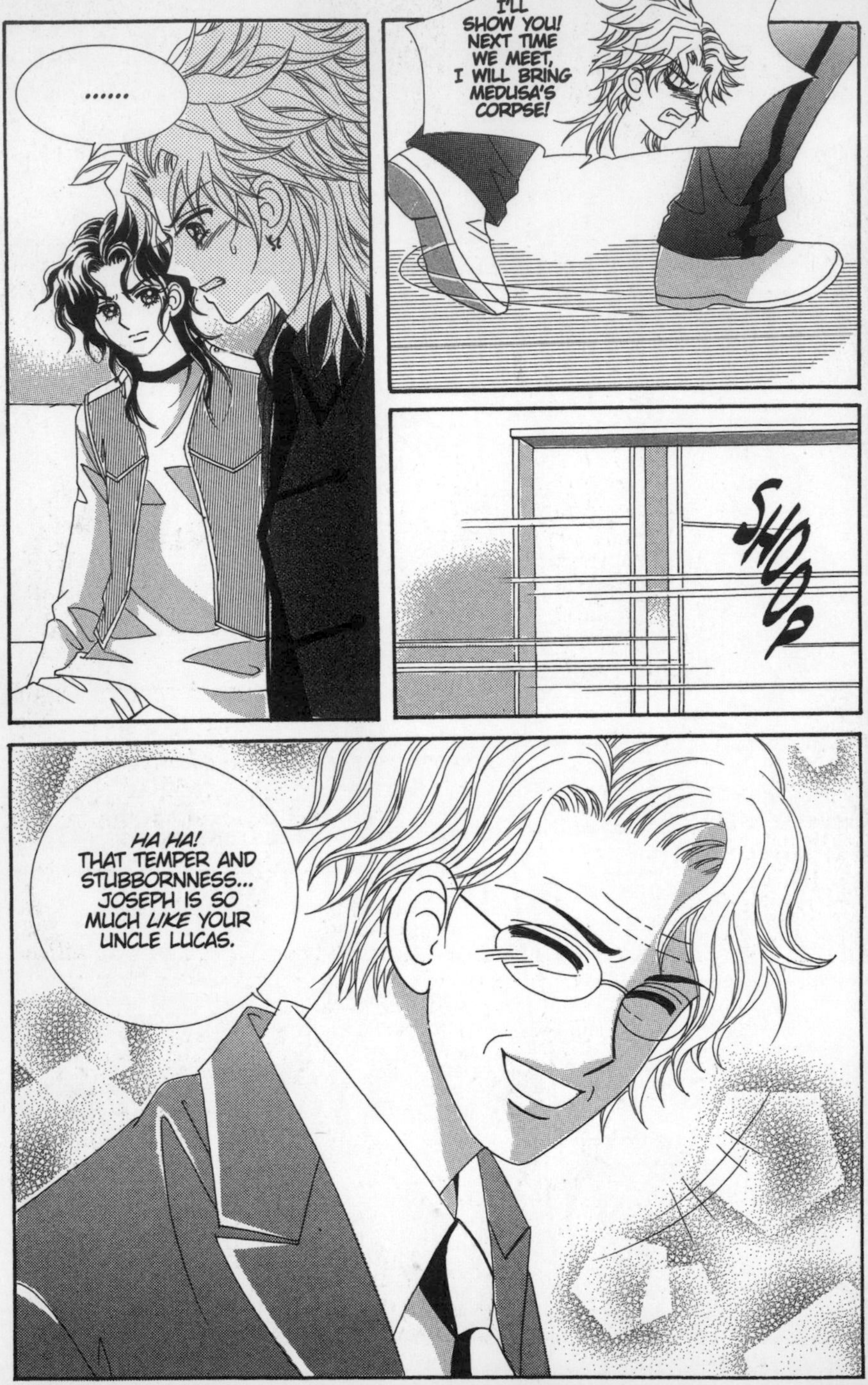
......
I'LL SHOW YOU! NEXT TIME WE MEET, I WILL BRING MEDUSA'S CORPSE!
SHOOP
HA HA! THAT TEMPER AND STUBBORNNESS... JOSEPH IS SO MUCH LIKE YOUR UNCLE LUCAS.

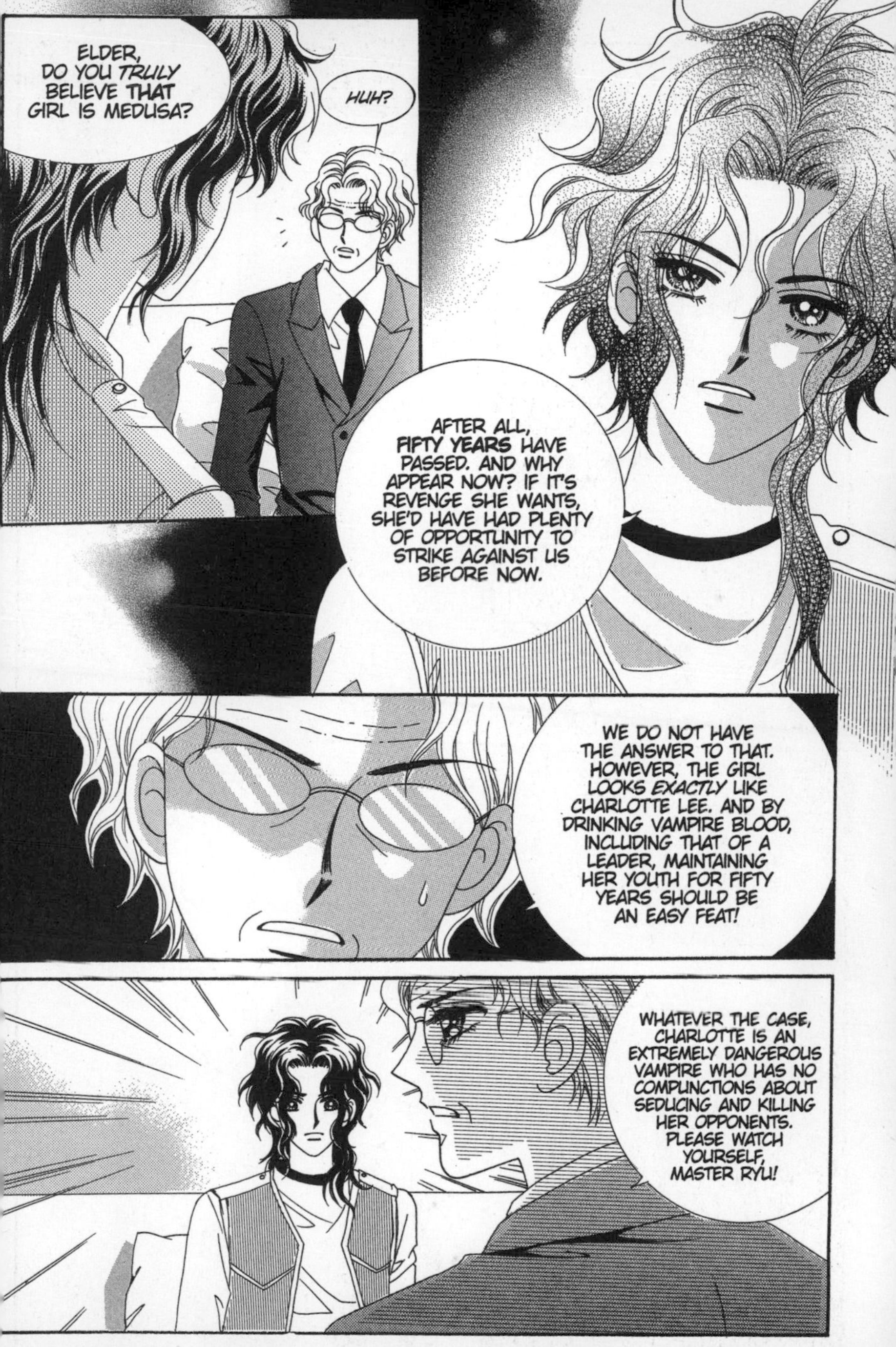
ELDER, DO YOU *TRULY* BELIEVE THAT GIRL IS MEDUSA?
*HUH?*
AFTER ALL, **FIFTY YEARS** HAVE PASSED. AND WHY APPEAR NOW? IF IT'S REVENGE SHE WANTS, SHE'D HAVE HAD PLENTY OF OPPORTUNITY TO STRIKE AGAINST US BEFORE NOW.
WE DO NOT HAVE THE ANSWER TO THAT. HOWEVER, THE GIRL LOOKS *EXACTLY* LIKE CHARLOTTE LEE. AND BY DRINKING VAMPIRE BLOOD, INCLUDING THAT OF A LEADER, MAINTAINING HER YOUTH FOR FIFTY YEARS SHOULD BE AN EASY FEAT!
WHATEVER THE CASE, CHARLOTTE IS AN EXTREMELY DANGEROUS VAMPIRE WHO HAS NO COMPUNCTIONS ABOUT SEDUCING AND KILLING HER OPPONENTS. PLEASE WATCH YOURSELF, MASTER RYU!

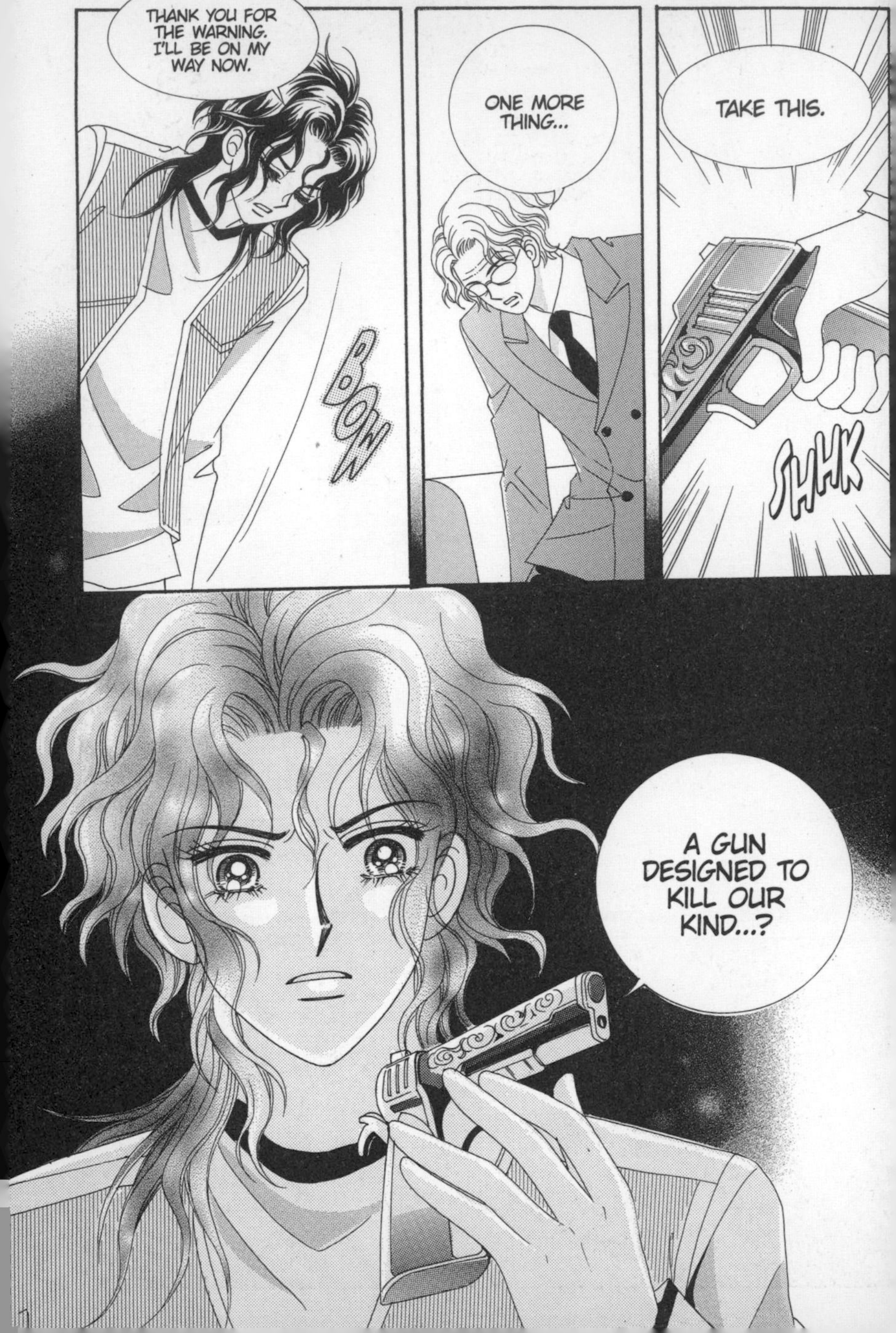
THANK YOU FOR THE WARNING. I'LL BE ON MY WAY NOW.
BOW
ONE MORE THING...
TAKE THIS.
SHHK
A GUN DESIGNED TO KILL OUR KIND...?

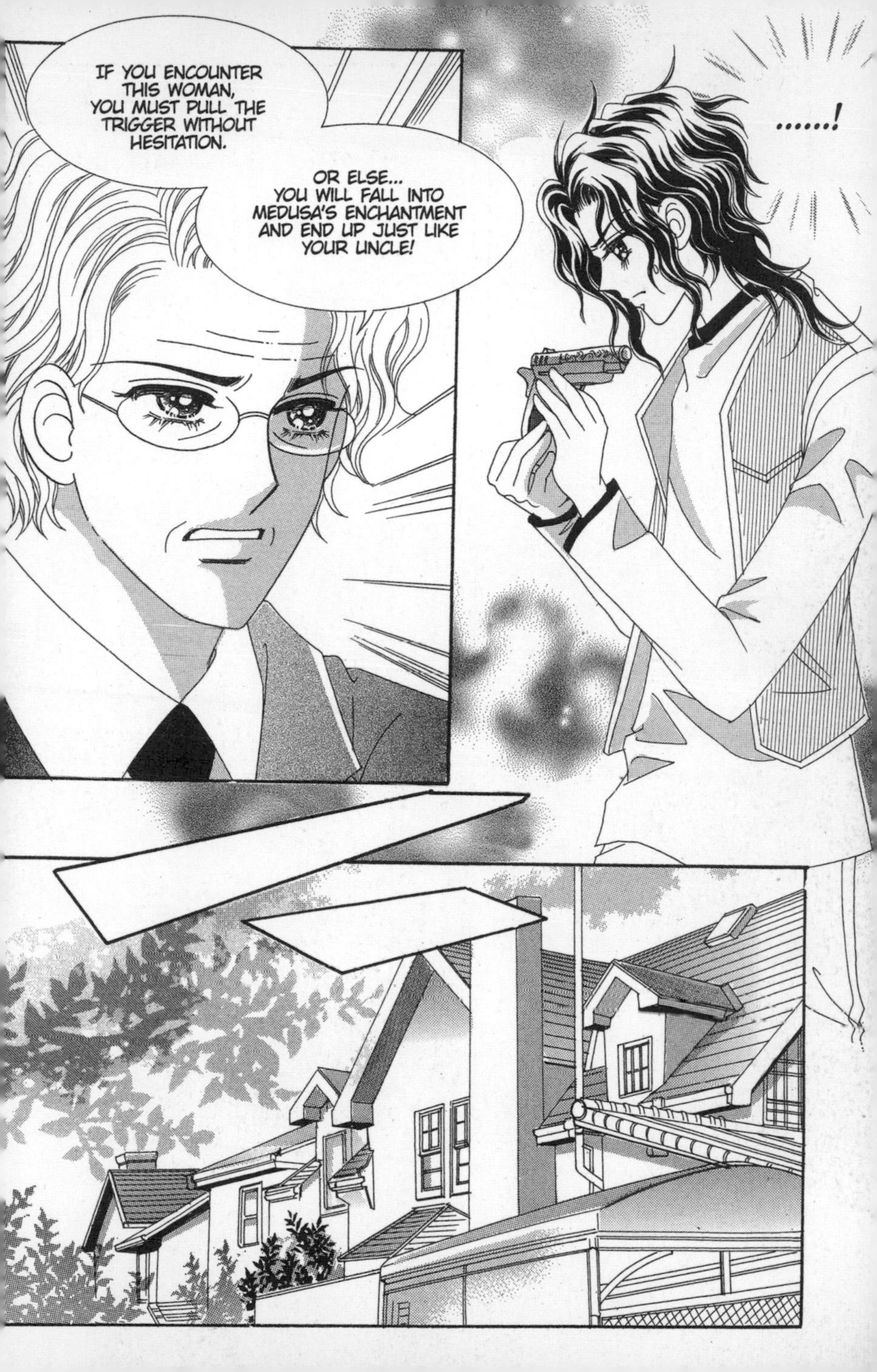
IF YOU ENCOUNTER THIS WOMAN, YOU MUST PULL THE TRIGGER WITHOUT HESITATION.
OR ELSE... YOU WILL FALL INTO MEDUSA'S ENCHANTMENT AND END UP JUST LIKE YOUR UNCLE!
......!

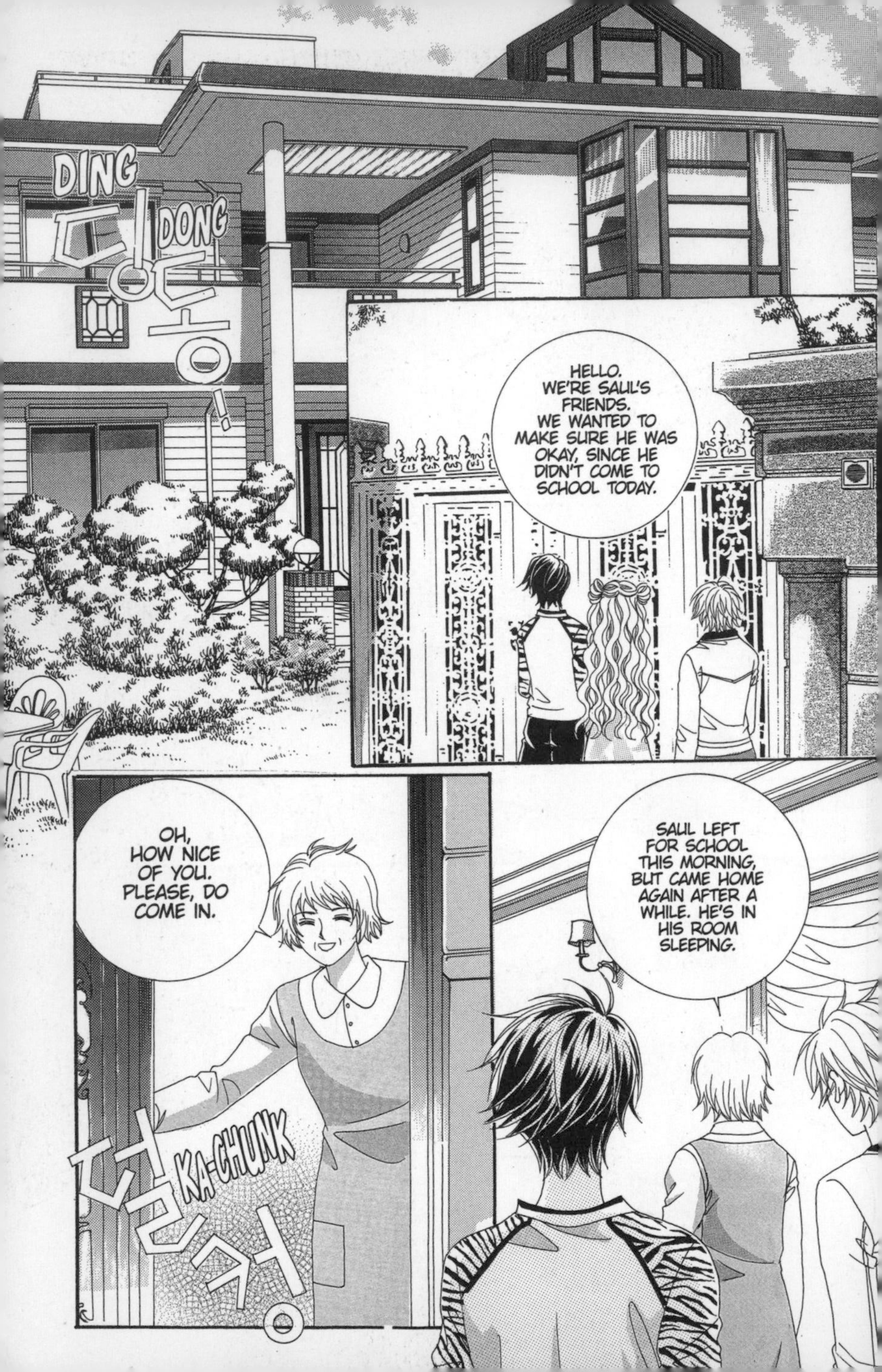
DING DONG
HELLO. WE'RE SAUL'S FRIENDS. WE WANTED TO MAKE SURE HE WAS OKAY, SINCE HE DIDN'T COME TO SCHOOL TODAY.
OH, HOW NICE OF YOU. PLEASE, DO COME IN.
KA-CHUNK
SAUL LEFT FOR SCHOOL THIS MORNING, BUT CAME HOME AGAIN AFTER A WHILE. HE'S IN HIS ROOM SLEEPING.

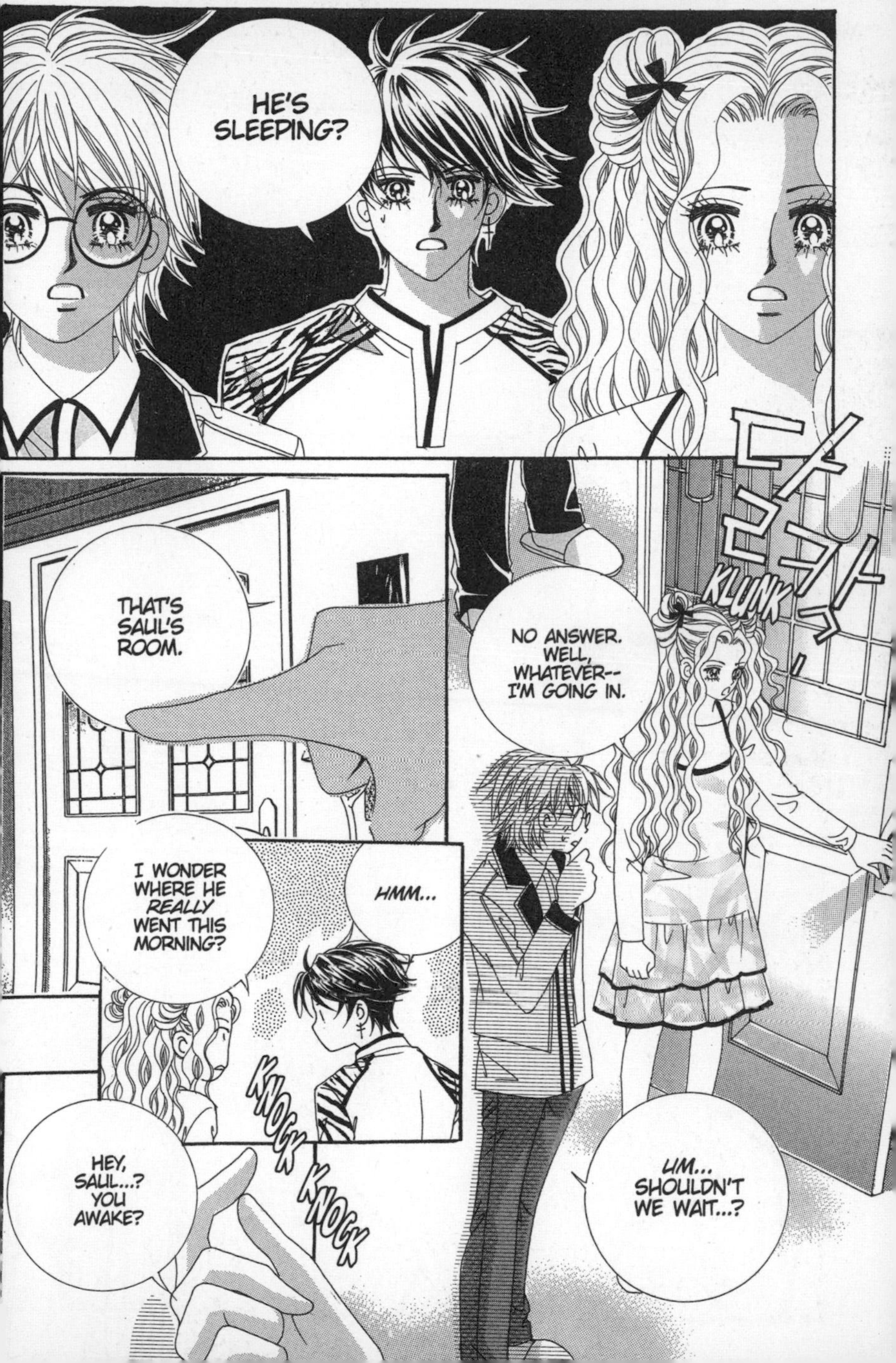
HE'S SLEEPING?
THAT'S SAUL'S ROOM.
I WONDER WHERE HE *REALLY* WENT THIS MORNING?
*HMM...*
KNOCK
KNOCK
HEY, SAUL...? YOU AWAKE?
KLUNK
NO ANSWER. WELL, WHATEVER-- I'M GOING IN.
UM... SHOULDN'T WE WAIT...?

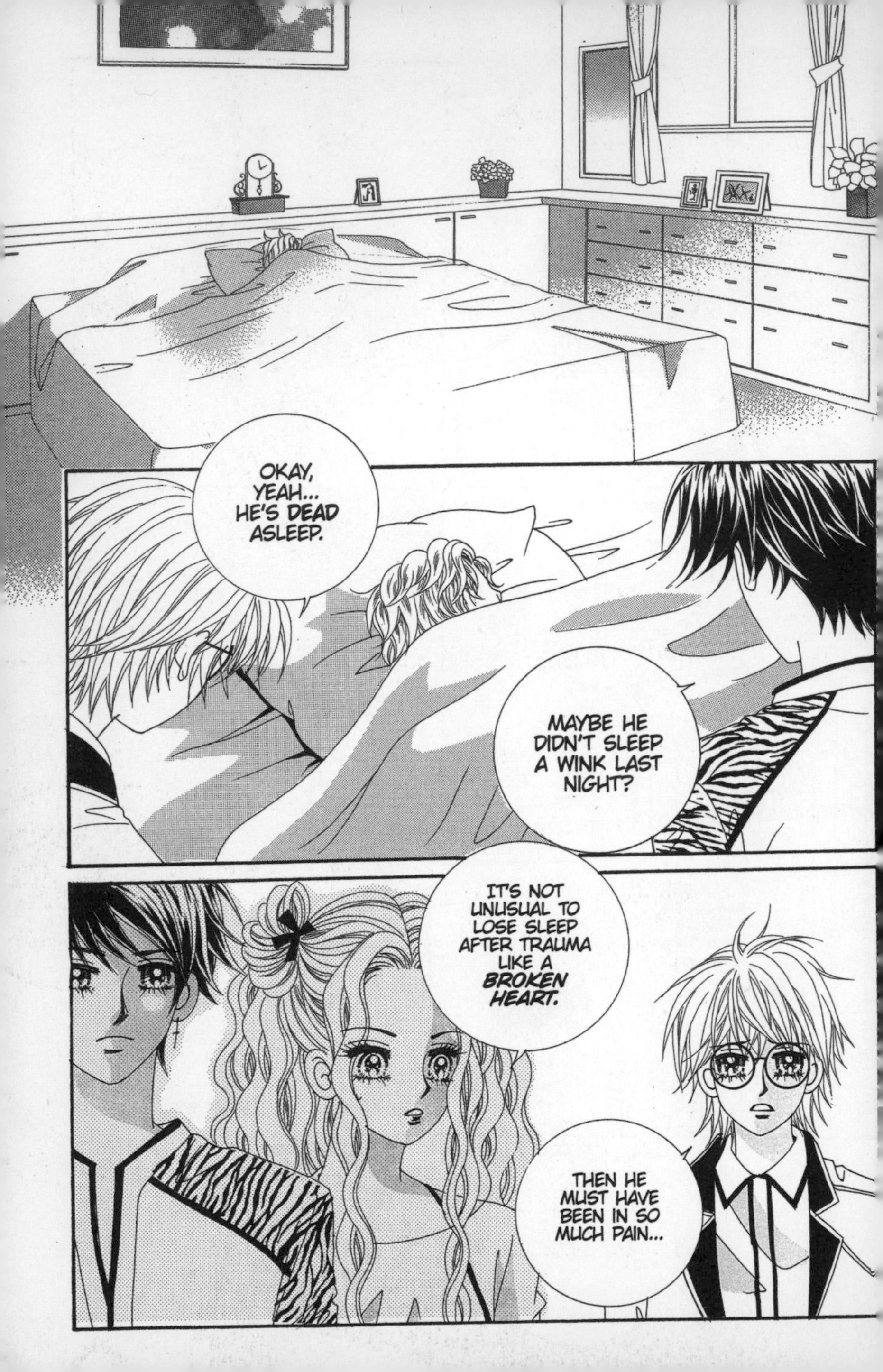
OKAY, YEAH... HE'S DEAD ASLEEP.
MAYBE HE DIDN'T SLEEP A WINK LAST NIGHT?
IT'S NOT UNUSUAL TO LOSE SLEEP AFTER TRAUMA LIKE A BROKEN HEART.
THEN HE MUST HAVE BEEN IN SO MUCH PAIN...

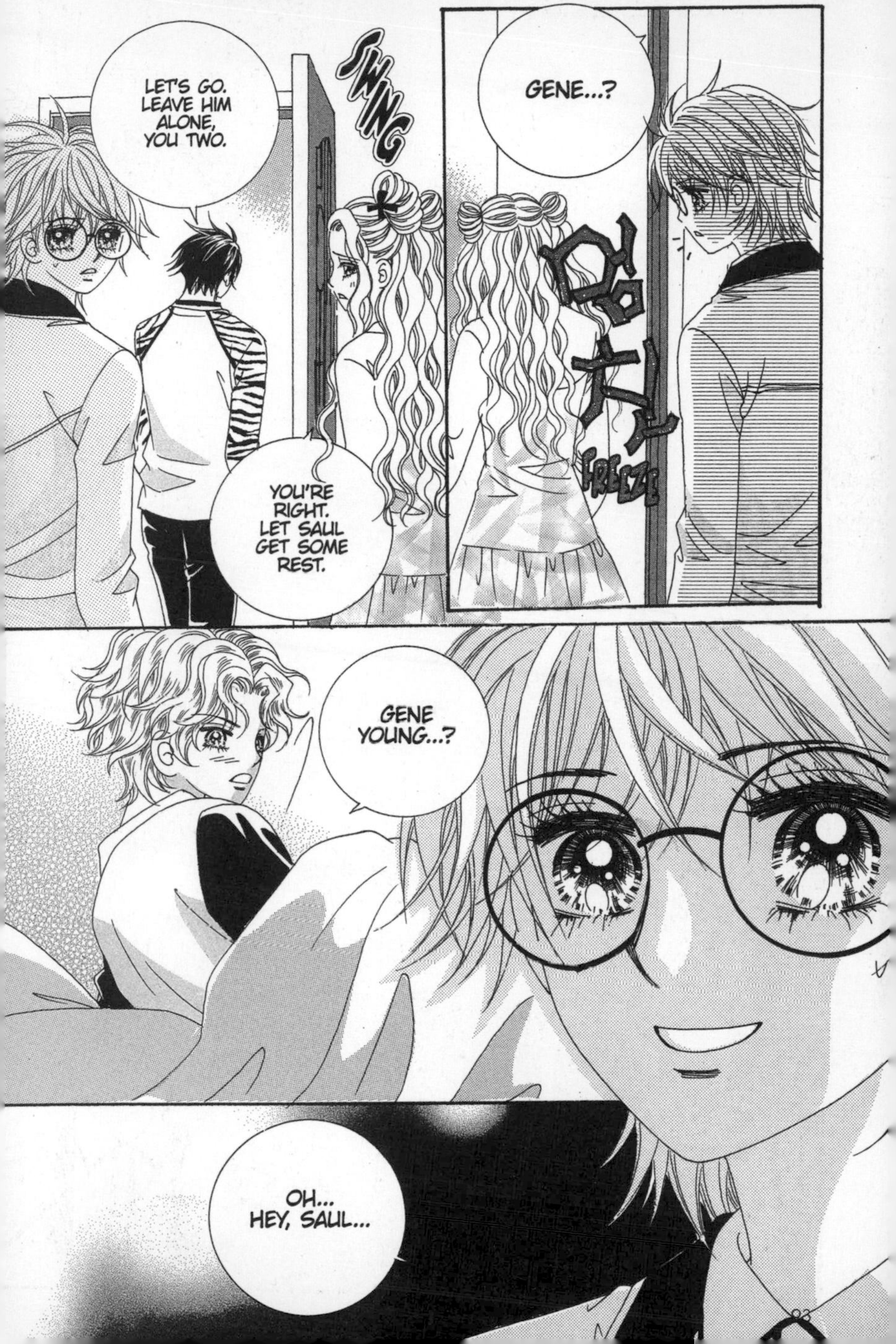
LET'S GO. LEAVE HIM ALONE, YOU TWO.
SWING
YOU'RE RIGHT. LET SAUL GET SOME REST.
GENE...?
FREEZE
GENE YOUNG...?
OH... HEY, SAUL...

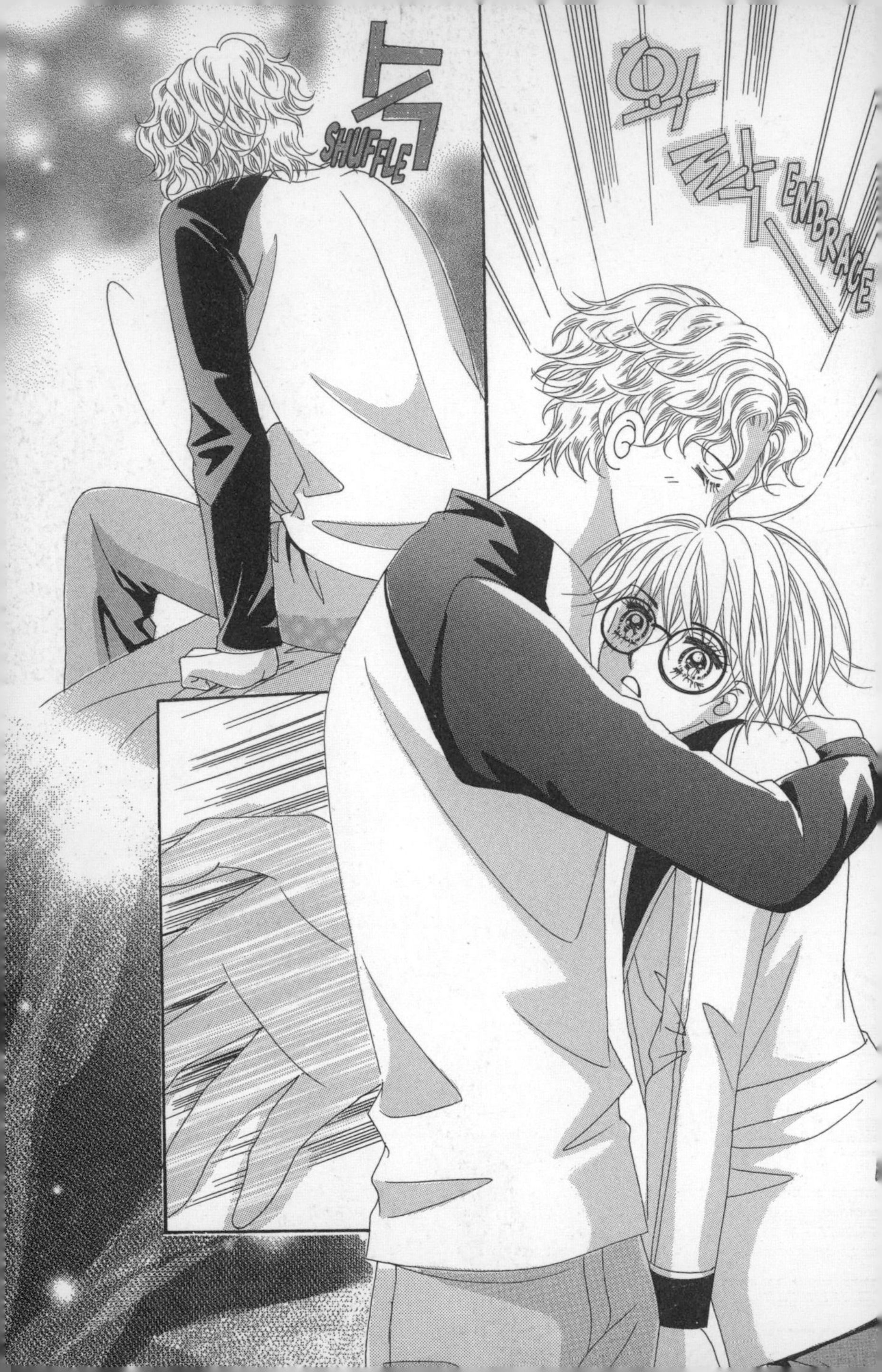
SHUFFLE
EMBRACE

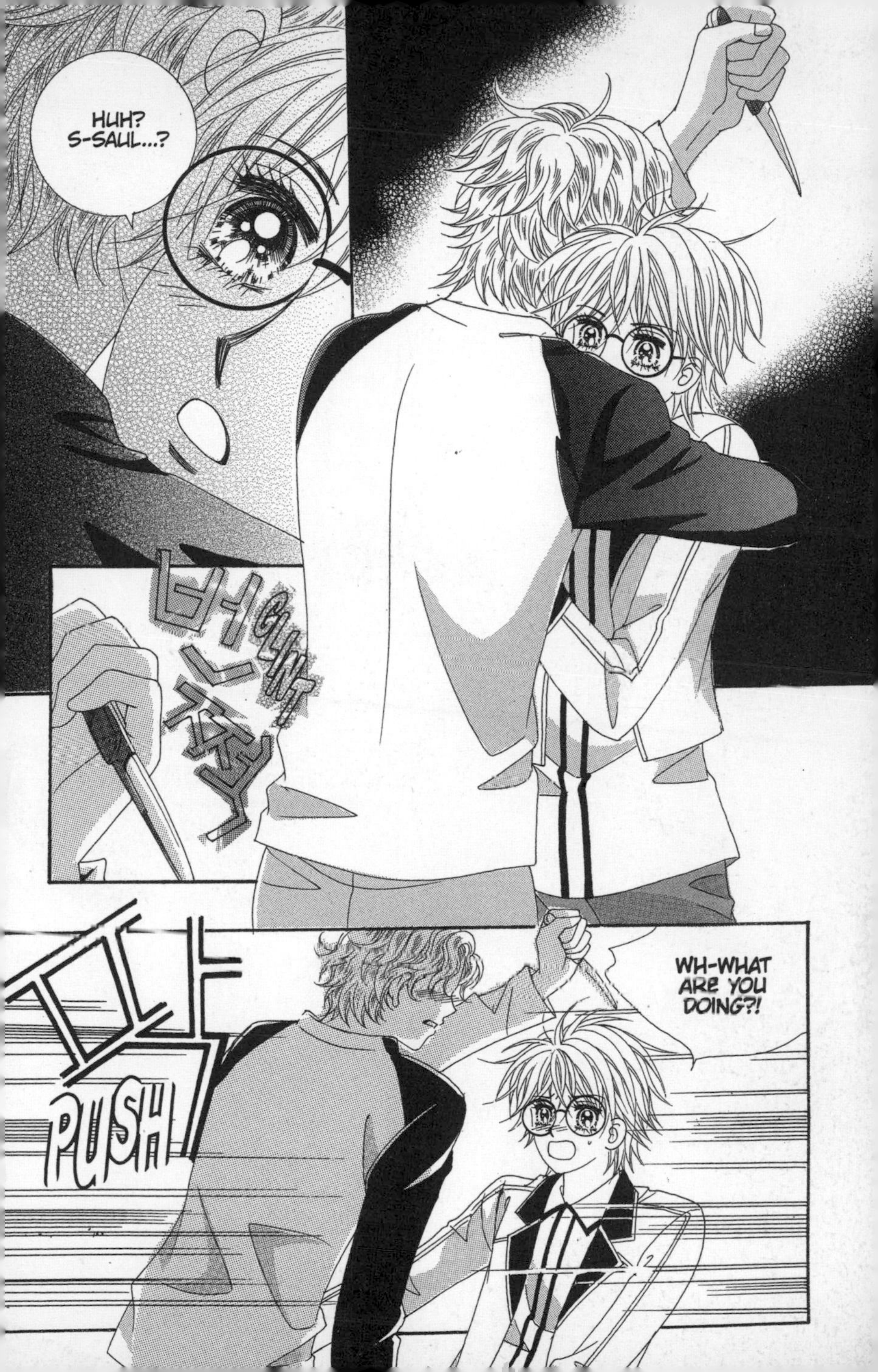
HUH? S-SAUL...?
GLINT
PUSH
WH-WHAT ARE YOU DOING?!

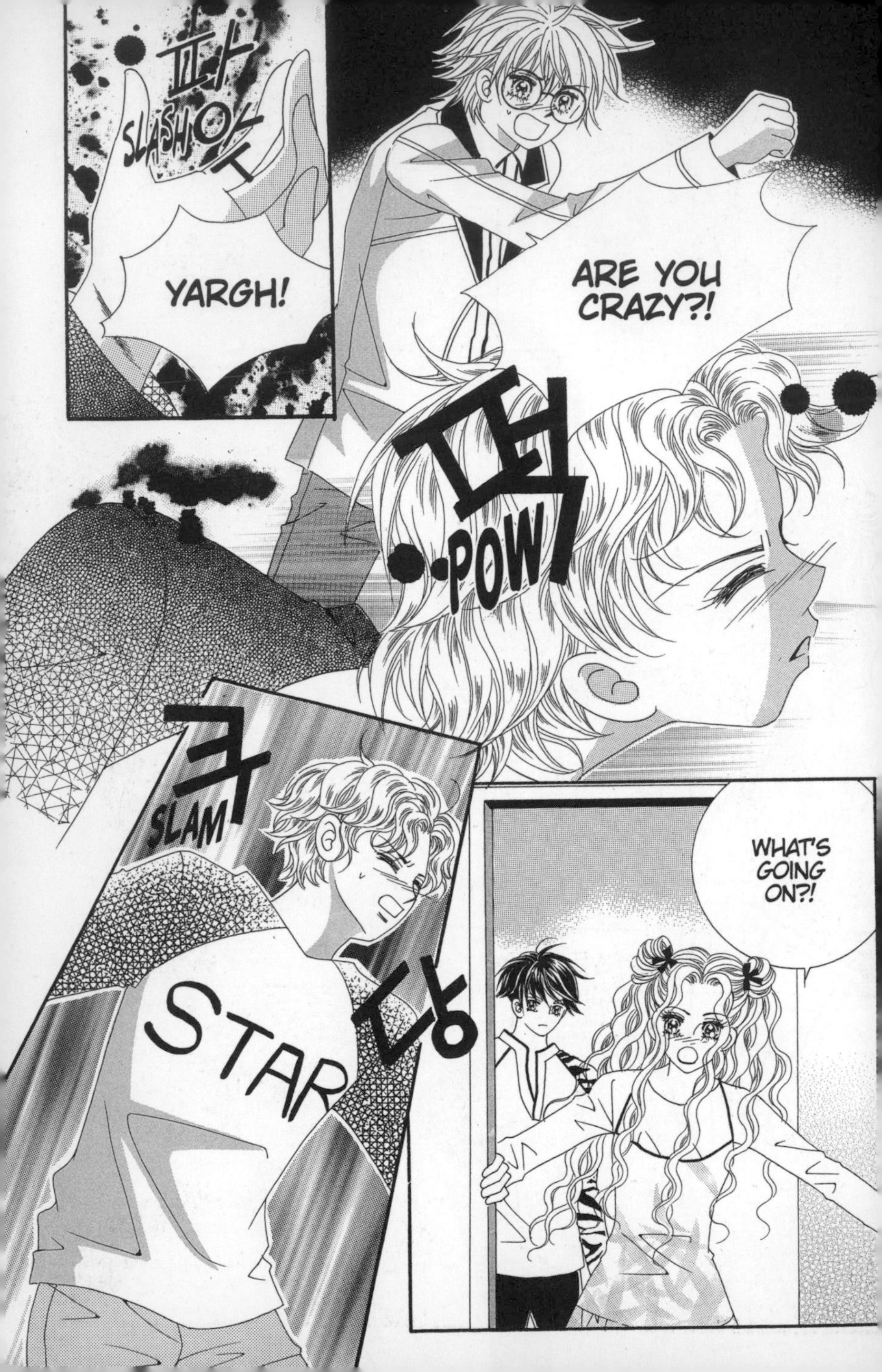
SLASH
YARGH!
ARE YOU CRAZY?!
POW
SLAM
STAR
WHAT'S GOING ON?!

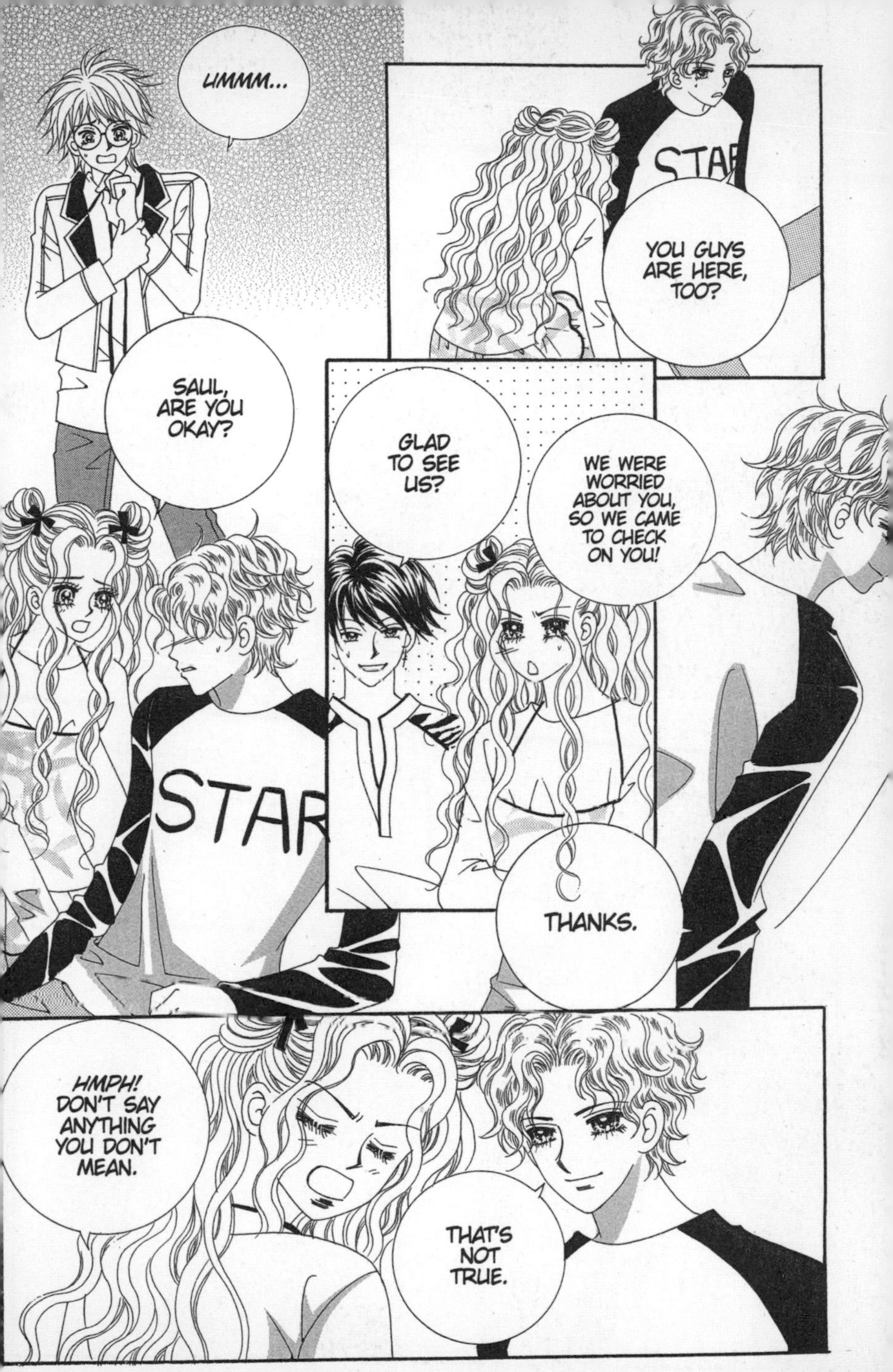
UMMM...
YOU GUYS ARE HERE, TOO?
SAUL, ARE YOU OKAY?
GLAD TO SEE US?
WE WERE WORRIED ABOUT YOU, SO WE CAME TO CHECK ON YOU!
THANKS.
HMPH! DON'T SAY ANYTHING YOU DON'T MEAN.
THAT'S NOT TRUE.

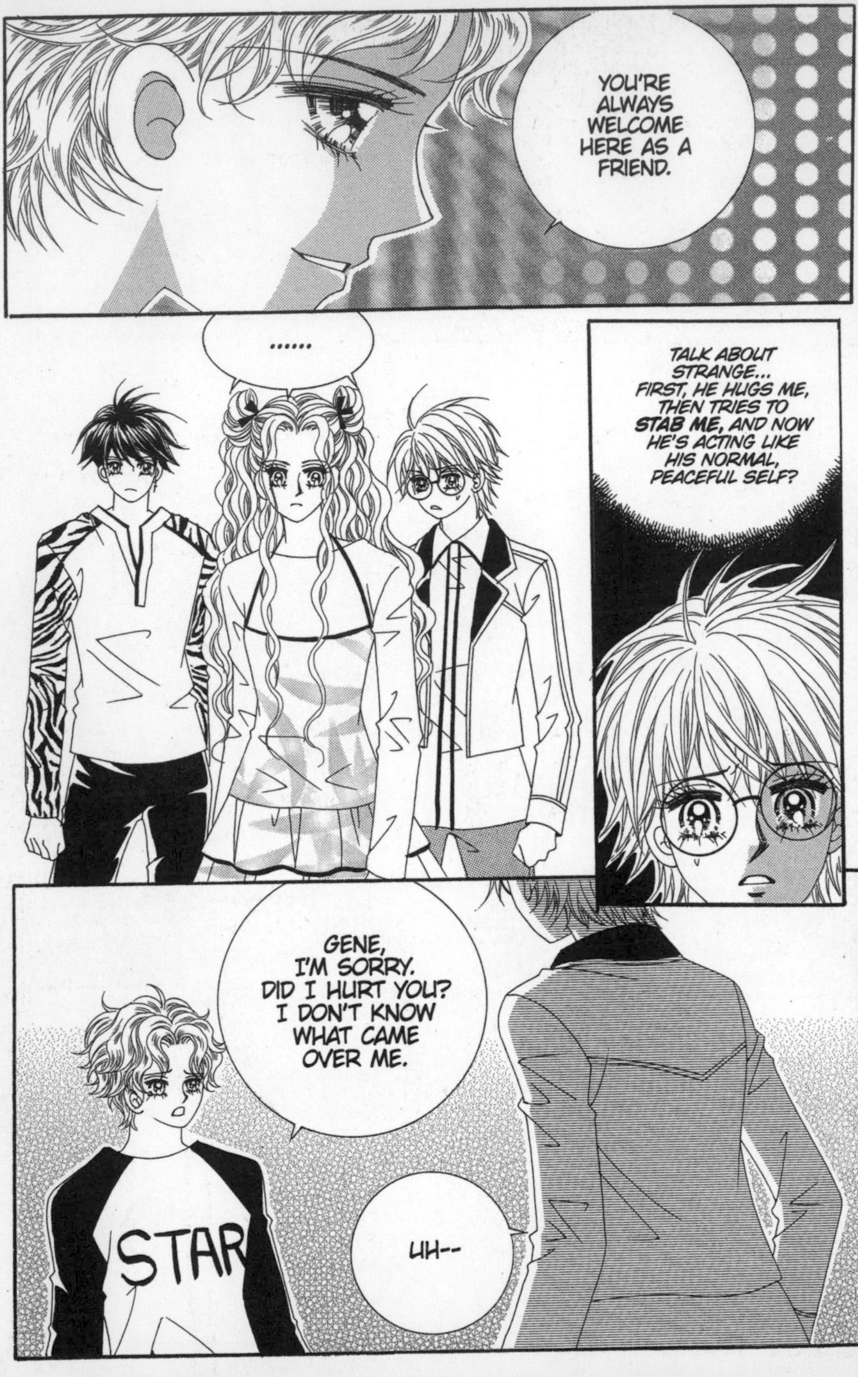
YOU'RE ALWAYS WELCOME HERE AS A FRIEND.
......
TALK ABOUT STRANGE... FIRST, HE HUGS ME, THEN TRIES TO **STAB ME,** AND NOW HE'S ACTING LIKE HIS NORMAL, PEACEFUL SELF?
GENE, I'M SORRY. DID I HURT YOU? I DON'T KNOW WHAT CAME OVER ME.
STAR
UH--

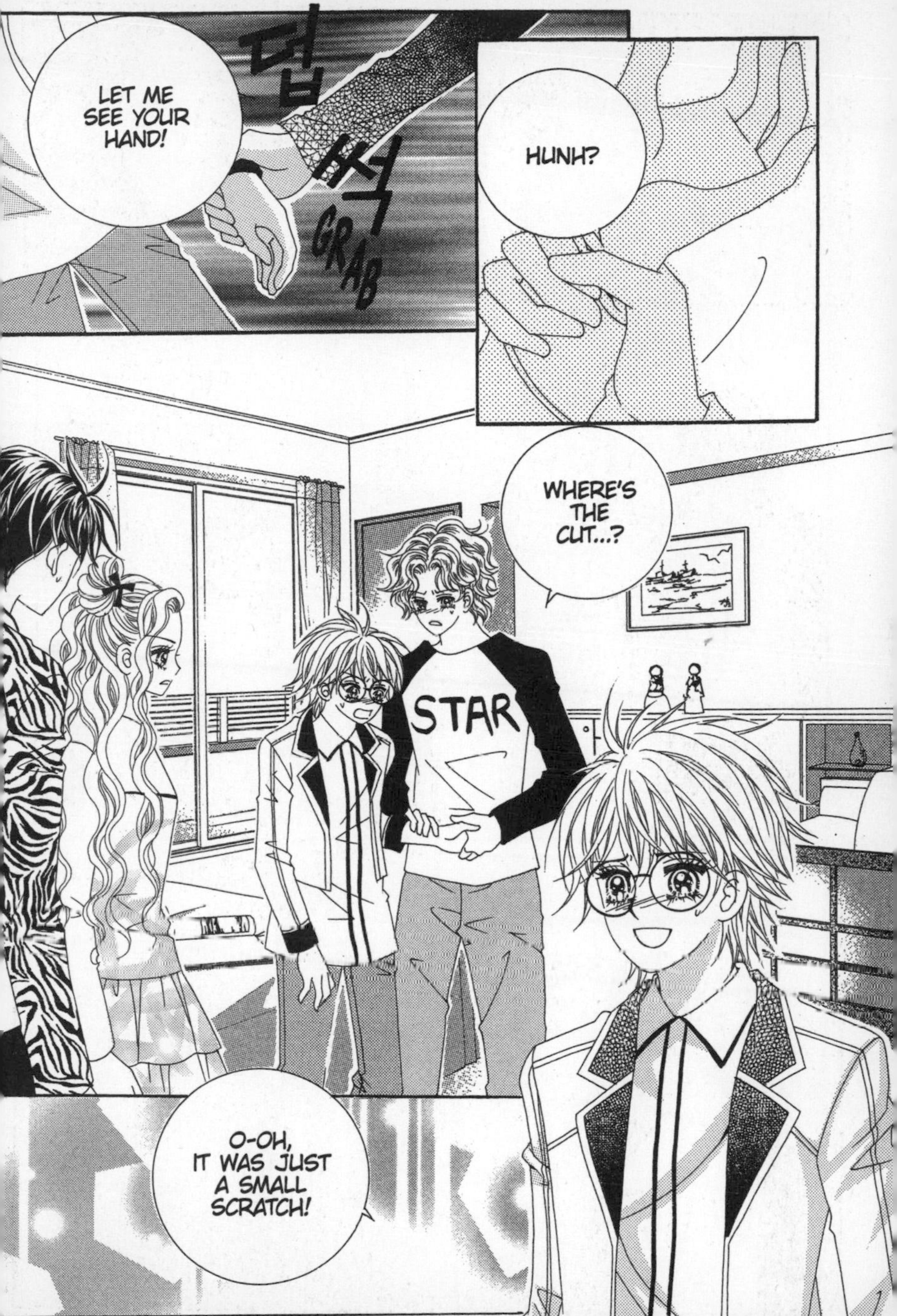
LET ME SEE YOUR HAND!
덥썩
GRAB
HUNH?
WHERE'S THE CUT...?
O-OH, IT WAS JUST A SMALL SCRATCH!

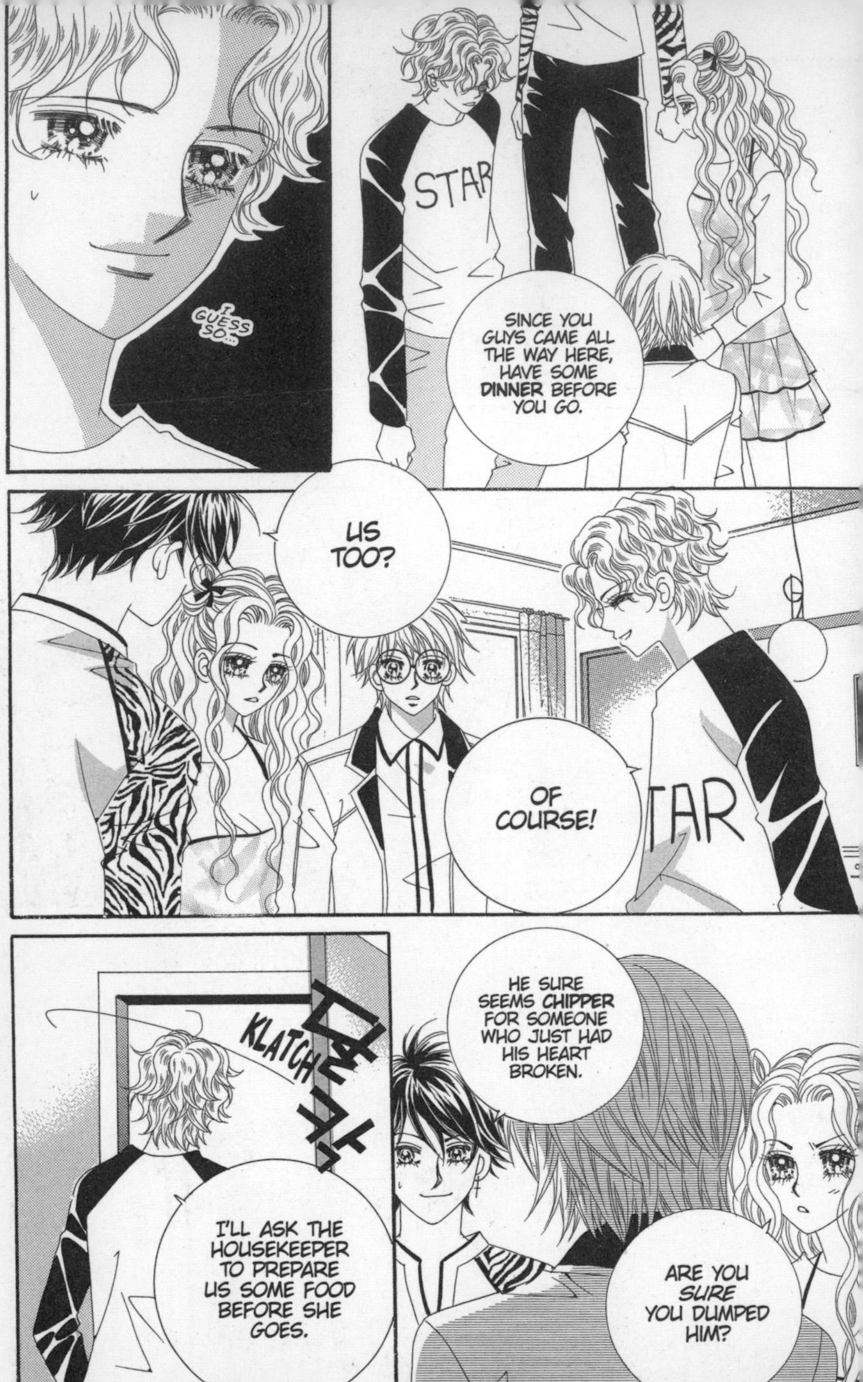
I GUESS SO...
SINCE YOU GUYS CAME ALL THE WAY HERE, HAVE SOME DINNER BEFORE YOU GO.
US TOO?
OF COURSE!
KLATCH
I'LL ASK THE HOUSEKEEPER TO PREPARE US SOME FOOD BEFORE SHE GOES.
HE SURE SEEMS CHIPPER FOR SOMEONE WHO JUST HAD HIS HEART BROKEN.
ARE YOU SURE YOU DUMPED HIM?

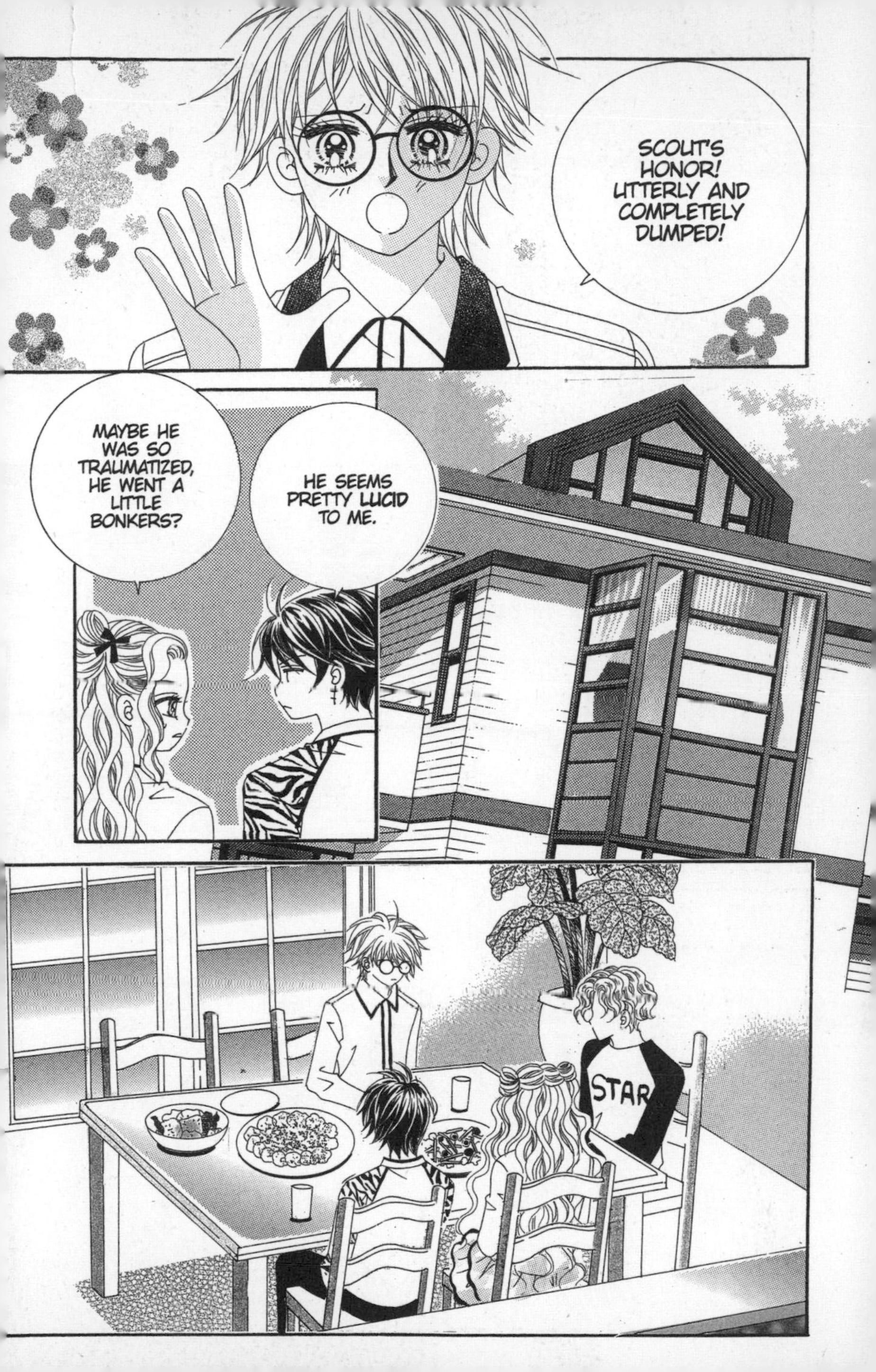
SCOUT'S HONOR! UTTERLY AND COMPLETELY DUMPED!
MAYBE HE WAS SO TRAUMATIZED, HE WENT A LITTLE BONKERS?
HE SEEMS PRETTY LUCID TO ME.
STAR

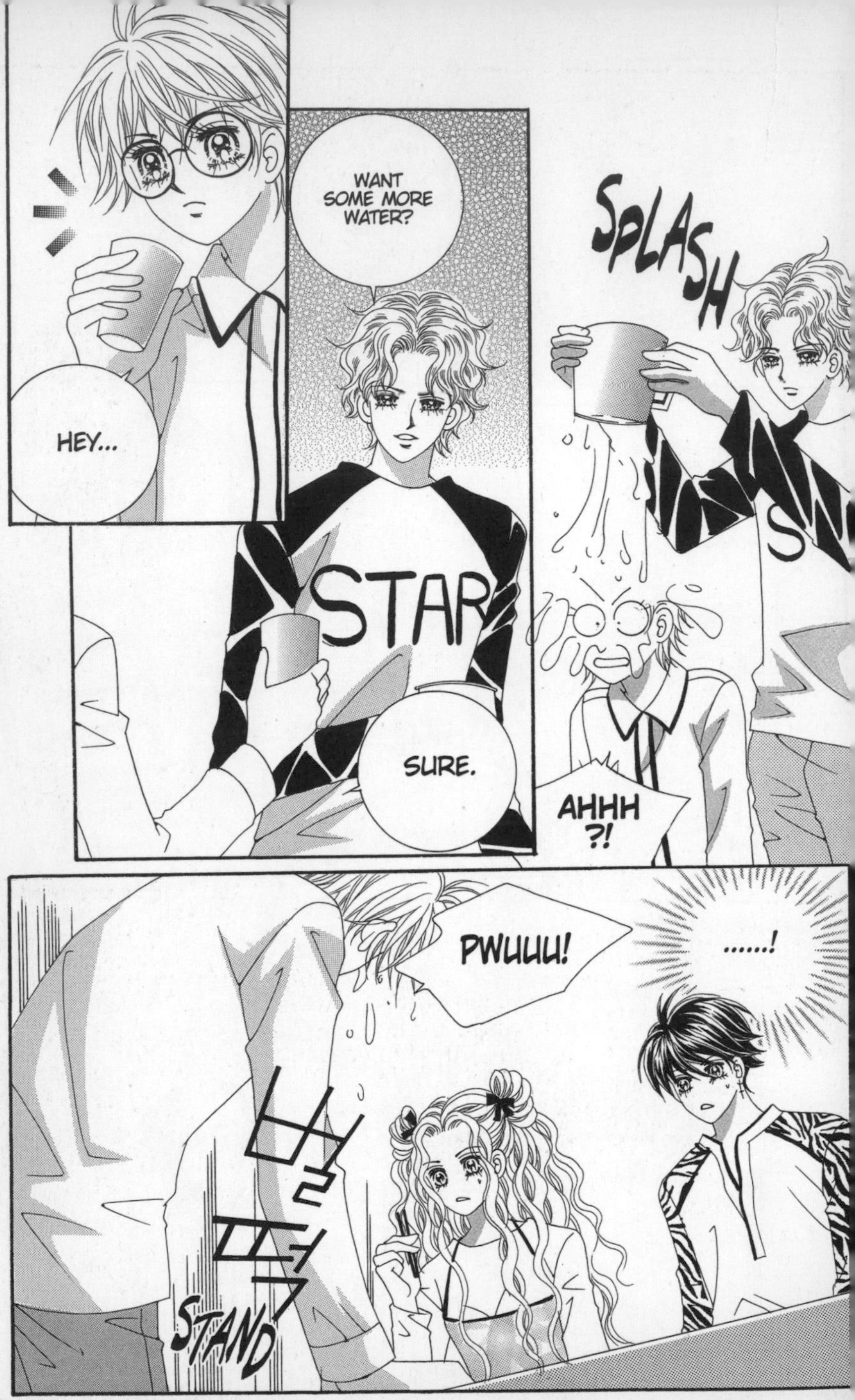

HEY...
WANT SOME MORE WATER?
STAR
SURE.
SPLASH
S
AHHH ?!
PWUUU!
......!
벌떡
STAND

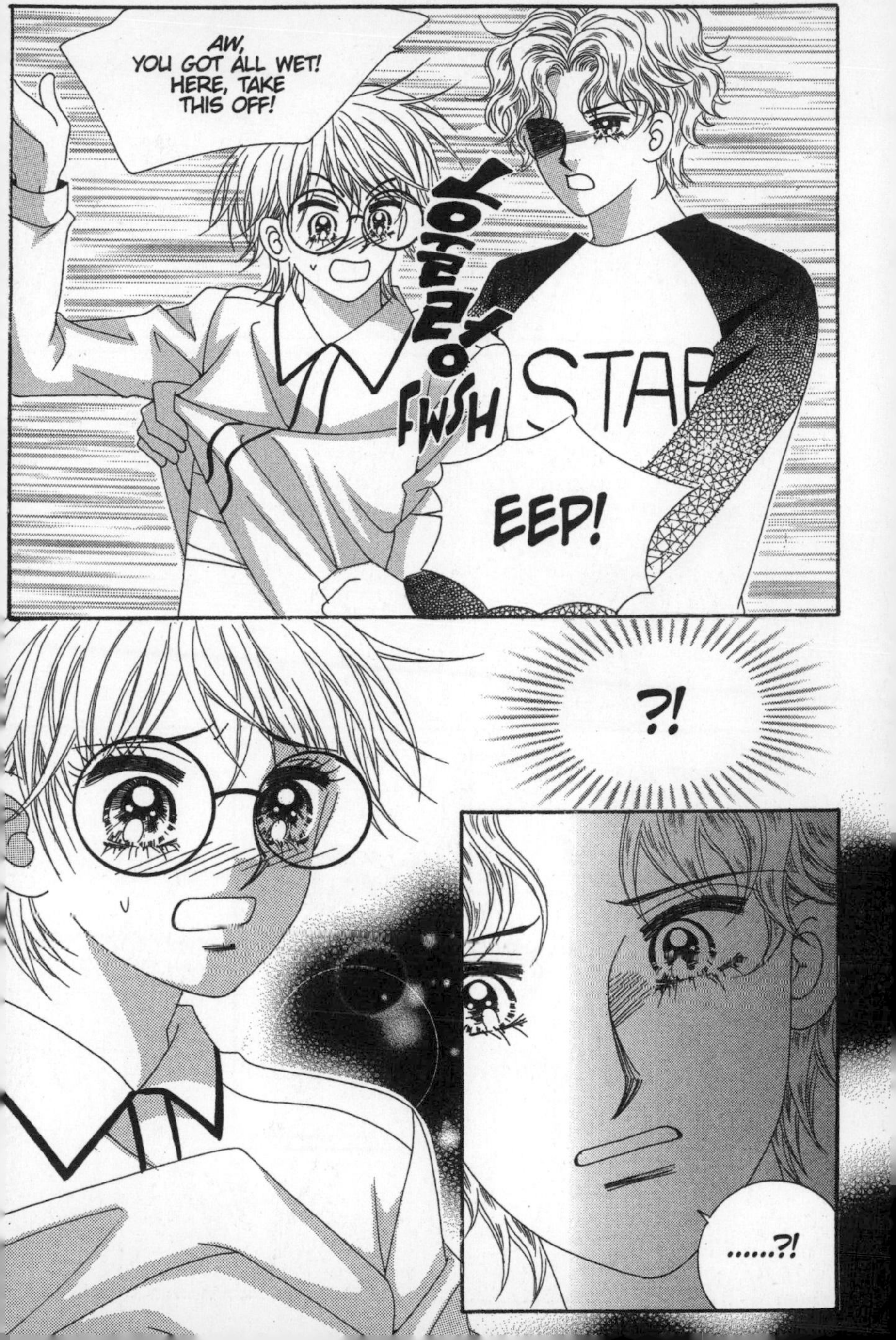
AW, YOU GOT ALL WET! HERE, TAKE THIS OFF!
FWSH
EEP!
?!
......?!

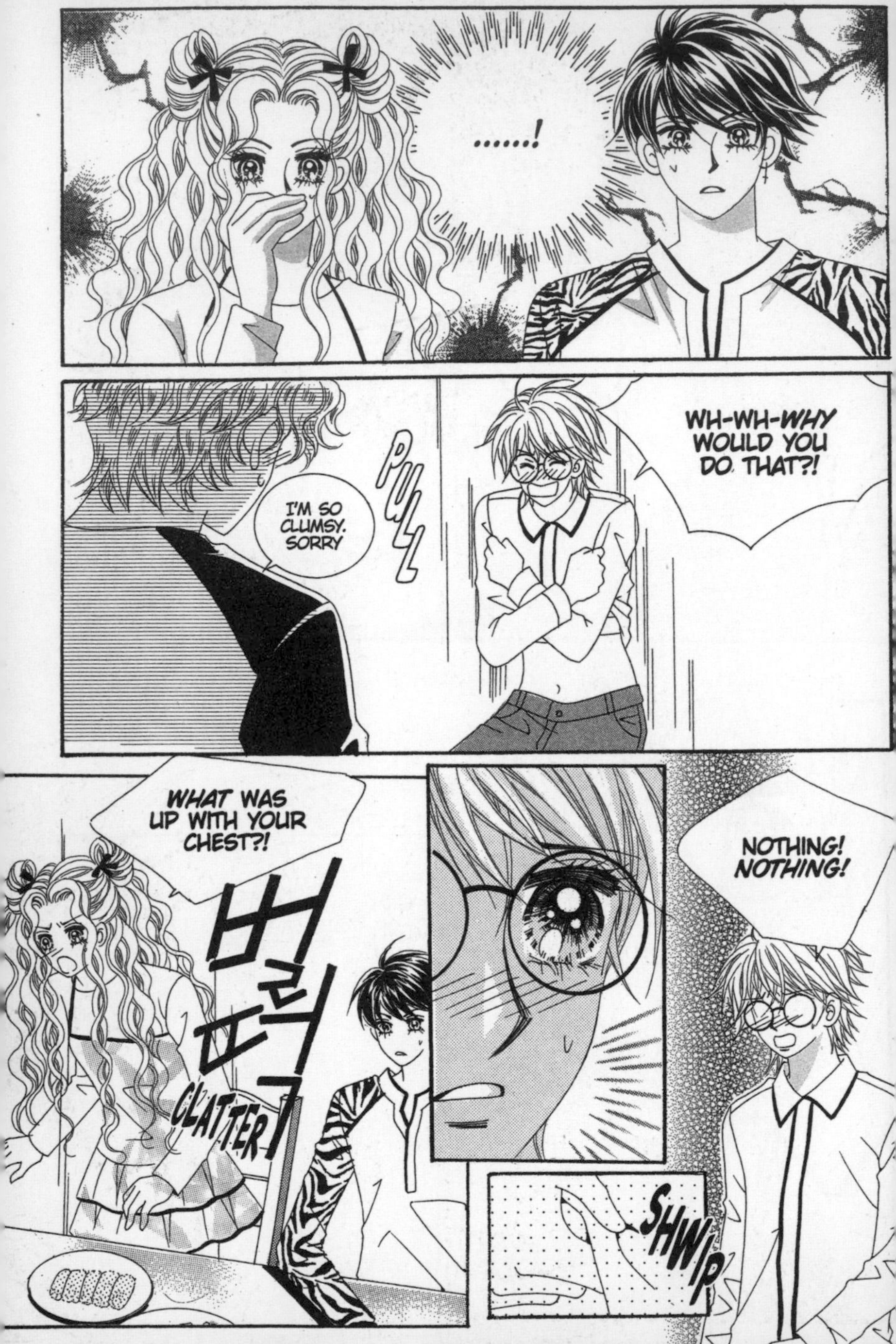
......!
I'M SO CLUMSY. SORRY
PULL
WH-WH-*WHY* WOULD YOU DO THAT?!
*WHAT* WAS UP WITH YOUR CHEST?!
벌떡
CLATTER
NOTHING! *NOTHING!*
SHWIP

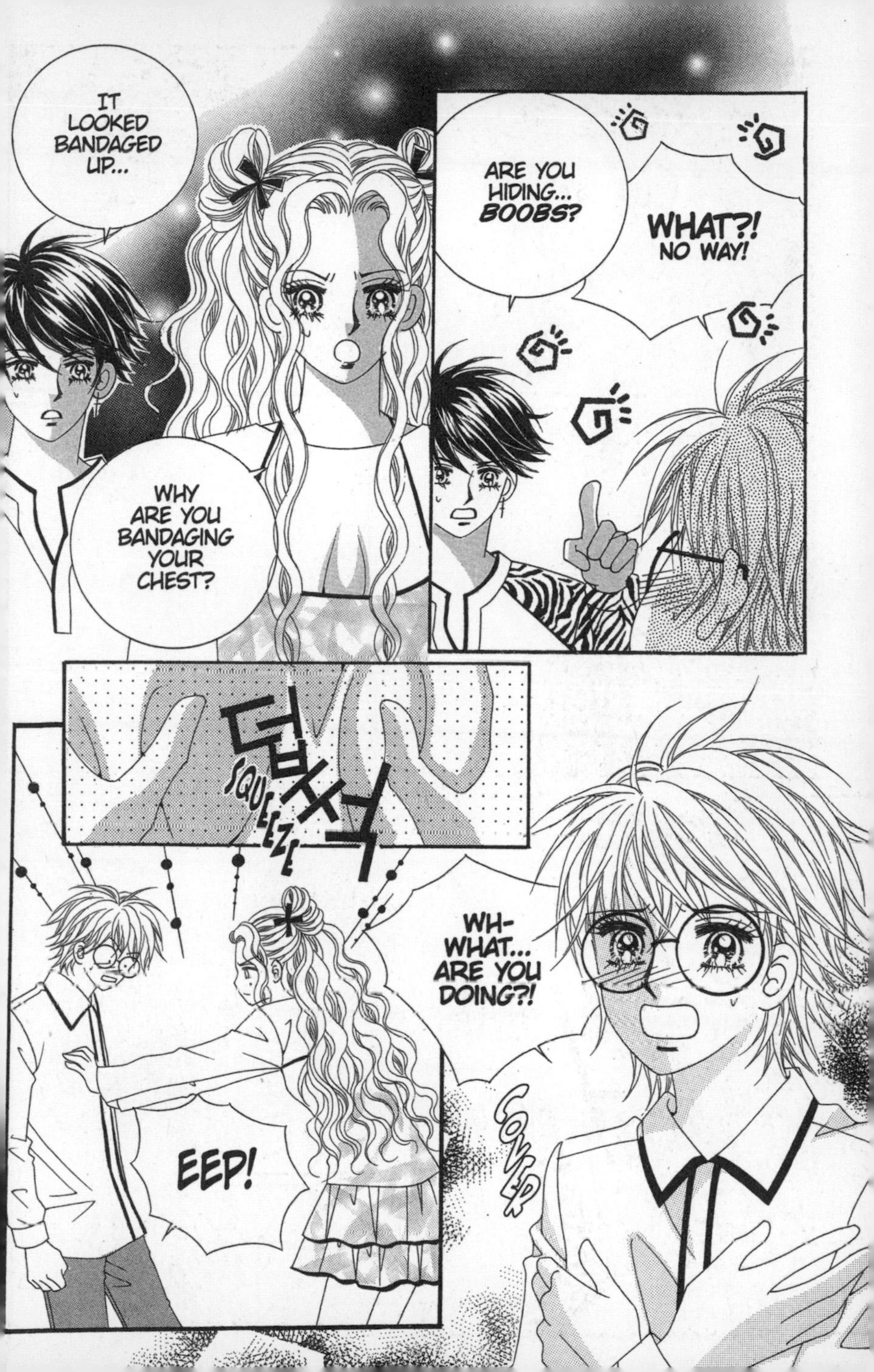
IT LOOKED BANDAGED UP...
WHY ARE YOU BANDAGING YOUR CHEST?
ARE YOU HIDING... BOOBS?
WHAT?! NO WAY!
SQUEEZE
EEP!
WH-WHAT... ARE YOU DOING?!
COVER

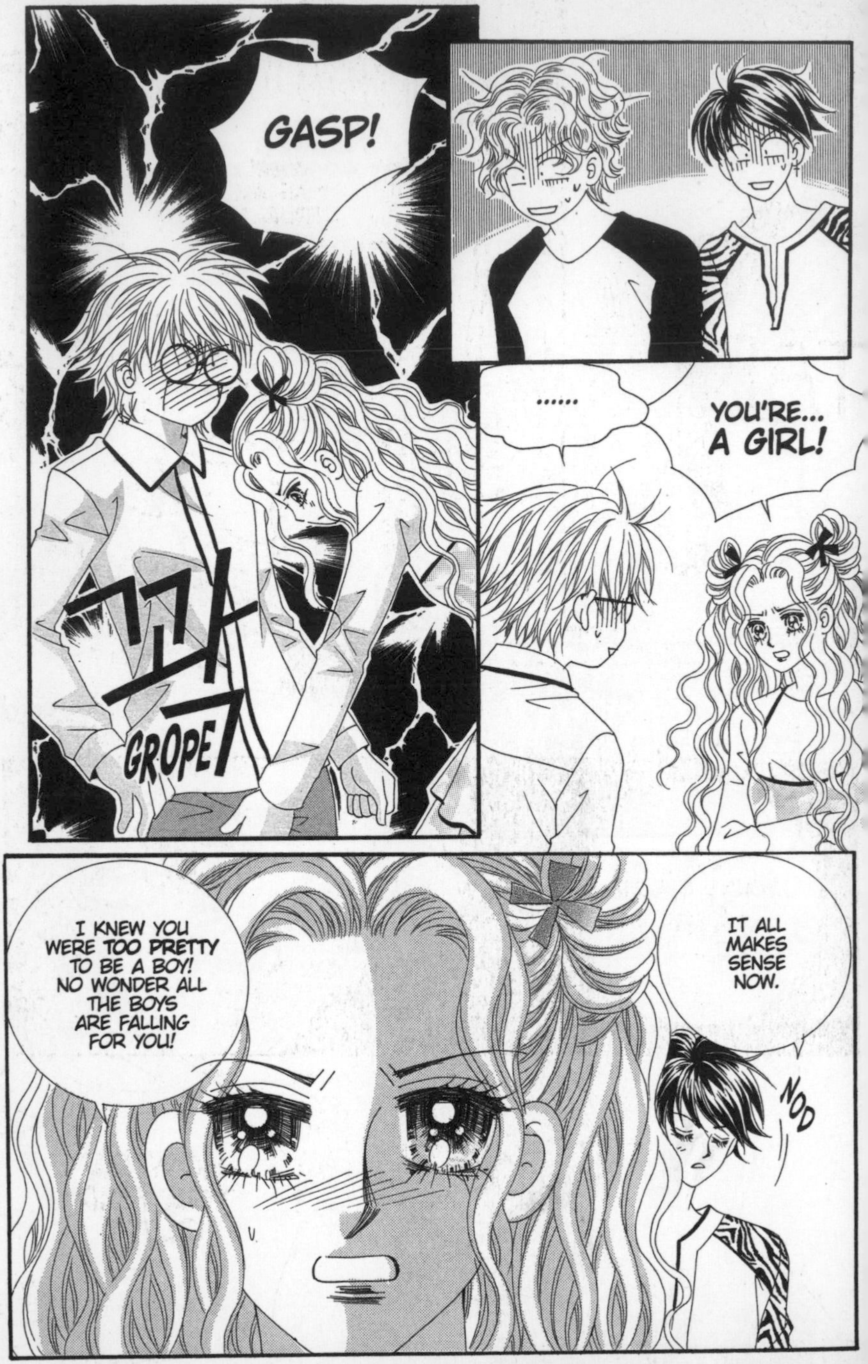
GASP!
GROPE
......
YOU'RE... A GIRL!
I KNEW YOU WERE TOO PRETTY TO BE A BOY! NO WONDER ALL THE BOYS ARE FALLING FOR YOU!
IT ALL MAKES SENSE NOW.
NOD

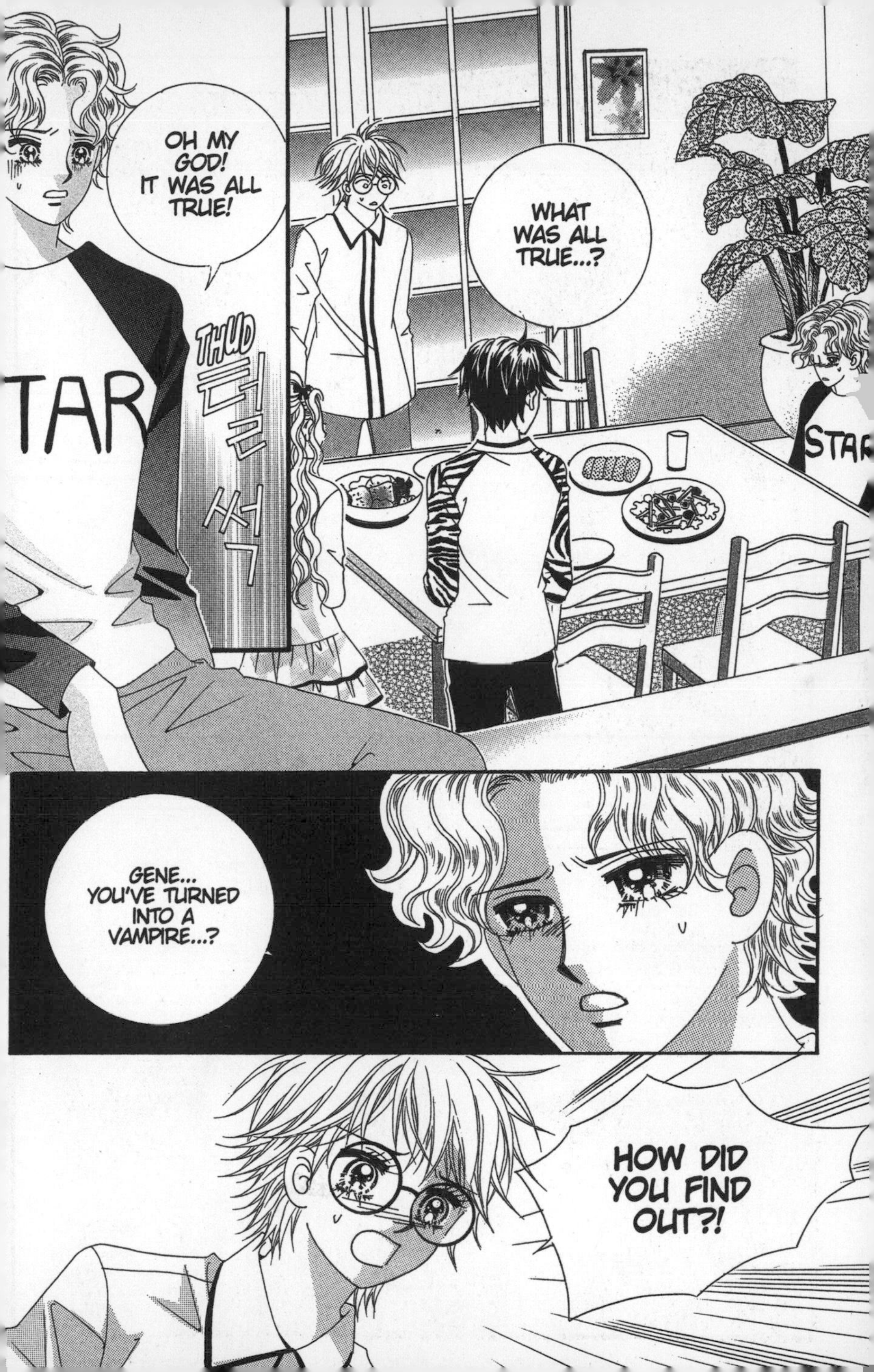
OH MY GOD! IT WAS ALL TRUE!
TAR
THUD
털썩
WHAT WAS ALL TRUE...?
STAR
GENE... YOU'VE TURNED INTO A VAMPIRE...?
HOW DID YOU FIND OUT?!

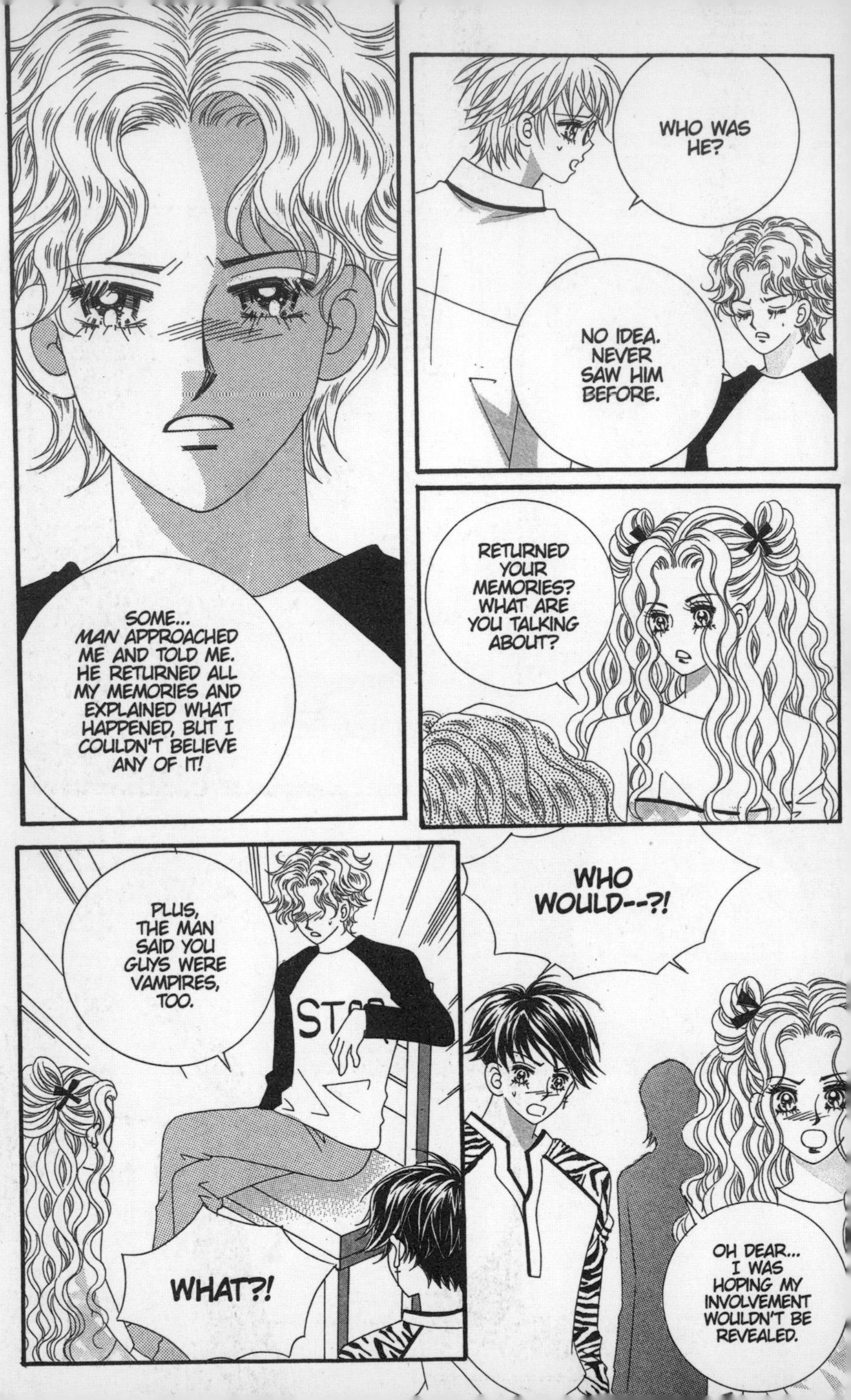

SOME... MAN APPROACHED ME AND TOLD ME. HE RETURNED ALL MY MEMORIES AND EXPLAINED WHAT HAPPENED, BUT I COULDN'T BELIEVE ANY OF IT!
WHO WAS HE?
NO IDEA. NEVER SAW HIM BEFORE.
RETURNED YOUR MEMORIES? WHAT ARE YOU TALKING ABOUT?
PLUS, THE MAN SAID YOU GUYS WERE VAMPIRES, TOO.
WHAT?!
WHO WOULD--?!
OH DEAR... I WAS HOPING MY INVOLVEMENT WOULDN'T BE REVEALED.

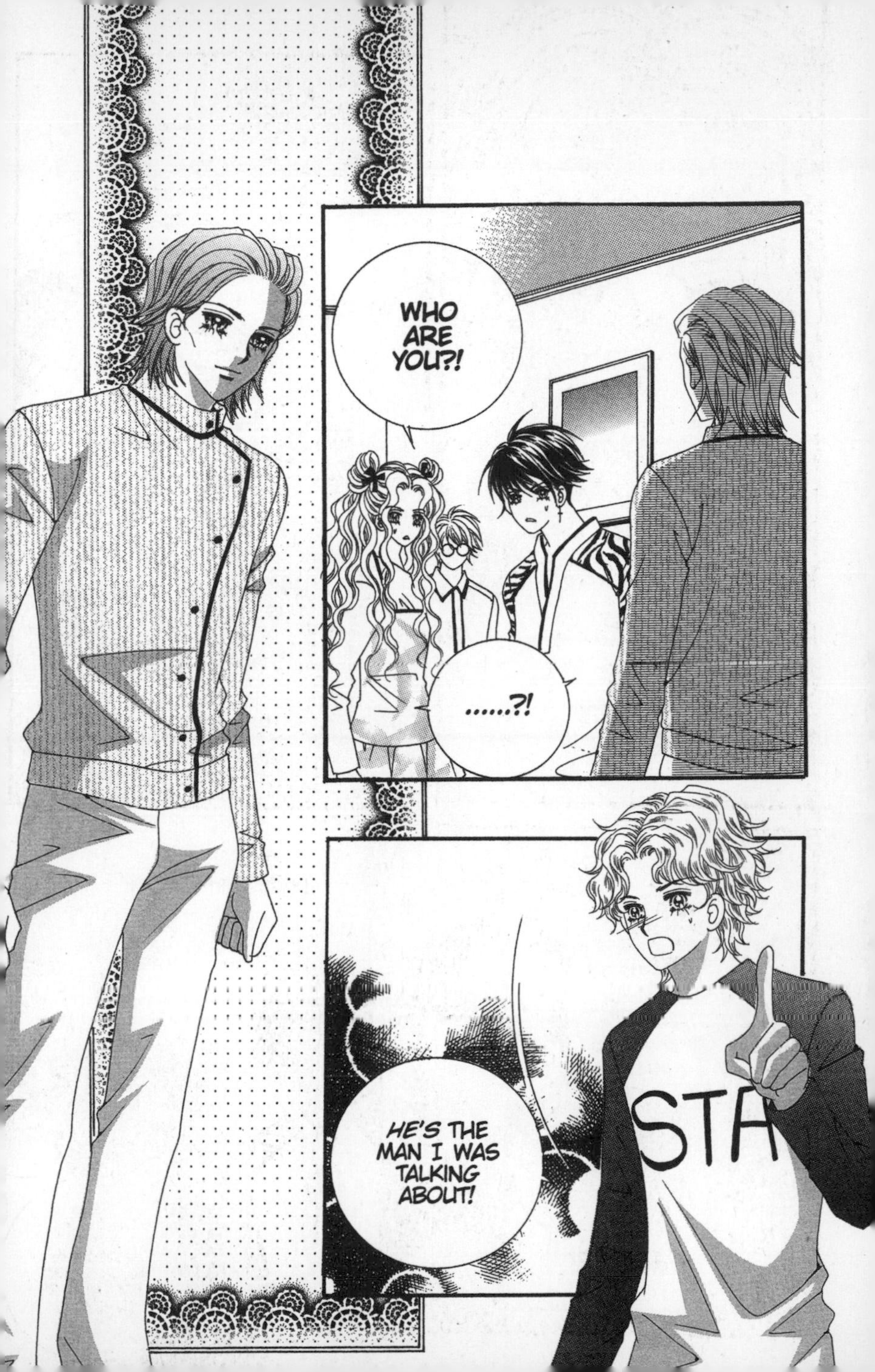
WHO ARE YOU?!
......?!
HE'S THE MAN I WAS TALKING ABOUT!
STA

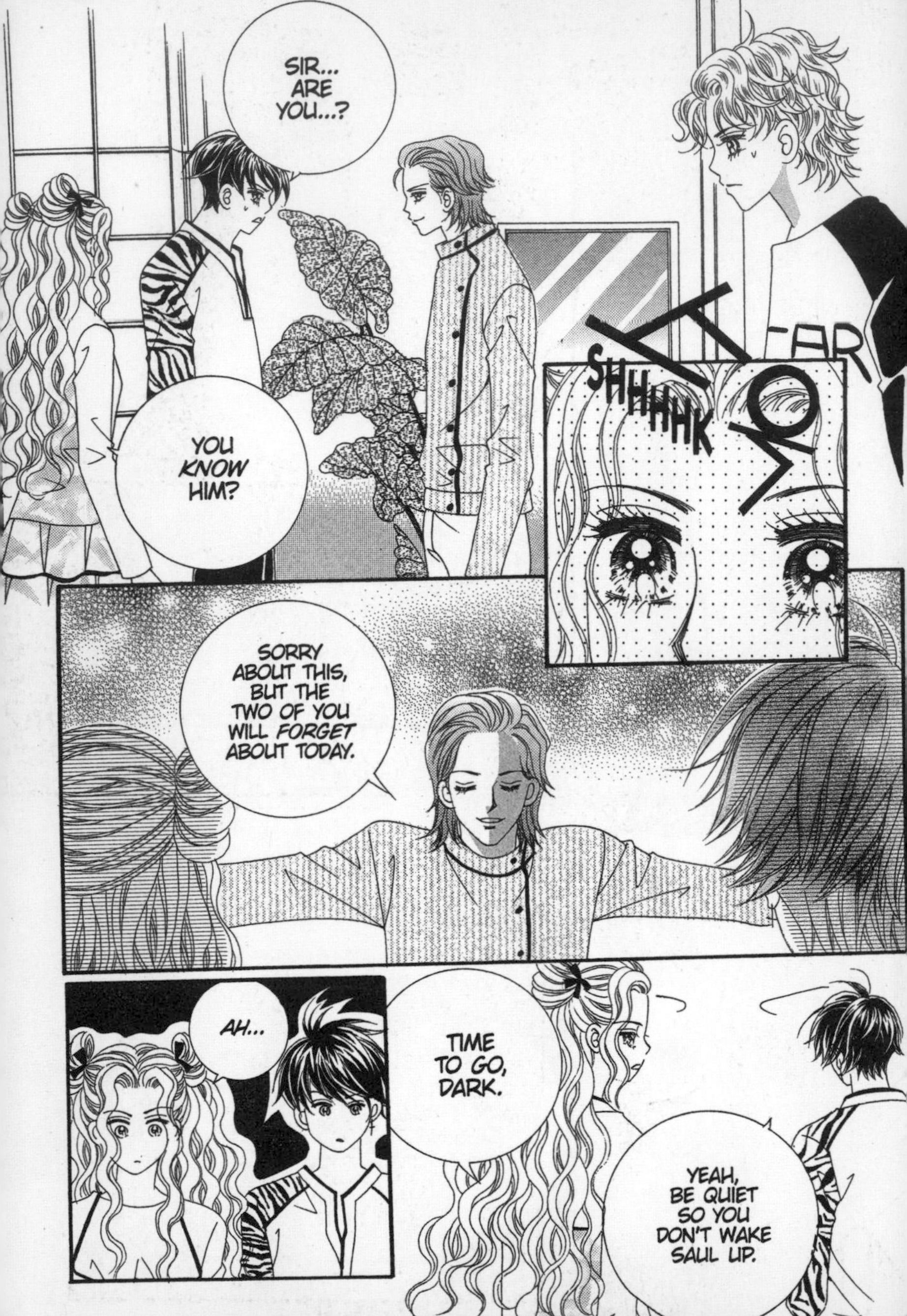
SIR... ARE YOU...?
YOU KNOW HIM?
SHHHHK
SORRY ABOUT THIS, BUT THE TWO OF YOU WILL FORGET ABOUT TODAY.
AH...
TIME TO GO, DARK.
YEAH, BE QUIET SO YOU DON'T WAKE SAUL UP.

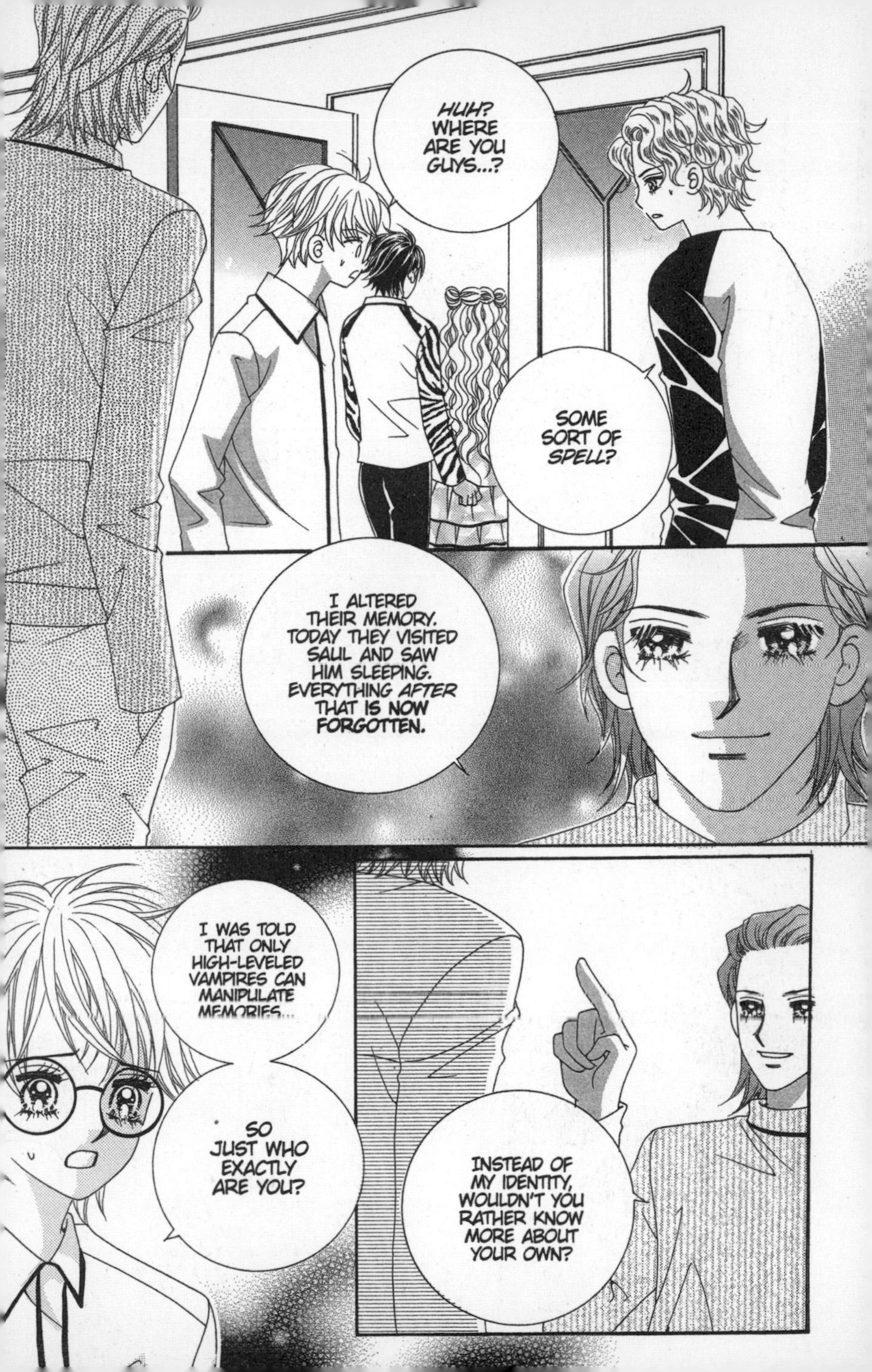
HUH? WHERE ARE YOU GUYS...?
SOME SORT OF SPELL?
I ALTERED THEIR MEMORY. TODAY THEY VISITED SAUL AND SAW HIM SLEEPING. EVERYTHING AFTER THAT IS NOW FORGOTTEN.
I WAS TOLD THAT ONLY HIGH-LEVELED VAMPIRES CAN MANIPULATE MEMORIES...
SO JUST WHO EXACTLY ARE YOU?
INSTEAD OF MY IDENTITY, WOULDN'T YOU RATHER KNOW MORE ABOUT YOUR OWN?

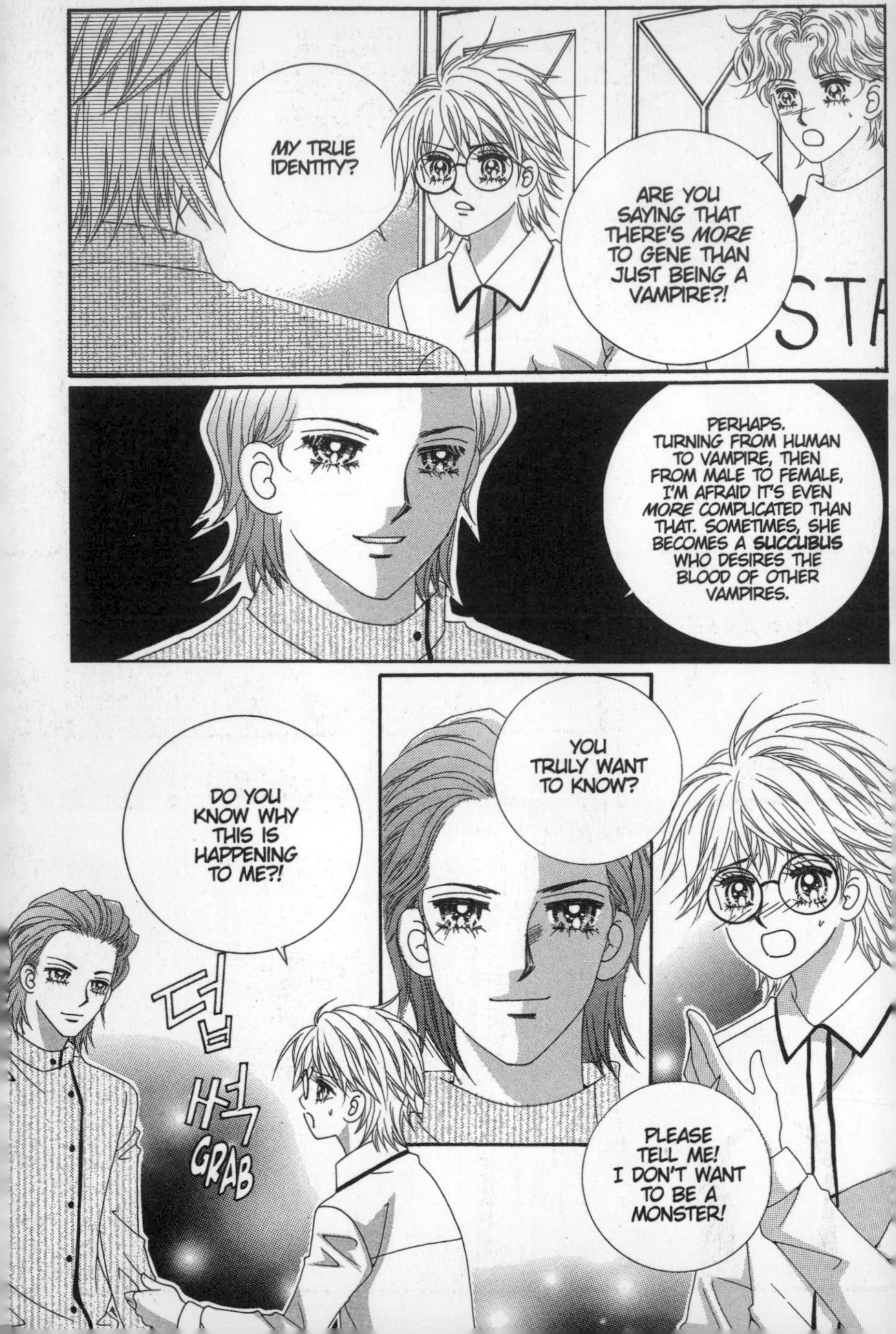
MY TRUE IDENTITY?
ARE YOU SAYING THAT THERE'S *MORE* TO GENE THAN JUST BEING A VAMPIRE?!
PERHAPS. TURNING FROM HUMAN TO VAMPIRE, THEN FROM MALE TO FEMALE, I'M AFRAID IT'S EVEN *MORE* COMPLICATED THAN THAT. SOMETIMES, SHE BECOMES A **SUCCUBUS** WHO DESIRES THE BLOOD OF OTHER VAMPIRES.
DO YOU KNOW WHY THIS IS HAPPENING TO ME?!
덥석
GRAB
YOU TRULY WANT TO KNOW?
PLEASE TELL ME! I DON'T WANT TO BE A MONSTER!

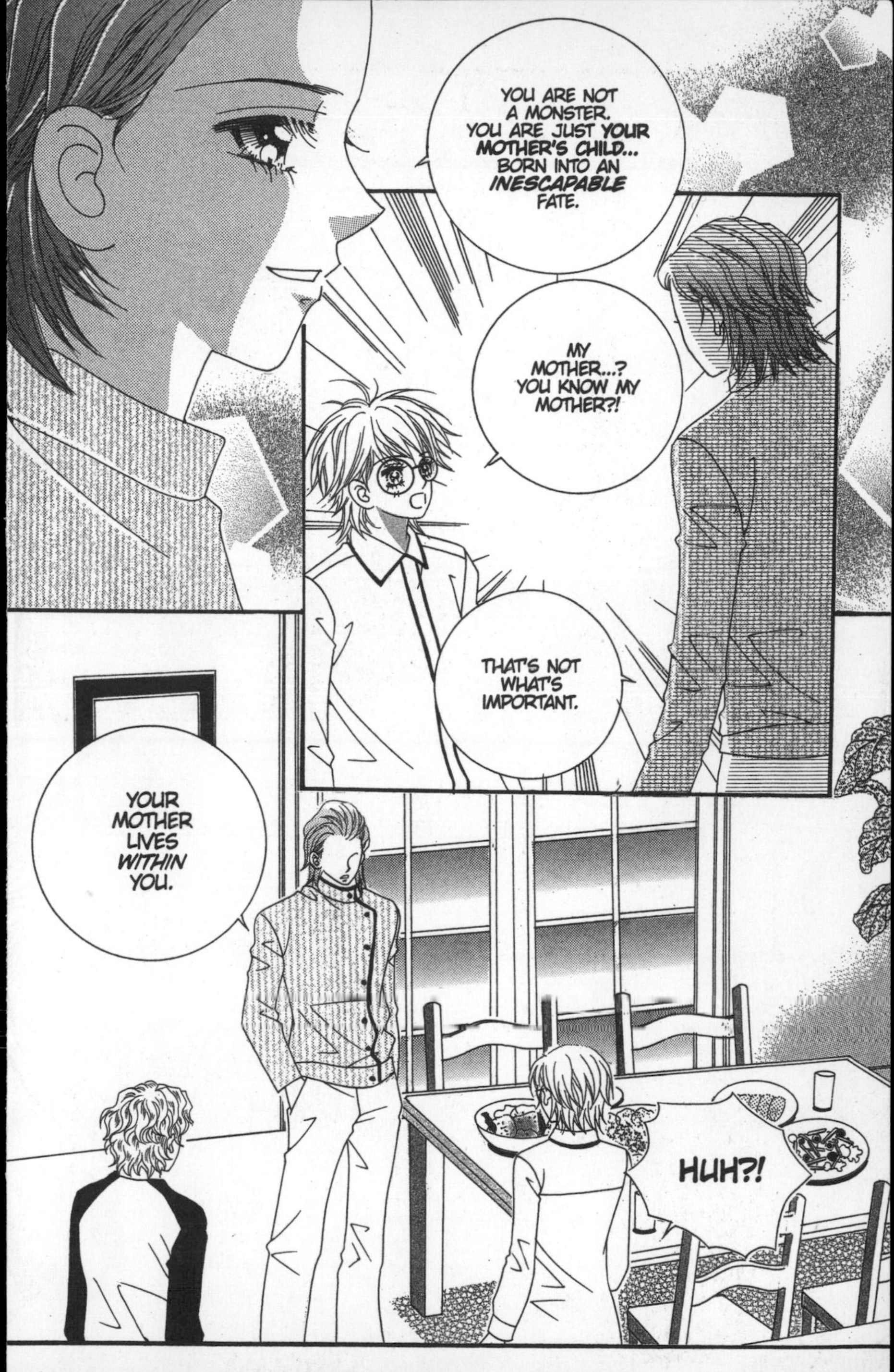
YOU ARE NOT A MONSTER. YOU ARE JUST YOUR MOTHER'S CHILD... BORN INTO AN INESCAPABLE FATE.
MY MOTHER...? YOU KNOW MY MOTHER?!
THAT'S NOT WHAT'S IMPORTANT.
YOUR MOTHER LIVES WITHIN YOU.
HUH?!

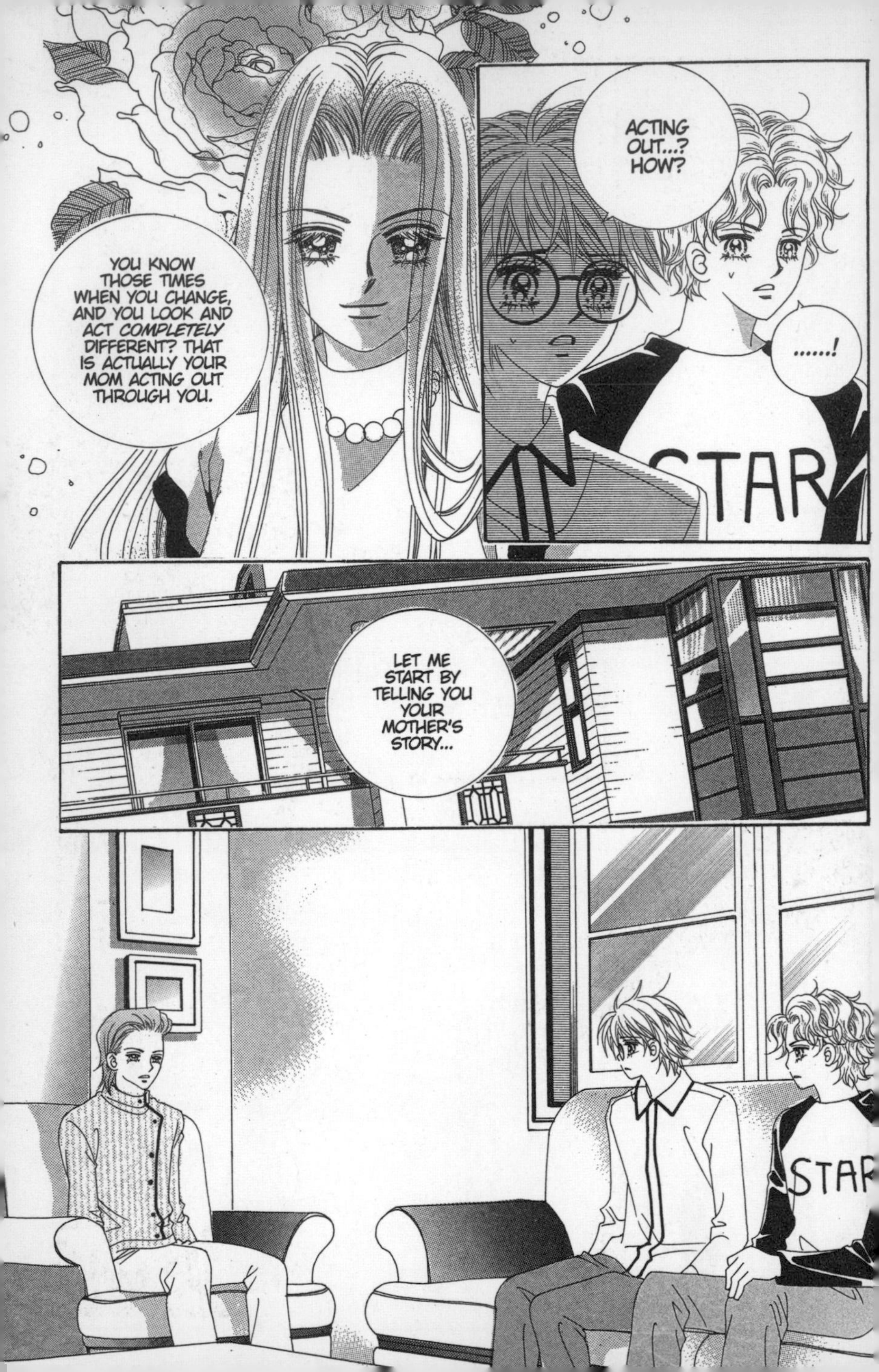
YOU KNOW THOSE TIMES WHEN YOU CHANGE, AND YOU LOOK AND ACT *COMPLETELY* DIFFERENT? THAT IS ACTUALLY YOUR MOM ACTING OUT THROUGH YOU.
ACTING OUT...? HOW?
......!
STAR
LET ME START BY TELLING YOU YOUR MOTHER'S STORY...
STAR

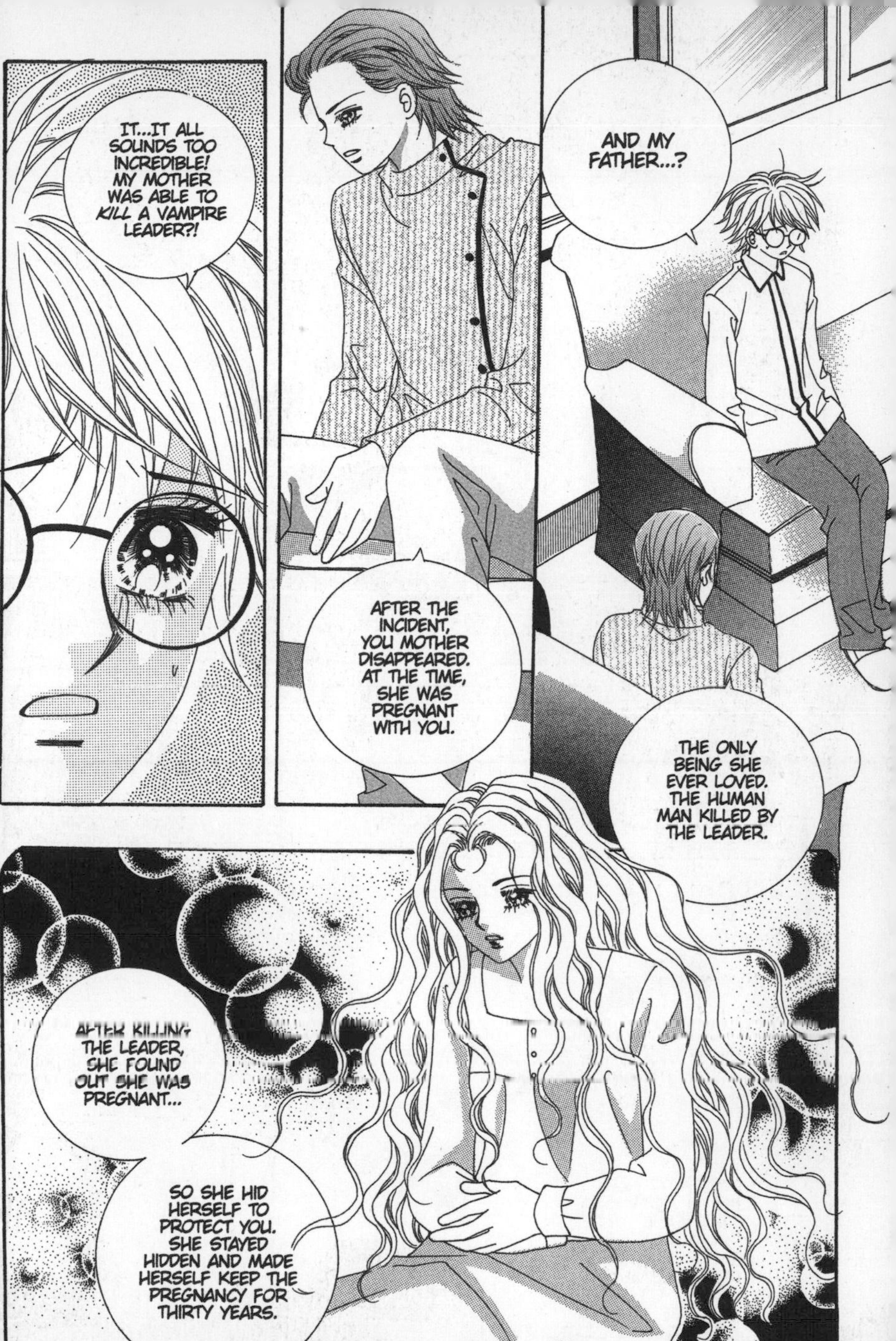
IT...IT ALL SOUNDS TOO INCREDIBLE! MY MOTHER WAS ABLE TO KILL A VAMPIRE LEADER?!
AFTER THE INCIDENT, YOU MOTHER DISAPPEARED. AT THE TIME, SHE WAS PREGNANT WITH YOU.
AND MY FATHER...?
THE ONLY BEING SHE EVER LOVED. THE HUMAN MAN KILLED BY THE LEADER.
AFTER KILLING THE LEADER, SHE FOUND OUT SHE WAS PREGNANT...
SO SHE HID HERSELF TO PROTECT YOU. SHE STAYED HIDDEN AND MADE HERSELF KEEP THE PREGNANCY FOR THIRTY YEARS.

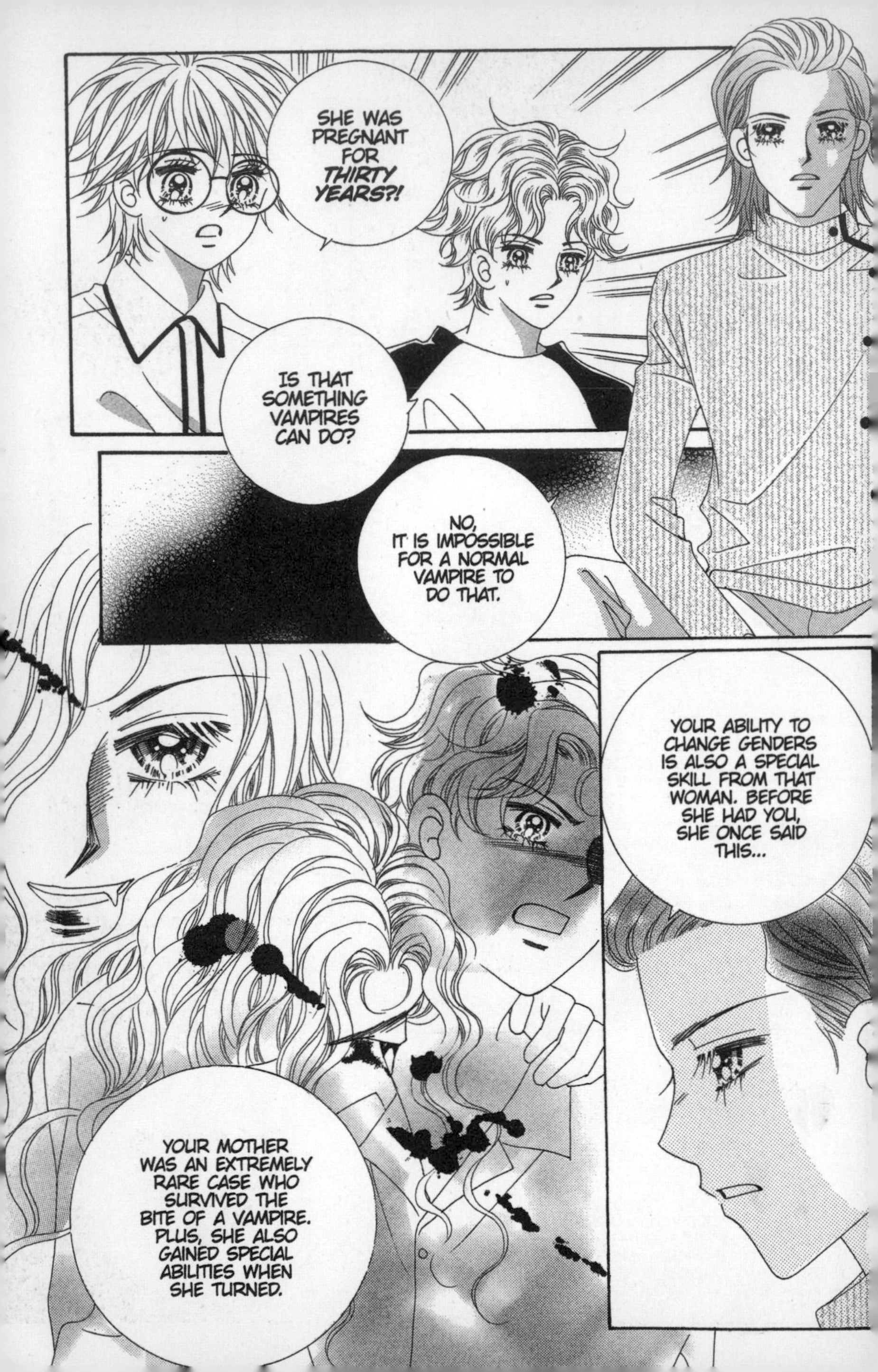
SHE WAS PREGNANT FOR *THIRTY YEARS?!*
IS THAT SOMETHING VAMPIRES CAN DO?
NO, IT IS IMPOSSIBLE FOR A NORMAL VAMPIRE TO DO THAT.
YOUR MOTHER WAS AN EXTREMELY RARE CASE WHO SURVIVED THE BITE OF A VAMPIRE. PLUS, SHE ALSO GAINED SPECIAL ABILITIES WHEN SHE TURNED.
YOUR ABILITY TO CHANGE GENDERS IS ALSO A SPECIAL SKILL FROM THAT WOMAN. BEFORE SHE HAD YOU, SHE ONCE SAID THIS...

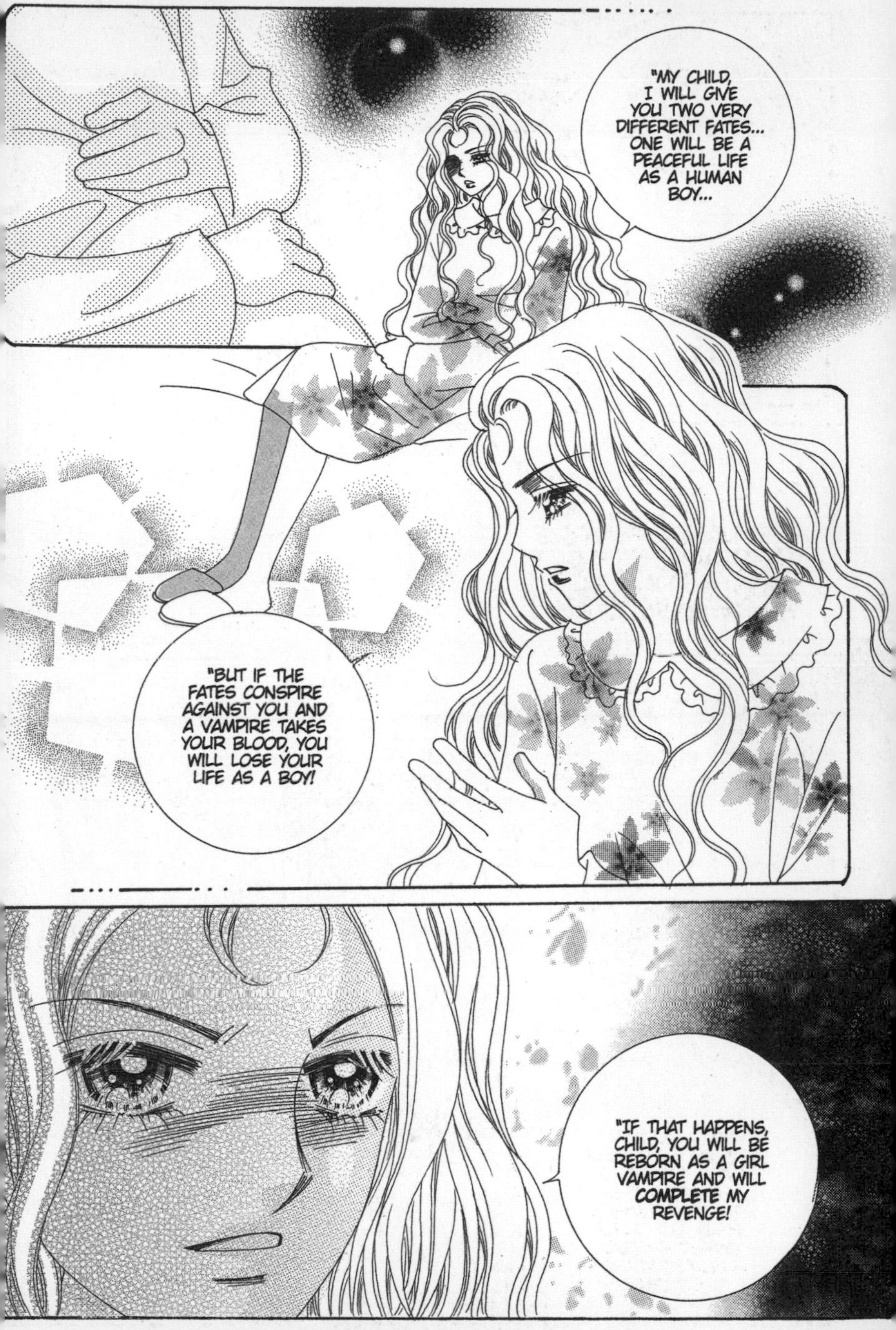
"MY CHILD, I WILL GIVE YOU TWO VERY DIFFERENT FATES... ONE WILL BE A PEACEFUL LIFE AS A HUMAN BOY...
"BUT IF THE FATES CONSPIRE AGAINST YOU AND A VAMPIRE TAKES YOUR BLOOD, YOU WILL LOSE YOUR LIFE AS A BOY!
"IF THAT HAPPENS, CHILD, YOU WILL BE REBORN AS A GIRL VAMPIRE AND WILL COMPLETE MY REVENGE!

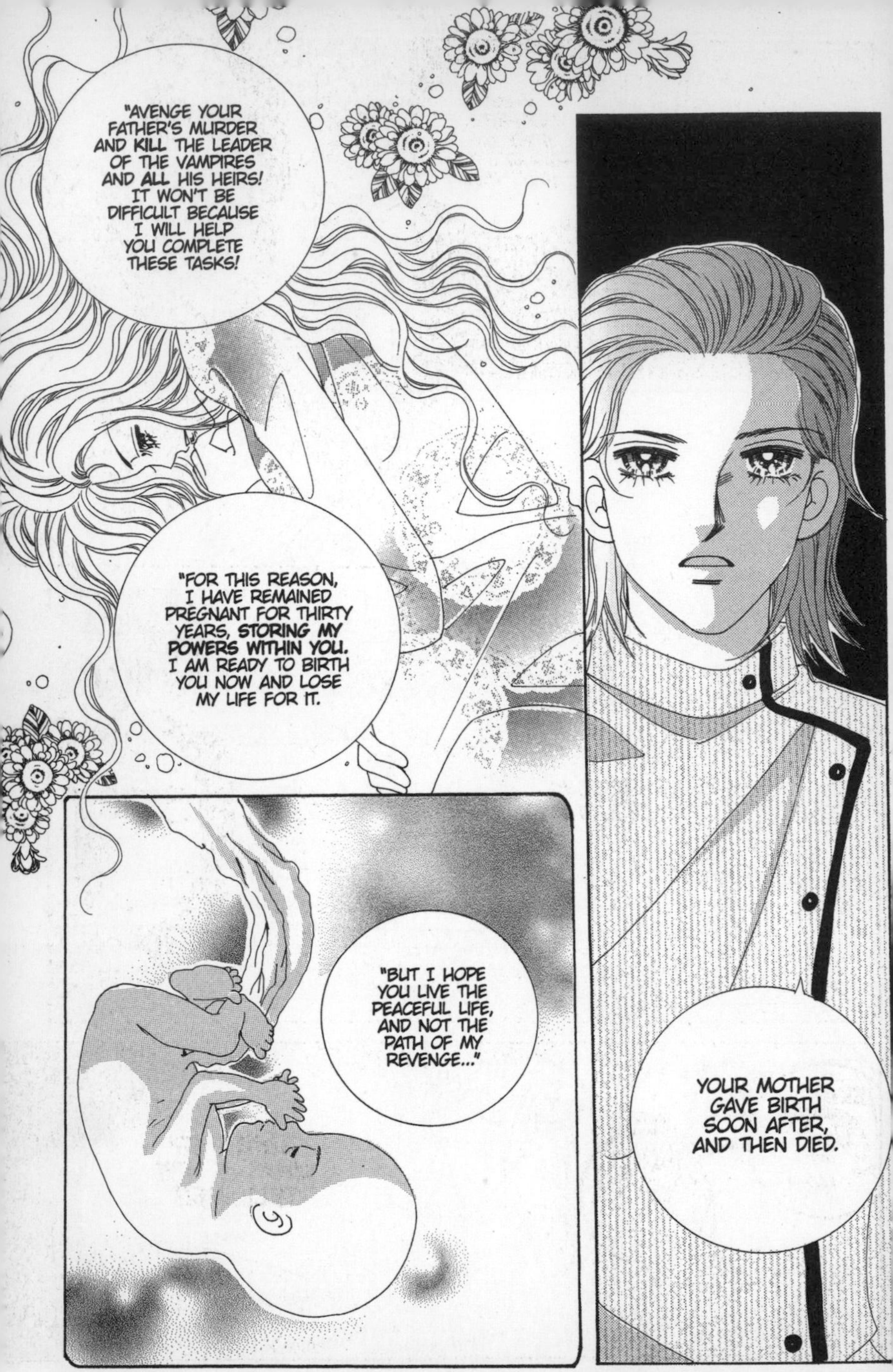
"AVENGE YOUR FATHER'S MURDER AND KILL THE LEADER OF THE VAMPIRES AND ALL HIS HEIRS! IT WON'T BE DIFFICULT BECAUSE I WILL HELP YOU COMPLETE THESE TASKS!
"FOR THIS REASON, I HAVE REMAINED PREGNANT FOR THIRTY YEARS, STORING MY POWERS WITHIN YOU. I AM READY TO BIRTH YOU NOW AND LOSE MY LIFE FOR IT.
"BUT I HOPE YOU LIVE THE PEACEFUL LIFE, AND NOT THE PATH OF MY REVENGE..."
YOUR MOTHER GAVE BIRTH SOON AFTER, AND THEN DIED.

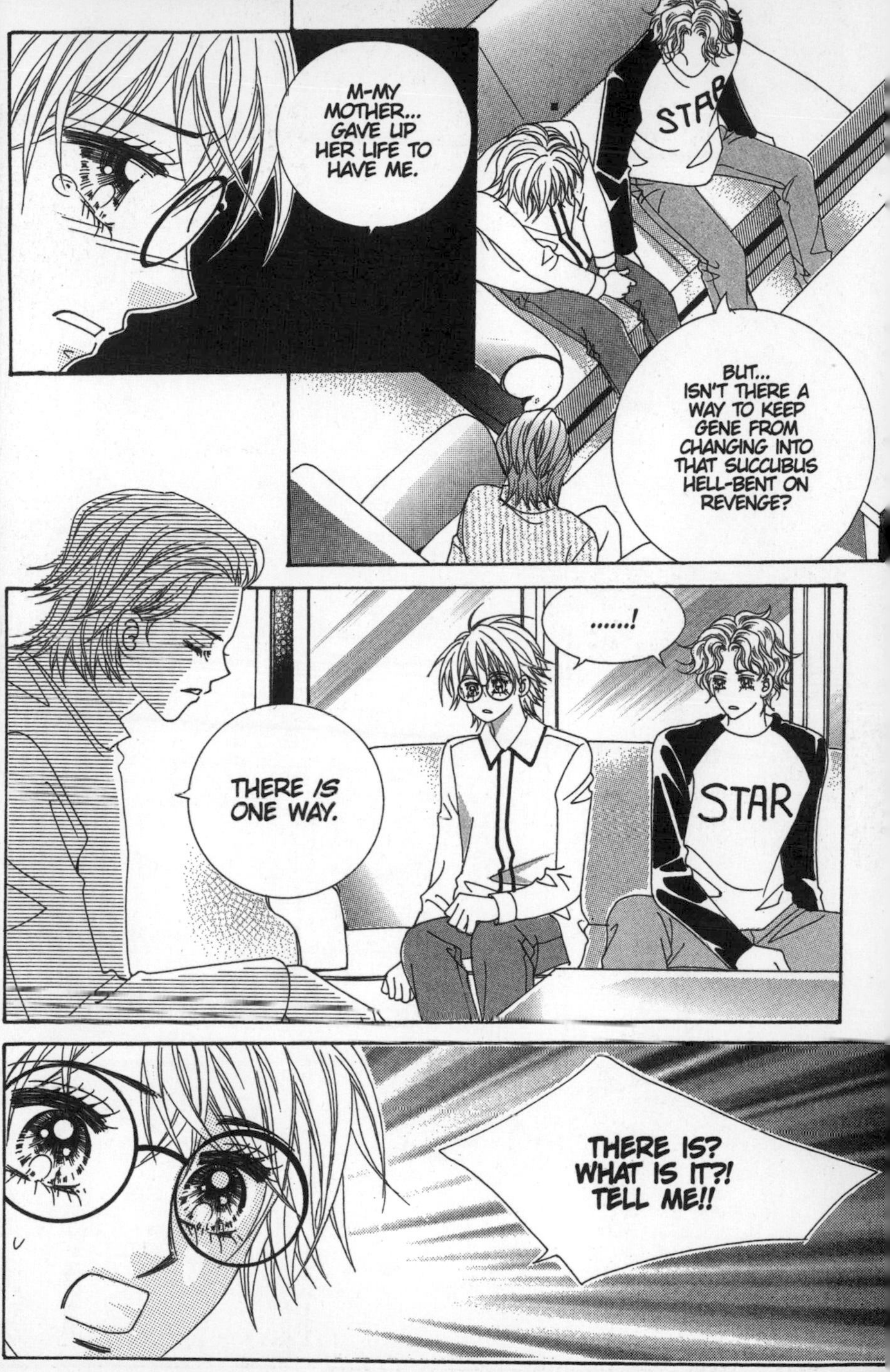
M-MY MOTHER... GAVE UP HER LIFE TO HAVE ME.
STAR
BUT... ISN'T THERE A WAY TO KEEP GENE FROM CHANGING INTO THAT SUCCUBUS HELL-BENT ON REVENGE?
......!
THERE IS ONE WAY.
STAR
THERE IS? WHAT IS IT?! TELL ME!!

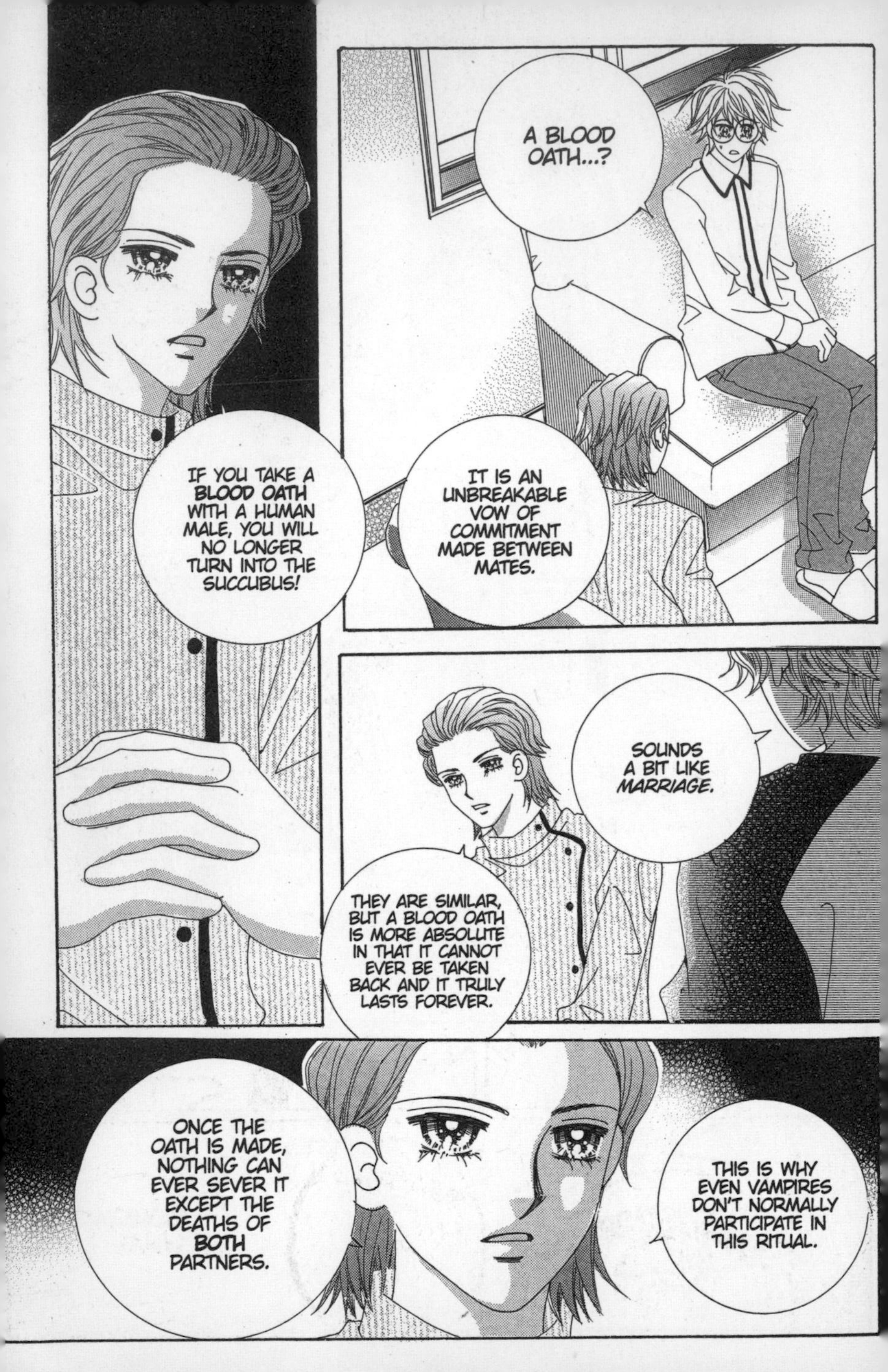
IF YOU TAKE A BLOOD OATH WITH A HUMAN MALE, YOU WILL NO LONGER TURN INTO THE SUCCUBUS!
A BLOOD OATH...?
IT IS AN UNBREAKABLE VOW OF COMMITMENT MADE BETWEEN MATES.
SOUNDS A BIT LIKE MARRIAGE.
THEY ARE SIMILAR, BUT A BLOOD OATH IS MORE ABSOLUTE IN THAT IT CANNOT EVER BE TAKEN BACK AND IT TRULY LASTS FOREVER.
ONCE THE OATH IS MADE, NOTHING CAN EVER SEVER IT EXCEPT THE DEATHS OF BOTH PARTNERS.
THIS IS WHY EVEN VAMPIRES DON'T NORMALLY PARTICIPATE IN THIS RITUAL.

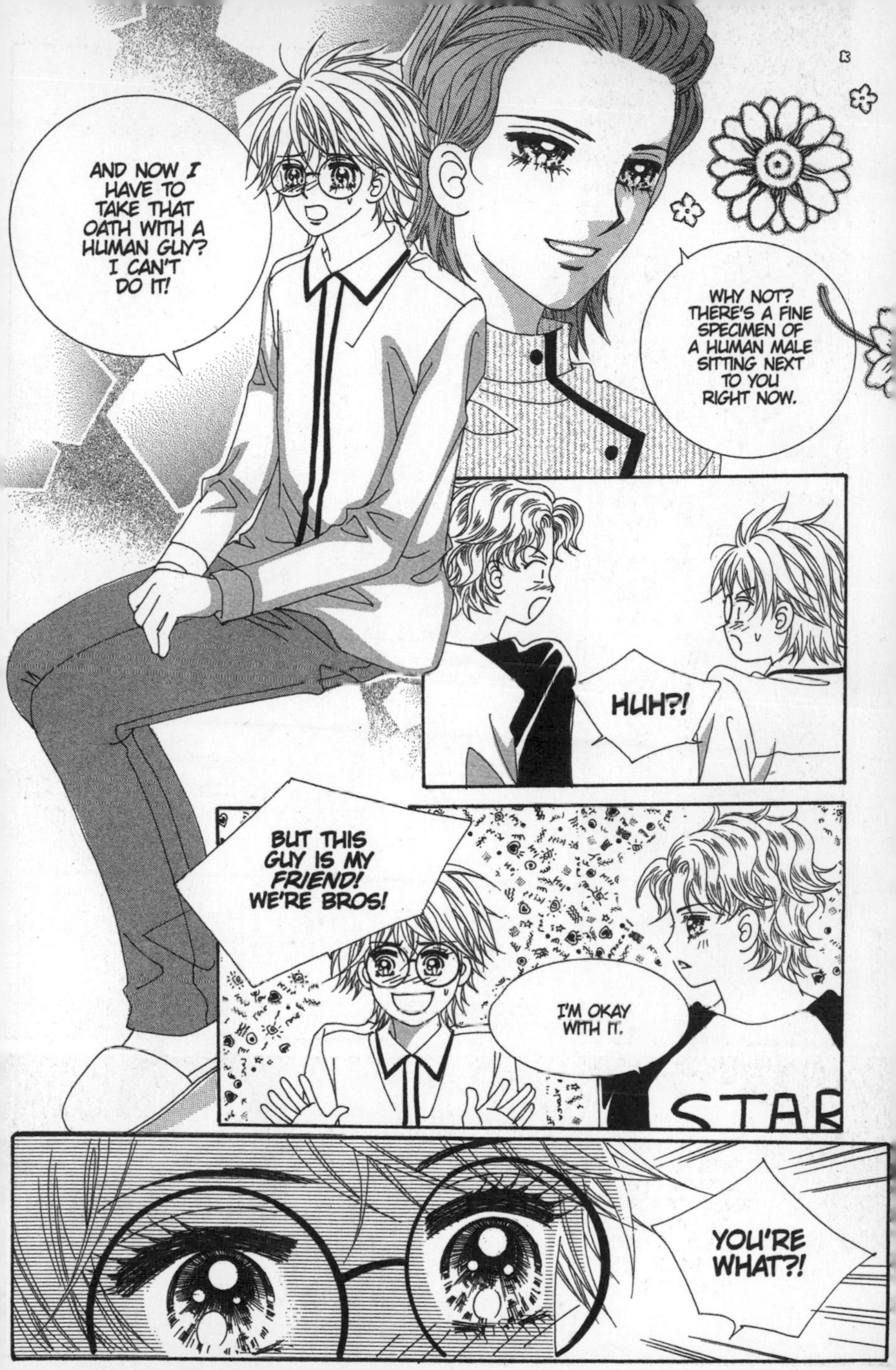
AND NOW I HAVE TO TAKE THAT OATH WITH A HUMAN GUY? I CAN'T DO IT!
WHY NOT? THERE'S A FINE SPECIMEN OF A HUMAN MALE SITTING NEXT TO YOU RIGHT NOW.
HUH?!
BUT THIS GUY IS MY FRIEND! WE'RE BROS!
I'M OKAY WITH IT.
STAR
YOU'RE WHAT?!

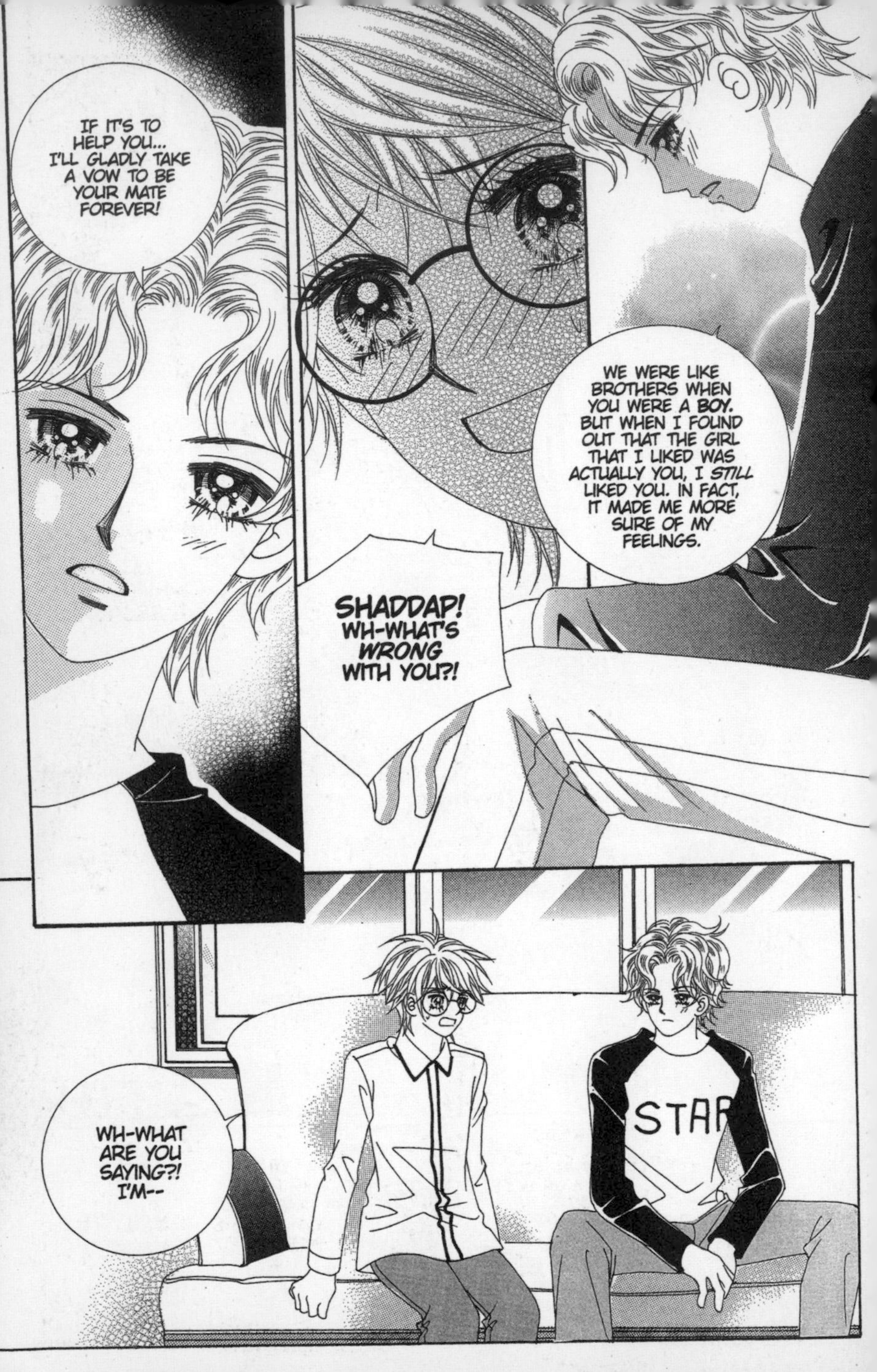
IF IT'S TO HELP YOU... I'LL GLADLY TAKE A VOW TO BE YOUR MATE FOREVER!
SHADDAP! WH-WHAT'S WRONG WITH YOU?!
WE WERE LIKE BROTHERS WHEN YOU WERE A BOY. BUT WHEN I FOUND OUT THAT THE GIRL THAT I LIKED WAS ACTUALLY YOU, I STILL LIKED YOU. IN FACT, IT MADE ME MORE SURE OF MY FEELINGS.
WH-WHAT ARE YOU SAYING?! I'M--
STAR

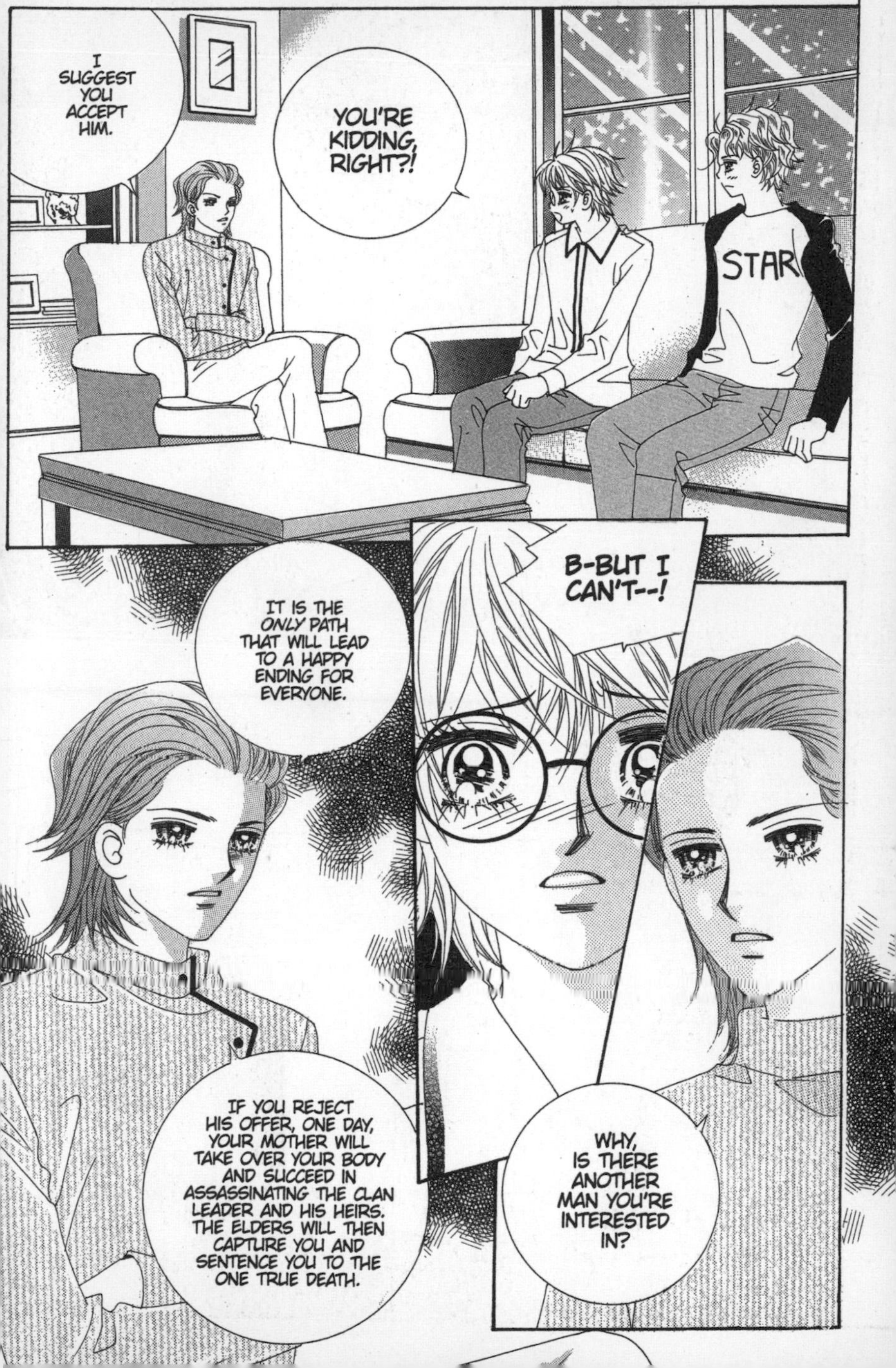
I SUGGEST YOU ACCEPT HIM.
YOU'RE KIDDING, RIGHT?!
STAR
IT IS THE *ONLY* PATH THAT WILL LEAD TO A HAPPY ENDING FOR EVERYONE.
B-BUT I CAN'T--!
IF YOU REJECT HIS OFFER, ONE DAY, YOUR MOTHER WILL TAKE OVER YOUR BODY AND SUCCEED IN ASSASSINATING THE CLAN LEADER AND HIS HEIRS. THE ELDERS WILL THEN CAPTURE YOU AND SENTENCE YOU TO THE ONE TRUE DEATH.
WHY, IS THERE ANOTHER MAN YOU'RE INTERESTED IN?

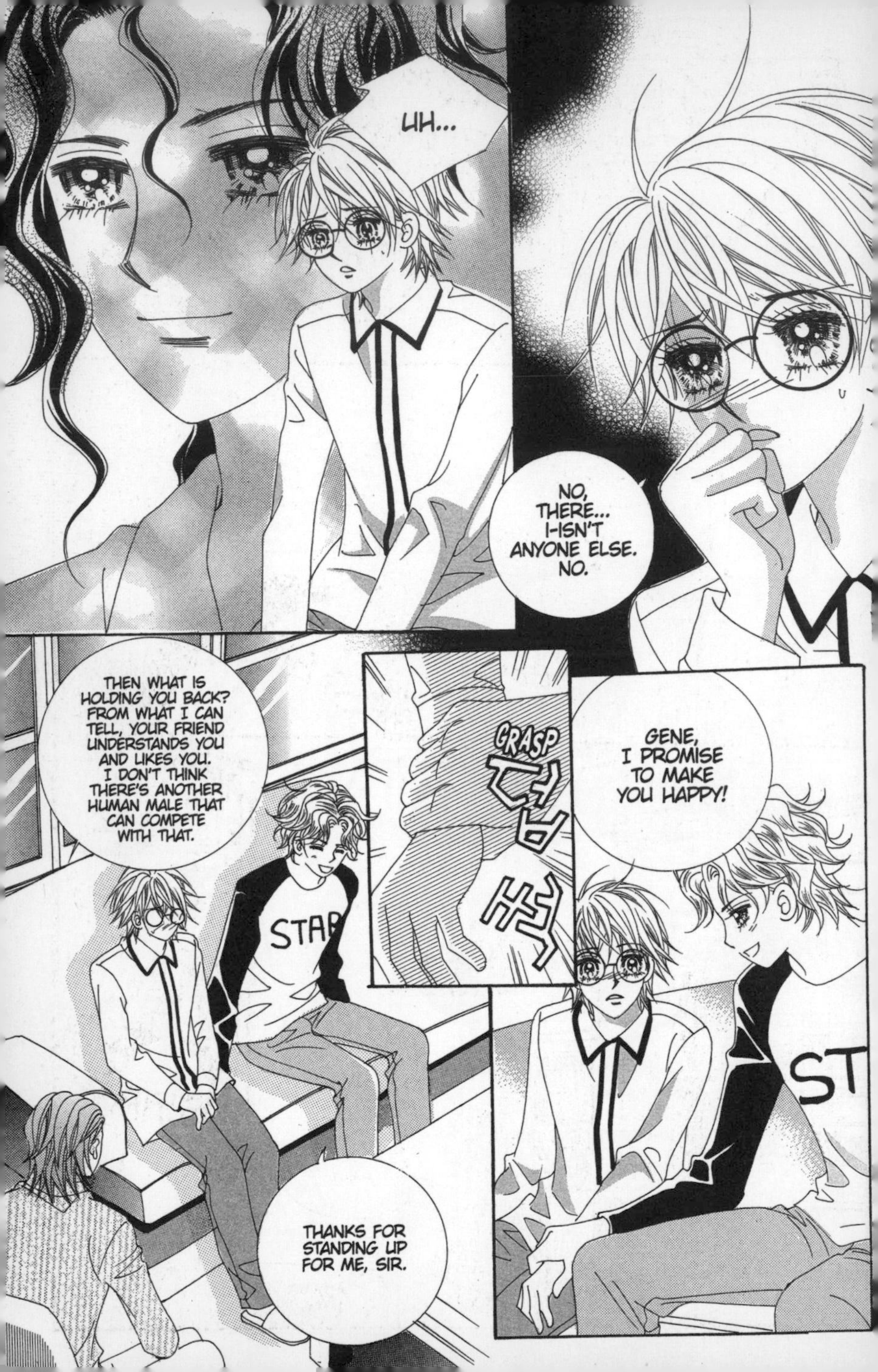
UH...
NO, THERE... I-ISN'T ANYONE ELSE. NO.
THEN WHAT IS HOLDING YOU BACK? FROM WHAT I CAN TELL, YOUR FRIEND UNDERSTANDS YOU AND LIKES YOU. I DON'T THINK THERE'S ANOTHER HUMAN MALE THAT CAN COMPETE WITH THAT.
GRASP
GENE, I PROMISE TO MAKE YOU HAPPY!
THANKS FOR STANDING UP FOR ME, SIR.

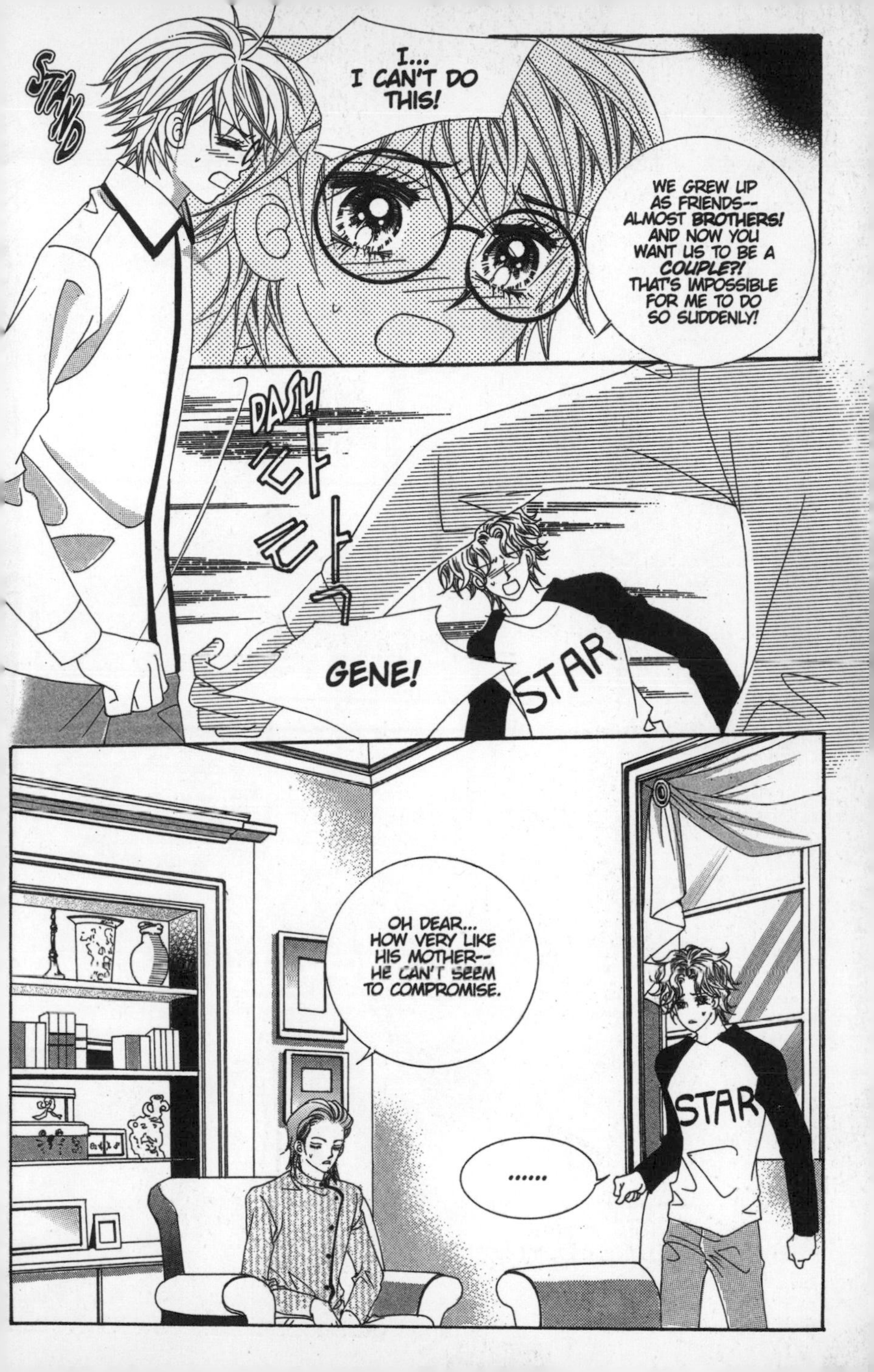
STAND
I... I CAN'T DO THIS!
WE GREW UP AS FRIENDS-- ALMOST BROTHERS! AND NOW YOU WANT US TO BE A COUPLE?! THAT'S IMPOSSIBLE FOR ME TO DO SO SUDDENLY!
DASH
GENE!
STAR
OH DEAR... HOW VERY LIKE HIS MOTHER-- HE CAN'T SEEM TO COMPROMISE.
......
STAR

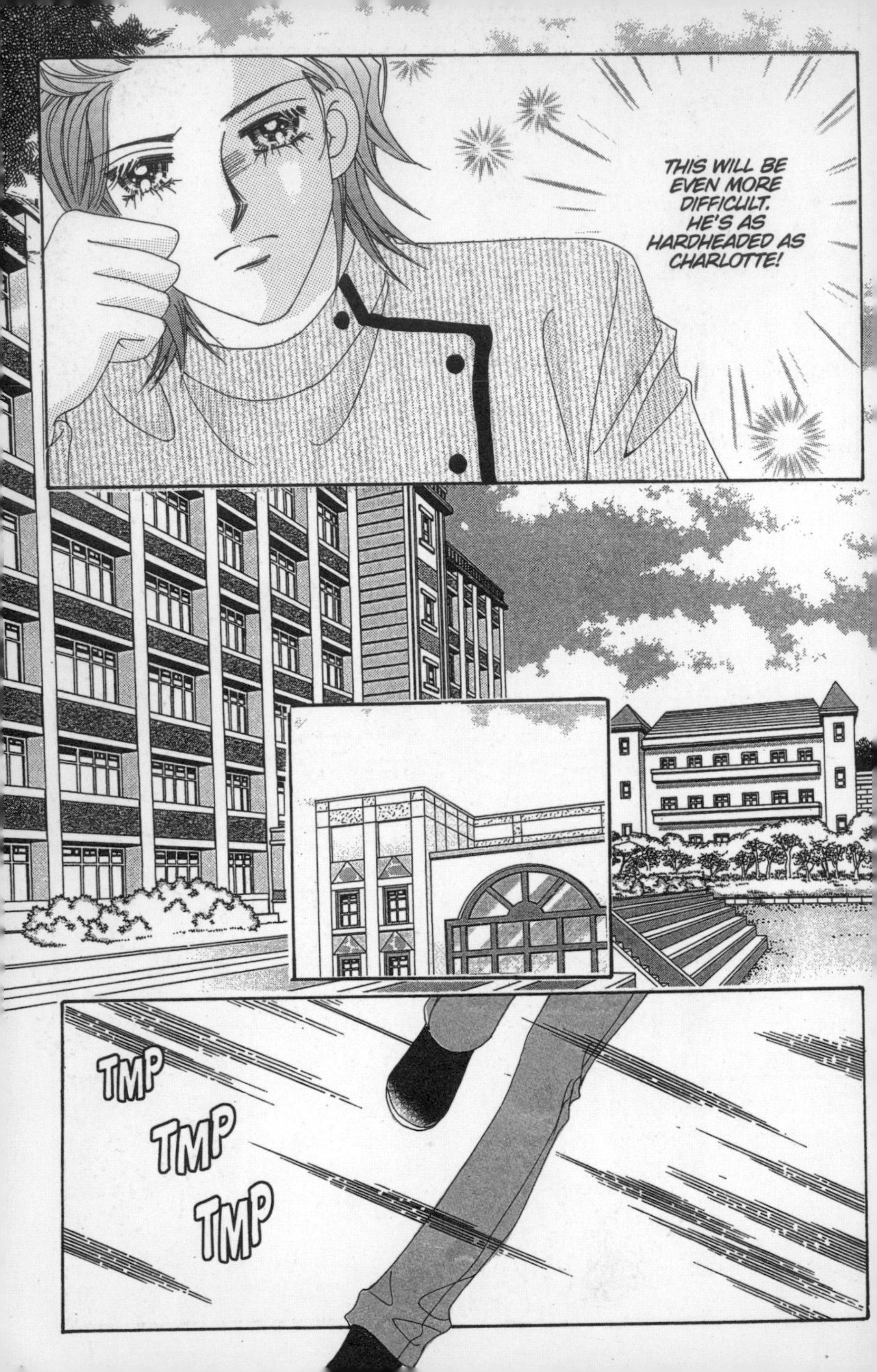
THIS WILL BE EVEN MORE DIFFICULT. HE'S AS HARDHEADED AS CHARLOTTE!
TMP
TMP
TMP

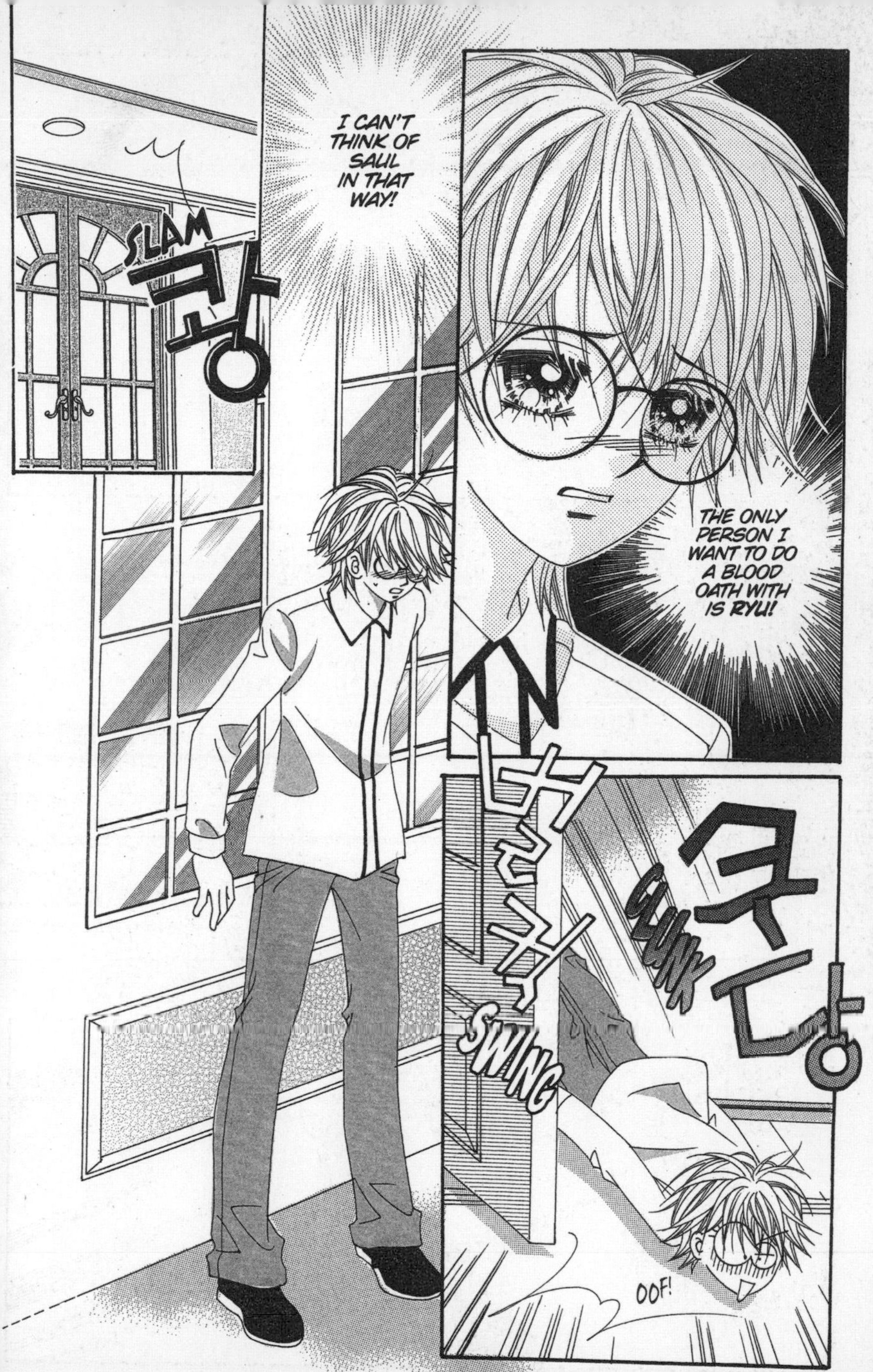
SLAM
쾅
I CAN'T THINK OF SAUL IN THAT WAY!
THE ONLY PERSON I WANT TO DO A BLOOD OATH WITH IS RYU!
SWING
CLUNK
OOF!

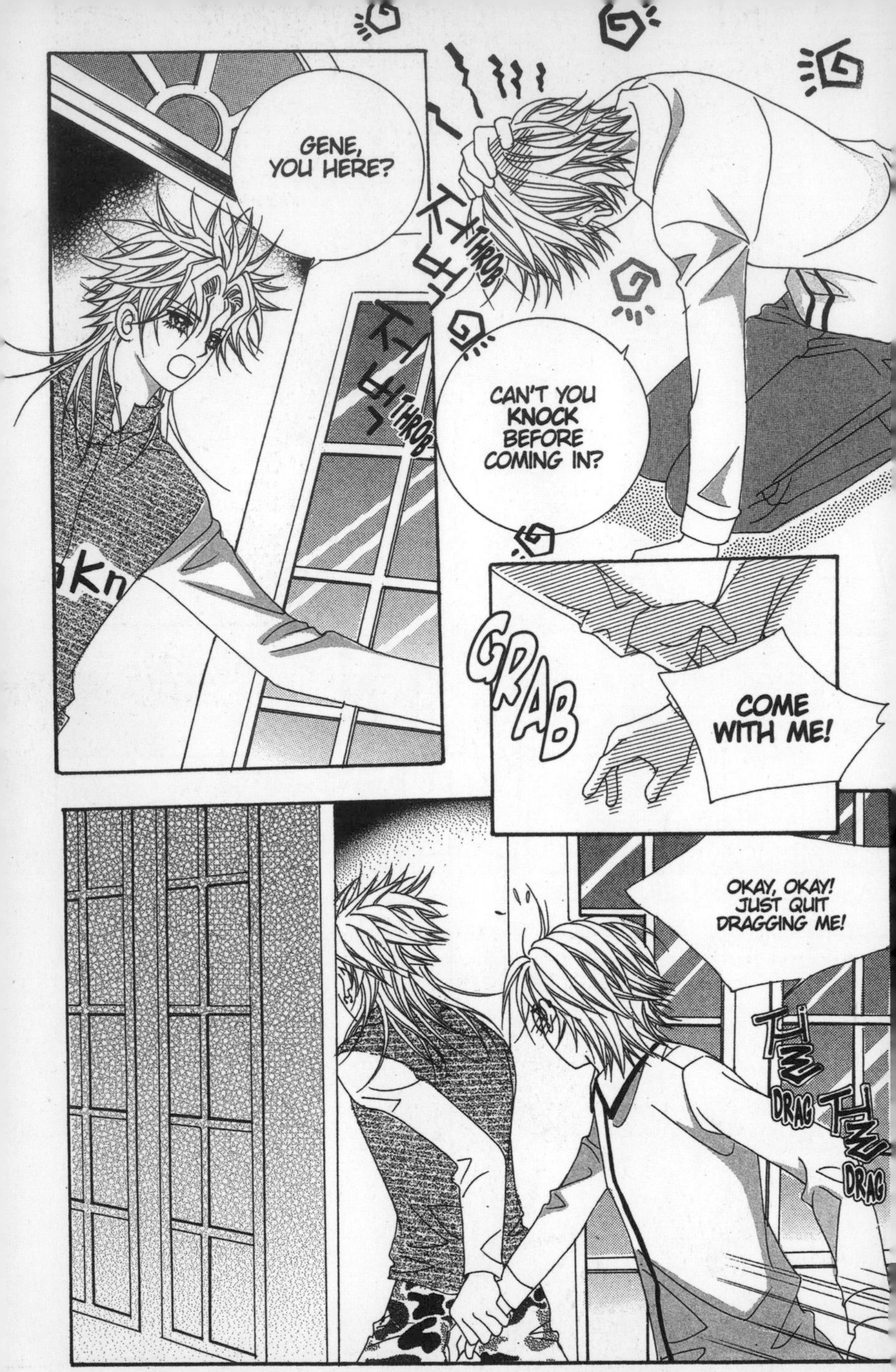
GENE, YOU HERE?
THROB
THROB
CAN'T YOU KNOCK BEFORE COMING IN?
GRAB
COME WITH ME!
OKAY, OKAY! JUST QUIT DRAGGING ME!
DRAG
DRAG

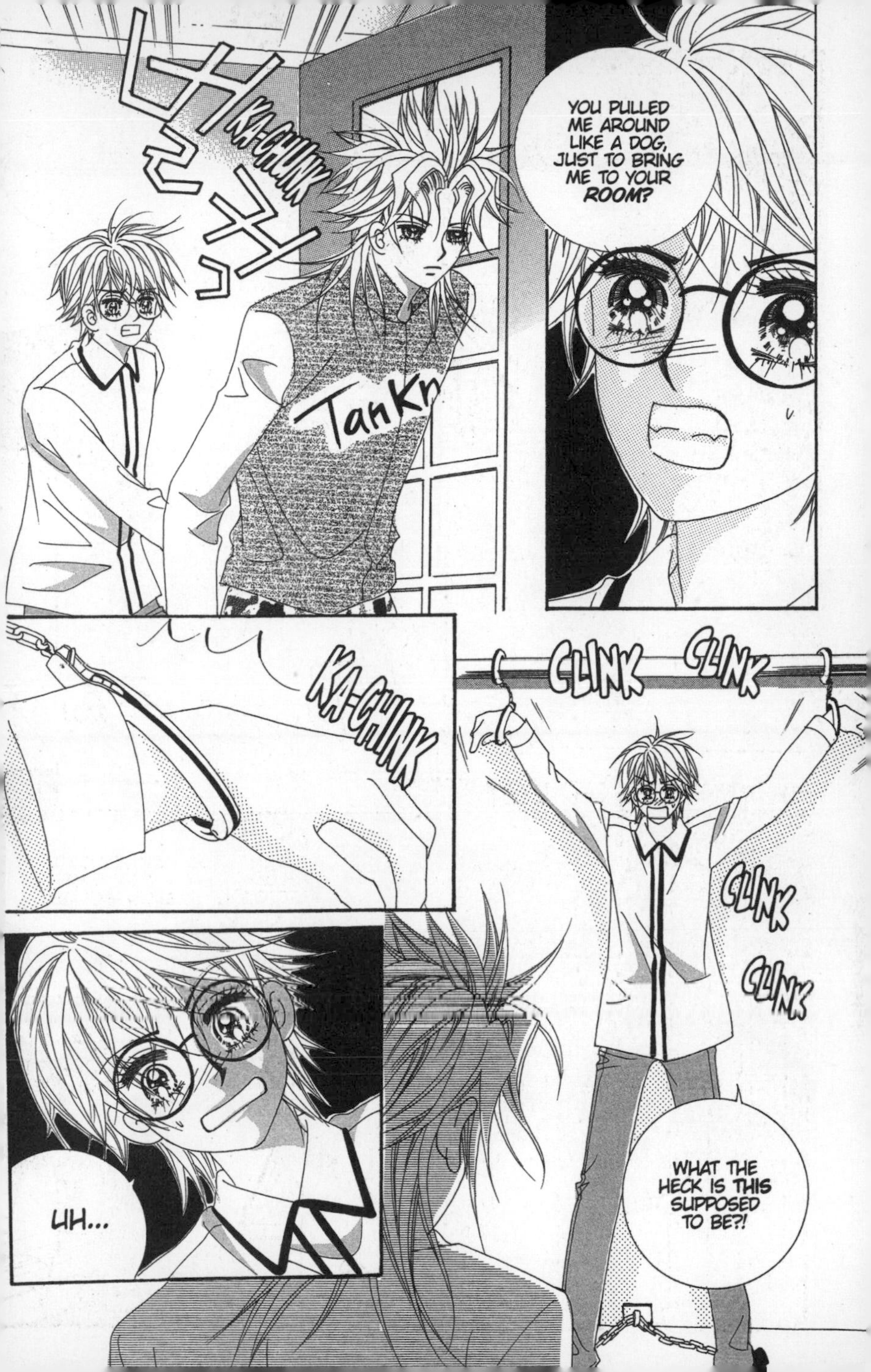
KA-CHUNK
YOU PULLED ME AROUND LIKE A DOG, JUST TO BRING ME TO YOUR *ROOM?*
KA-CHUNK
UH...
CLINK
CLINK
CLINK
CLINK
WHAT THE HECK IS THIS SUPPOSED TO BE?!

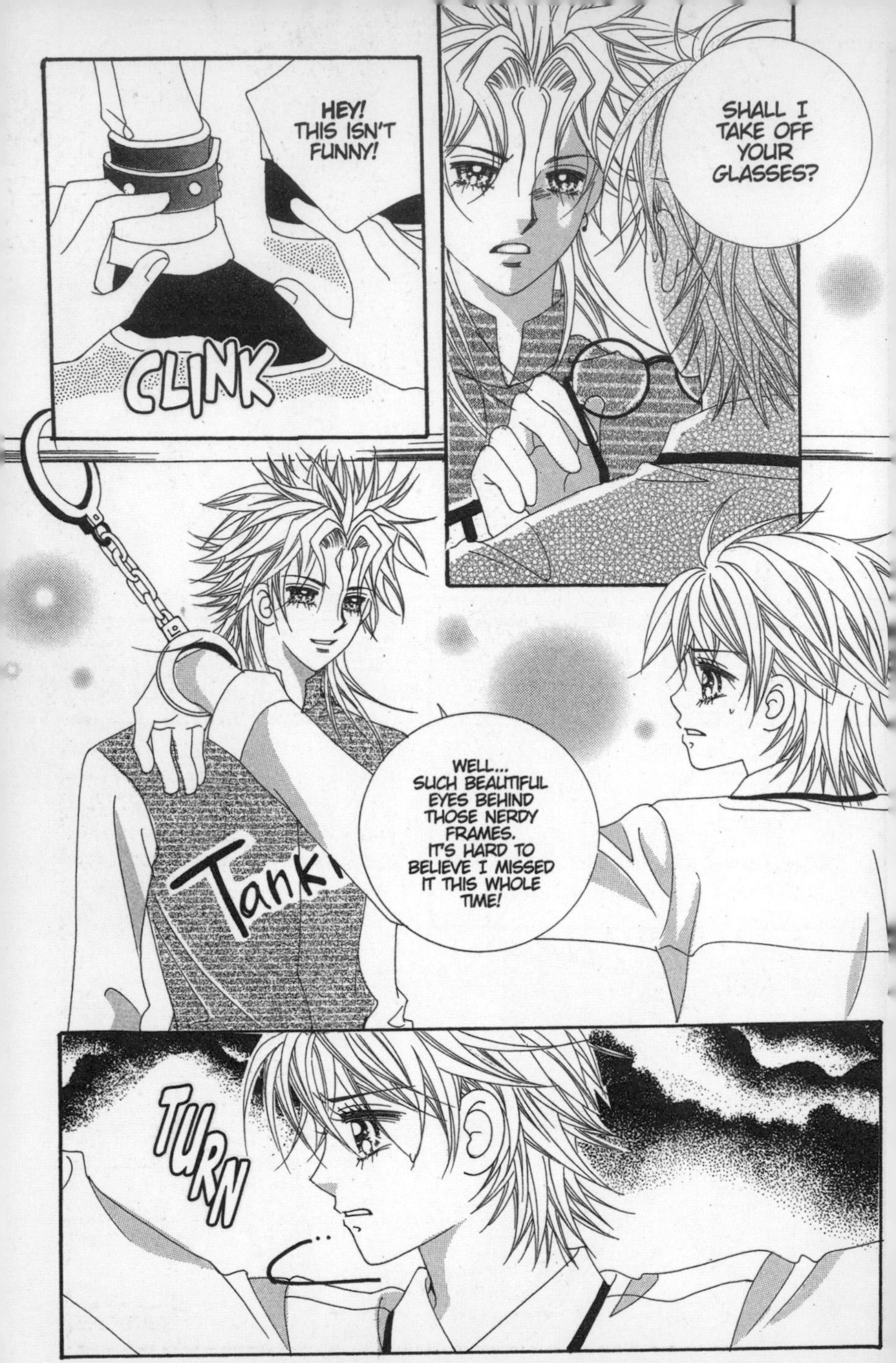
HEY! THIS ISN'T FUNNY!
CLINK
SHALL I TAKE OFF YOUR GLASSES?
Tank
WELL... SUCH BEAUTIFUL EYES BEHIND THOSE NERDY FRAMES. IT'S HARD TO BELIEVE I MISSED IT THIS WHOLE TIME!
TURN

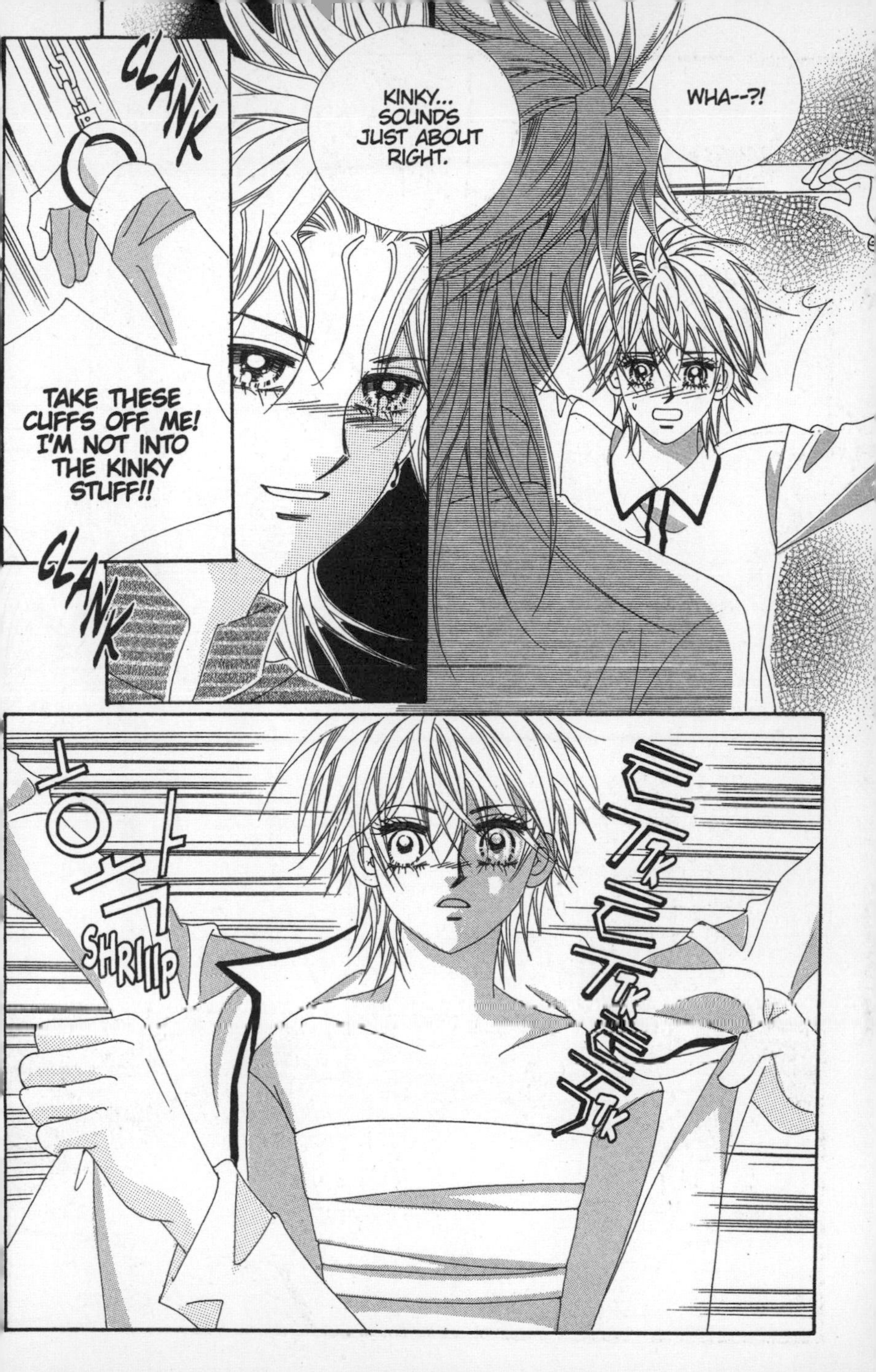
CLANK
TAKE THESE CUFFS OFF ME! I'M NOT INTO THE KINKY STUFF!!
CLANK
KINKY... SOUNDS JUST ABOUT RIGHT.
WHA--?!
SHRIIIP
TK TK TK TK

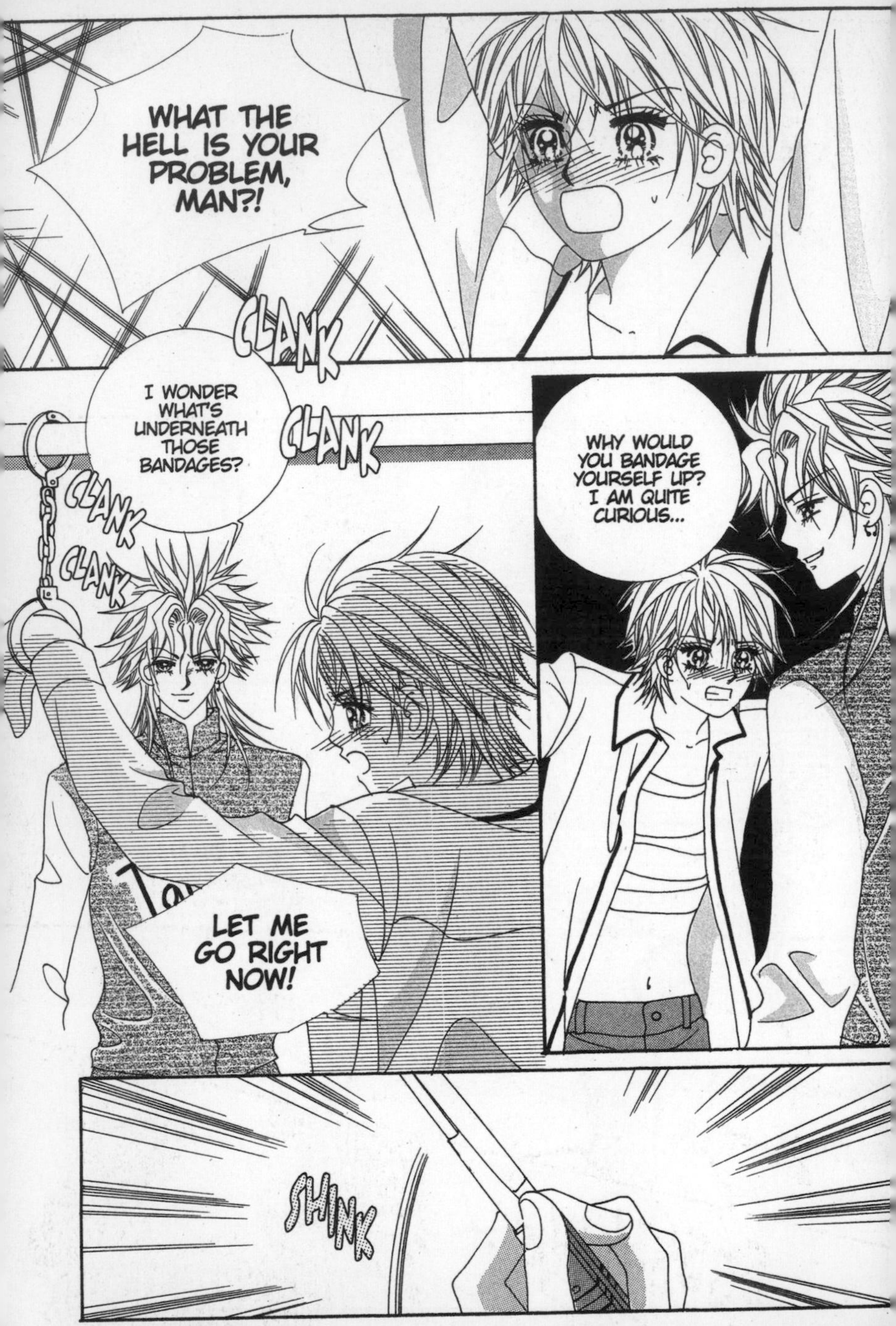
WHAT THE HELL IS YOUR PROBLEM, MAN?!
CLANK
I WONDER WHAT'S UNDERNEATH THOSE BANDAGES?
CLANK
CLANK
CLANK
LET ME GO RIGHT NOW!
WHY WOULD YOU BANDAGE YOURSELF UP? I AM QUITE CURIOUS...
SHINK

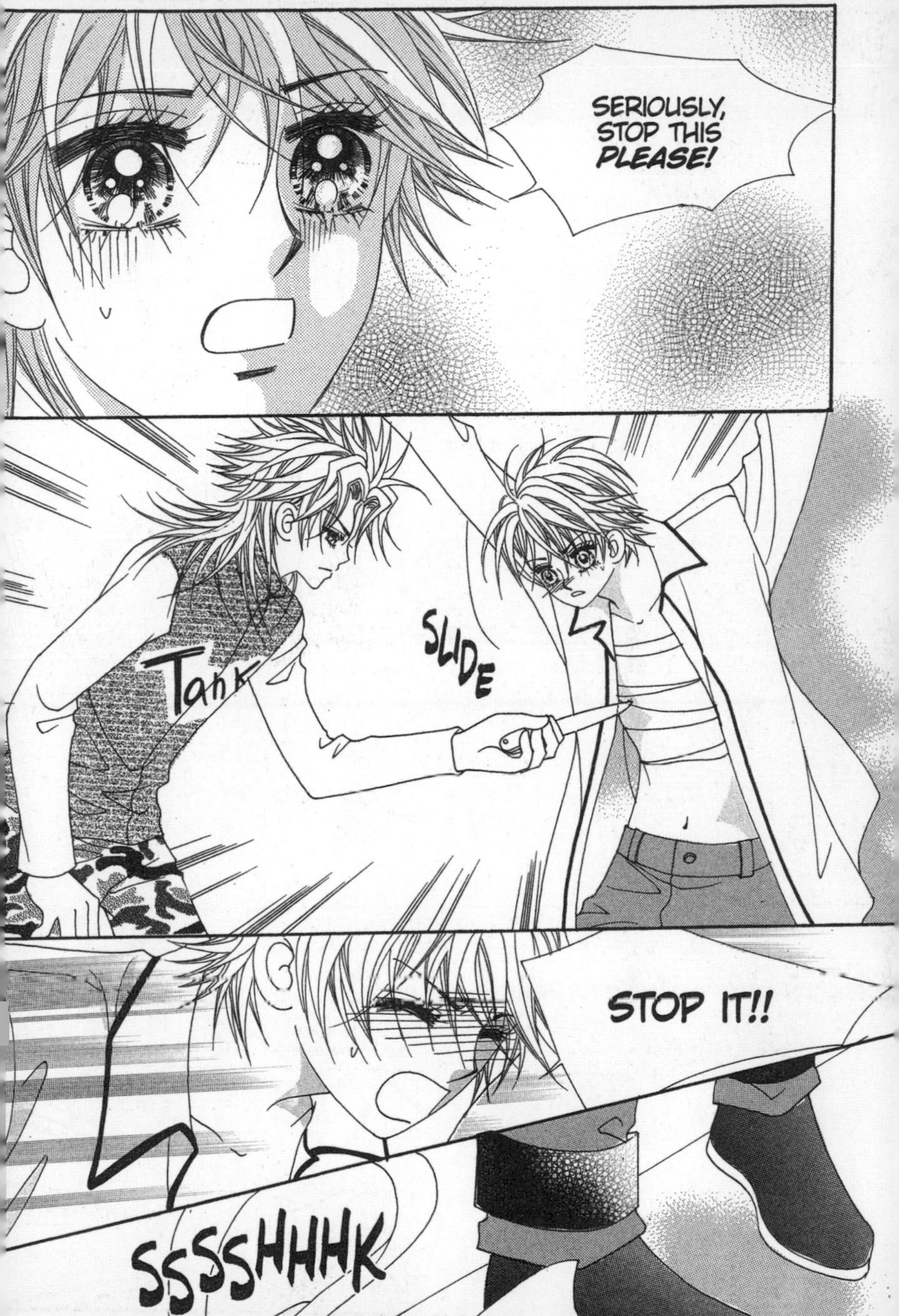
SERIOUSLY, STOP THIS PLEASE!
Tank
SLIDE
STOP IT!!
SSSSHHHK

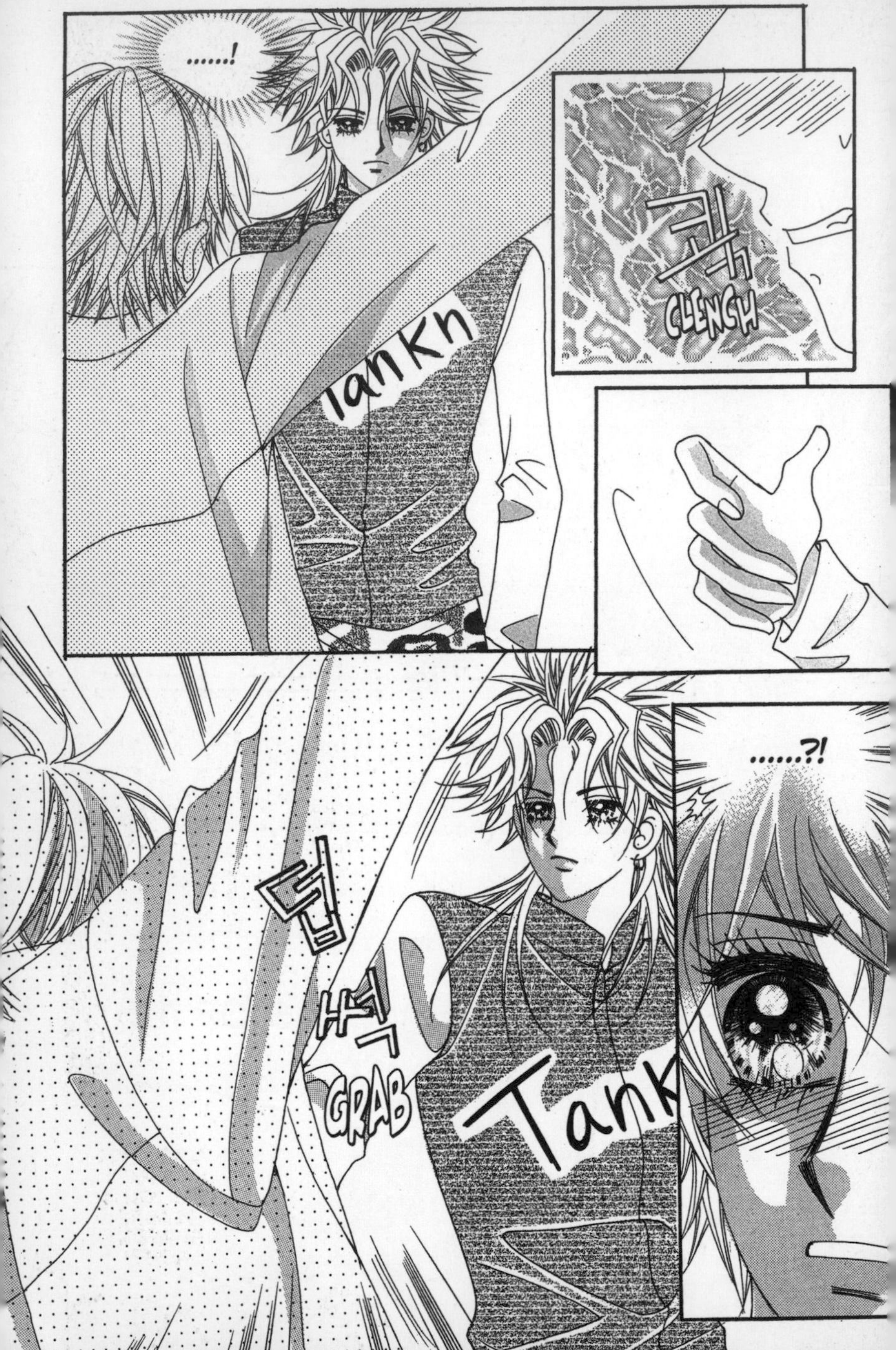
......!
Tankn
CLENCH
GRAB
Tank
......?!

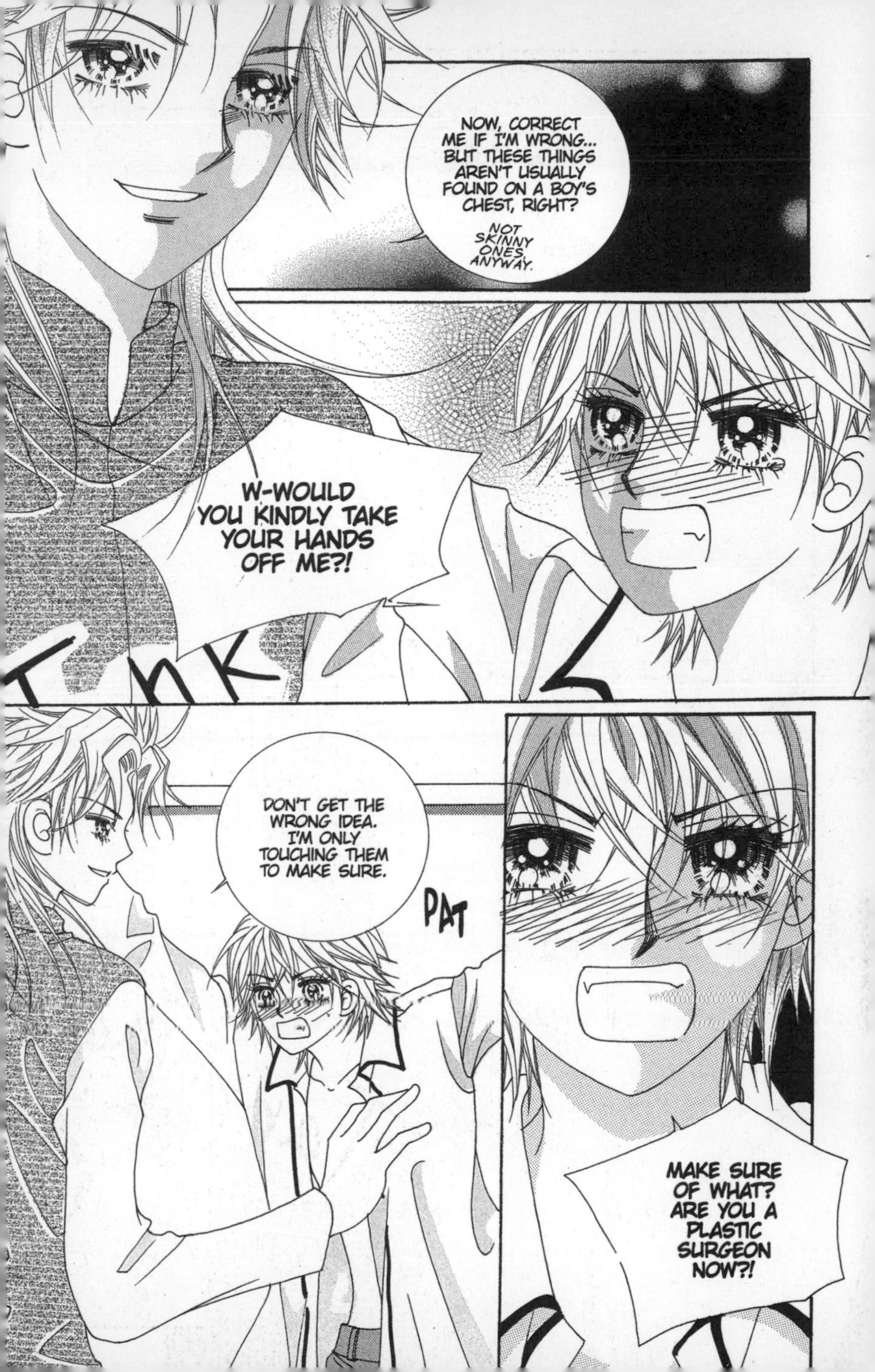
NOW, CORRECT ME IF I'M WRONG... BUT THESE THINGS AREN'T USUALLY FOUND ON A BOY'S CHEST, RIGHT?
NOT SKINNY ONES, ANYWAY.
W-WOULD YOU KINDLY TAKE YOUR HANDS OFF ME?!
TINK
DON'T GET THE WRONG IDEA. I'M ONLY TOUCHING THEM TO MAKE SURE.
PAT
MAKE SURE OF WHAT? ARE YOU A PLASTIC SURGEON NOW?!

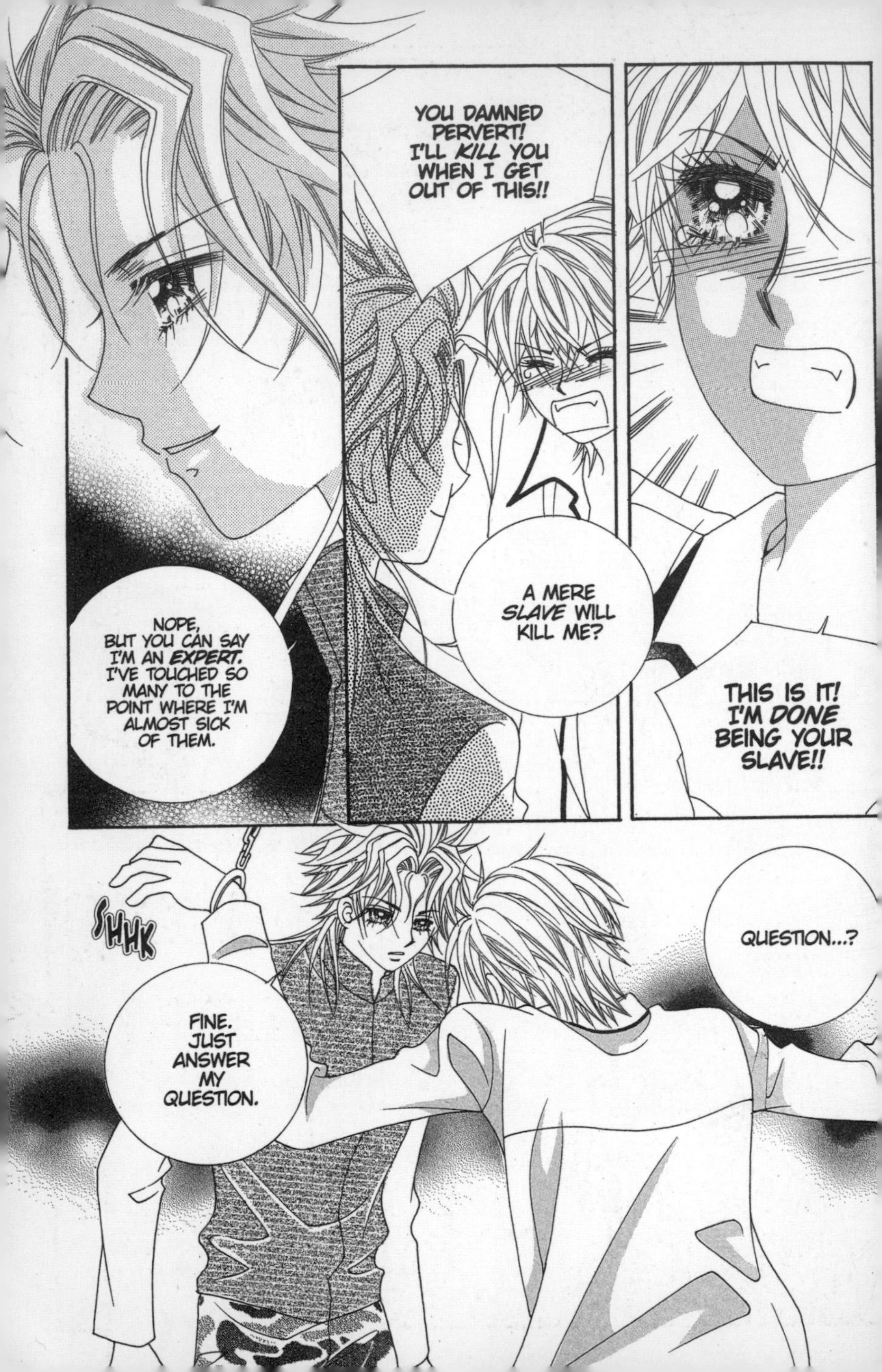
NOPE, BUT YOU CAN SAY I'M AN *EXPERT.* I'VE TOUCHED SO MANY TO THE POINT WHERE I'M ALMOST SICK OF THEM.
YOU DAMNED PERVERT! I'LL *KILL* YOU WHEN I GET OUT OF THIS!!
A MERE *SLAVE* WILL KILL ME?
THIS IS IT! I'M *DONE* BEING YOUR SLAVE!!
SHHK
FINE. JUST ANSWER MY QUESTION.
QUESTION...?

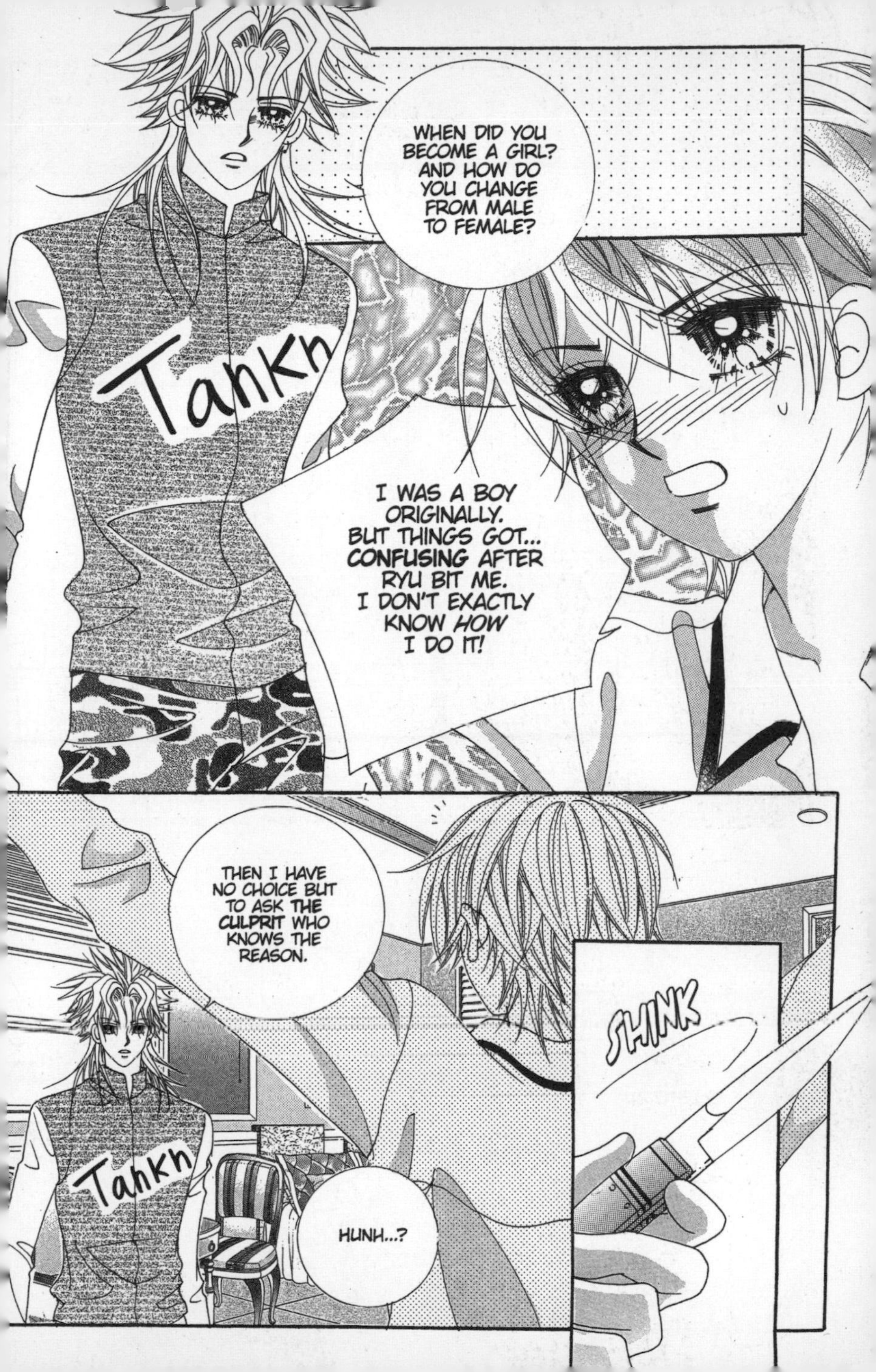
WHEN DID YOU BECOME A GIRL? AND HOW DO YOU CHANGE FROM MALE TO FEMALE?
Tankh
I WAS A BOY ORIGINALLY. BUT THINGS GOT... **CONFUSING** AFTER RYU BIT ME. I DON'T EXACTLY KNOW *HOW* I DO IT!
THEN I HAVE NO CHOICE BUT TO ASK **THE CULPRIT** WHO KNOWS THE REASON.
Tankh
HUNH...?
SHINK

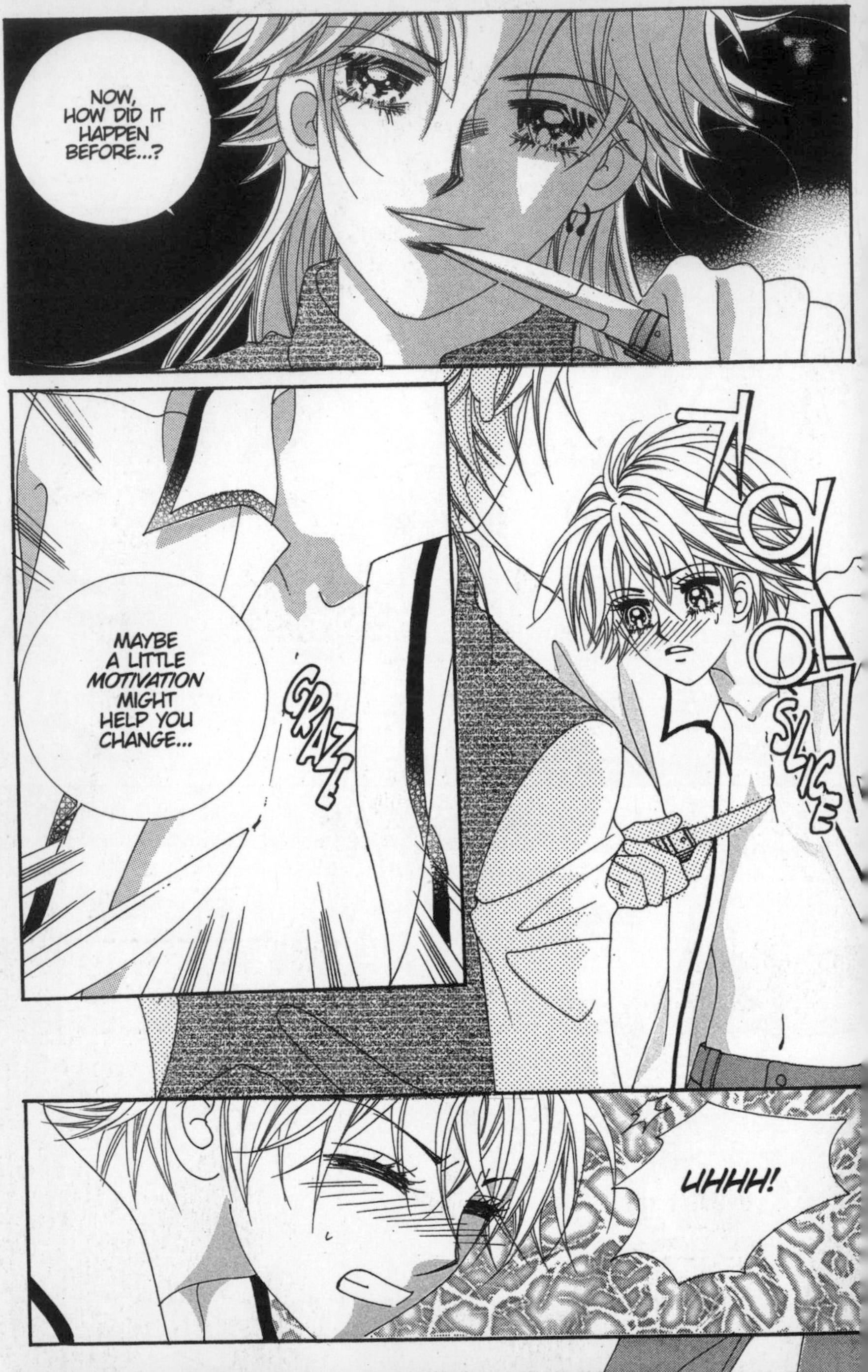
NOW, HOW DID IT HAPPEN BEFORE...?
MAYBE A LITTLE *MOTIVATION* MIGHT HELP YOU CHANGE...
GRAZE
SLICE
UHHH!

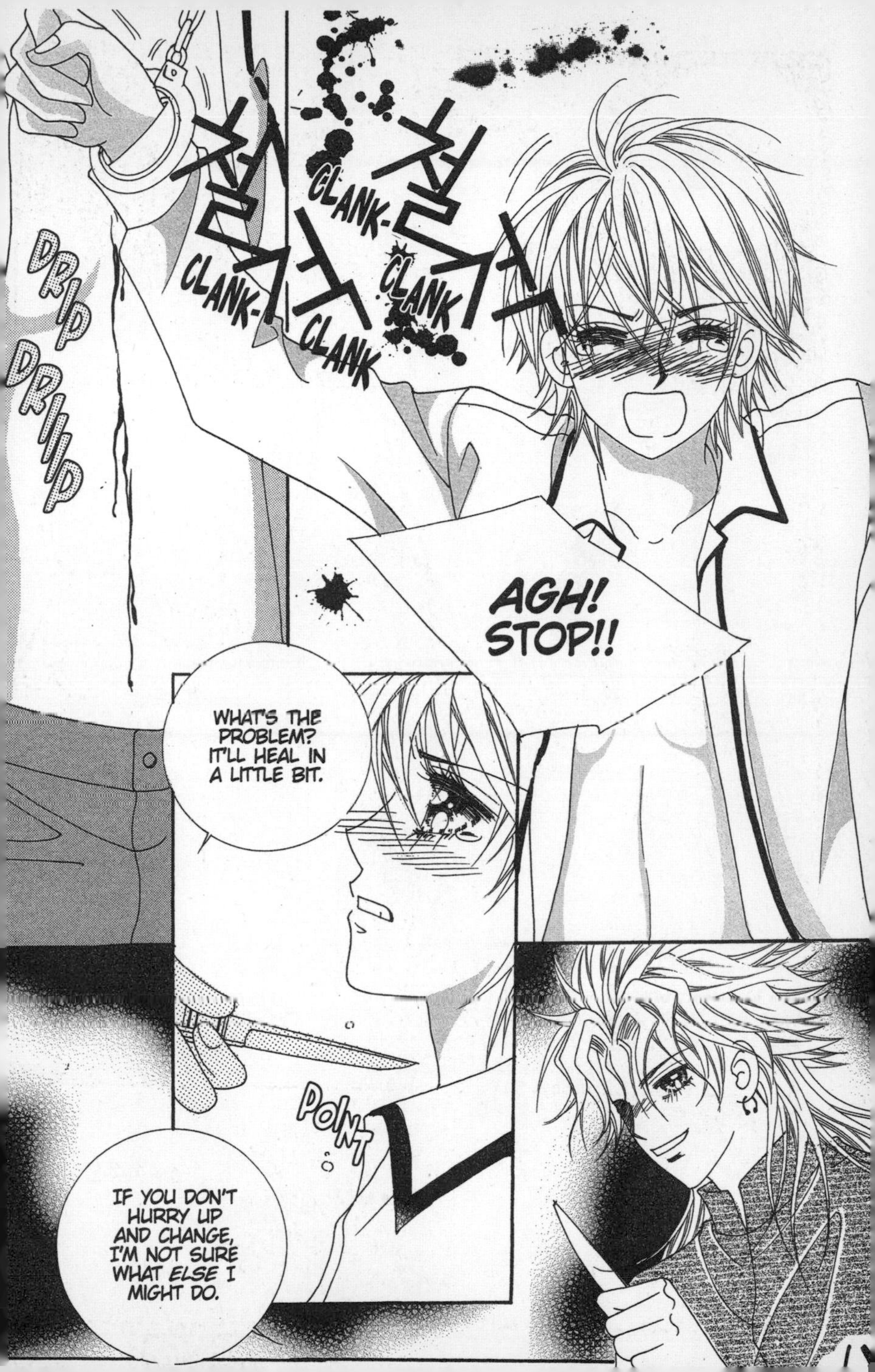
DRIP DRIIIP
철컥
CLANK-CLANK-
CLANK-CLANK
철컥
AGH! STOP!!
WHAT'S THE PROBLEM? IT'LL HEAL IN A LITTLE BIT.
IF YOU DON'T HURRY UP AND CHANGE, I'M NOT SURE WHAT *ELSE* I MIGHT DO.
POINT

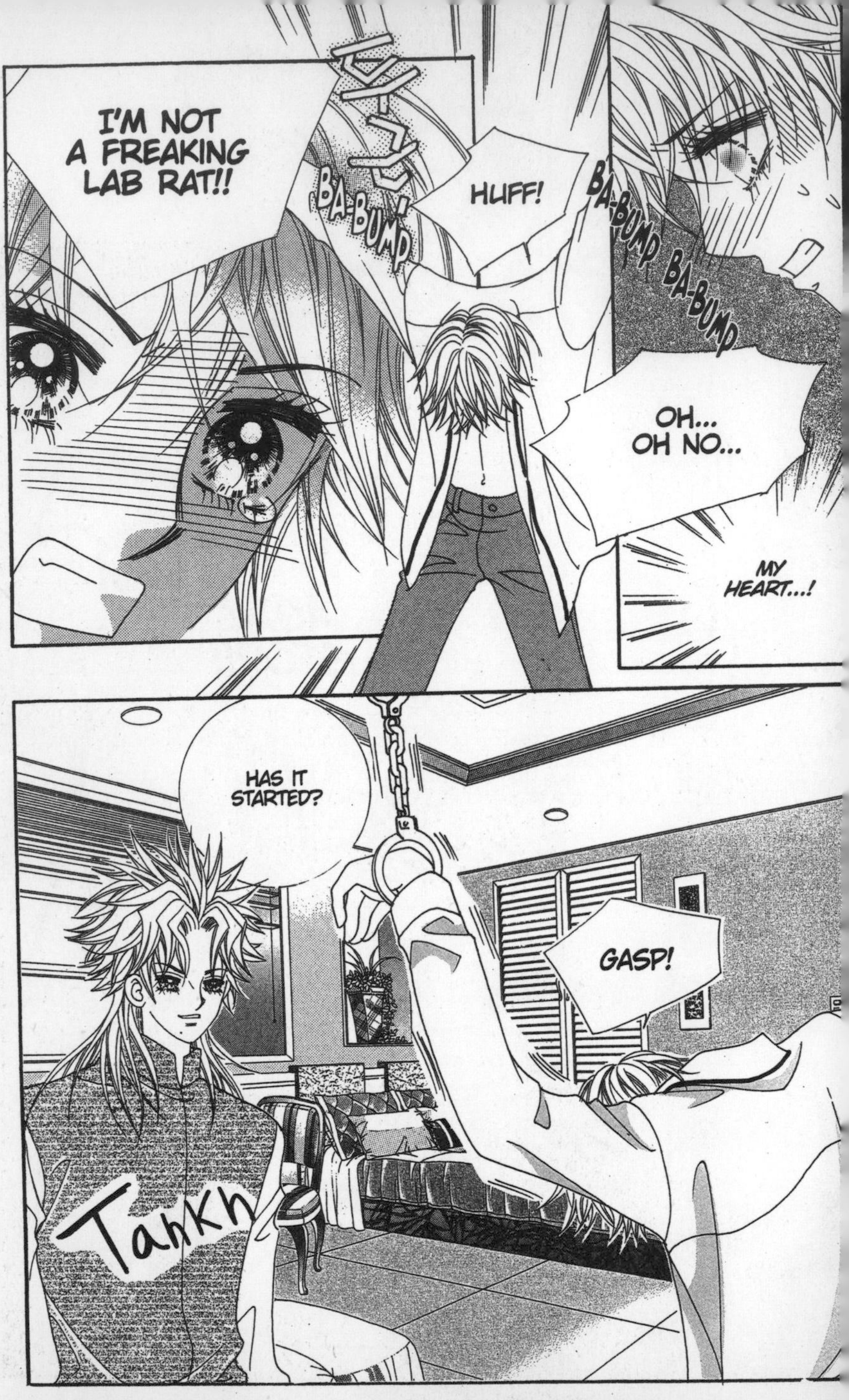
I'M NOT A FREAKING LAB RAT!!
BA-BUMP
HUFF!
BA-BUMP BA-BUMP
OH... OH NO...
MY HEART...!
HAS IT STARTED?
GASP!
Tahkh

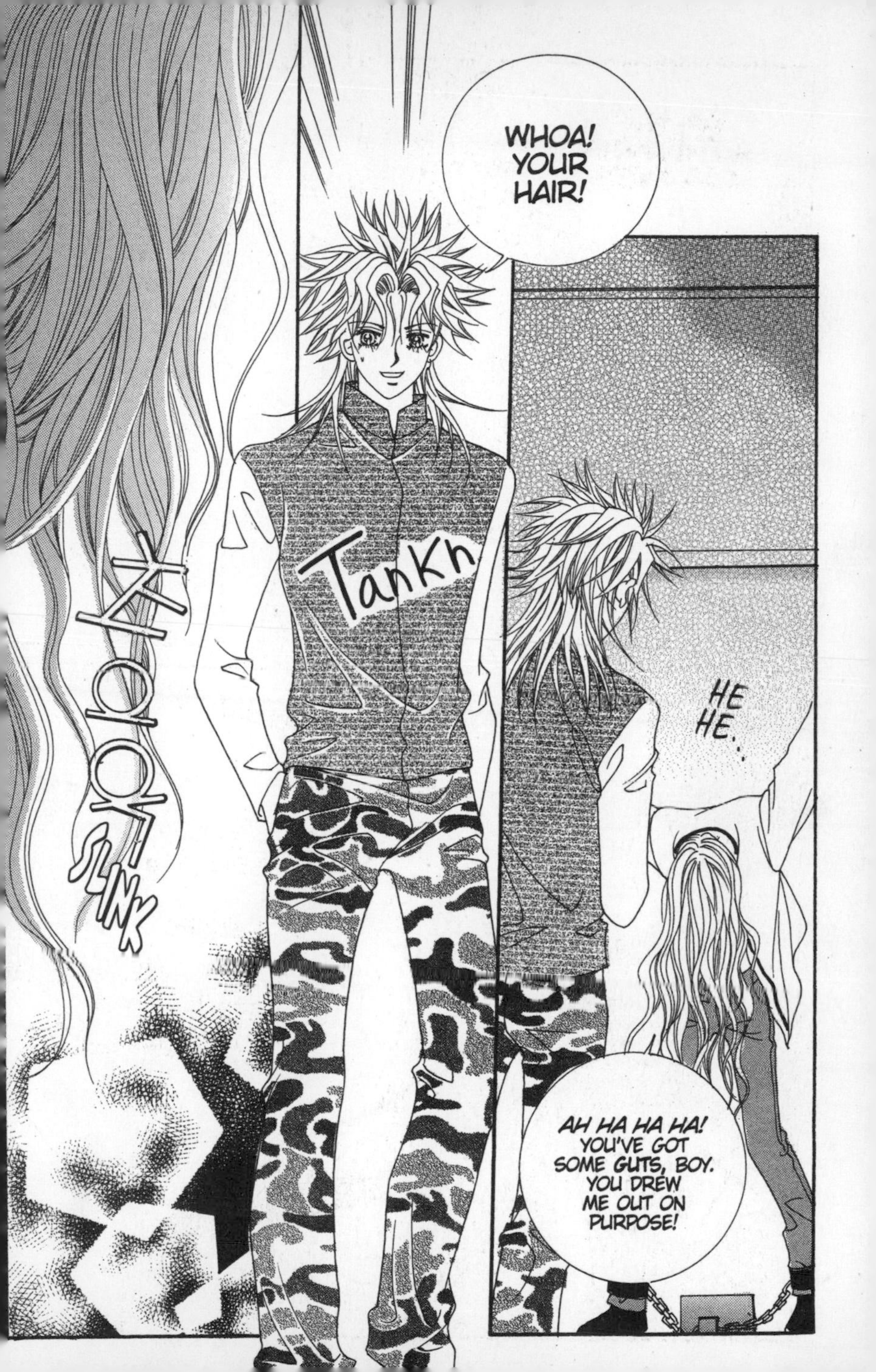
SLINK
WHOA! YOUR HAIR!
Tankn
HE HE...
AH HA HA HA! YOU'VE GOT SOME GUTS, BOY. YOU DREW ME OUT ON PURPOSE!

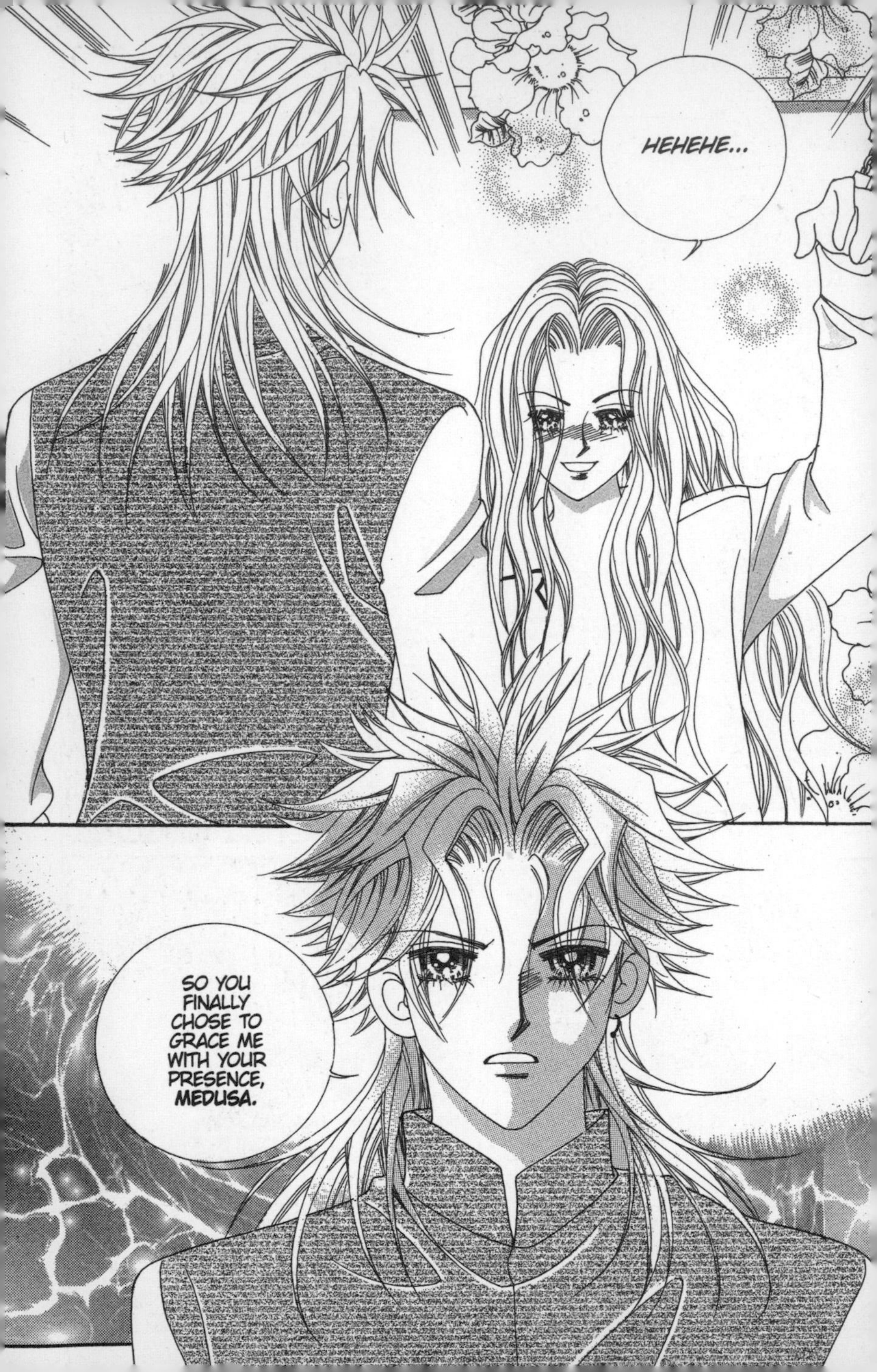
HEHEHE...
SO YOU FINALLY CHOSE TO GRACE ME WITH YOUR PRESENCE, MEDUSA.

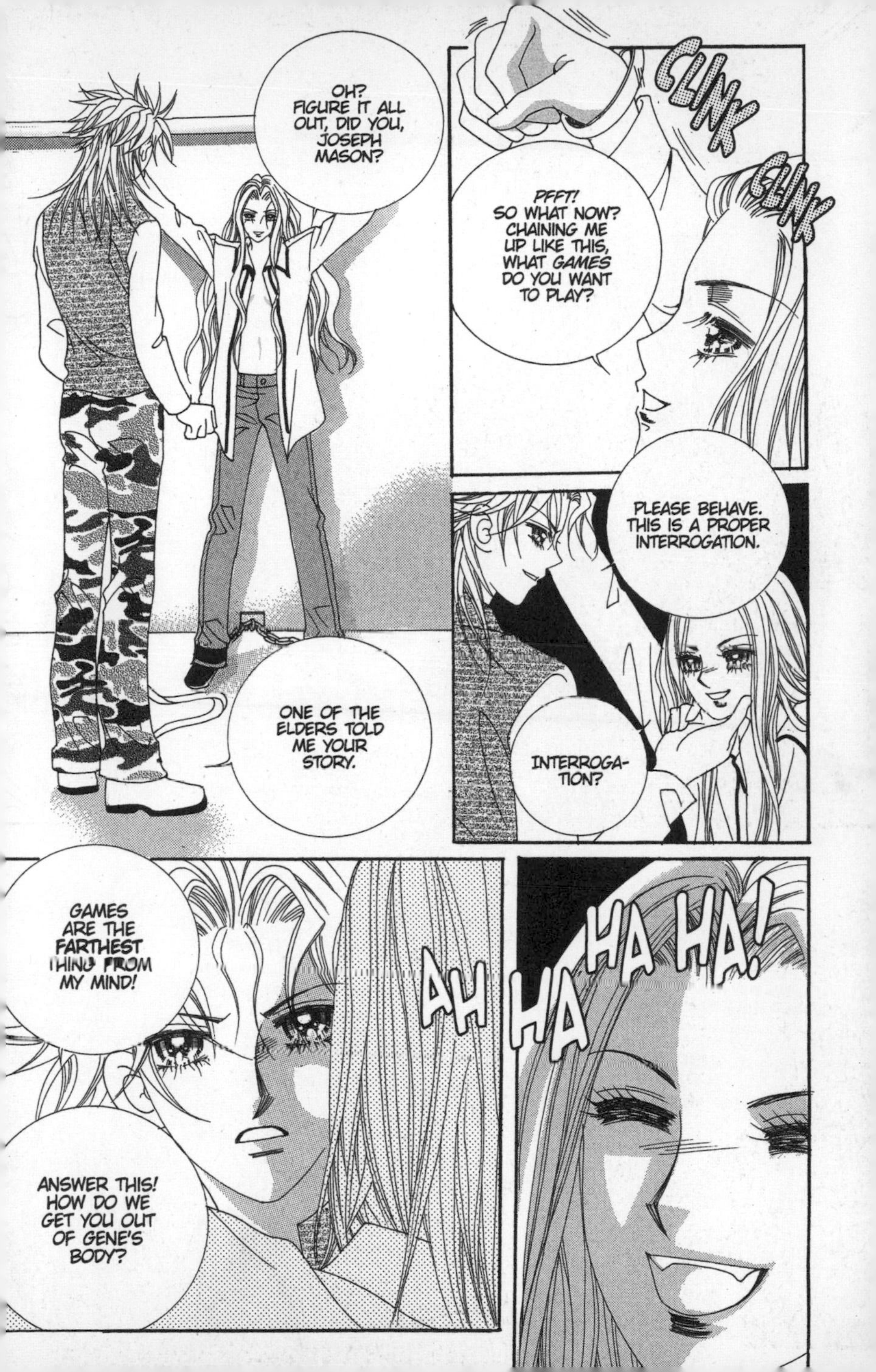
OH? FIGURE IT ALL OUT, DID YOU, JOSEPH MASON?
ONE OF THE ELDERS TOLD ME YOUR STORY.
CLINK
CLINK
PFFT! SO WHAT NOW? CHAINING ME UP LIKE THIS, WHAT *GAMES* DO YOU WANT TO PLAY?
PLEASE BEHAVE. THIS IS A PROPER INTERROGATION.
INTERROGA-TION?
GAMES ARE THE FARTHEST THING FROM MY MIND!
ANSWER THIS! HOW DO WE GET YOU OUT OF GENE'S BODY?
AH HA HA HA HA!

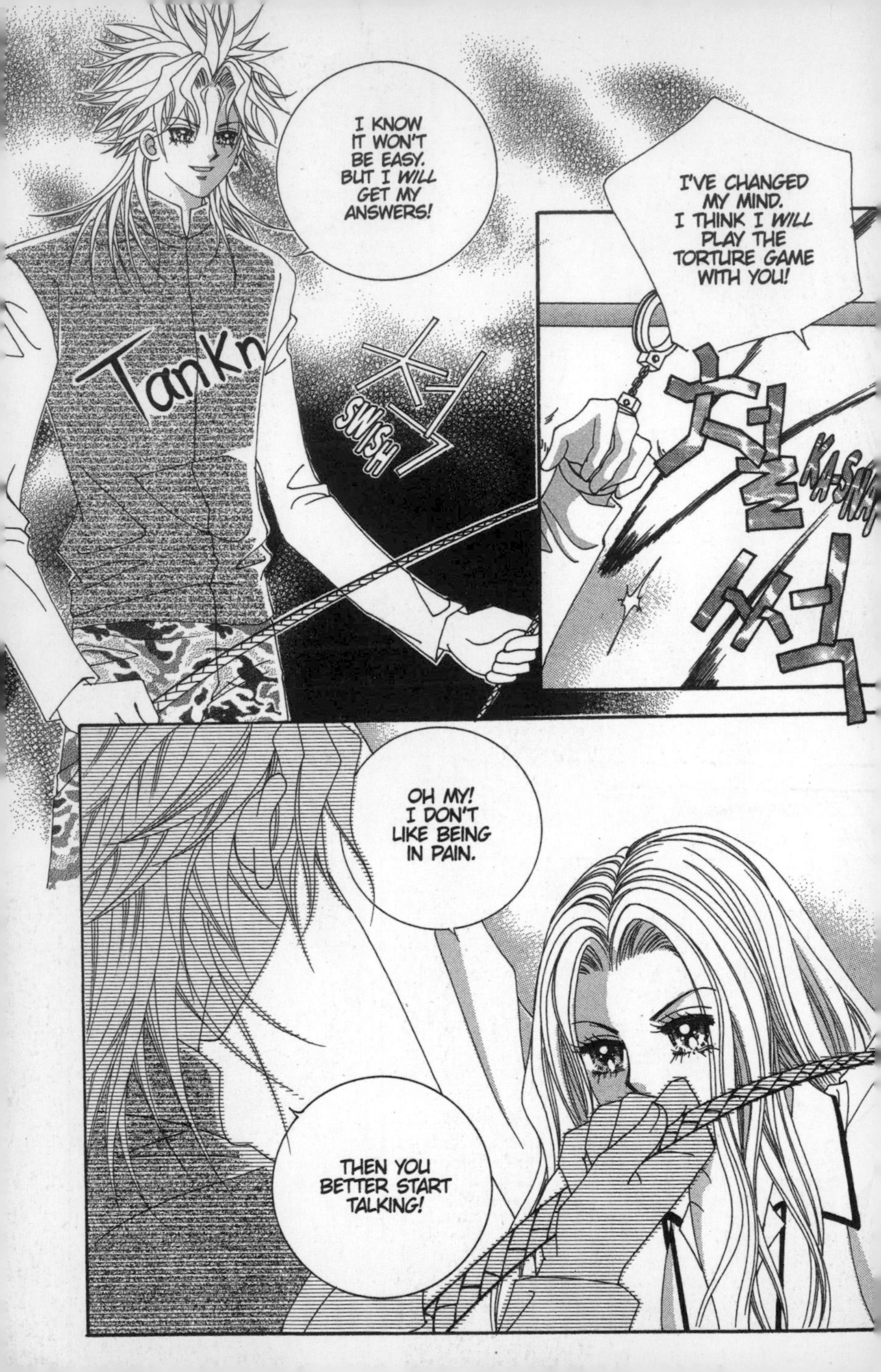
I KNOW IT WON'T BE EASY. BUT I *WILL* GET MY ANSWERS!
Tankn
SWISH
I'VE CHANGED MY MIND. I THINK I *WILL* PLAY THE TORTURE GAME WITH YOU!
KA-SHA
OH MY! I DON'T LIKE BEING IN PAIN.
THEN YOU BETTER START TALKING!

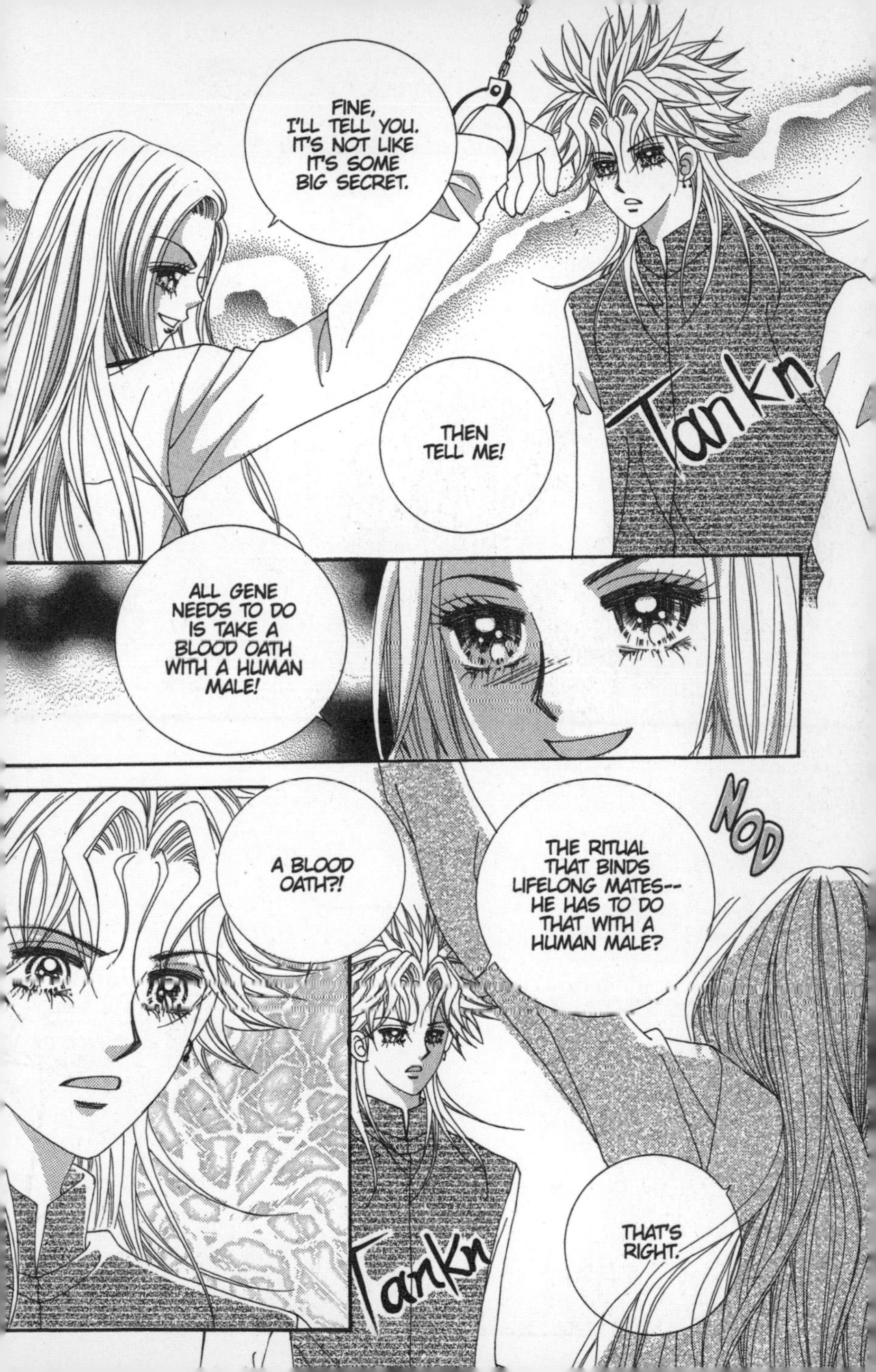
FINE, I'LL TELL YOU. IT'S NOT LIKE IT'S SOME BIG SECRET.
THEN TELL ME!
Tankn
ALL GENE NEEDS TO DO IS TAKE A BLOOD OATH WITH A HUMAN MALE!
A BLOOD OATH?!
NOD
THE RITUAL THAT BINDS LIFELONG MATES-- HE HAS TO DO THAT WITH A HUMAN MALE?
Tankn
THAT'S RIGHT.

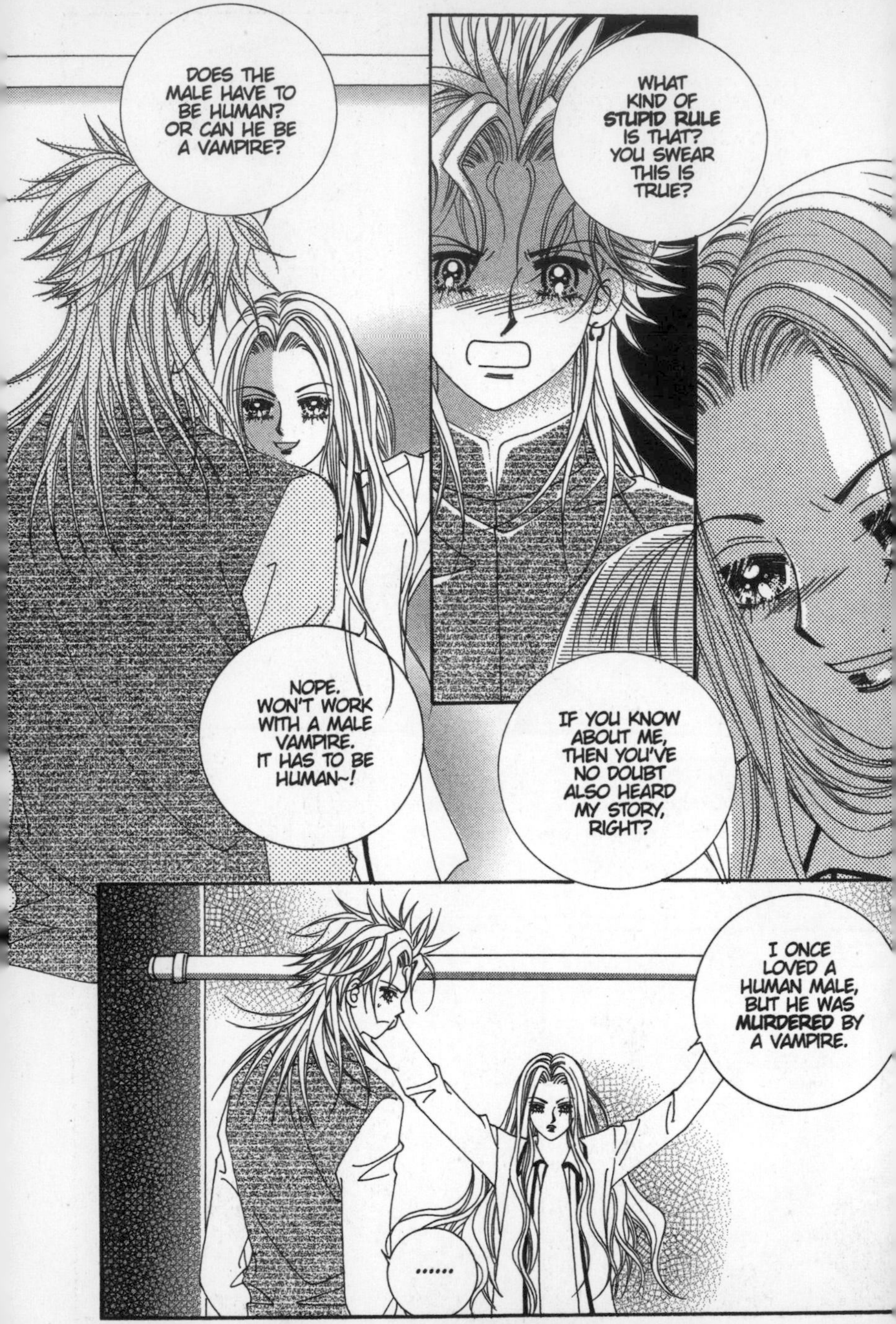
DOES THE MALE HAVE TO BE HUMAN? OR CAN HE BE A VAMPIRE?
NOPE. WON'T WORK WITH A MALE VAMPIRE. IT HAS TO BE HUMAN~!
WHAT KIND OF STUPID RULE IS THAT? YOU SWEAR THIS IS TRUE?
IF YOU KNOW ABOUT ME, THEN YOU'VE NO DOUBT ALSO HEARD MY STORY, RIGHT?
I ONCE LOVED A HUMAN MALE, BUT HE WAS MURDERED BY A VAMPIRE.
......

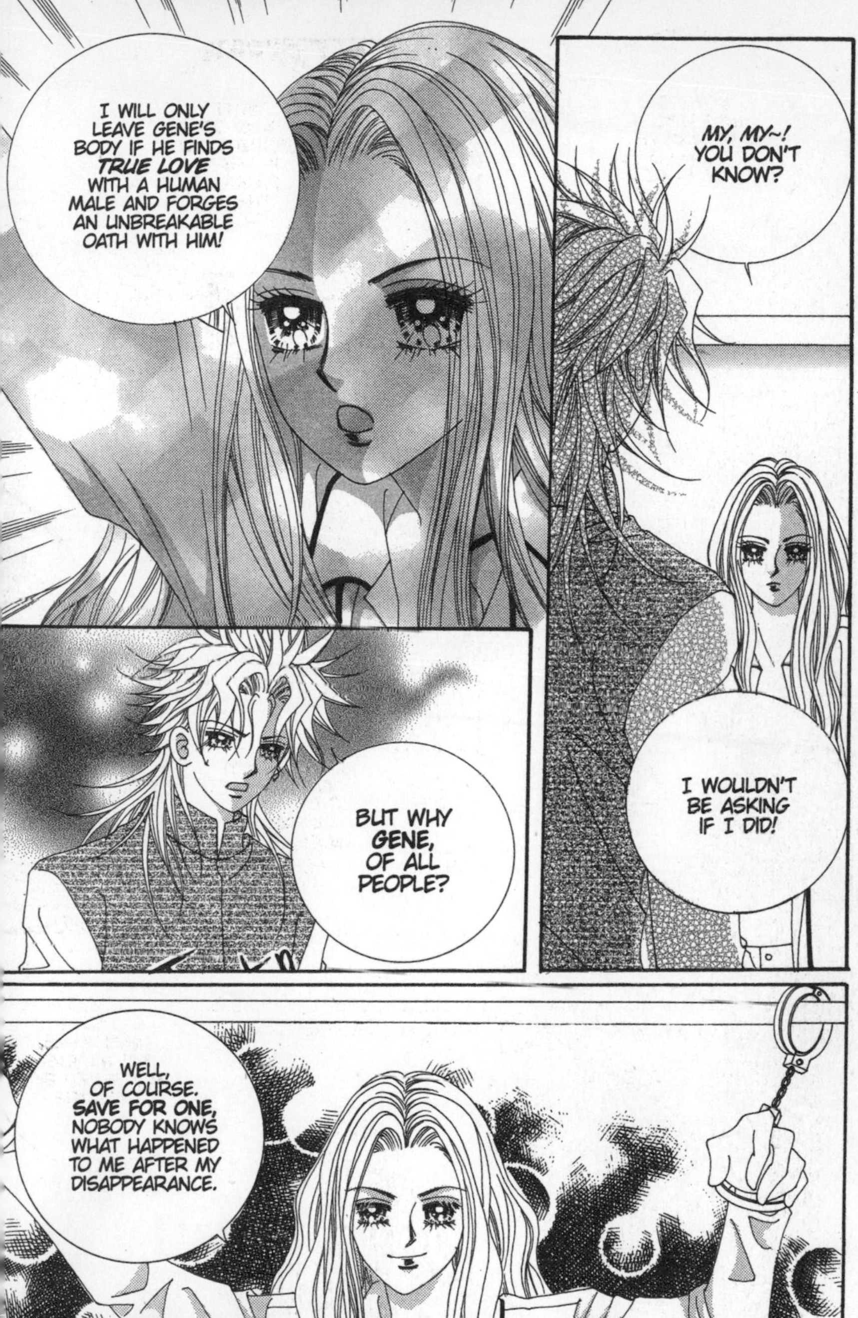
I WILL ONLY LEAVE GENE'S BODY IF HE FINDS ***TRUE LOVE*** WITH A HUMAN MALE AND FORGES AN UNBREAKABLE OATH WITH HIM!
BUT WHY GENE, OF ALL PEOPLE?
*MY, MY~!* YOU DON'T KNOW?
I WOULDN'T BE ASKING IF I DID!
WELL, OF COURSE. SAVE FOR ONE, NOBODY KNOWS WHAT HAPPENED TO ME AFTER MY DISAPPEARANCE.

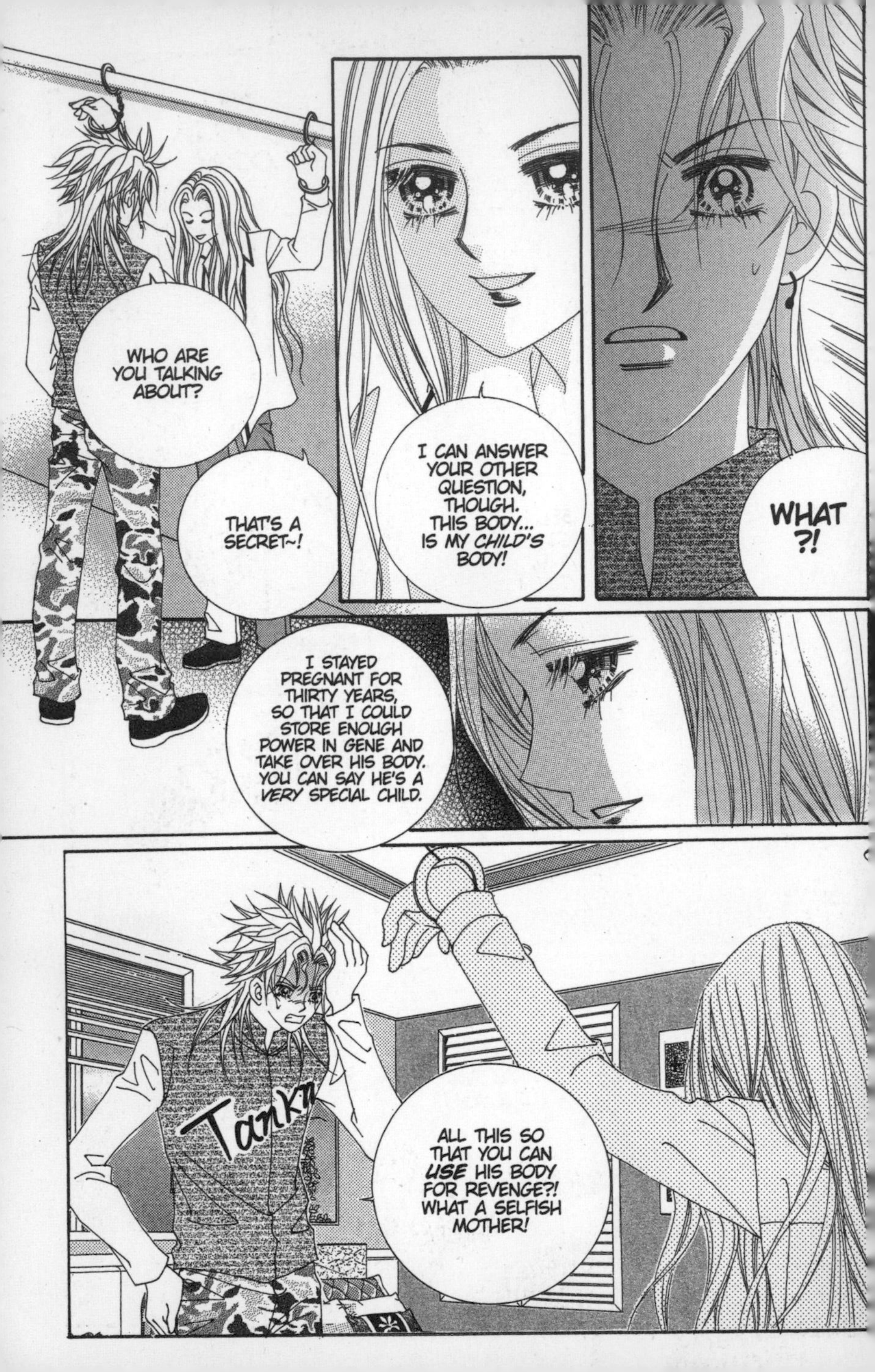
WHO ARE YOU TALKING ABOUT?
THAT'S A SECRET~!
I CAN ANSWER YOUR OTHER QUESTION, THOUGH. THIS BODY... IS MY *CHILD'S* BODY!
WHAT?!
I STAYED PREGNANT FOR THIRTY YEARS, SO THAT I COULD STORE ENOUGH POWER IN GENE AND TAKE OVER HIS BODY. YOU CAN SAY HE'S A *VERY* SPECIAL CHILD.
Tanka
ALL THIS SO THAT YOU CAN ***USE*** HIS BODY FOR REVENGE?! WHAT A SELFISH MOTHER!

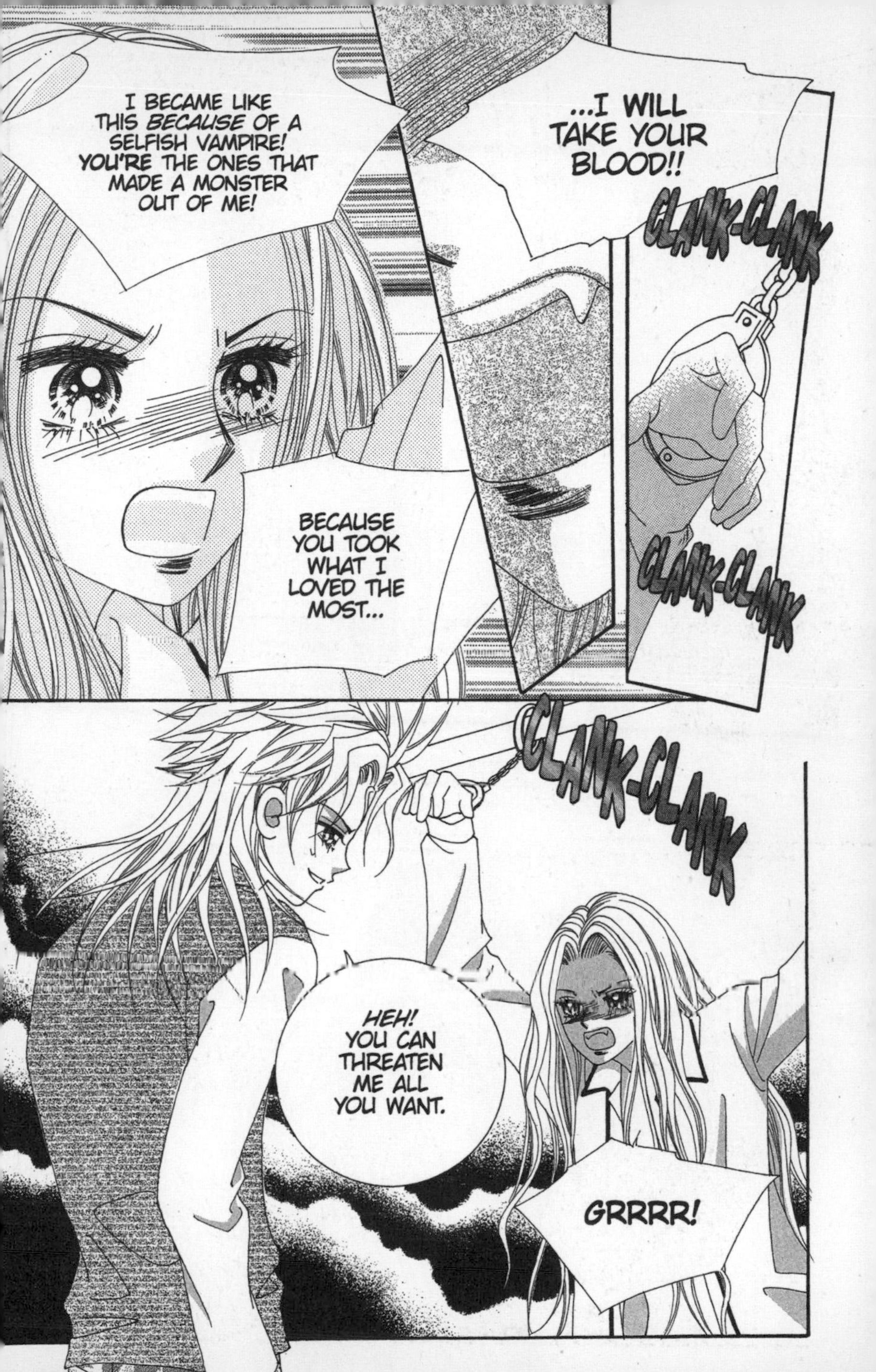
I BECAME LIKE THIS *BECAUSE* OF A SELFISH VAMPIRE! YOU'RE THE ONES THAT MADE A MONSTER OUT OF ME!
BECAUSE YOU TOOK WHAT I LOVED THE MOST...
...I WILL TAKE YOUR BLOOD!!
CLANK-CLANK
CLANK-CLANK
CLANK-CLANK
*HEH!* YOU CAN THREATEN ME ALL YOU WANT.
GRRRR!

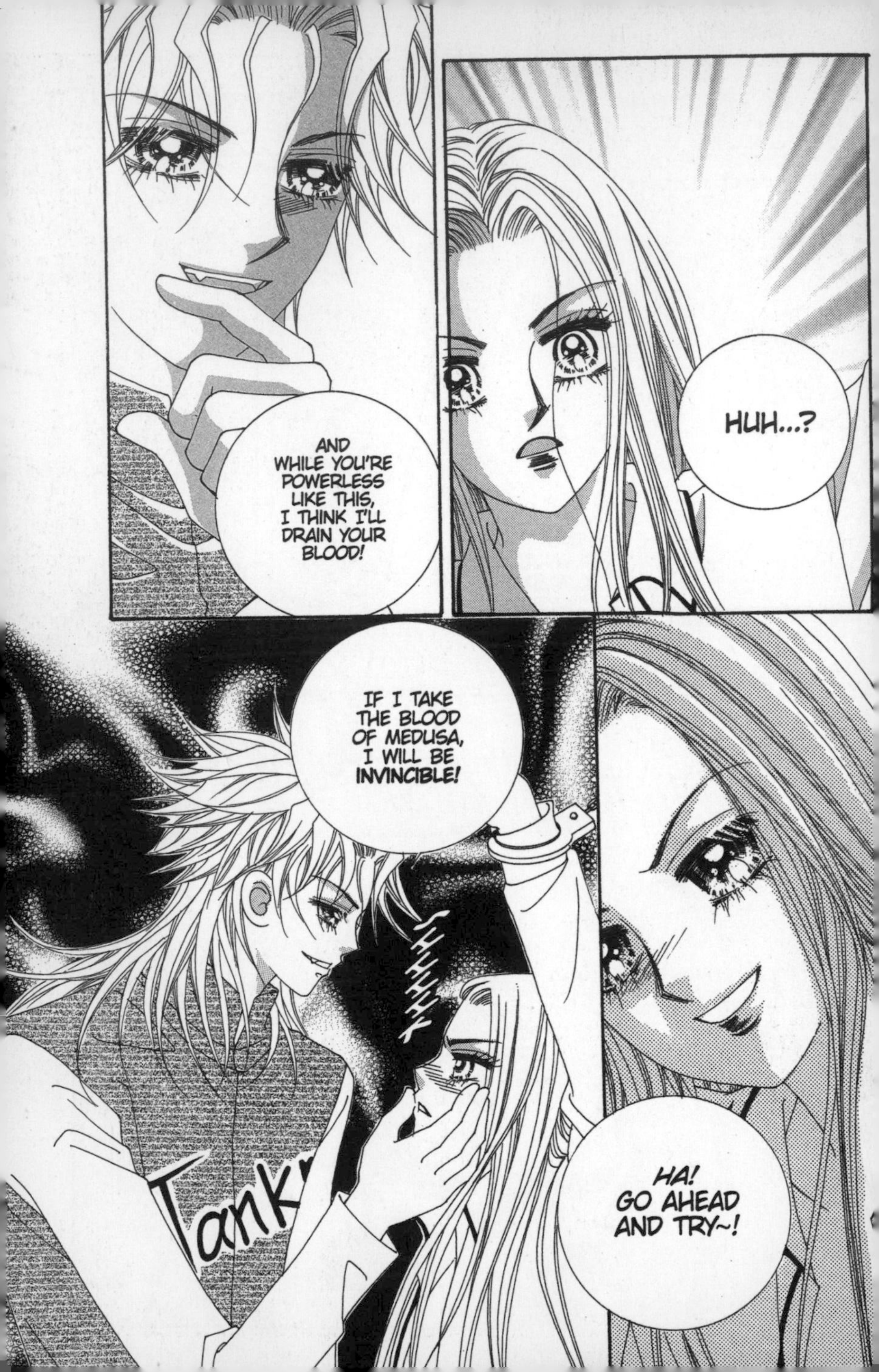
AND WHILE YOU'RE POWERLESS LIKE THIS, I THINK I'LL DRAIN YOUR BLOOD!
HUH...?
IF I TAKE THE BLOOD OF MEDUSA, I WILL BE INVINCIBLE!
SHHHHHK
Tank
HA! GO AHEAD AND TRY~!

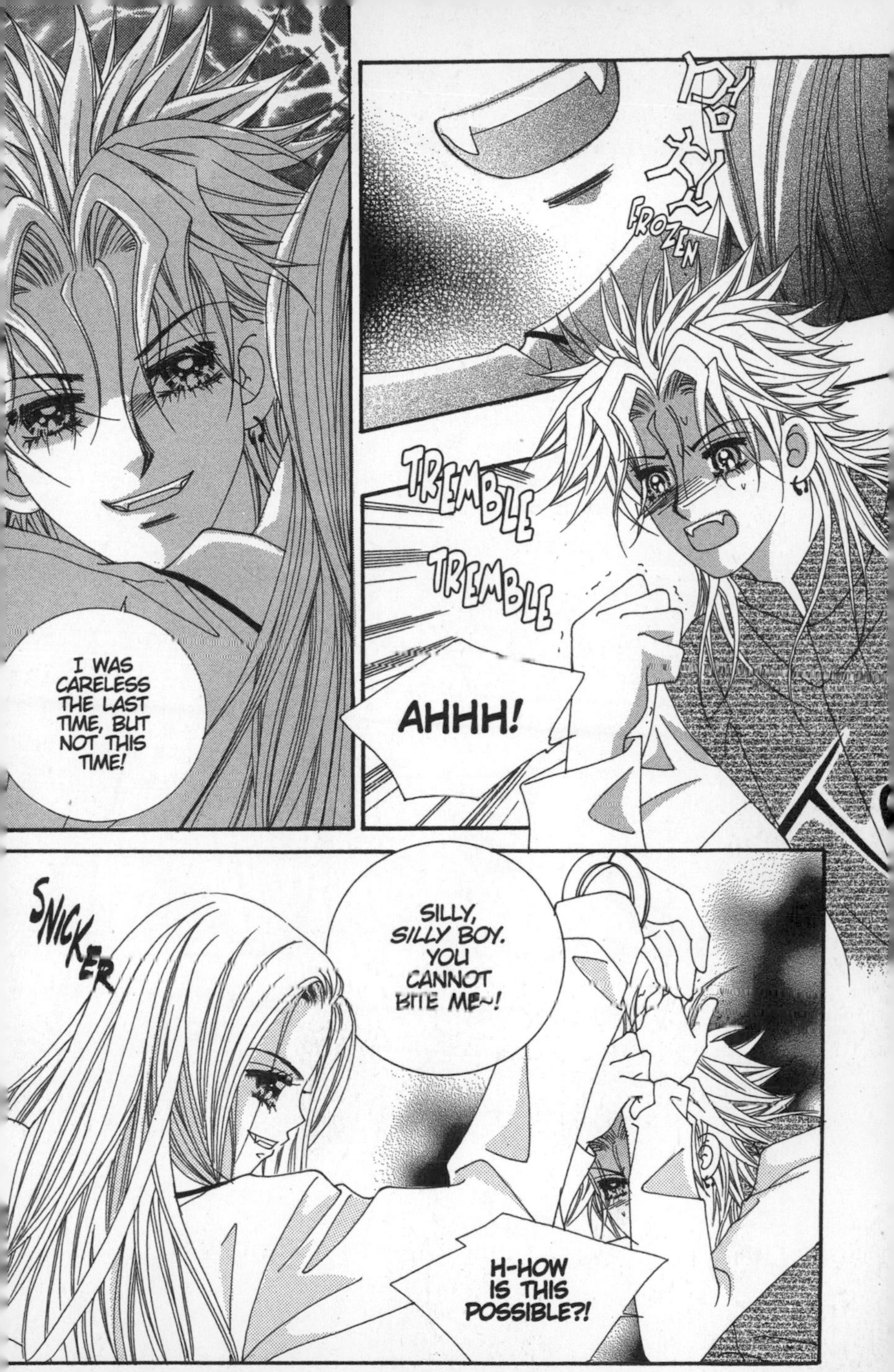
I WAS CARELESS THE LAST TIME, BUT NOT THIS TIME!
FROZEN
TREMBLE
TREMBLE
AHHH!
SNICKER
SILLY, SILLY BOY. YOU CANNOT BITE ME~!
H-HOW IS THIS POSSIBLE?!

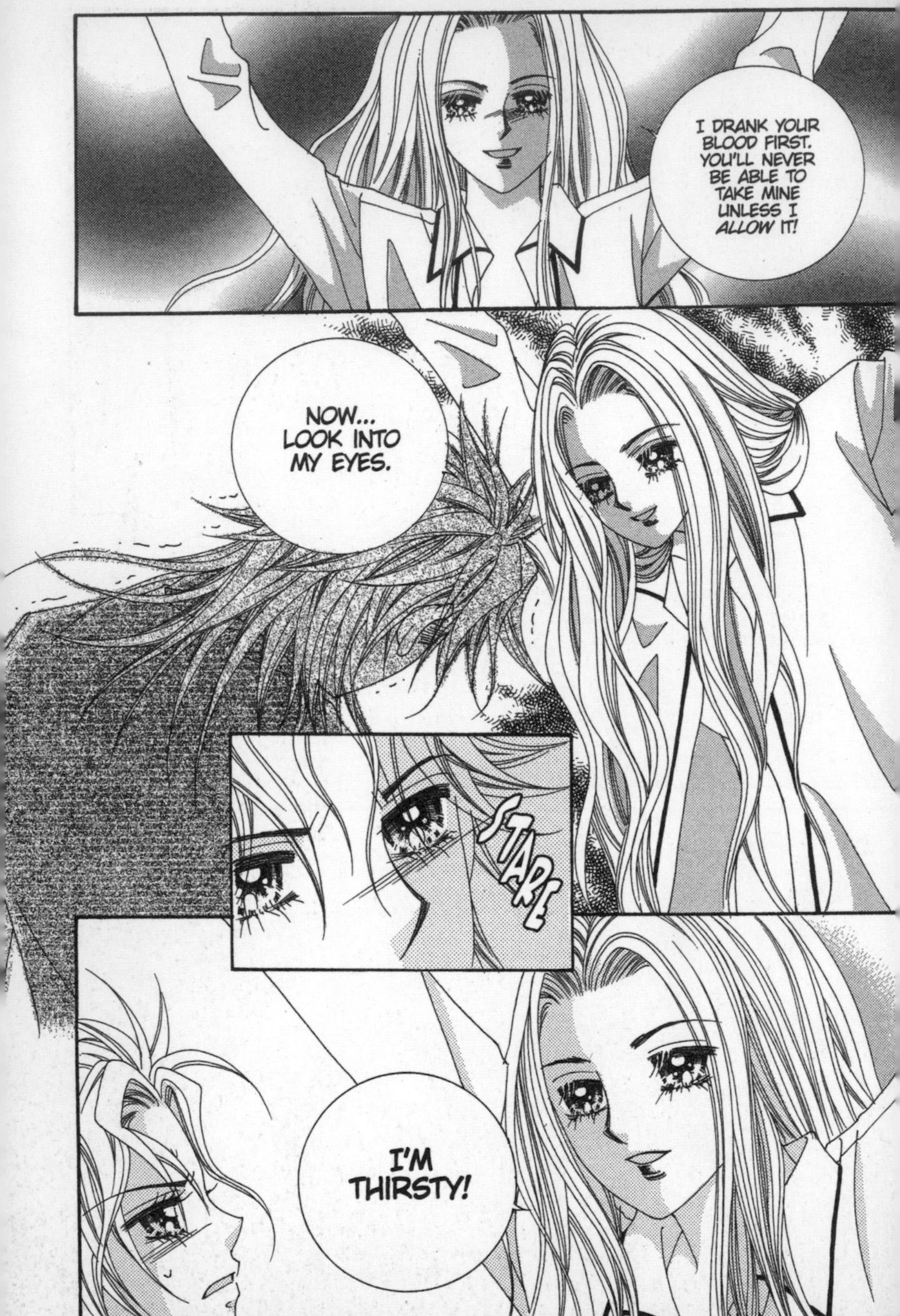
I DRANK YOUR BLOOD FIRST. YOU'LL NEVER BE ABLE TO TAKE MINE UNLESS I *ALLOW* IT!
NOW... LOOK INTO MY EYES.
STARE
I'M THIRSTY!

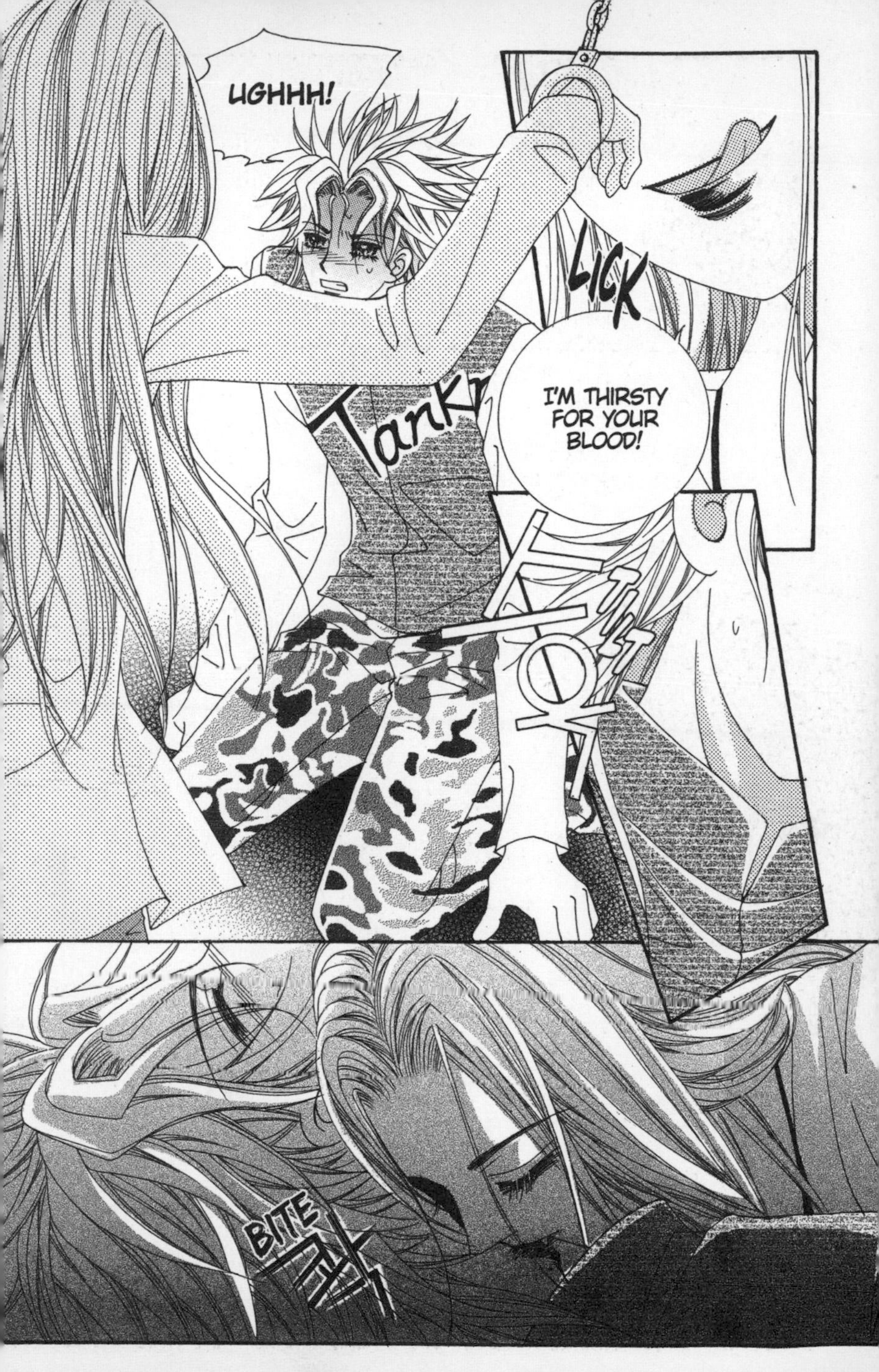
UGHHH!
LICK
I'M THIRSTY FOR YOUR BLOOD!
BITE

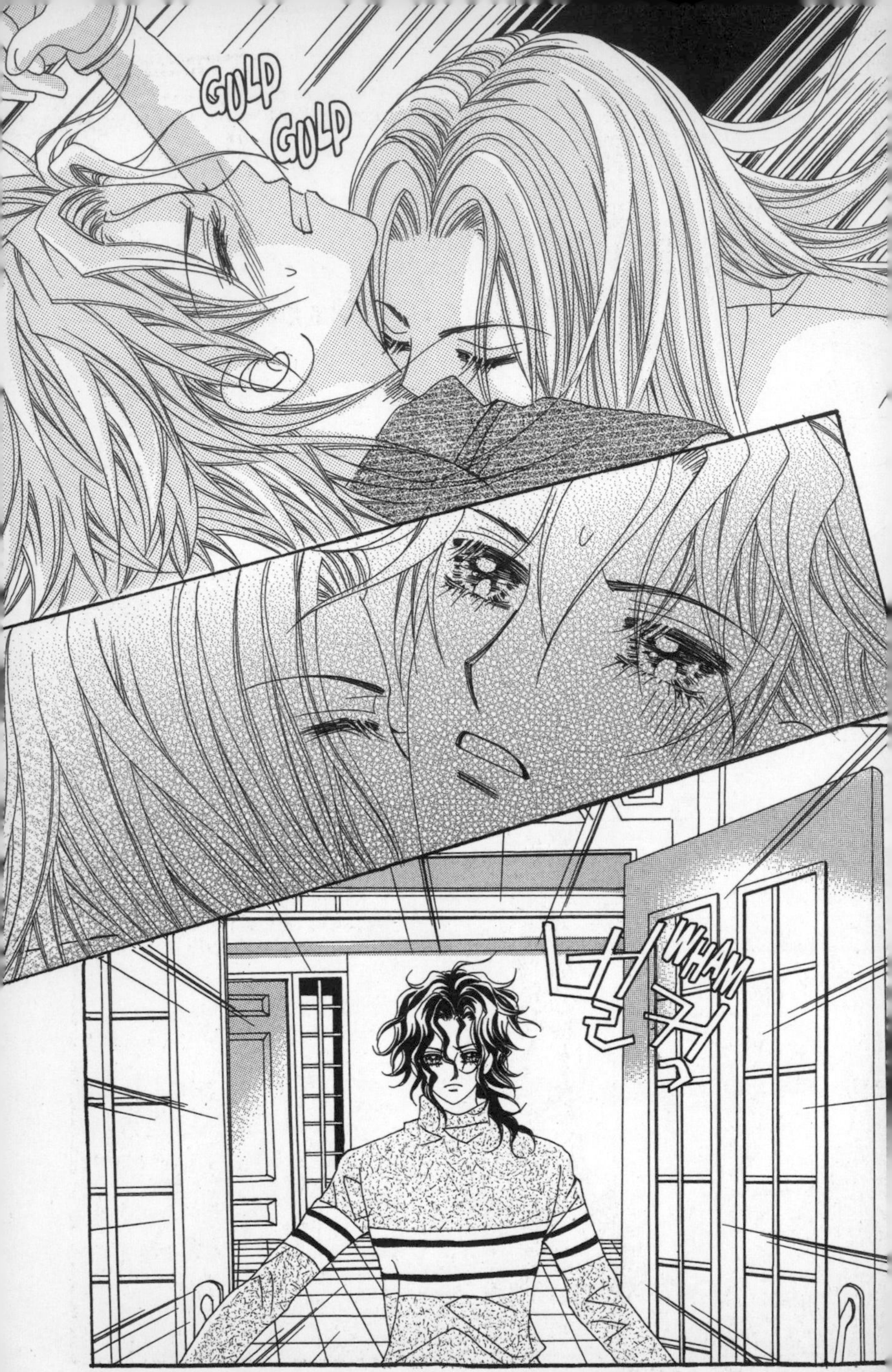
GULP
GULP
WHAM

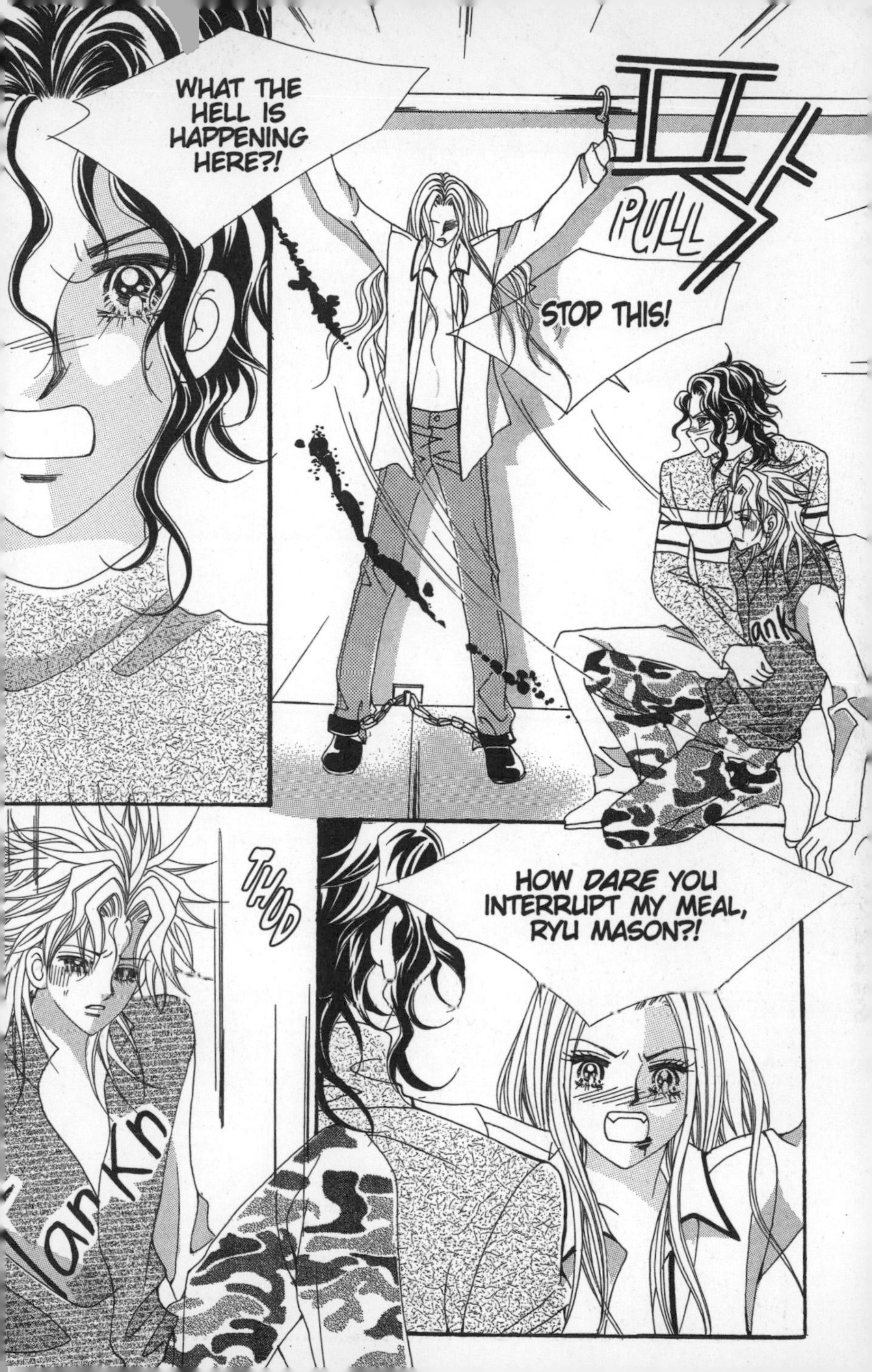
WHAT THE HELL IS HAPPENING HERE?!
PULL
STOP THIS!
THUD
HOW DARE YOU INTERRUPT MY MEAL, RYU MASON?!

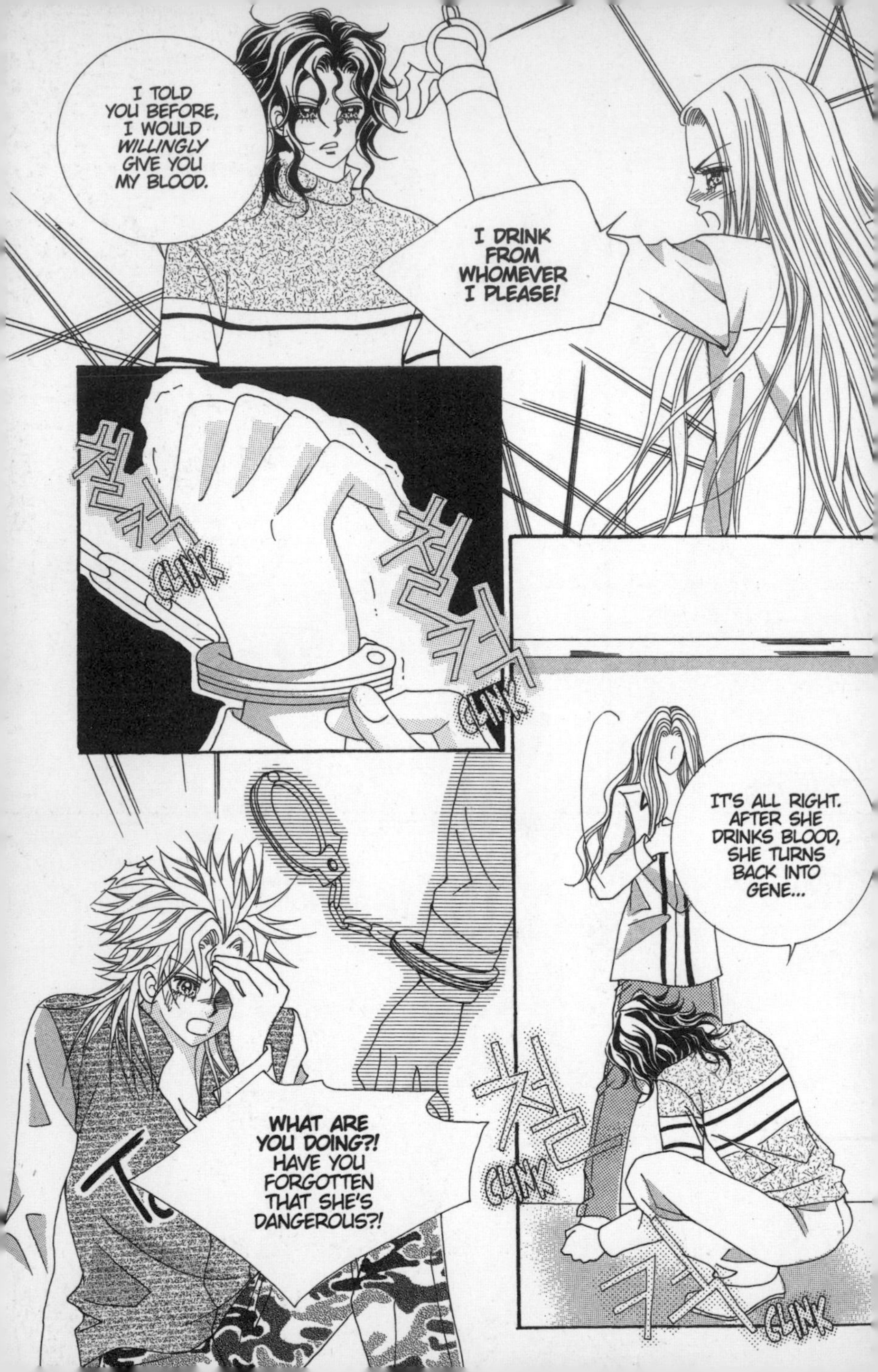
I TOLD YOU BEFORE, I WOULD *WILLINGLY* GIVE YOU MY BLOOD.
I DRINK FROM WHOMEVER I PLEASE!
CLINK
CLINK
WHAT ARE YOU DOING?! HAVE YOU FORGOTTEN THAT SHE'S DANGEROUS?!
IT'S ALL RIGHT. AFTER SHE DRINKS BLOOD, SHE TURNS BACK INTO GENE...
CLINK
CLINK

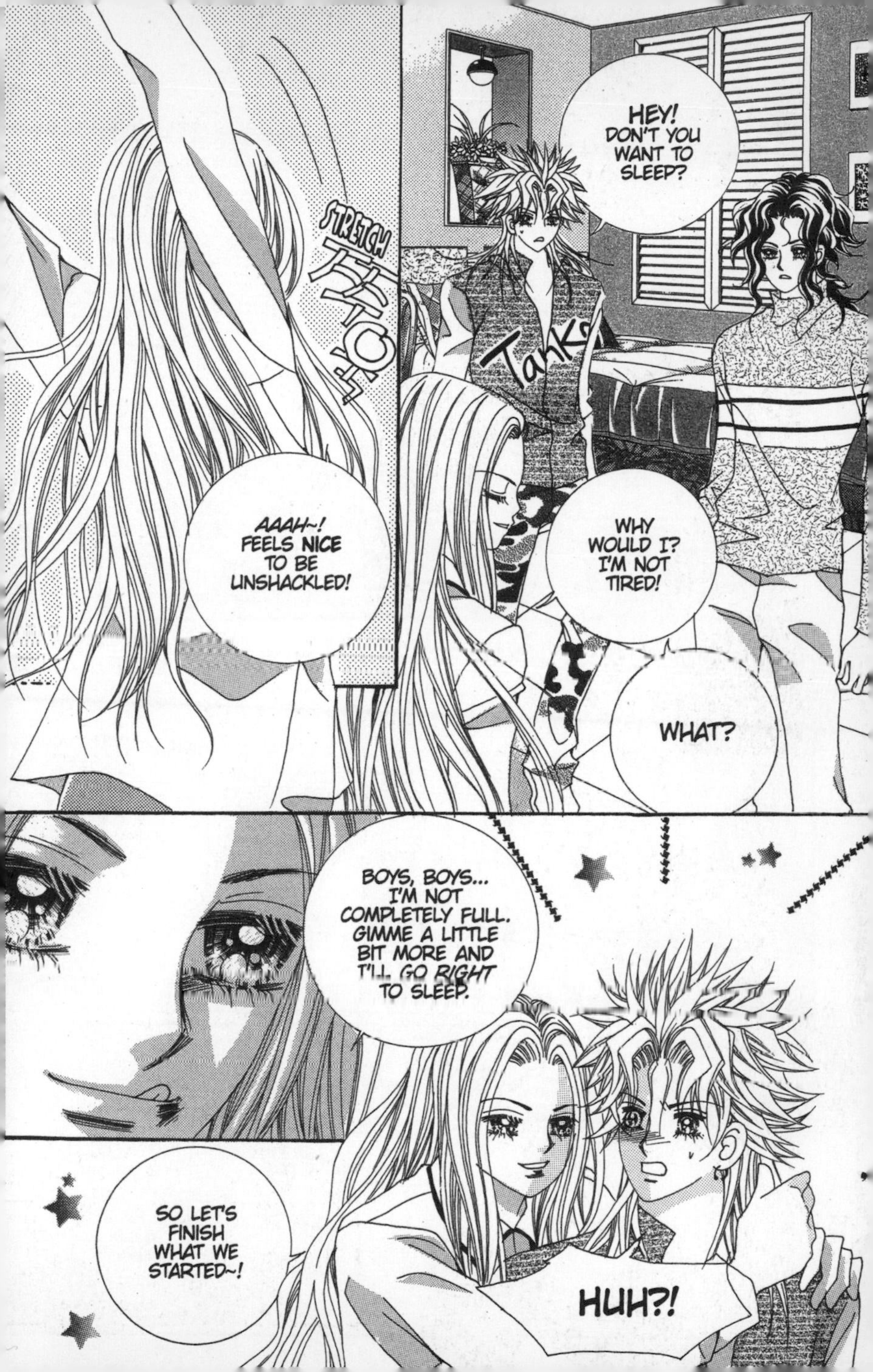
STRETCH
AAAH~! FEELS NICE TO BE UNSHACKLED!
HEY! DON'T YOU WANT TO SLEEP?
Tanks
WHY WOULD I? I'M NOT TIRED!
WHAT?
BOYS, BOYS... I'M NOT COMPLETELY FULL. GIMME A LITTLE BIT MORE AND I'LL GO RIGHT TO SLEEP.
SO LET'S FINISH WHAT WE STARTED~!
HUH?!

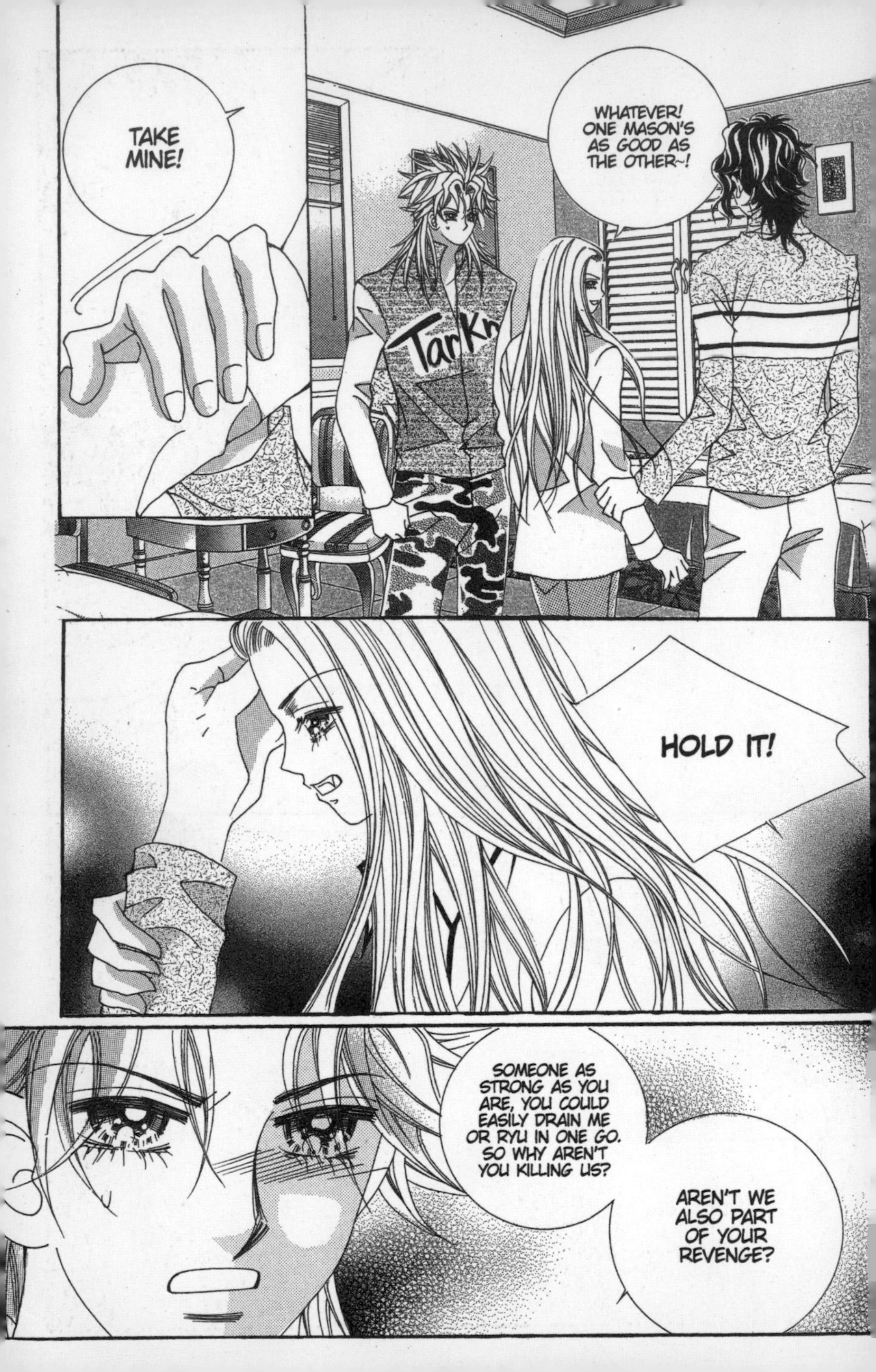
TAKE MINE!
WHATEVER! ONE MASON'S AS GOOD AS THE OTHER~!
TarKn
HOLD IT!
SOMEONE AS STRONG AS YOU ARE, YOU COULD EASILY DRAIN ME OR RYU IN ONE GO. SO WHY AREN'T YOU KILLING US?
AREN'T WE ALSO PART OF YOUR REVENGE?

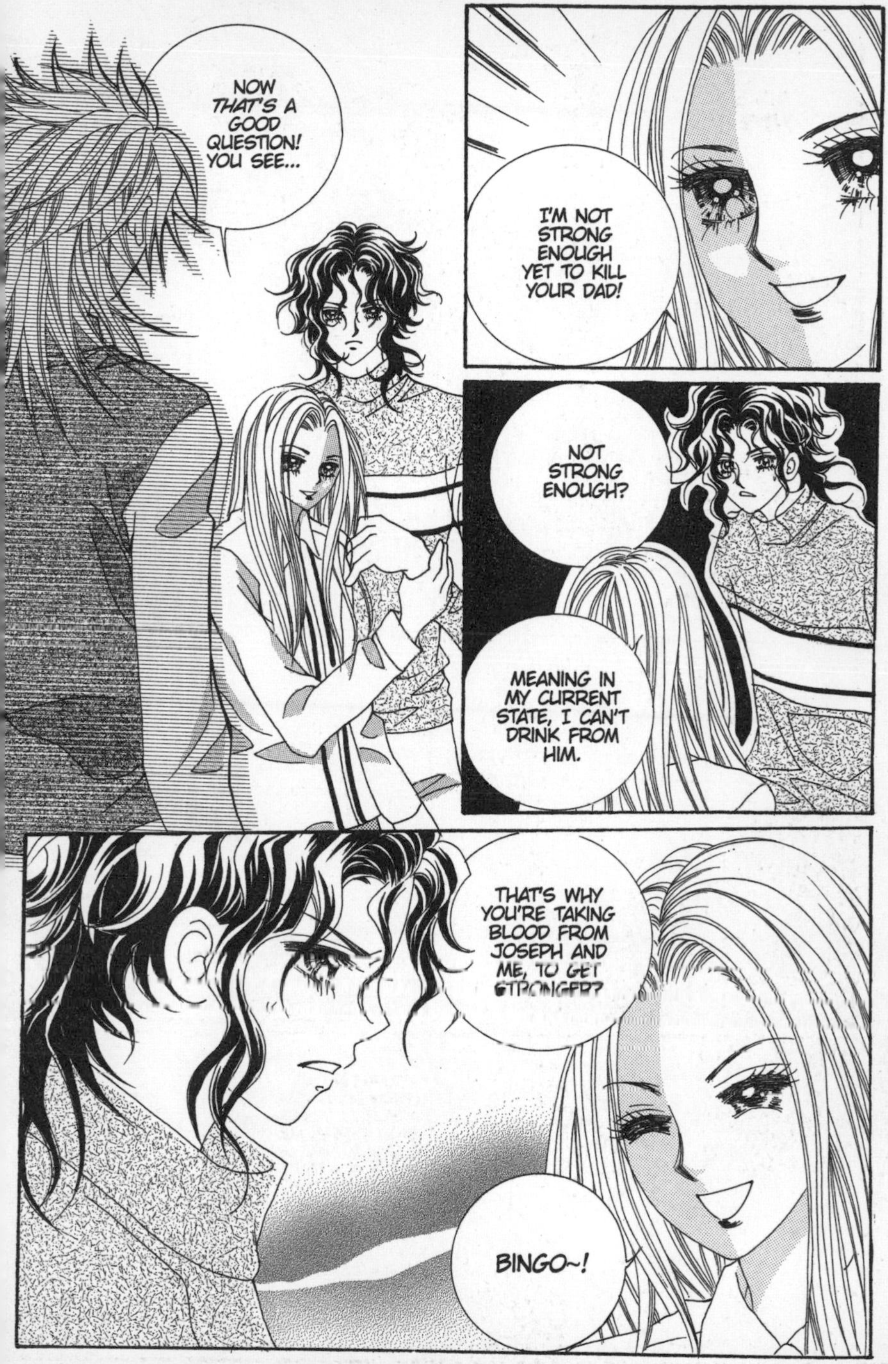
NOW THAT'S A GOOD QUESTION! YOU SEE...
I'M NOT STRONG ENOUGH YET TO KILL YOUR DAD!
NOT STRONG ENOUGH?
MEANING IN MY CURRENT STATE, I CAN'T DRINK FROM HIM.
THAT'S WHY YOU'RE TAKING BLOOD FROM JOSEPH AND ME, TO GET STRONGER?
BINGO~!

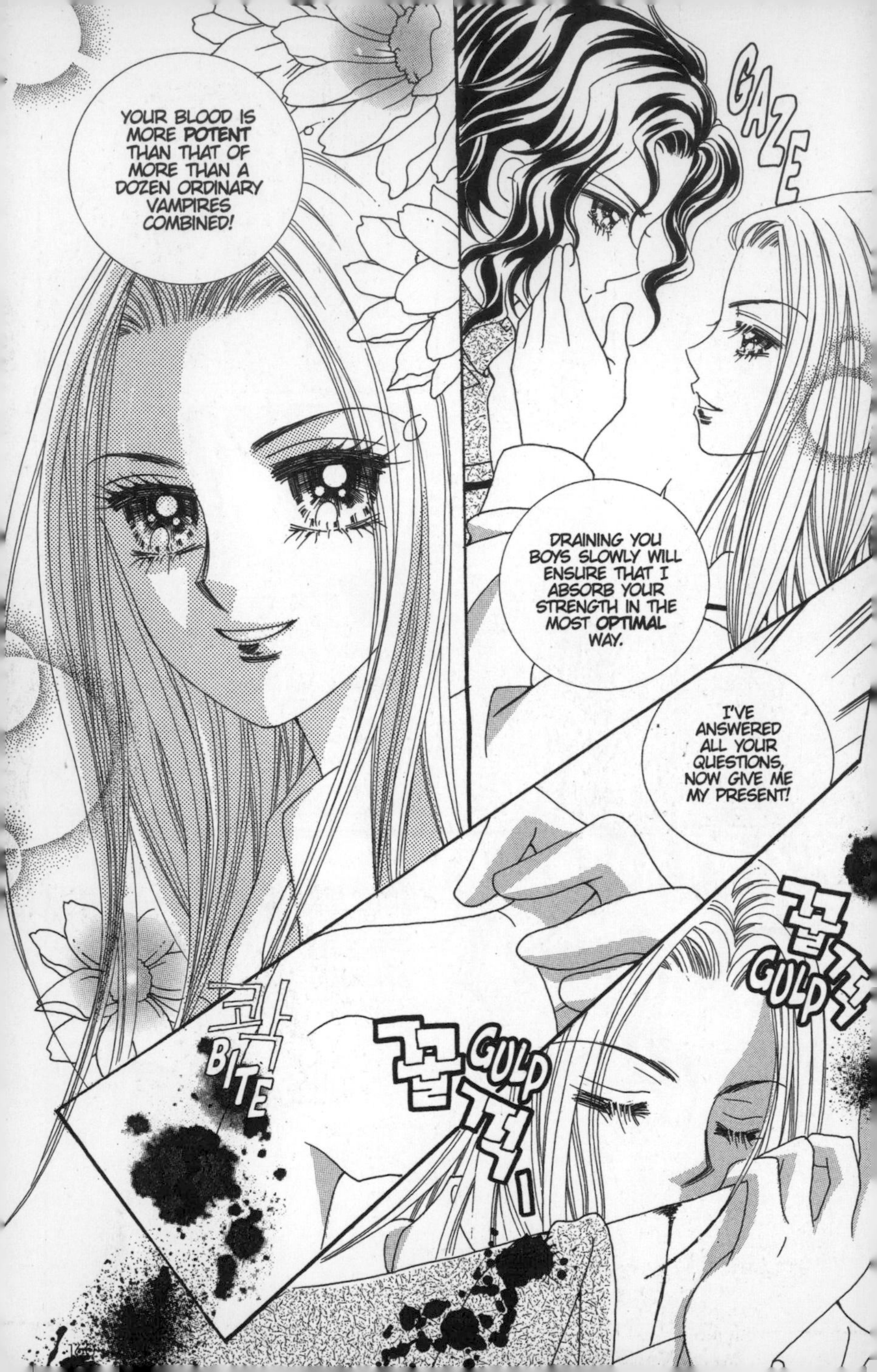
YOUR BLOOD IS MORE POTENT THAN THAT OF MORE THAN A DOZEN ORDINARY VAMPIRES COMBINED!
GAZE
DRAINING YOU BOYS SLOWLY WILL ENSURE THAT I ABSORB YOUR STRENGTH IN THE MOST OPTIMAL WAY.
I'VE ANSWERED ALL YOUR QUESTIONS, NOW GIVE ME MY PRESENT!
BITE
GULP
GULP

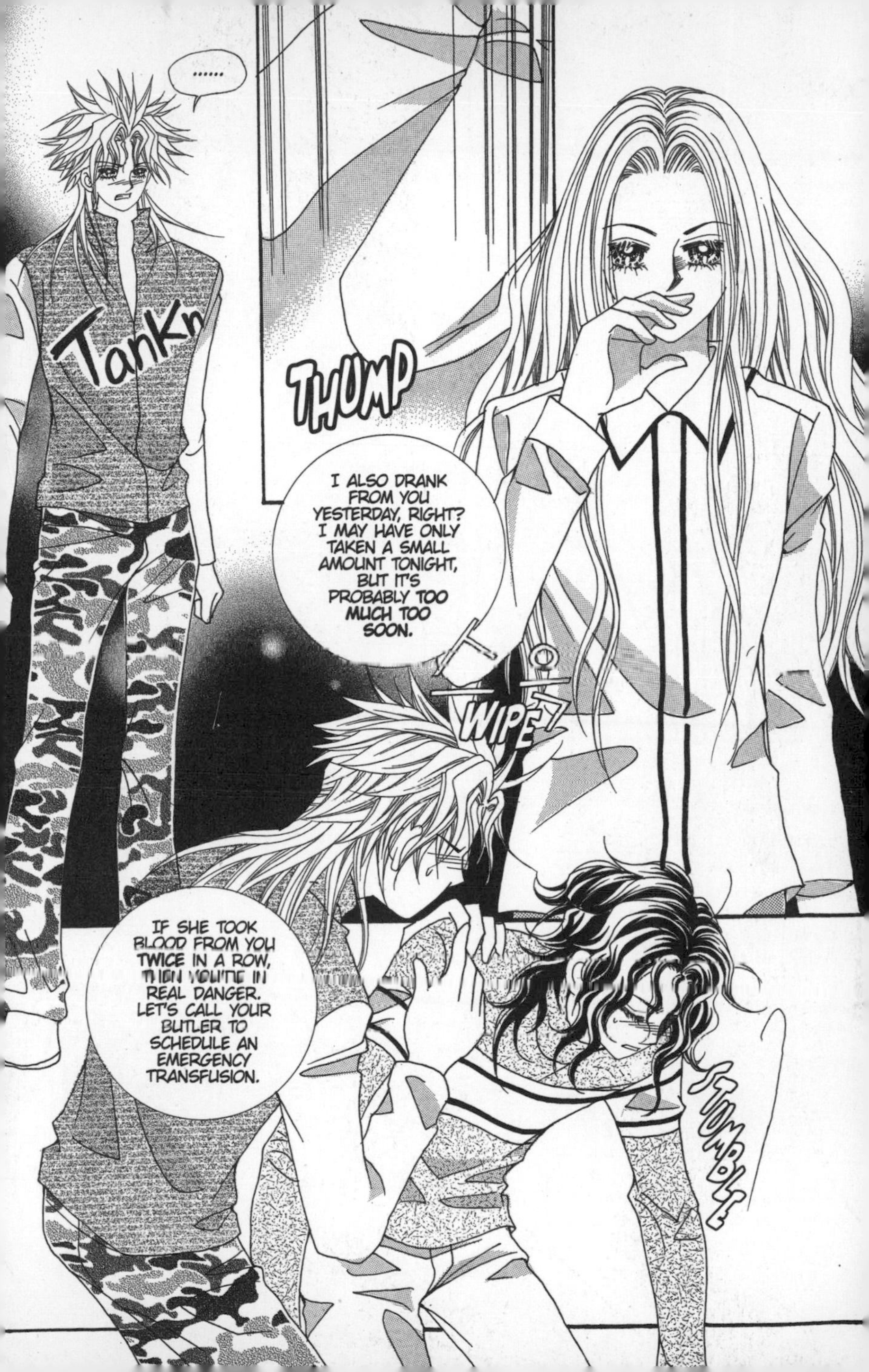
......
THUMP
I ALSO DRANK FROM YOU YESTERDAY, RIGHT? I MAY HAVE ONLY TAKEN A SMALL AMOUNT TONIGHT, BUT IT'S PROBABLY TOO MUCH TOO SOON.
WIPE
IF SHE TOOK BLOOD FROM YOU TWICE IN A ROW, THEN YOU'RE IN REAL DANGER. LET'S CALL YOUR BUTLER TO SCHEDULE AN EMERGENCY TRANSFUSION.
STUMBLE

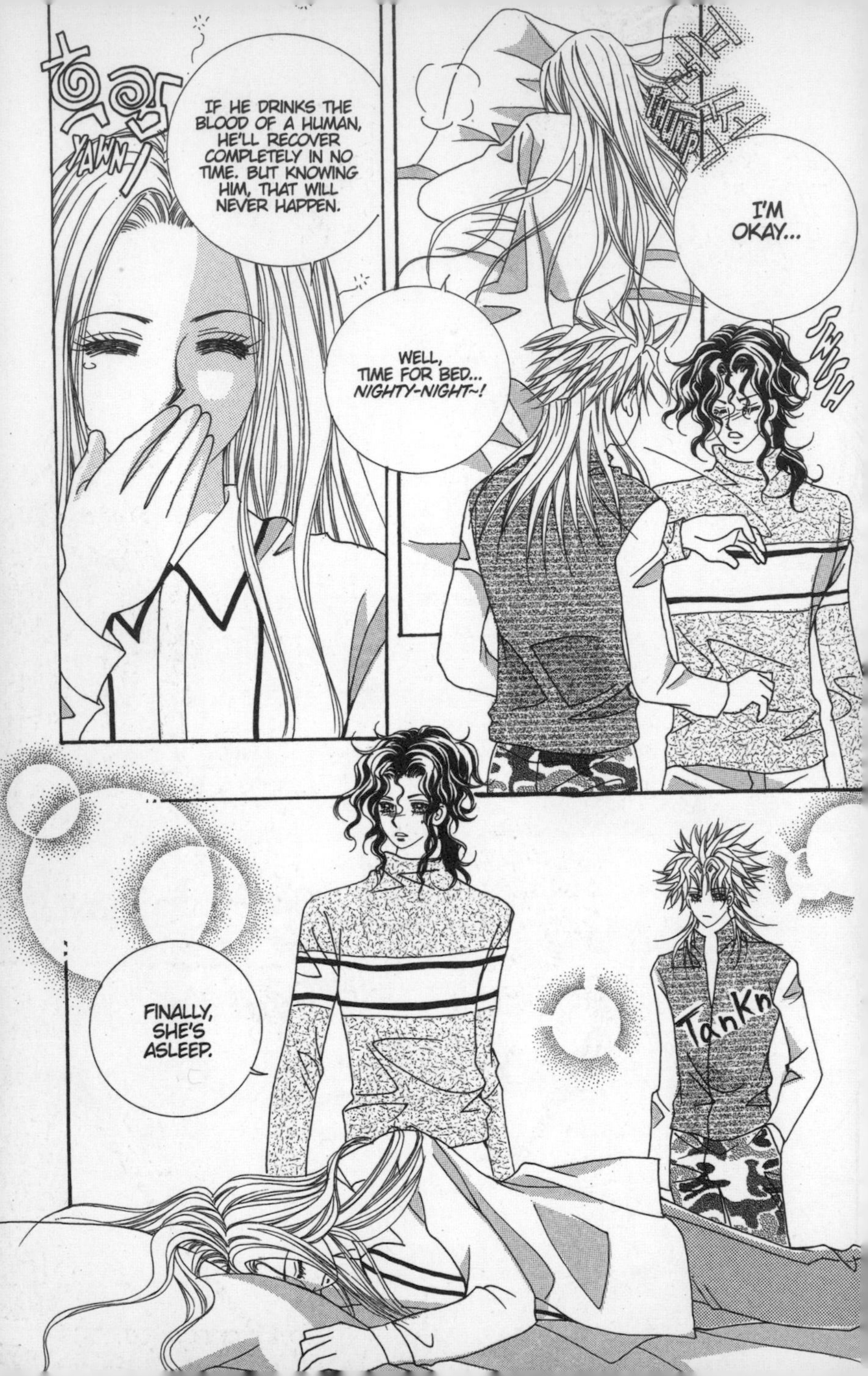
YAWN
IF HE DRINKS THE BLOOD OF A HUMAN, HE'LL RECOVER COMPLETELY IN NO TIME. BUT KNOWING HIM, THAT WILL NEVER HAPPEN.
WELL, TIME FOR BED... *NIGHTY-NIGHT~!*
THUMP
I'M OKAY...
SWISH
FINALLY, SHE'S ASLEEP.
TanKn

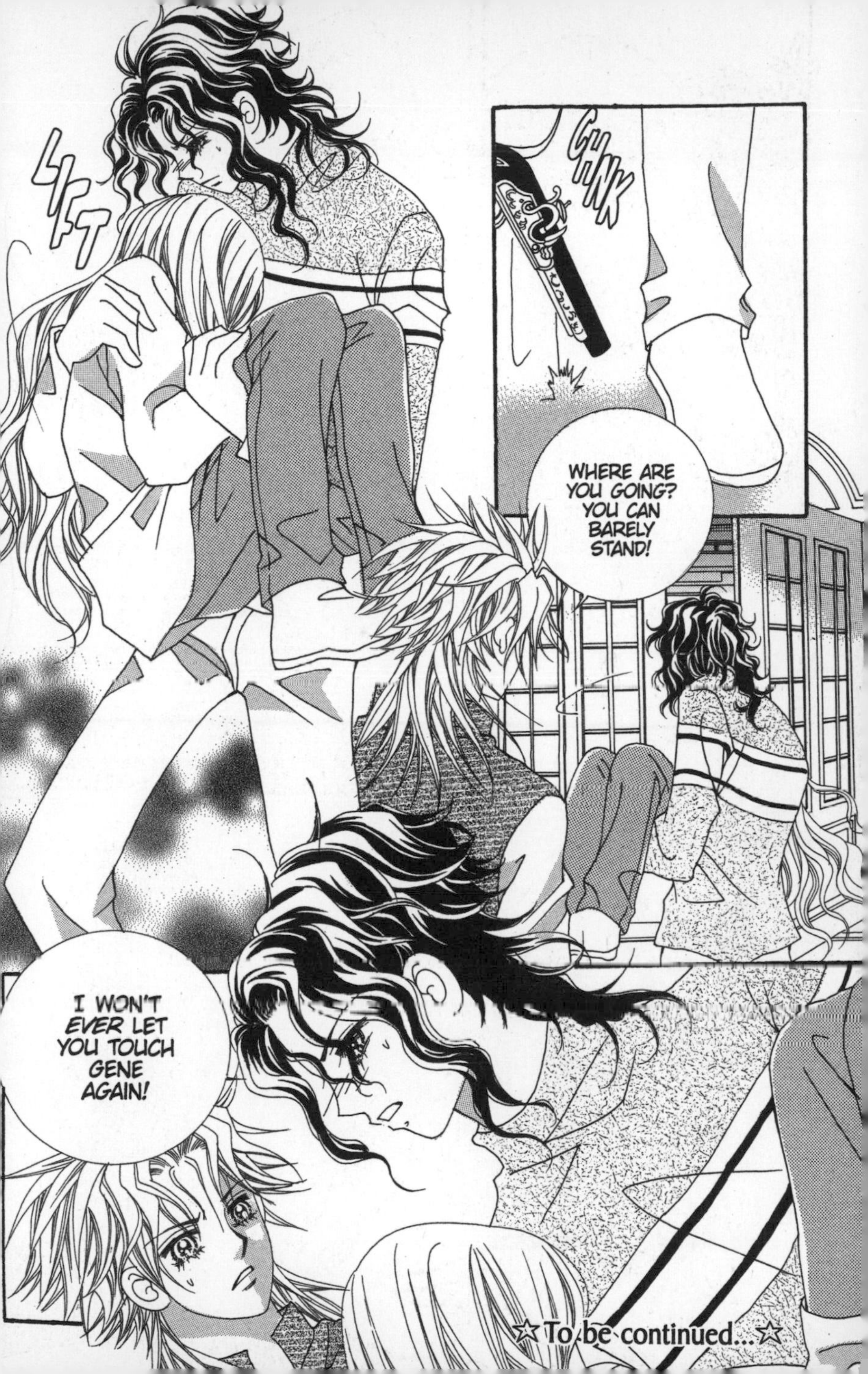
LIFT
CHINK
WHERE ARE YOU GOING? YOU CAN BARELY STAND!
I WON'T *EVER* LET YOU TOUCH GENE AGAIN!
☆To be continued...☆

My Boyfriend is a

VAMPIRE

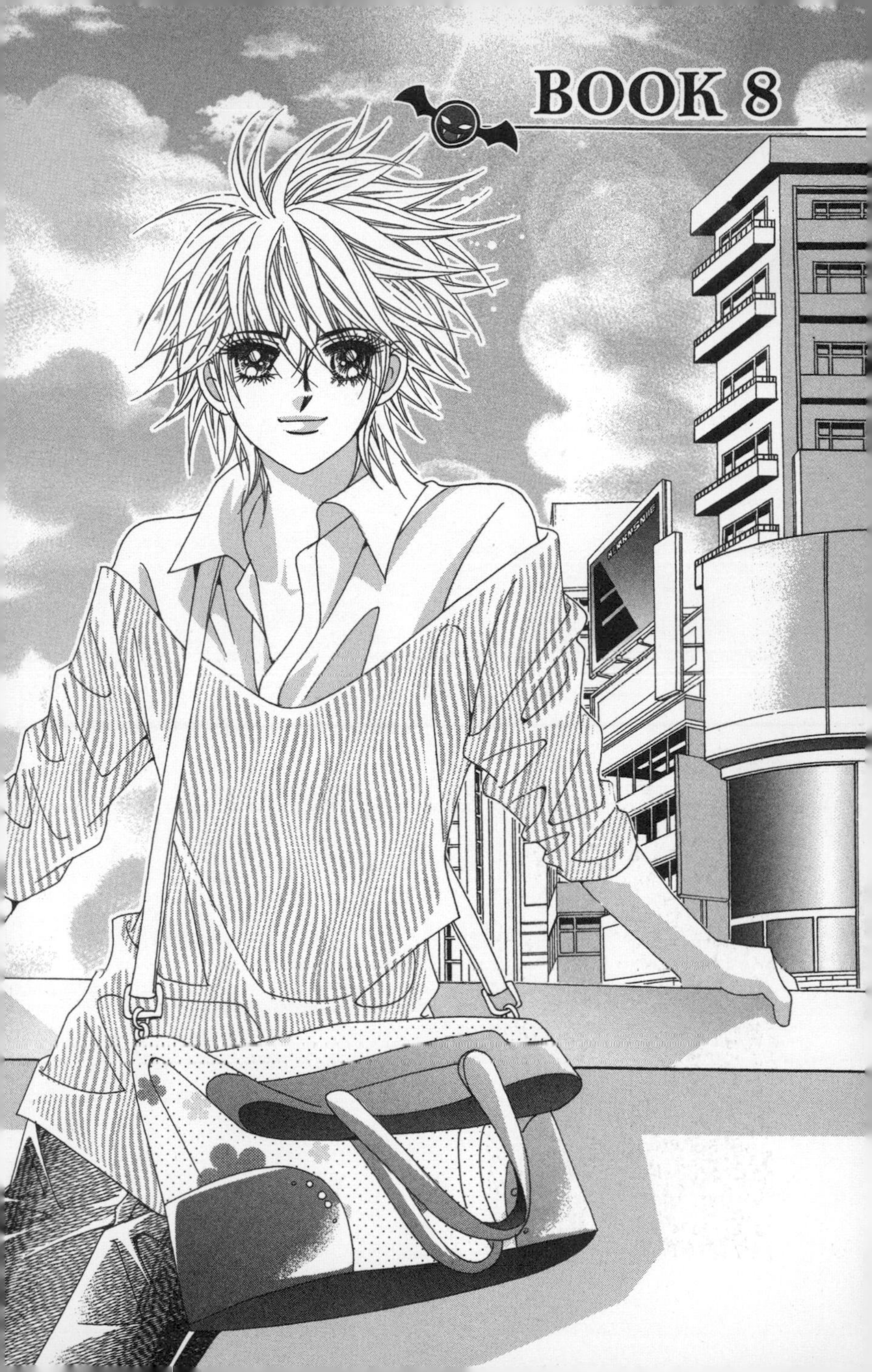
BOOK 8

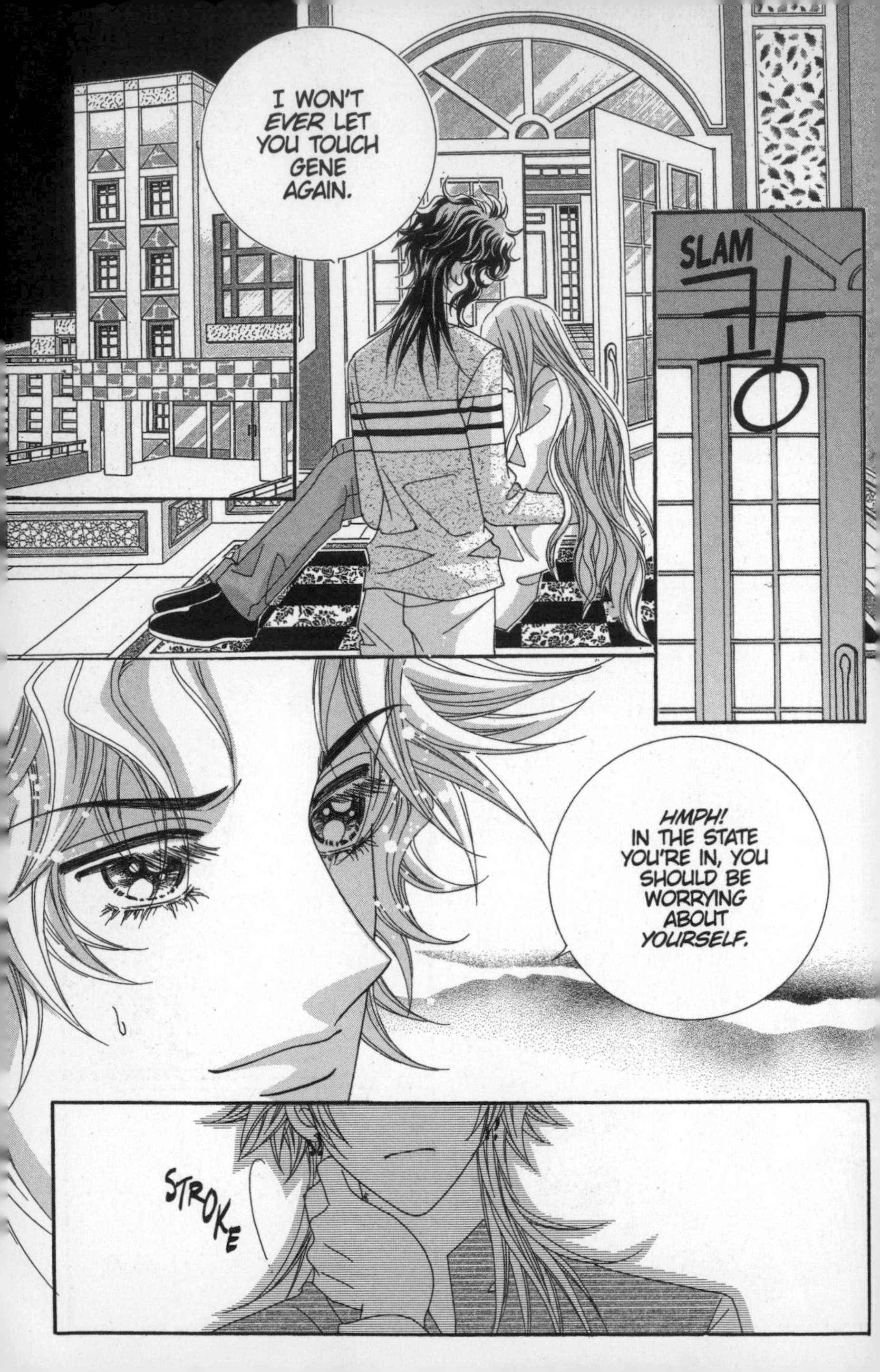
I WON'T EVER LET YOU TOUCH GENE AGAIN.
SLAM
쾅
HMPH! IN THE STATE YOU'RE IN, YOU SHOULD BE WORRYING ABOUT YOURSELF.
STROKE

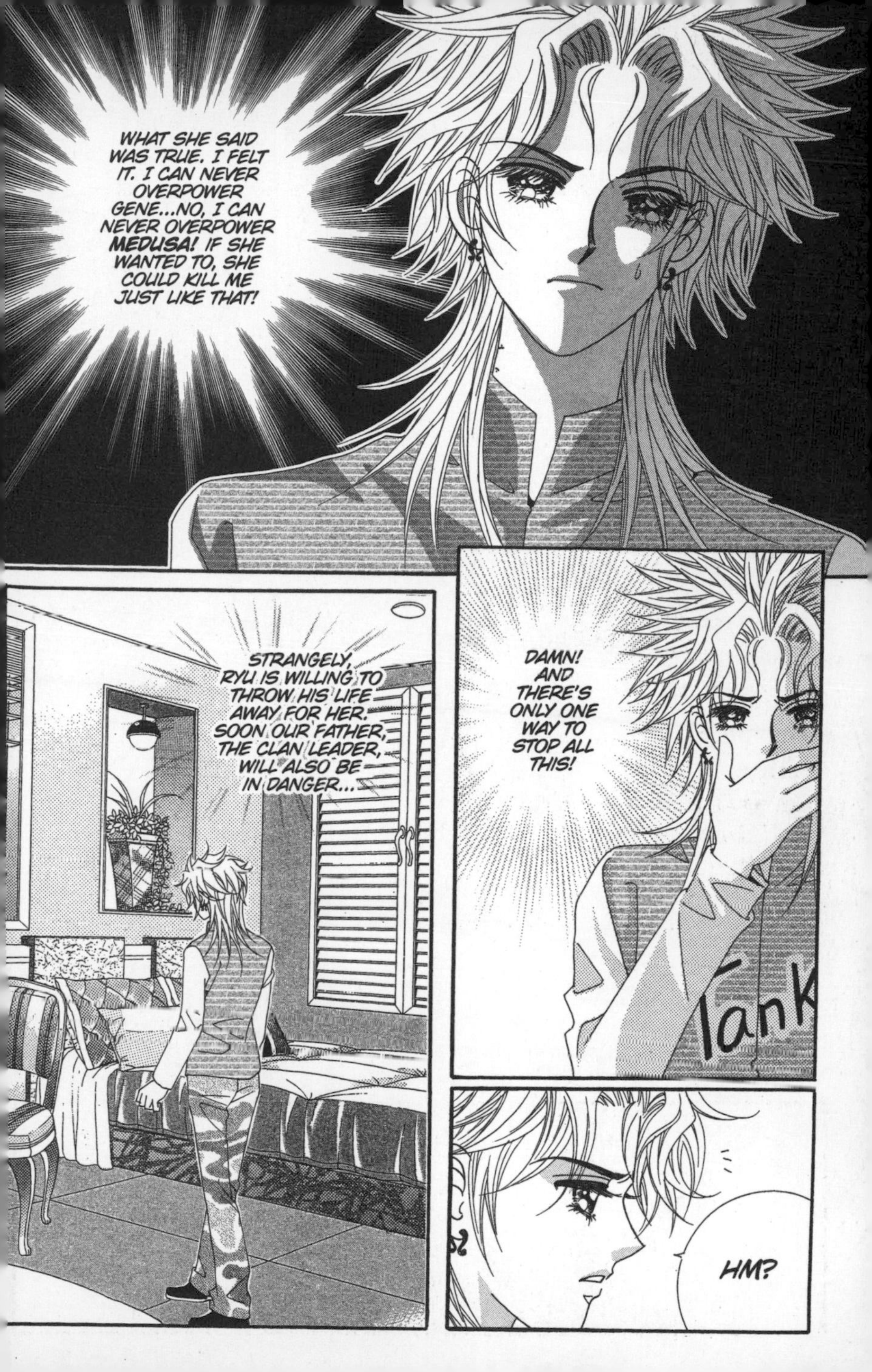
WHAT SHE SAID WAS TRUE. I FELT IT. I CAN NEVER OVERPOWER GENE...NO, I CAN NEVER OVERPOWER **MEDUSA!** IF SHE WANTED TO, SHE COULD KILL ME JUST LIKE THAT!
STRANGELY, RYU IS WILLING TO THROW HIS LIFE AWAY FOR HER. SOON OUR FATHER, THE CLAN LEADER, WILL ALSO BE IN DANGER...
DAMN! AND THERE'S ONLY ONE WAY TO STOP ALL THIS!
Tank
HM?

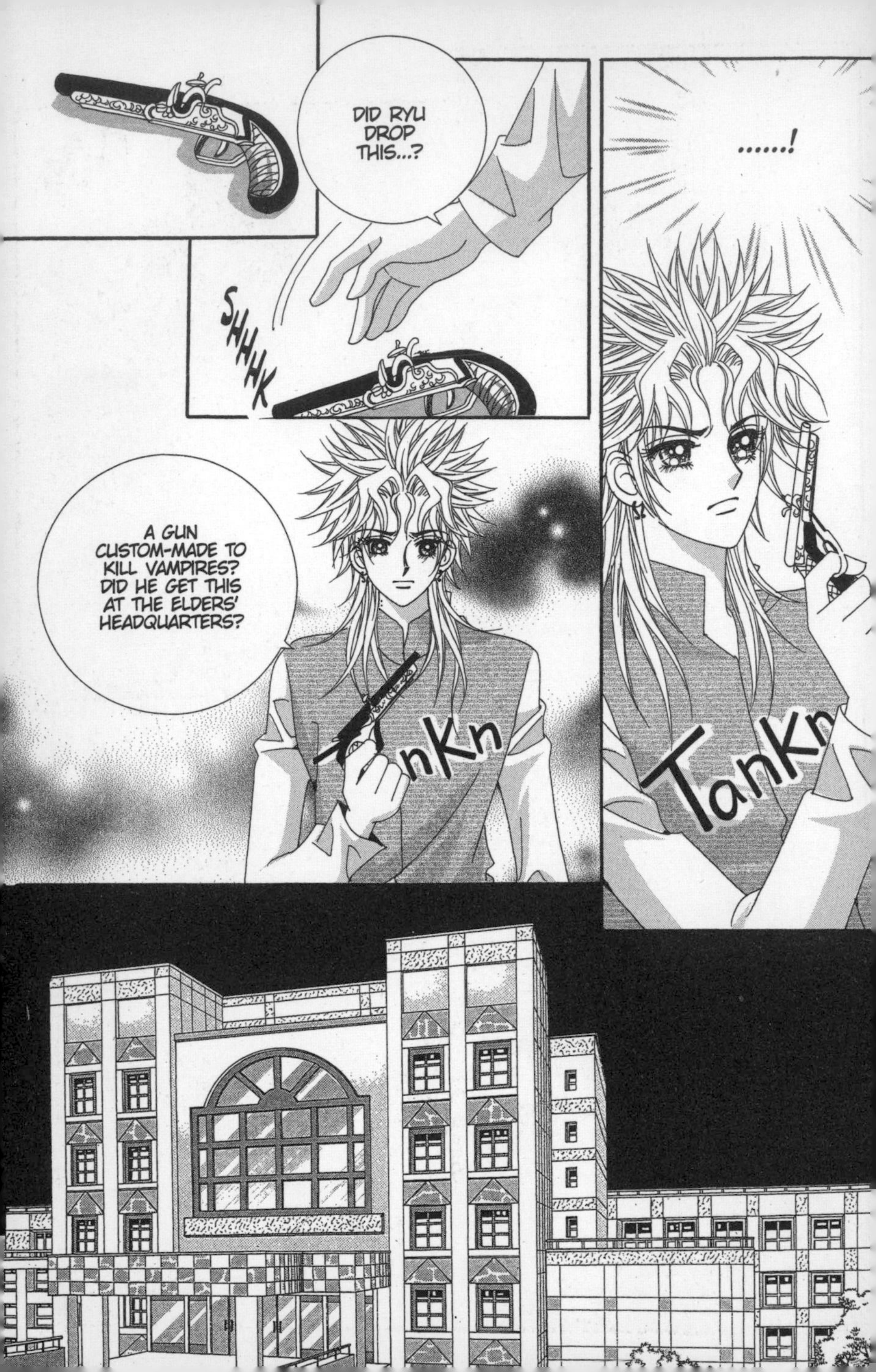
DID RYU DROP THIS...?
SHHHK
A GUN CUSTOM-MADE TO KILL VAMPIRES? DID HE GET THIS AT THE ELDERS' HEADQUARTERS?
......!

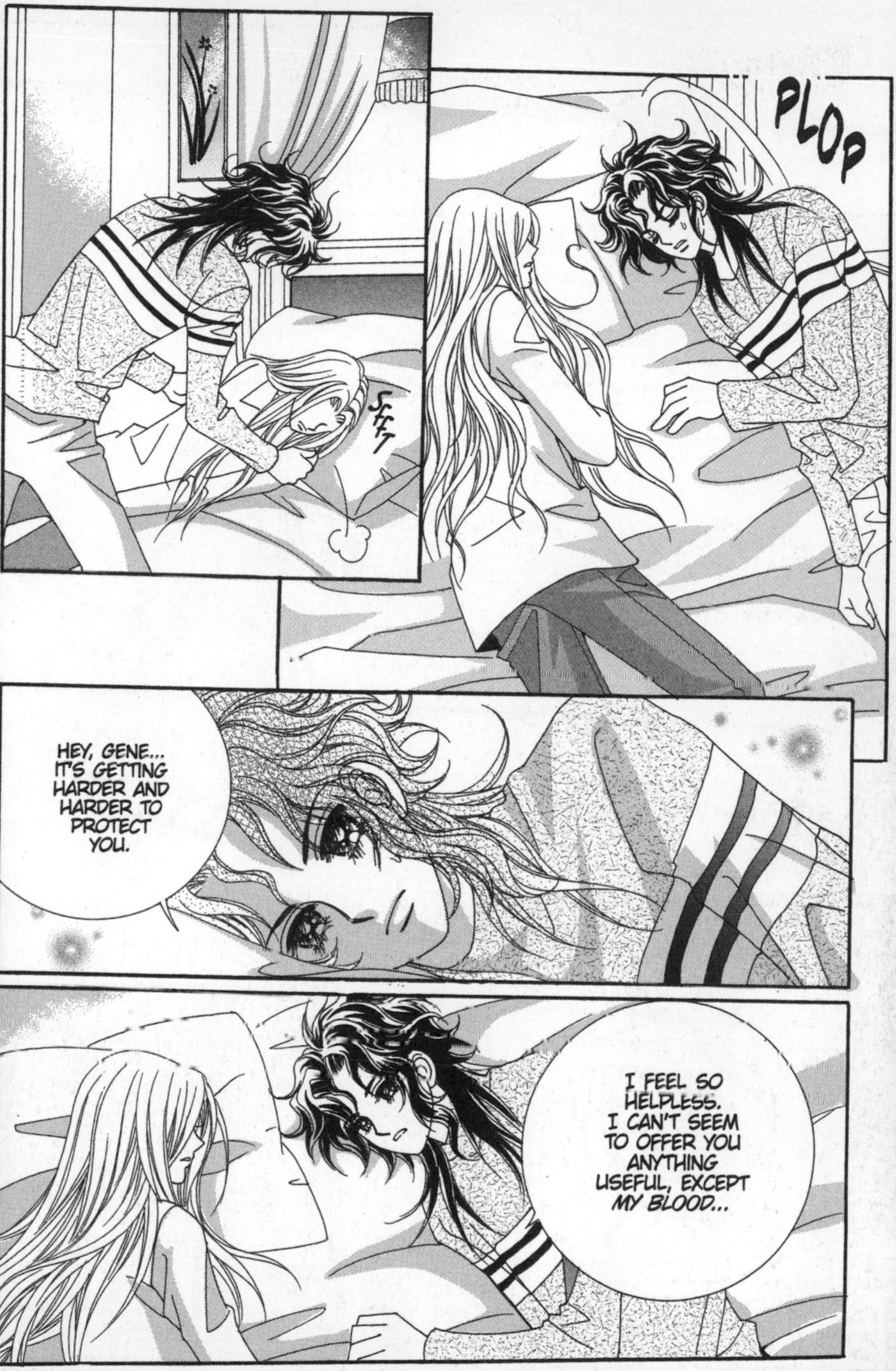
SFFT
PLOP
HEY, GENE... IT'S GETTING HARDER AND HARDER TO PROTECT YOU.
I FEEL SO HELPLESS. I CAN'T SEEM TO OFFER YOU ANYTHING USEFUL, EXCEPT *MY BLOOD*...

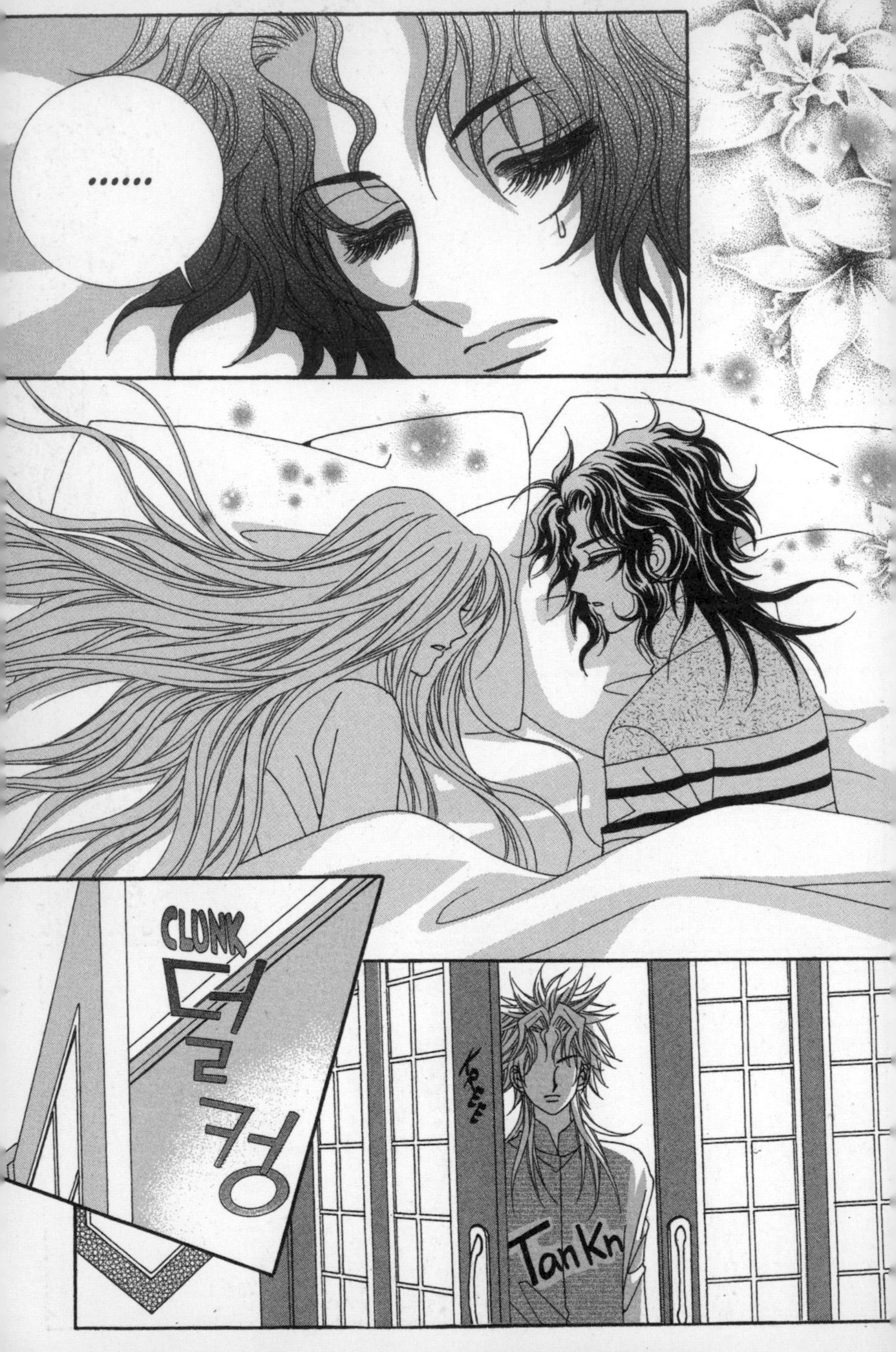
......
CLUNK
덜컹
TanKn

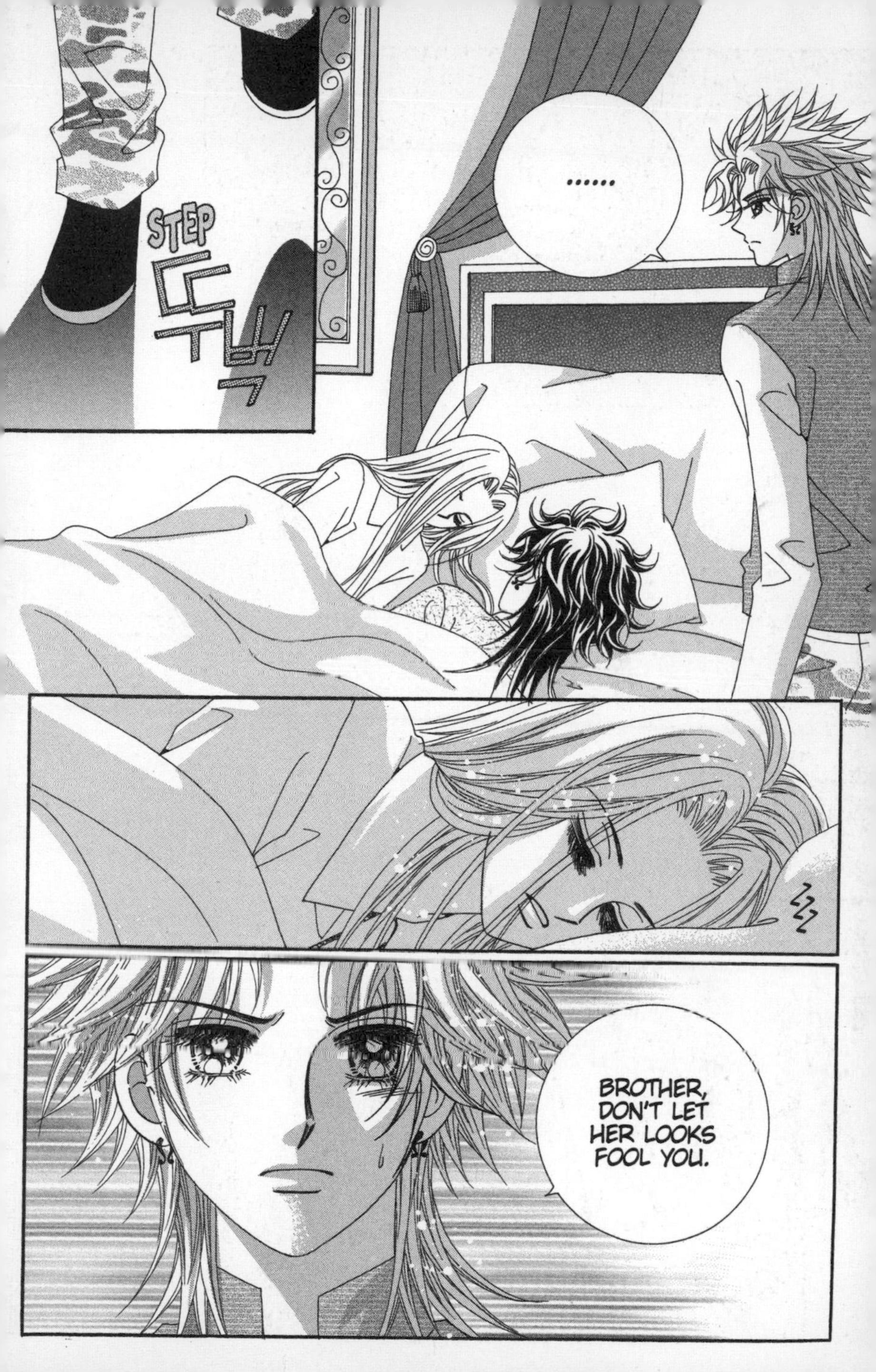
STEP
......
ZZZ
BROTHER, DON'T LET HER LOOKS FOOL YOU.

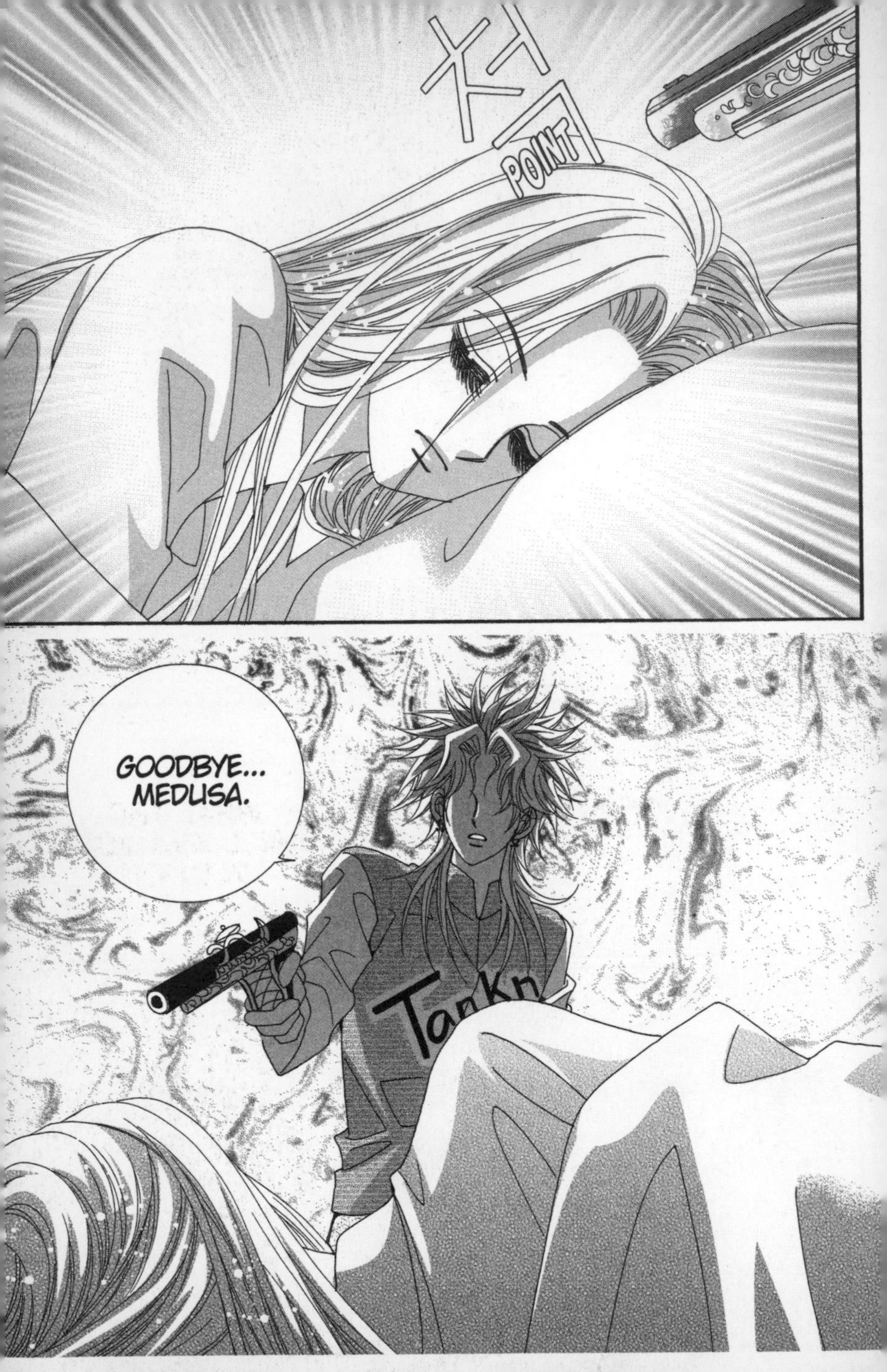
POINT
GOODBYE... MEDUSA.
Tankn

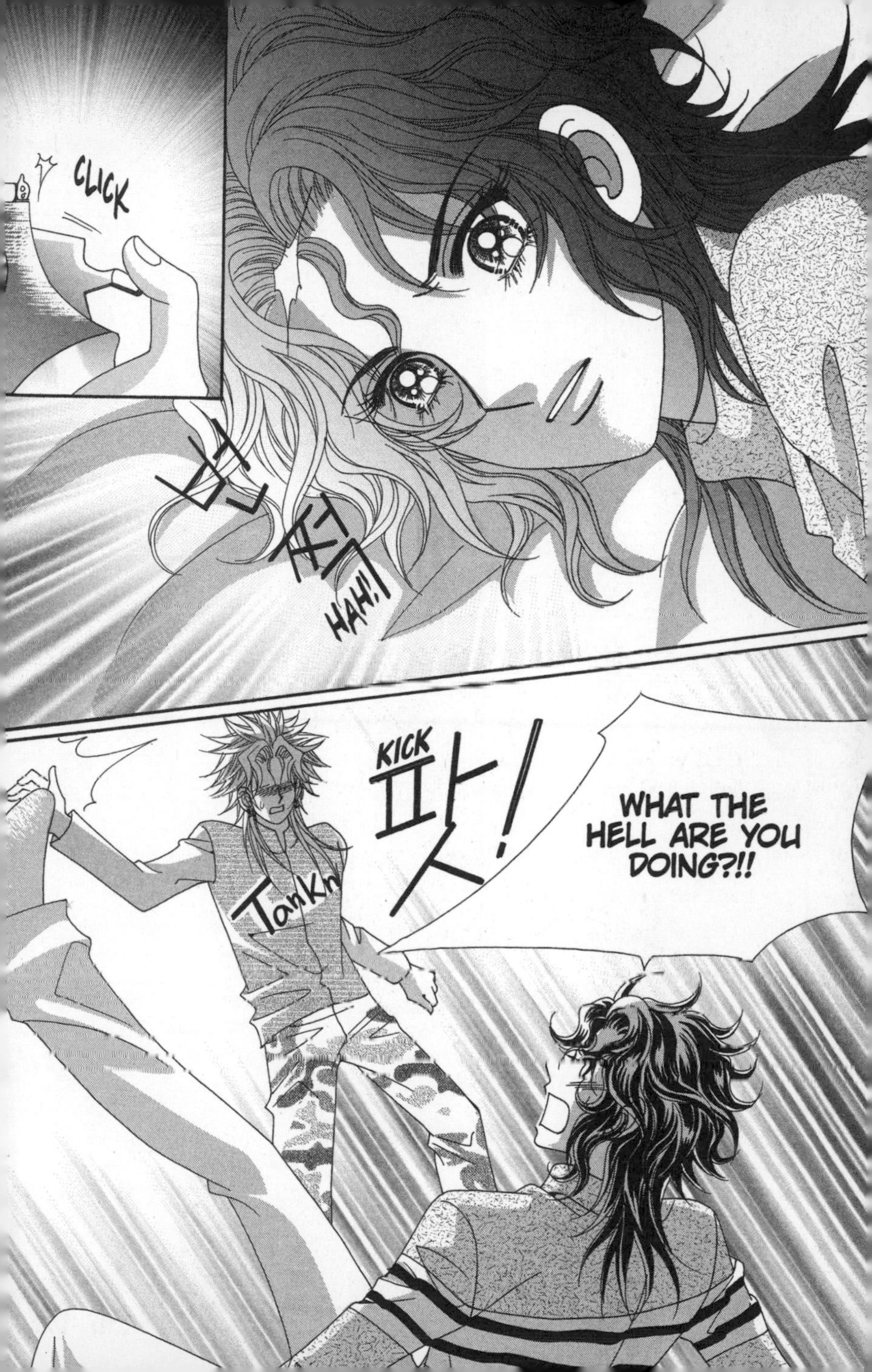
CLICK
헉
HAH!
KICK
팍!
Tankn
WHAT THE HELL ARE YOU DOING?!!

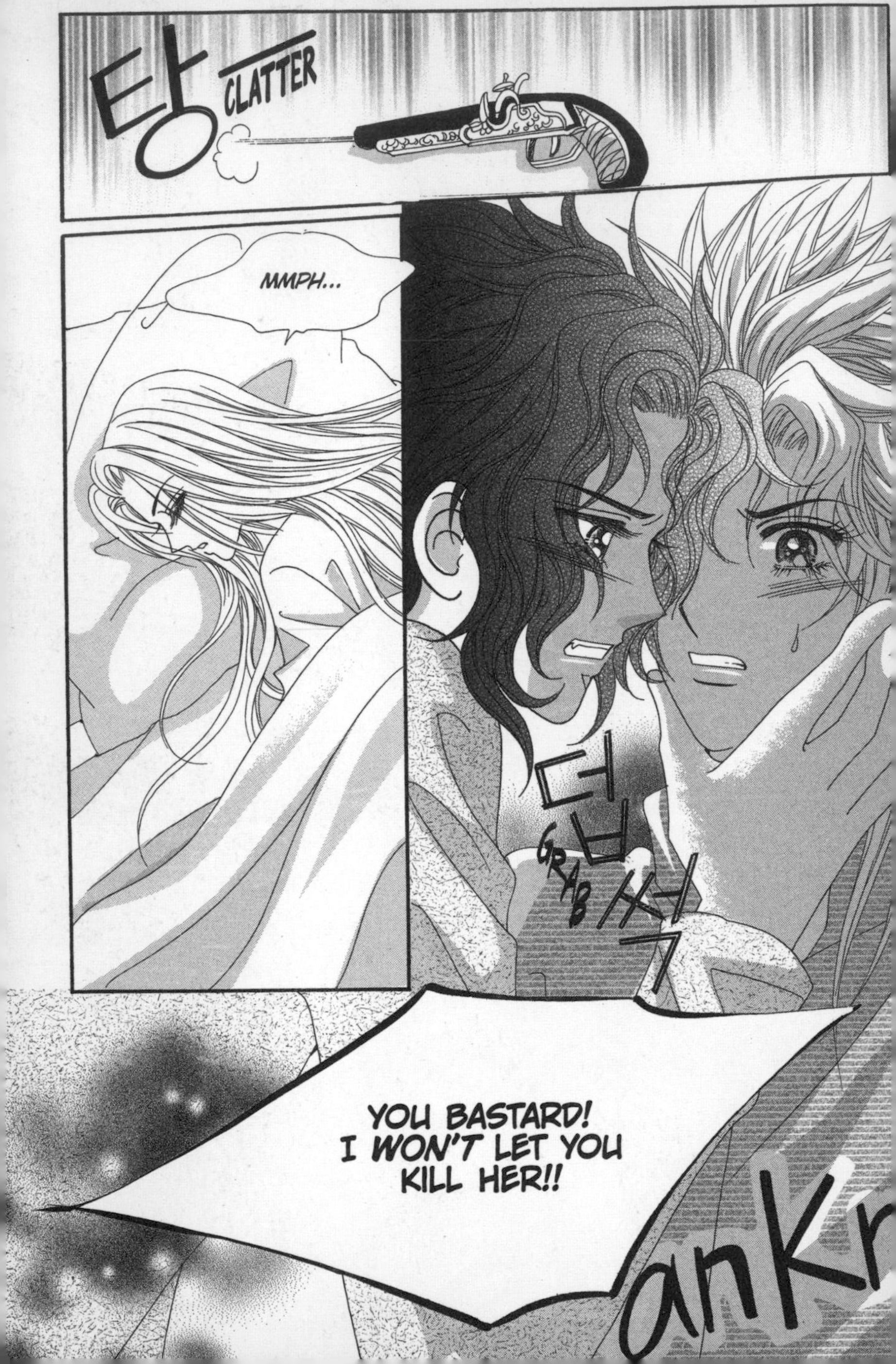
탕
CLATTER
MMPH...
GRAB
YOU BASTARD! I WON'T LET YOU KILL HER!!

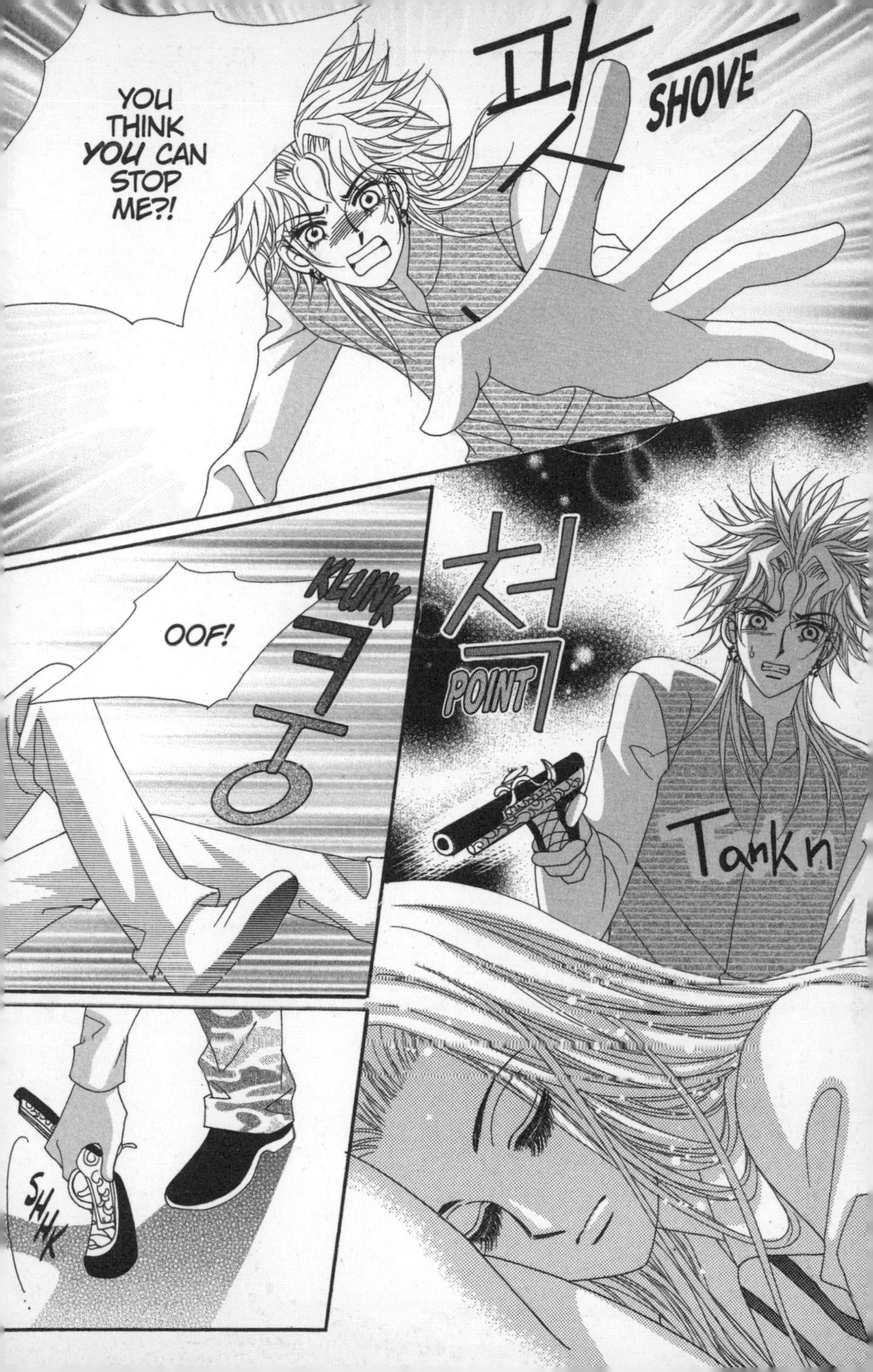
YOU THINK YOU CAN STOP ME?!
팟
SHOVE
OOF!
KLUNK
쿵
척
POINT
Tankn
SHK

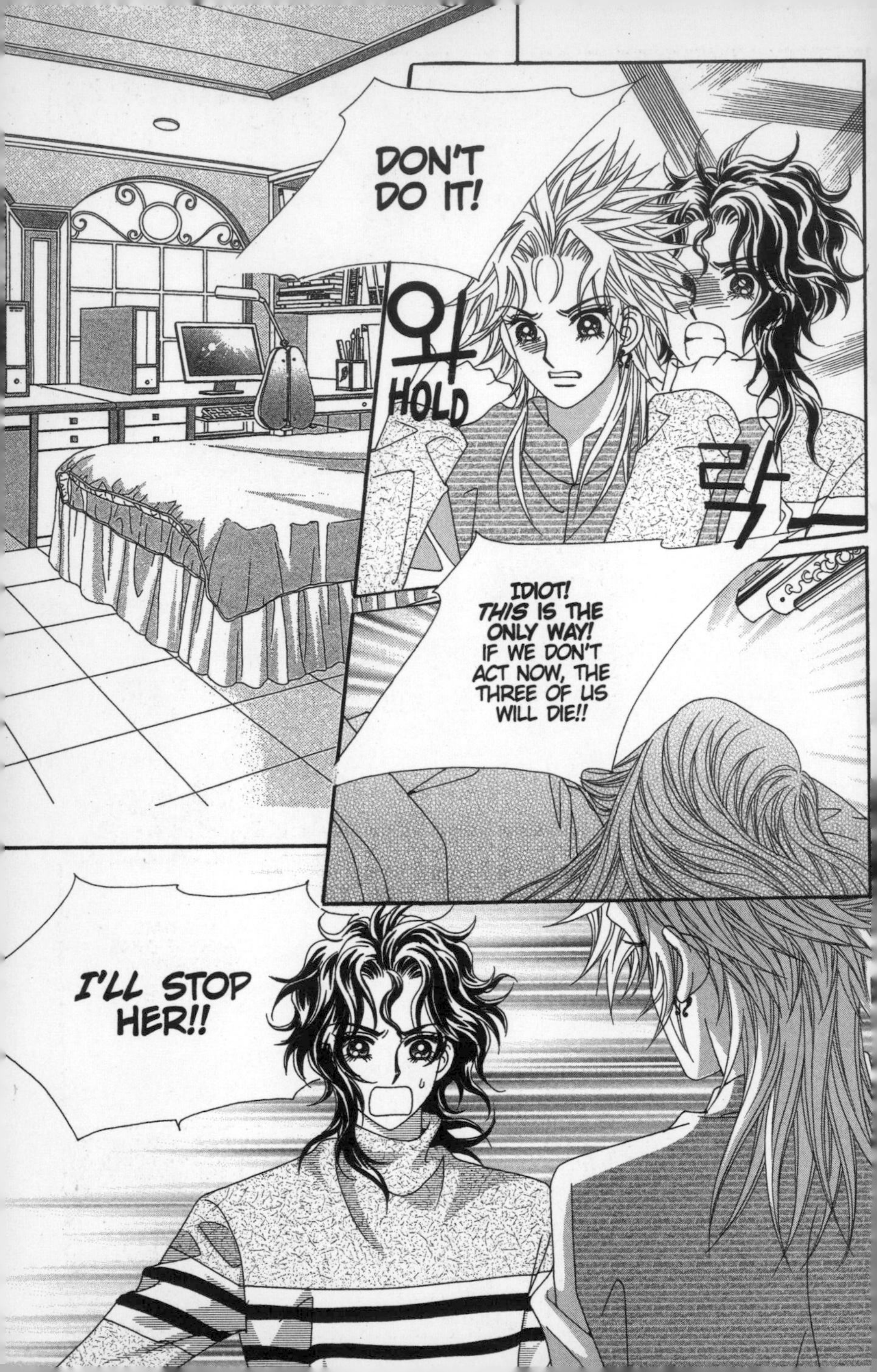
DON'T DO IT!
와
HOLD
락
IDIOT! THIS IS THE ONLY WAY! IF WE DON'T ACT NOW, THE THREE OF US WILL DIE!!
I'LL STOP HER!!

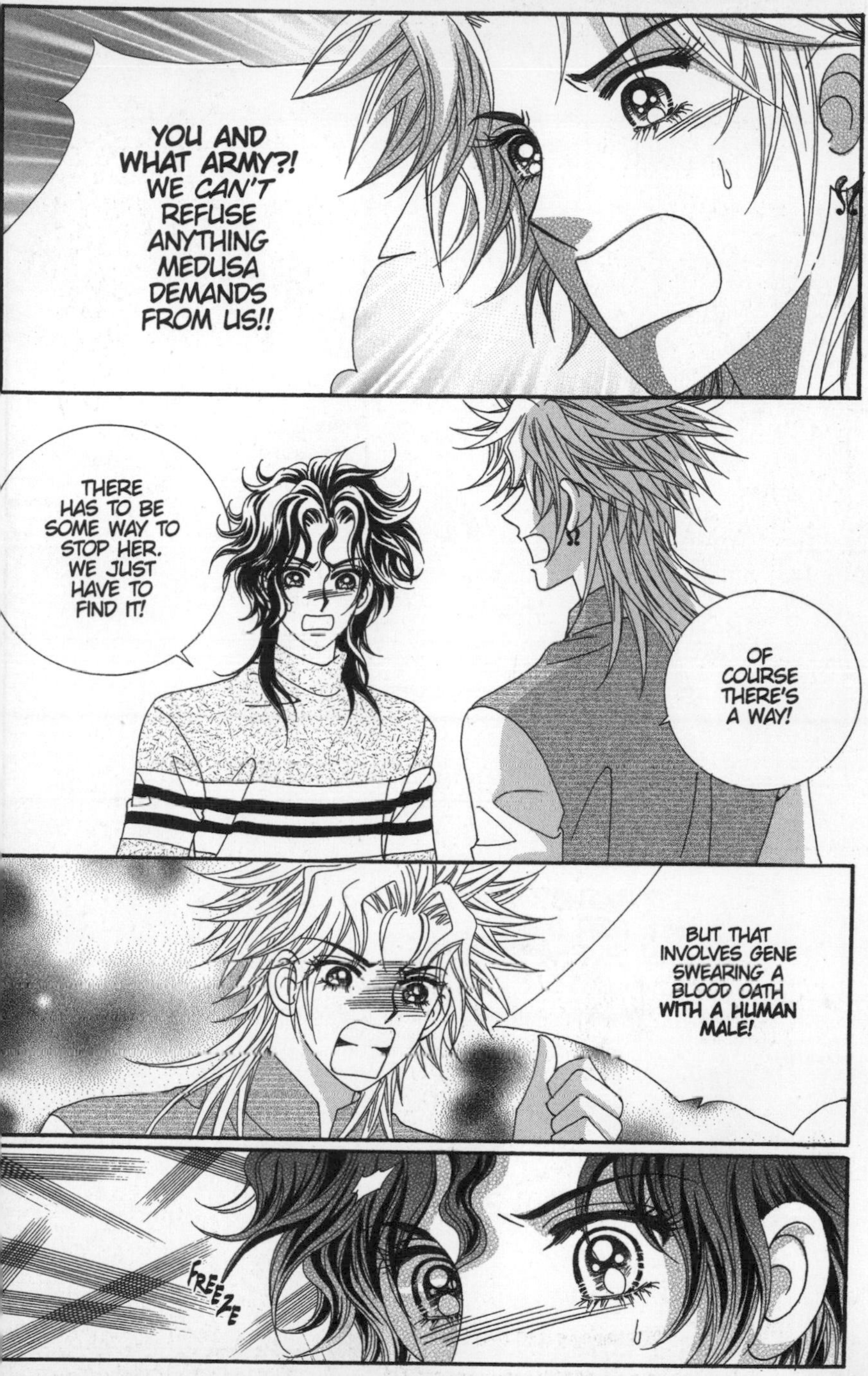
YOU AND WHAT ARMY?! WE CAN'T REFUSE ANYTHING MEDUSA DEMANDS FROM US!!
THERE HAS TO BE SOME WAY TO STOP HER. WE JUST HAVE TO FIND IT!
OF COURSE THERE'S A WAY!
BUT THAT INVOLVES GENE SWEARING A BLOOD OATH WITH A HUMAN MALE!
FREEZE

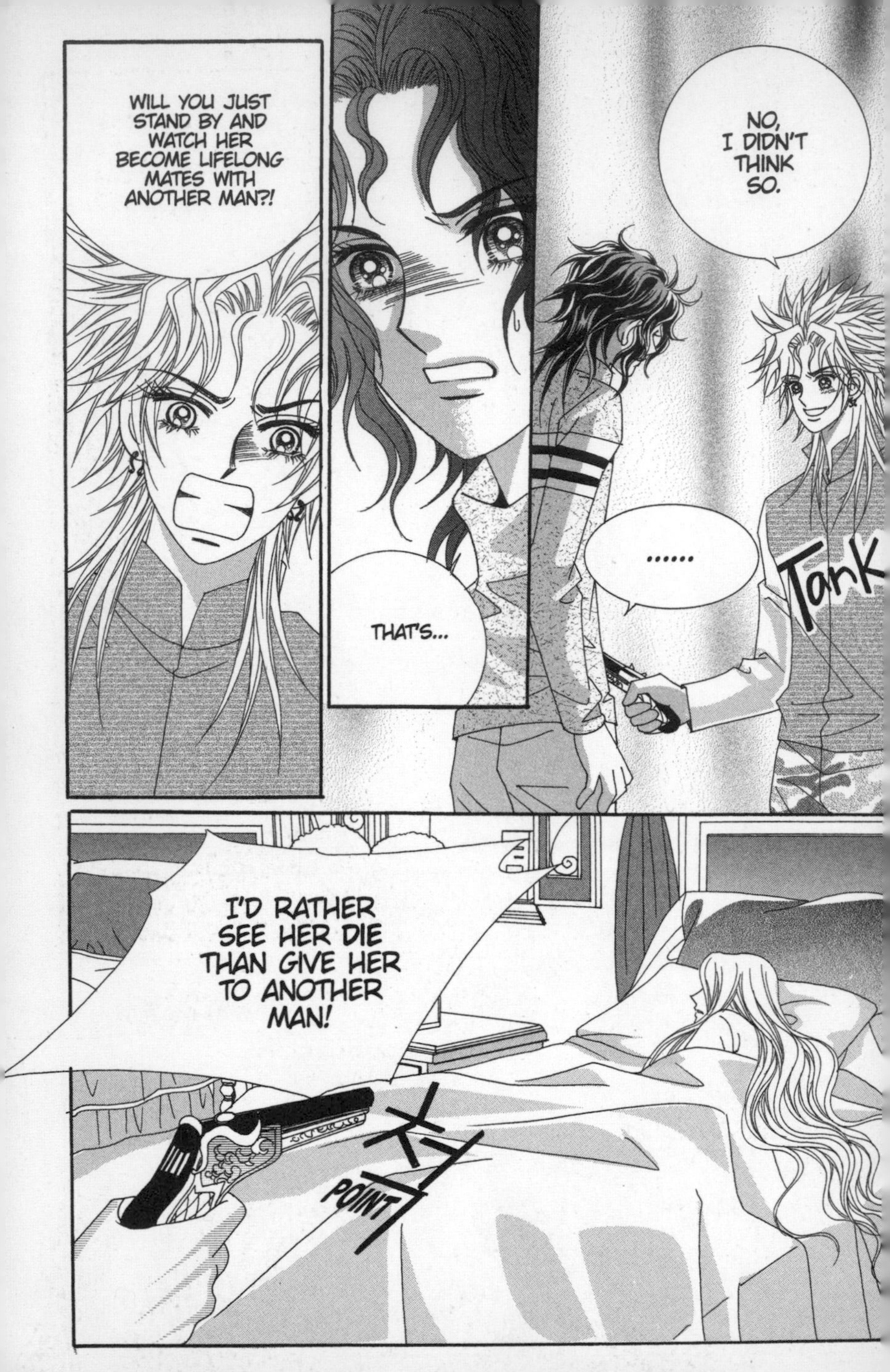
WILL YOU JUST STAND BY AND WATCH HER BECOME LIFELONG MATES WITH ANOTHER MAN?!
THAT'S...
NO, I DIDN'T THINK SO.
......
Tank
I'D RATHER SEE HER DIE THAN GIVE HER TO ANOTHER MAN!
POINT

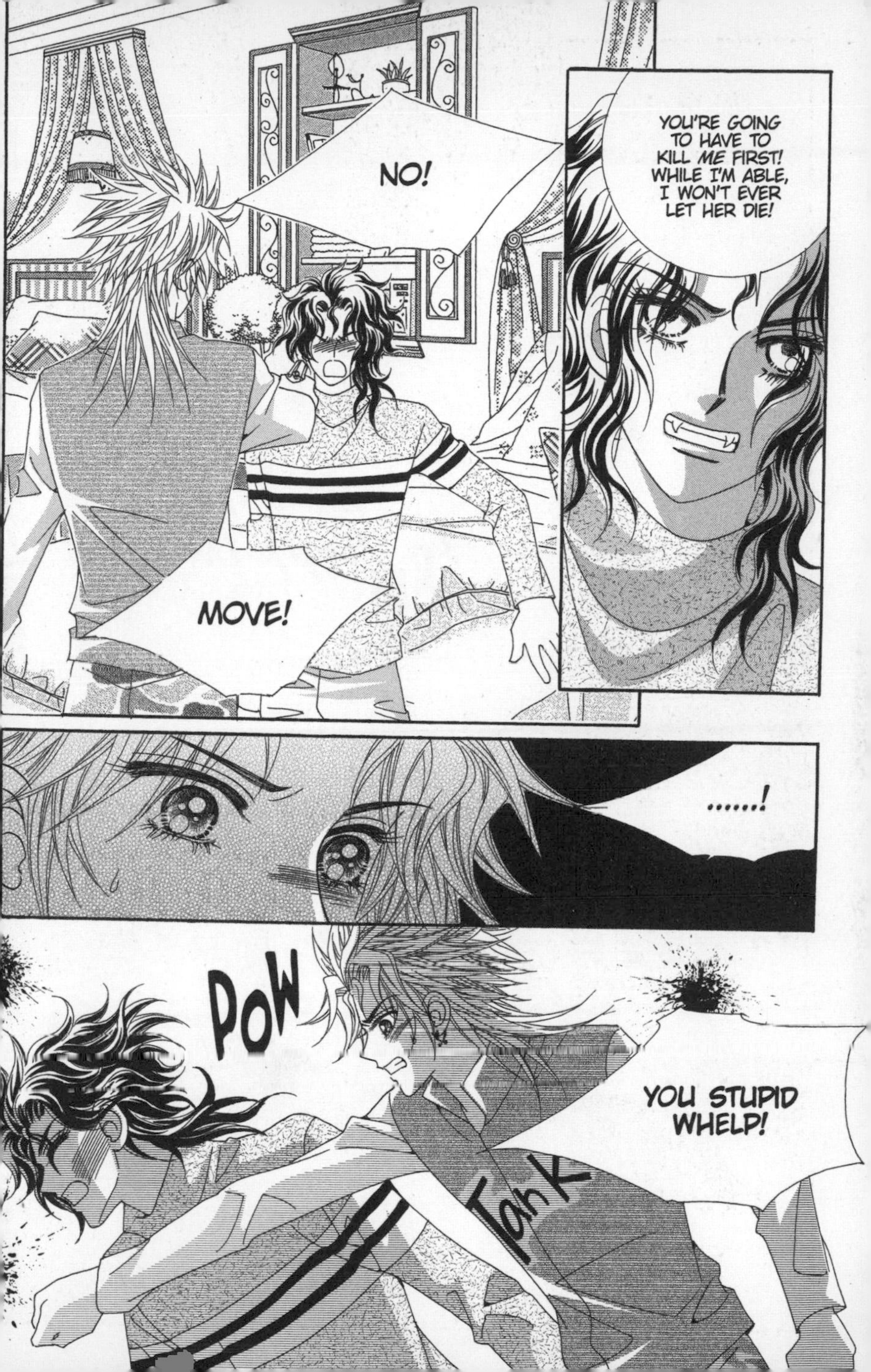
NO!
MOVE!
YOU'RE GOING TO HAVE TO KILL *ME* FIRST! WHILE I'M ABLE, I WON'T EVER LET HER DIE!
......!
POW
YOU STUPID WHELP!
TANK

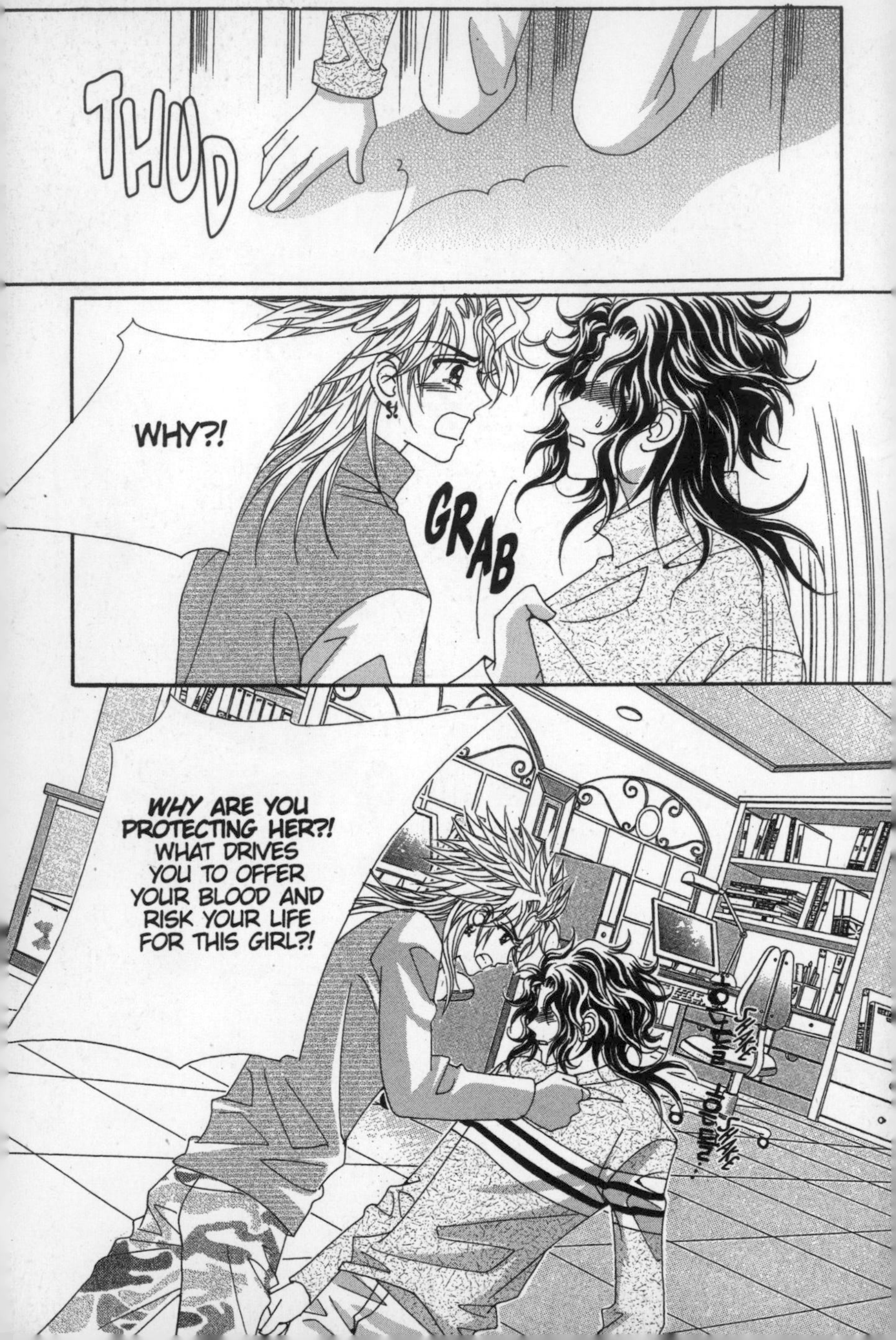
THUD
WHY?!
GRAB
*WHY* ARE YOU PROTECTING HER?! WHAT DRIVES YOU TO OFFER YOUR BLOOD AND RISK YOUR LIFE FOR THIS GIRL?!
SHAKE
SHAKE

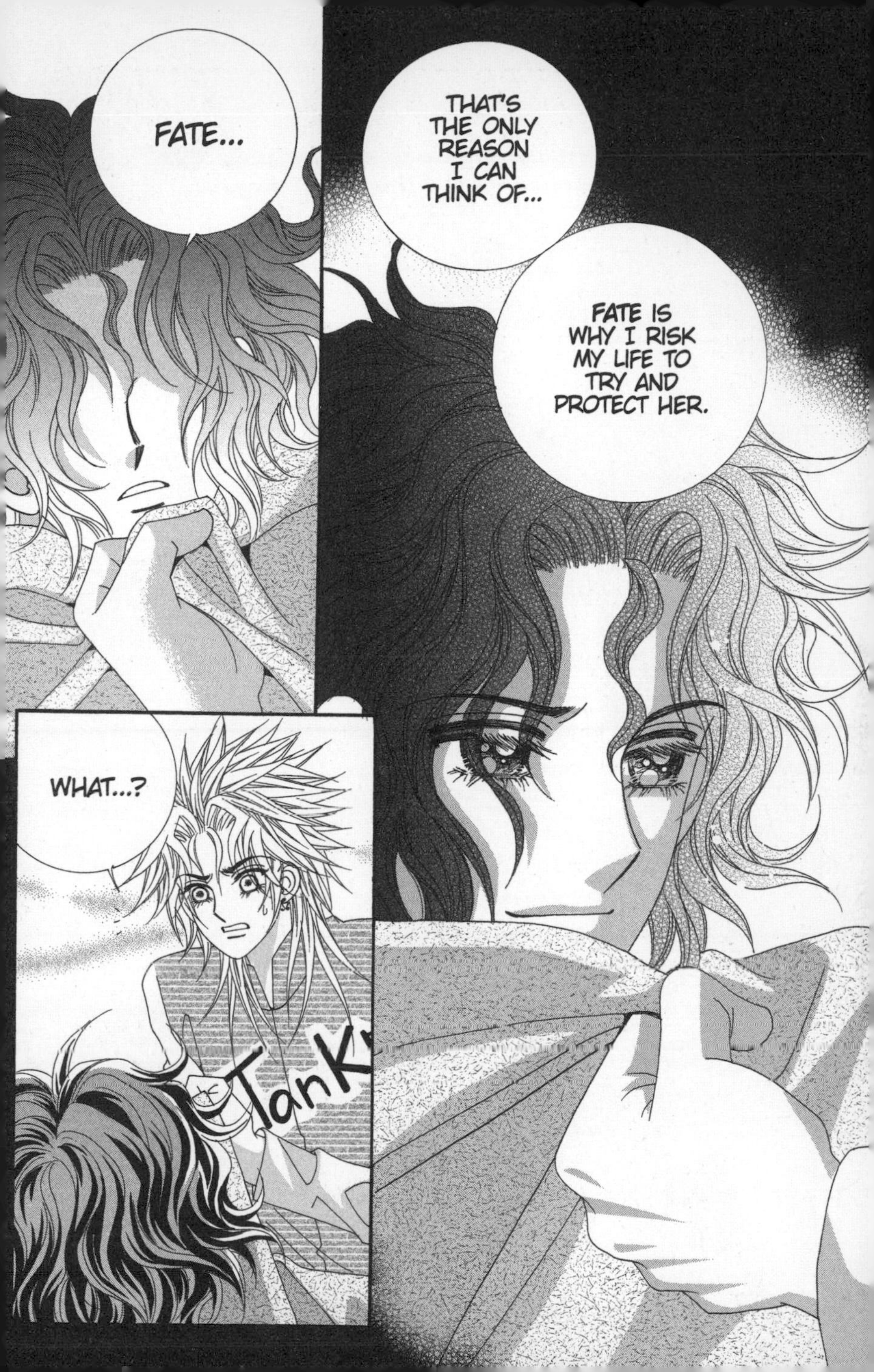
FATE...
WHAT...?
TanK
THAT'S THE ONLY REASON I CAN THINK OF...
FATE IS WHY I RISK MY LIFE TO TRY AND PROTECT HER.

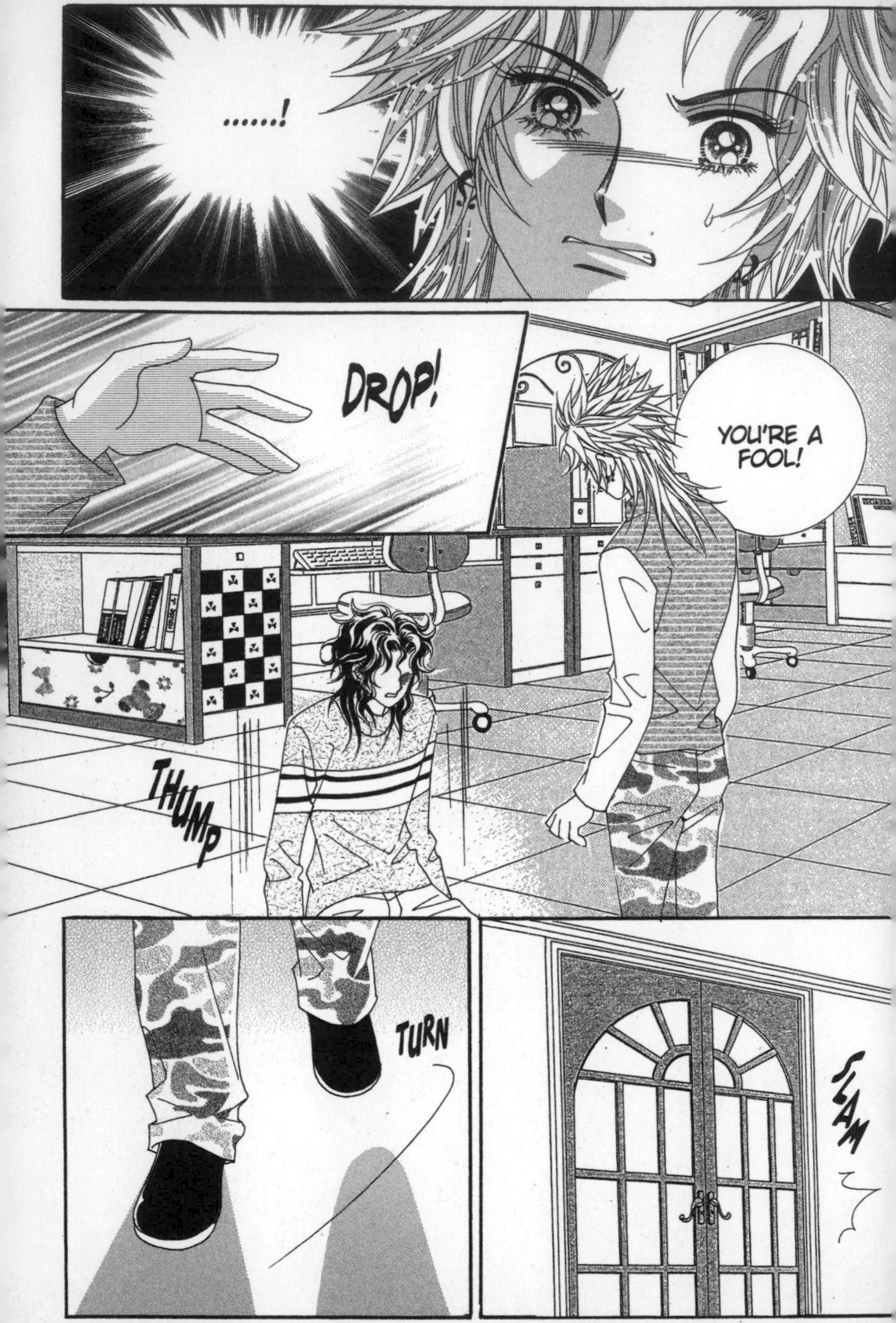

......!
DROP!
YOU'RE A FOOL!
THUMP
TURN
SLAM

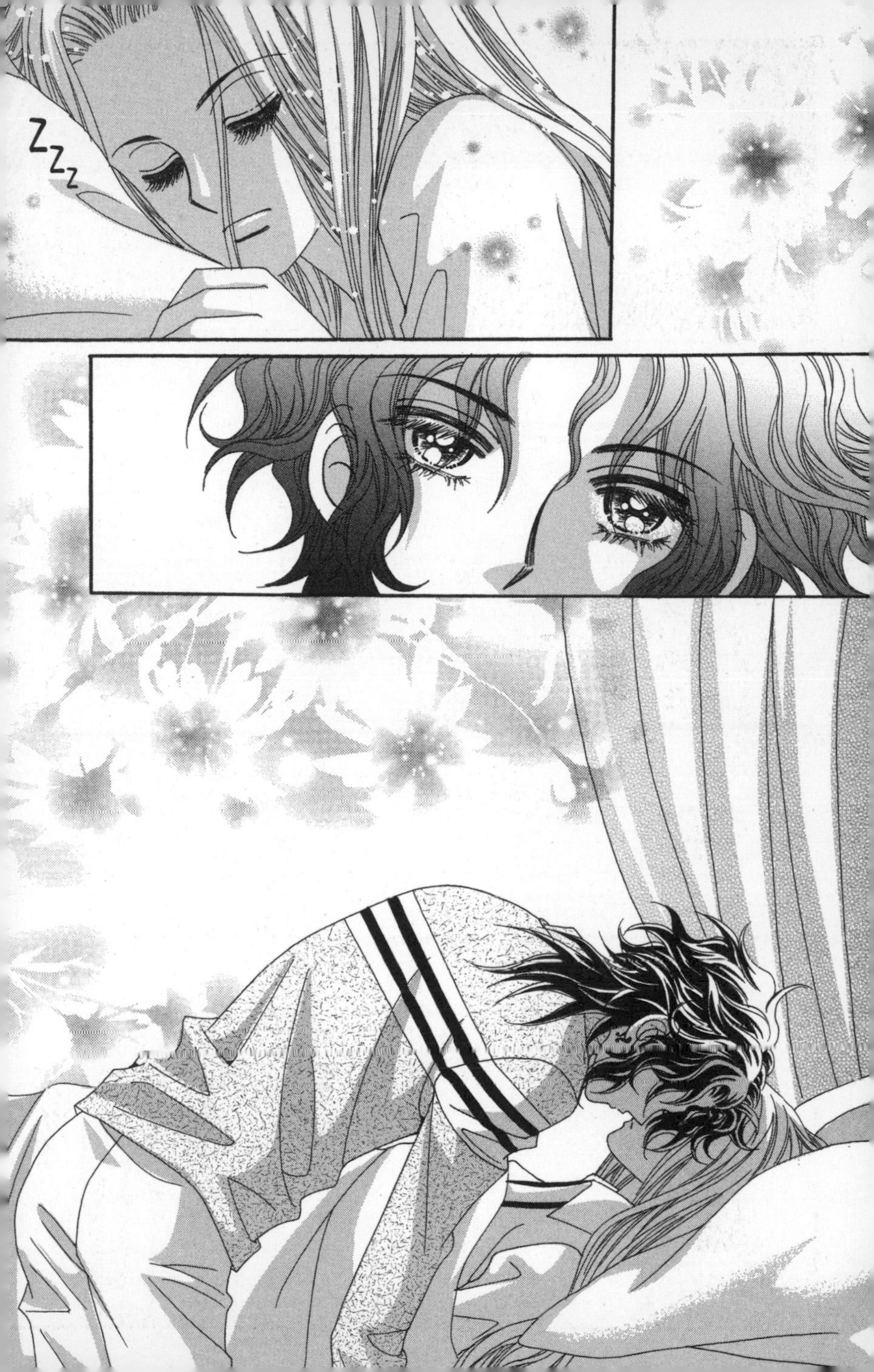
ZZZ

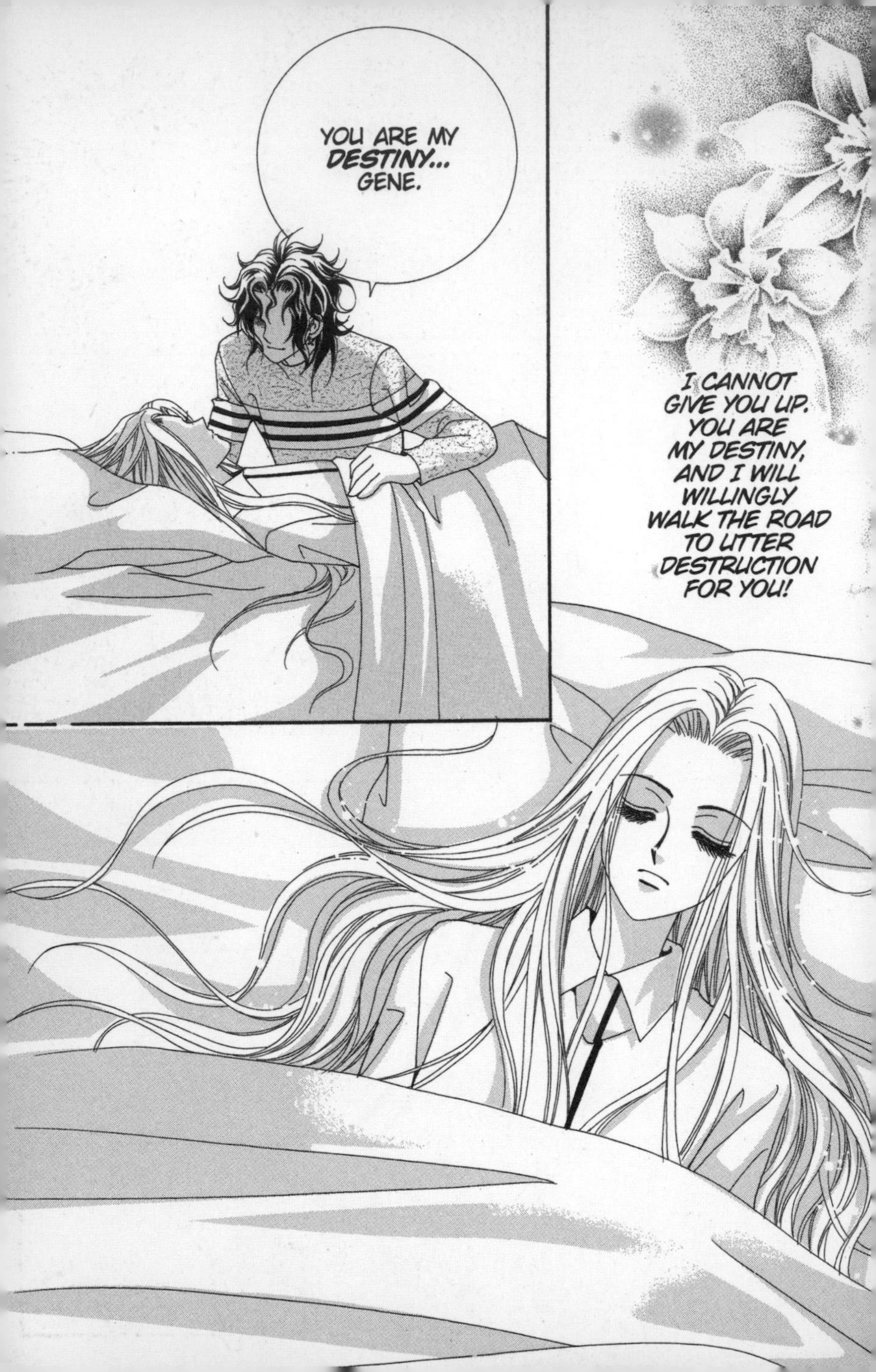
YOU ARE MY DESTINY... GENE.
I CANNOT GIVE YOU UP. YOU ARE MY DESTINY, AND I WILL WILLINGLY WALK THE ROAD TO UTTER DESTRUCTION FOR YOU!

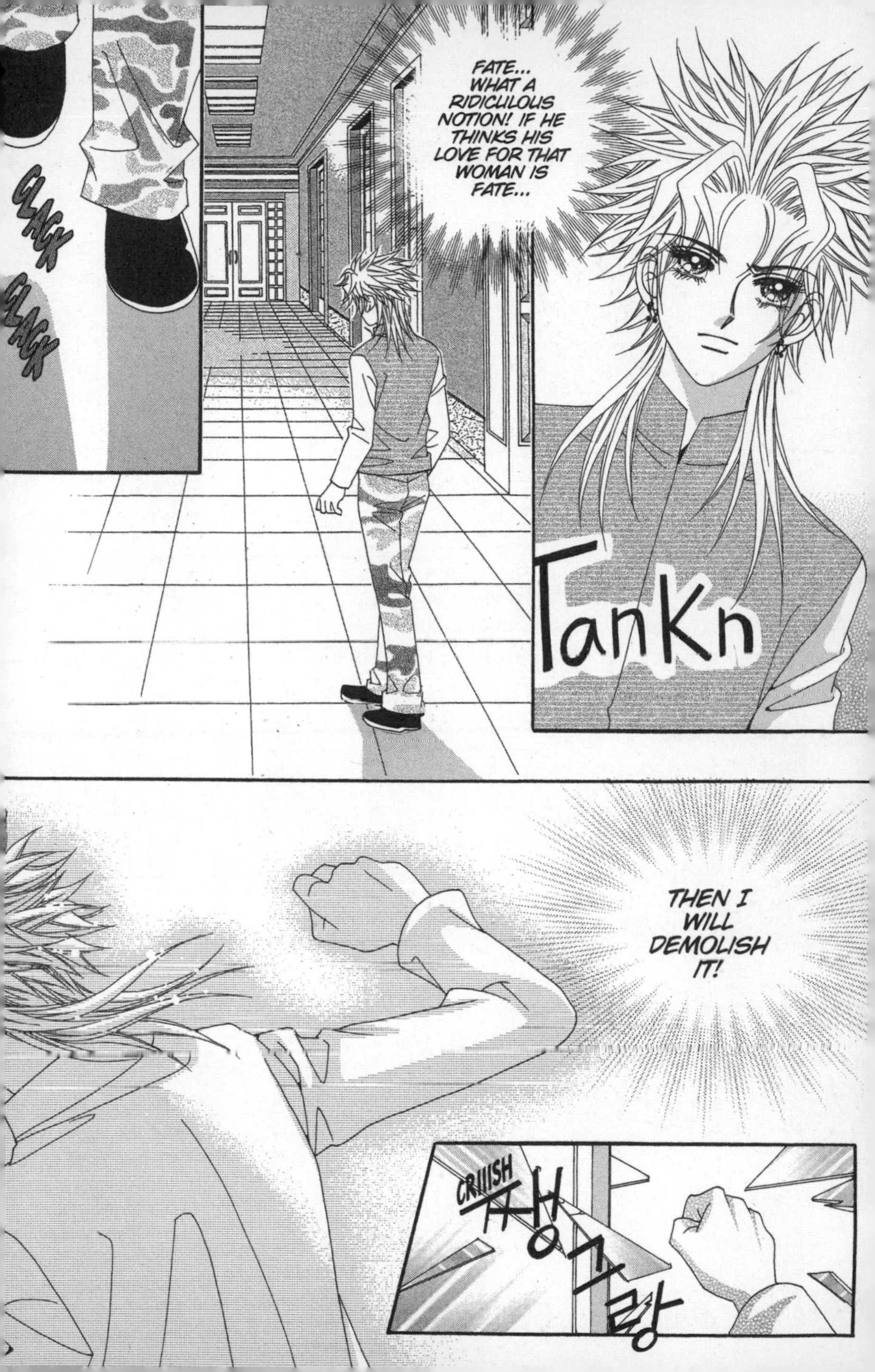
CLACK
CLACK
CLACK
FATE... WHAT A RIDICULOUS NOTION! IF HE THINKS HIS LOVE FOR THAT WOMAN IS FATE...
TanKn
THEN I WILL DEMOLISH IT!
CRIIISH
쨍그랑

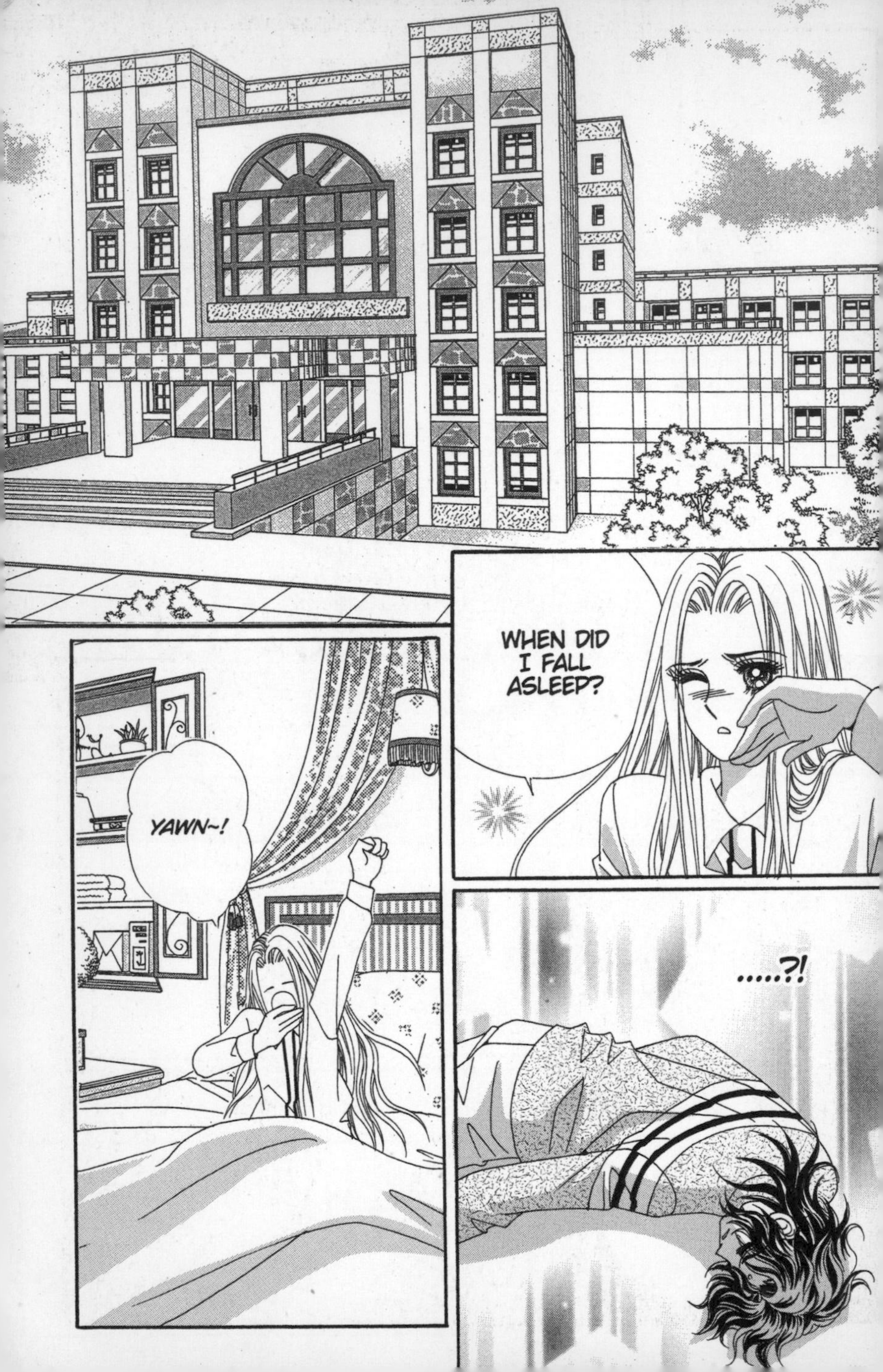
YAWN~!
WHEN DID I FALL ASLEEP?
.....?!

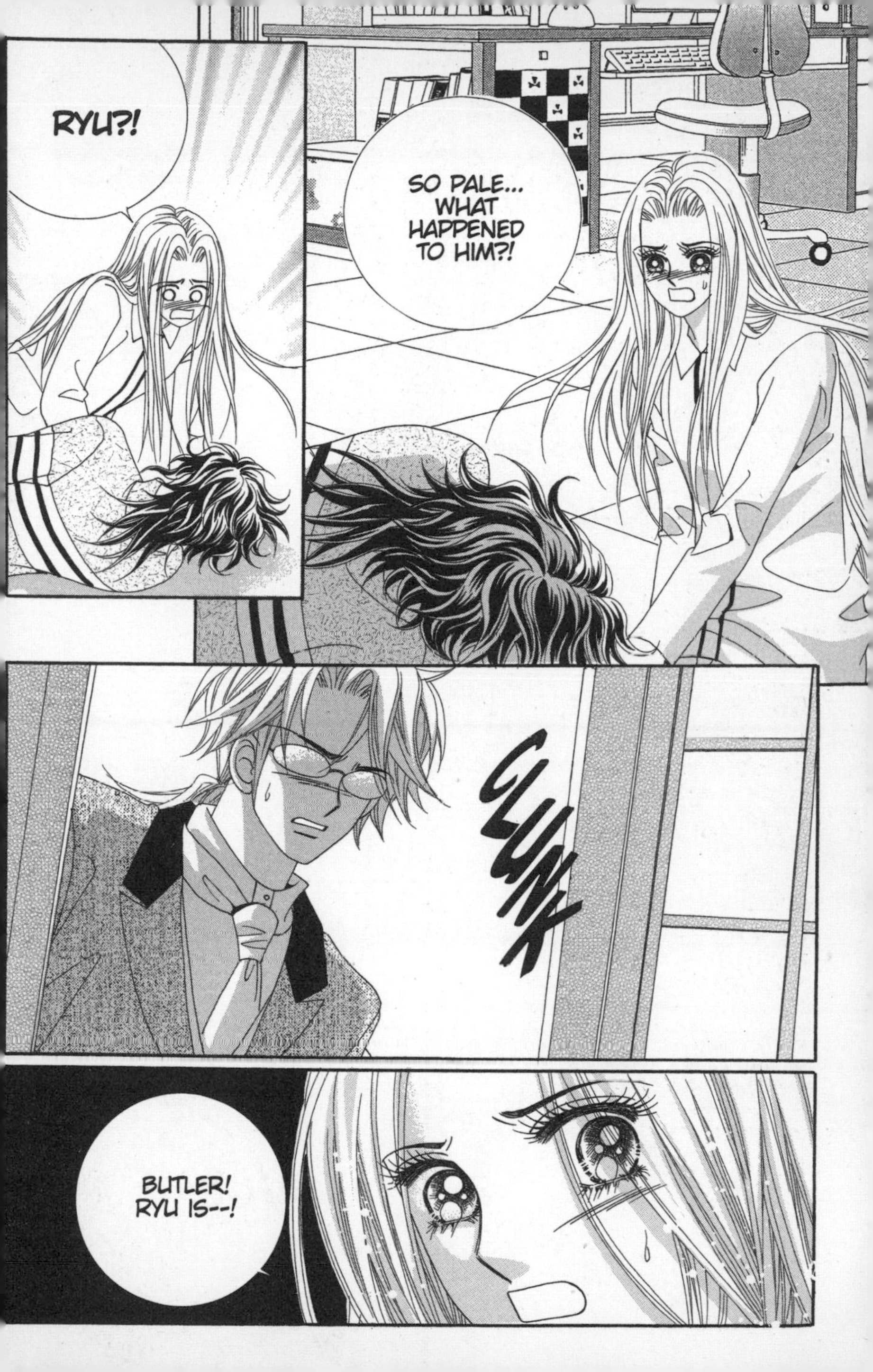
RYU?!
SO PALE... WHAT HAPPENED TO HIM?!
CLUNK
BUTLER! RYU IS--!

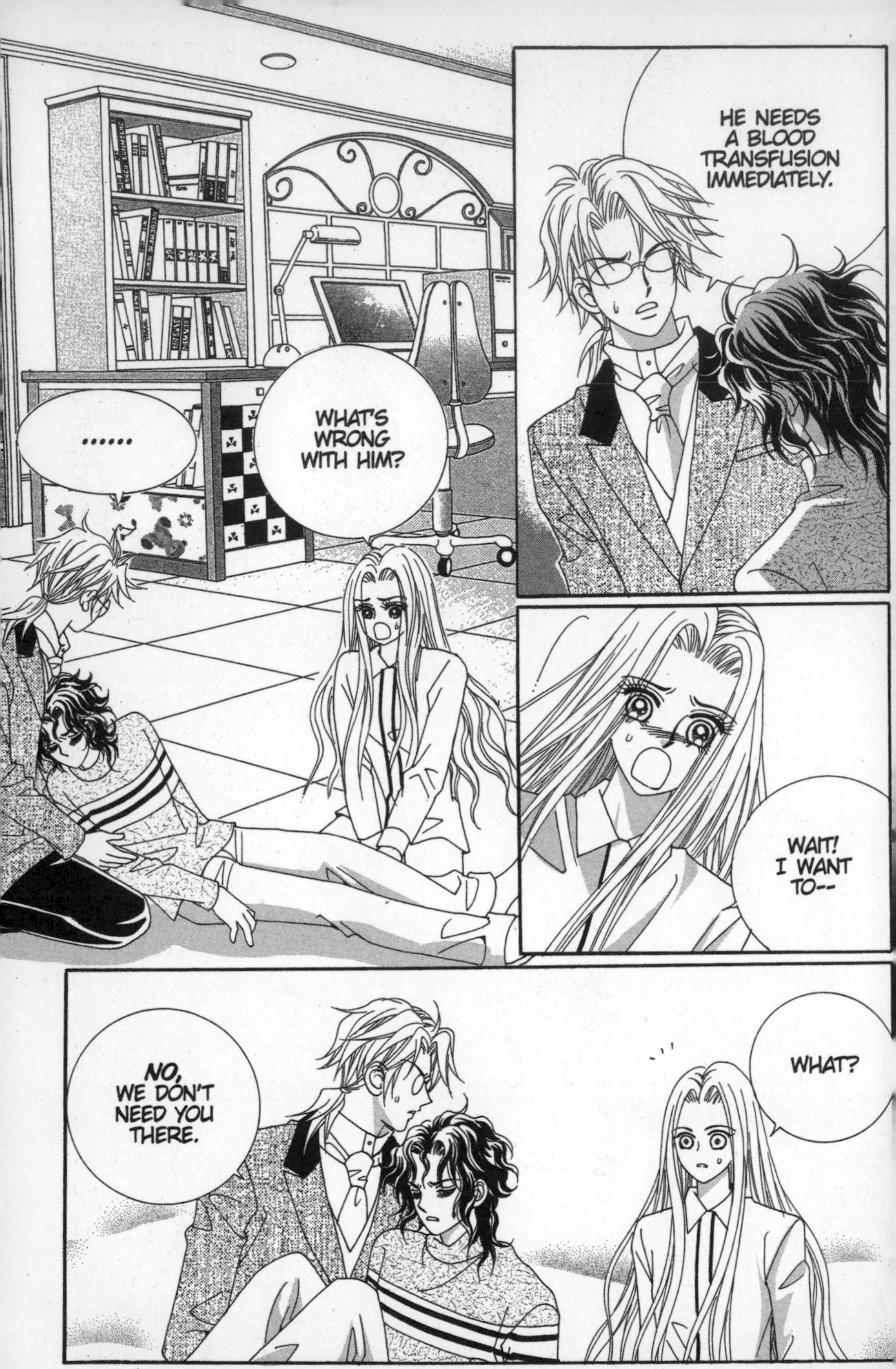
......
WHAT'S WRONG WITH HIM?
HE NEEDS A BLOOD TRANSFUSION IMMEDIATELY.
WAIT! I WANT TO--
NO, WE DON'T NEED YOU THERE.
WHAT?

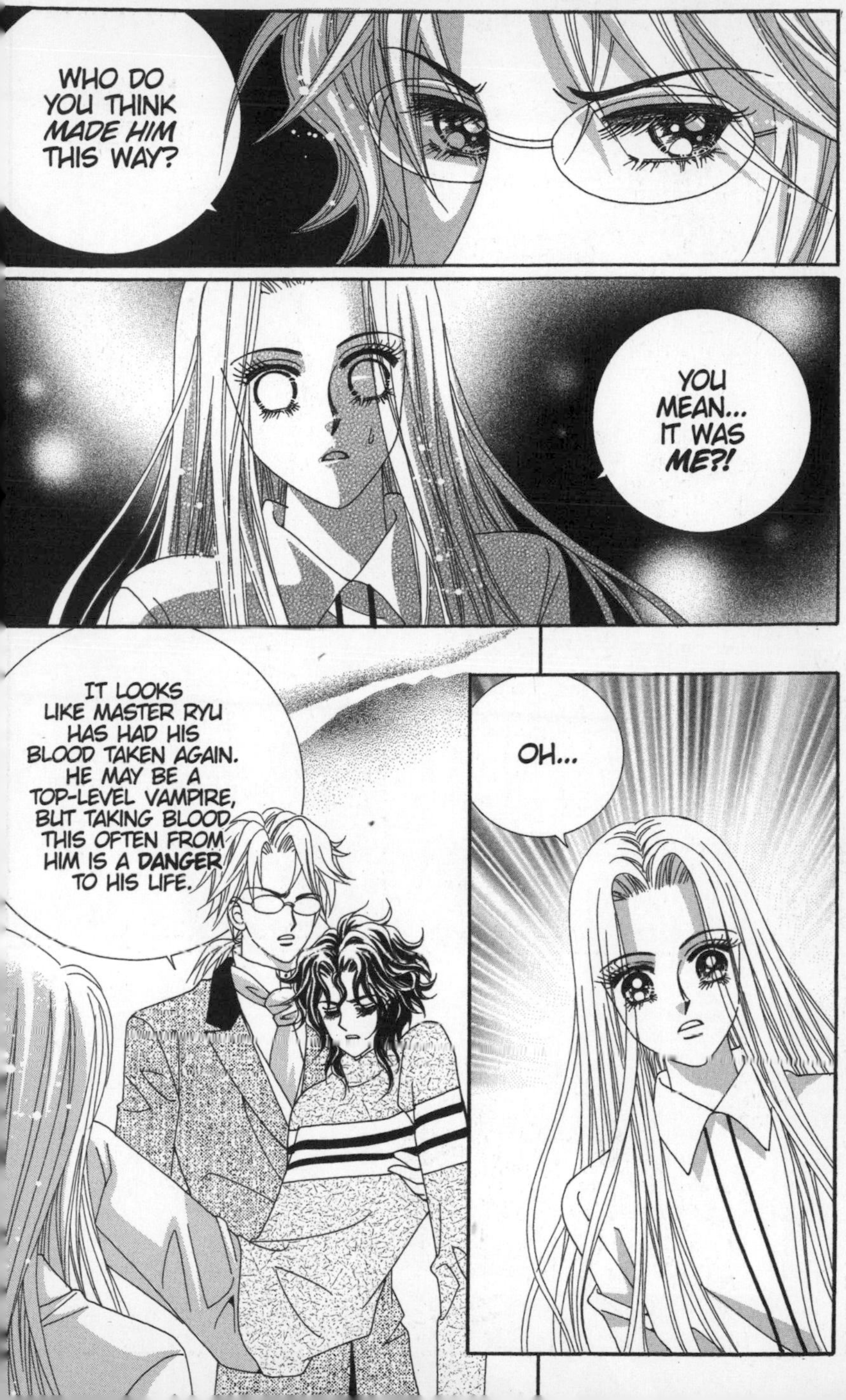
WHO DO YOU THINK *MADE HIM* THIS WAY?
YOU MEAN... IT WAS **ME?!**
IT LOOKS LIKE MASTER RYU HAS HAD HIS BLOOD TAKEN AGAIN. HE MAY BE A TOP-LEVEL VAMPIRE, BUT TAKING BLOOD THIS OFTEN FROM HIM IS A **DANGER** TO HIS LIFE.
OH...

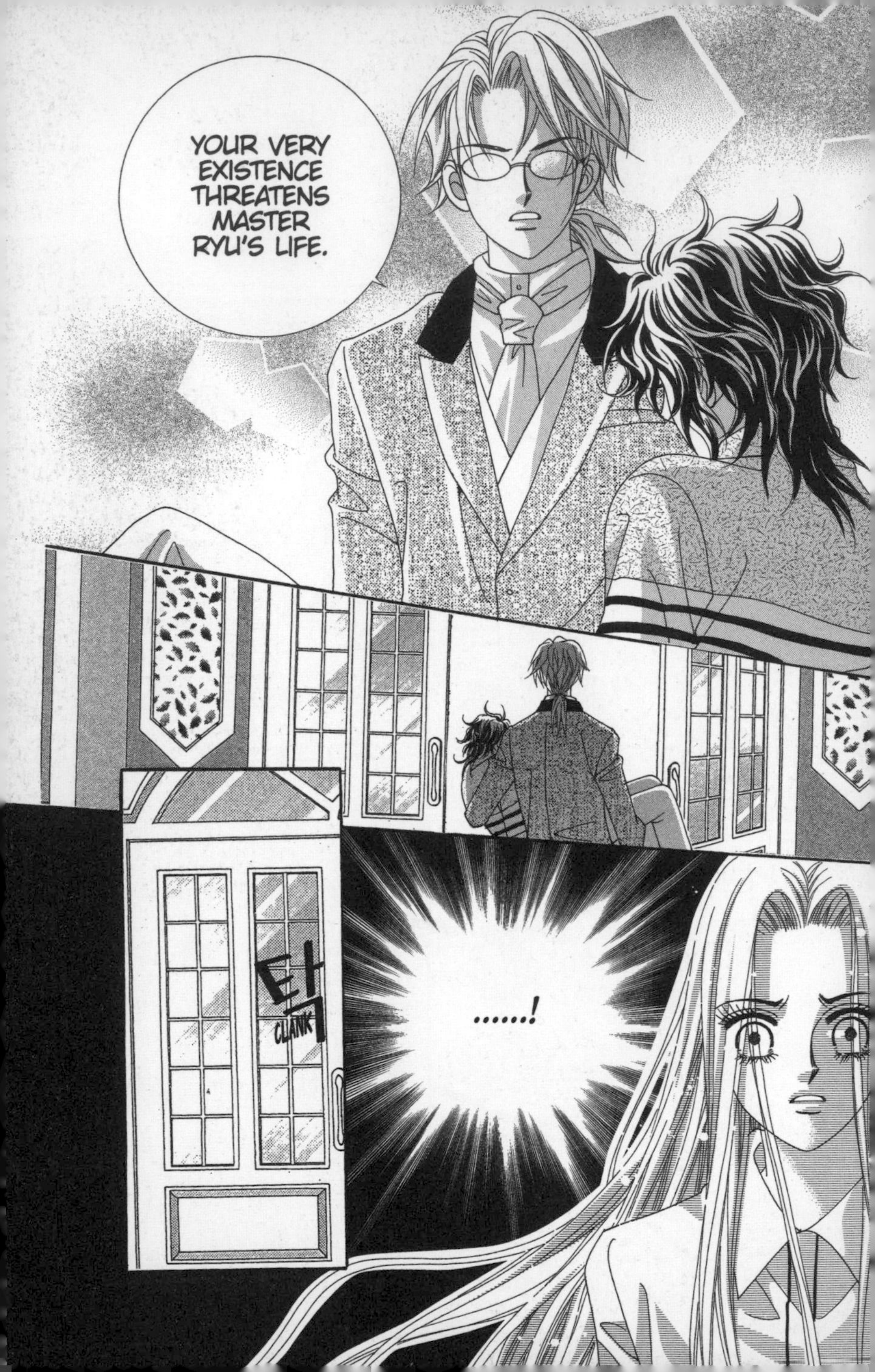
YOUR VERY EXISTENCE THREATENS MASTER RYU'S LIFE.
CLANK
......!

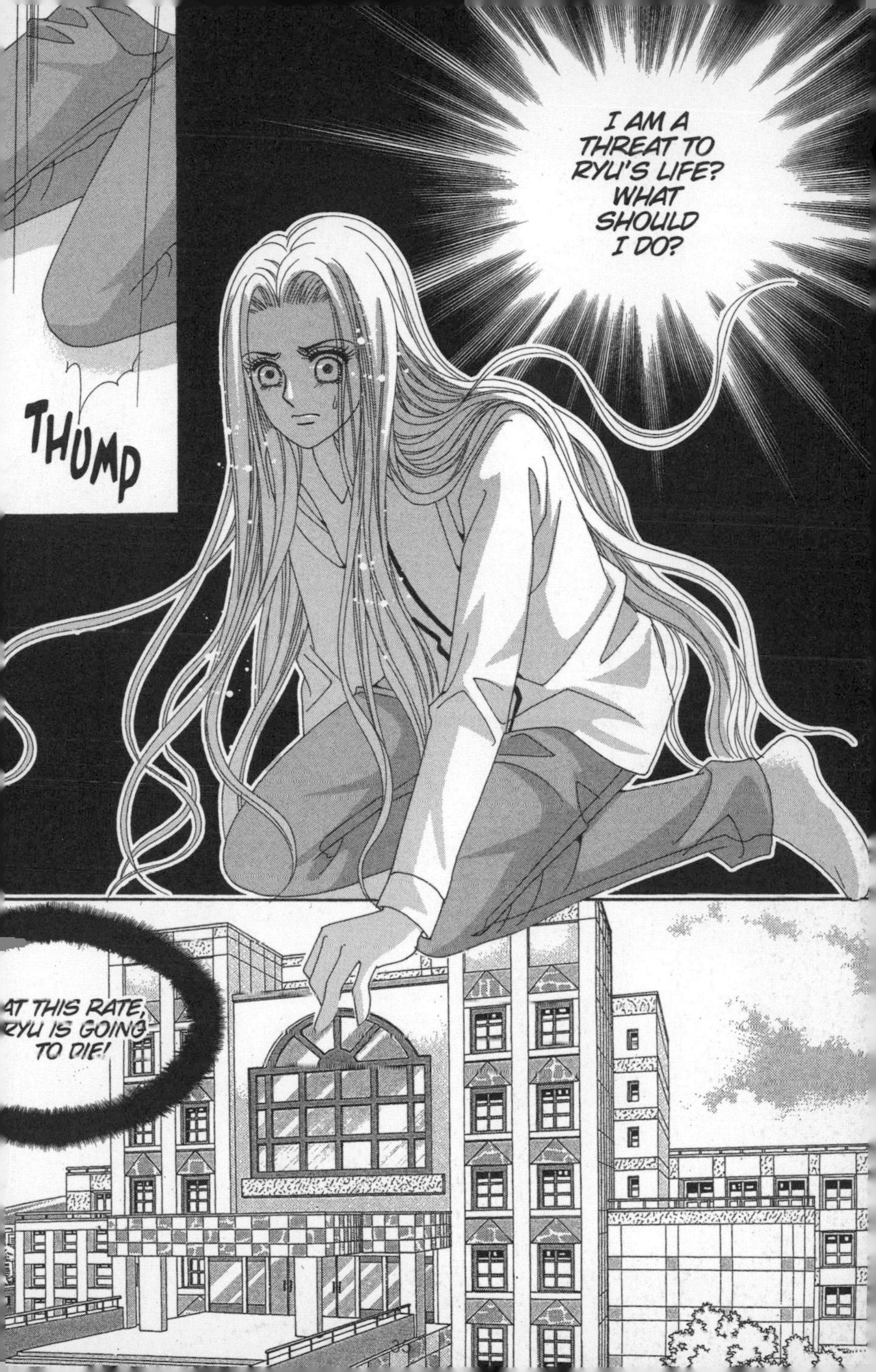

THUMP
I AM A THREAT TO RYU'S LIFE? WHAT SHOULD I DO?
AT THIS RATE, RYU IS GOING TO DIE!

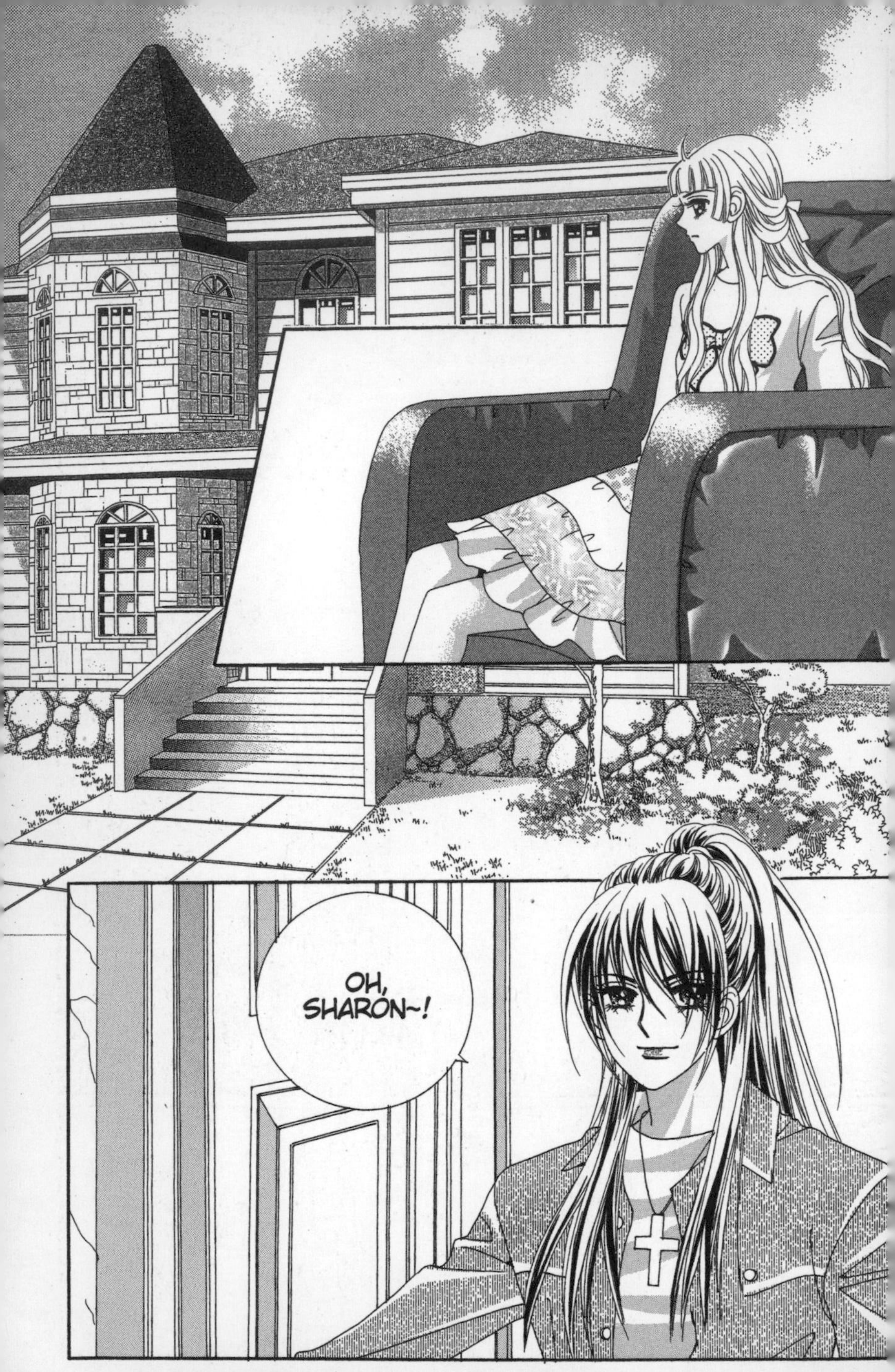
OH, SHARON~!

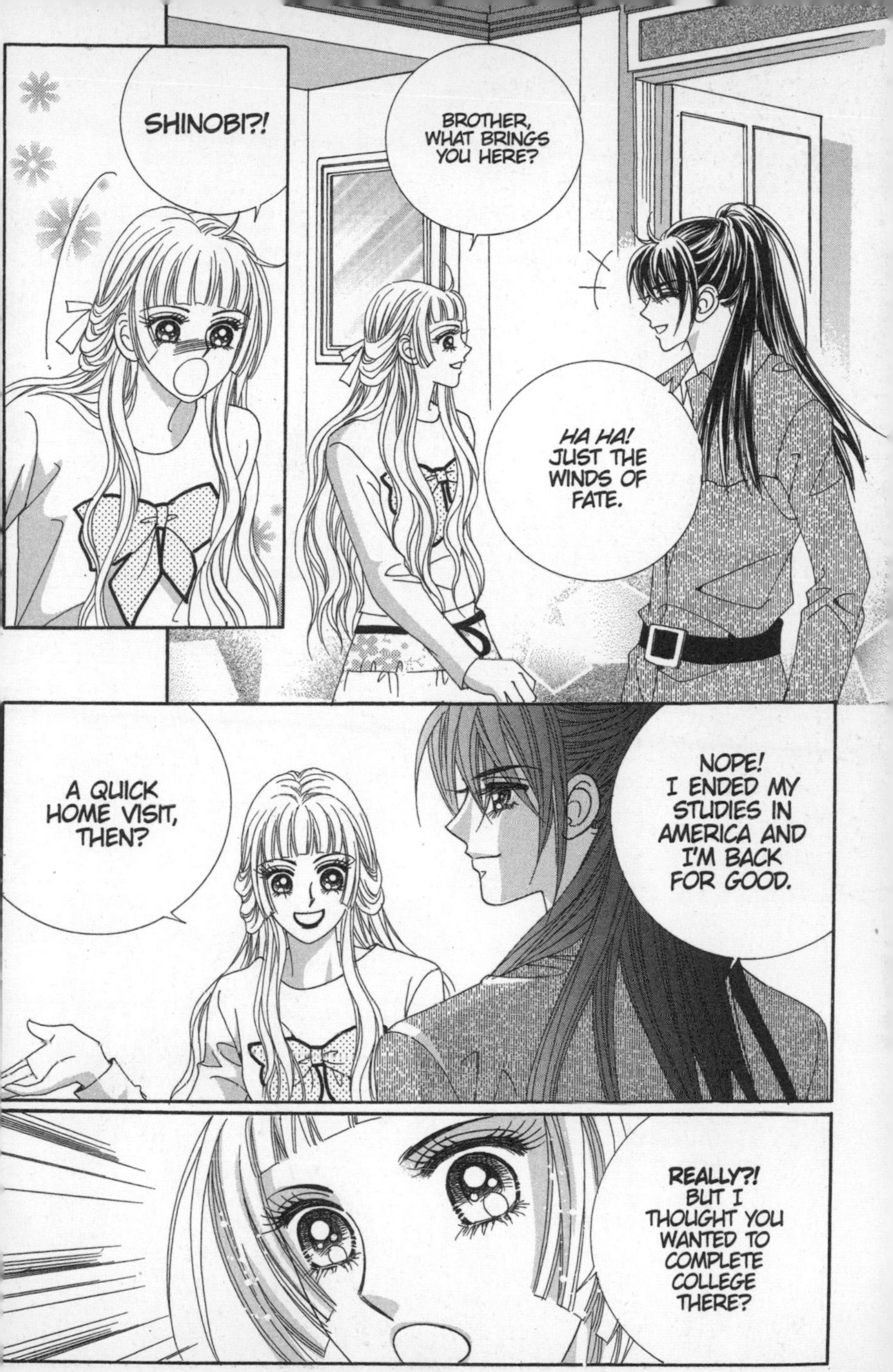
SHINOBI?!
BROTHER, WHAT BRINGS YOU HERE?
HA HA! JUST THE WINDS OF FATE.
A QUICK HOME VISIT, THEN?
NOPE! I ENDED MY STUDIES IN AMERICA AND I'M BACK FOR GOOD.
REALLY?! BUT I THOUGHT YOU WANTED TO COMPLETE COLLEGE THERE?

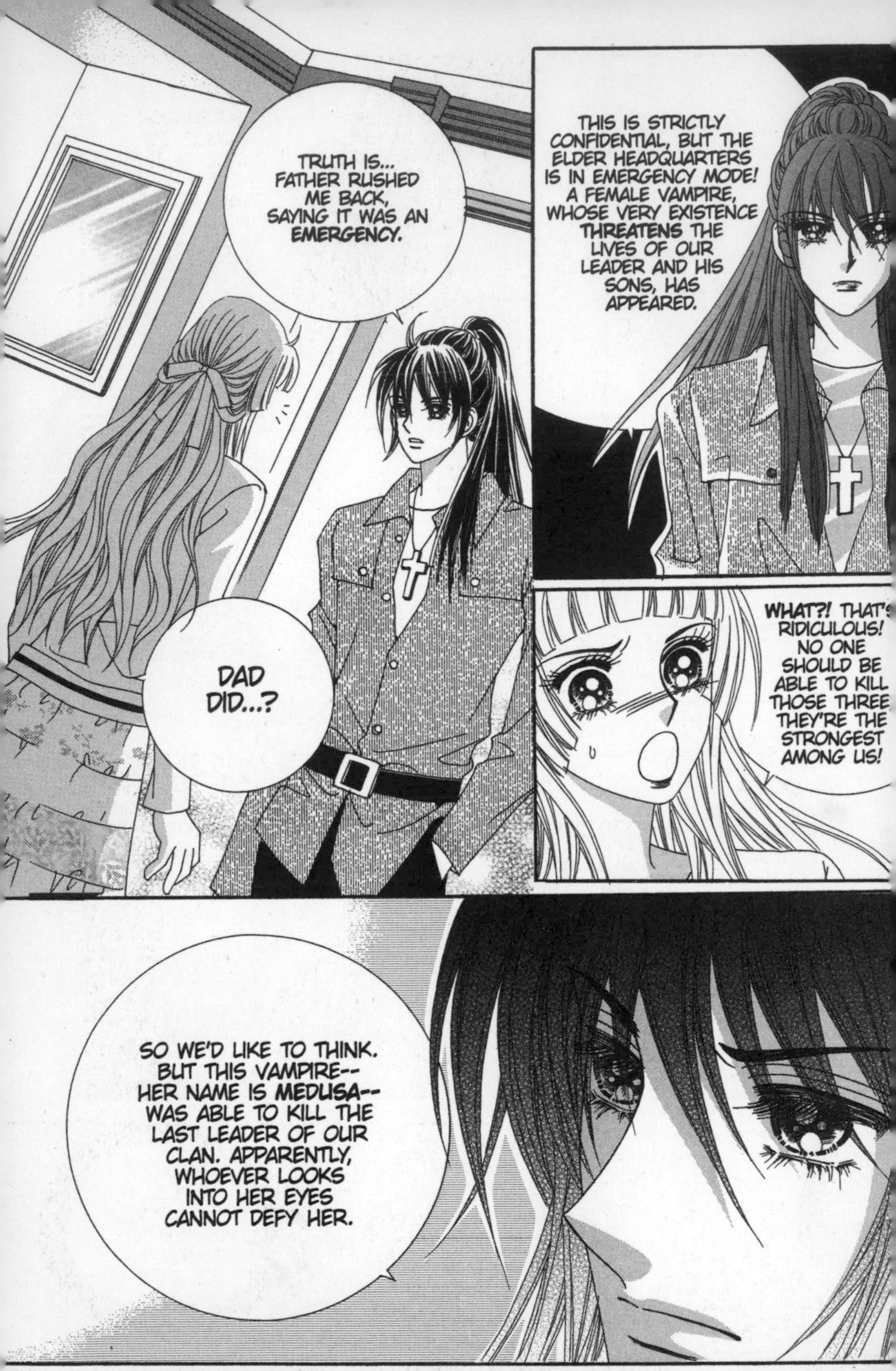
TRUTH IS... FATHER RUSHED ME BACK, SAYING IT WAS AN EMERGENCY.
DAD DID...?
THIS IS STRICTLY CONFIDENTIAL, BUT THE ELDER HEADQUARTERS IS IN EMERGENCY MODE! A FEMALE VAMPIRE, WHOSE VERY EXISTENCE THREATENS THE LIVES OF OUR LEADER AND HIS SONS, HAS APPEARED.
WHAT?! THAT'S RIDICULOUS! NO ONE SHOULD BE ABLE TO KILL THOSE THREE THEY'RE THE STRONGEST AMONG US!
SO WE'D LIKE TO THINK. BUT THIS VAMPIRE-- HER NAME IS MEDUSA-- WAS ABLE TO KILL THE LAST LEADER OF OUR CLAN. APPARENTLY, WHOEVER LOOKS INTO HER EYES CANNOT DEFY HER.

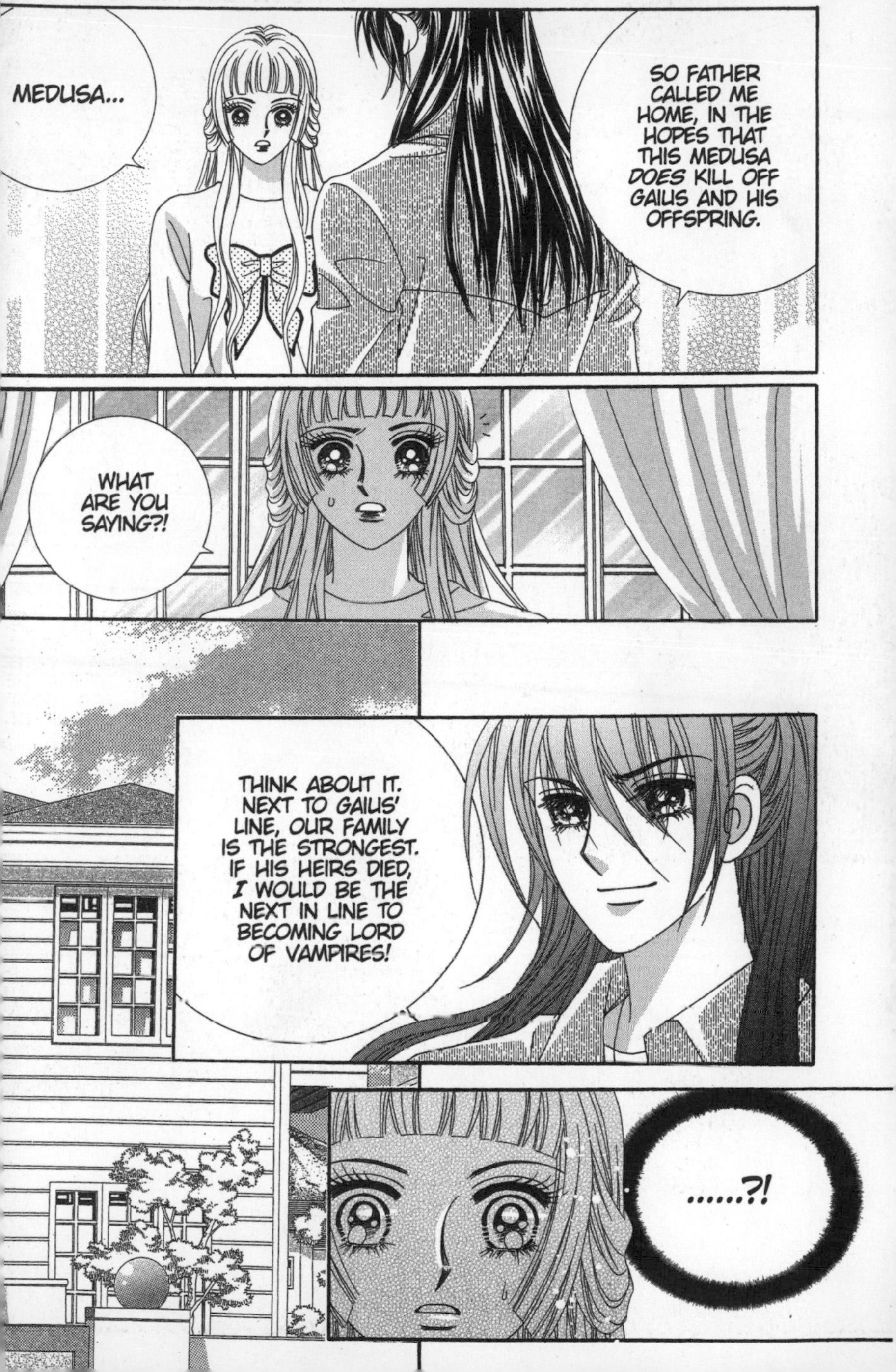
MEDUSA...
SO FATHER CALLED ME HOME, IN THE HOPES THAT THIS MEDUSA *DOES* KILL OFF GAIUS AND HIS OFFSPRING.
WHAT ARE YOU SAYING?!
THINK ABOUT IT. NEXT TO GAIUS' LINE, OUR FAMILY IS THE STRONGEST. IF HIS HEIRS DIED, *I* WOULD BE THE NEXT IN LINE TO BECOMING LORD OF VAMPIRES!
......?!

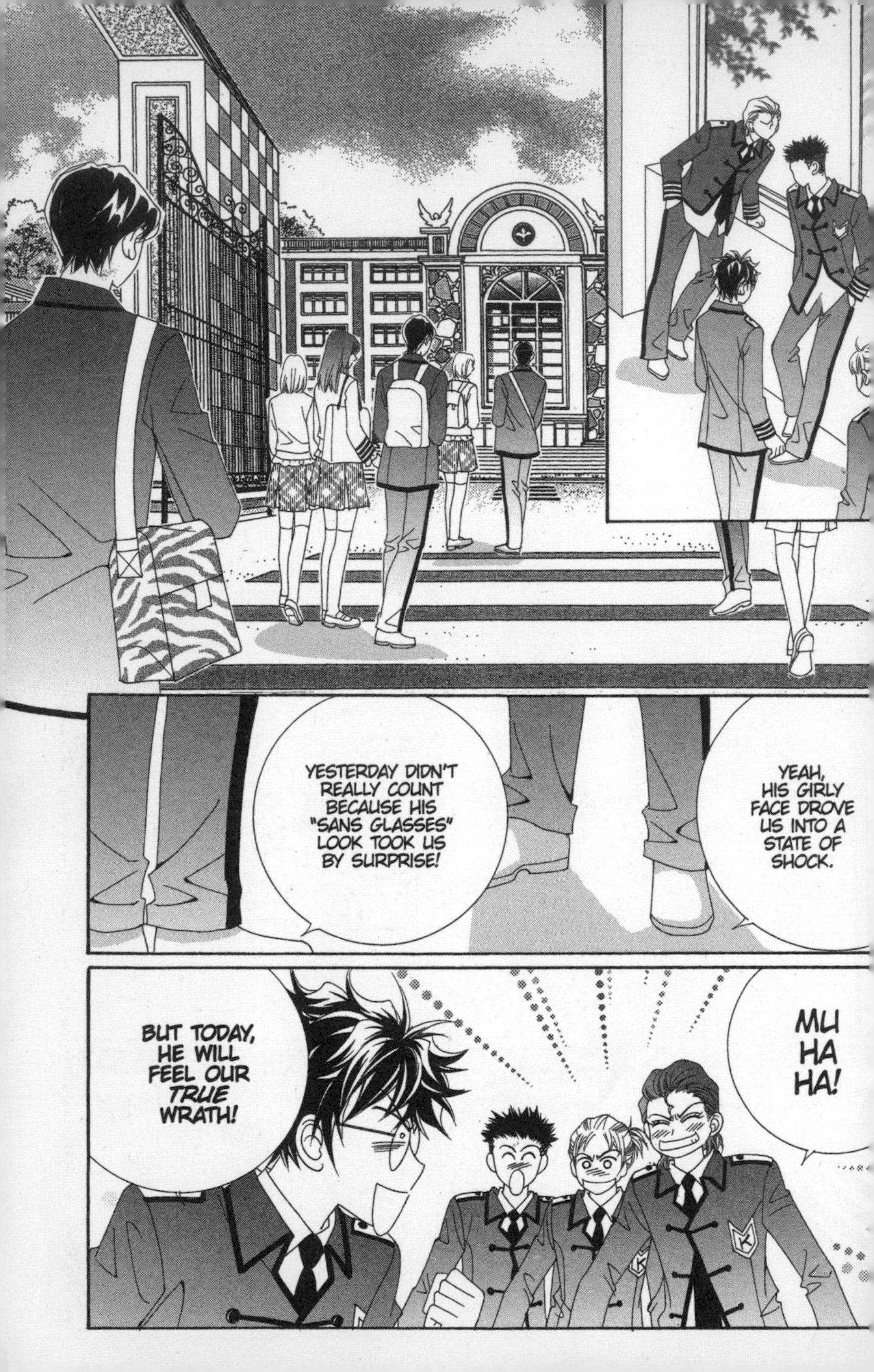
YESTERDAY DIDN'T REALLY COUNT BECAUSE HIS "SANS GLASSES" LOOK TOOK US BY SURPRISE!
YEAH, HIS GIRLY FACE DROVE US INTO A STATE OF SHOCK.
BUT TODAY, HE WILL FEEL OUR *TRUE* WRATH!
MU HA HA!

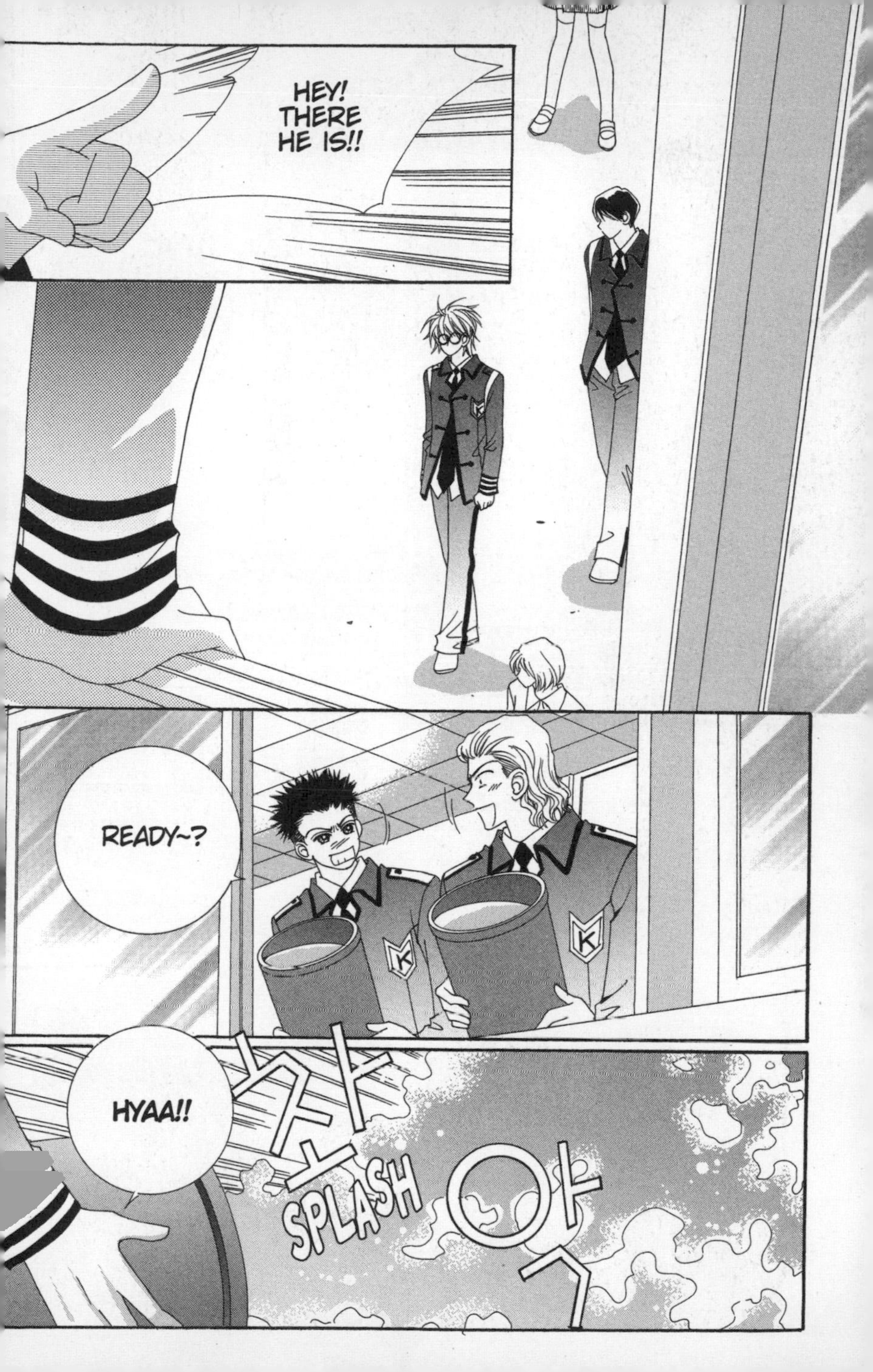
HEY! THERE HE IS!!
READY~?
HYAA!!
SPLASH

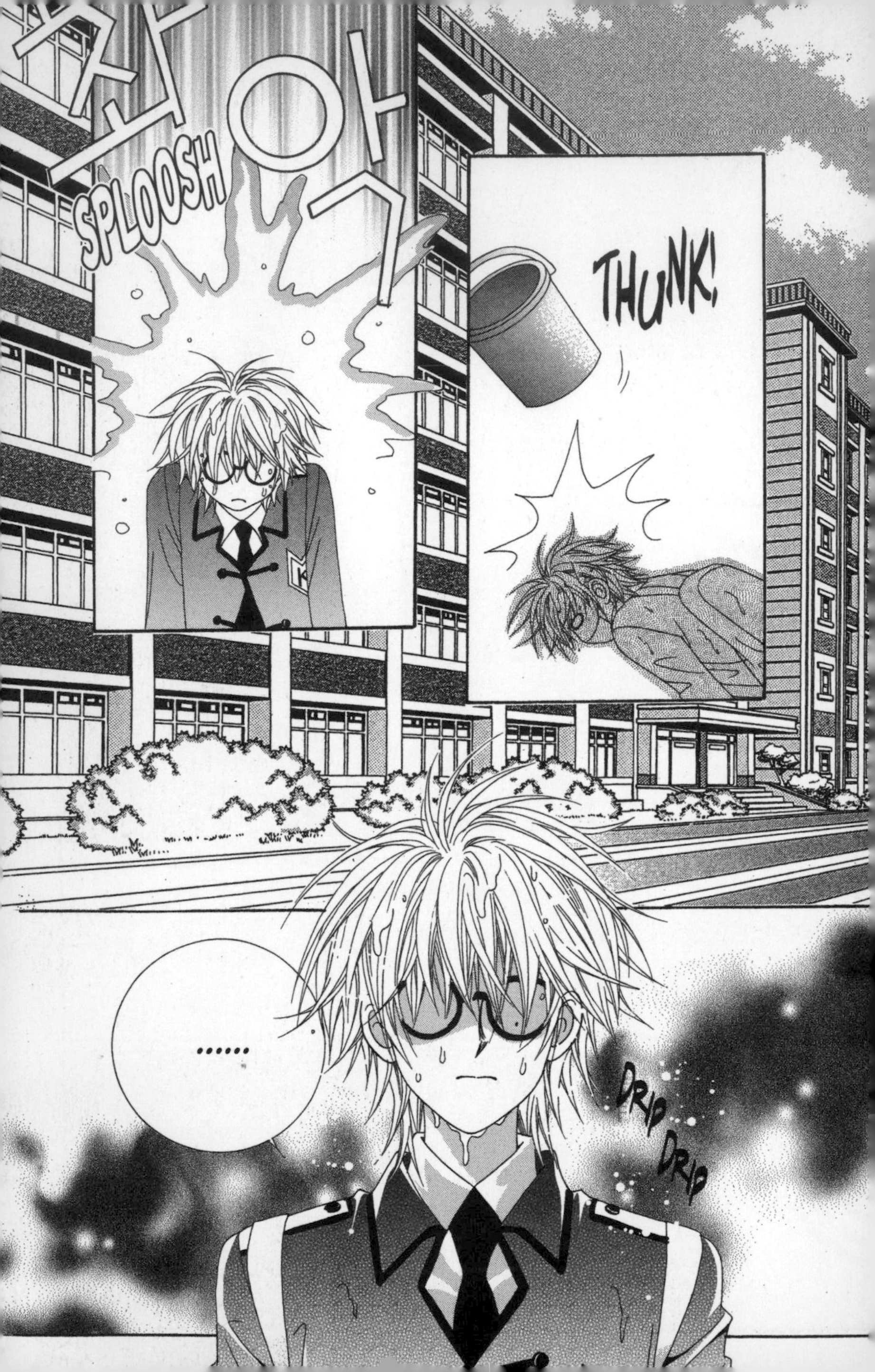
SPLOOSH
THUNK!
......
DRIP
DRIP

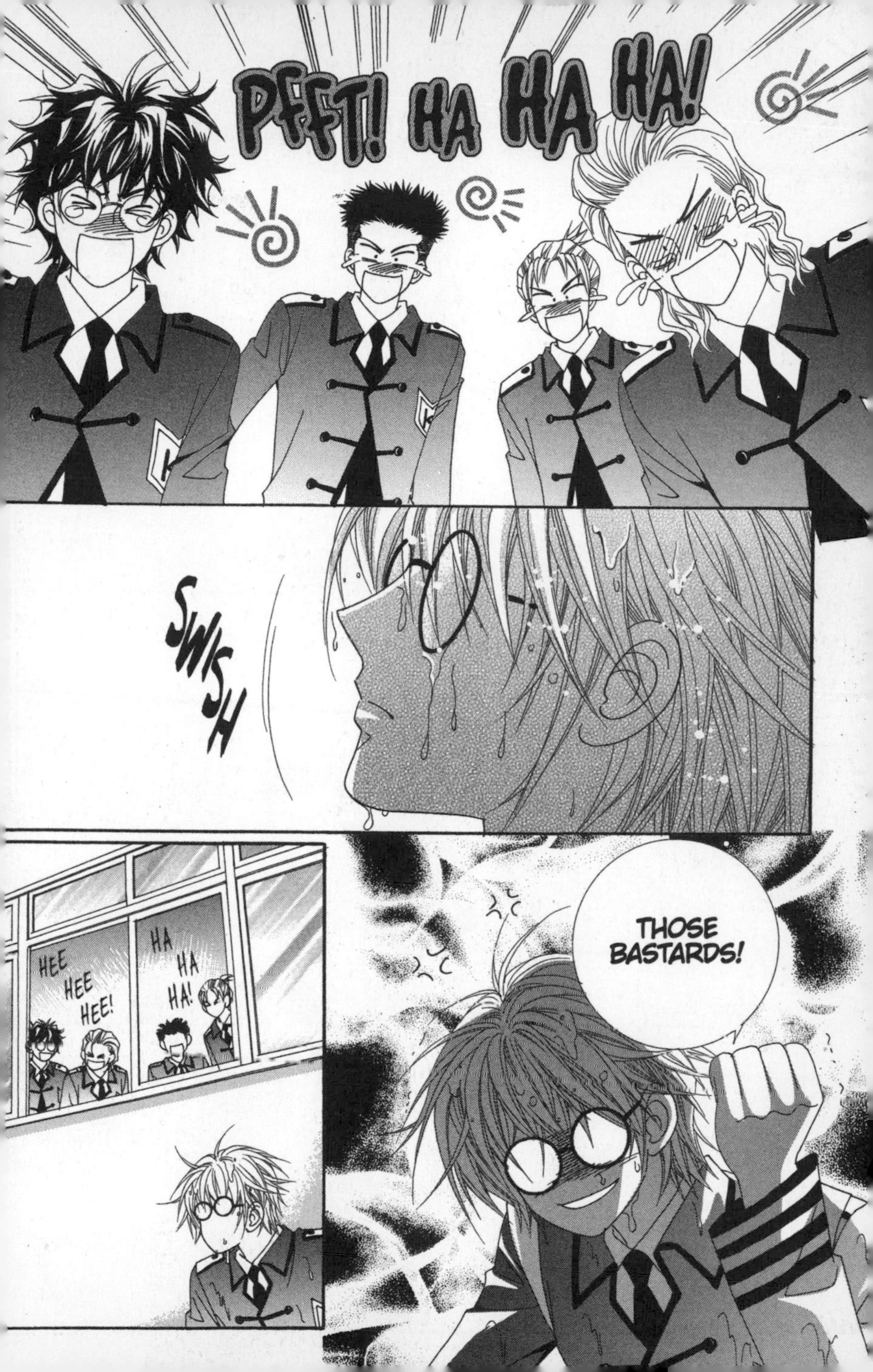
PFFT! HA HA HA!
SWISH
HEE HEE HEE!
HA HA HA!
THOSE BASTARDS!

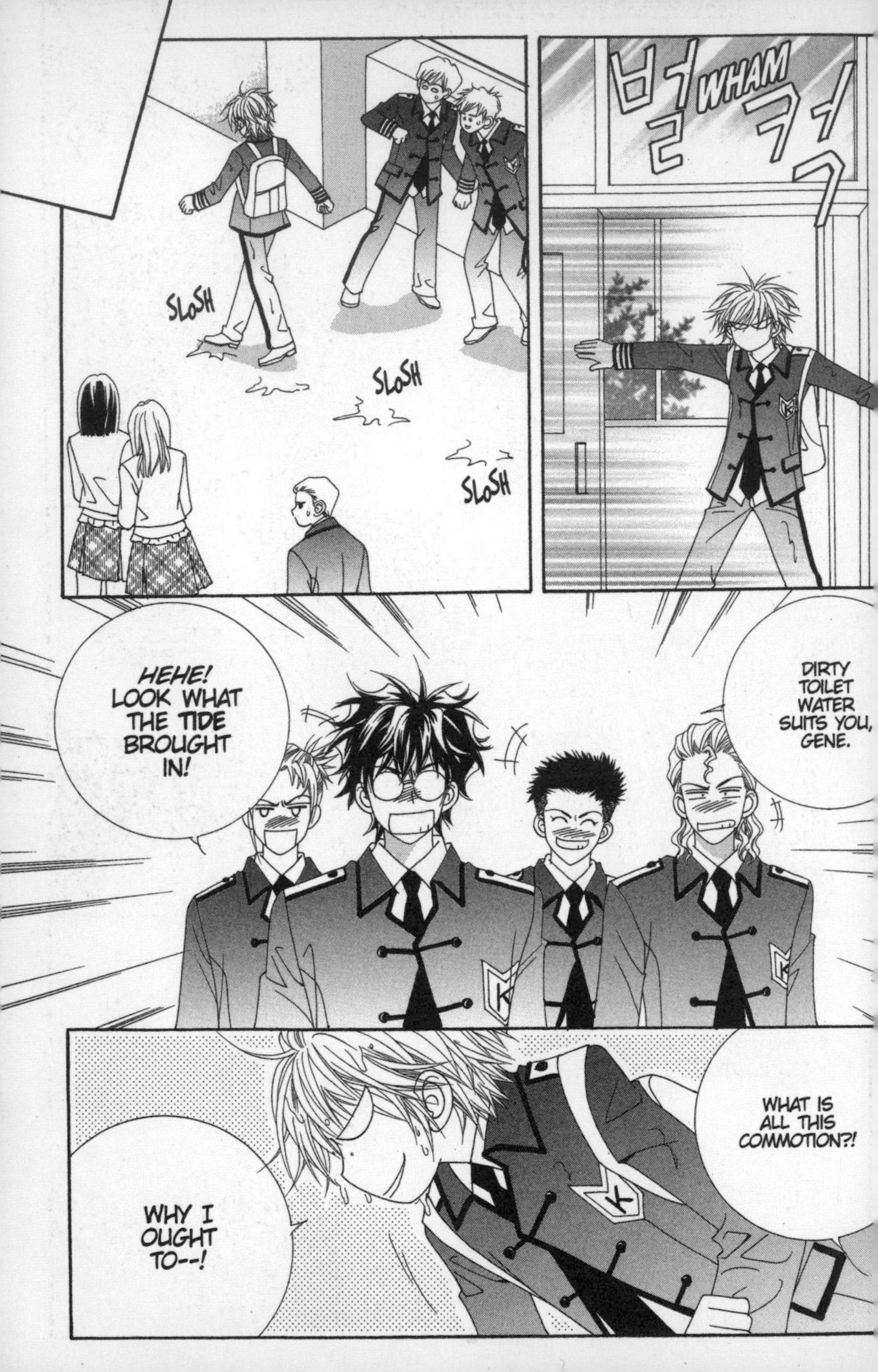
SLOSH
SLOSH
SLOSH
WHAM
HEHE! LOOK WHAT THE TIDE BROUGHT IN!
DIRTY TOILET WATER SUITS YOU, GENE.
WHY I OUGHT TO--!
WHAT IS ALL THIS COMMOTION?!

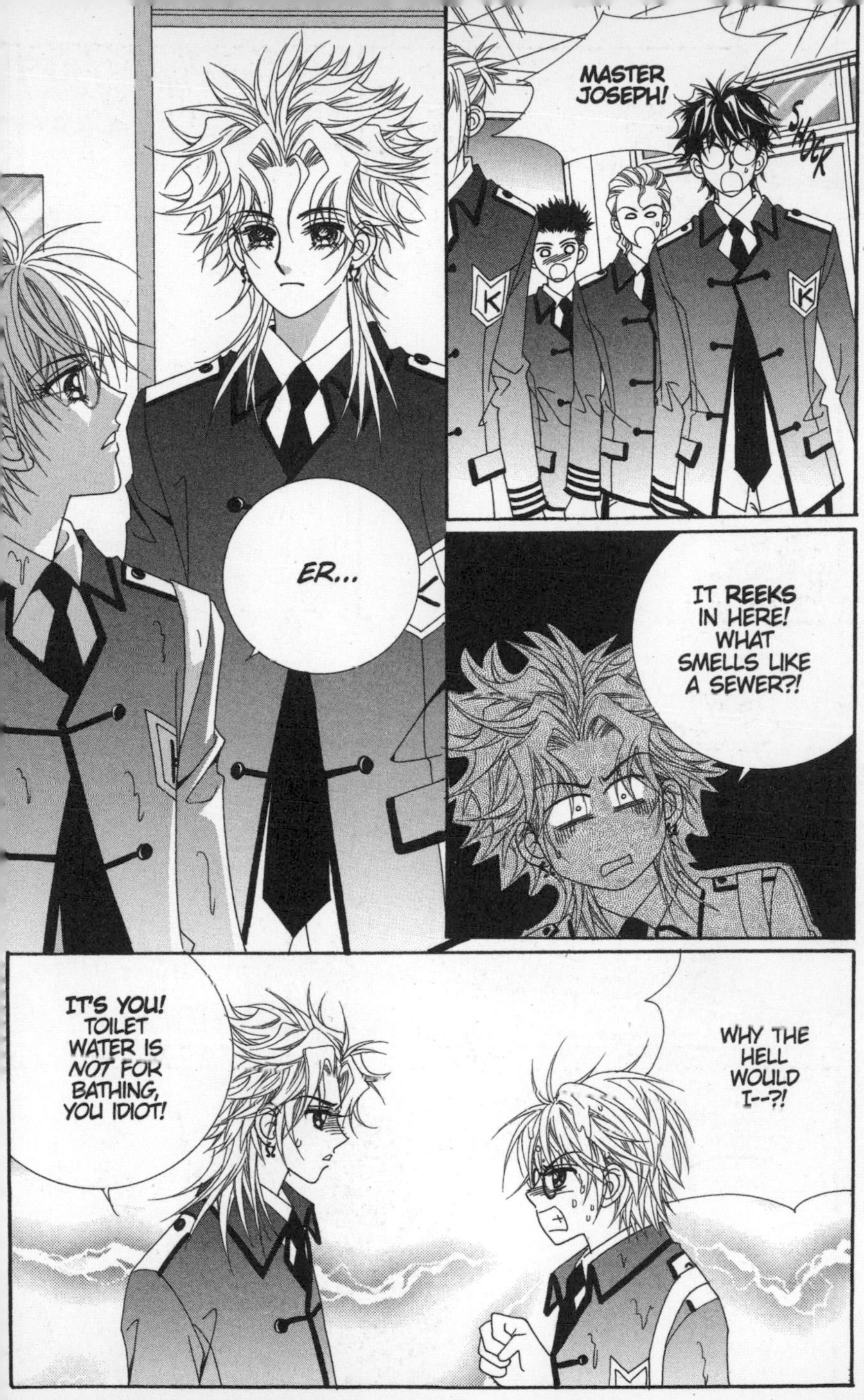
ER...
MASTER JOSEPH!
SHOCK
IT REEKS IN HERE! WHAT SMELLS LIKE A SEWER?!
IT'S YOU! TOILET WATER IS *NOT* FOR BATHING, YOU IDIOT!
WHY THE HELL WOULD I--?!

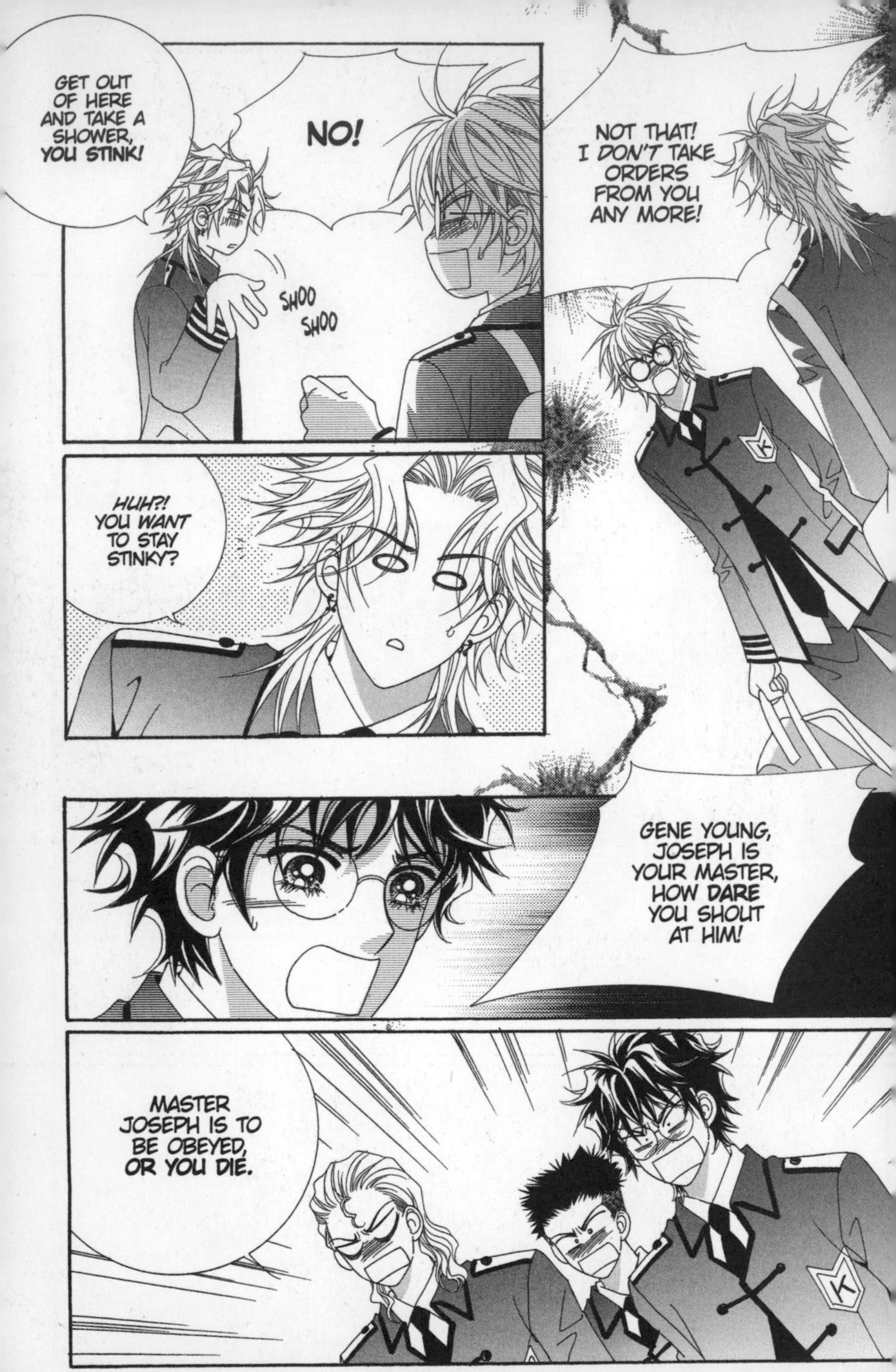
GET OUT OF HERE AND TAKE A SHOWER, YOU STINK!
NO!
SHOO SHOO
NOT THAT! I *DON'T* TAKE ORDERS FROM YOU ANY MORE!
*HUH?!* YOU *WANT* TO STAY STINKY?
GENE YOUNG, JOSEPH IS YOUR MASTER, HOW DARE YOU SHOUT AT HIM!
MASTER JOSEPH IS TO BE OBEYED, OR YOU DIE.

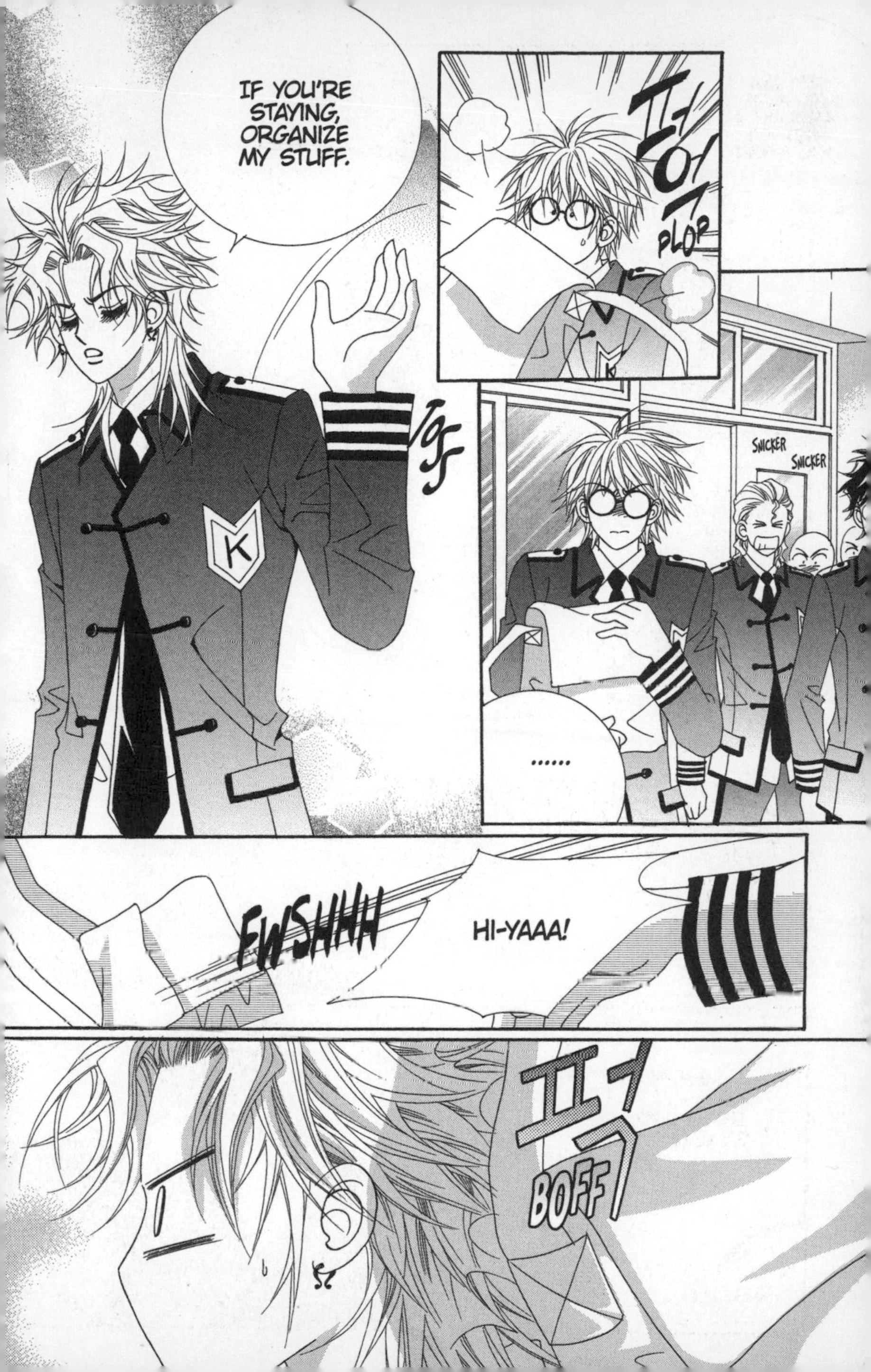
IF YOU'RE STAYING, ORGANIZE MY STUFF.
TOSS
PLOP
SNICKER
SNICKER
......
FWSHHH
HI-YAAA!
BOFF

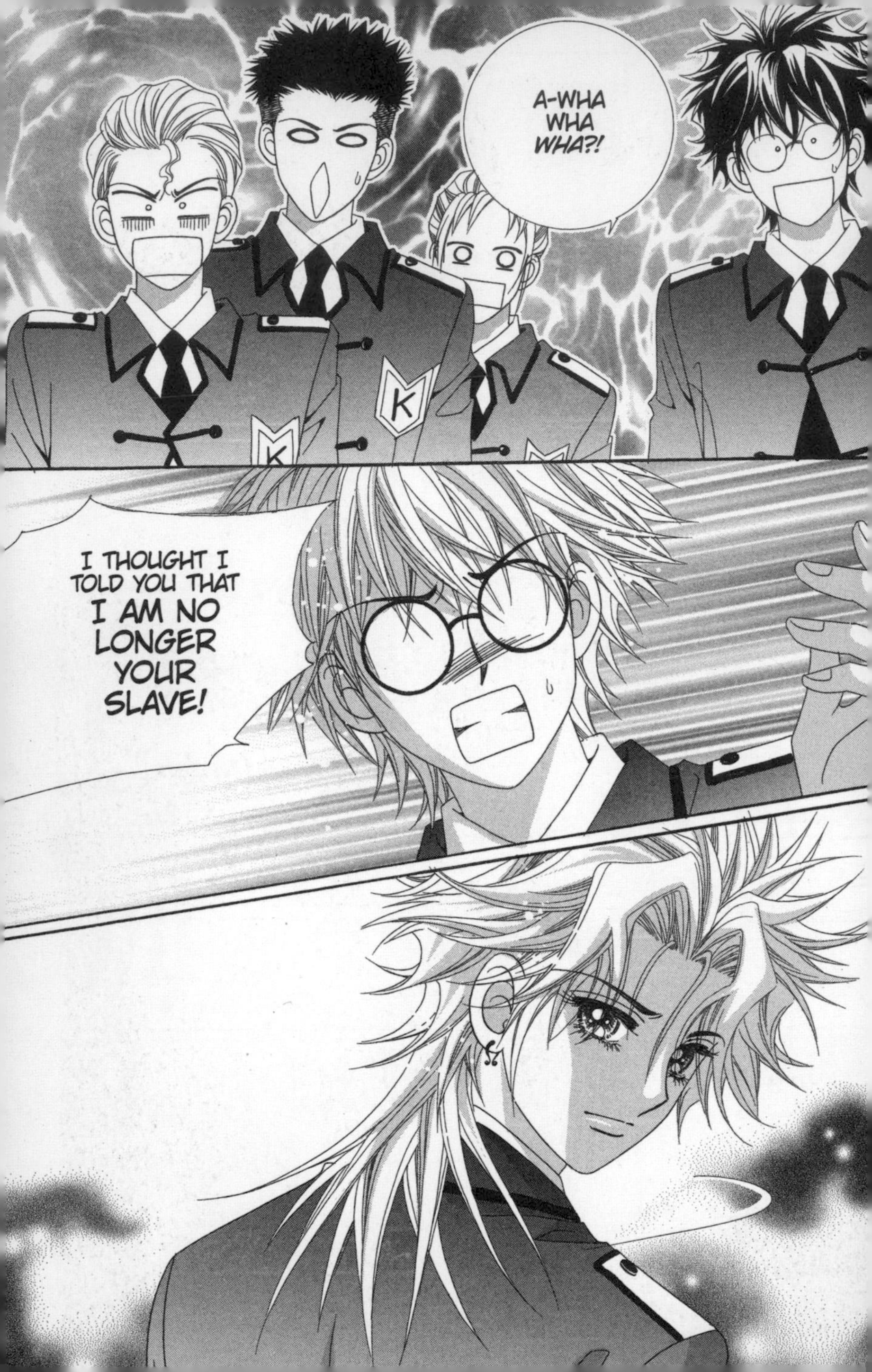
A-WHA WHA WHA?!
I THOUGHT I TOLD YOU THAT I AM NO LONGER YOUR SLAVE!

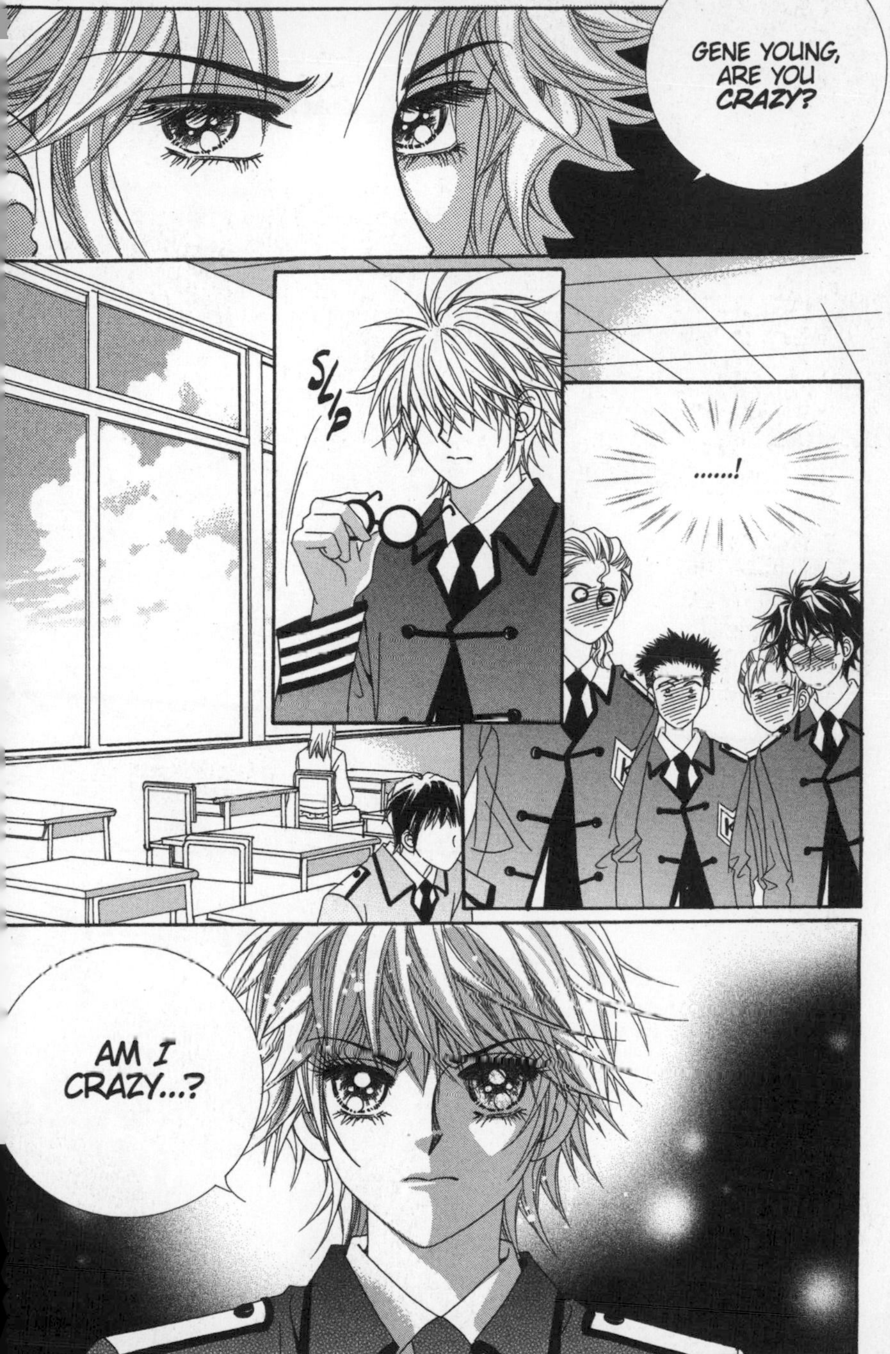
GENE YOUNG, ARE YOU CRAZY?
SLIP
......!
AM I CRAZY...?

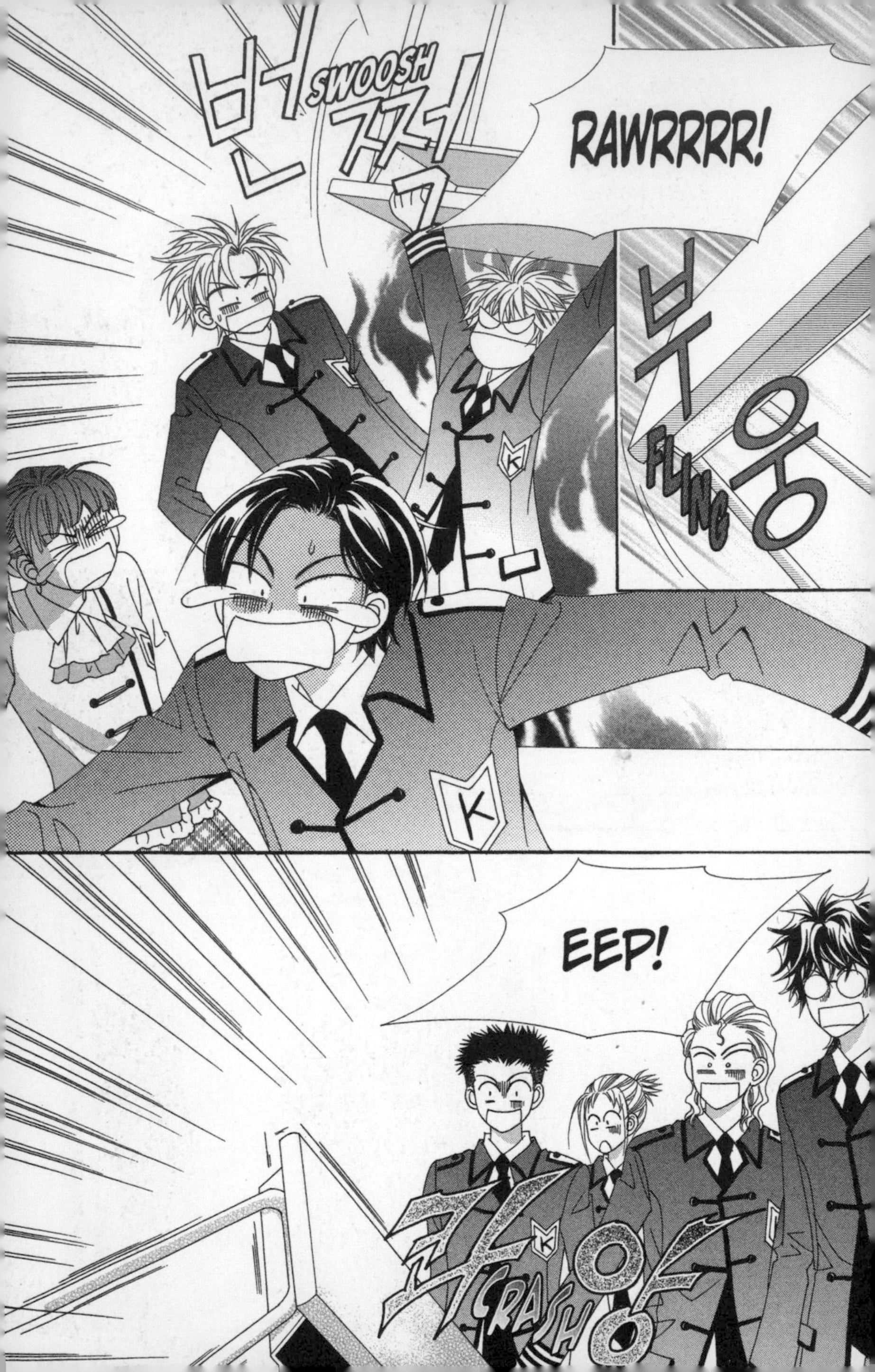
SWOOSH
RAWRRRR!
FLING
EEP!
CRASH

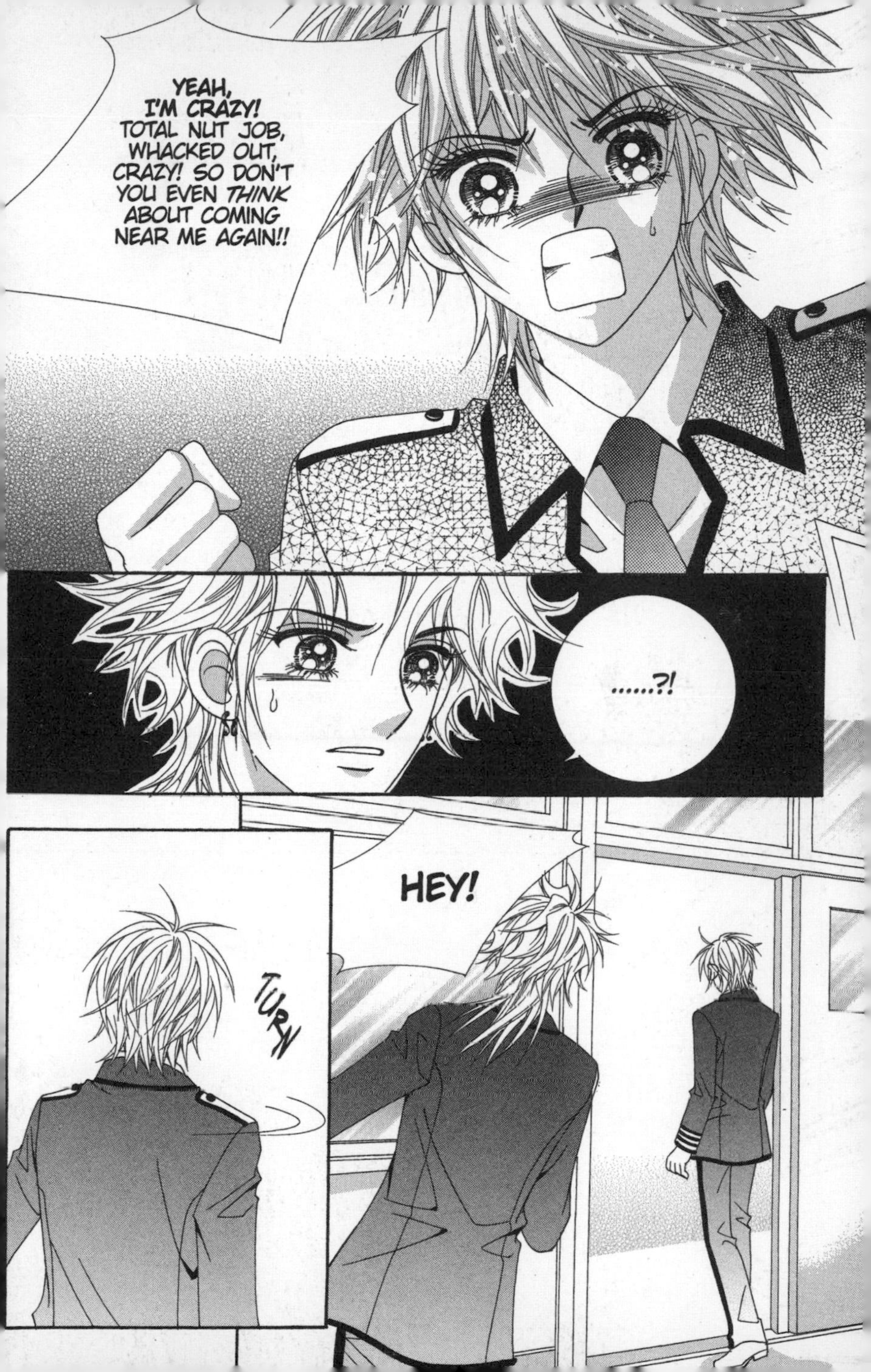
YEAH, I'M CRAZY! TOTAL NUT JOB, WHACKED OUT, CRAZY! SO DON'T YOU EVEN *THINK* ABOUT COMING NEAR ME AGAIN!!
......?!
HEY!
TURN

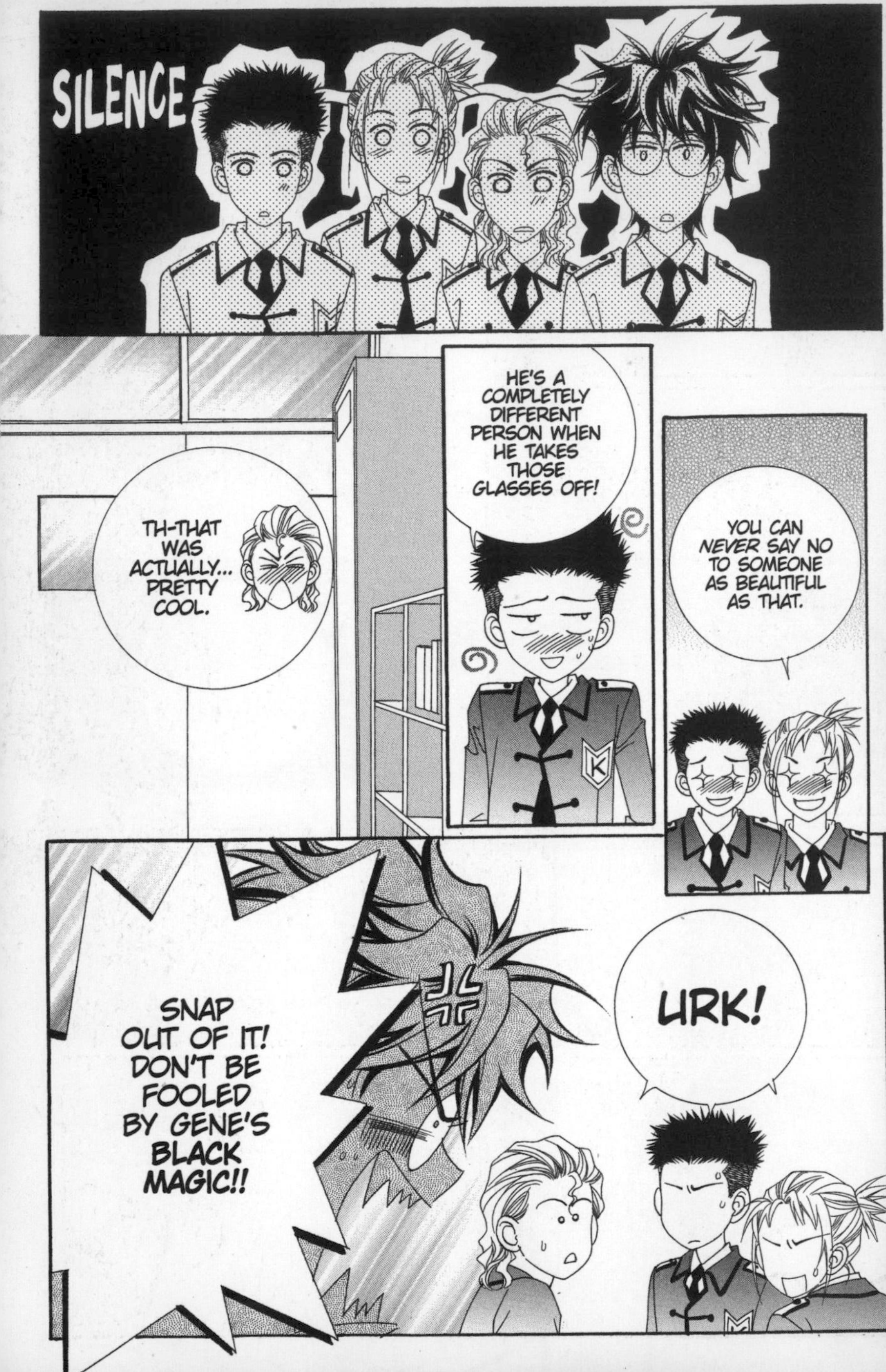
SILENCE
TH-THAT WAS ACTUALLY... PRETTY COOL.
HE'S A COMPLETELY DIFFERENT PERSON WHEN HE TAKES THOSE GLASSES OFF!
YOU CAN NEVER SAY NO TO SOMEONE AS BEAUTIFUL AS THAT.
SNAP OUT OF IT! DON'T BE FOOLED BY GENE'S BLACK MAGIC!!
URK!

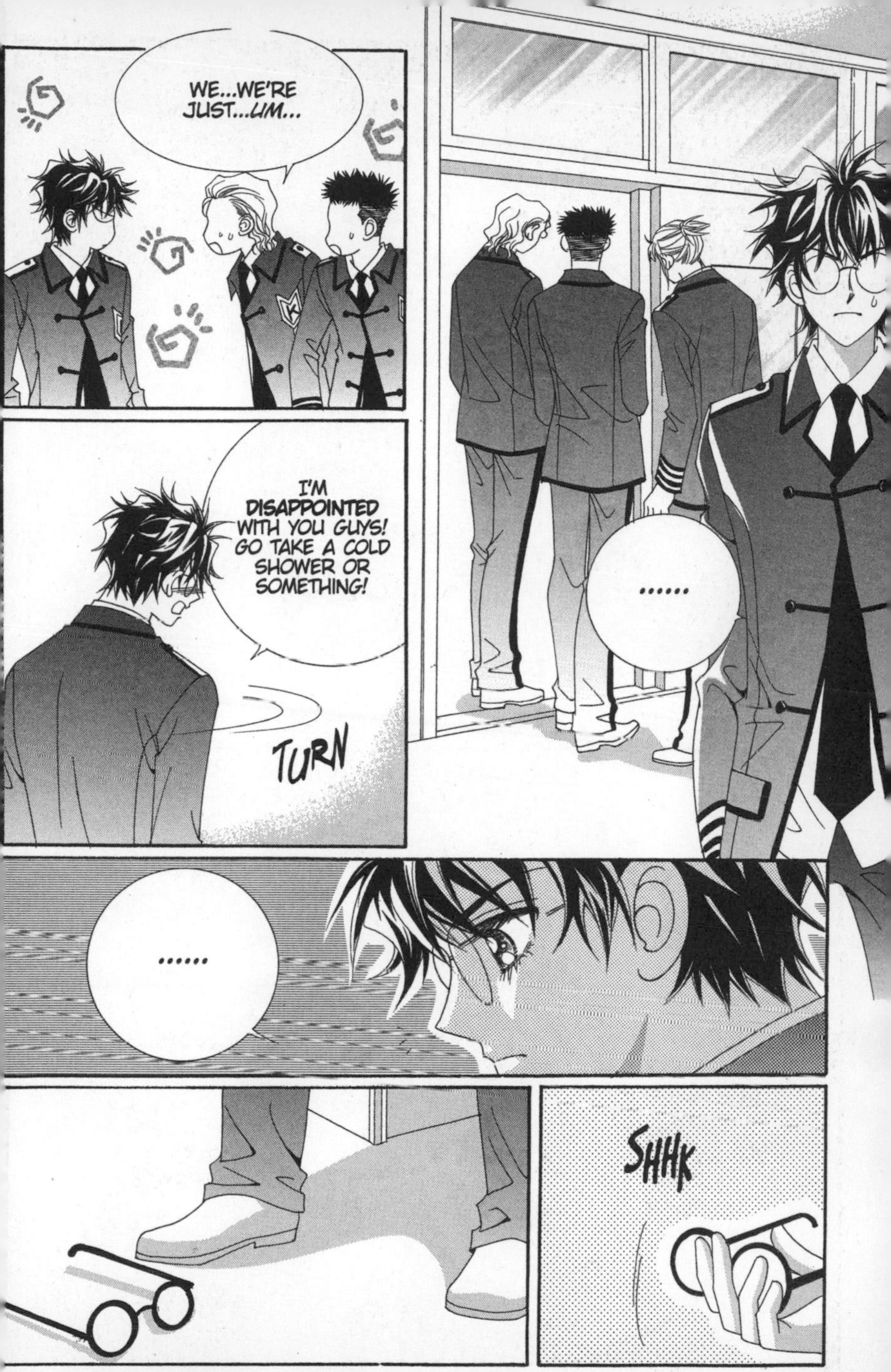
WE...WE'RE JUST...UM...
I'M DISAPPOINTED WITH YOU GUYS! GO TAKE A COLD SHOWER OR SOMETHING!
TURN
......
......
SHHK

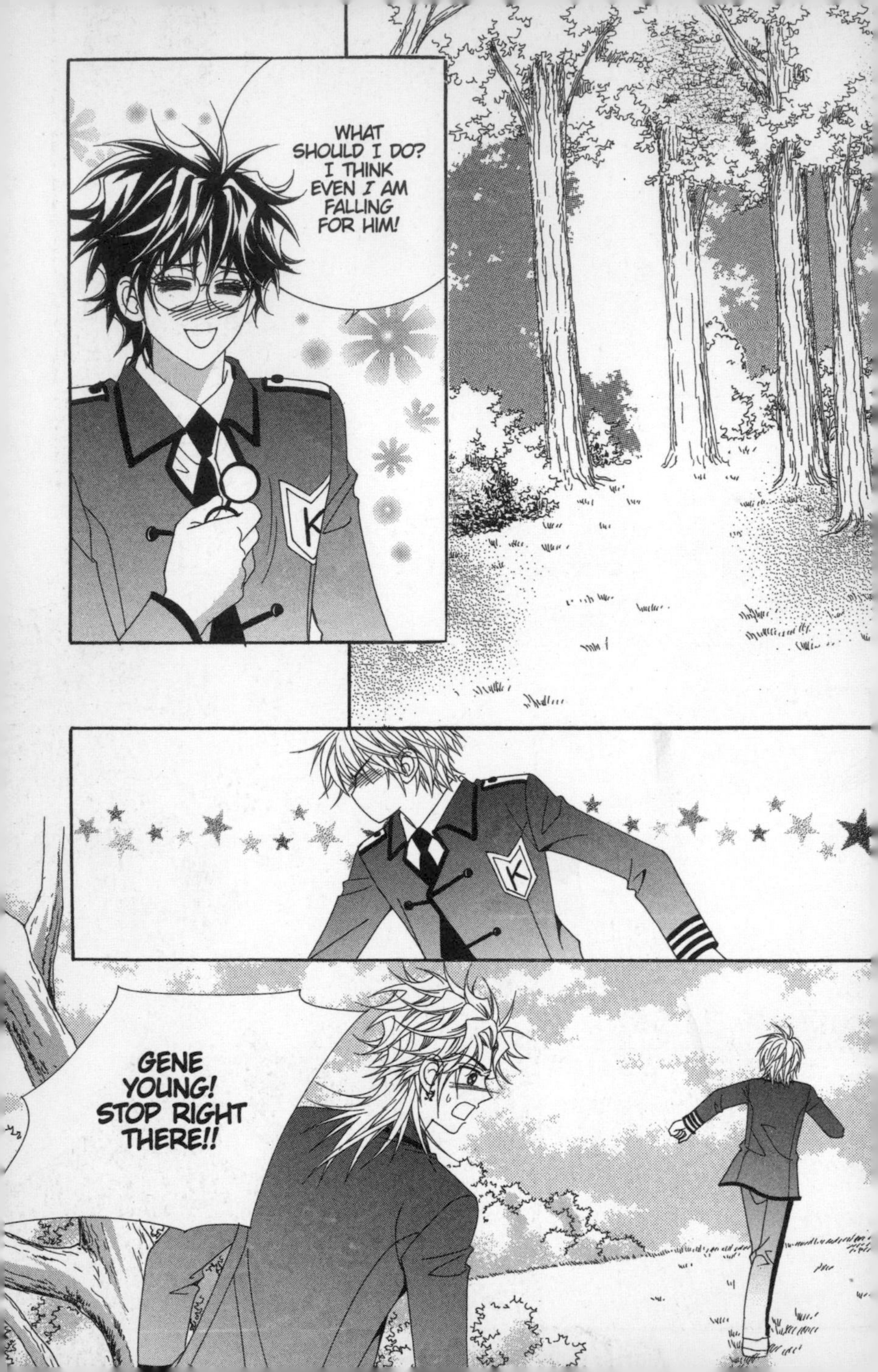
WHAT SHOULD I DO? I THINK EVEN I AM FALLING FOR HIM!
GENE YOUNG! STOP RIGHT THERE!!

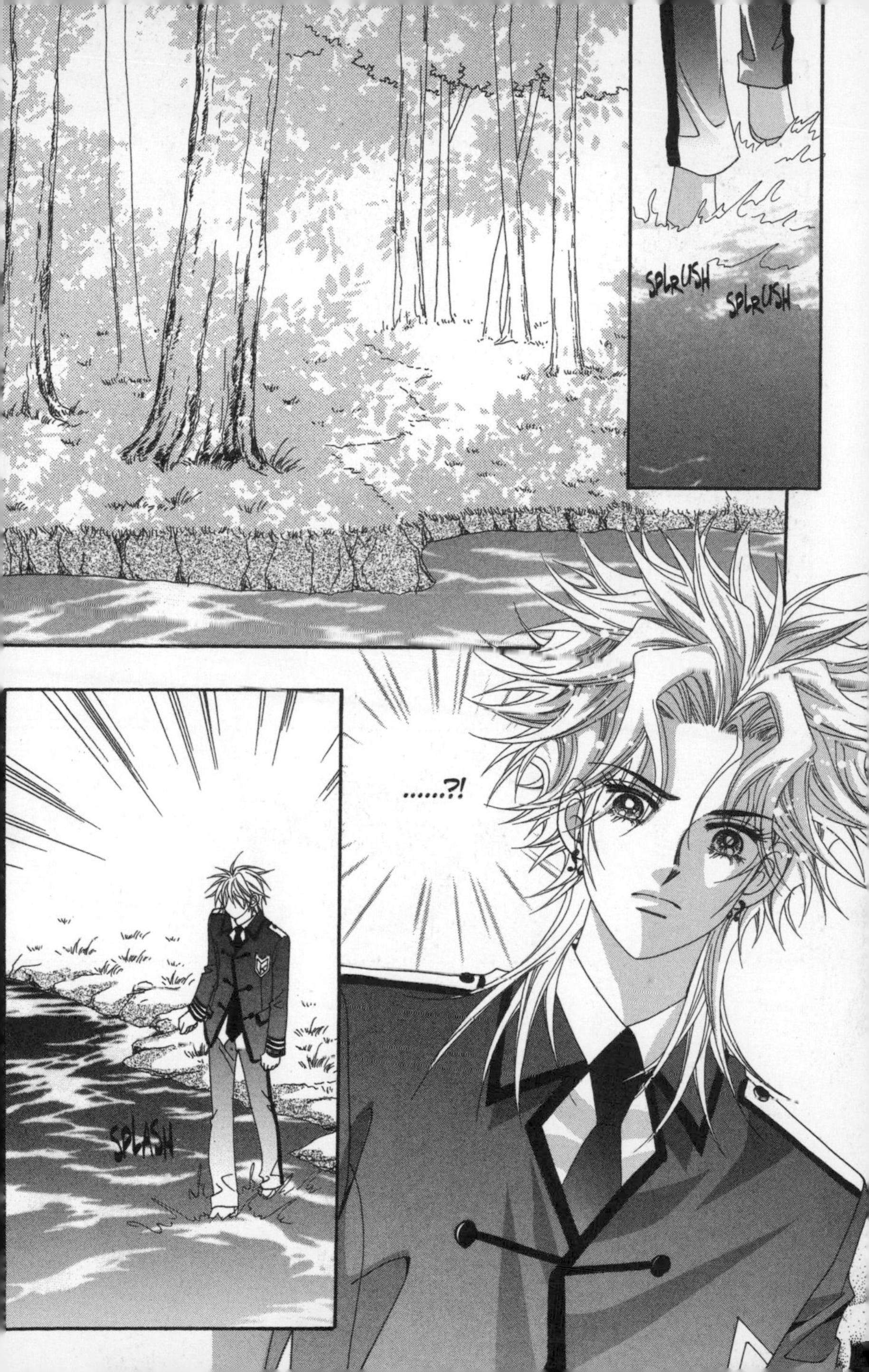
SPLRUSH
SPLRUSH
SPLASH
......?!

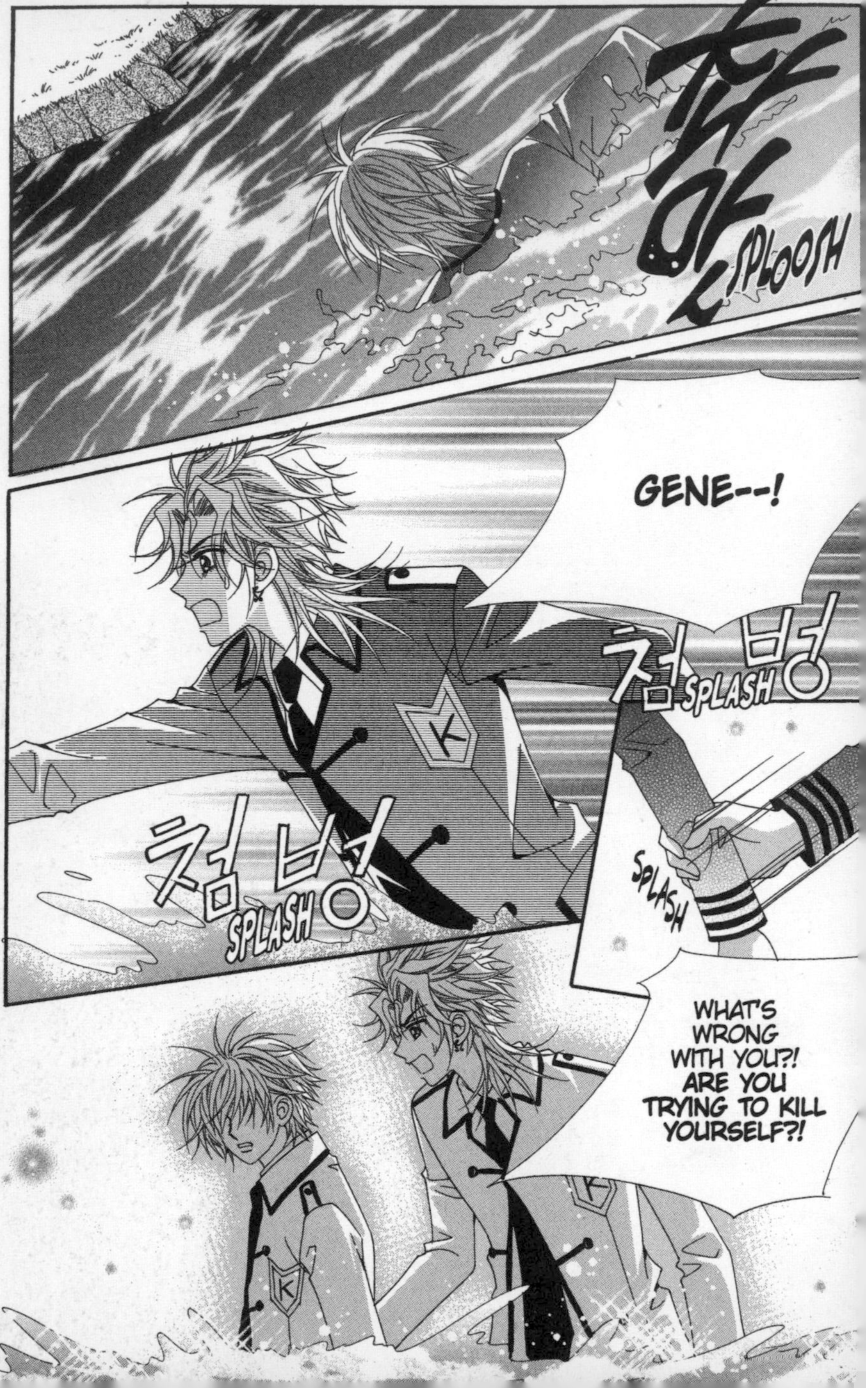
SPLOOSH
GENE--!
첨벙
SPLASH
첨벙
SPLASH
SPLASH
WHAT'S WRONG WITH YOU?! ARE YOU TRYING TO KILL YOURSELF?!

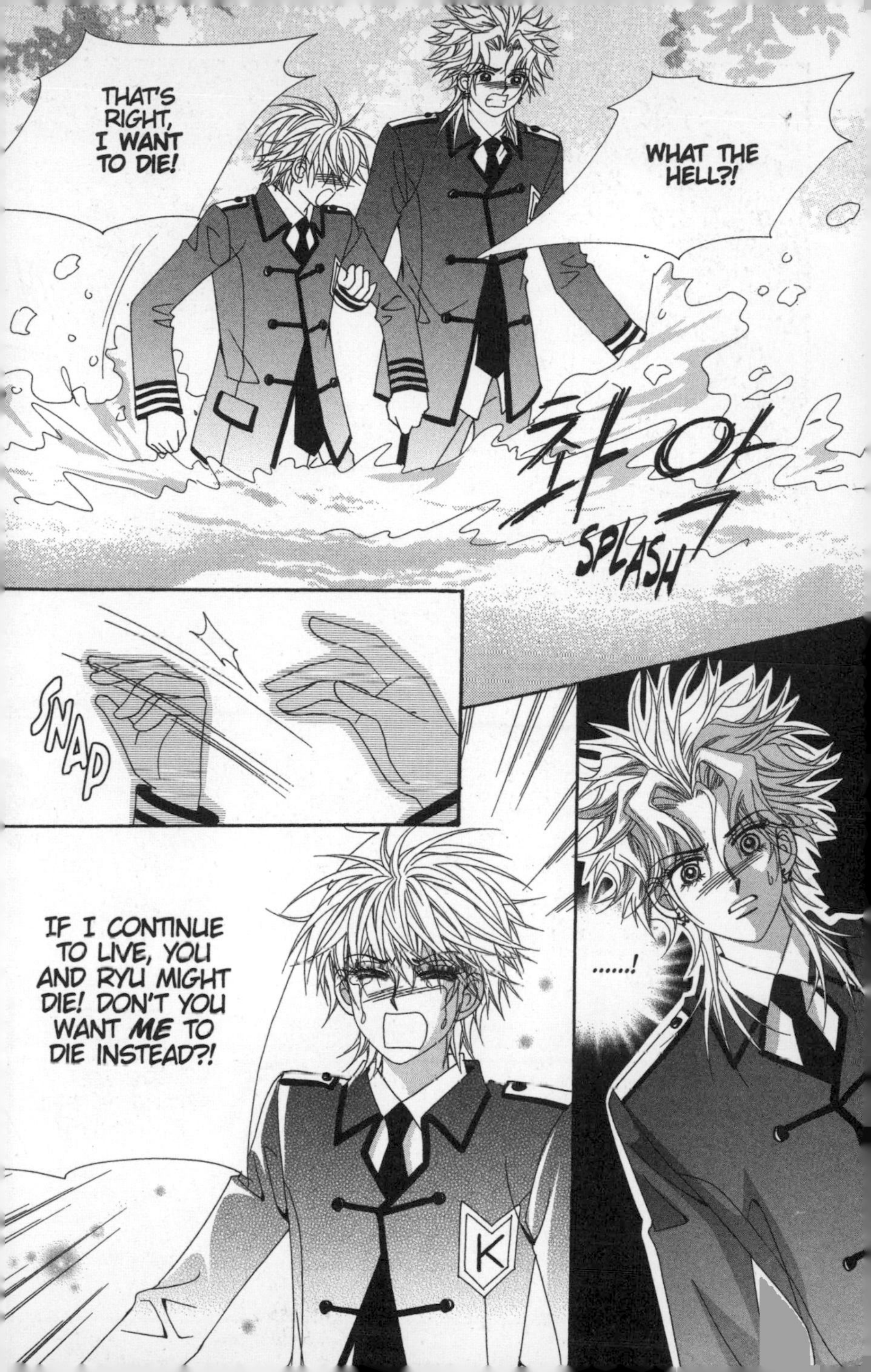
THAT'S RIGHT, I WANT TO DIE!
WHAT THE HELL?!
화아
SPLASH
SNAP
IF I CONTINUE TO LIVE, YOU AND RYU MIGHT DIE! DON'T YOU WANT *ME* TO DIE INSTEAD?!
......!
K

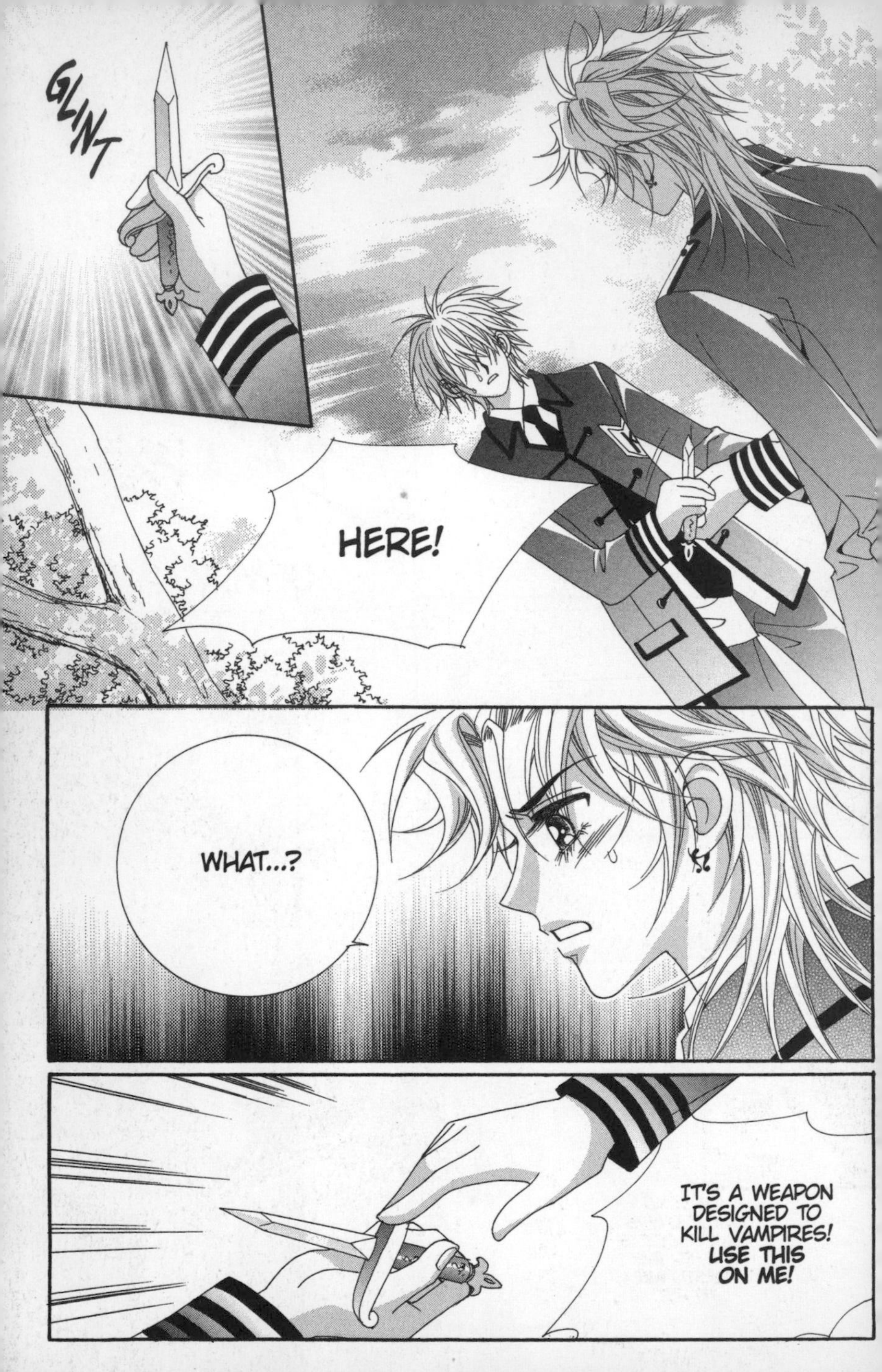
GLINT
HERE!
WHAT...?
IT'S A WEAPON DESIGNED TO KILL VAMPIRES! USE THIS ON ME!

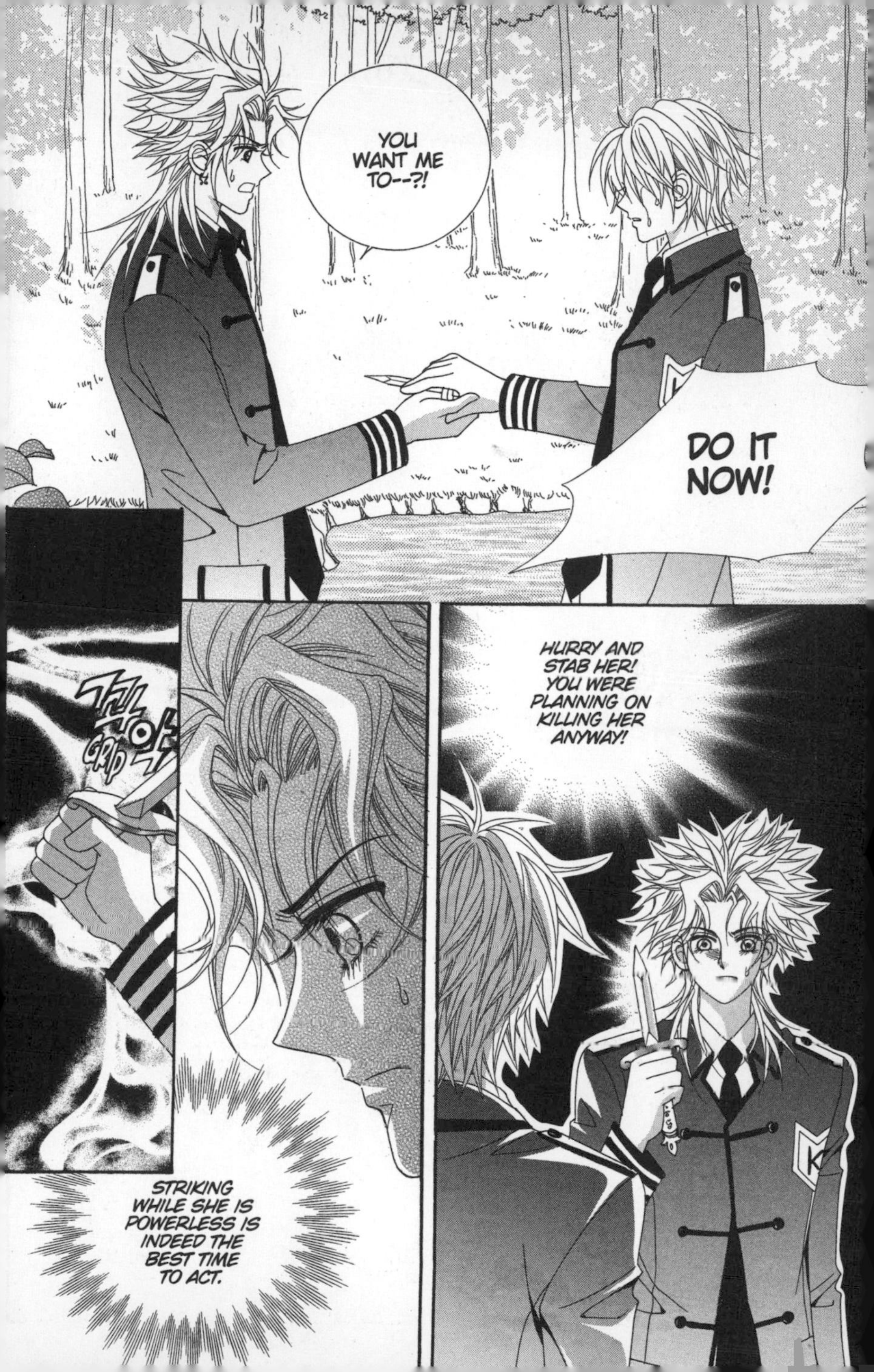
YOU WANT ME TO--?!
DO IT NOW!
GRIP
STRIKING WHILE SHE IS POWERLESS IS INDEED THE BEST TIME TO ACT.
HURRY AND STAB HER! YOU WERE PLANNING ON KILLING HER ANYWAY!

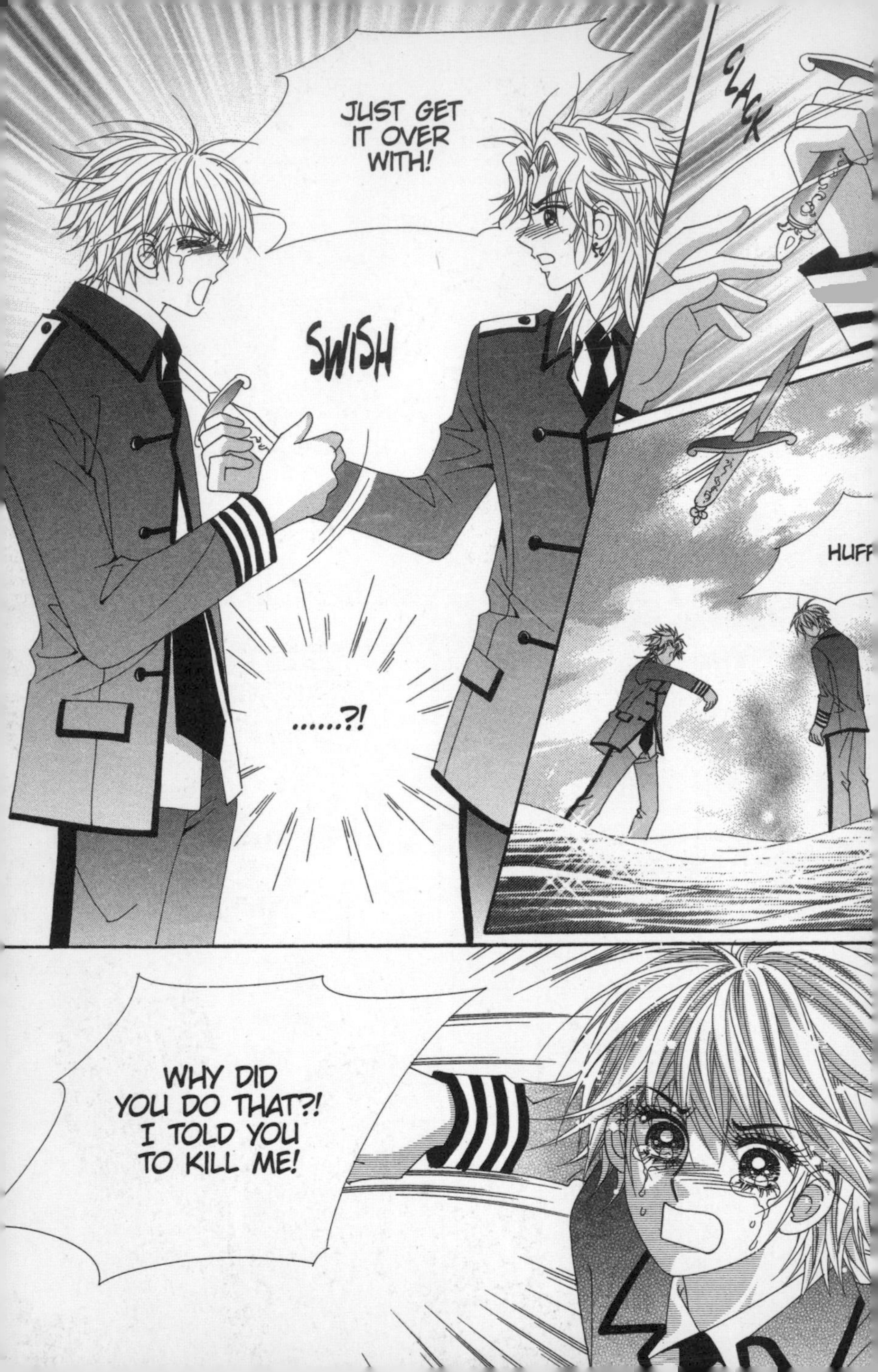
JUST GET IT OVER WITH!
SWISH
......?!
CLACK
HUFF
WHY DID YOU DO THAT?! I TOLD YOU TO KILL ME!

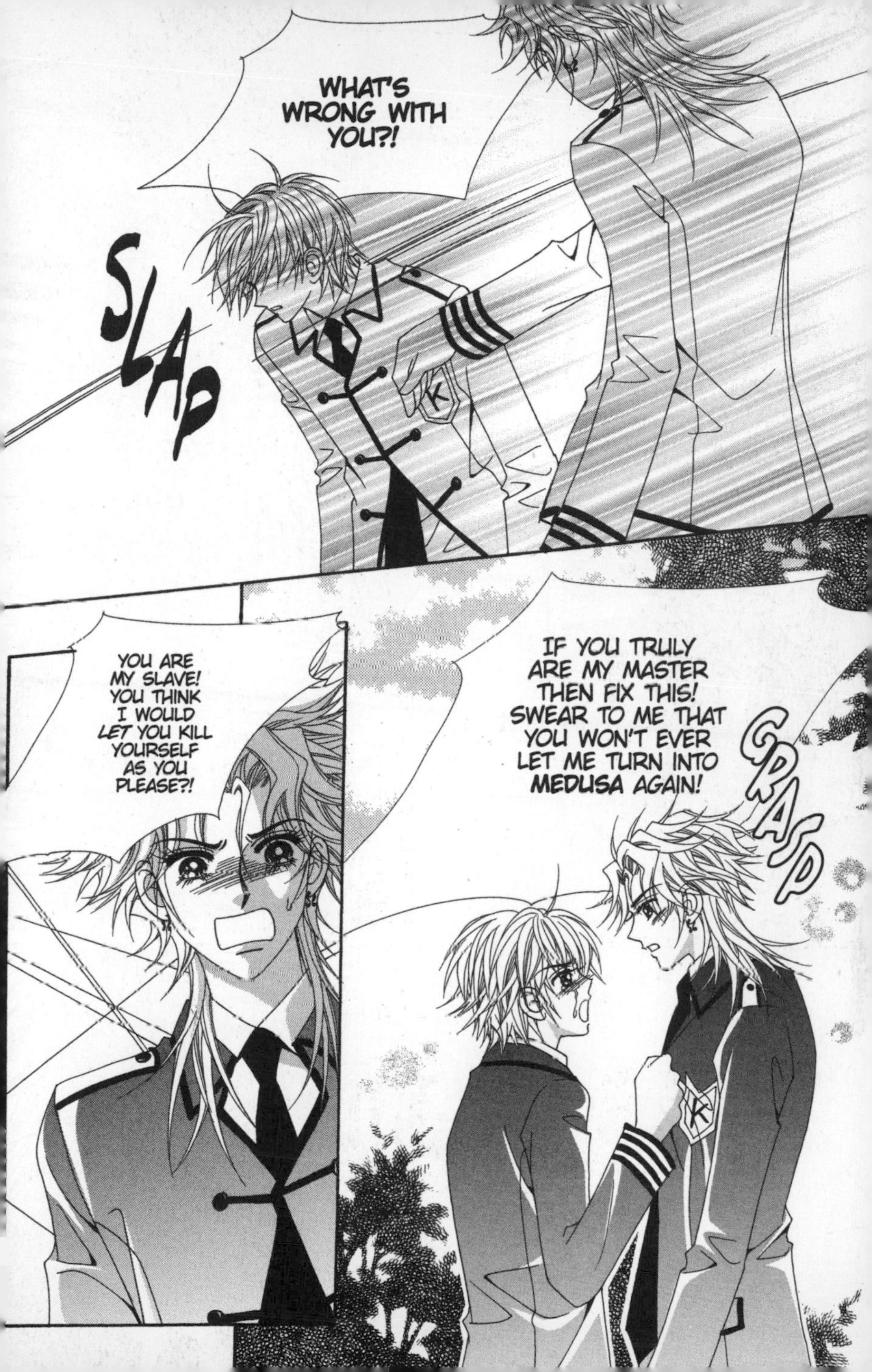
WHAT'S WRONG WITH YOU?!
SLAP
YOU ARE MY SLAVE! YOU THINK I WOULD LET YOU KILL YOURSELF AS YOU PLEASE?!
IF YOU TRULY ARE MY MASTER THEN FIX THIS! SWEAR TO ME THAT YOU WON'T EVER LET ME TURN INTO MEDUSA AGAIN!
GRASP

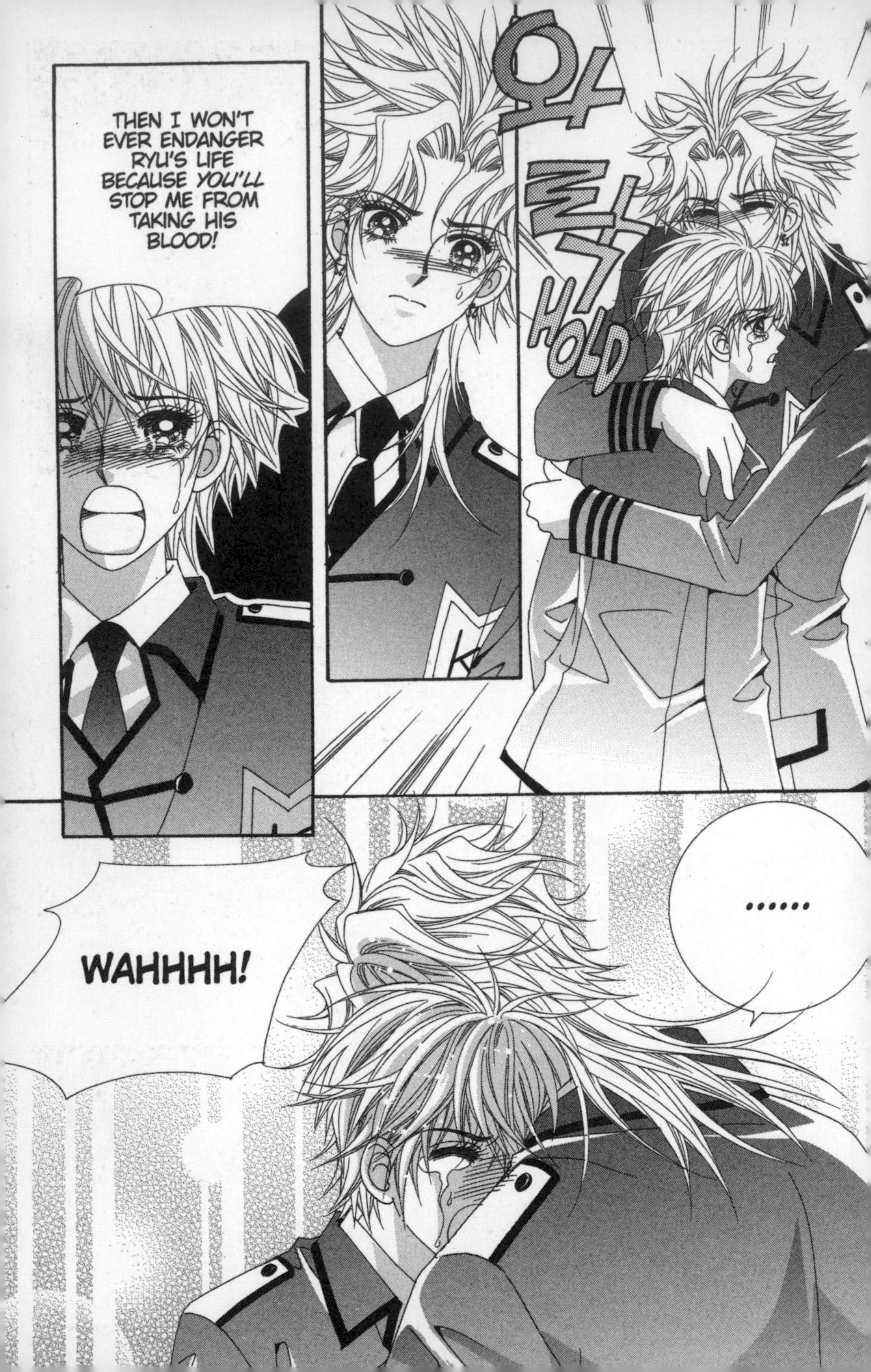
THEN I WON'T EVER ENDANGER RYU'S LIFE BECAUSE *YOU'LL* STOP ME FROM TAKING HIS BLOOD!
HOLD
WAHHHH!
......

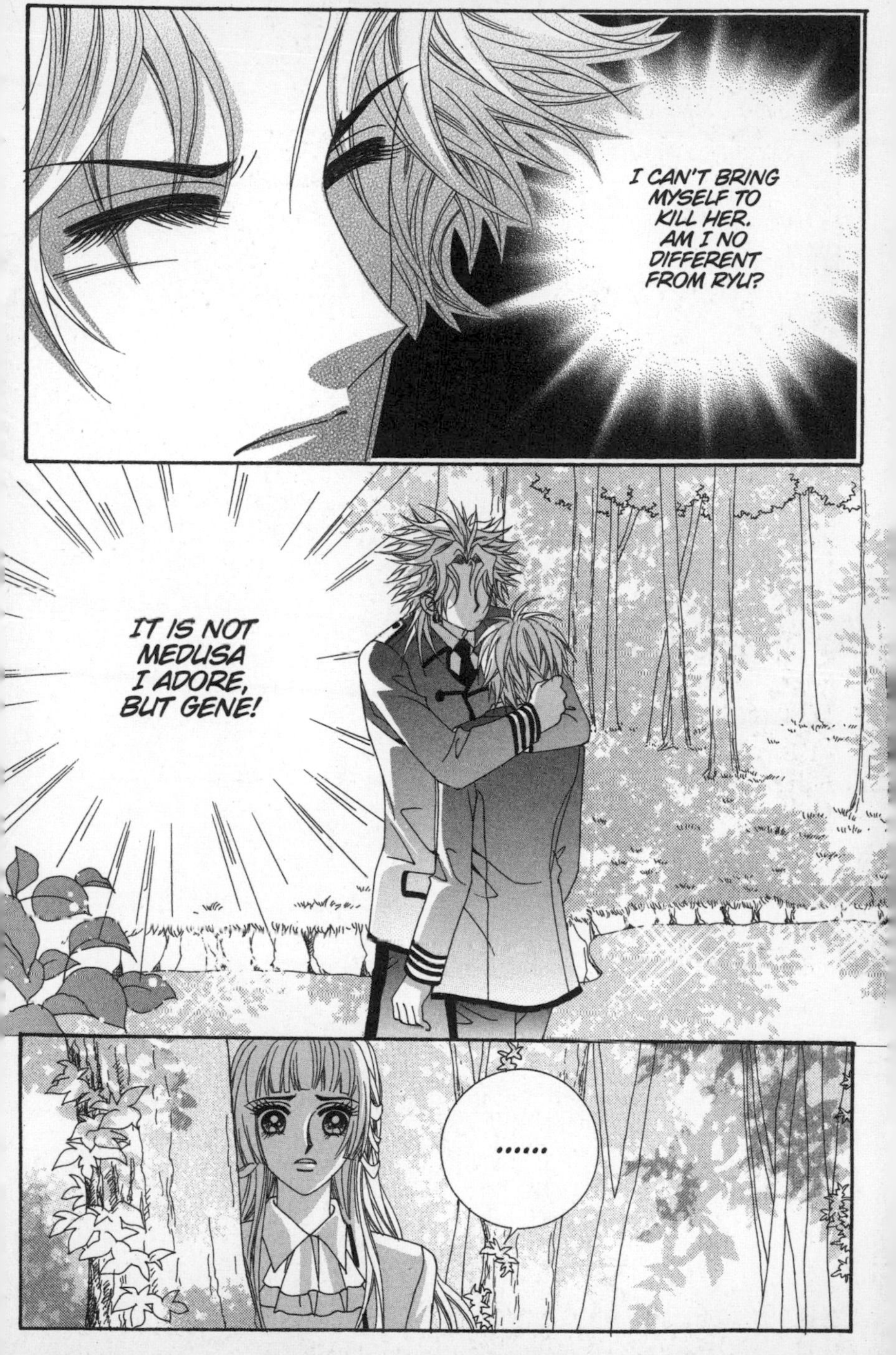
I CAN'T BRING MYSELF TO KILL HER. AM I NO DIFFERENT FROM RYU?
IT IS NOT MEDUSA I ADORE, BUT GENE!
......

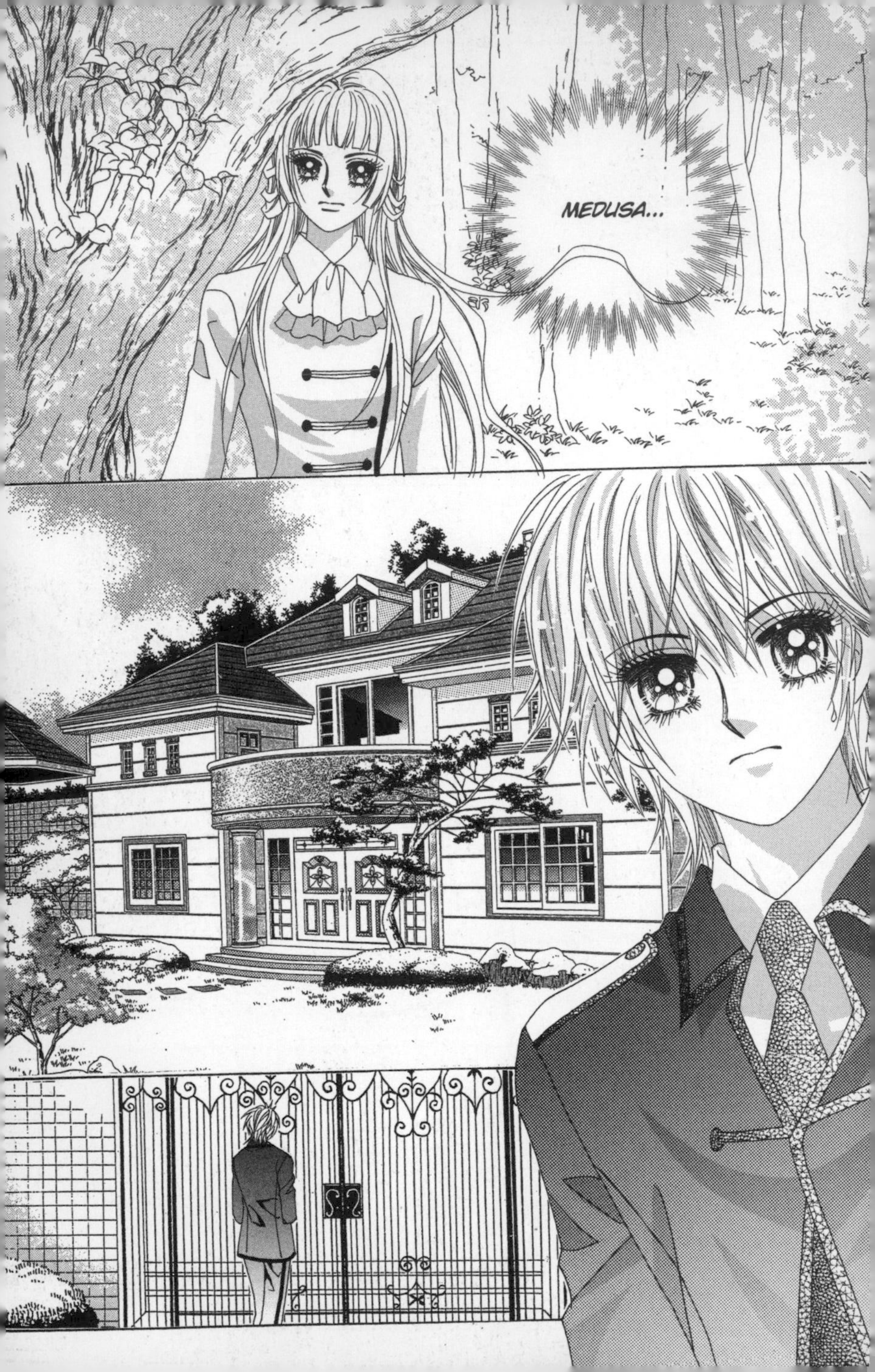
MEDUSA...

HE PROBABLY WOULDN'T LIKE ME VISITING RYU.

Hesitate

YOUR VERY EXISTENCE THREATENS MASTER RYU'S LIFE.

DROP

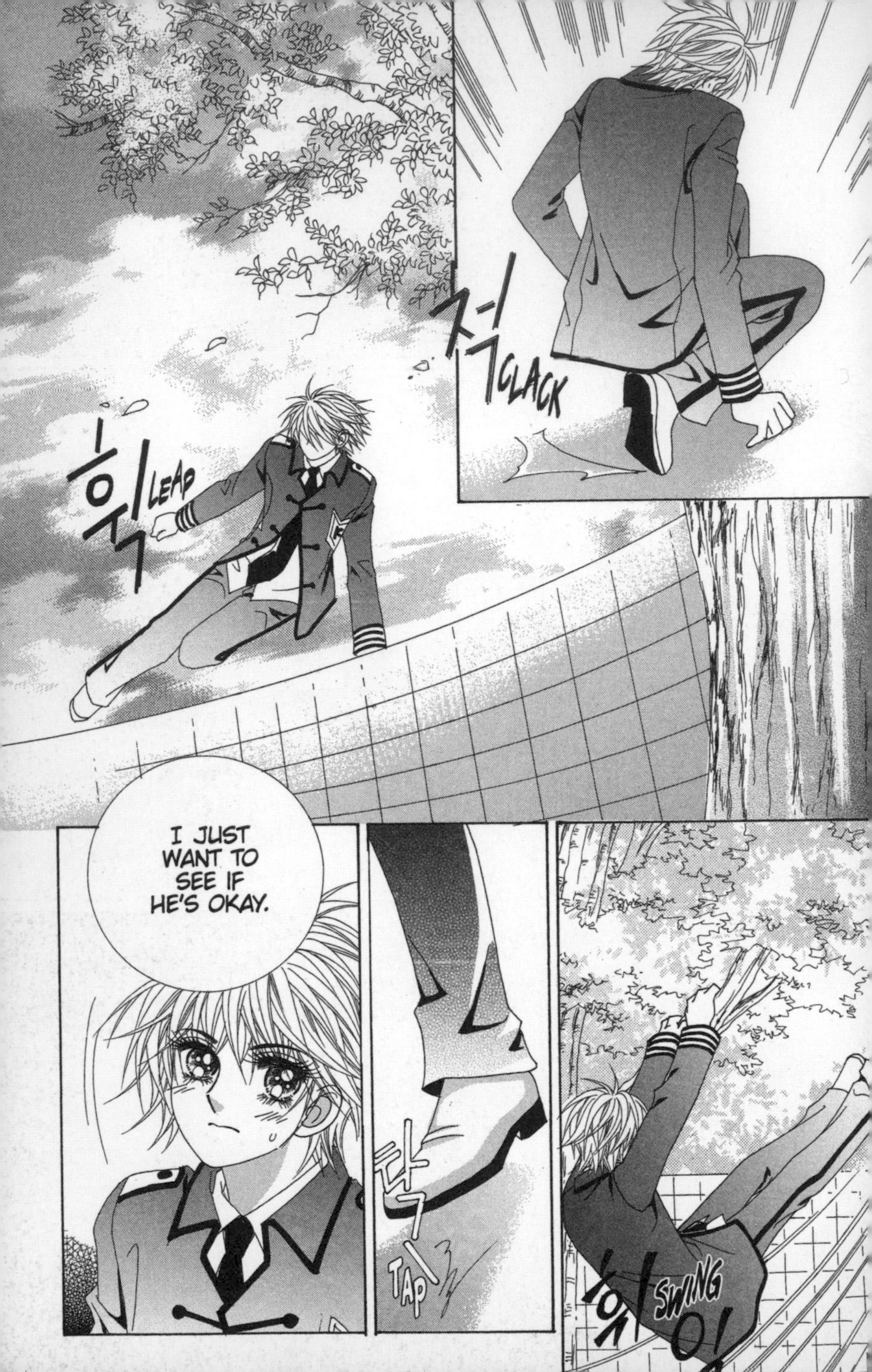
LEAP
CLACK
I JUST WANT TO SEE IF HE'S OKAY.
TAP
SWING

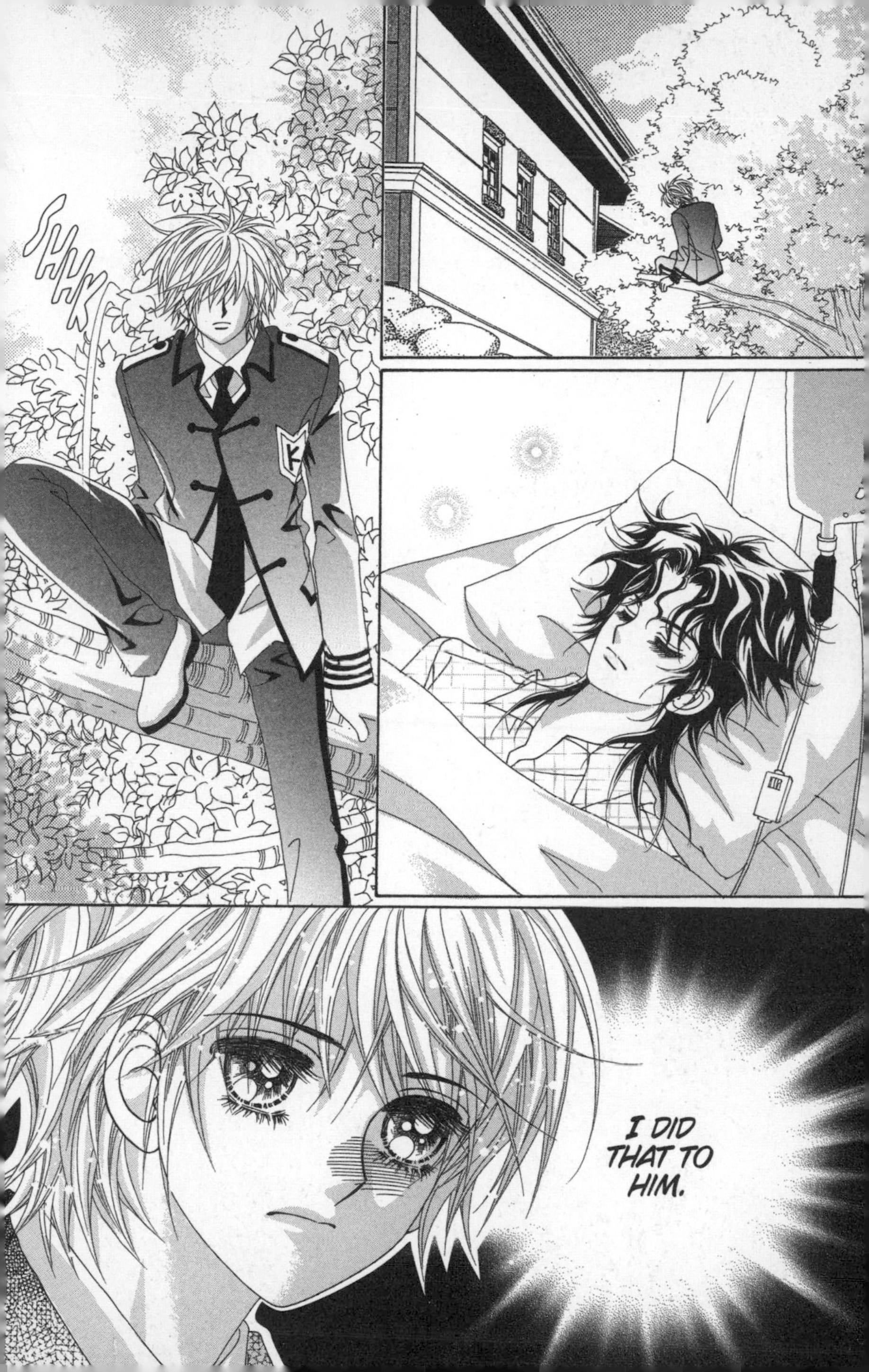
SHHK
I DID THAT TO HIM.

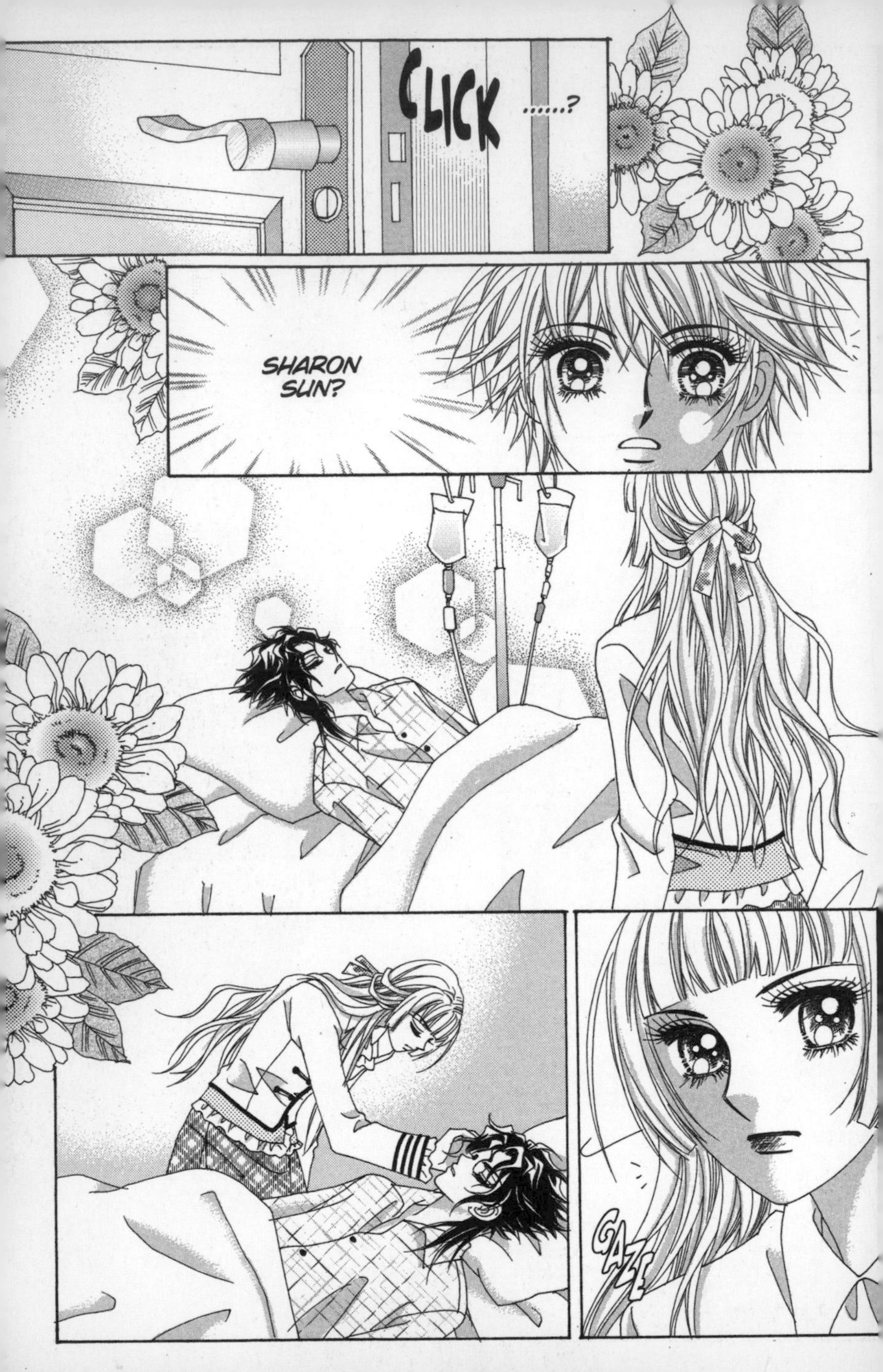
CLICK
......?
SHARON SUN?
GAZE

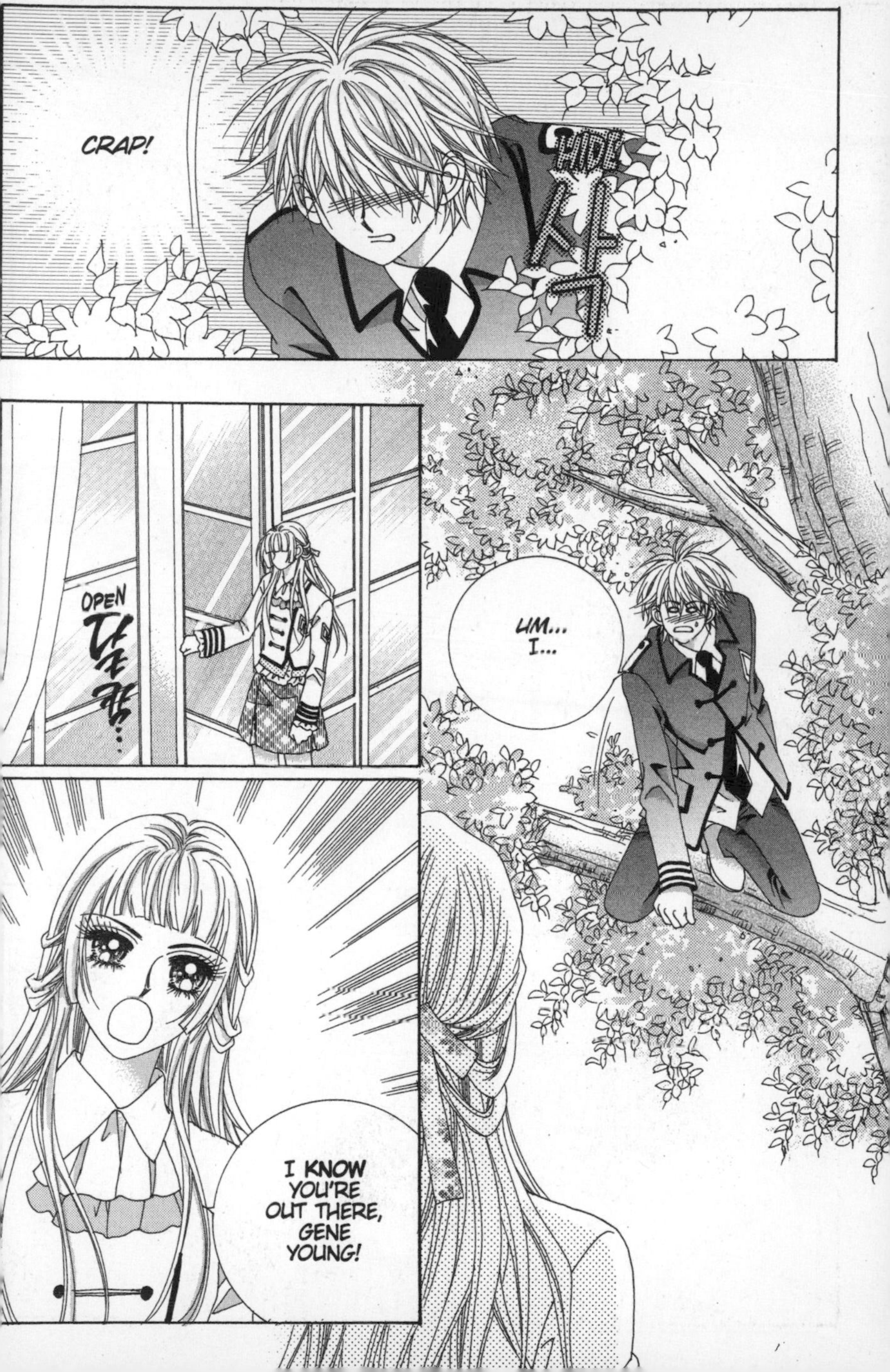
CRAP!
HIDE
OPEN
UM... I...
I KNOW YOU'RE OUT THERE, GENE YOUNG!

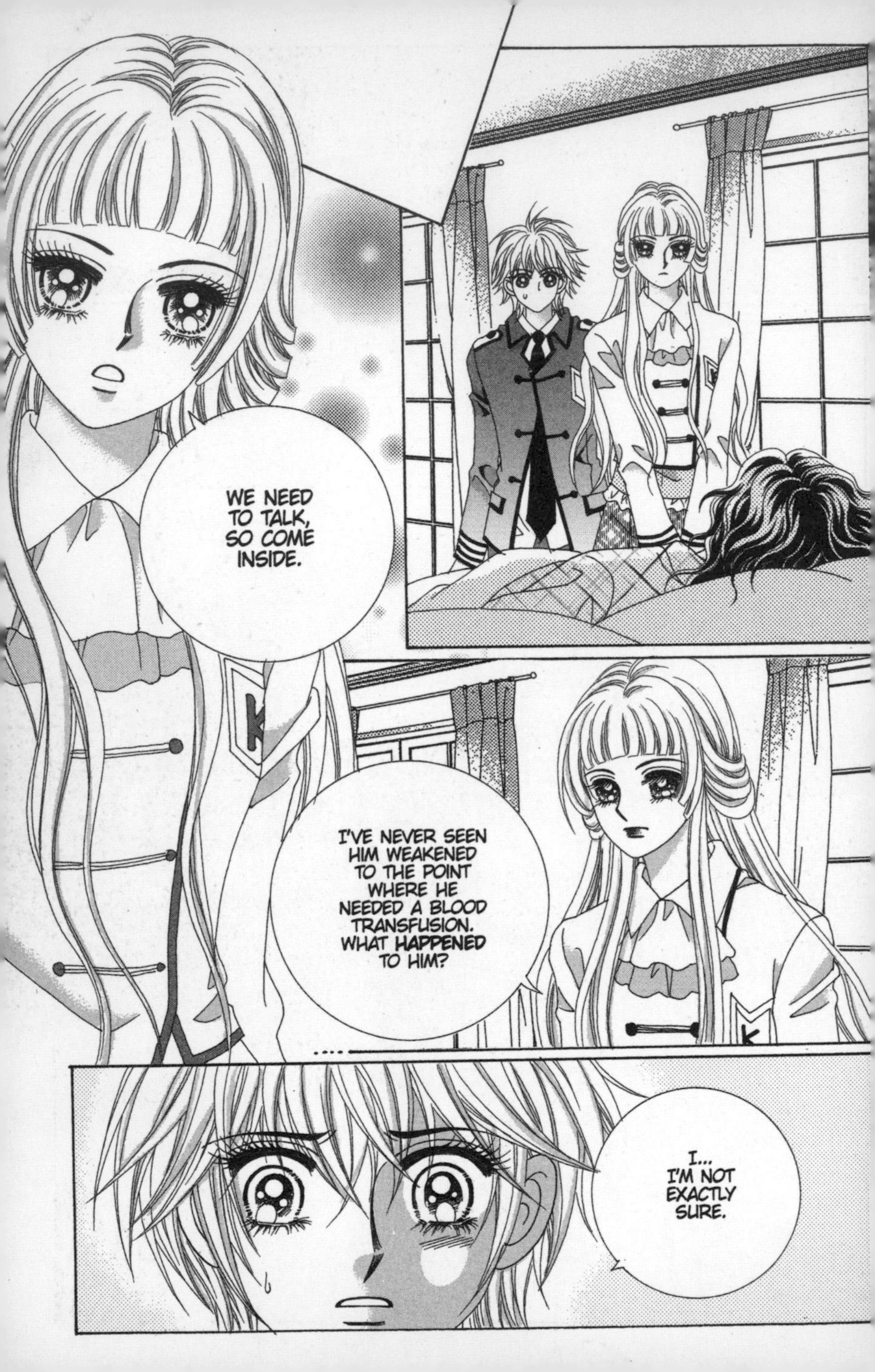
WE NEED TO TALK, SO COME INSIDE.
I'VE NEVER SEEN HIM WEAKENED TO THE POINT WHERE HE NEEDED A BLOOD TRANSFUSION. WHAT HAPPENED TO HIM?
....
I... I'M NOT EXACTLY SURE.

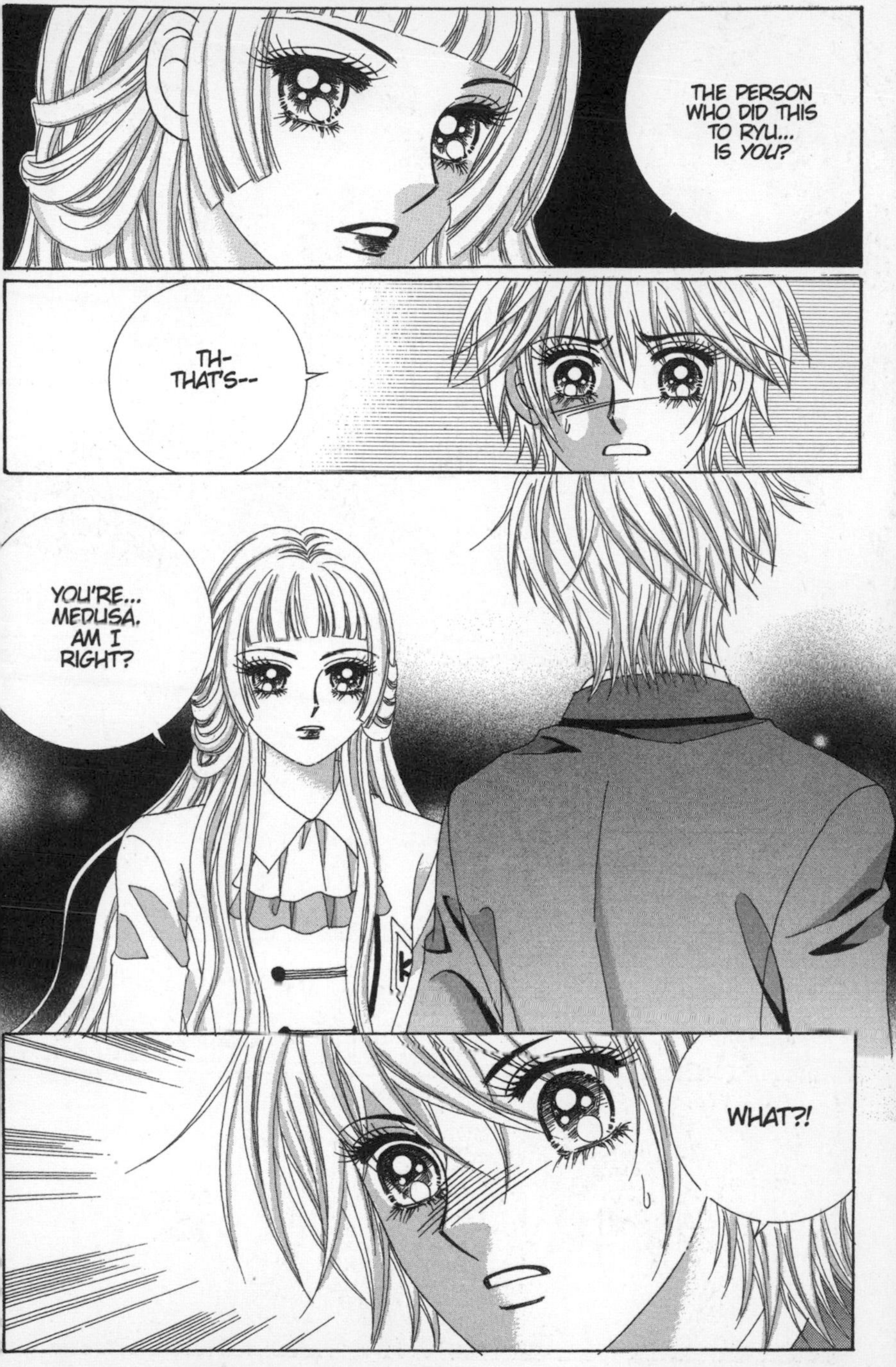
THE PERSON WHO DID THIS TO RYU... IS *YOU*?
TH-THAT'S--
YOU'RE... MEDUSA. AM I RIGHT?
WHAT?!

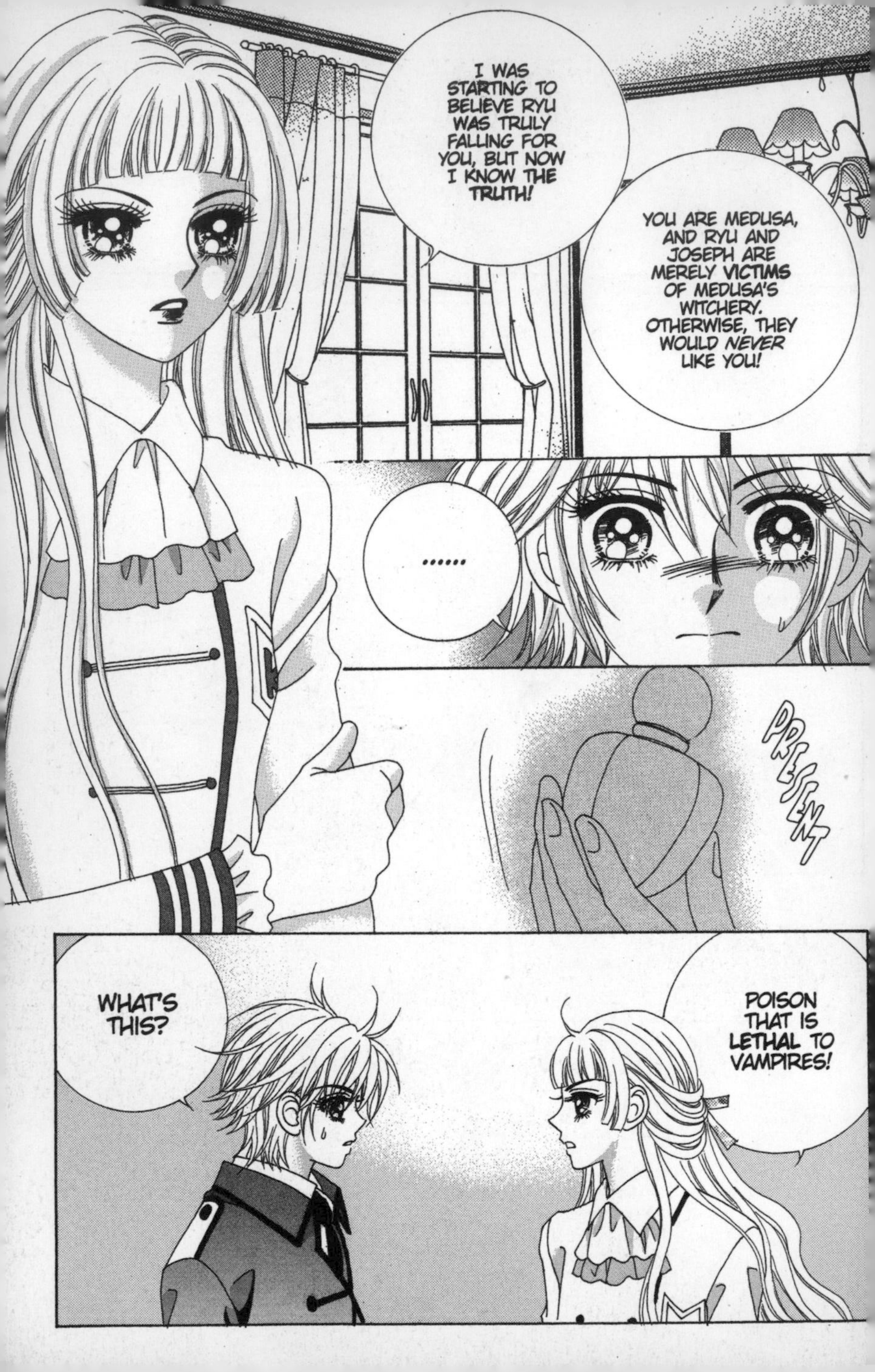
I WAS STARTING TO BELIEVE RYU WAS TRULY FALLING FOR YOU, BUT NOW I KNOW THE TRUTH!
YOU ARE MEDUSA, AND RYU AND JOSEPH ARE MERELY VICTIMS OF MEDUSA'S WITCHERY. OTHERWISE, THEY WOULD *NEVER* LIKE YOU!
......
PRESENT
WHAT'S THIS?
POISON THAT IS LETHAL TO VAMPIRES!

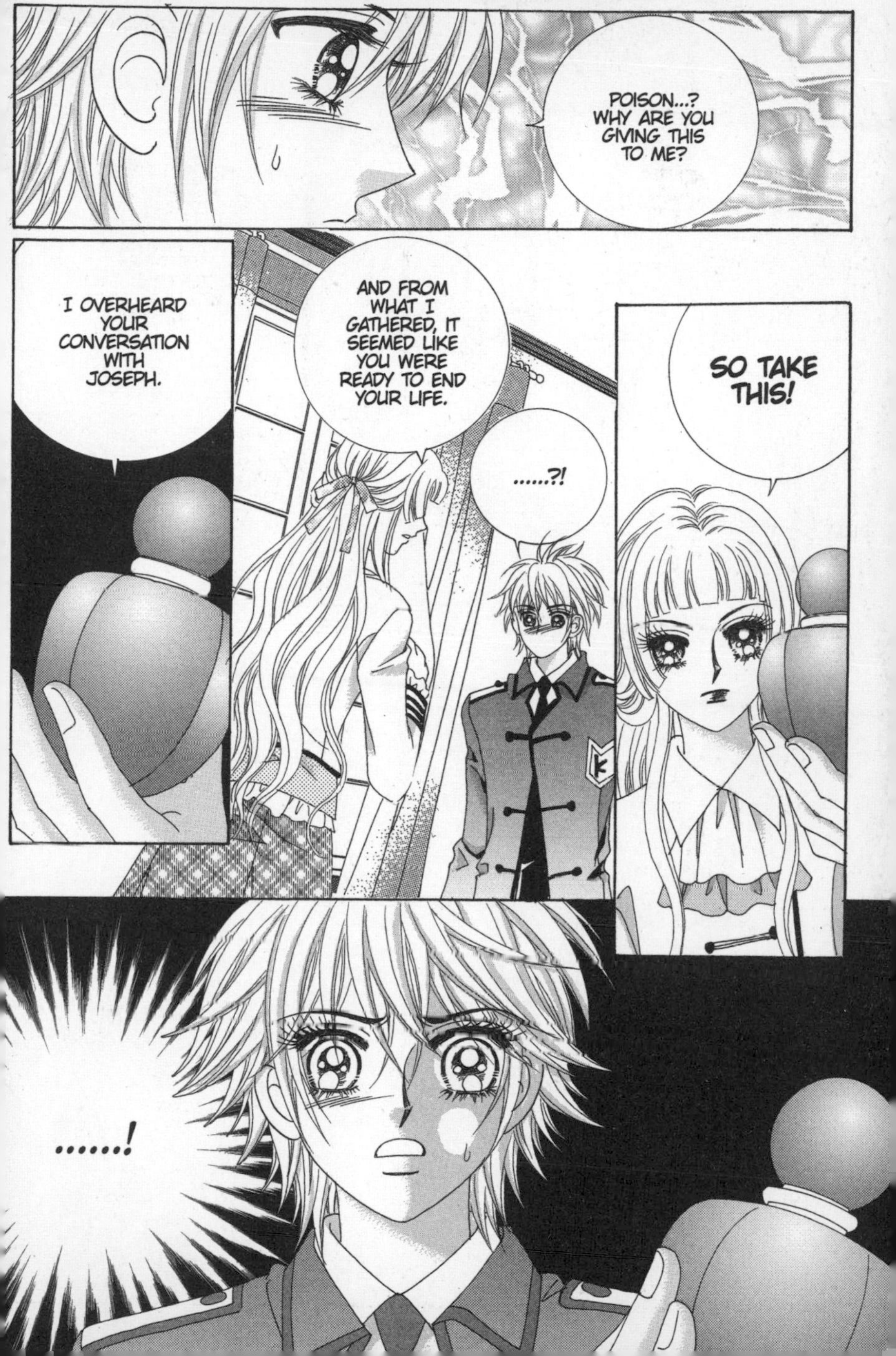
POISON...? WHY ARE YOU GIVING THIS TO ME?
I OVERHEARD YOUR CONVERSATION WITH JOSEPH.
AND FROM WHAT I GATHERED, IT SEEMED LIKE YOU WERE READY TO END YOUR LIFE.
......?!
SO TAKE THIS!
......!

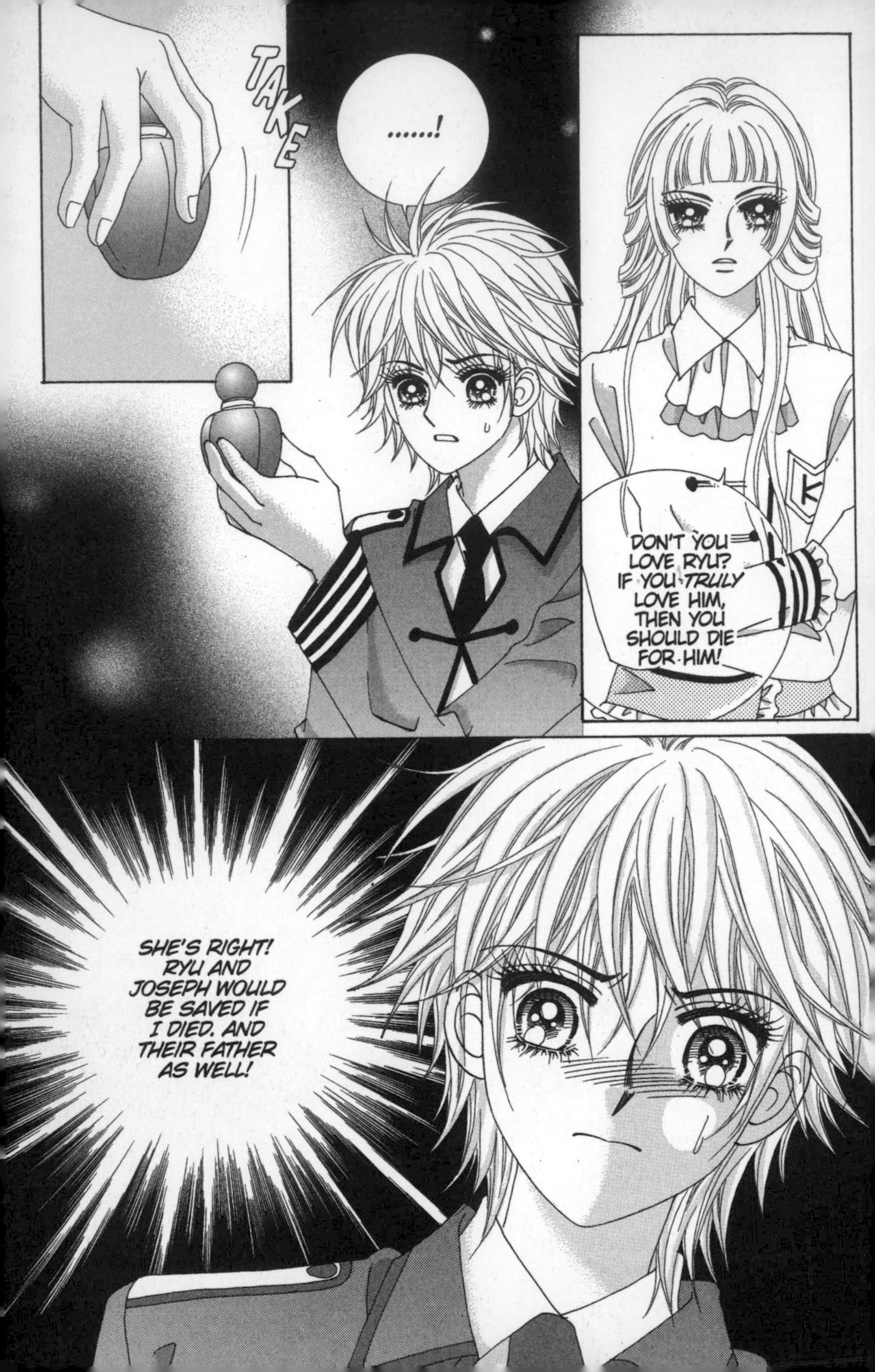
TAKE
......!
DON'T YOU LOVE RYU? IF YOU *TRULY* LOVE HIM, THEN YOU SHOULD DIE FOR HIM!
SHE'S RIGHT! RYU AND JOSEPH WOULD BE SAVED IF I DIED. AND THEIR FATHER AS WELL!

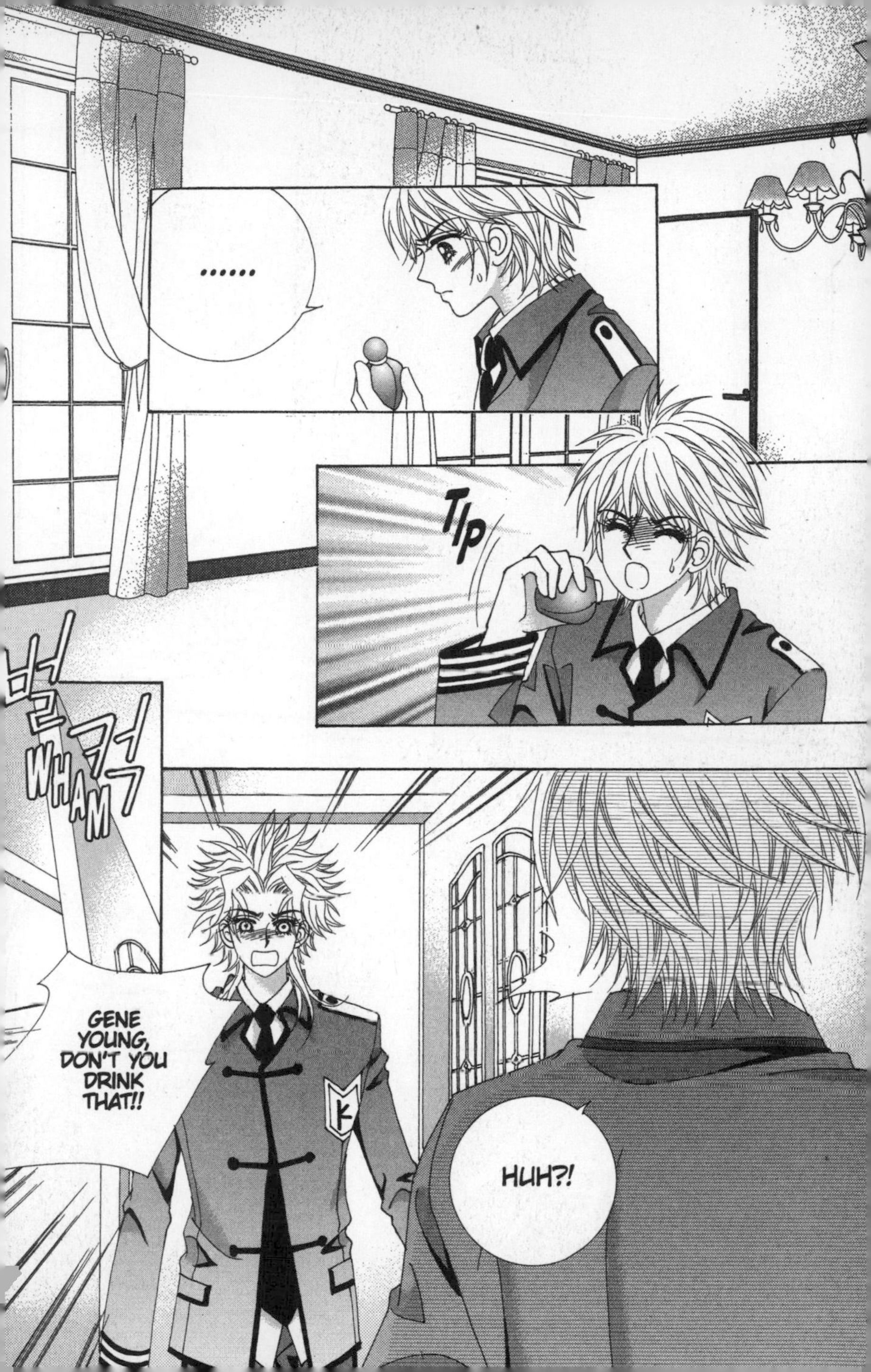
......
TIP
벌컥
WHAM
GENE YOUNG, DON'T YOU DRINK THAT!!
HUH?!

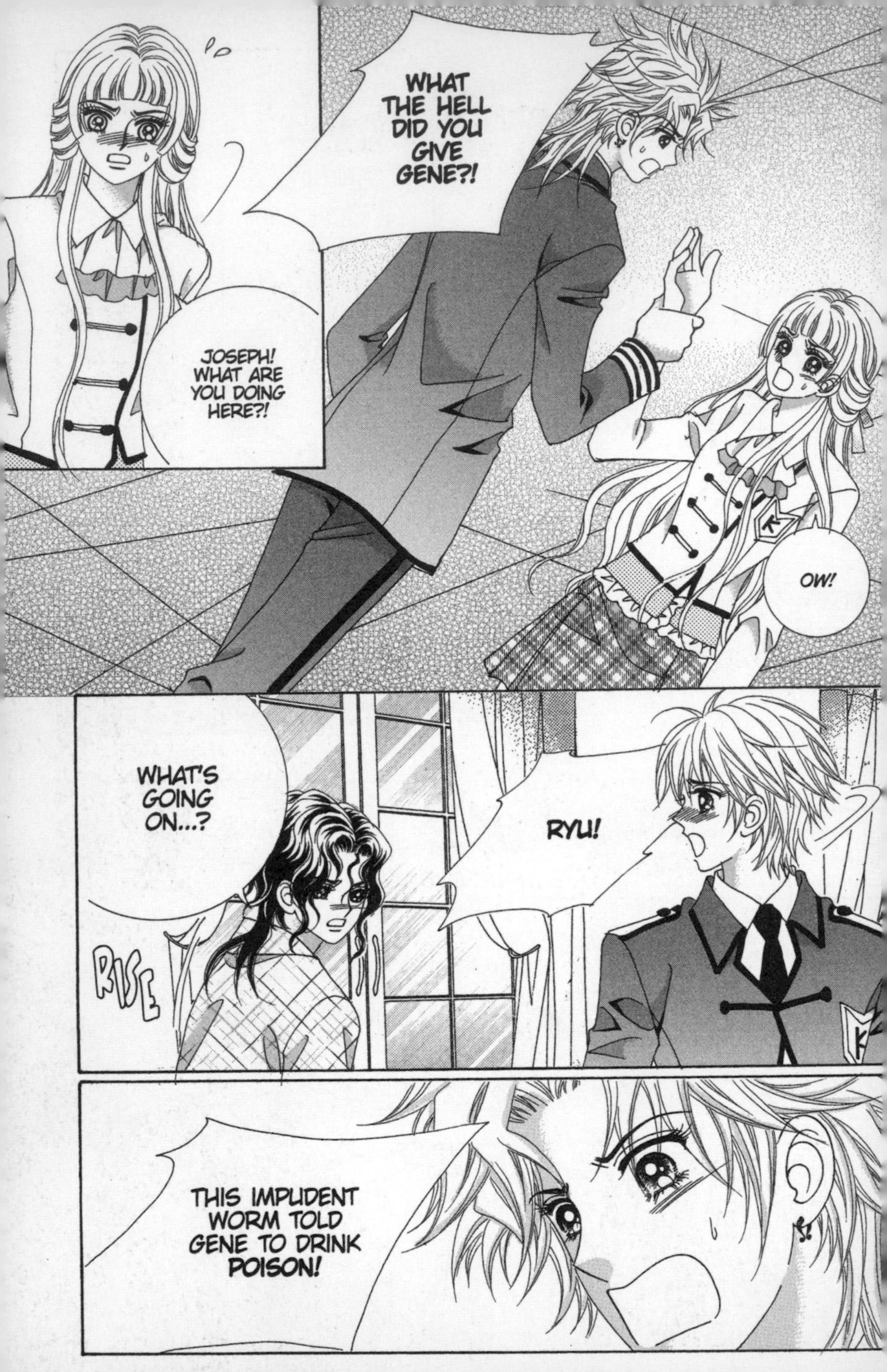
JOSEPH! WHAT ARE YOU DOING HERE?!
WHAT THE HELL DID YOU GIVE GENE?!
OW!
WHAT'S GOING ON...?
RISE
RYU!
THIS IMPUDENT WORM TOLD GENE TO DRINK POISON!

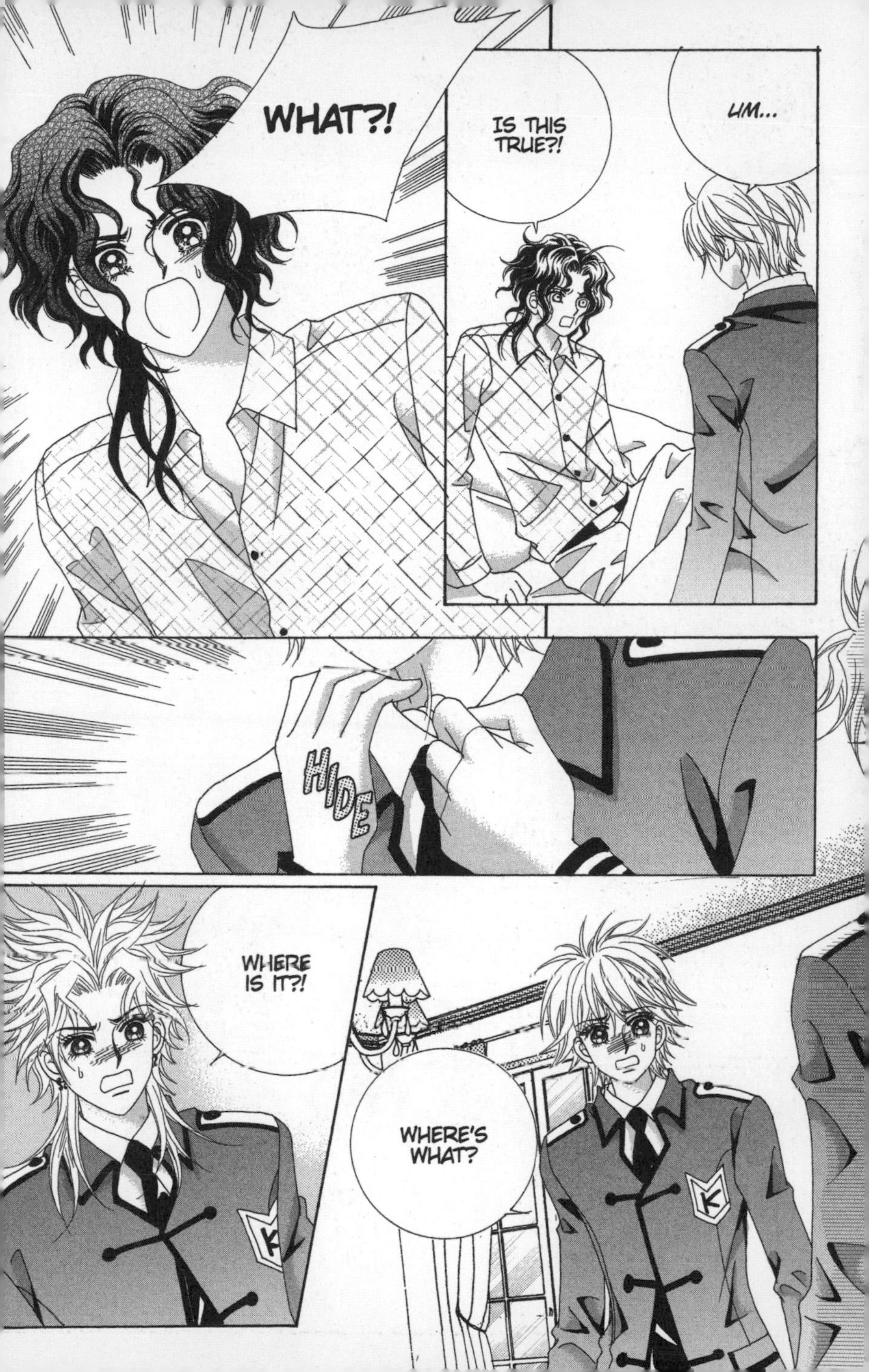
WHAT?!
IS THIS TRUE?!
UM...
HIDE
WHERE IS IT?!
WHERE'S WHAT?

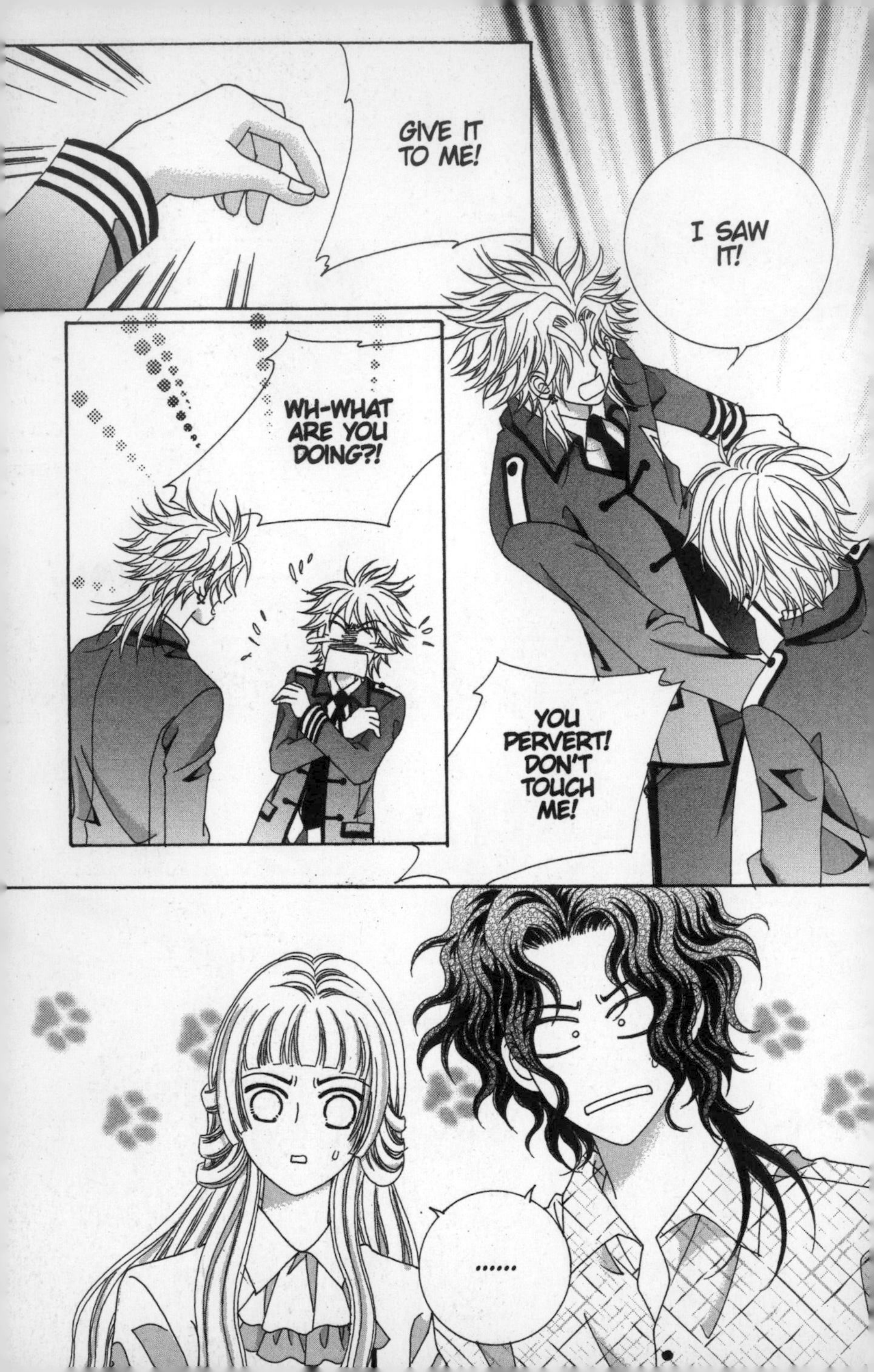
I SAW IT!
GIVE IT TO ME!
YOU PERVERT! DON'T TOUCH ME!
WH-WHAT ARE YOU DOING?!
......

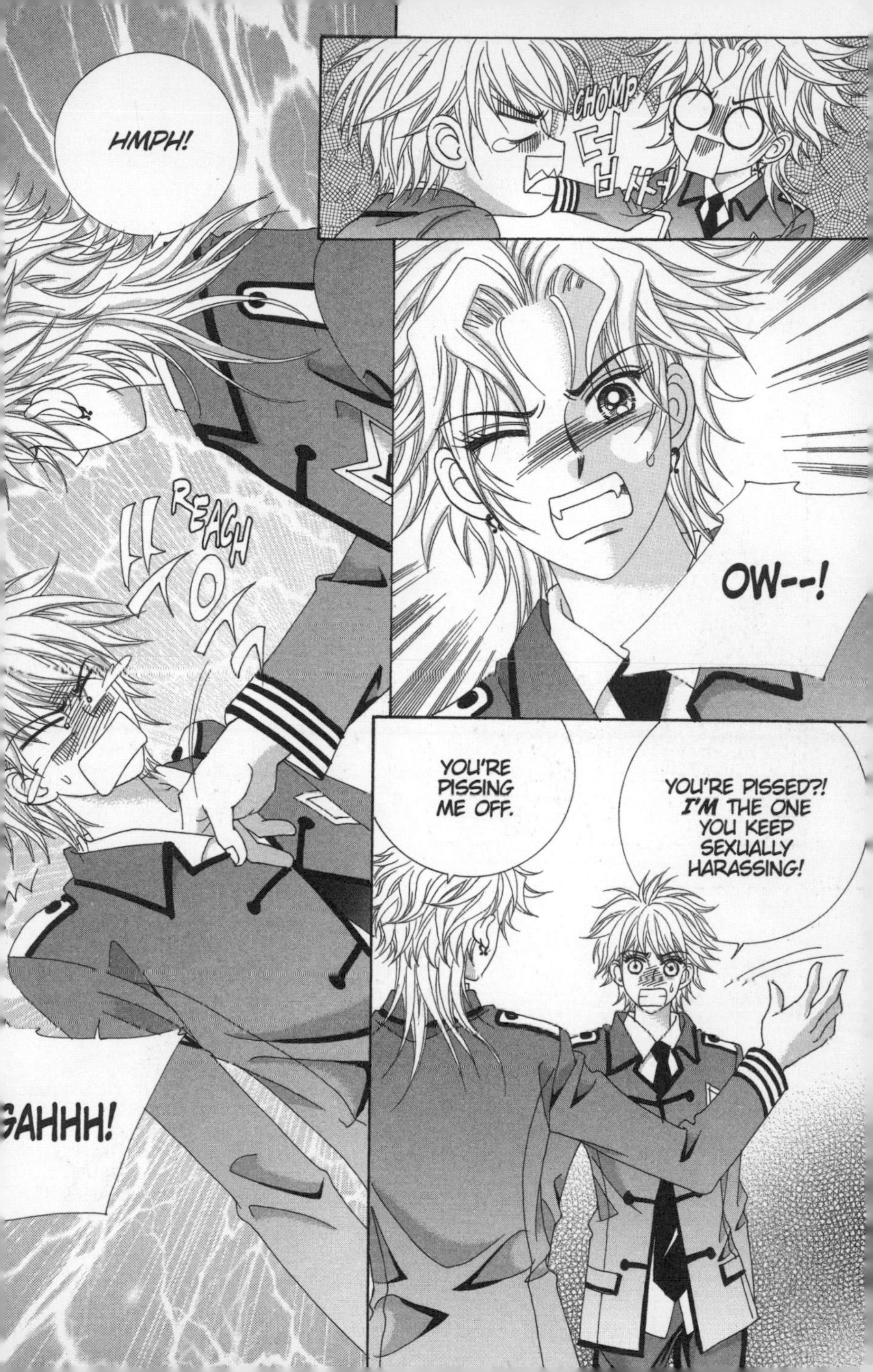
HMPH!
REACH
GAHHH!
CHOMP
OW--!
YOU'RE PISSING ME OFF.
YOU'RE PISSED?! ***I'M*** THE ONE YOU KEEP SEXUALLY HARASSING!

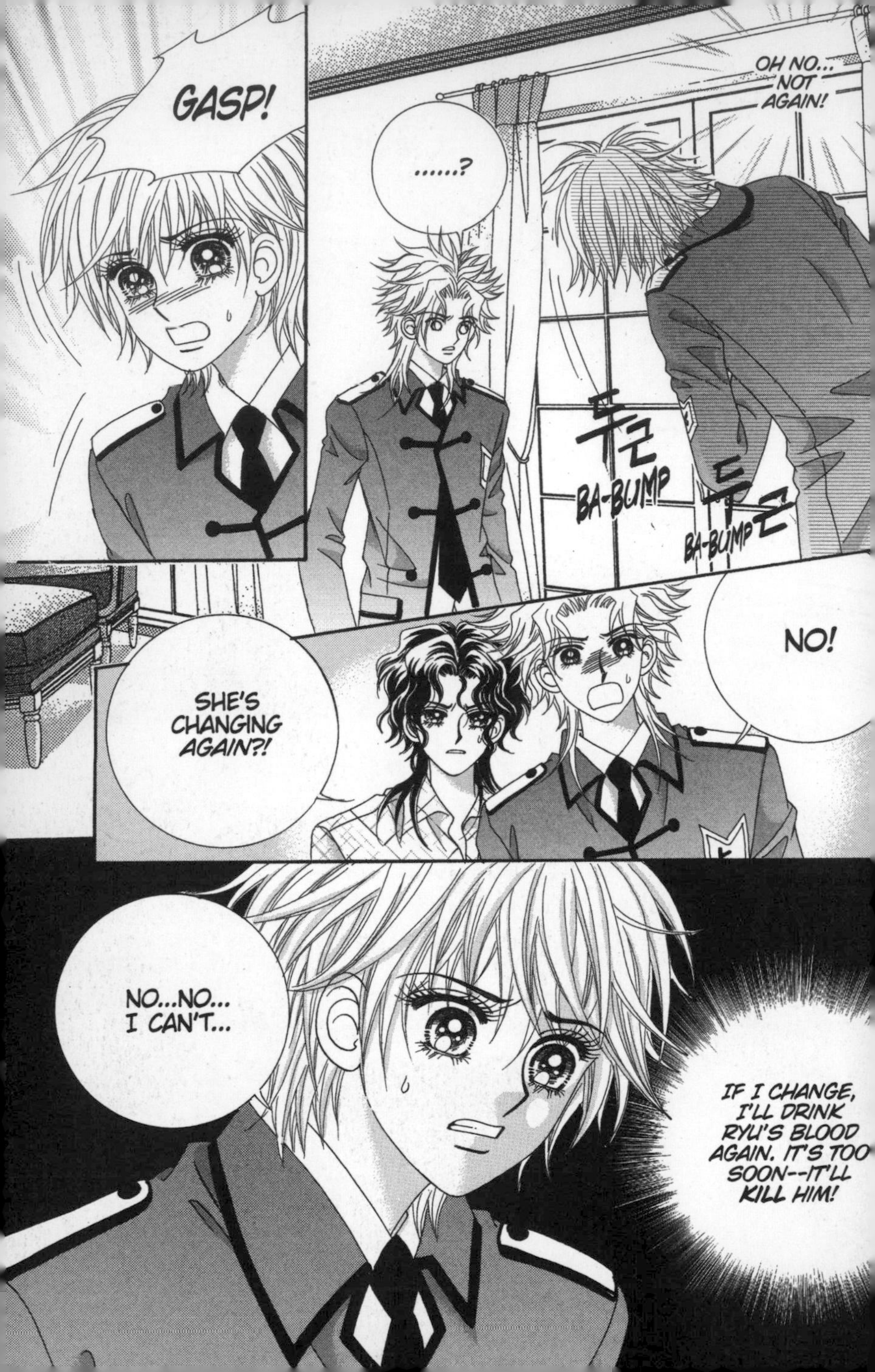
GASP!
......?
OH NO... NOT AGAIN!
두근
BA-BUMP
두근
BA-BUMP
SHE'S CHANGING AGAIN?!
NO!
NO...NO... I CAN'T...
IF I CHANGE, I'LL DRINK RYU'S BLOOD AGAIN. IT'S TOO SOON--IT'LL KILL HIM!

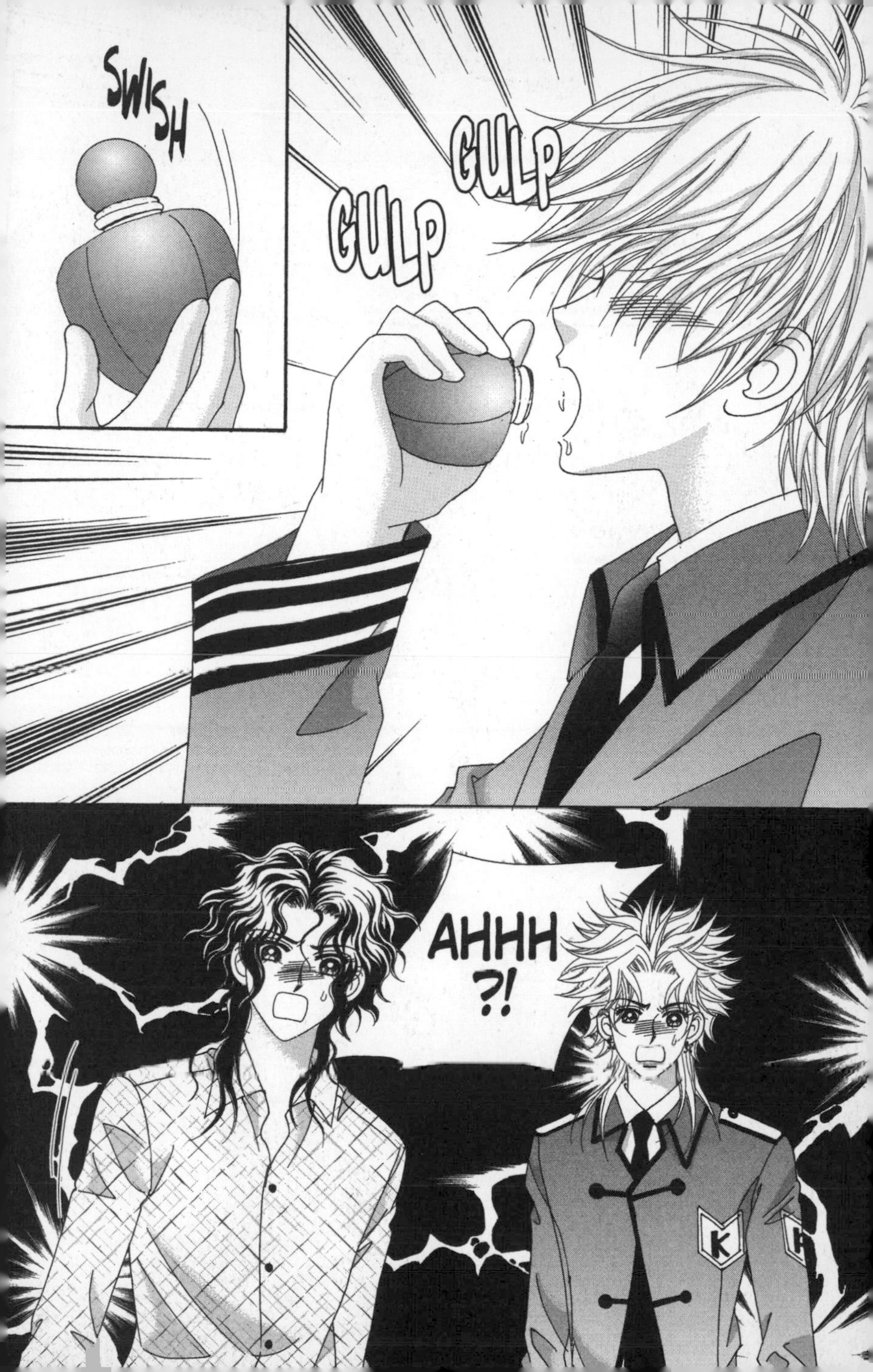
SWISH
GULP
GULP
AHHH ?!

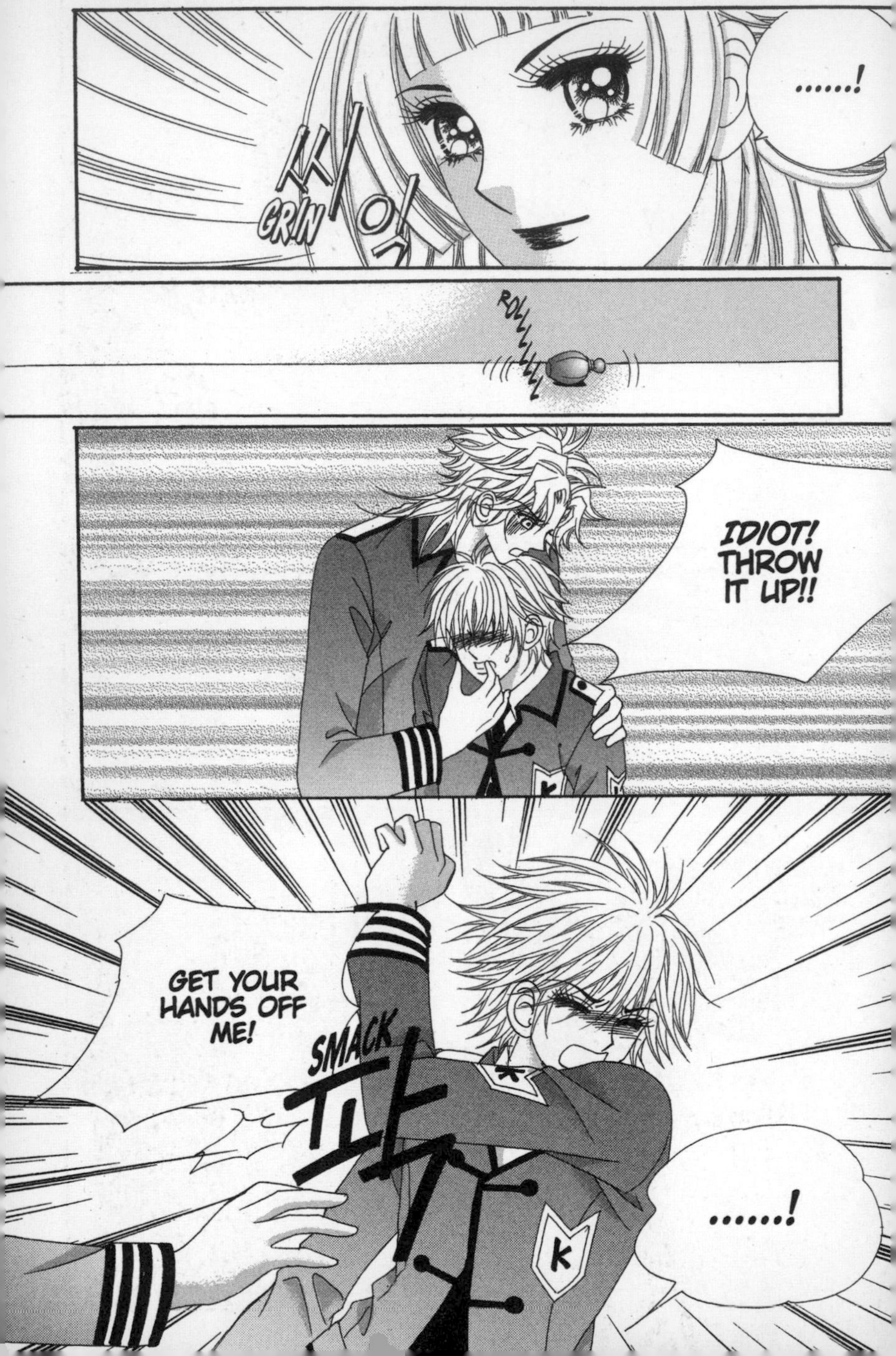
씨익
GRIN
......!
ROLLLLLLL
IDIOT! THROW IT UP!!
GET YOUR HANDS OFF ME!
SMACK
짝
......!

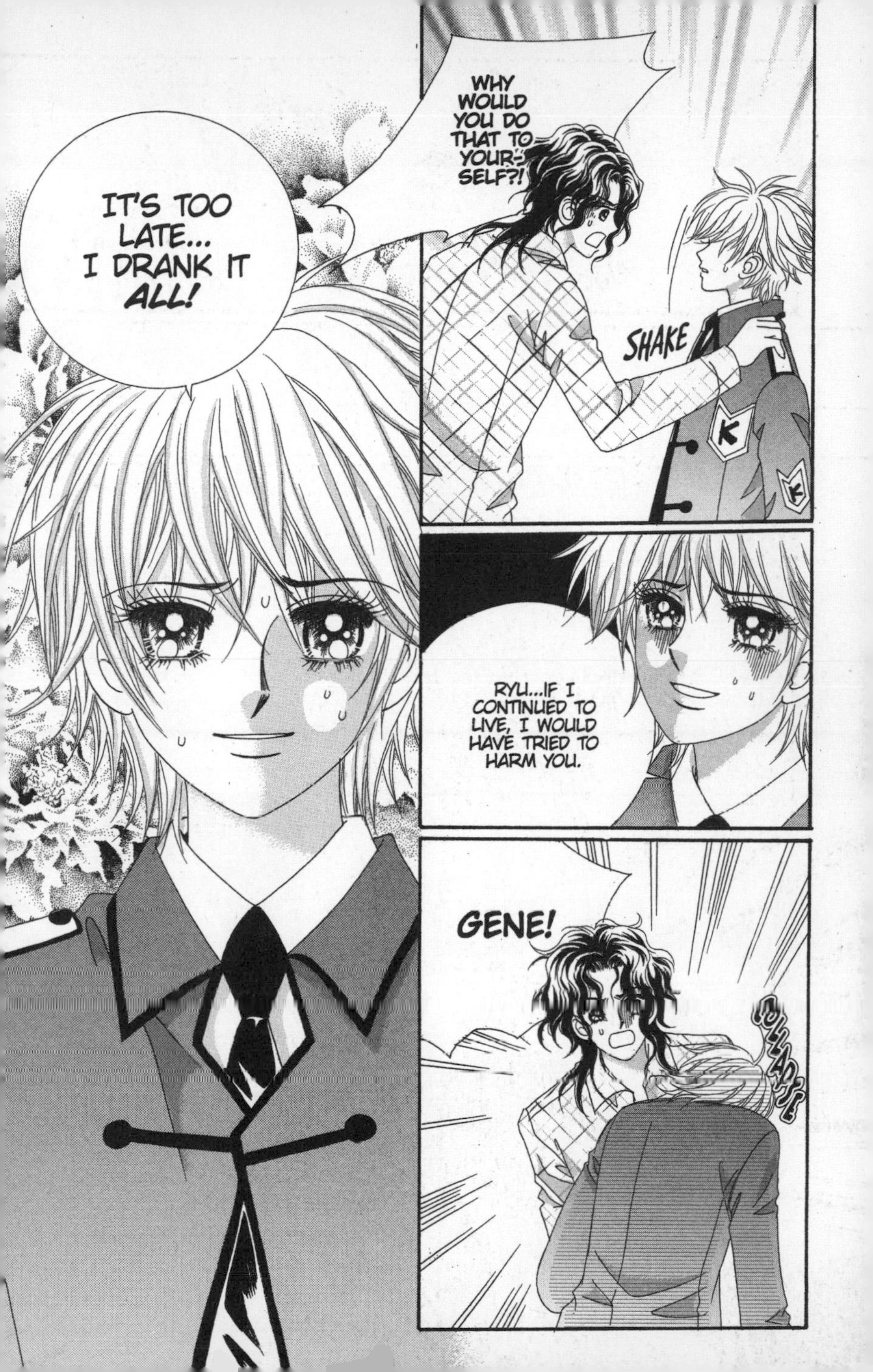
IT'S TOO LATE... I DRANK IT ALL!
WHY WOULD YOU DO THAT TO YOURSELF?!
SHAKE
RYU...IF I CONTINUED TO LIVE, I WOULD HAVE TRIED TO HARM YOU.
GENE!
COLLAPSE

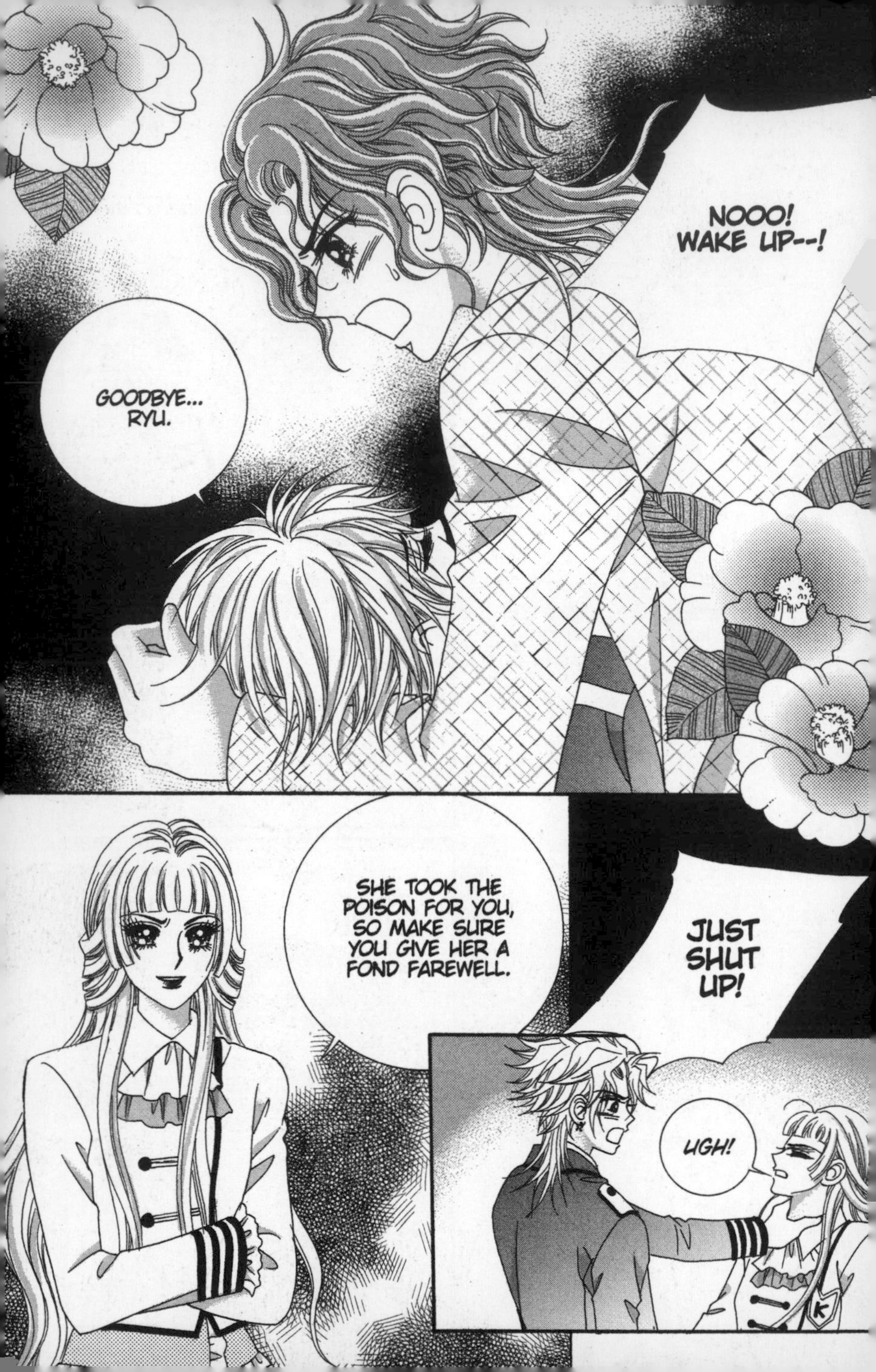
GOODBYE... RYU.
NOOO! WAKE UP--!
SHE TOOK THE POISON FOR YOU, SO MAKE SURE YOU GIVE HER A FOND FAREWELL.
JUST SHUT UP!
UGH!

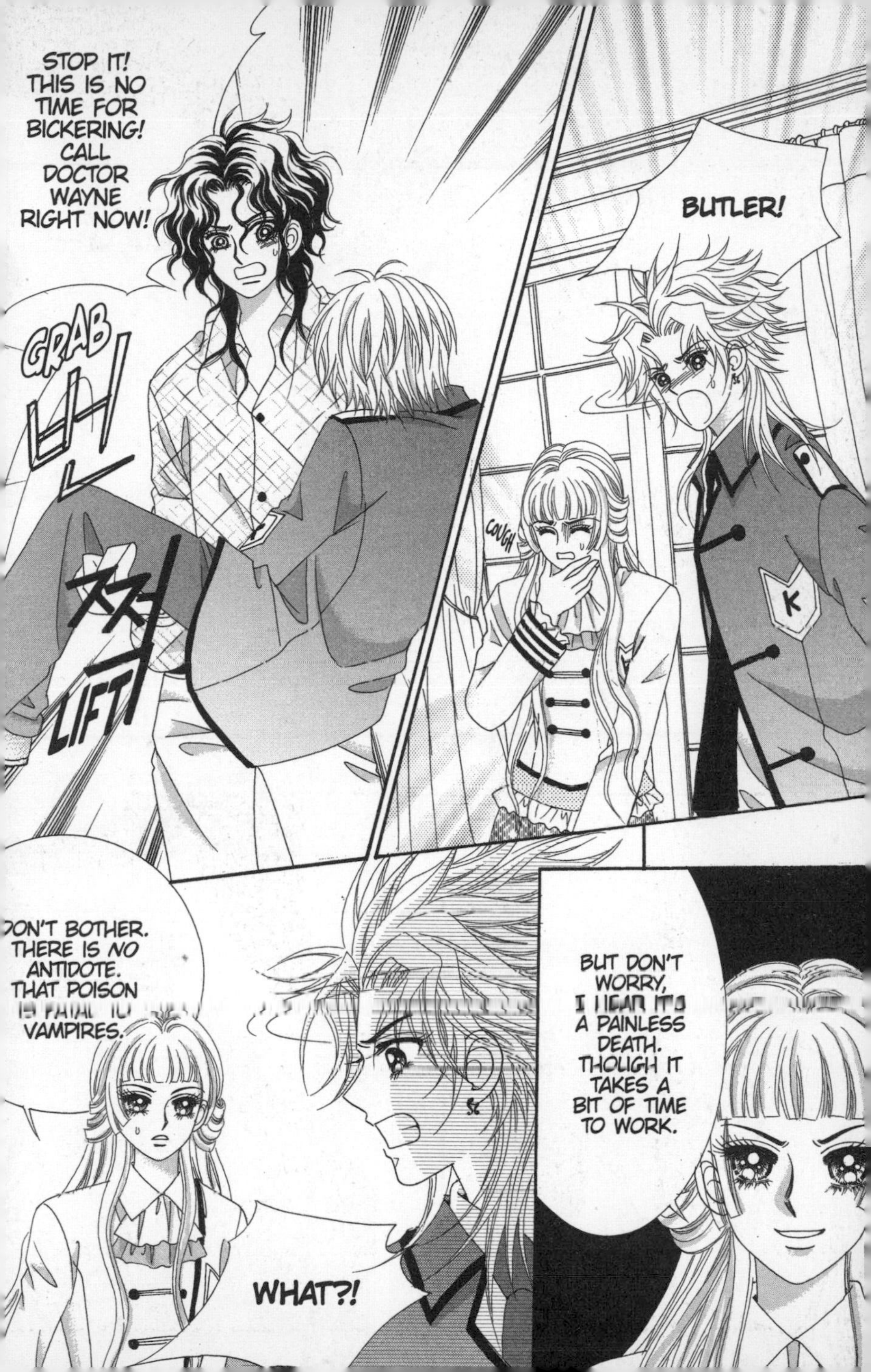
STOP IT! THIS IS NO TIME FOR BICKERING! CALL DOCTOR WAYNE RIGHT NOW!
GRAB
LIFT
BUTLER!
COUGH
DON'T BOTHER. THERE IS NO ANTIDOTE. THAT POISON IS FATAL TO VAMPIRES.
WHAT?!
BUT DON'T WORRY, I HEAR IT'S A PAINLESS DEATH. THOUGH IT TAKES A BIT OF TIME TO WORK.

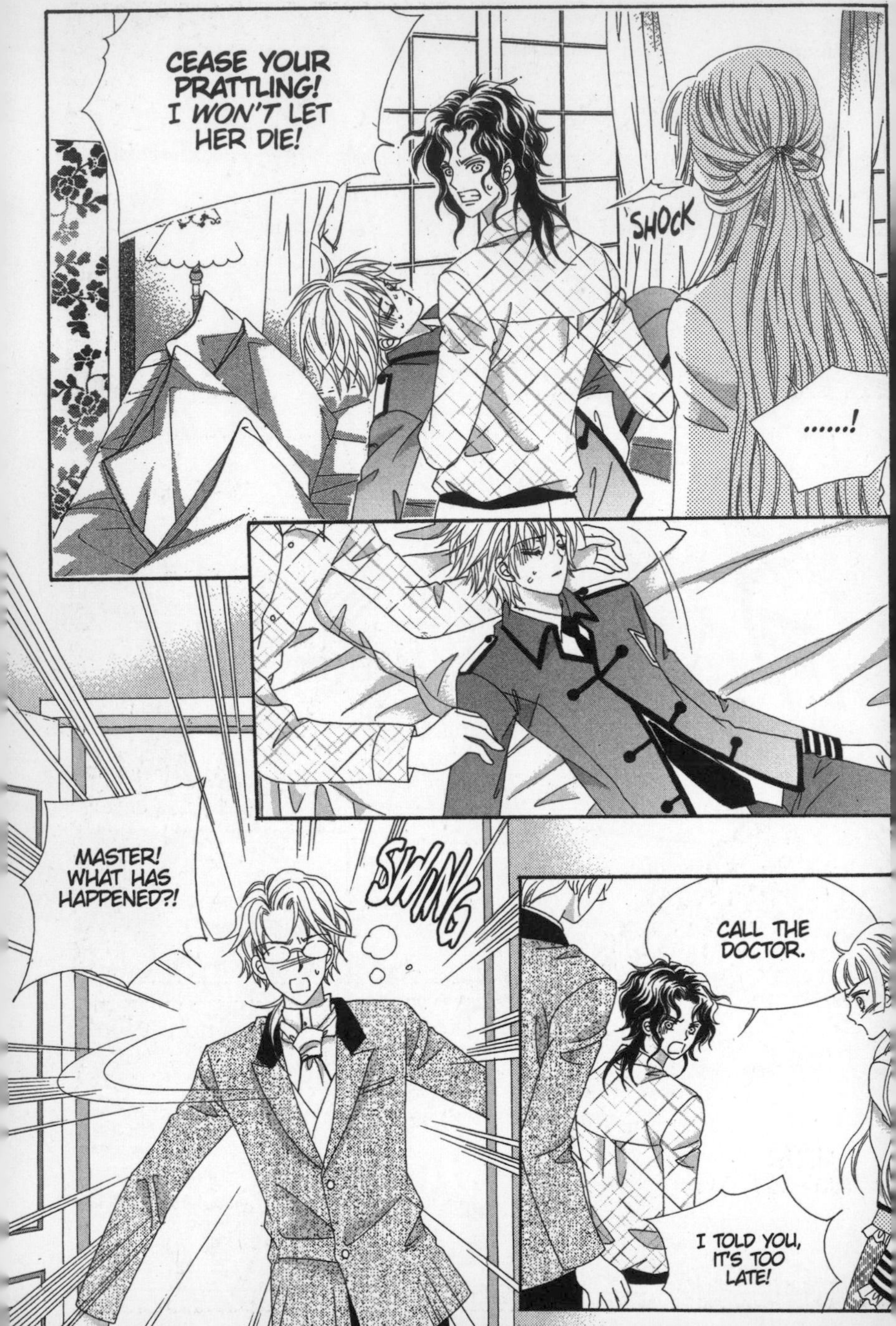
CEASE YOUR PRATTLING! I WON'T LET HER DIE!
SHOCK
......!
MASTER! WHAT HAS HAPPENED?!
SWING
CALL THE DOCTOR.
I TOLD YOU, IT'S TOO LATE!

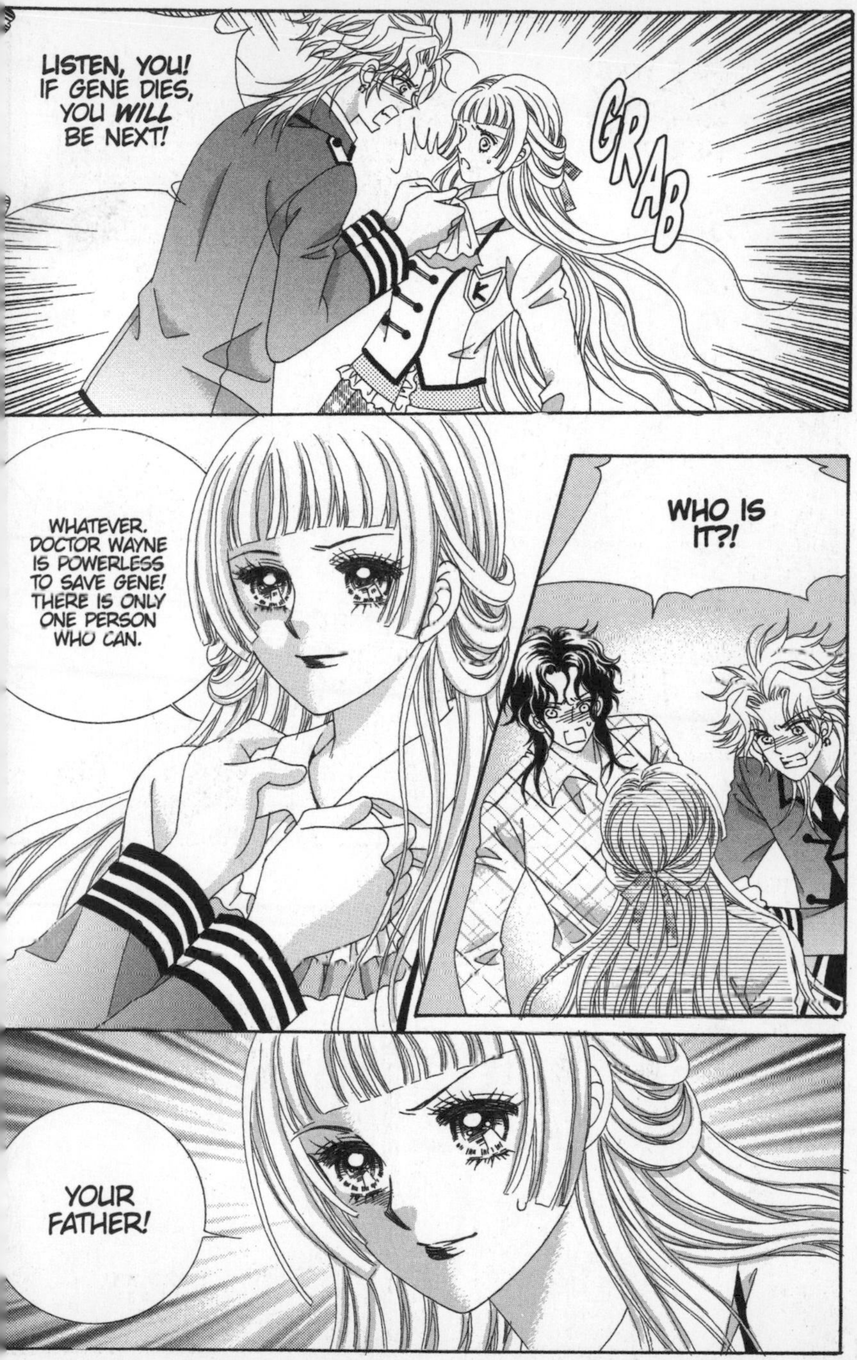
LISTEN, YOU! IF GENE DIES, YOU WILL BE NEXT!
GRAB
WHATEVER. DOCTOR WAYNE IS POWERLESS TO SAVE GENE! THERE IS ONLY ONE PERSON WHO CAN.
WHO IS IT?!
YOUR FATHER!

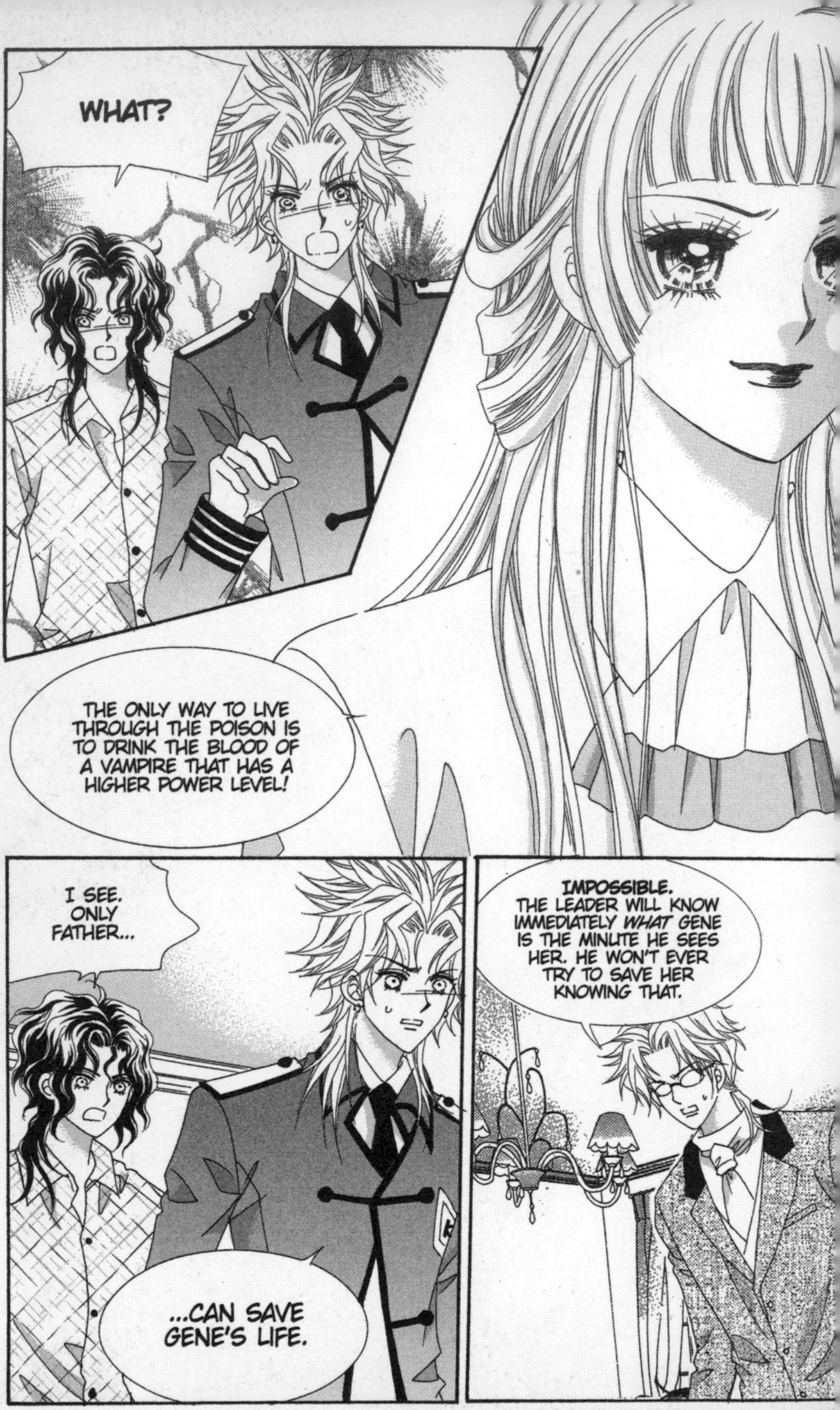
WHAT?
THE ONLY WAY TO LIVE THROUGH THE POISON IS TO DRINK THE BLOOD OF A VAMPIRE THAT HAS A HIGHER POWER LEVEL!
I SEE. ONLY FATHER...
...CAN SAVE GENE'S LIFE.
IMPOSSIBLE. THE LEADER WILL KNOW IMMEDIATELY *WHAT* GENE IS THE MINUTE HE SEES HER. HE WON'T EVER TRY TO SAVE HER KNOWING THAT.

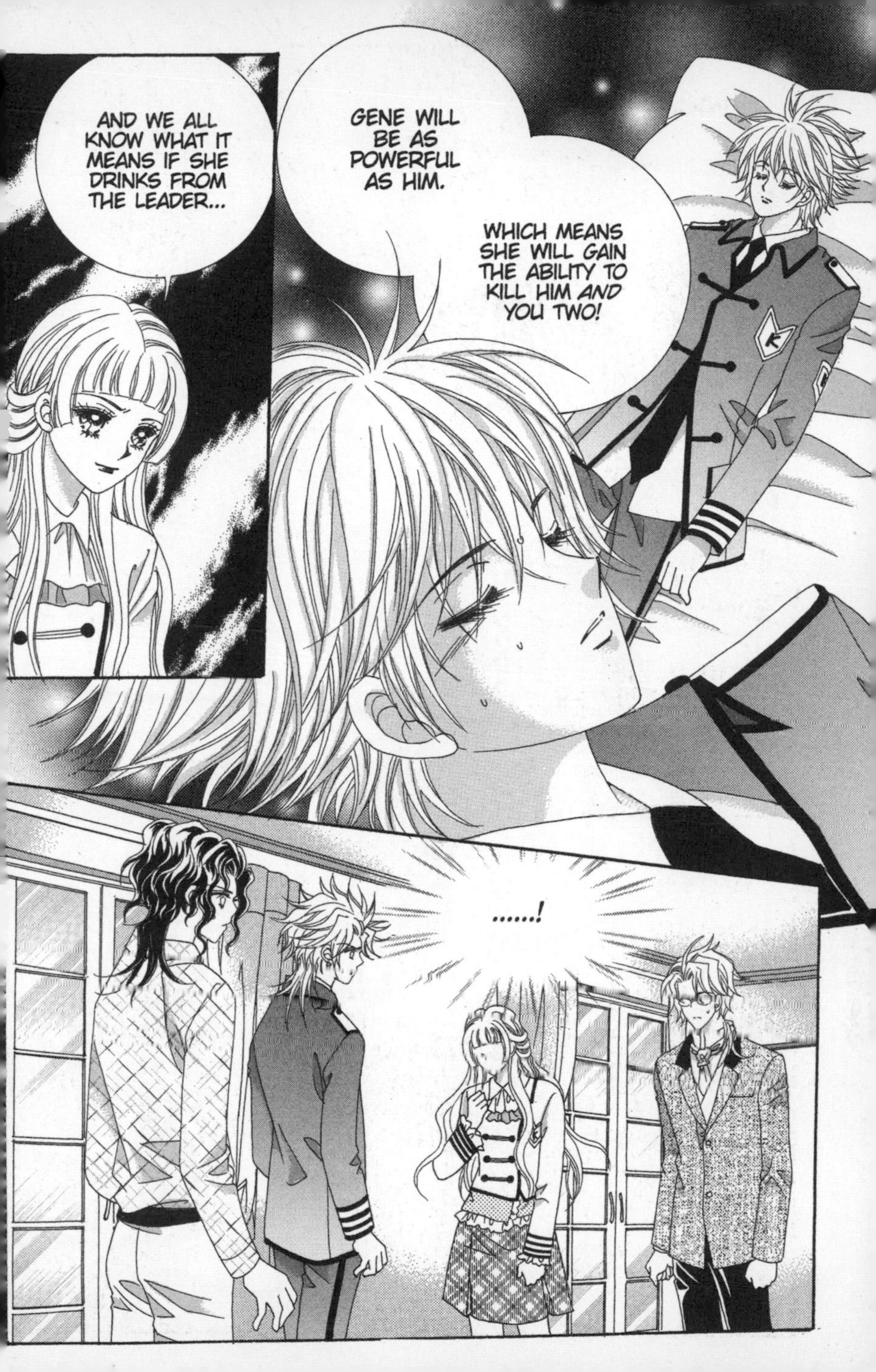
AND WE ALL KNOW WHAT IT MEANS IF SHE DRINKS FROM THE LEADER...
GENE WILL BE AS POWERFUL AS HIM.
WHICH MEANS SHE WILL GAIN THE ABILITY TO KILL HIM *AND* YOU TWO!
......!

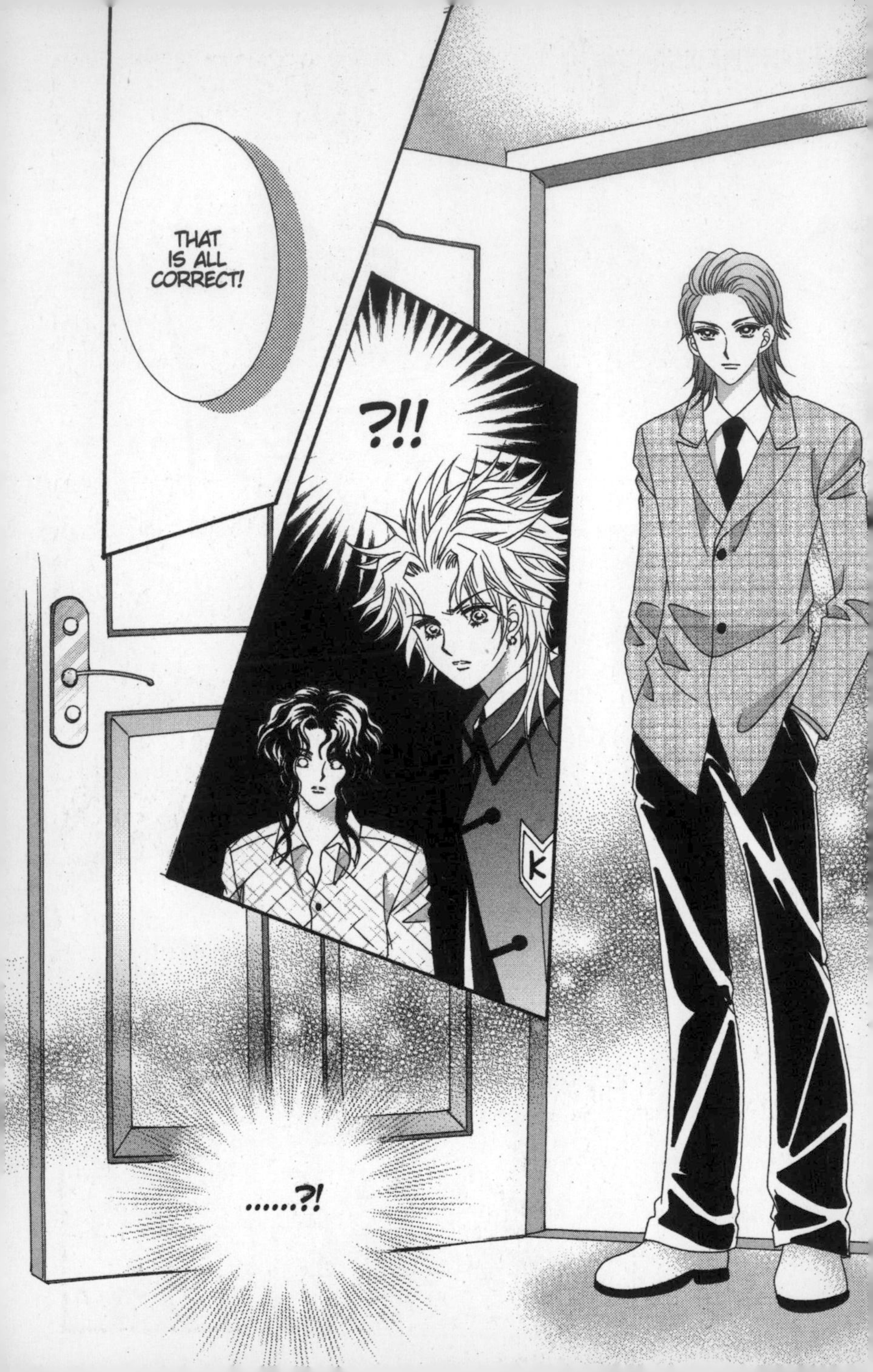
THAT IS ALL CORRECT!
?!!
......?!

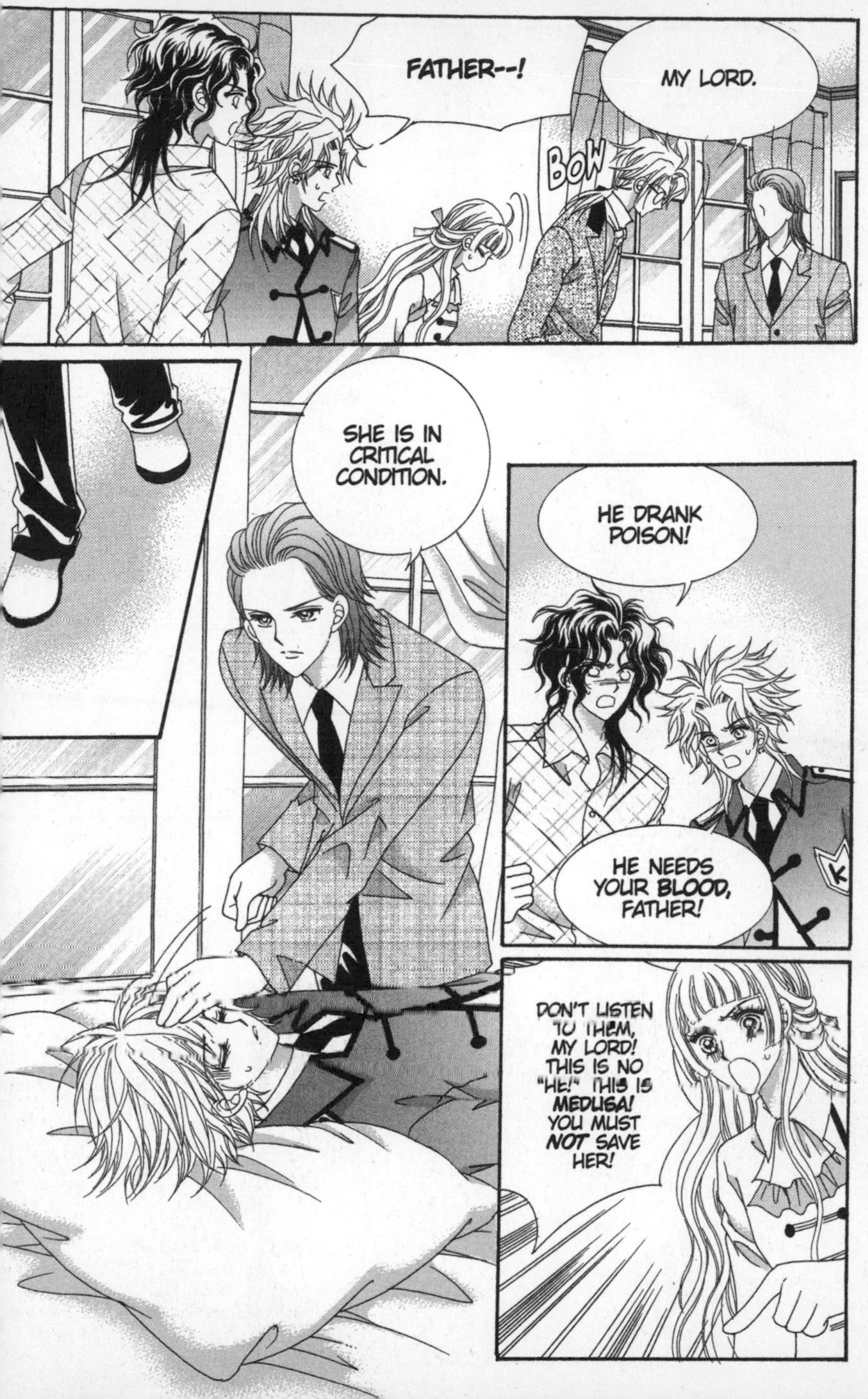
FATHER--!
BOW
MY LORD.
SHE IS IN CRITICAL CONDITION.
HE DRANK POISON!
HE NEEDS YOUR BLOOD, FATHER!
DON'T LISTEN TO THEM, MY LORD! THIS IS NO "HE!" THIS IS MEDUSA! YOU MUST NOT SAVE HER!

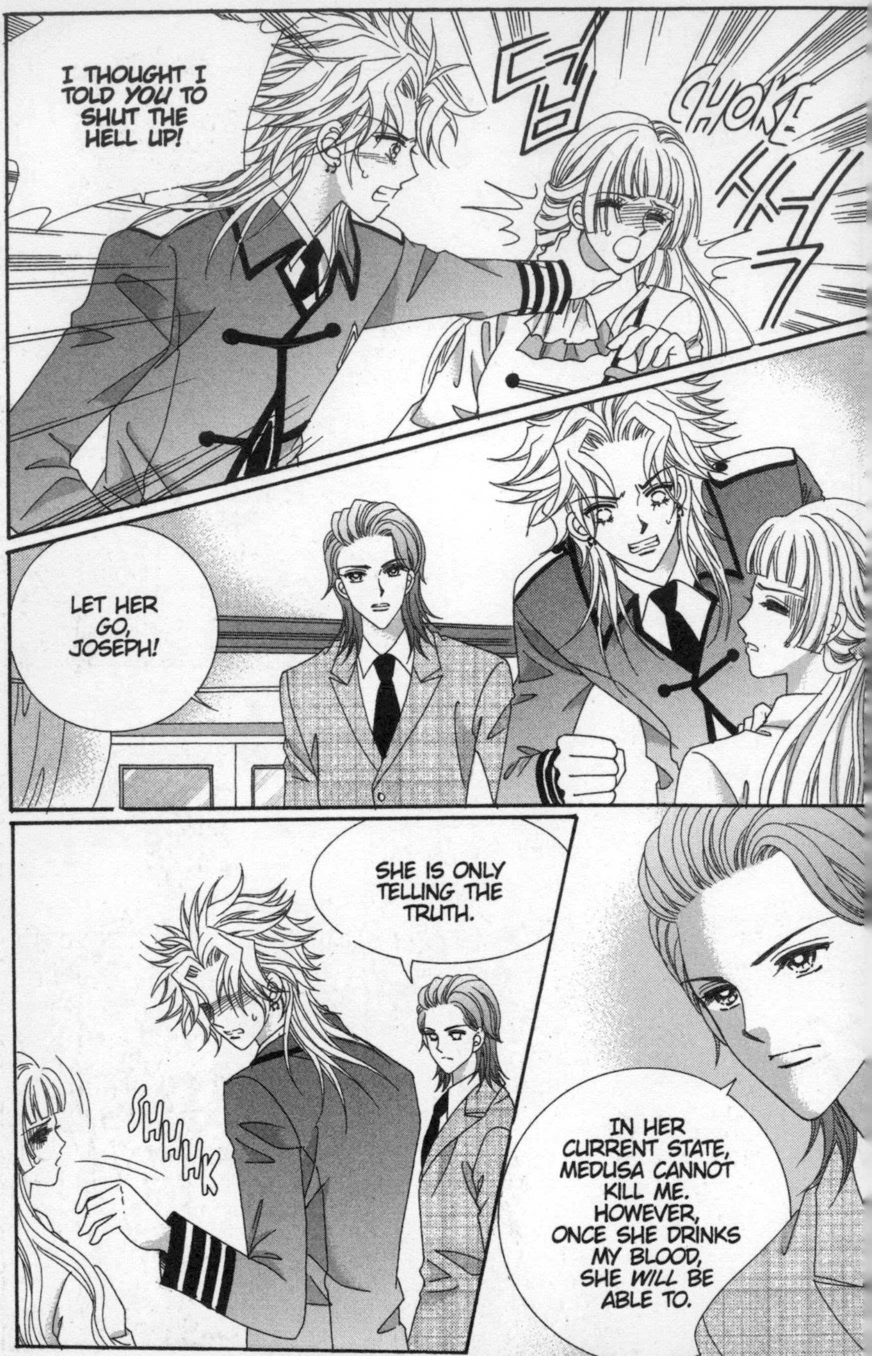

I THOUGHT I TOLD *YOU* TO SHUT THE HELL UP!
CHOKE
LET HER GO, JOSEPH!
SHE IS ONLY TELLING THE TRUTH.
SHHHK
IN HER CURRENT STATE, MEDUSA CANNOT KILL ME. HOWEVER, ONCE SHE DRINKS MY BLOOD, SHE *WILL* BE ABLE TO.

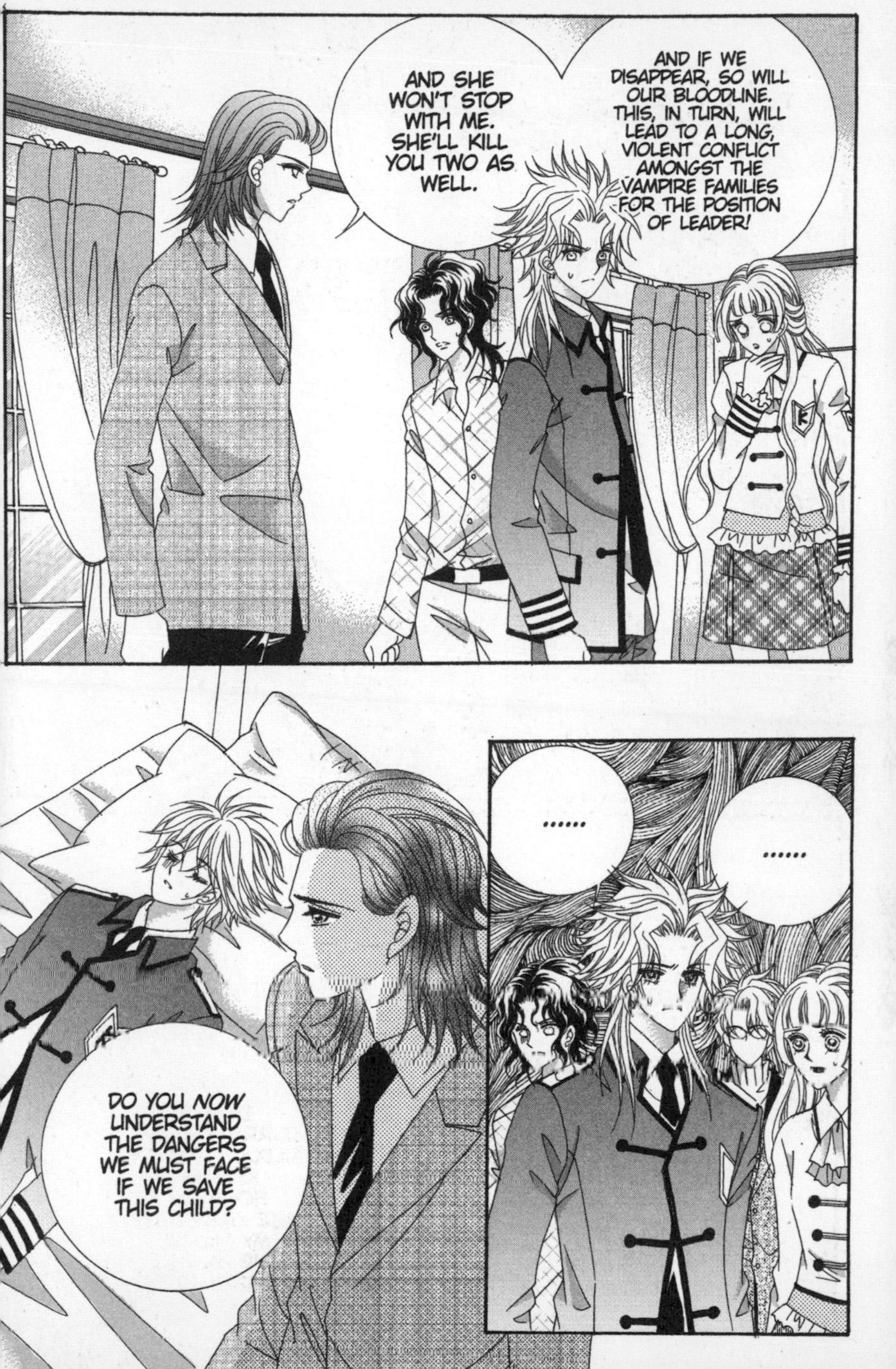
AND SHE WON'T STOP WITH ME. SHE'LL KILL YOU TWO AS WELL.
AND IF WE DISAPPEAR, SO WILL OUR BLOODLINE. THIS, IN TURN, WILL LEAD TO A LONG, VIOLENT CONFLICT AMONGST THE VAMPIRE FAMILIES FOR THE POSITION OF LEADER!
DO YOU *NOW* UNDERSTAND THE DANGERS WE MUST FACE IF WE SAVE THIS CHILD?
......
......

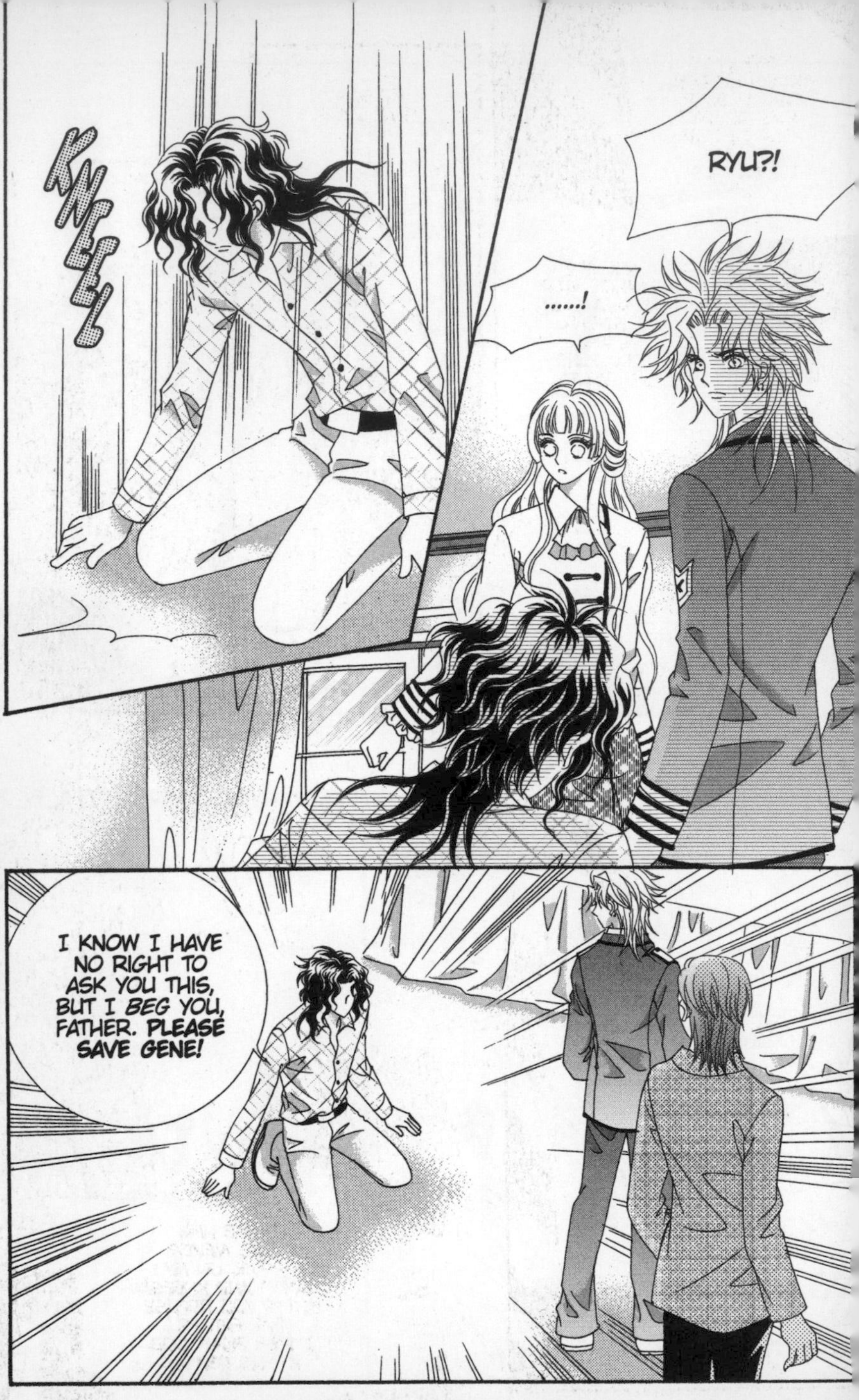
KNEEL
RYU?!
......!
I KNOW I HAVE NO RIGHT TO ASK YOU THIS, BUT I *BEG* YOU, FATHER. PLEASE SAVE GENE!

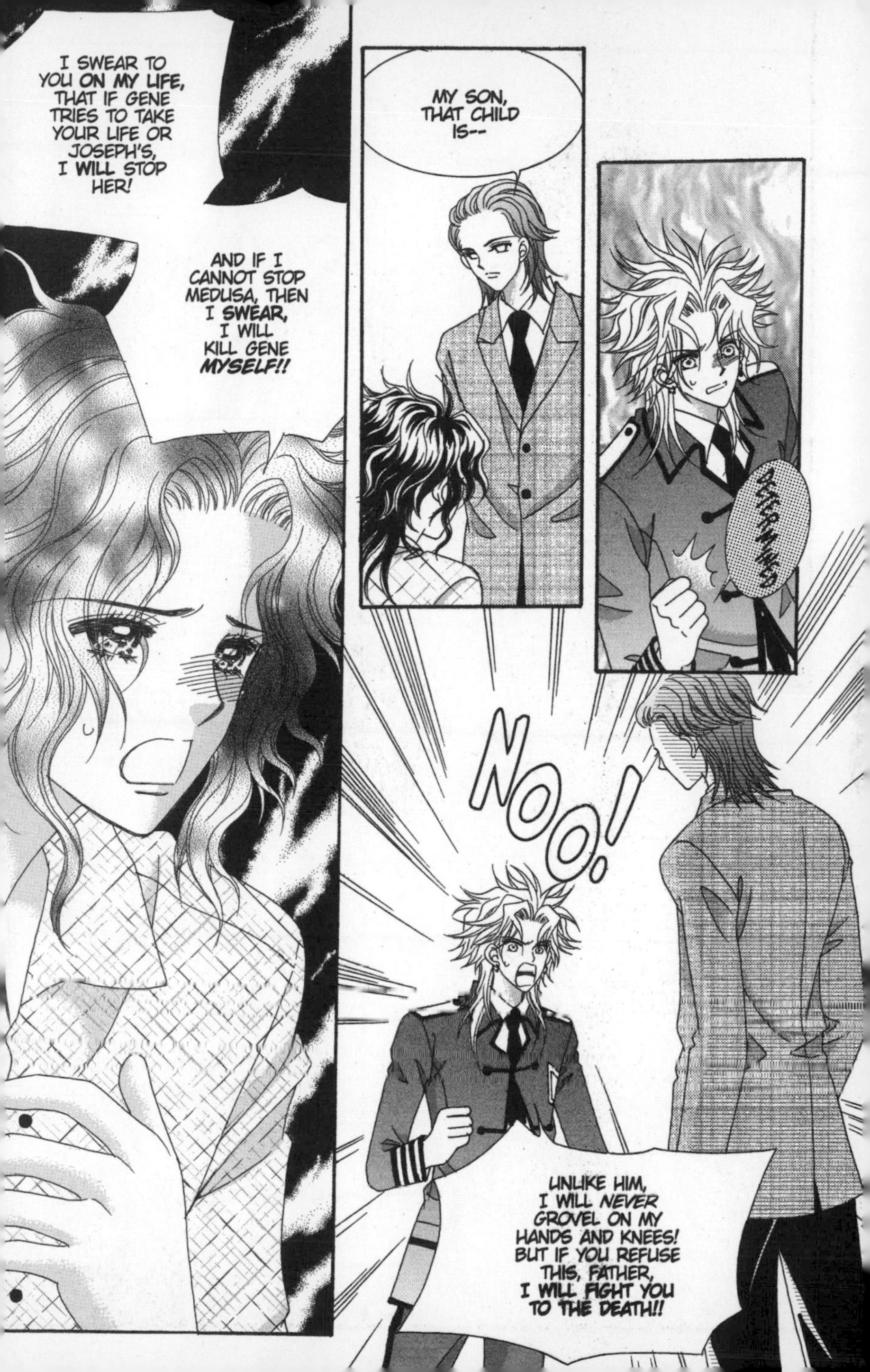
I SWEAR TO YOU ON MY LIFE, THAT IF GENE TRIES TO TAKE YOUR LIFE OR JOSEPH'S, I WILL STOP HER!
AND IF I CANNOT STOP MEDUSA, THEN I SWEAR, I WILL KILL GENE MYSELF!!
MY SON, THAT CHILD IS--
DETERMINED
NOO!
UNLIKE HIM, I WILL NEVER GROVEL ON MY HANDS AND KNEES! BUT IF YOU REFUSE THIS, FATHER, I WILL FIGHT YOU TO THE DEATH!!

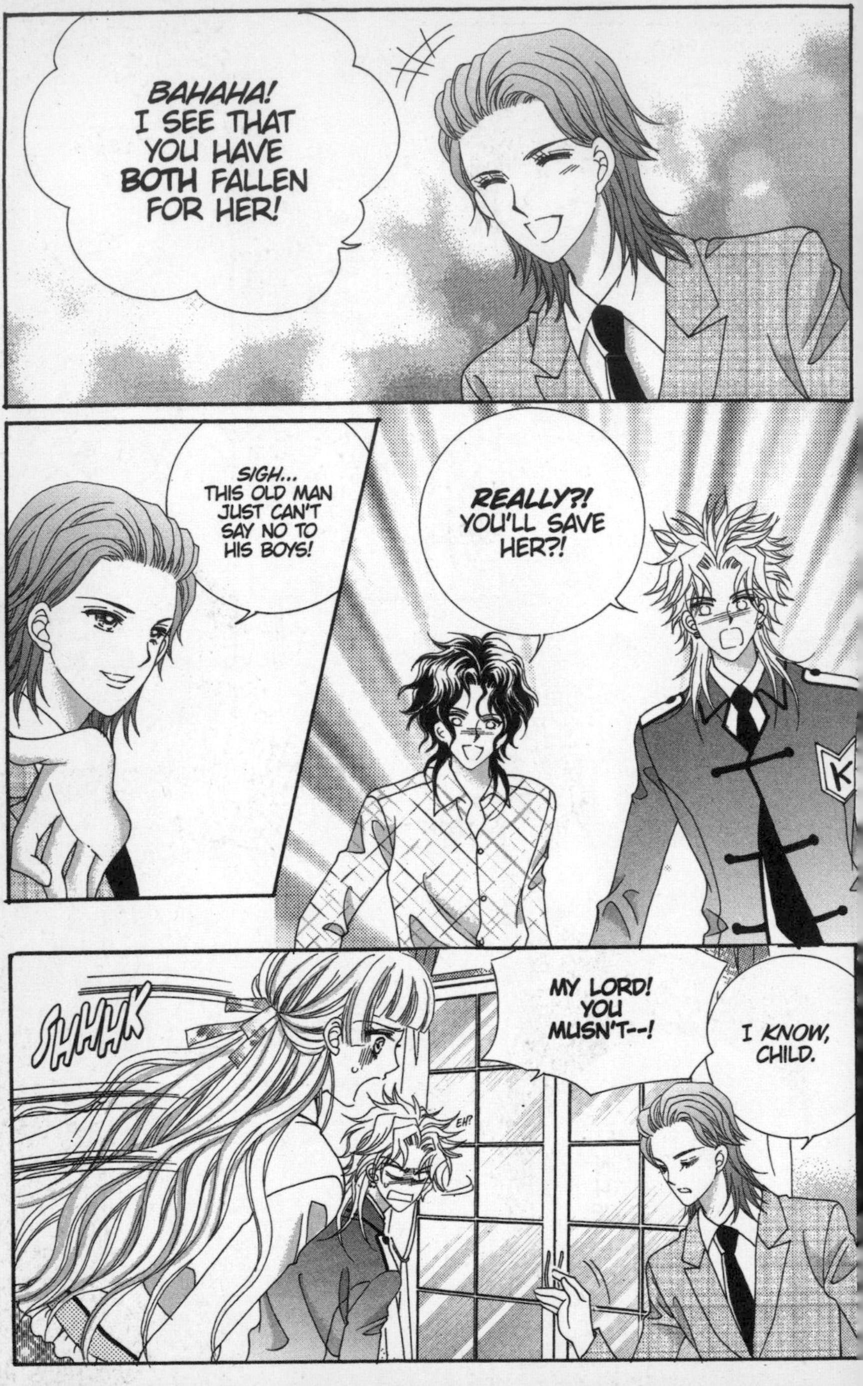
BAHAHA! I SEE THAT YOU HAVE BOTH FALLEN FOR HER!
SIGH... THIS OLD MAN JUST CAN'T SAY NO TO HIS BOYS!
REALLY?! YOU'LL SAVE HER?!
SHHHK
MY LORD! YOU MUSN'T--!
I KNOW, CHILD.
EH?

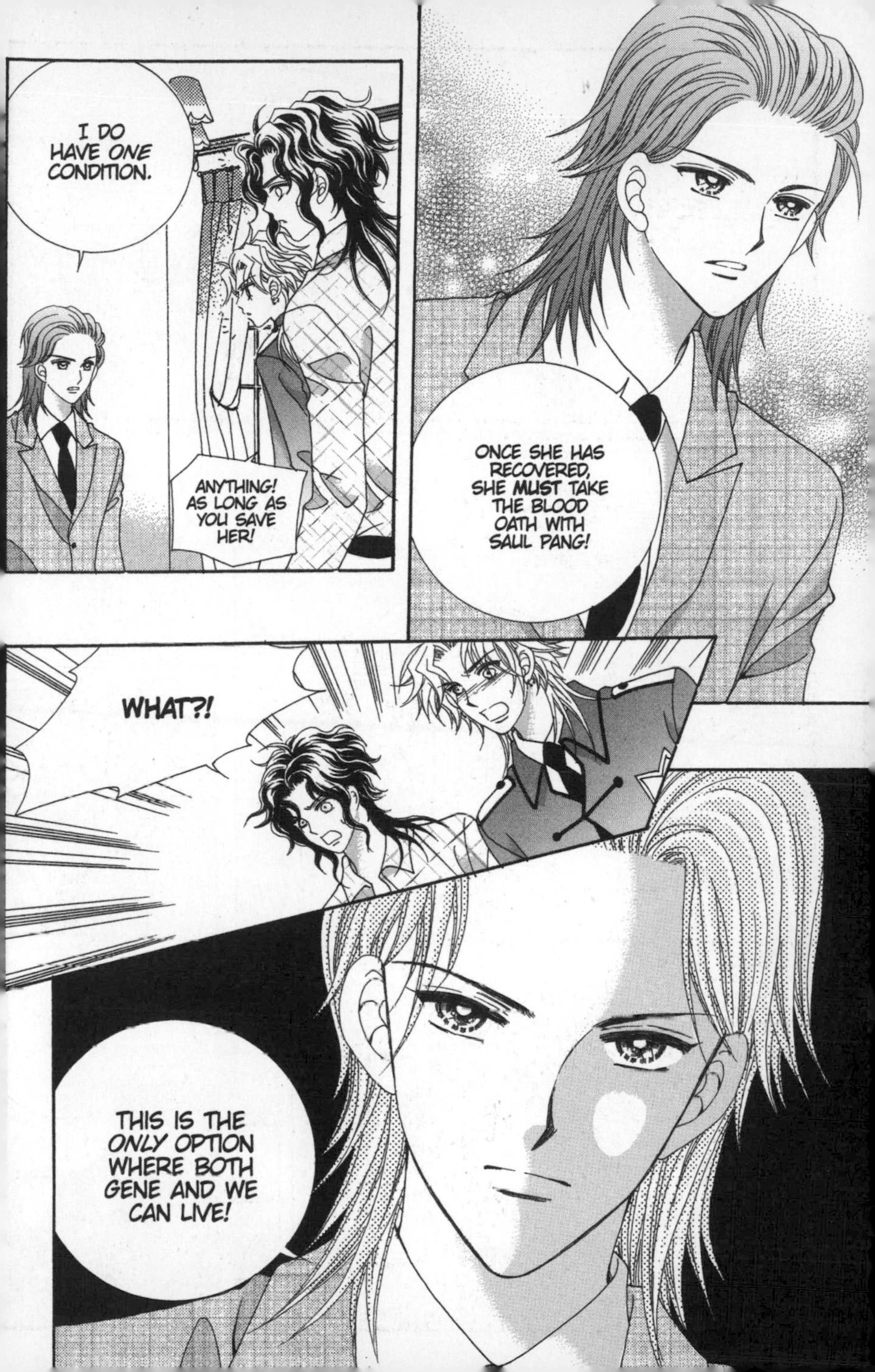
I DO HAVE *ONE* CONDITION.
ANYTHING! AS LONG AS YOU SAVE HER!
ONCE SHE HAS RECOVERED, SHE **MUST** TAKE THE BLOOD OATH WITH SAUL PANG!
WHAT?!
THIS IS THE *ONLY* OPTION WHERE BOTH GENE AND WE CAN LIVE!

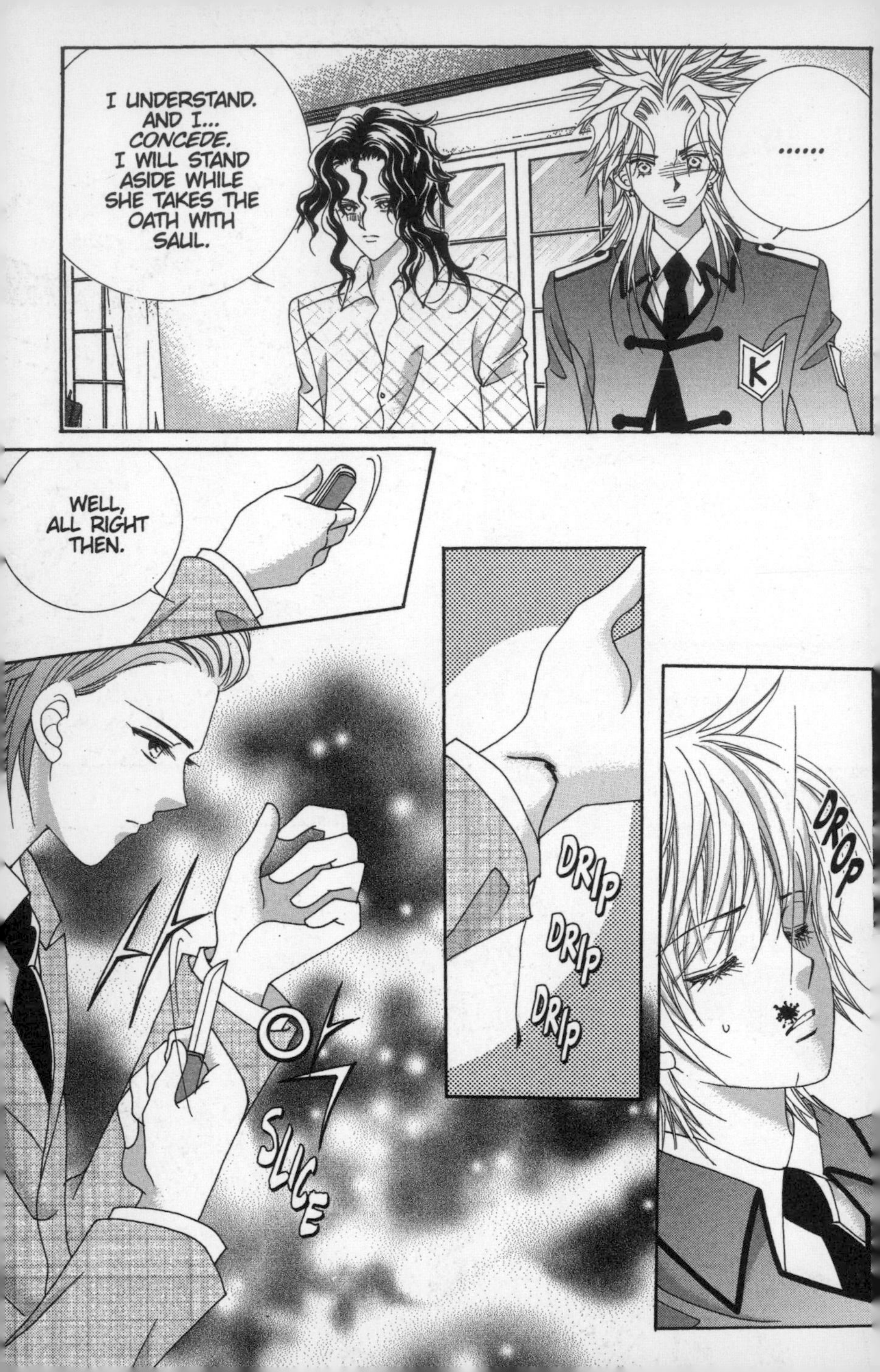
I UNDERSTAND. AND I... CONCEDE. I WILL STAND ASIDE WHILE SHE TAKES THE OATH WITH SAUL.
......
WELL, ALL RIGHT THEN.
SLICE
DRIP
DRIP
DRIP
DROP

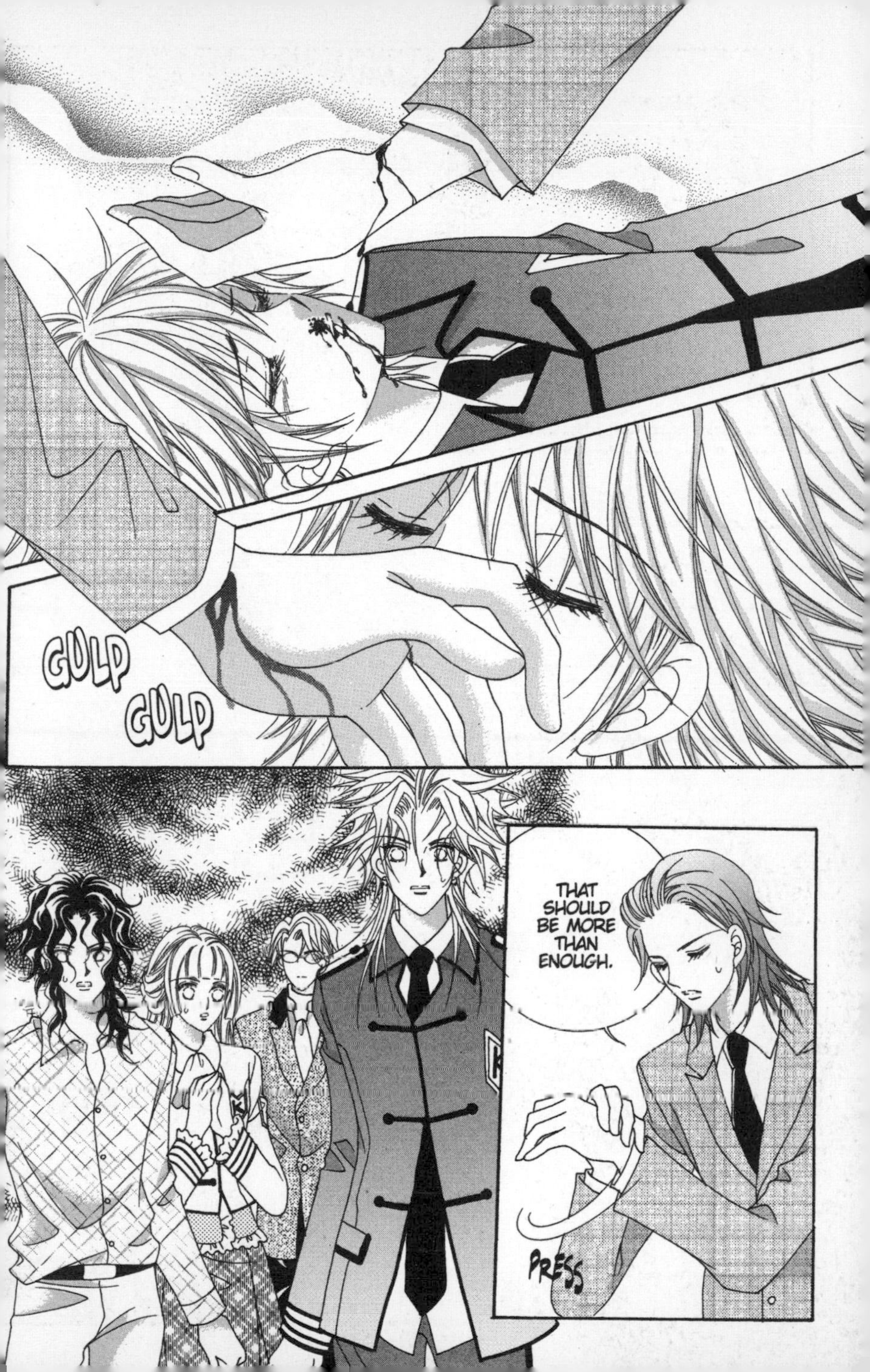
GULP GULP
THAT SHOULD BE MORE THAN ENOUGH.
PRESS

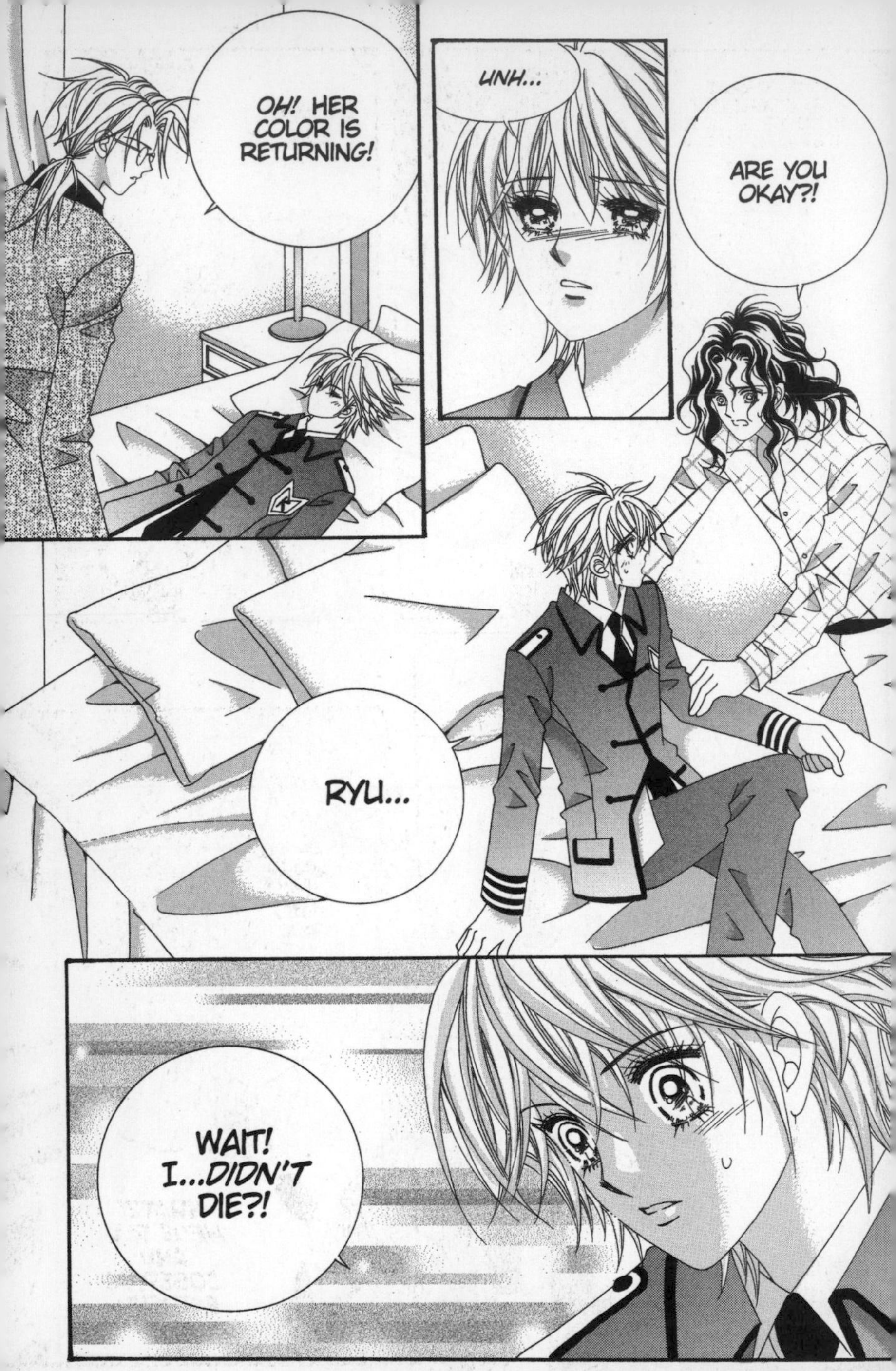
OH! HER COLOR IS RETURNING!
UNH...
ARE YOU OKAY?!
RYU...
WAIT! I...DIDN'T DIE?!

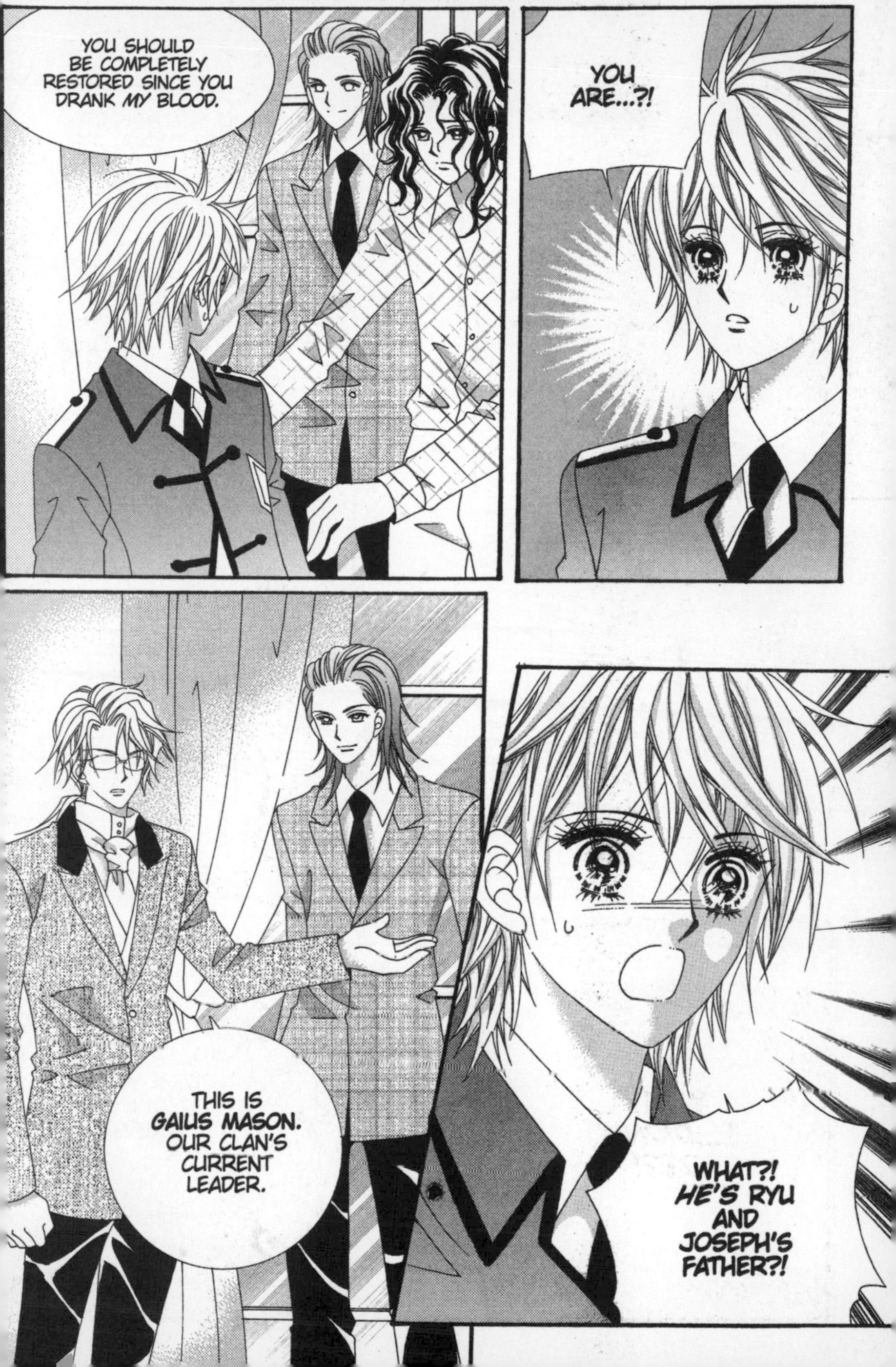
YOU SHOULD BE COMPLETELY RESTORED SINCE YOU DRANK MY BLOOD.
YOU ARE...?!
THIS IS GAIUS MASON. OUR CLAN'S CURRENT LEADER.
WHAT?! HE'S RYU AND JOSEPH'S FATHER?!

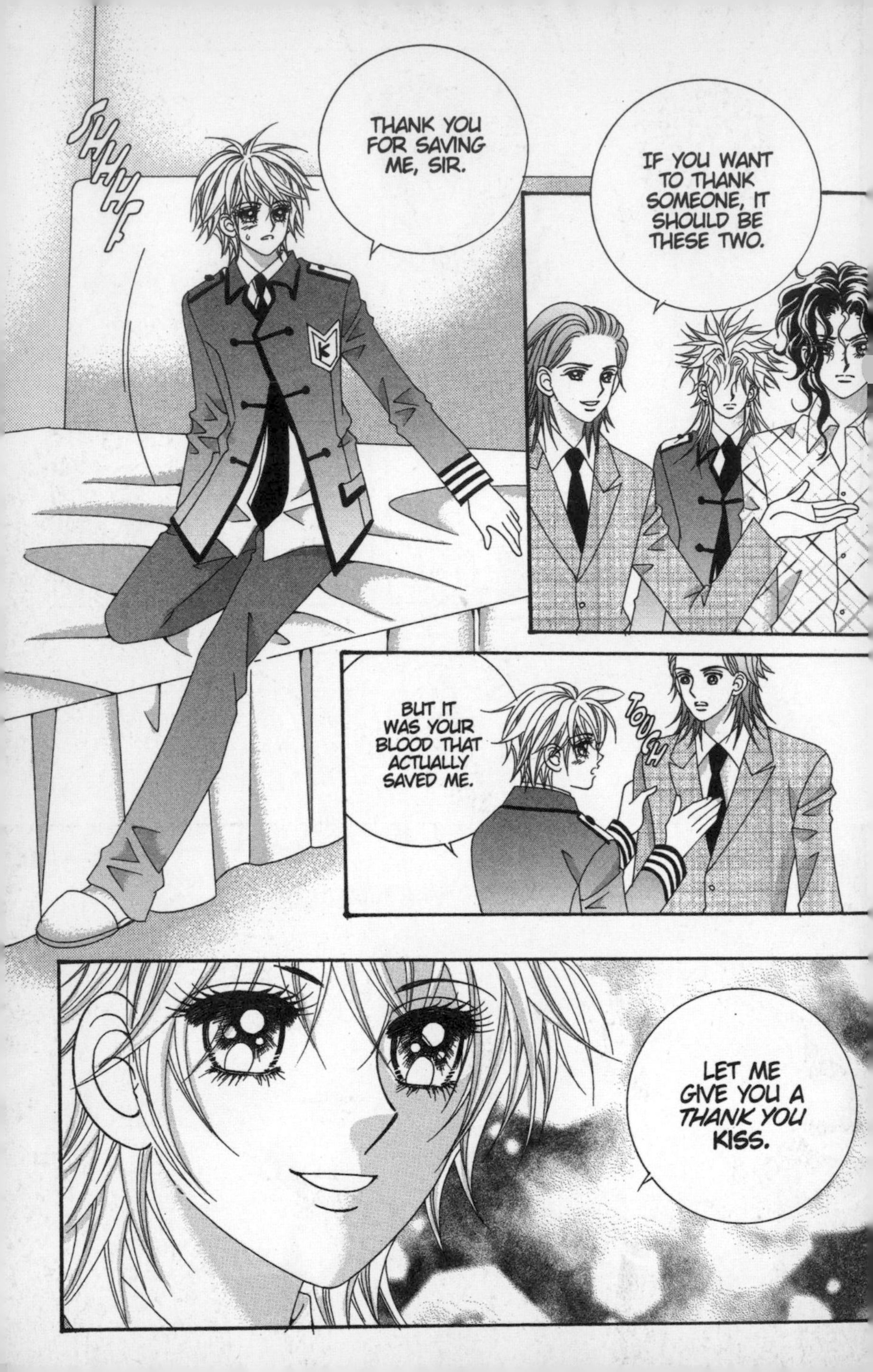
SHHHF
THANK YOU FOR SAVING ME, SIR.
IF YOU WANT TO THANK SOMEONE, IT SHOULD BE THESE TWO.
BUT IT WAS YOUR BLOOD THAT ACTUALLY SAVED ME.
TOUCH
LET ME GIVE YOU A *THANK YOU* KISS.

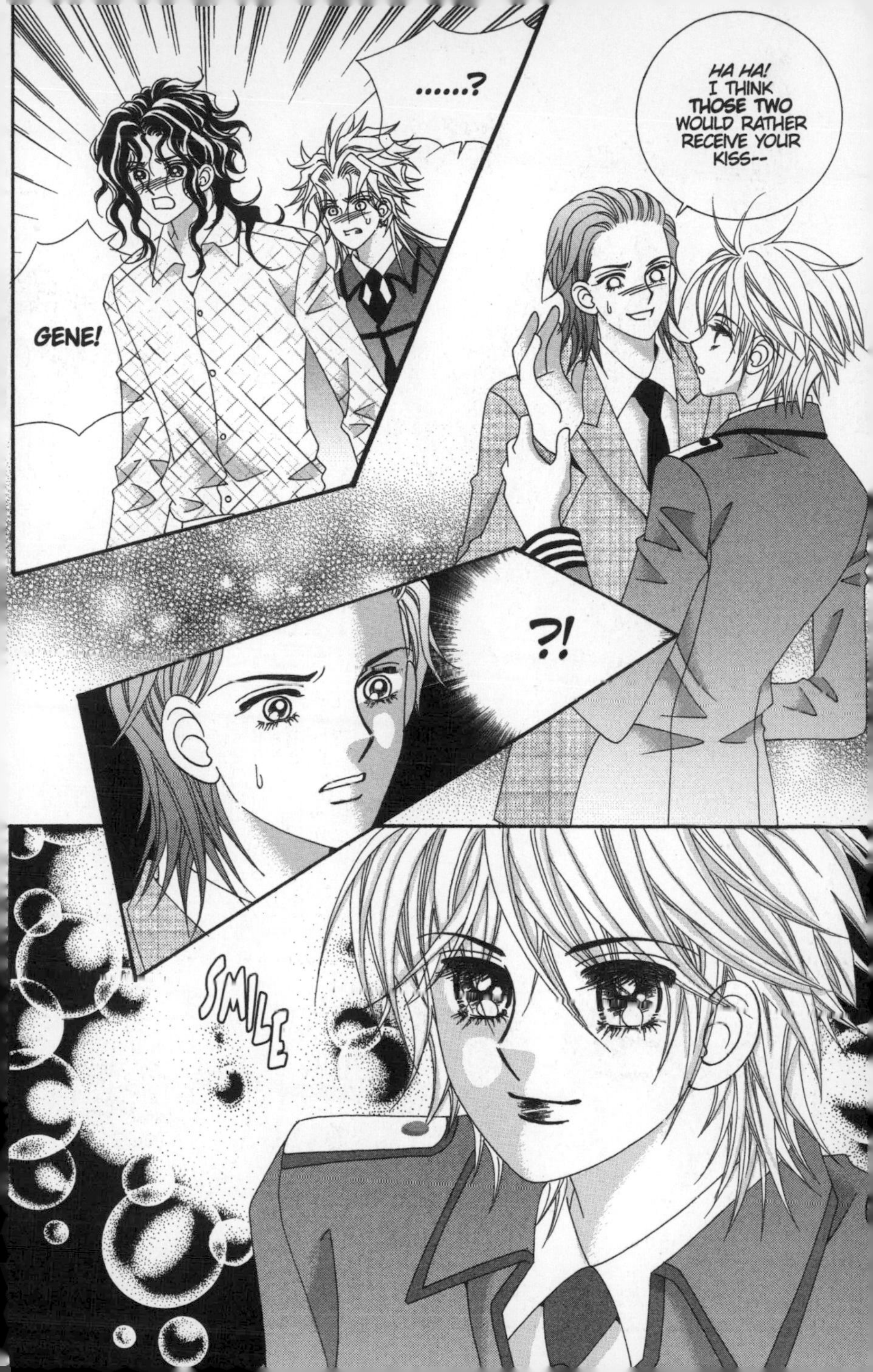
......?
GENE!
HA HA! I THINK THOSE TWO WOULD RATHER RECEIVE YOUR KISS--
?!
SMILE

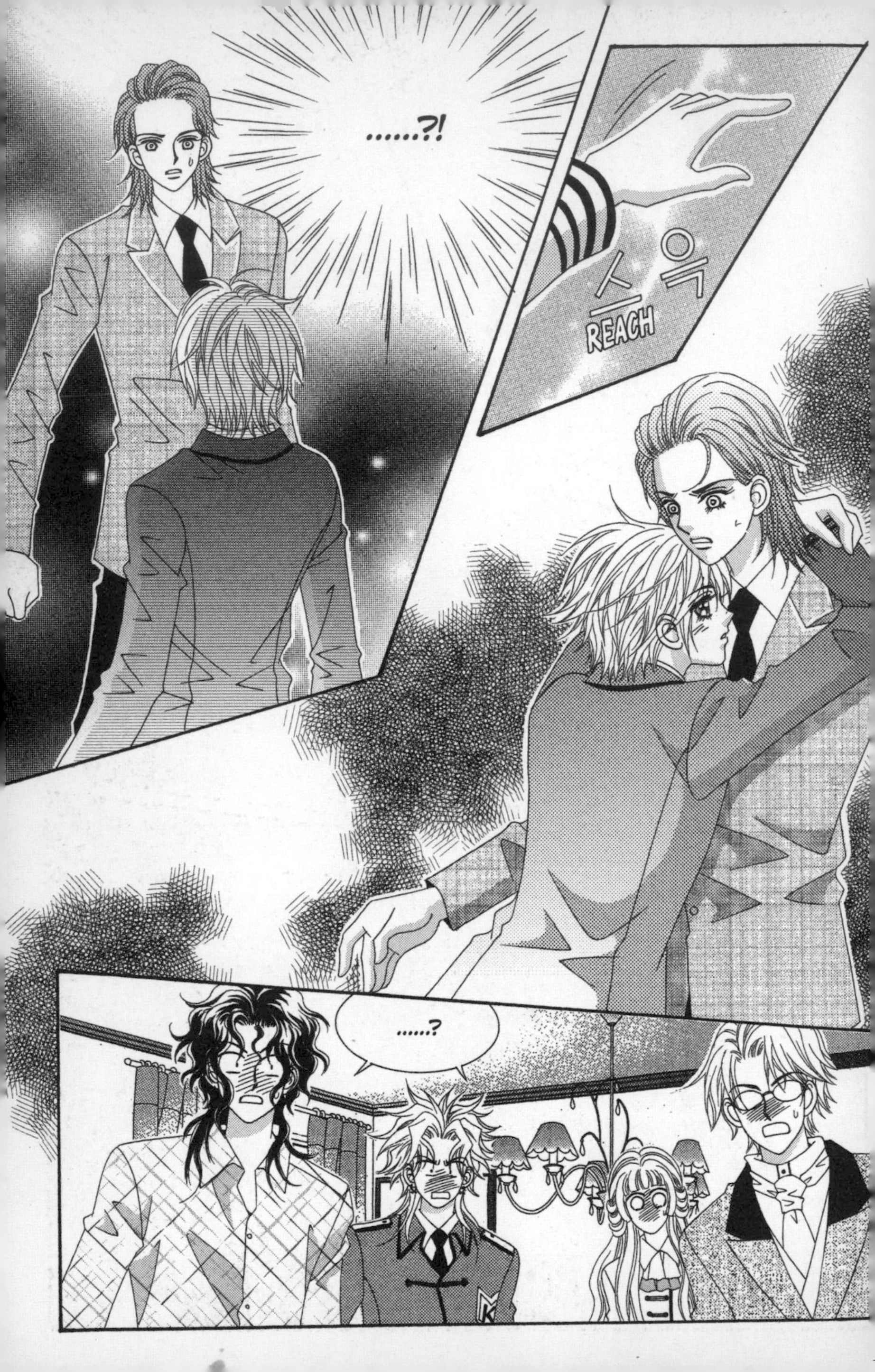
......?!
REACH
......?

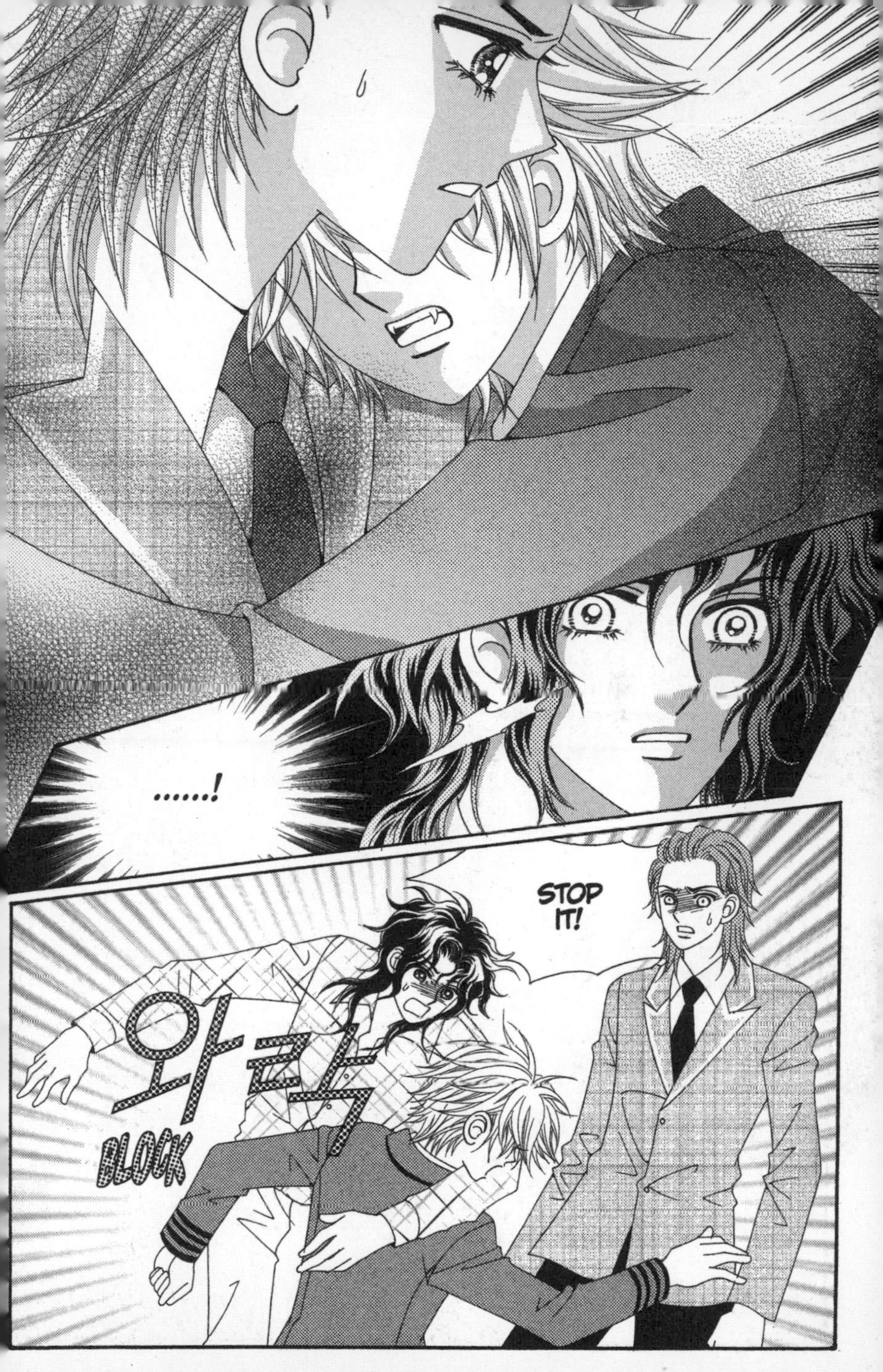

......!
STOP IT!
와락
BLOCK

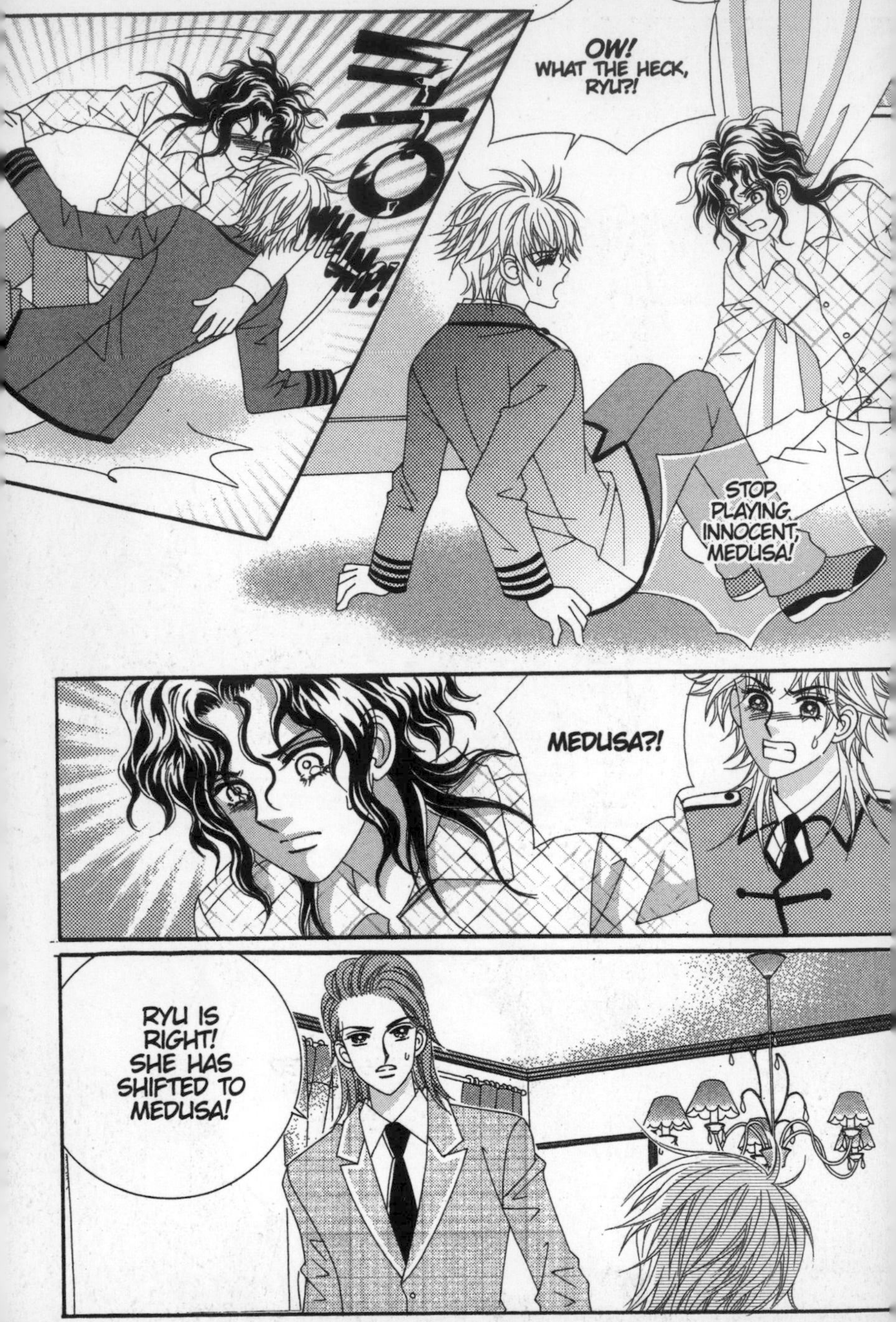
쿵
WHUMP!
OW! WHAT THE HECK, RYU?!
STOP PLAYING INNOCENT, MEDUSA!
MEDUSA?!
RYU IS RIGHT! SHE HAS SHIFTED TO MEDUSA!

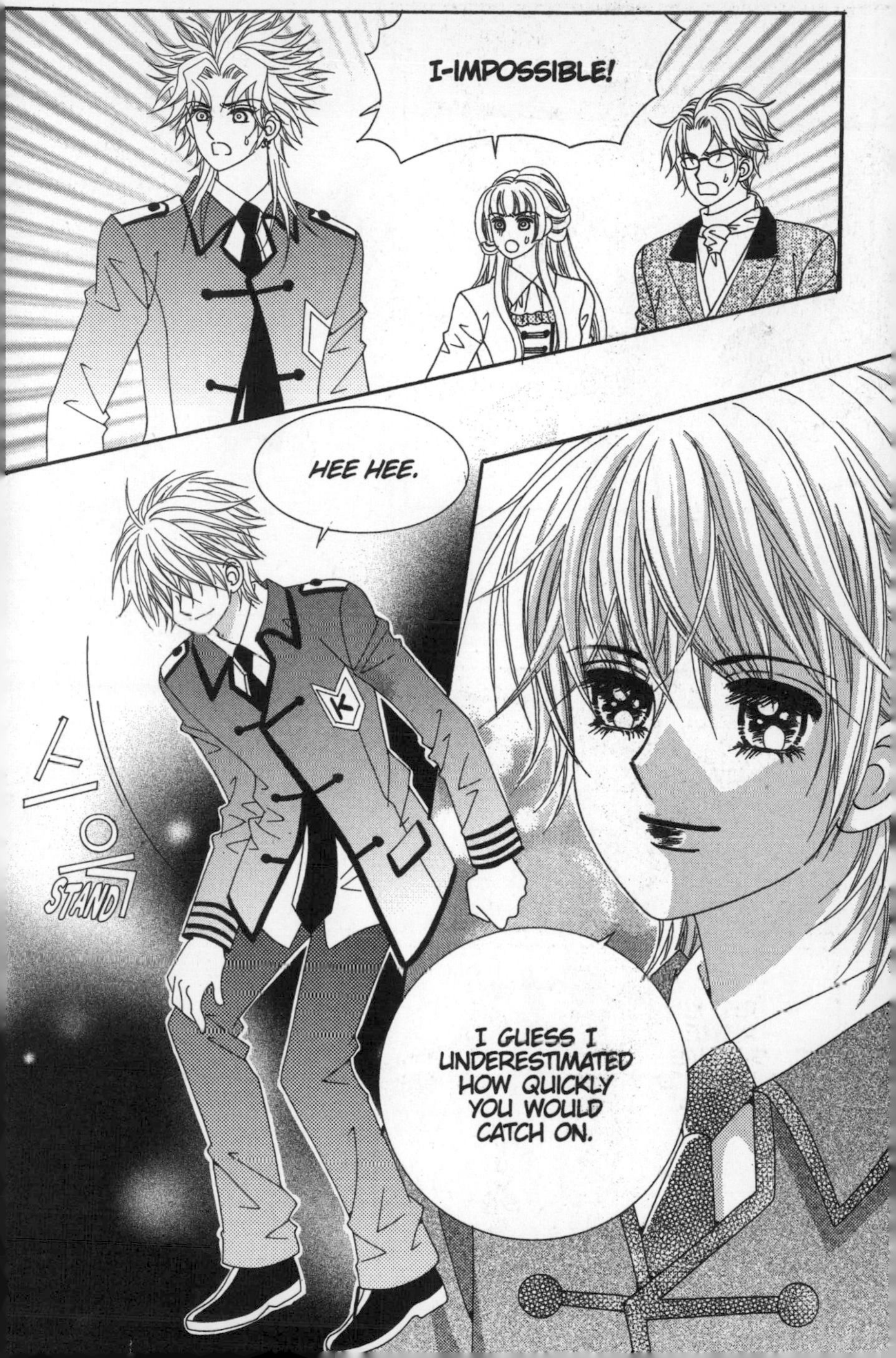
I-IMPOSSIBLE!
HEE HEE.
STAND
I GUESS I UNDERESTIMATED HOW QUICKLY YOU WOULD CATCH ON.

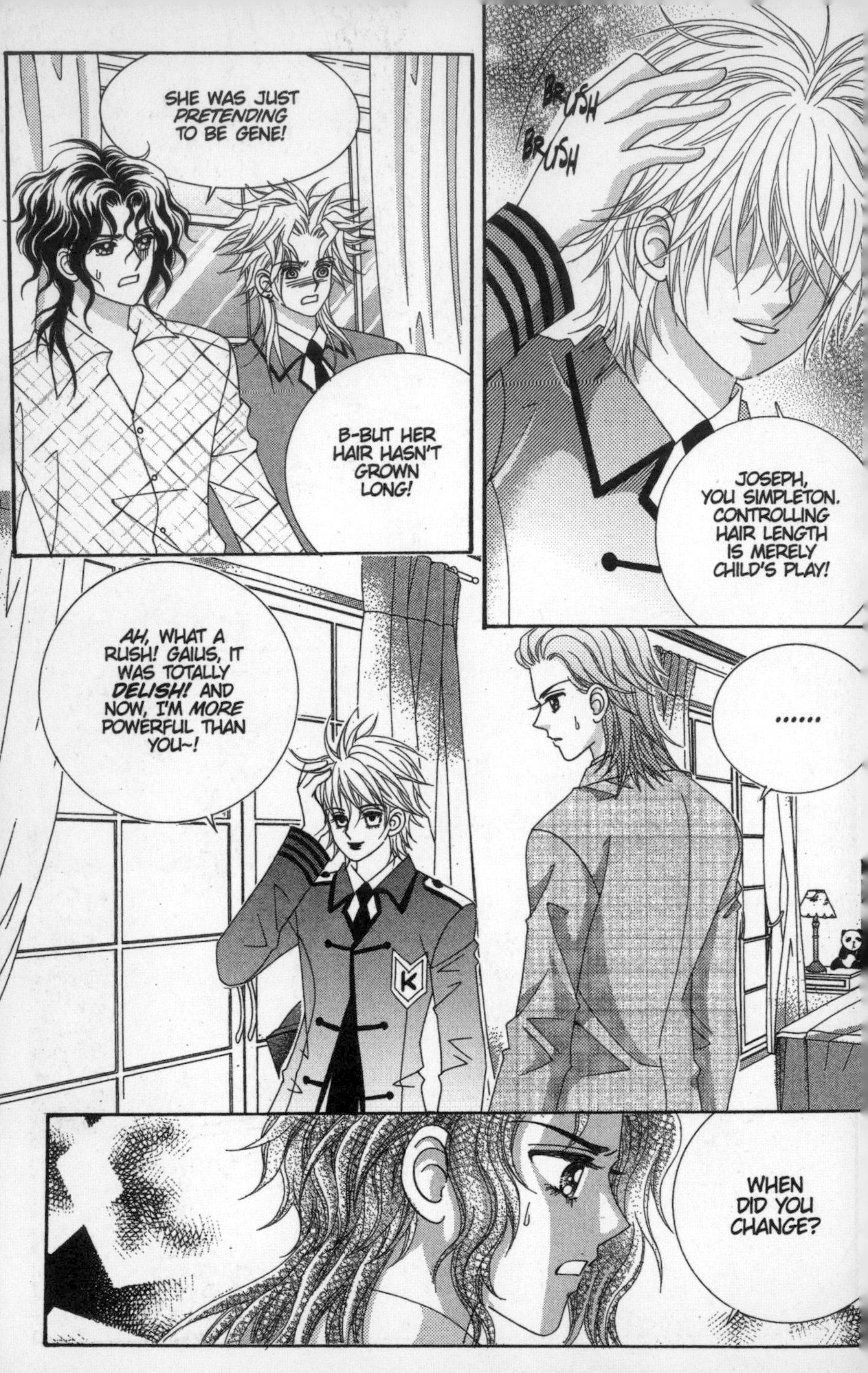
SHE WAS JUST *PRETENDING* TO BE GENE!
B-BUT HER HAIR HASN'T GROWN LONG!
BRUSH
BRUSH
JOSEPH, YOU SIMPLETON. CONTROLLING HAIR LENGTH IS MERELY CHILD'S PLAY!
*AH*, WHAT A RUSH! GAIUS, IT WAS TOTALLY ***DELISH!*** AND NOW, I'M *MORE* POWERFUL THAN YOU~!
......
WHEN DID YOU CHANGE?

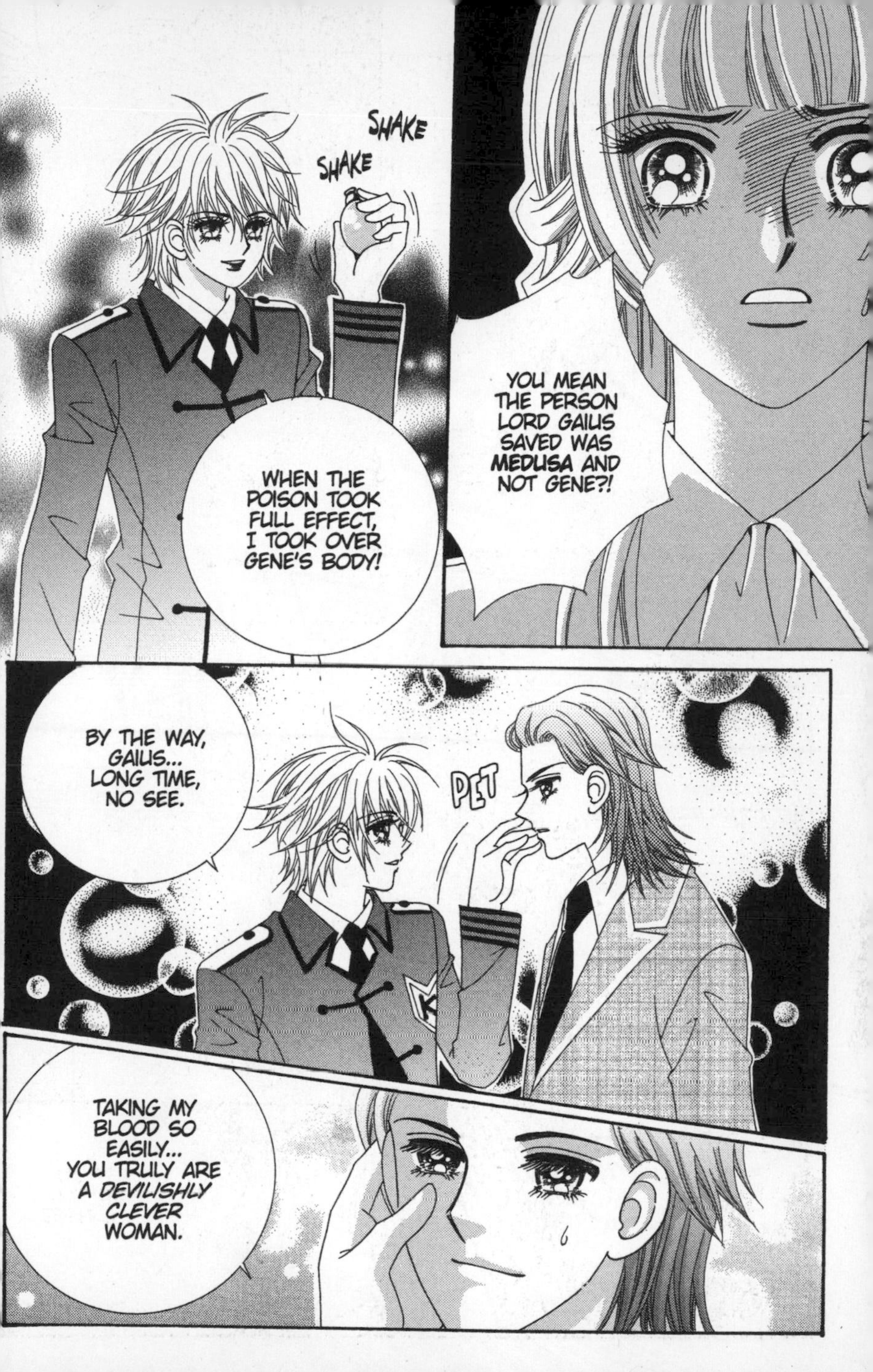
SHAKE
SHAKE
WHEN THE POISON TOOK FULL EFFECT, I TOOK OVER GENE'S BODY!
YOU MEAN THE PERSON LORD GAIUS SAVED WAS MEDUSA AND NOT GENE?!
BY THE WAY, GAIUS... LONG TIME, NO SEE.
PET
TAKING MY BLOOD SO EASILY... YOU TRULY ARE A *DEVILISHLY* CLEVER WOMAN.

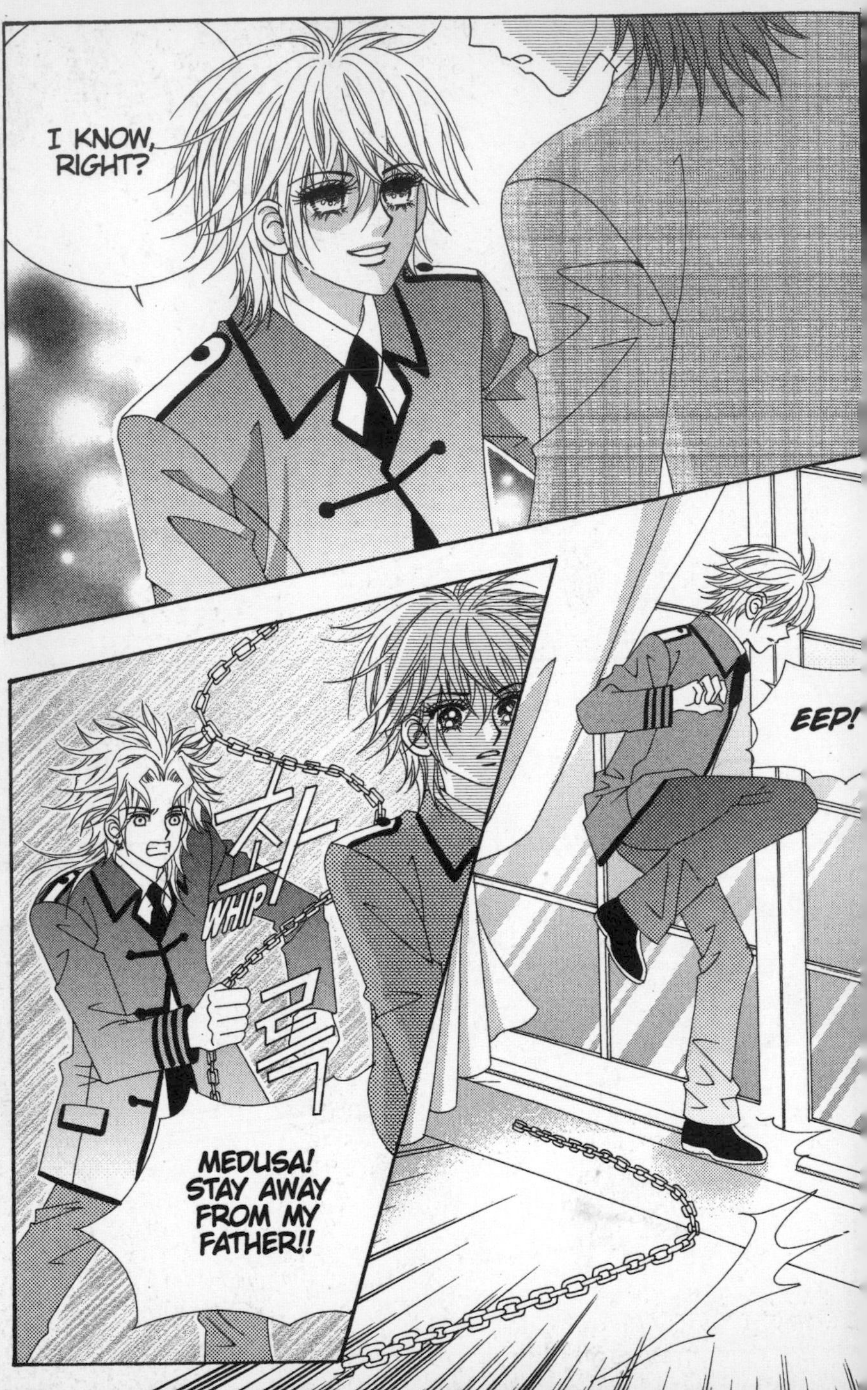
I KNOW, RIGHT?
WHIP
MEDUSA! STAY AWAY FROM MY FATHER!!
EEP!

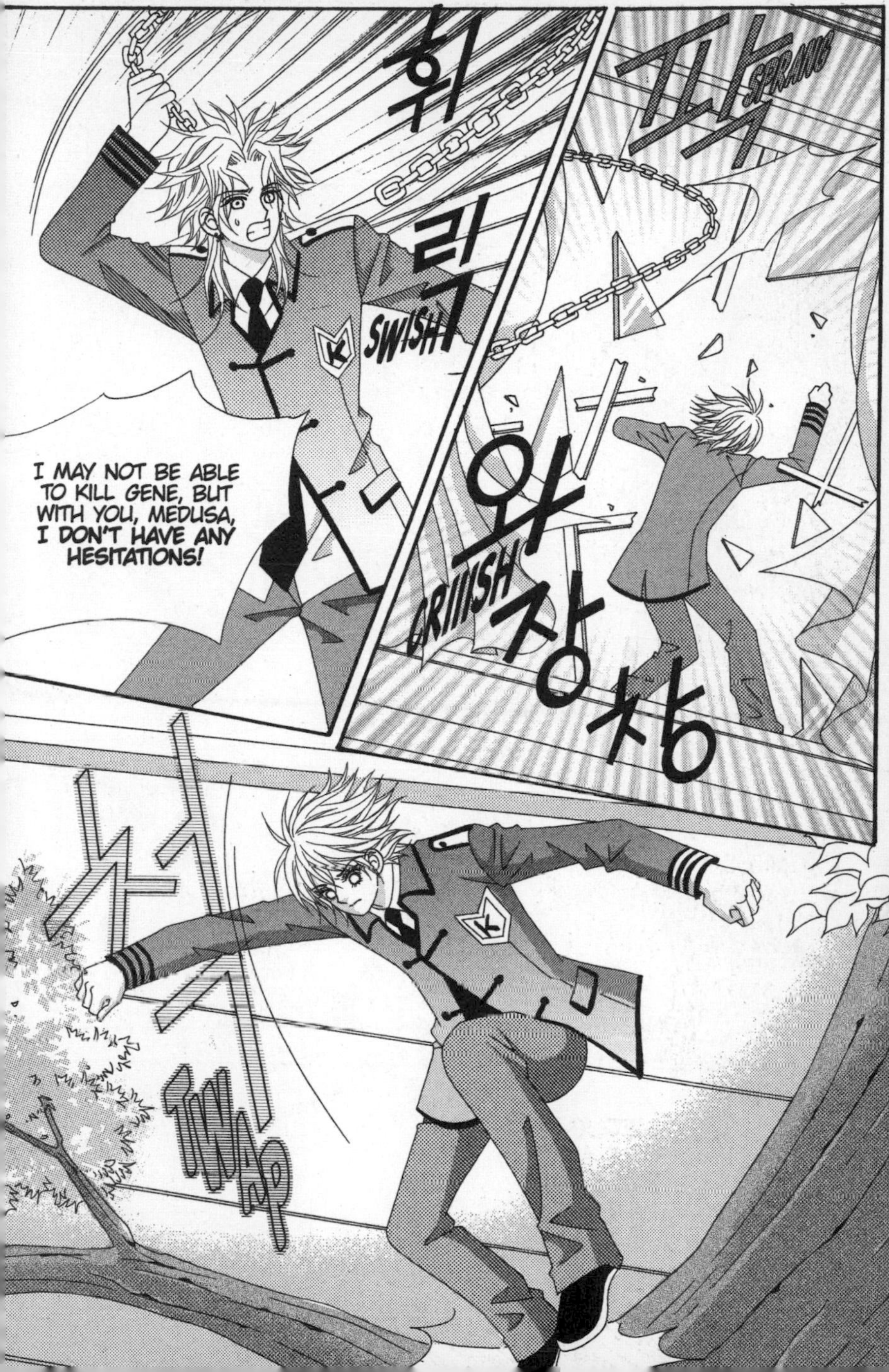
휘릭
SWISH
I MAY NOT BE ABLE TO KILL GENE, BUT WITH YOU, MEDUSA, I DON'T HAVE ANY HESITATIONS!
SPRANG
와장창
GRIIISH
TWAP

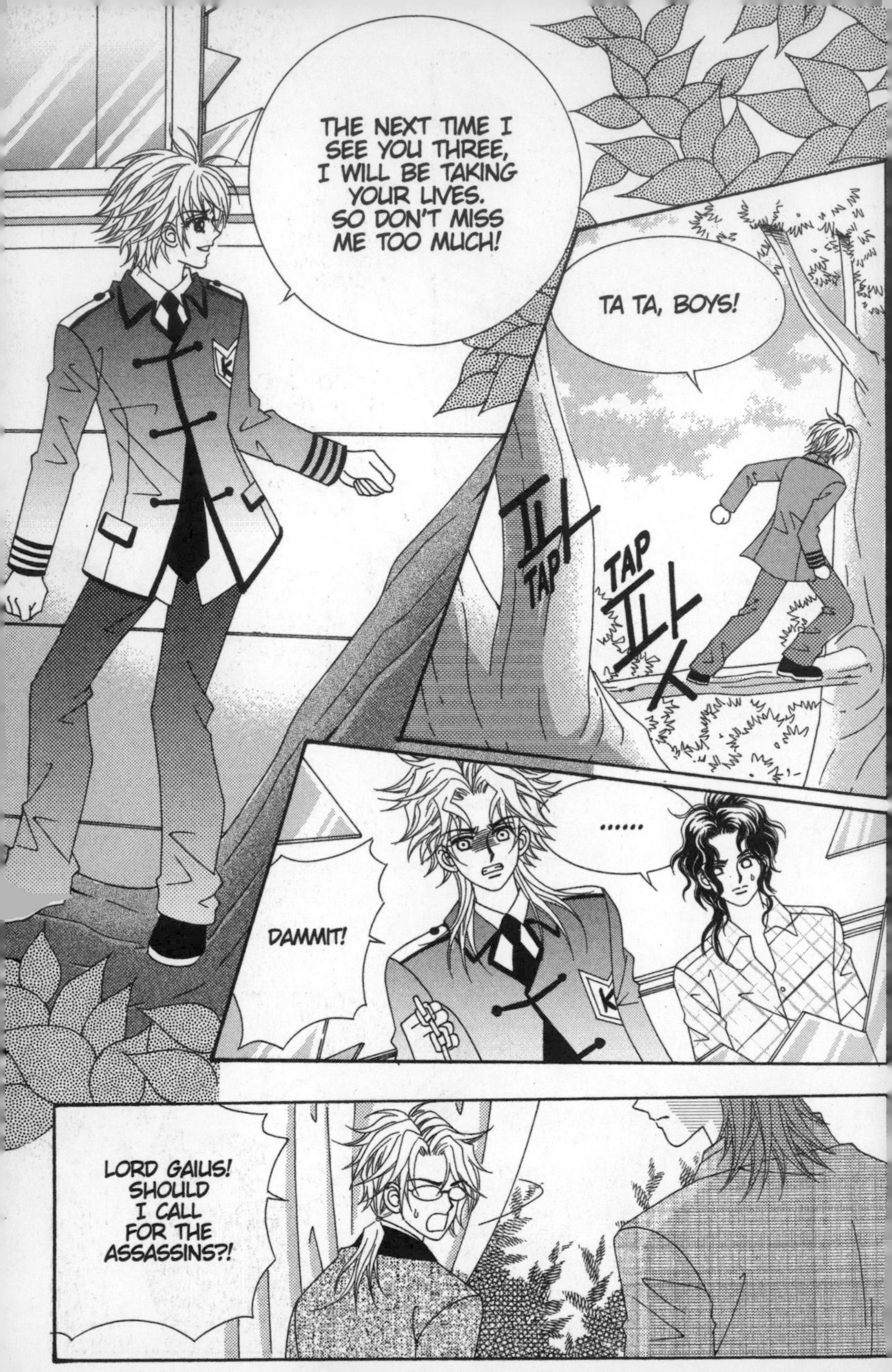
THE NEXT TIME I SEE YOU THREE, I WILL BE TAKING YOUR LIVES. SO DON'T MISS ME TOO MUCH!
TA TA, BOYS!
TAP
TAP
DAMMIT!
......
LORD GAIUS! SHOULD I CALL FOR THE ASSASSINS?!

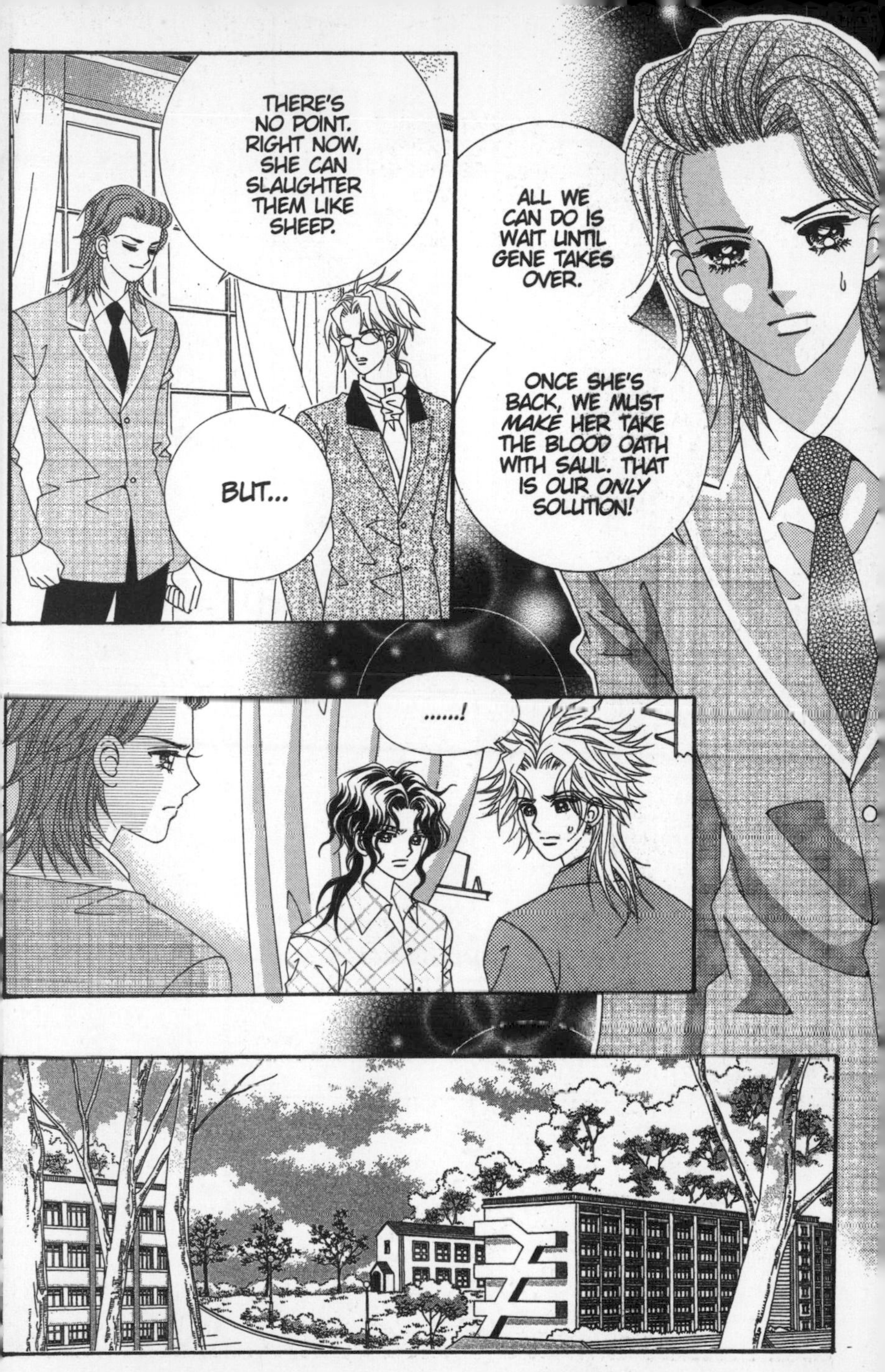
THERE'S NO POINT. RIGHT NOW, SHE CAN SLAUGHTER THEM LIKE SHEEP.
BUT...
ALL WE CAN DO IS WAIT UNTIL GENE TAKES OVER.
ONCE SHE'S BACK, WE MUST *MAKE* HER TAKE THE BLOOD OATH WITH SAUL. THAT IS OUR *ONLY* SOLUTION!
......!

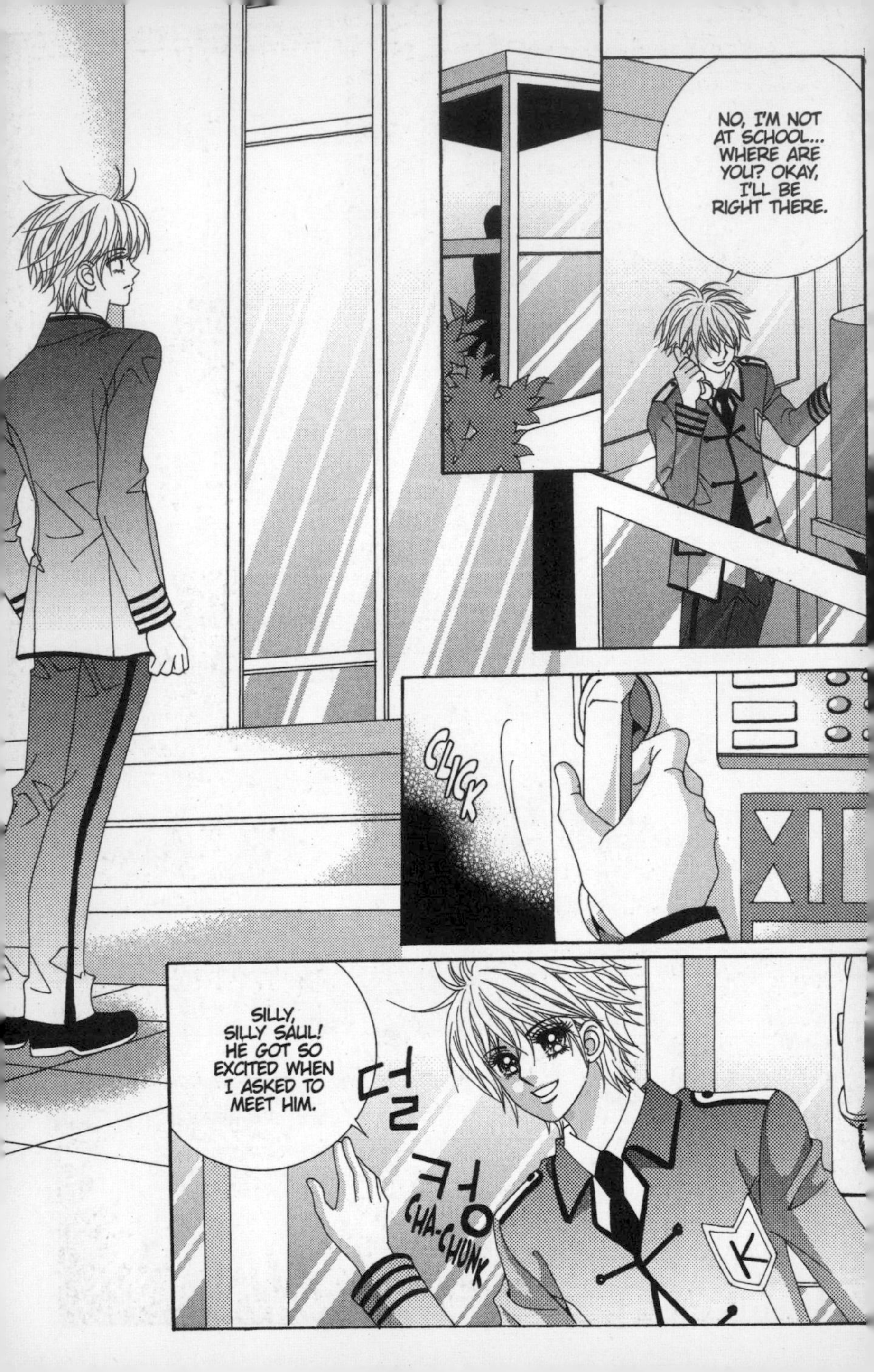
NO, I'M NOT AT SCHOOL... WHERE ARE YOU? OKAY, I'LL BE RIGHT THERE.
CLICK
SILLY, SILLY SAUL! HE GOT SO EXCITED WHEN I ASKED TO MEET HIM.
CHA-CHUNK

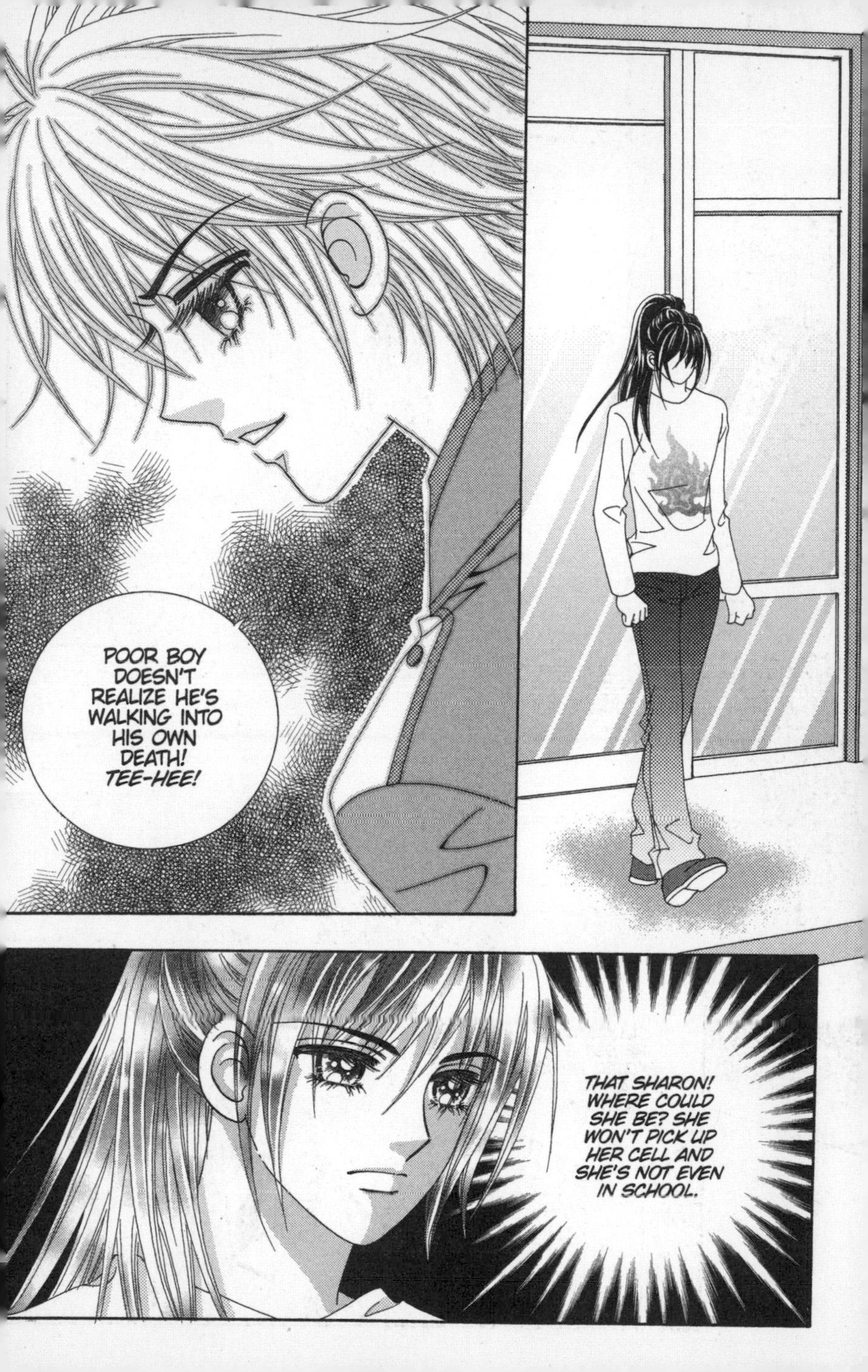
POOR BOY DOESN'T REALIZE HE'S WALKING INTO HIS OWN DEATH! TEE-HEE!
THAT SHARON! WHERE COULD SHE BE? SHE WON'T PICK UP HER CELL AND SHE'S NOT EVEN IN SCHOOL.

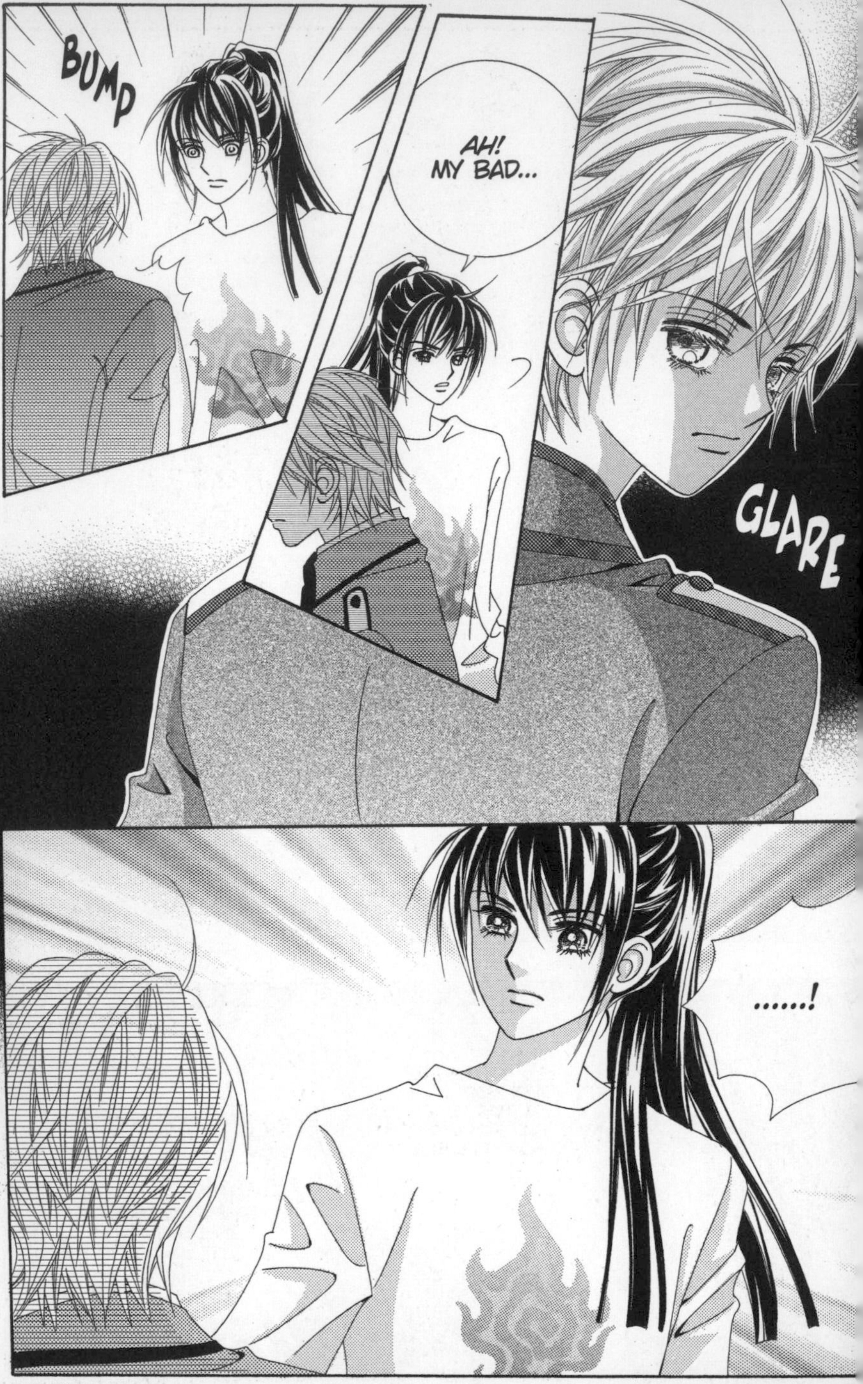
BUMP
AH! MY BAD...
GLARE
......!

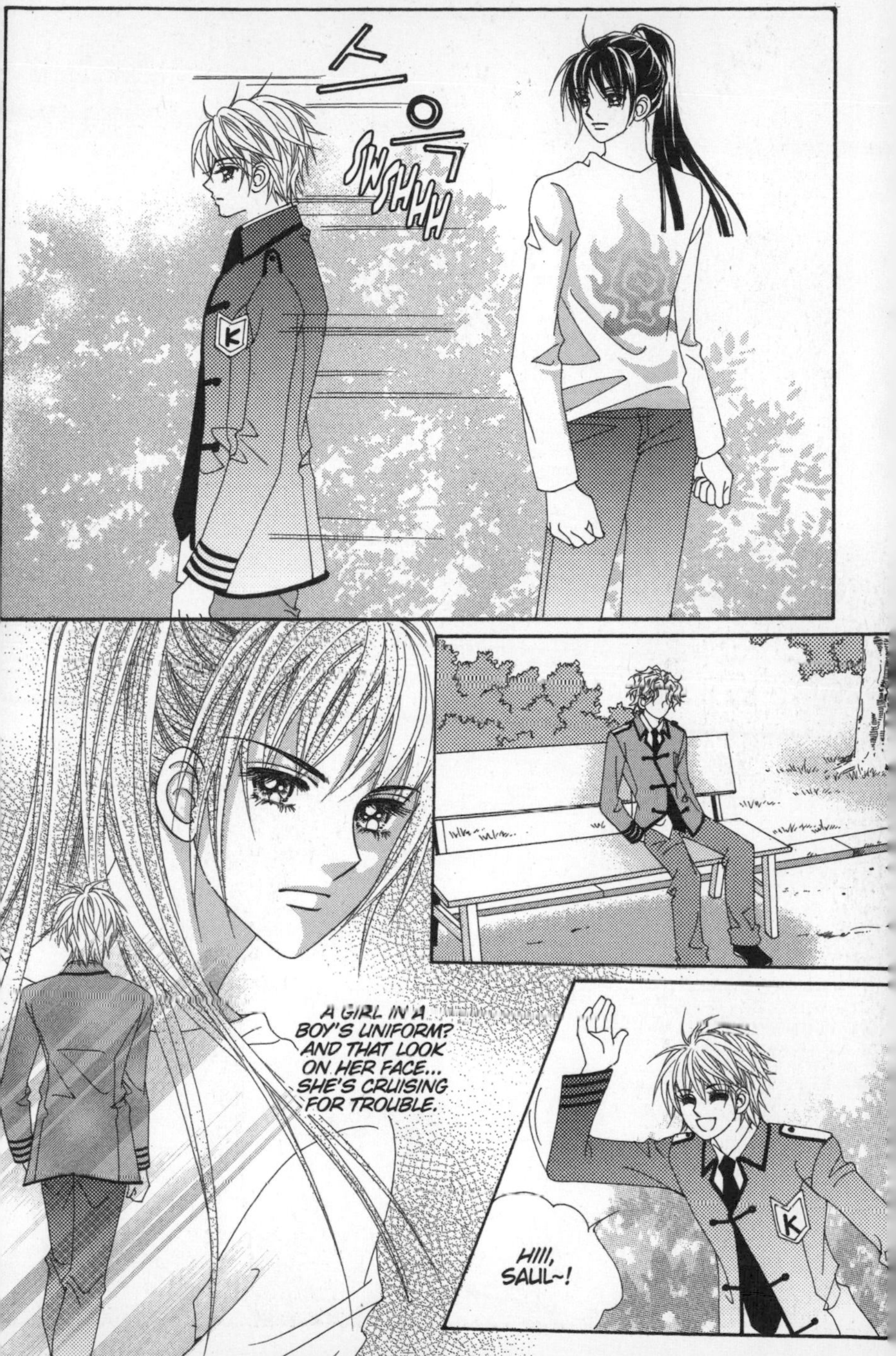
SWSHHH
A GIRL IN A BOY'S UNIFORM? AND THAT LOOK ON HER FACE... SHE'S CRUISING FOR TROUBLE.
HIII, SAUL~!

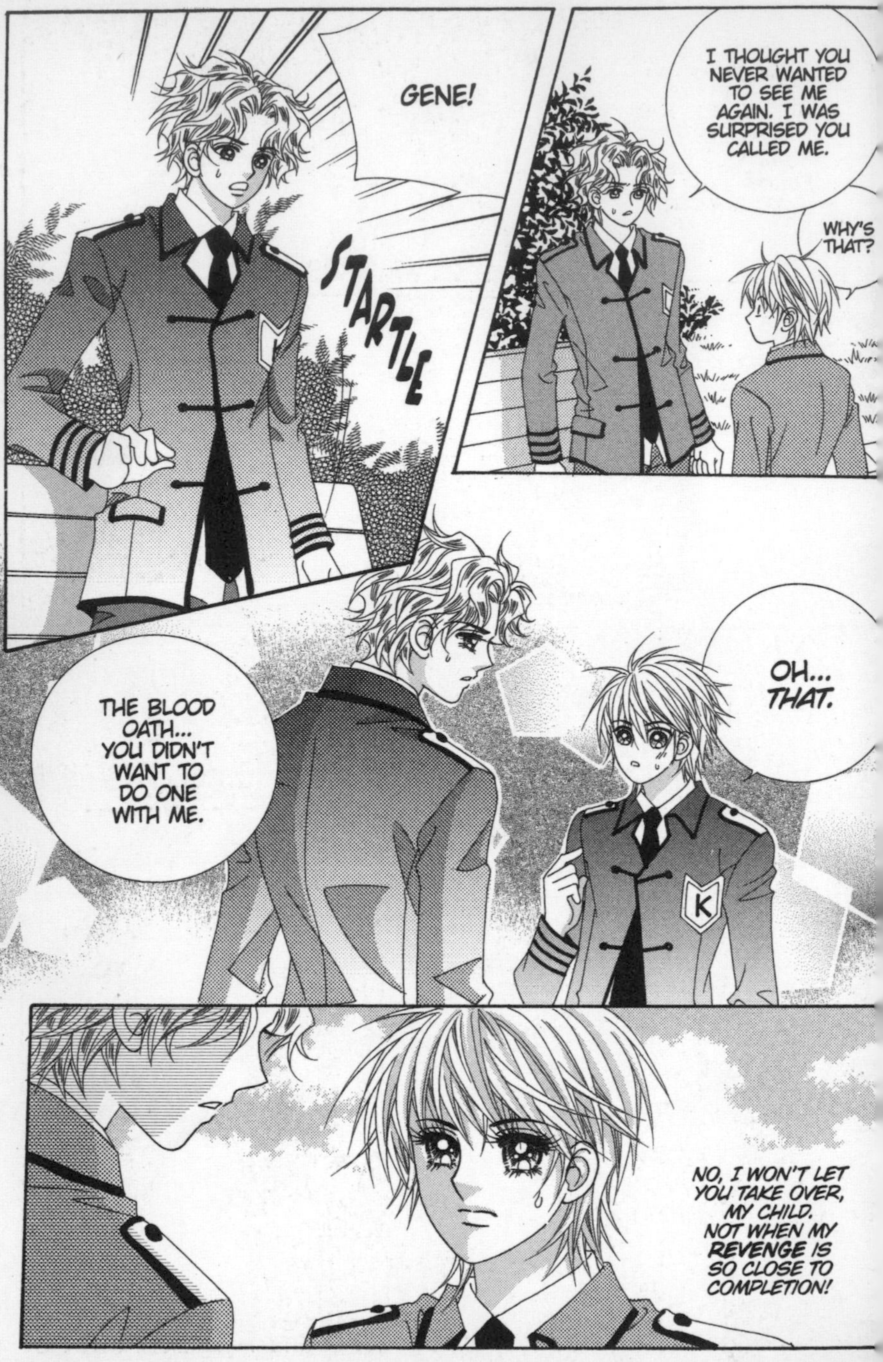
GENE!
STARTLE
I THOUGHT YOU NEVER WANTED TO SEE ME AGAIN. I WAS SURPRISED YOU CALLED ME.
WHY'S THAT?
THE BLOOD OATH... YOU DIDN'T WANT TO DO ONE WITH ME.
OH... THAT.
NO, I WON'T LET YOU TAKE OVER, MY CHILD. NOT WHEN MY REVENGE IS SO CLOSE TO COMPLETION!

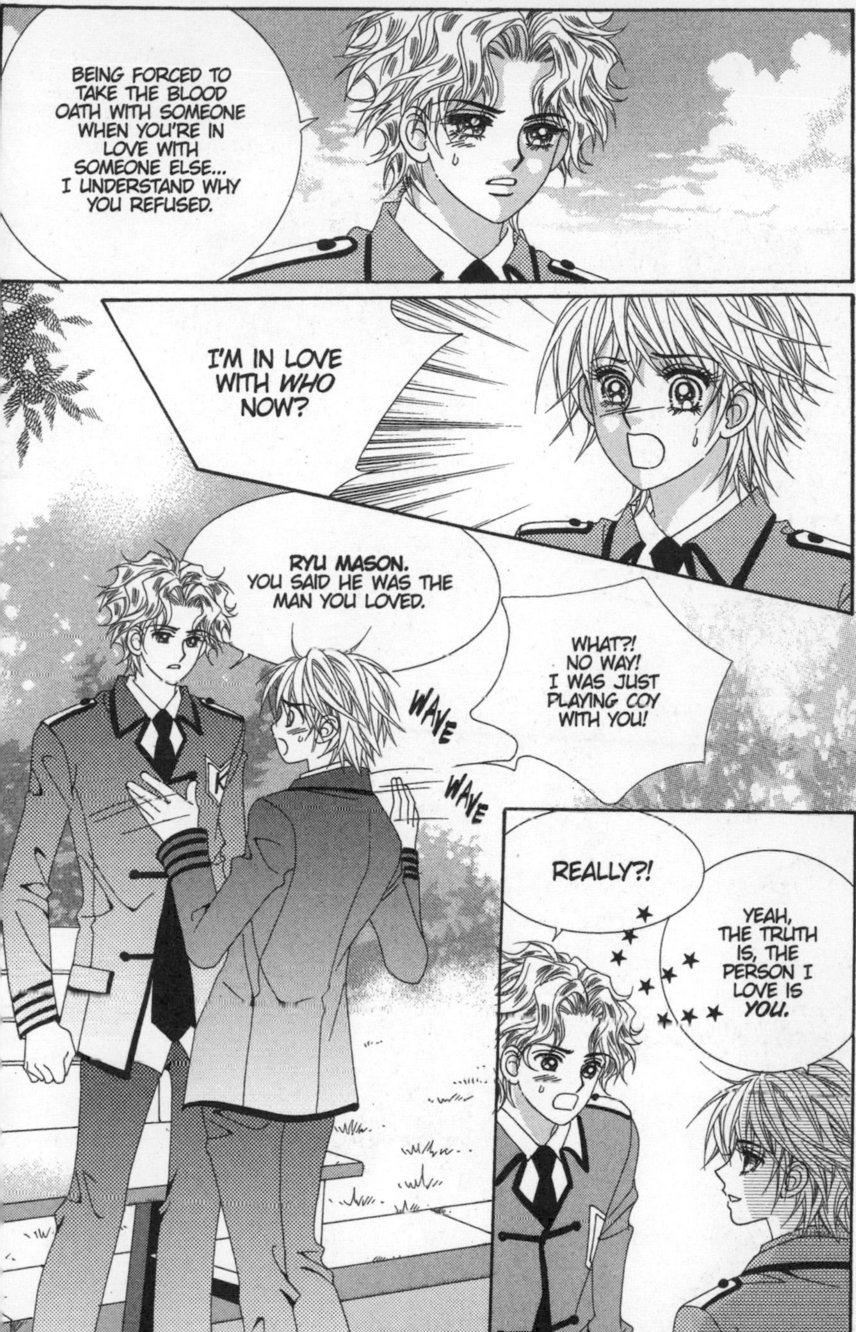
BEING FORCED TO TAKE THE BLOOD OATH WITH SOMEONE WHEN YOU'RE IN LOVE WITH SOMEONE ELSE... I UNDERSTAND WHY YOU REFUSED.
I'M IN LOVE WITH *WHO* NOW?
RYU MASON. YOU SAID HE WAS THE MAN YOU LOVED.
WHAT?! NO WAY! I WAS JUST PLAYING COY WITH YOU!
WAVE
WAVE
REALLY?!
YEAH, THE TRUTH IS, THE PERSON I LOVE IS *YOU*.

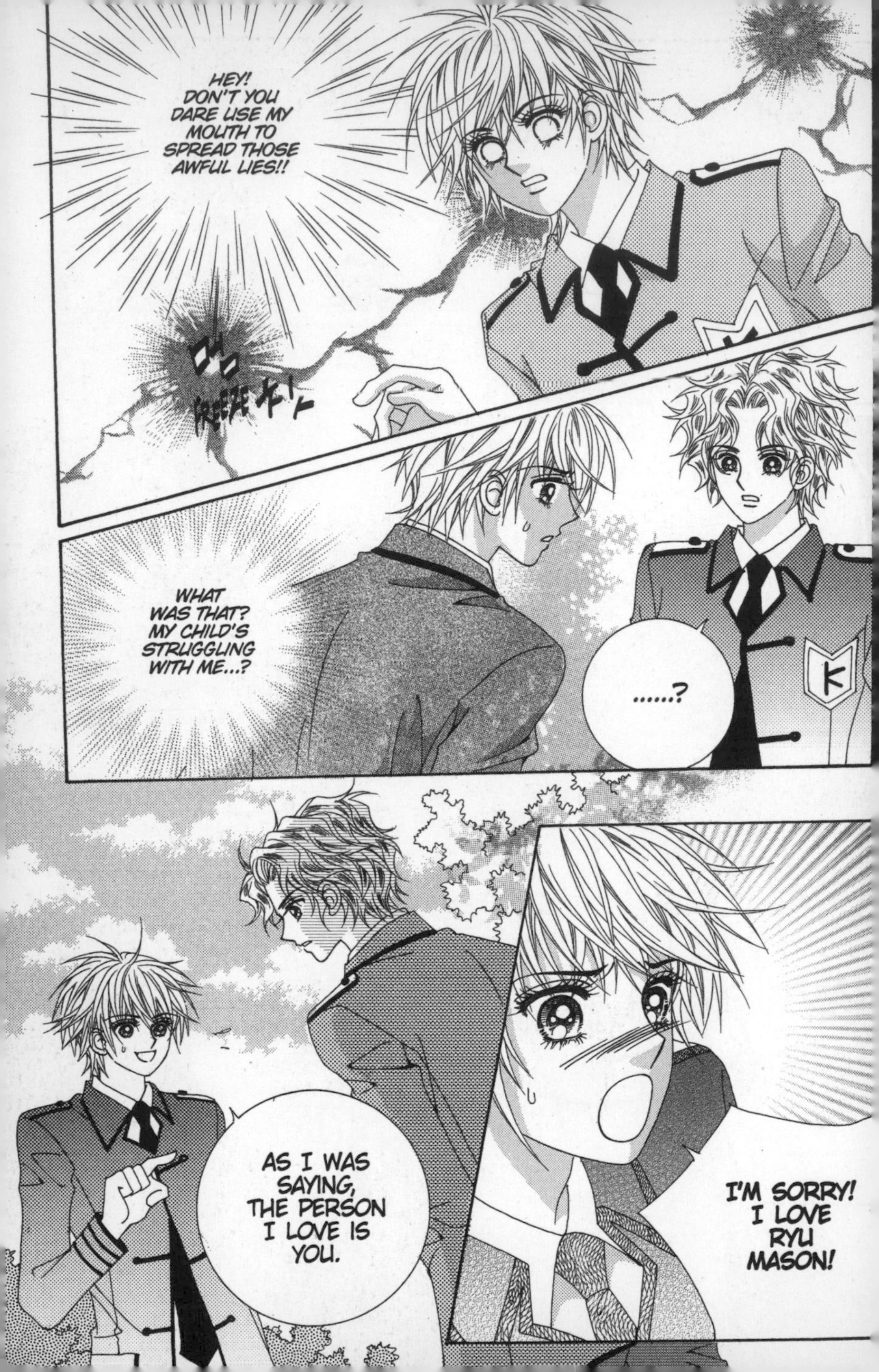
HEY! DON'T YOU DARE USE MY MOUTH TO SPREAD THOSE AWFUL LIES!!
FREEZE
WHAT WAS THAT? MY CHILD'S STRUGGLING WITH ME...?
......?
AS I WAS SAYING, THE PERSON I LOVE IS YOU.
I'M SORRY! I LOVE RYU MASON!

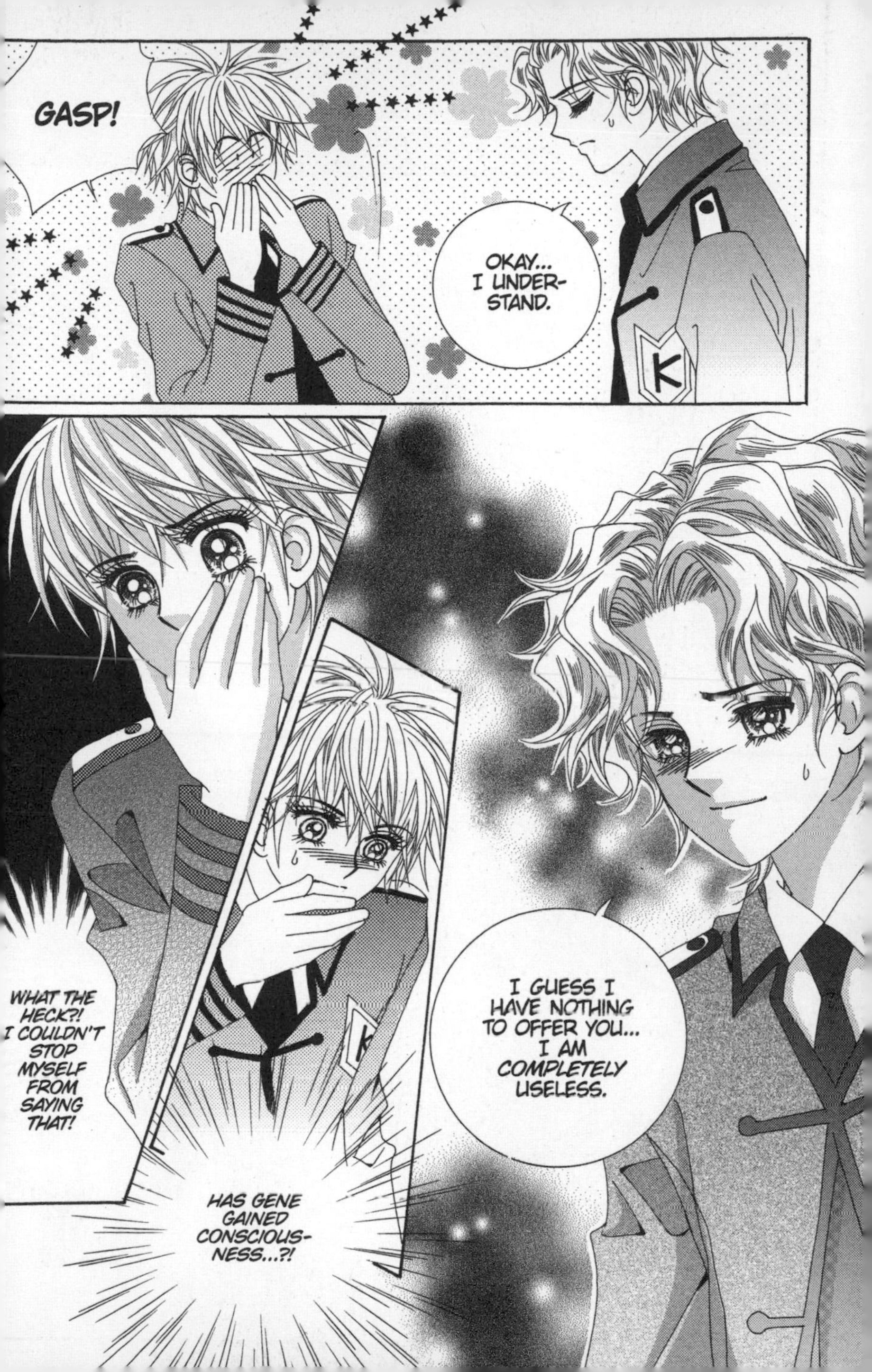
GASP!
OKAY... I UNDERSTAND.
WHAT THE HECK?! I COULDN'T STOP MYSELF FROM SAYING THAT!
HAS GENE GAINED CONSCIOUSNESS...?!
I GUESS I HAVE NOTHING TO OFFER YOU... I AM COMPLETELY USELESS.

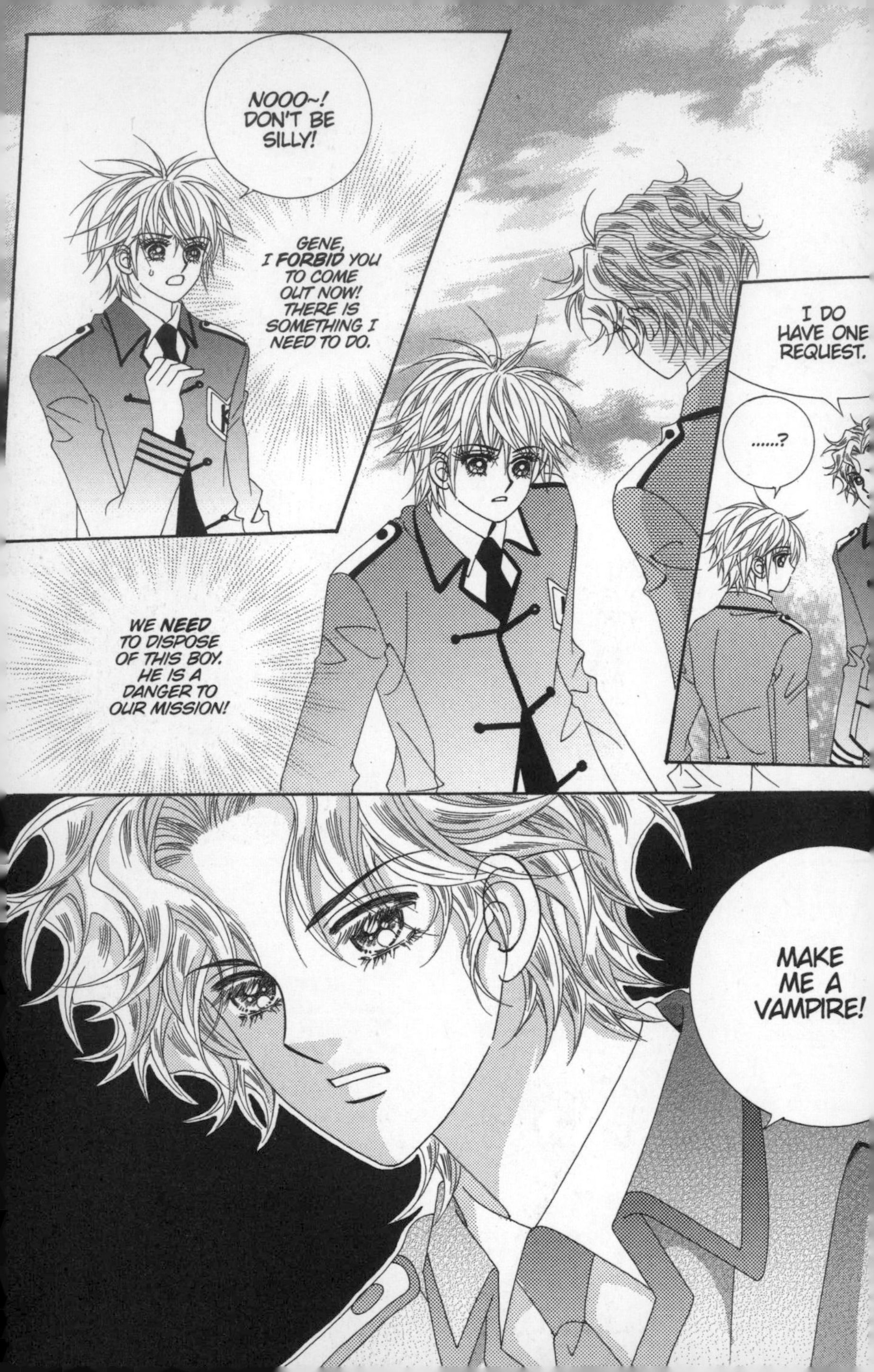
NOOO~! DON'T BE SILLY!
GENE, I FORBID YOU TO COME OUT NOW! THERE IS SOMETHING I NEED TO DO.
WE NEED TO DISPOSE OF THIS BOY. HE IS A DANGER TO OUR MISSION!
I DO HAVE ONE REQUEST.
......?
MAKE ME A VAMPIRE!

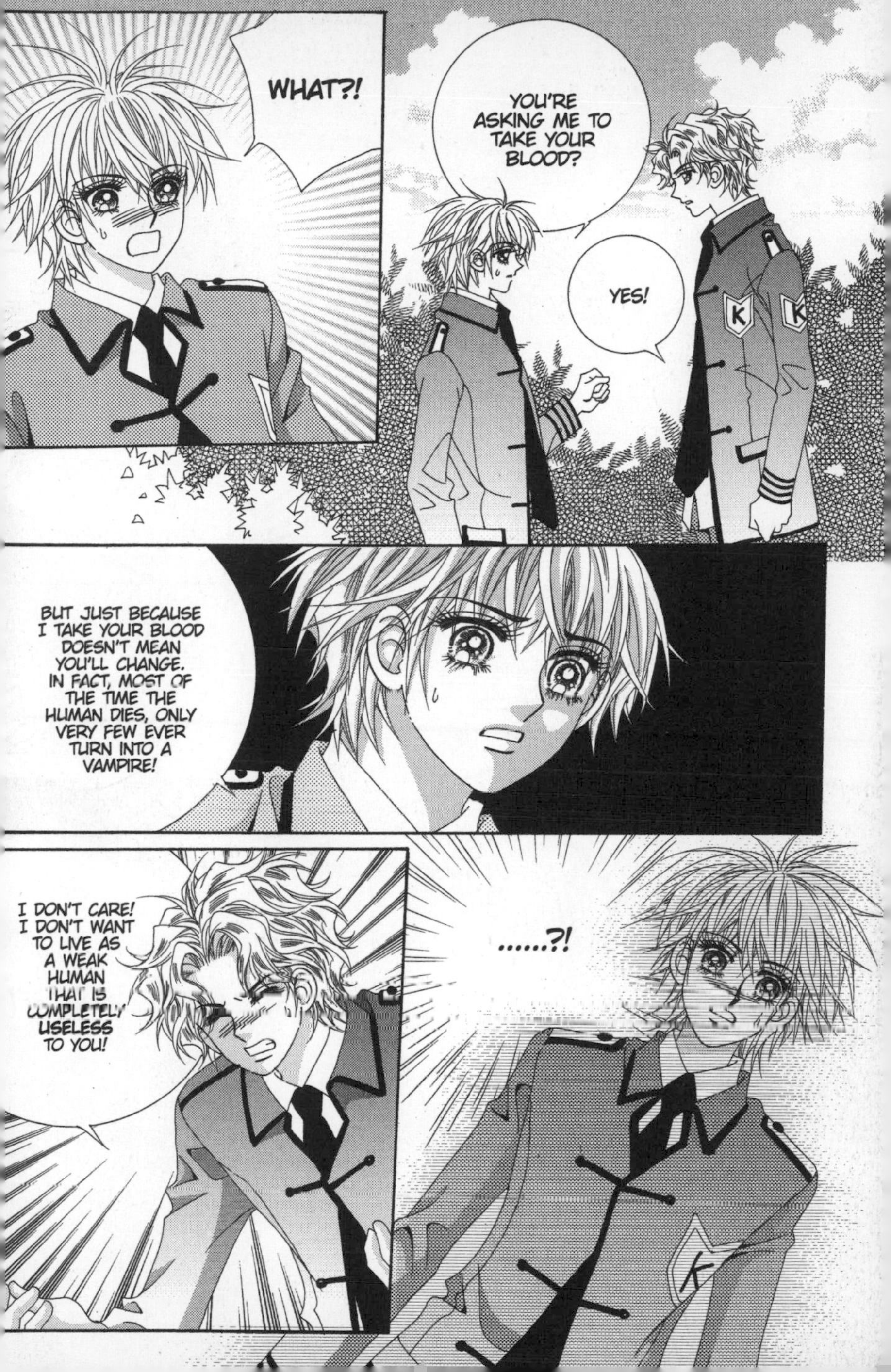
WHAT?!
YOU'RE ASKING ME TO TAKE YOUR BLOOD?
YES!
BUT JUST BECAUSE I TAKE YOUR BLOOD DOESN'T MEAN YOU'LL CHANGE. IN FACT, MOST OF THE TIME THE HUMAN DIES, ONLY VERY FEW EVER TURN INTO A VAMPIRE!
I DON'T CARE! I DON'T WANT TO LIVE AS A WEAK HUMAN THAT IS COMPLETELY USELESS TO YOU!
......?!

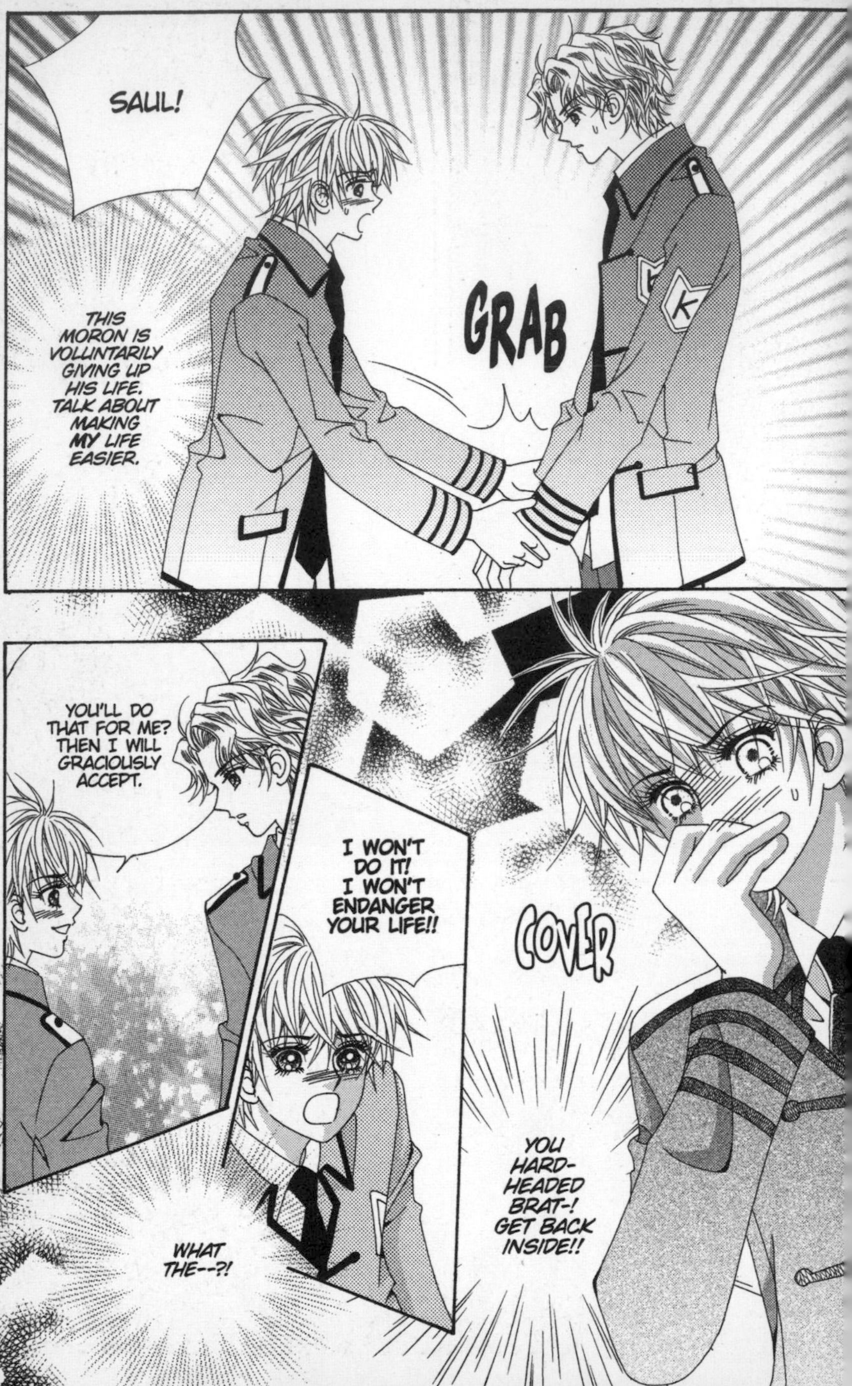
SAUL!
THIS MORON IS VOLUNTARILY GIVING UP HIS LIFE. TALK ABOUT MAKING MY LIFE EASIER.
GRAB
YOU'LL DO THAT FOR ME? THEN I WILL GRACIOUSLY ACCEPT.
I WON'T DO IT! I WON'T ENDANGER YOUR LIFE!!
WHAT THE--?!
COVER
YOU HARD-HEADED BRAT-! GET BACK INSIDE!!

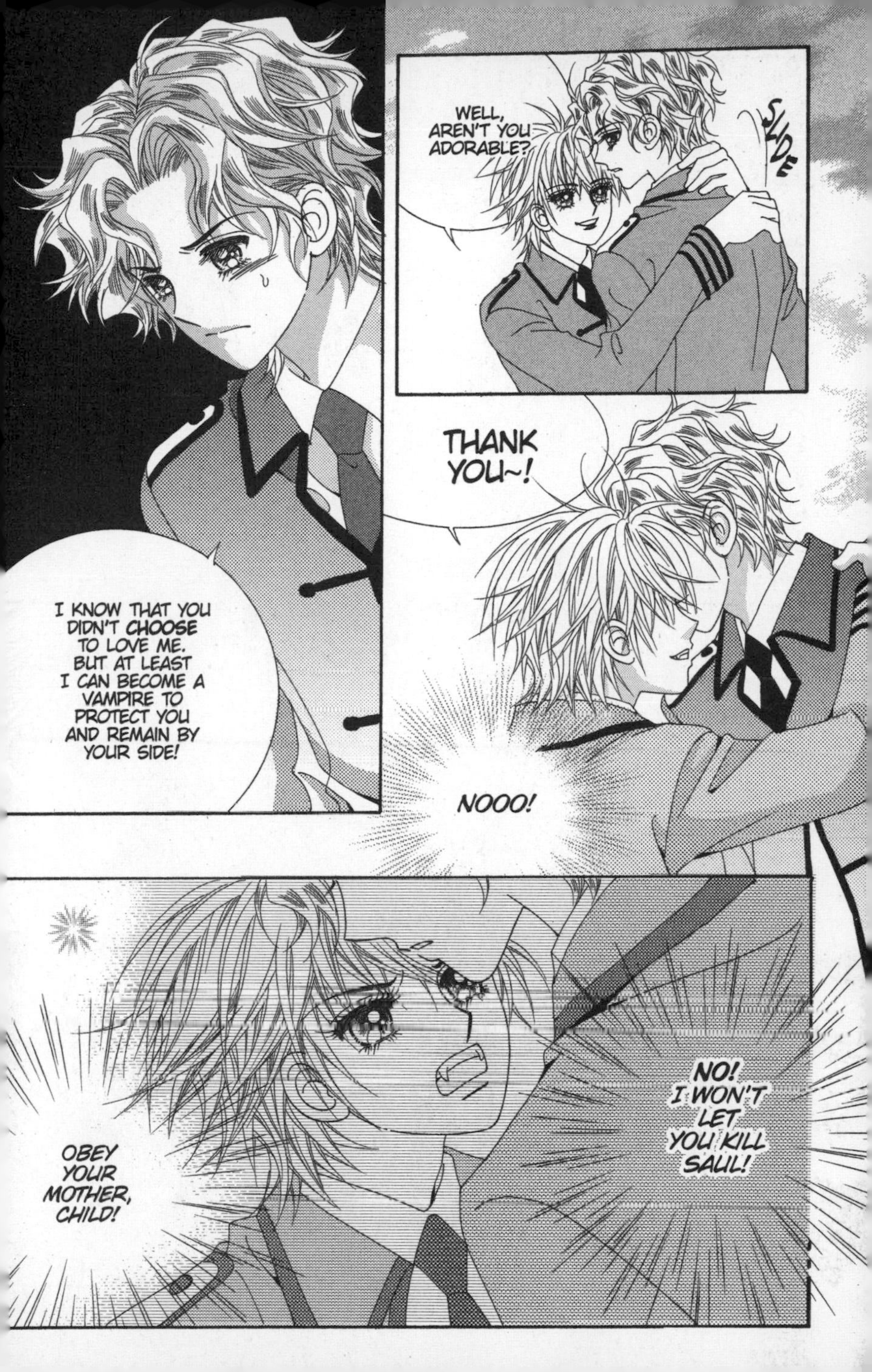
I KNOW THAT YOU DIDN'T CHOOSE TO LOVE ME. BUT AT LEAST I CAN BECOME A VAMPIRE TO PROTECT YOU AND REMAIN BY YOUR SIDE!
WELL, AREN'T YOU ADORABLE?
SLIDE
THANK YOU~!
NOOO!
OBEY YOUR MOTHER, CHILD!
NO! I WON'T LET YOU KILL SAUL!

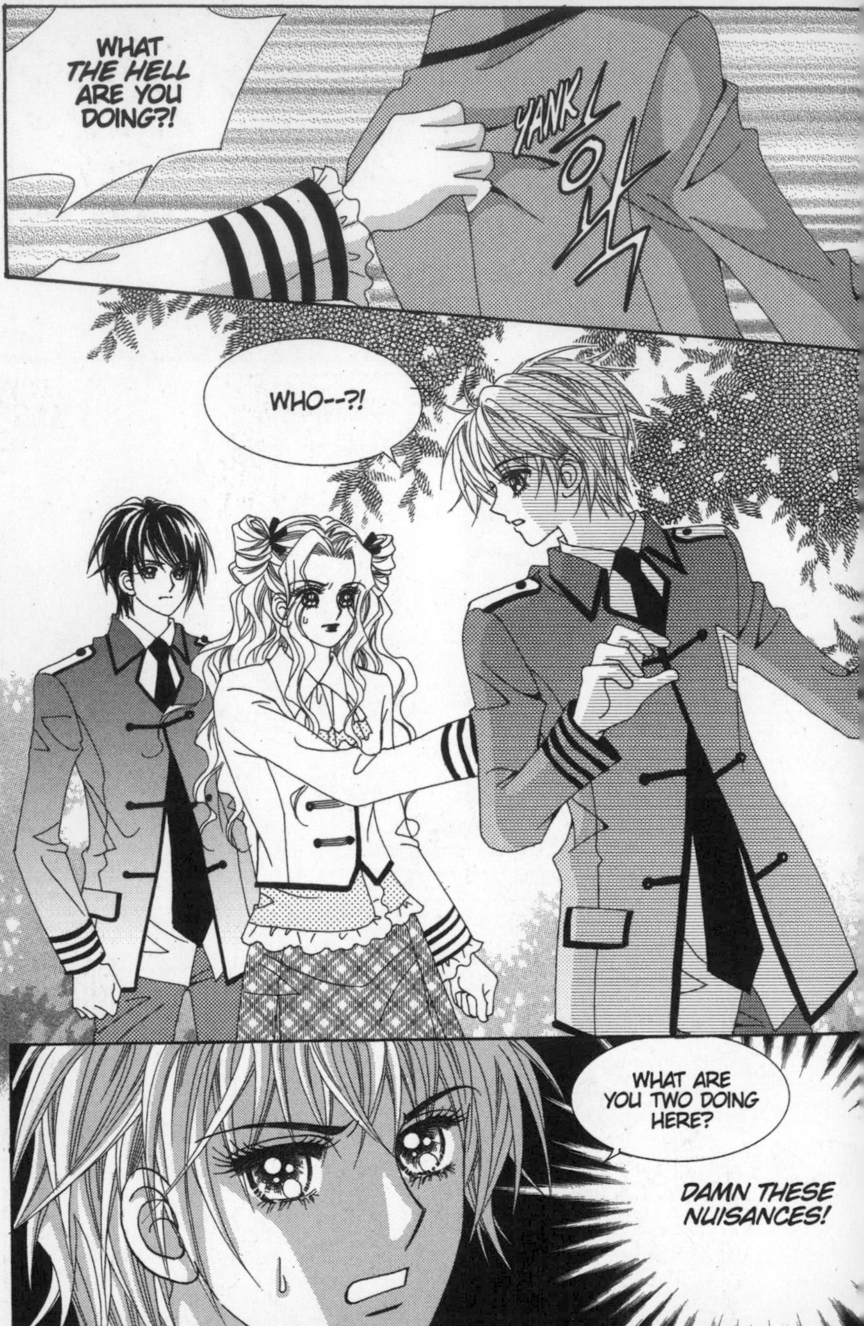
WHAT THE HELL ARE YOU DOING?!
YANK
WHO--?!
WHAT ARE YOU TWO DOING HERE?
DAMN THESE NUISANCES!

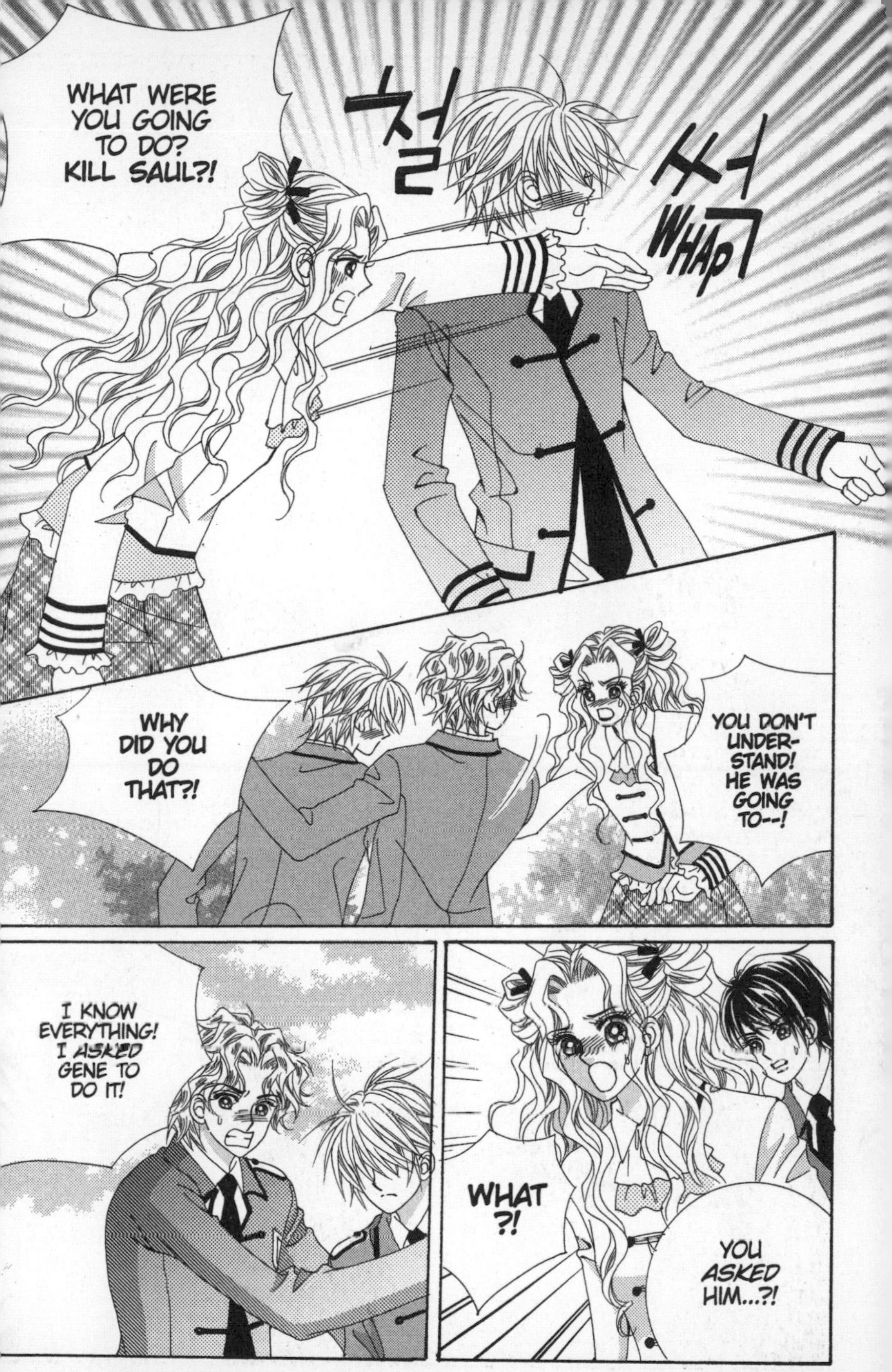
WHAT WERE YOU GOING TO DO? KILL SAUL?!
철썩
WHAP
WHY DID YOU DO THAT?!
YOU DON'T UNDER-STAND! HE WAS GOING TO--!
I KNOW EVERYTHING! I ASKED GENE TO DO IT!
WHAT?!
YOU ASKED HIM...?!

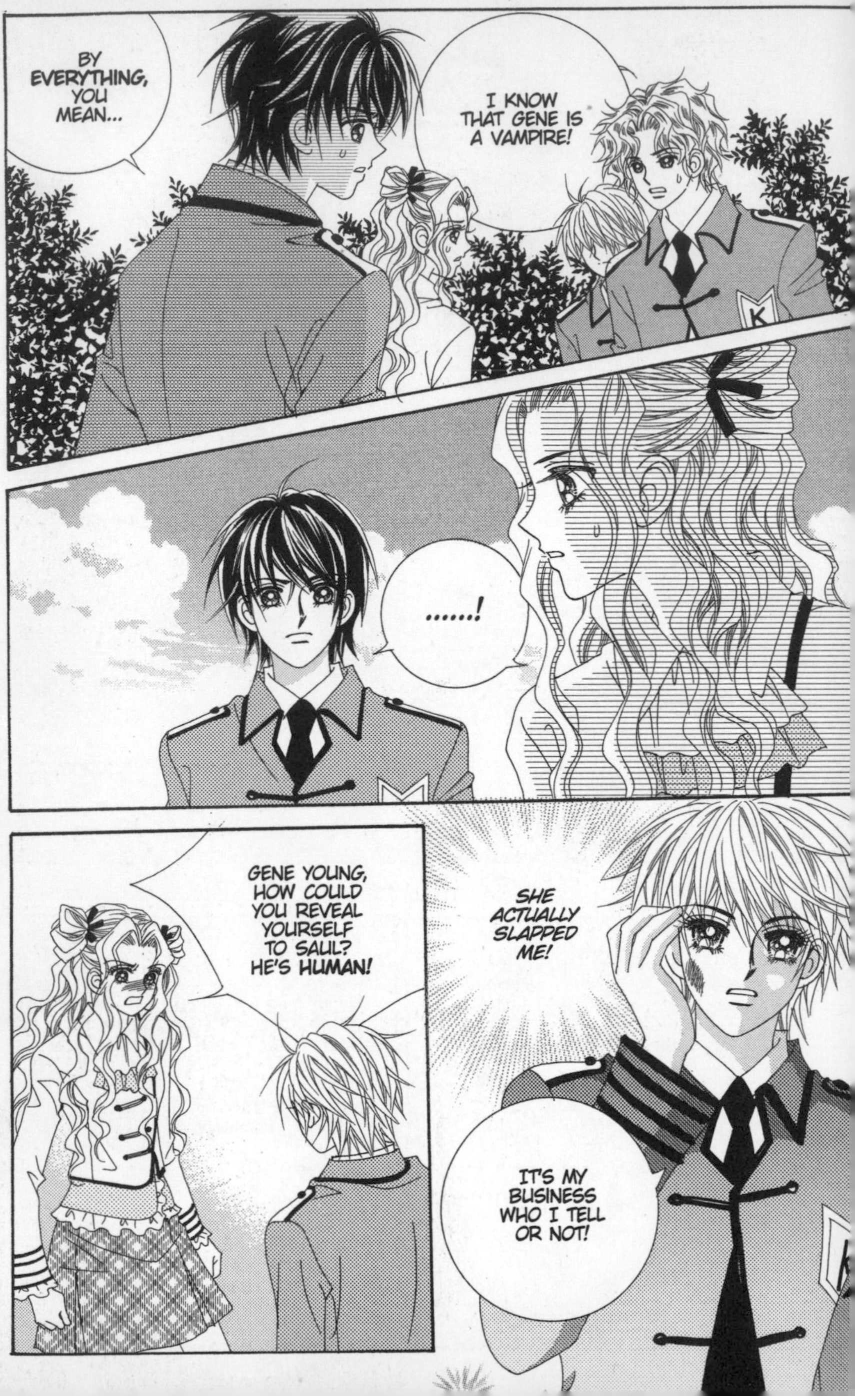
BY EVERYTHING, YOU MEAN...
I KNOW THAT GENE IS A VAMPIRE!
......!
GENE YOUNG, HOW COULD YOU REVEAL YOURSELF TO SAUL? HE'S HUMAN!
SHE ACTUALLY SLAPPED ME!
IT'S MY BUSINESS WHO I TELL OR NOT!

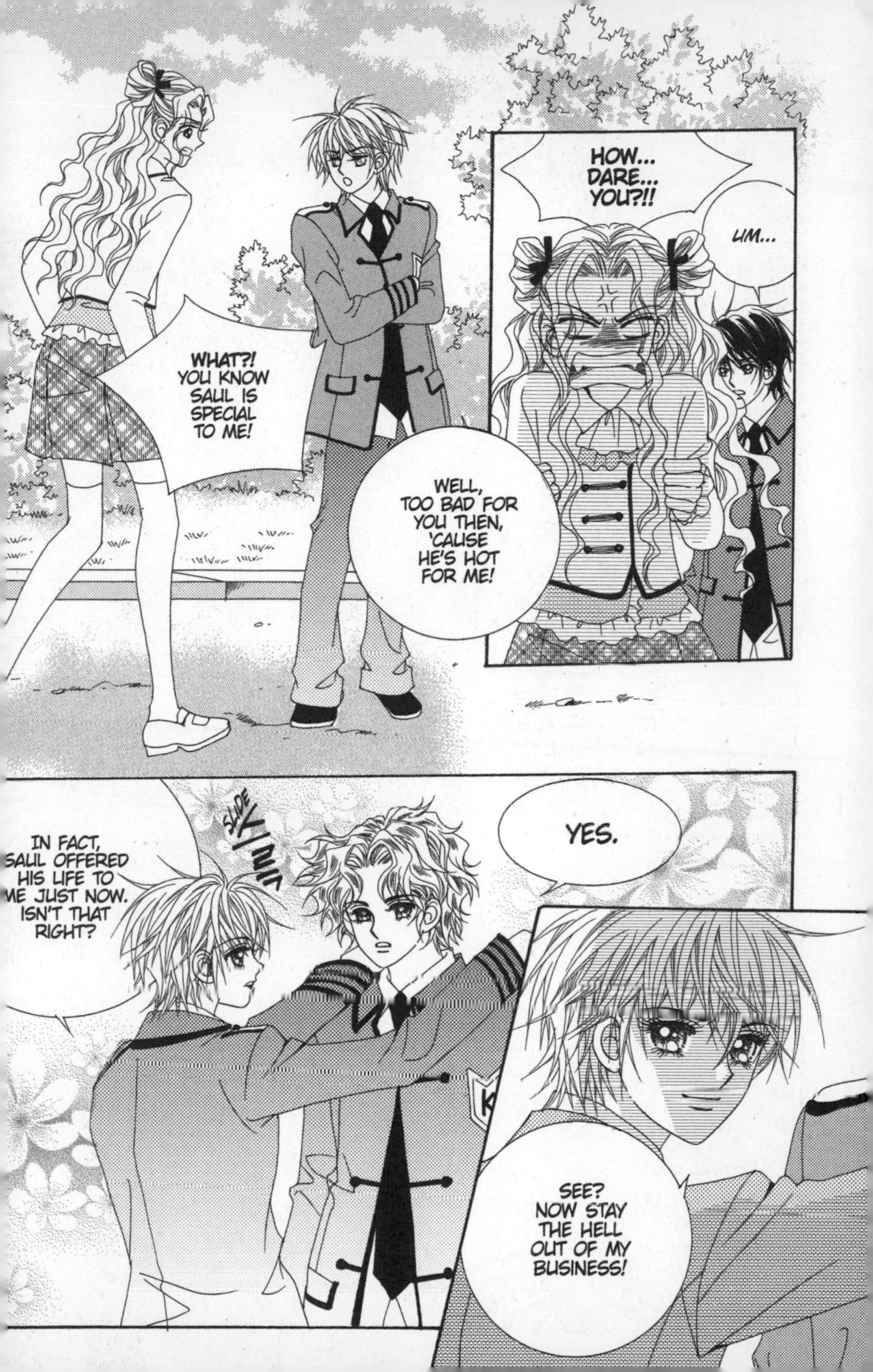

WHAT?! YOU KNOW SAUL IS SPECIAL TO ME!
WELL, TOO BAD FOR YOU THEN, 'CAUSE HE'S HOT FOR ME!
HOW... DARE... YOU?!!
UM...
IN FACT, SAUL OFFERED HIS LIFE TO ME JUST NOW. ISN'T THAT RIGHT?
SLIDE
YES.
SEE? NOW STAY THE HELL OUT OF MY BUSINESS!

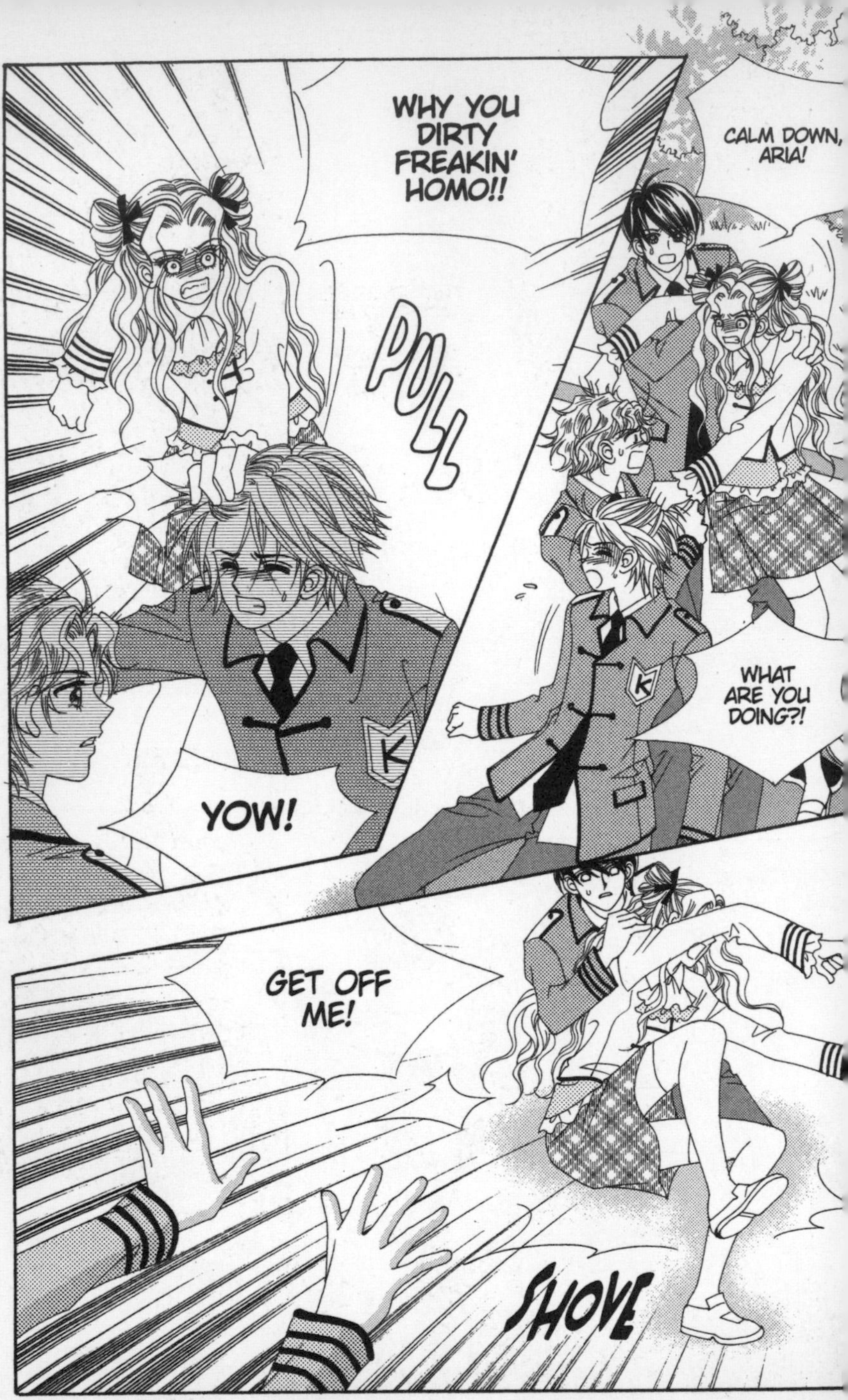
WHY YOU DIRTY FREAKIN' HOMO!!
PULL
YOW!
CALM DOWN, ARIA!
WHAT ARE YOU DOING?!
GET OFF ME!
SHOVE

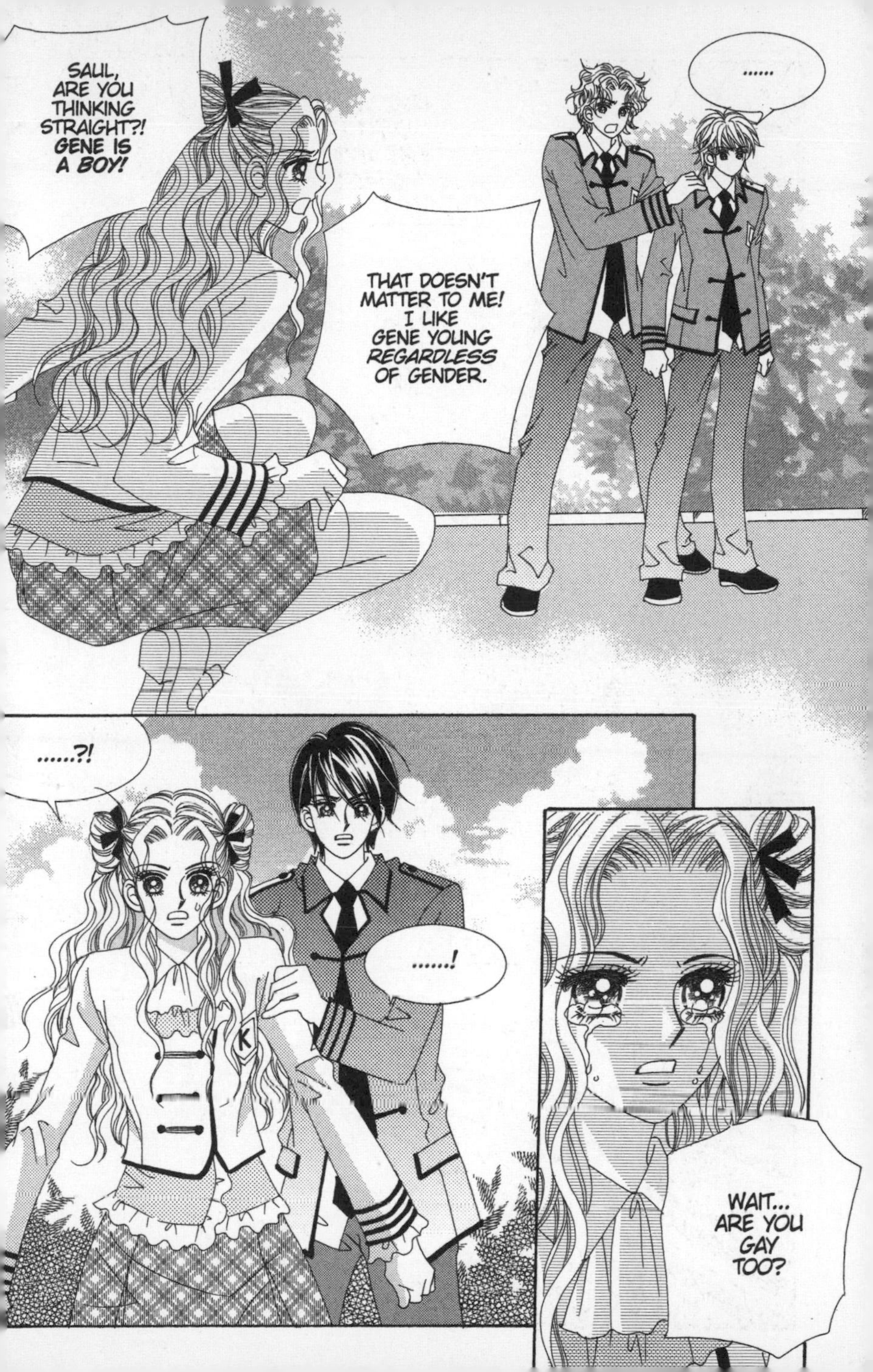
SAUL, ARE YOU THINKING STRAIGHT?! GENE IS A *BOY!*
THAT DOESN'T MATTER TO ME! I LIKE GENE YOUNG *REGARDLESS* OF GENDER.
......
......?!
......!
WAIT... ARE YOU GAY TOO?

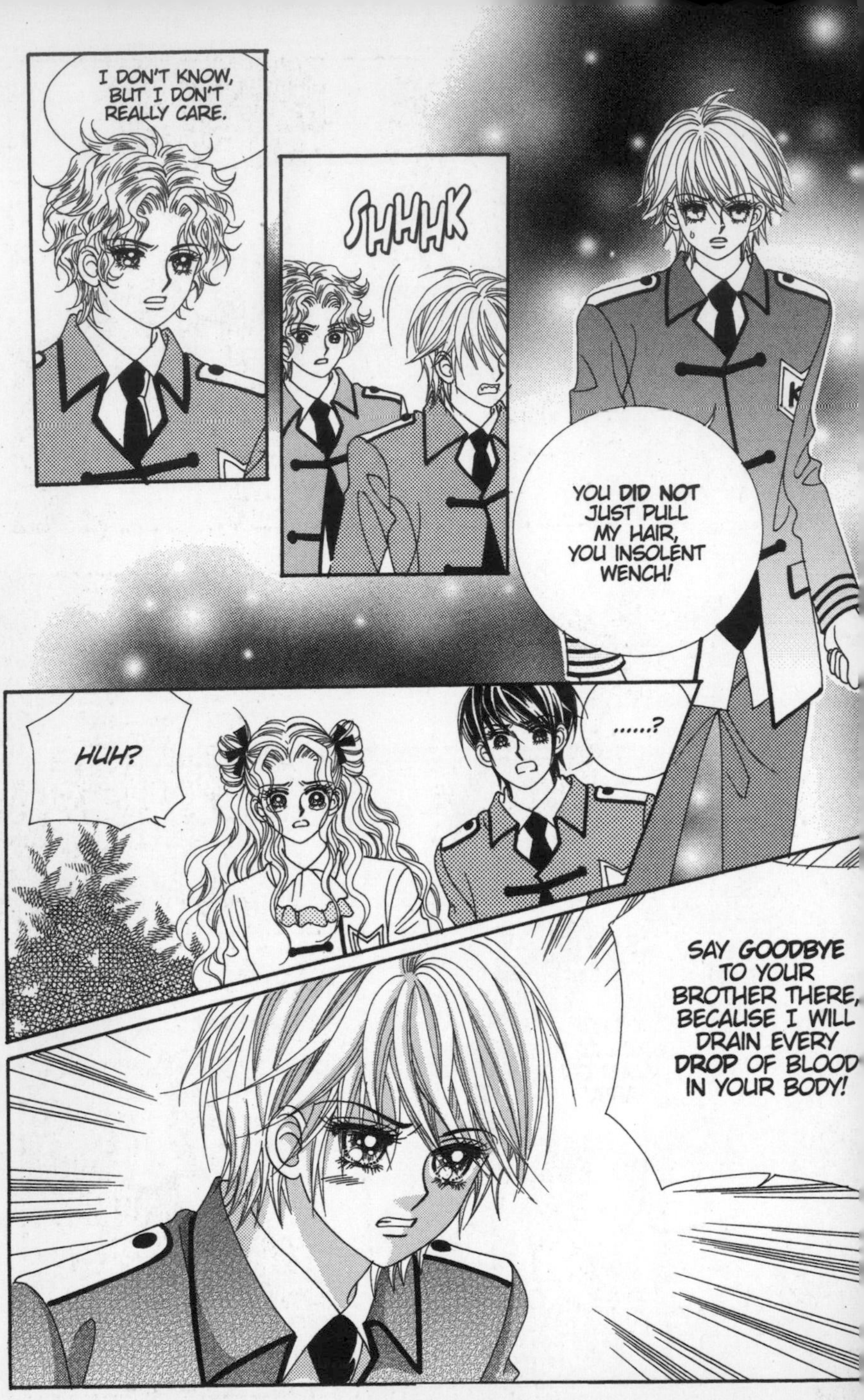
I DON'T KNOW, BUT I DON'T REALLY CARE.
SHHHK
YOU DID NOT JUST PULL MY HAIR, YOU INSOLENT WENCH!
HUH?
......?
SAY GOODBYE TO YOUR BROTHER THERE, BECAUSE I WILL DRAIN EVERY DROP OF BLOOD IN YOUR BODY!

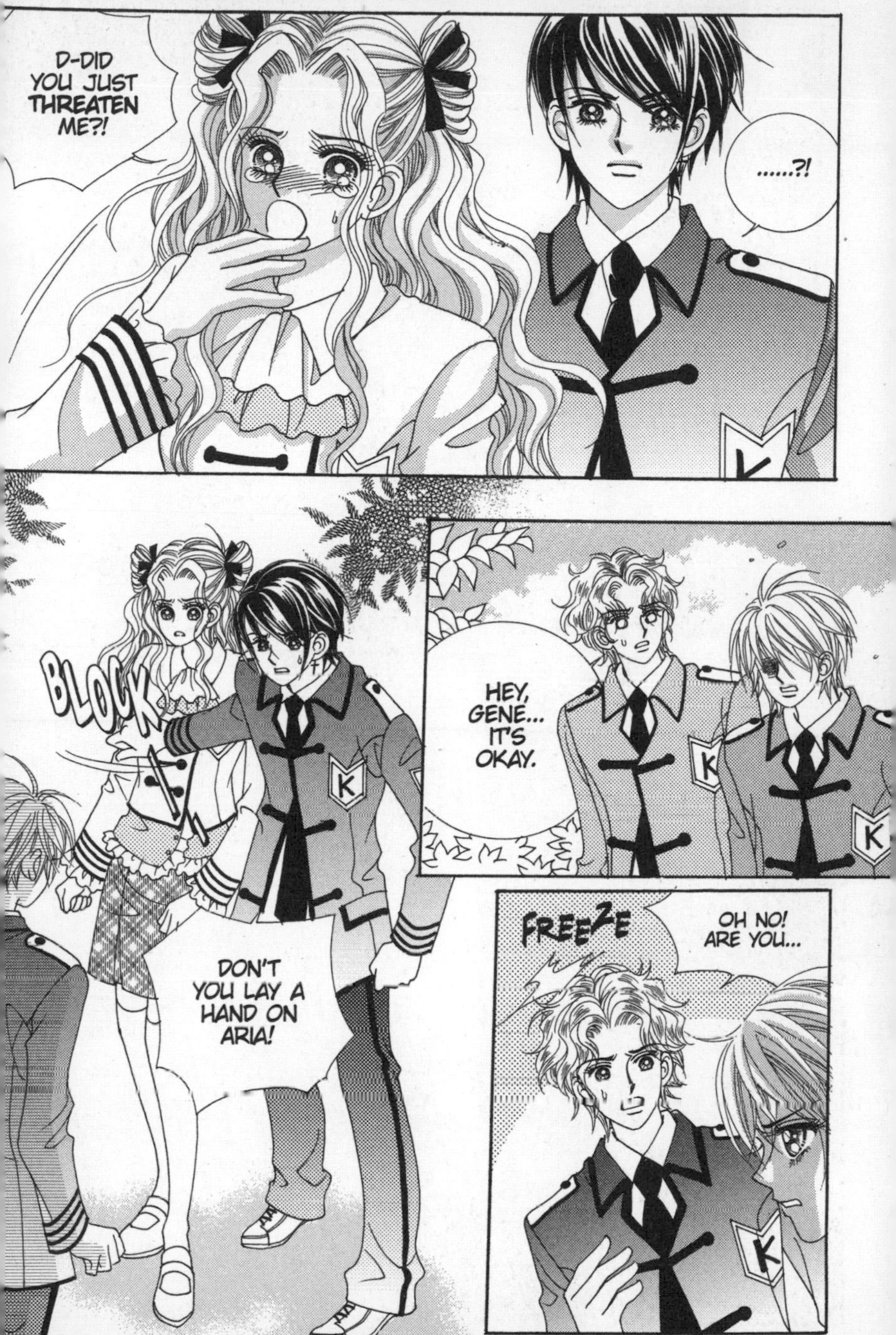
D-DID YOU JUST THREATEN ME?!
......?!
BLOCK
DON'T YOU LAY A HAND ON ARIA!
HEY, GENE... IT'S OKAY.
FREEZE
OH NO! ARE YOU...

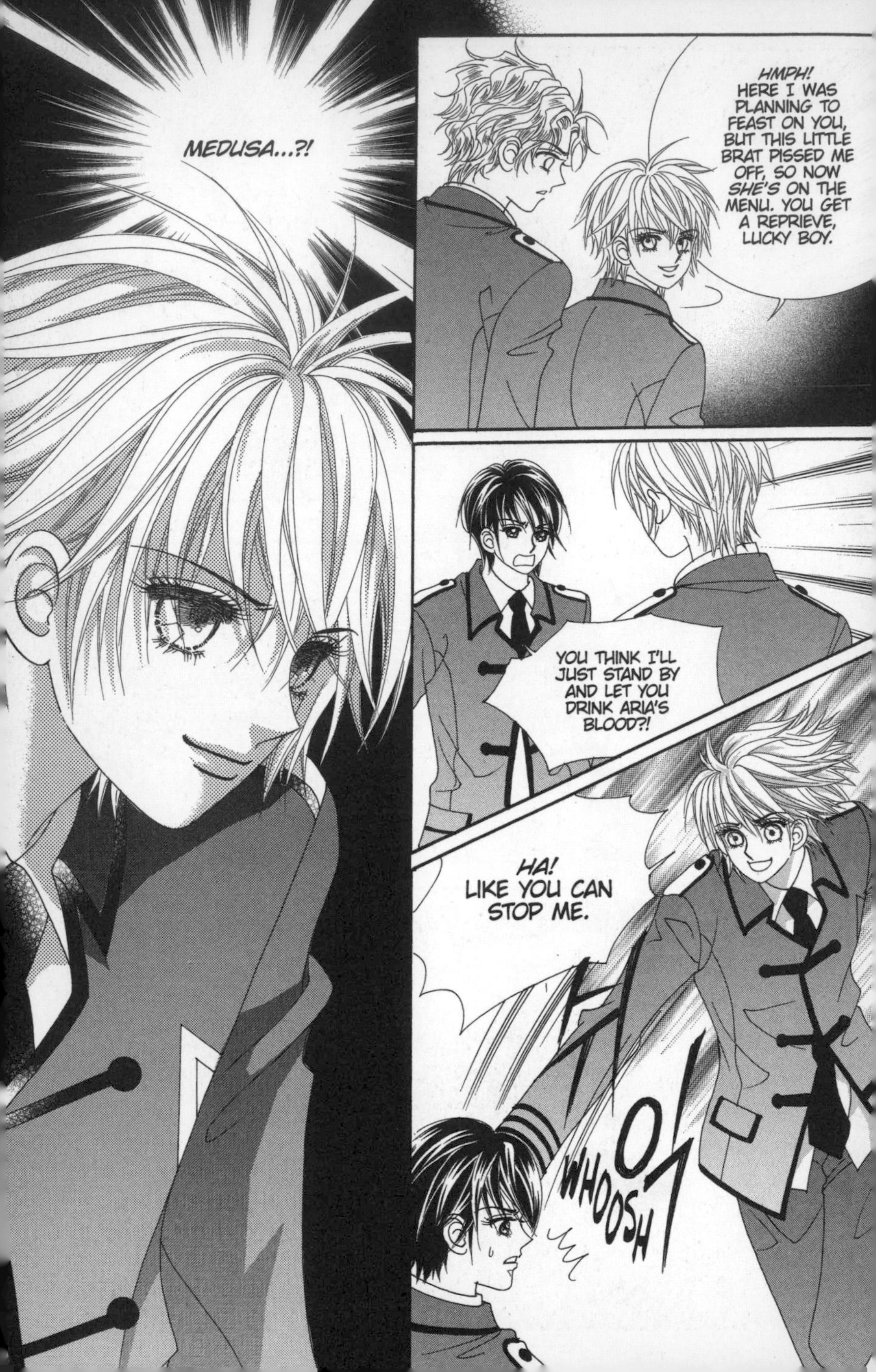
MEDUSA...?!
HMPH! HERE I WAS PLANNING TO FEAST ON YOU, BUT THIS LITTLE BRAT PISSED ME OFF, SO NOW SHE'S ON THE MENU. YOU GET A REPRIEVE, LUCKY BOY.
YOU THINK I'LL JUST STAND BY AND LET YOU DRINK ARIA'S BLOOD?!
HA! LIKE YOU CAN STOP ME.
WHOOSH

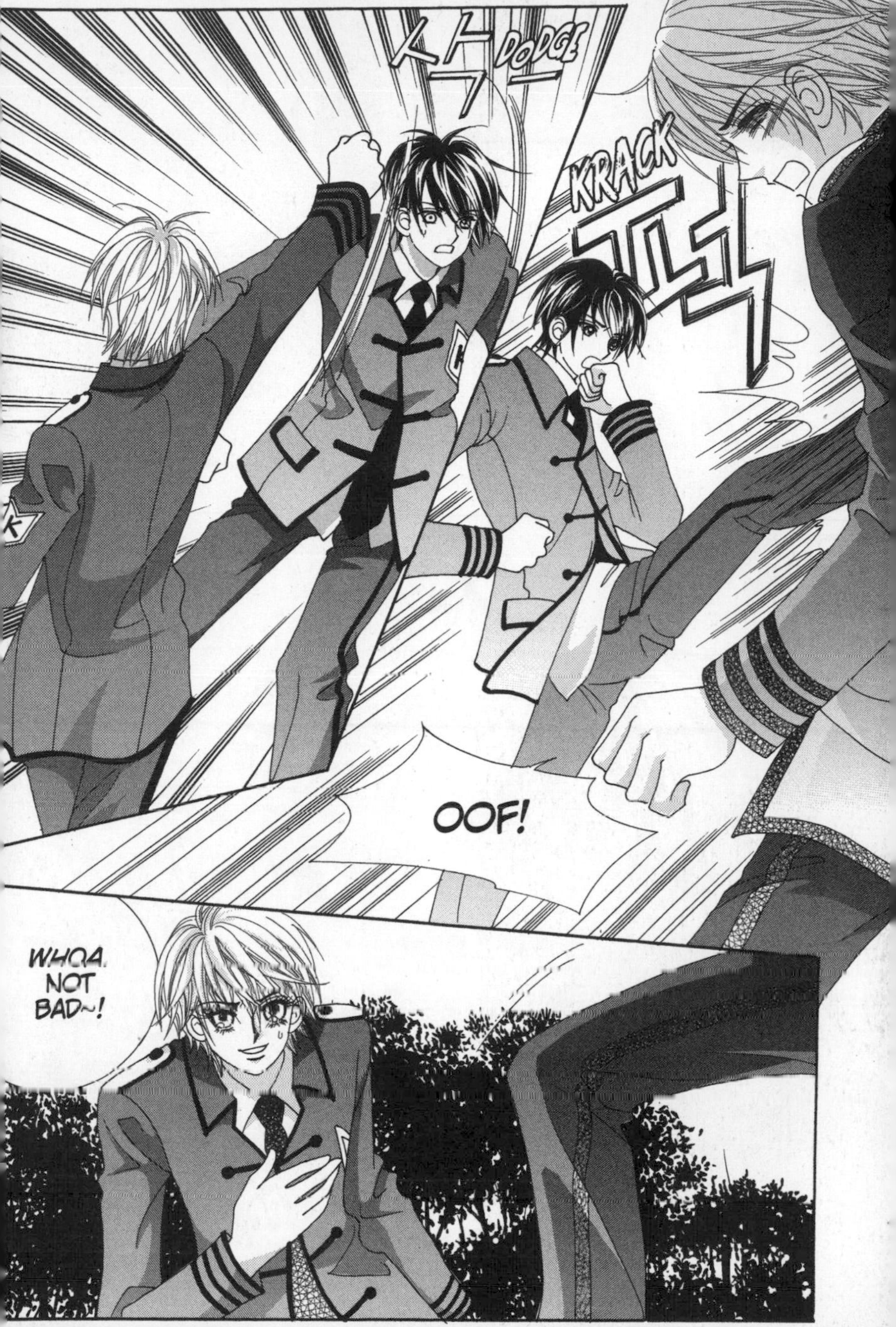
DODGE
KRACK
OOF!
WHOA, NOT BAD~!

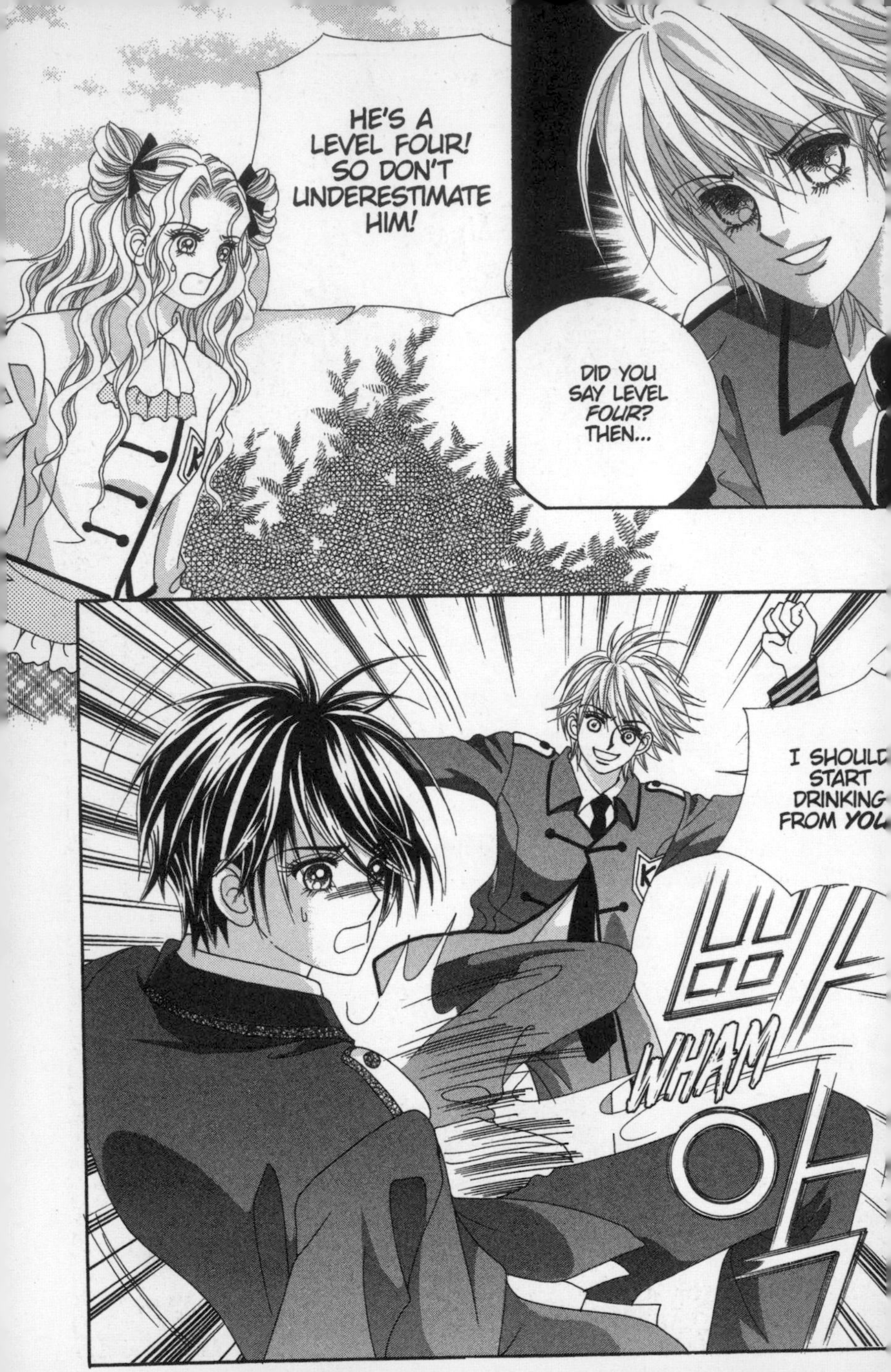
HE'S A LEVEL FOUR! SO DON'T UNDERESTIMATE HIM!
DID YOU SAY LEVEL FOUR? THEN...
I SHOULD START DRINKING FROM YOU
WHAM

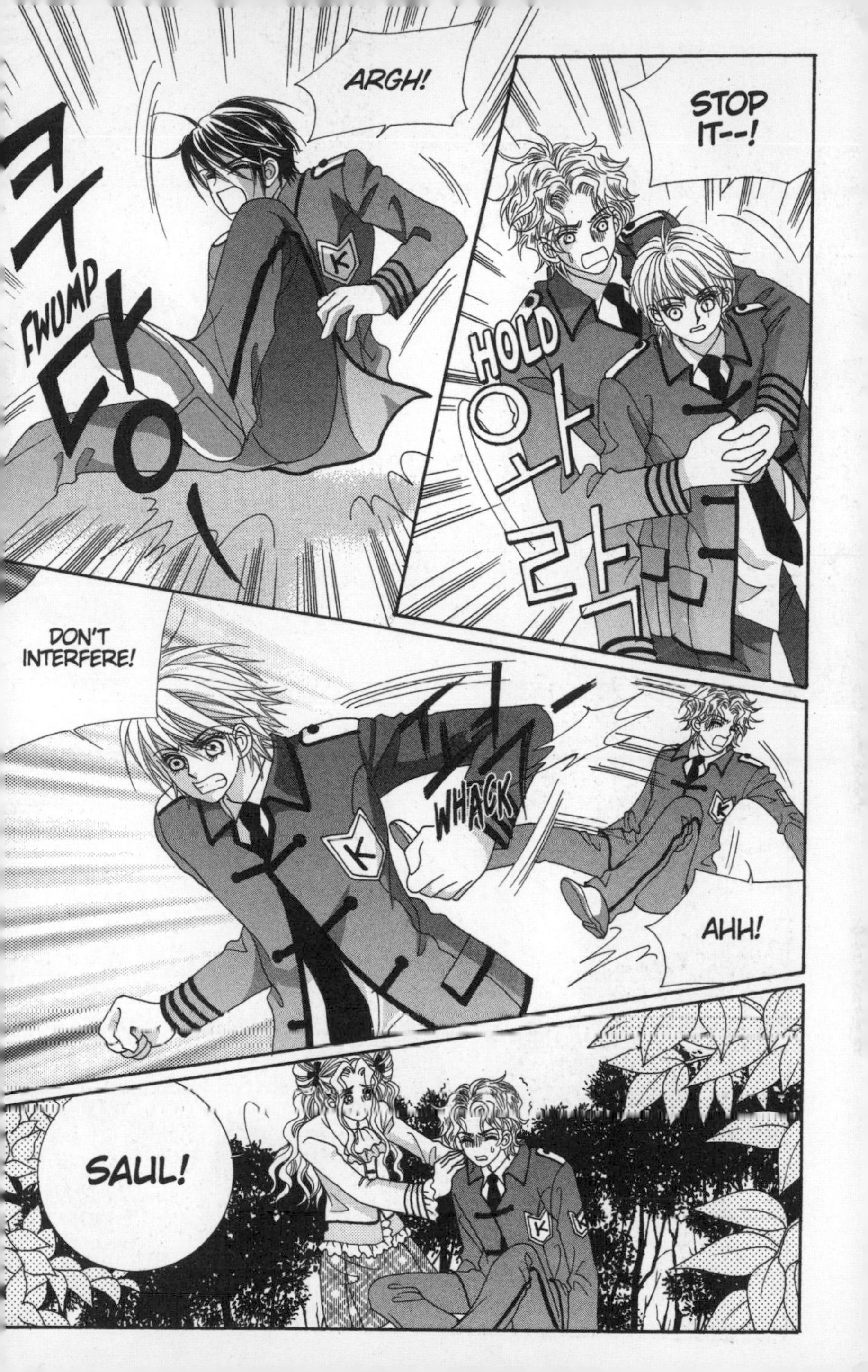

ARGH!
FWUMP
STOP IT--!
HOLD
DON'T INTERFERE!
WHACK
AHH!
SAUL!

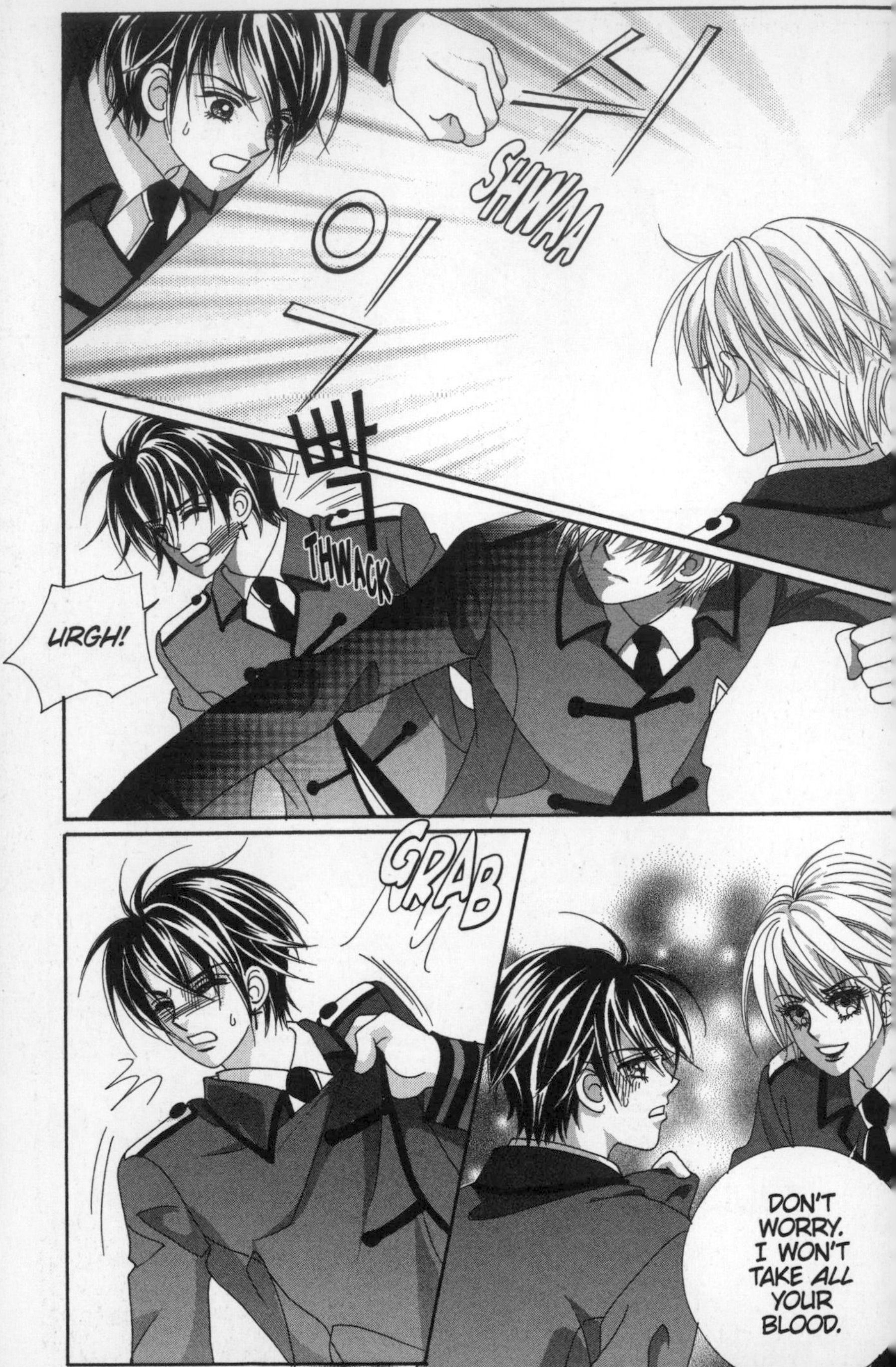
SHWAA
빡
THWACK
URGH!
GRAB
DON'T WORRY. I WON'T TAKE ALL YOUR BLOOD.

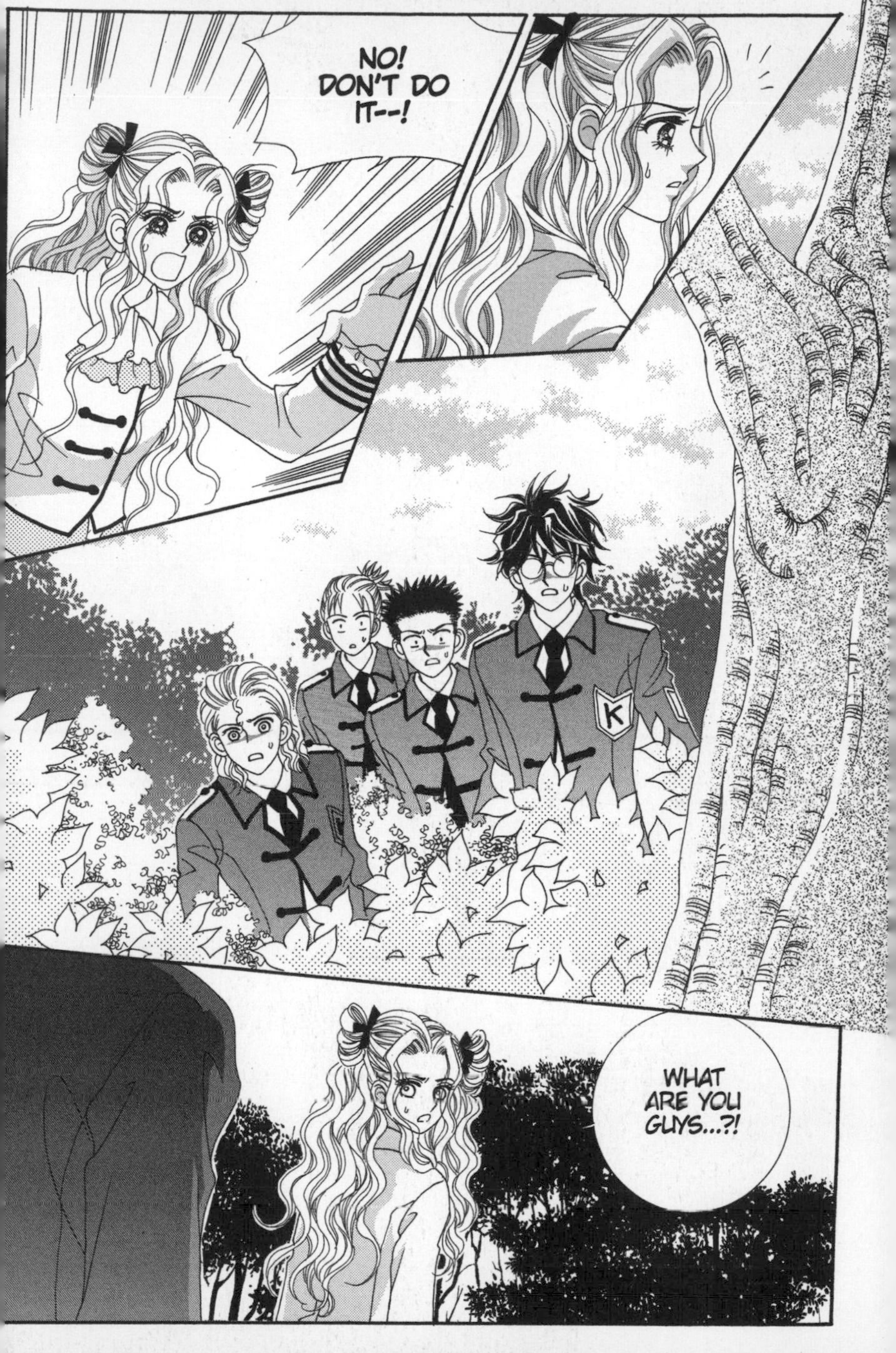
NO! DON'T DO IT--!
WHAT ARE YOU GUYS...?!

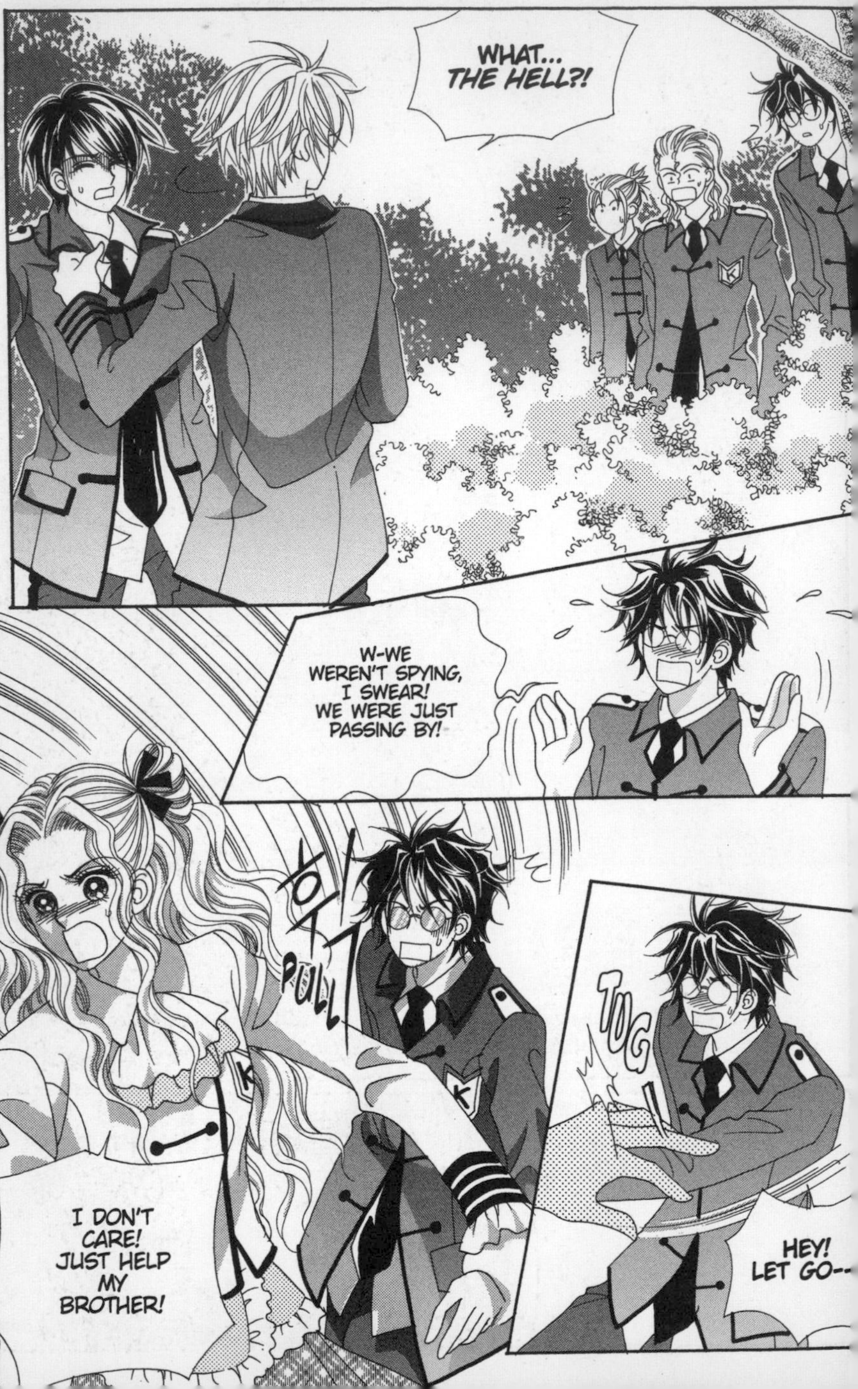
WHAT...
THE HELL?!
W-WE WEREN'T SPYING, I SWEAR! WE WERE JUST PASSING BY!
I DON'T CARE! JUST HELP MY BROTHER!
학
PULL
TUG
HEY! LET GO--

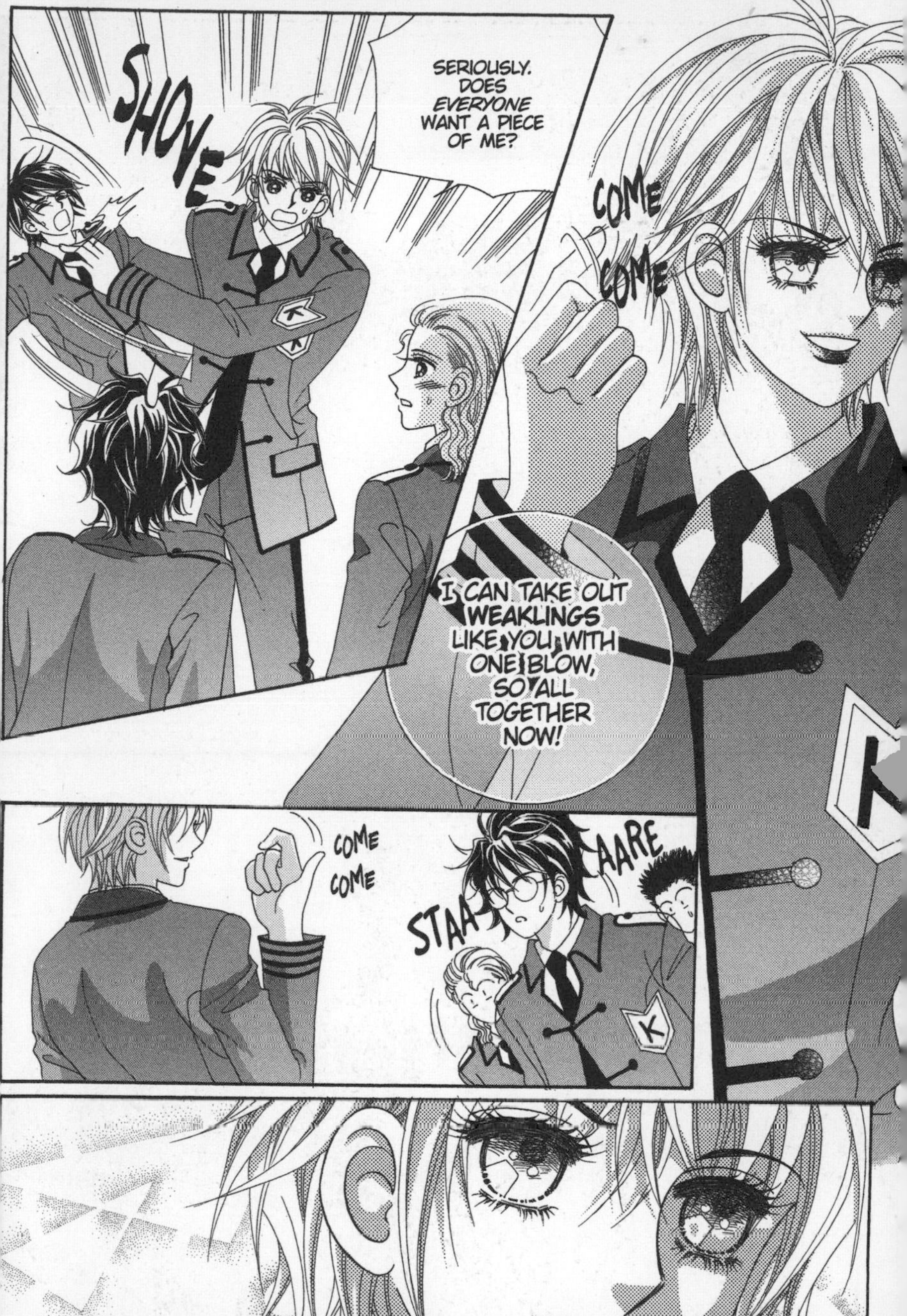
SHOVE
SERIOUSLY. DOES EVERYONE WANT A PIECE OF ME?
COME COME
I CAN TAKE OUT WEAKLINGS LIKE YOU WITH ONE BLOW, SO ALL TOGETHER NOW!
COME COME
STAA
AARE

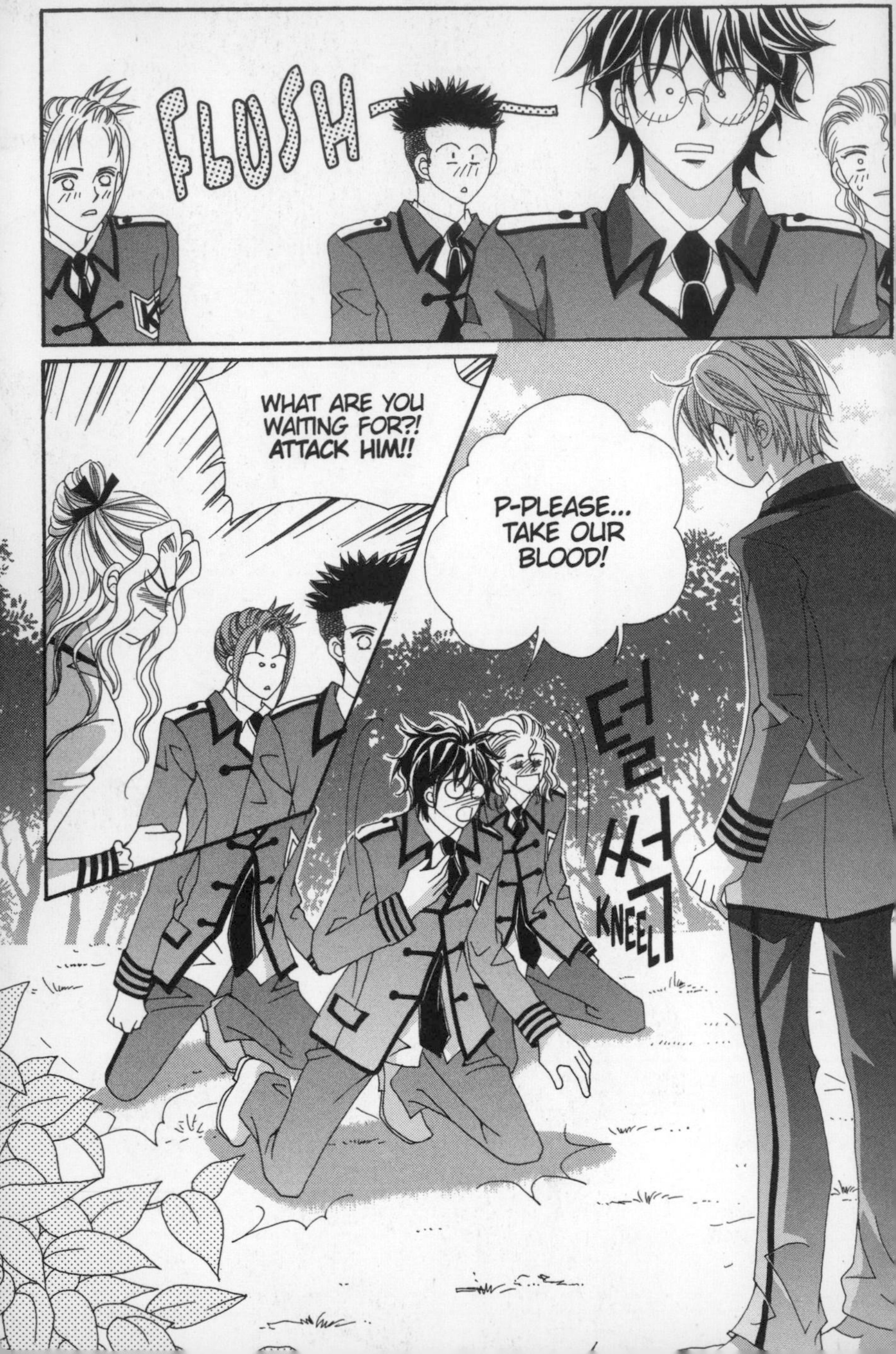
FLOSH
WHAT ARE YOU WAITING FOR?! ATTACK HIM!!
P-PLEASE... TAKE OUR BLOOD!
털썩
KNEEL

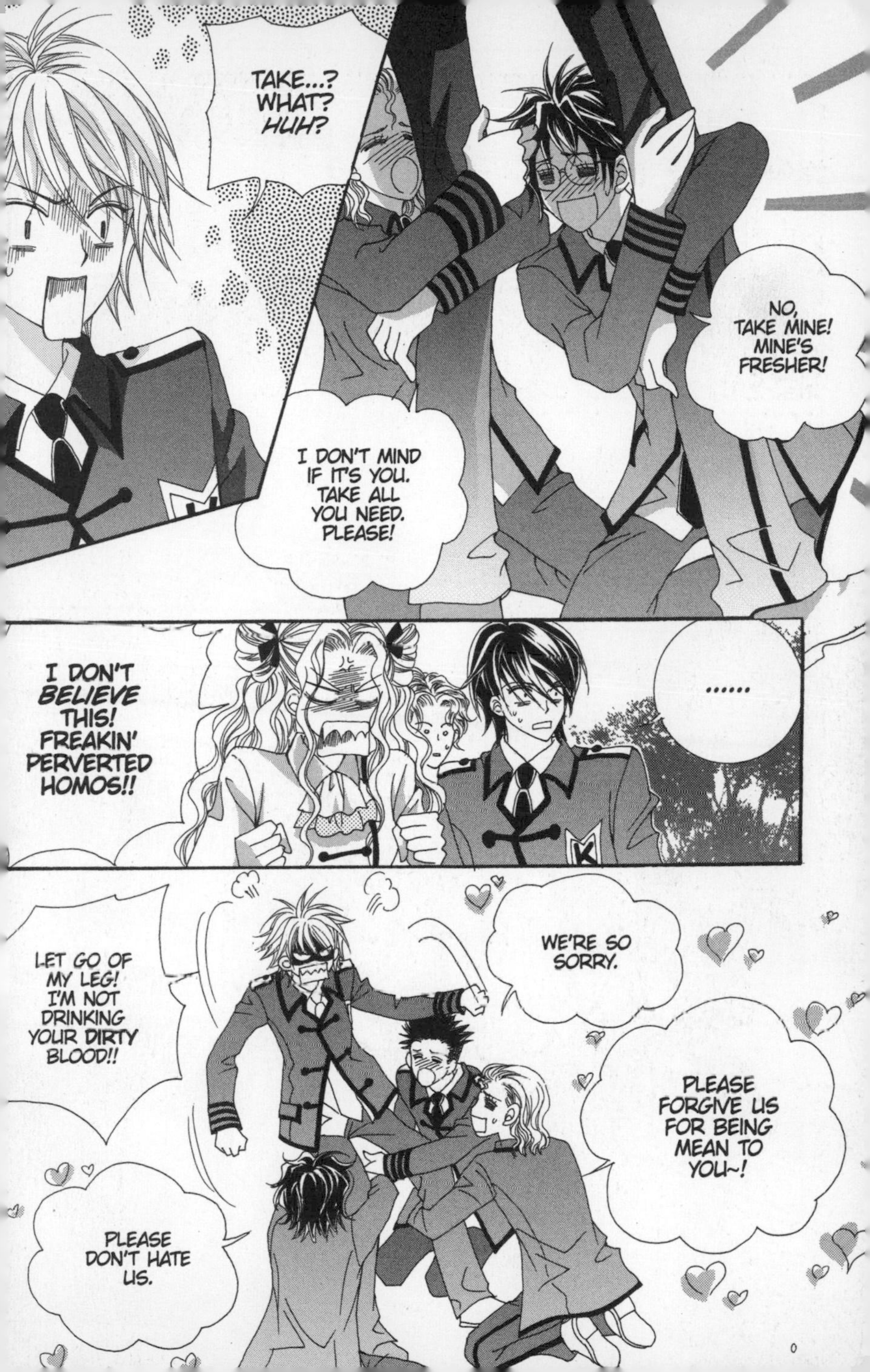
TAKE...? WHAT? *HUH?*
I DON'T MIND IF IT'S YOU. TAKE ALL YOU NEED. PLEASE!
NO, TAKE MINE! MINE'S FRESHER!
I DON'T *BELIEVE* THIS! FREAKIN' PERVERTED HOMOS!!
......
LET GO OF MY LEG! I'M NOT DRINKING YOUR DIRTY BLOOD!!
WE'RE SO SORRY.
PLEASE FORGIVE US FOR BEING MEAN TO YOU~!
PLEASE DON'T HATE US.

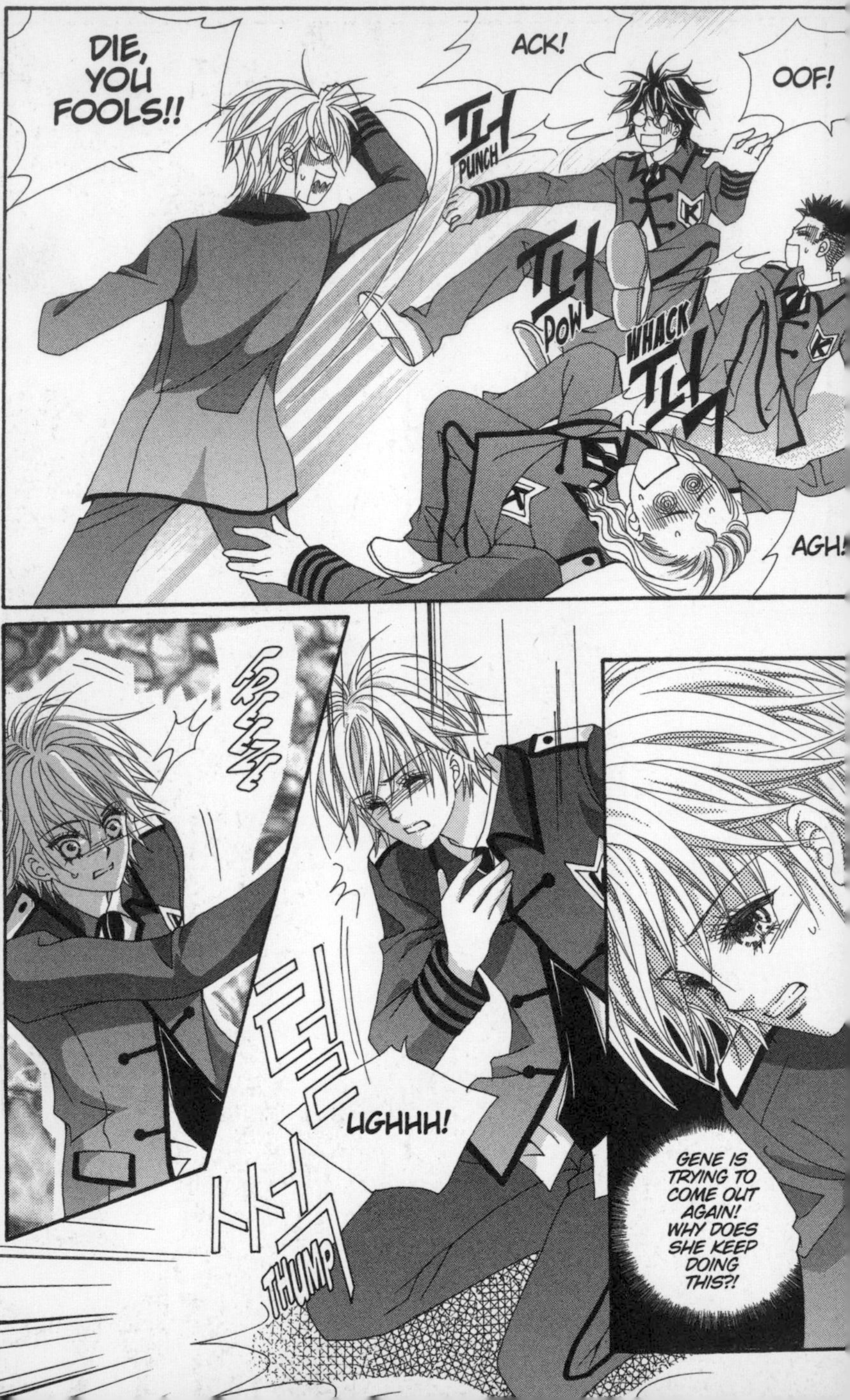
DIE, YOU FOOLS!!
PUNCH
ACK!
OOF!
POW
WHACK
AGH!
FREEZE
UGHHH!
THUMP
GENE IS TRYING TO COME OUT AGAIN! WHY DOES SHE KEEP DOING THIS?!

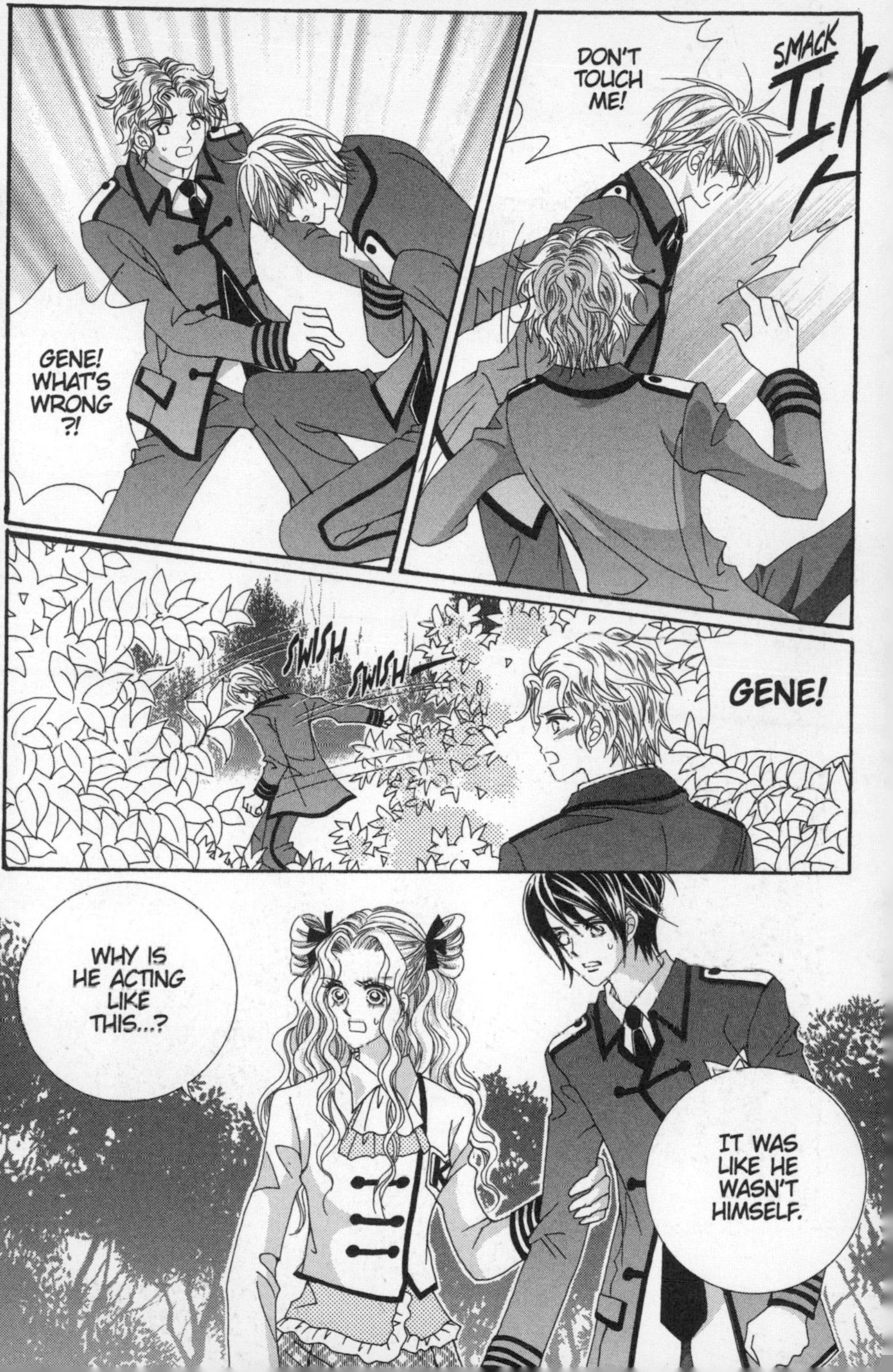
GENE! WHAT'S WRONG ?!
DON'T TOUCH ME!
SMACK
SWISH
SWISH
GENE!
WHY IS HE ACTING LIKE THIS...?
IT WAS LIKE HE WASN'T HIMSELF.

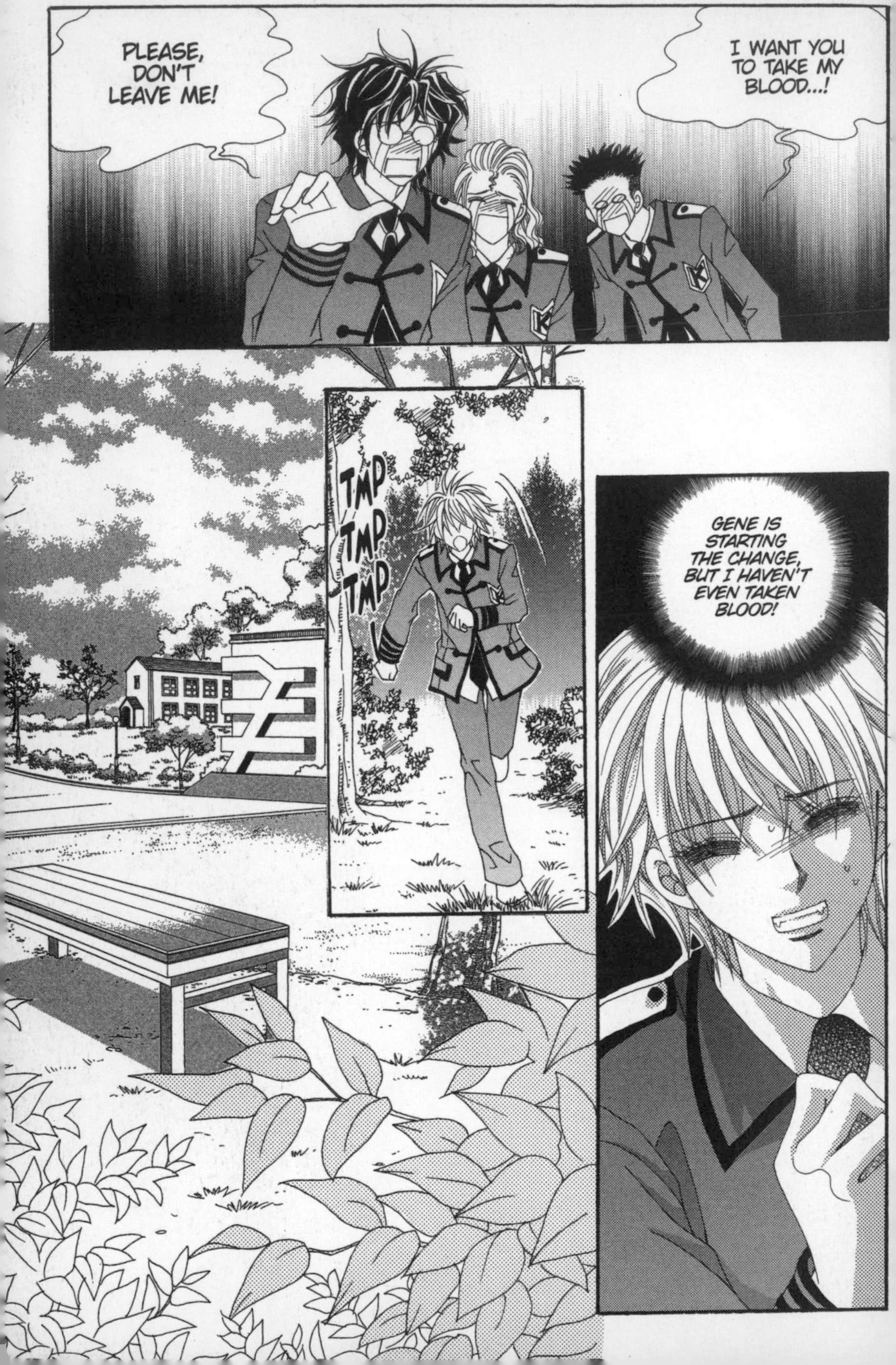
PLEASE, DON'T LEAVE ME!
I WANT YOU TO TAKE MY BLOOD...!
TMP TMP TMP
GENE IS STARTING THE CHANGE, BUT I HAVEN'T EVEN TAKEN BLOOD!

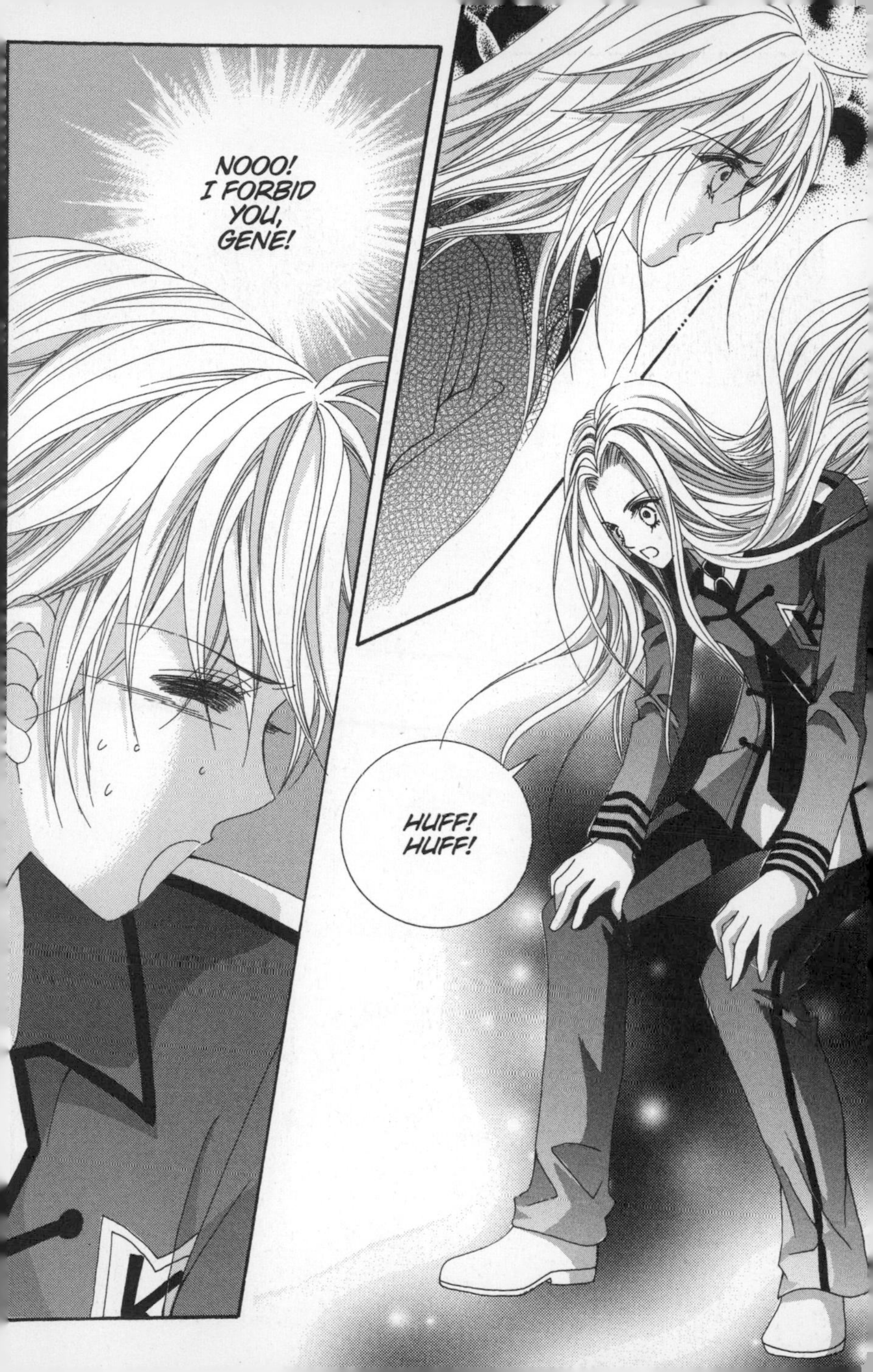
NOOO! I FORBID YOU, GENE!
HUFF! HUFF!

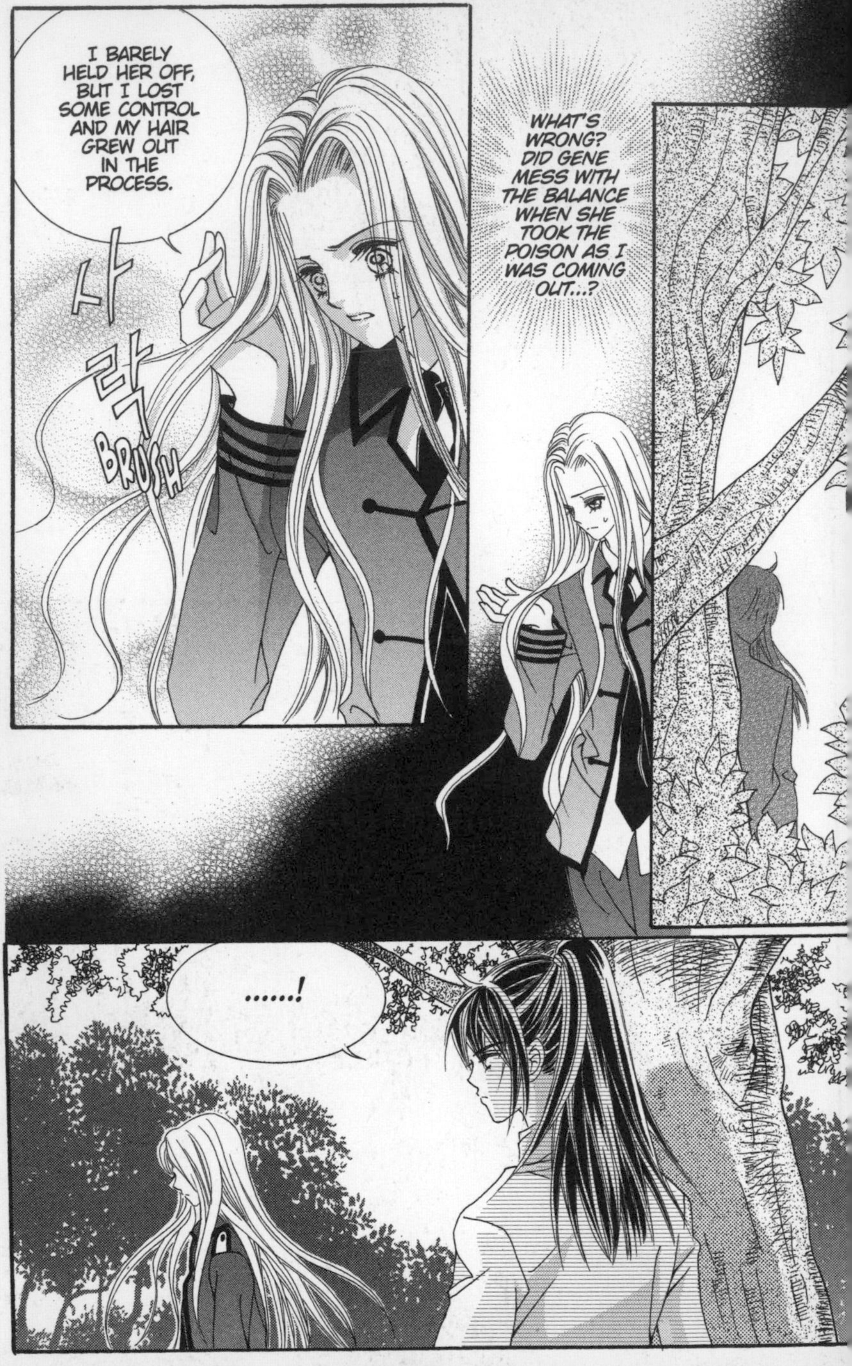
I BARELY HELD HER OFF, BUT I LOST SOME CONTROL AND MY HAIR GREW OUT IN THE PROCESS.
나 라
BRUSH
WHAT'S WRONG? DID GENE MESS WITH THE BALANCE WHEN SHE TOOK THE POISON AS I WAS COMING OUT...?
......!

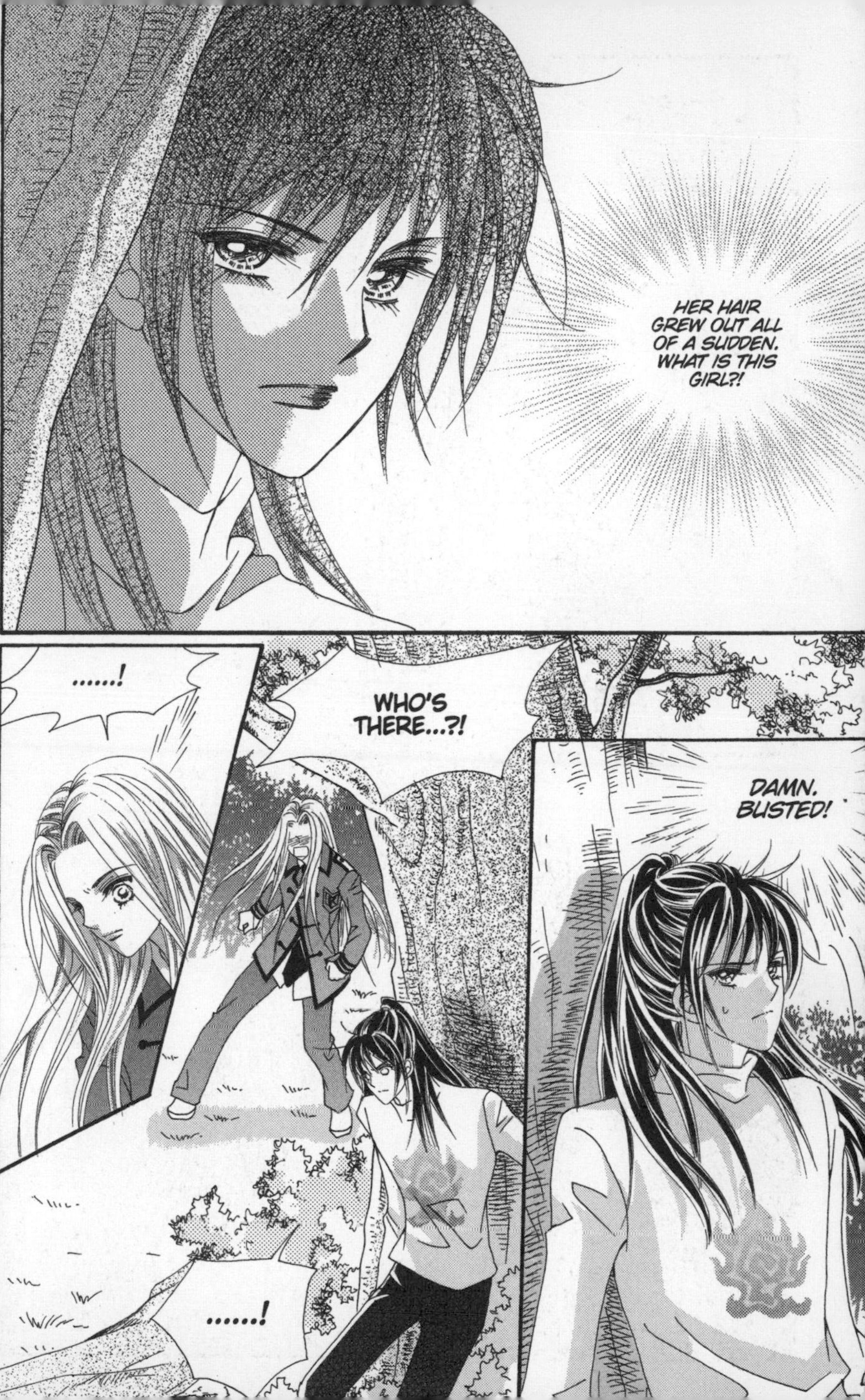
HER HAIR GREW OUT ALL OF A SUDDEN. WHAT IS THIS GIRL?!
......!
WHO'S THERE...?!
......!
DAMN. BUSTED!

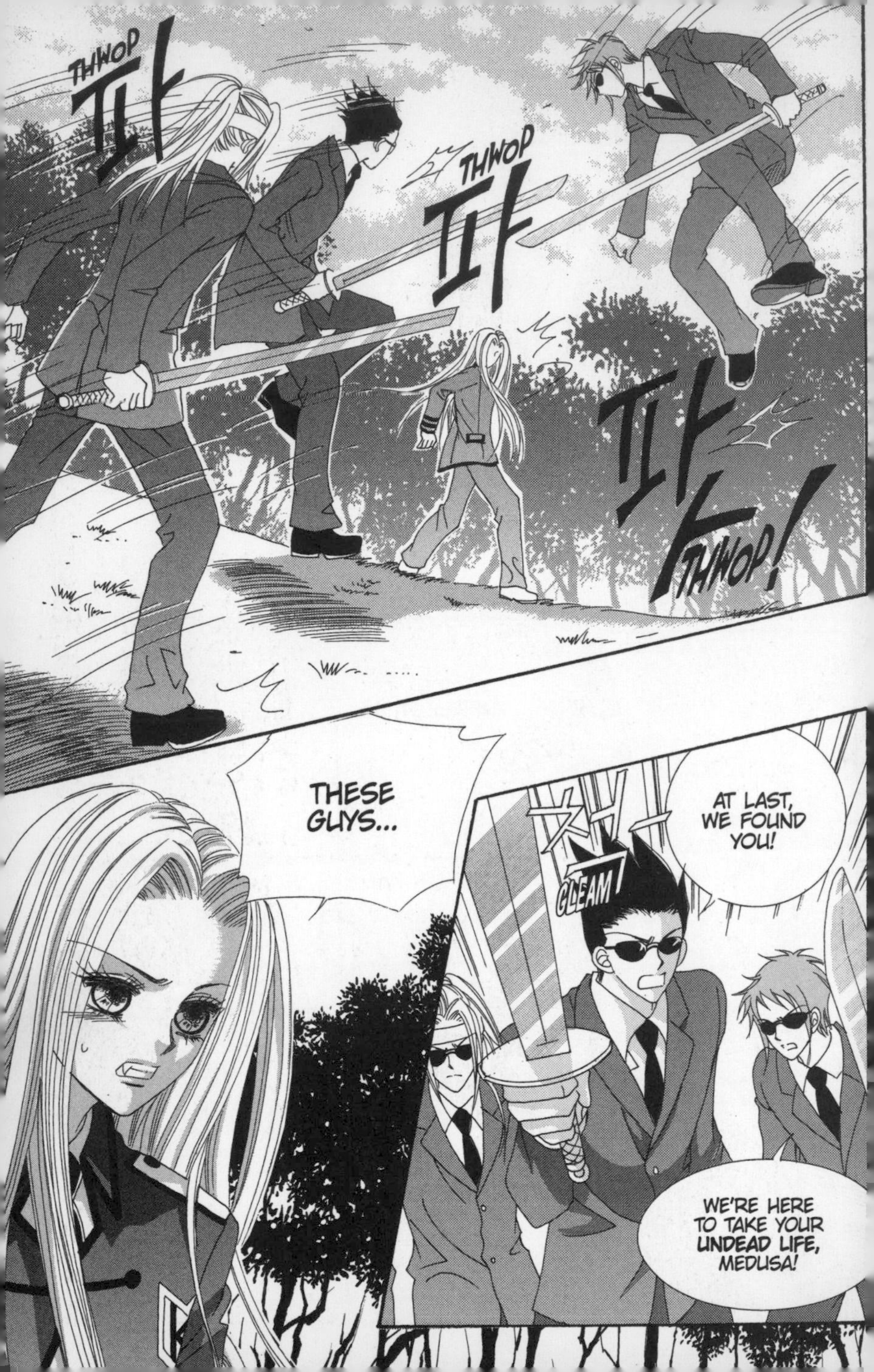
THWOP
THWOP
THWOP!
THESE GUYS...
GLEAM
AT LAST, WE FOUND YOU!
WE'RE HERE TO TAKE YOUR UNDEAD LIFE, MEDUSA!

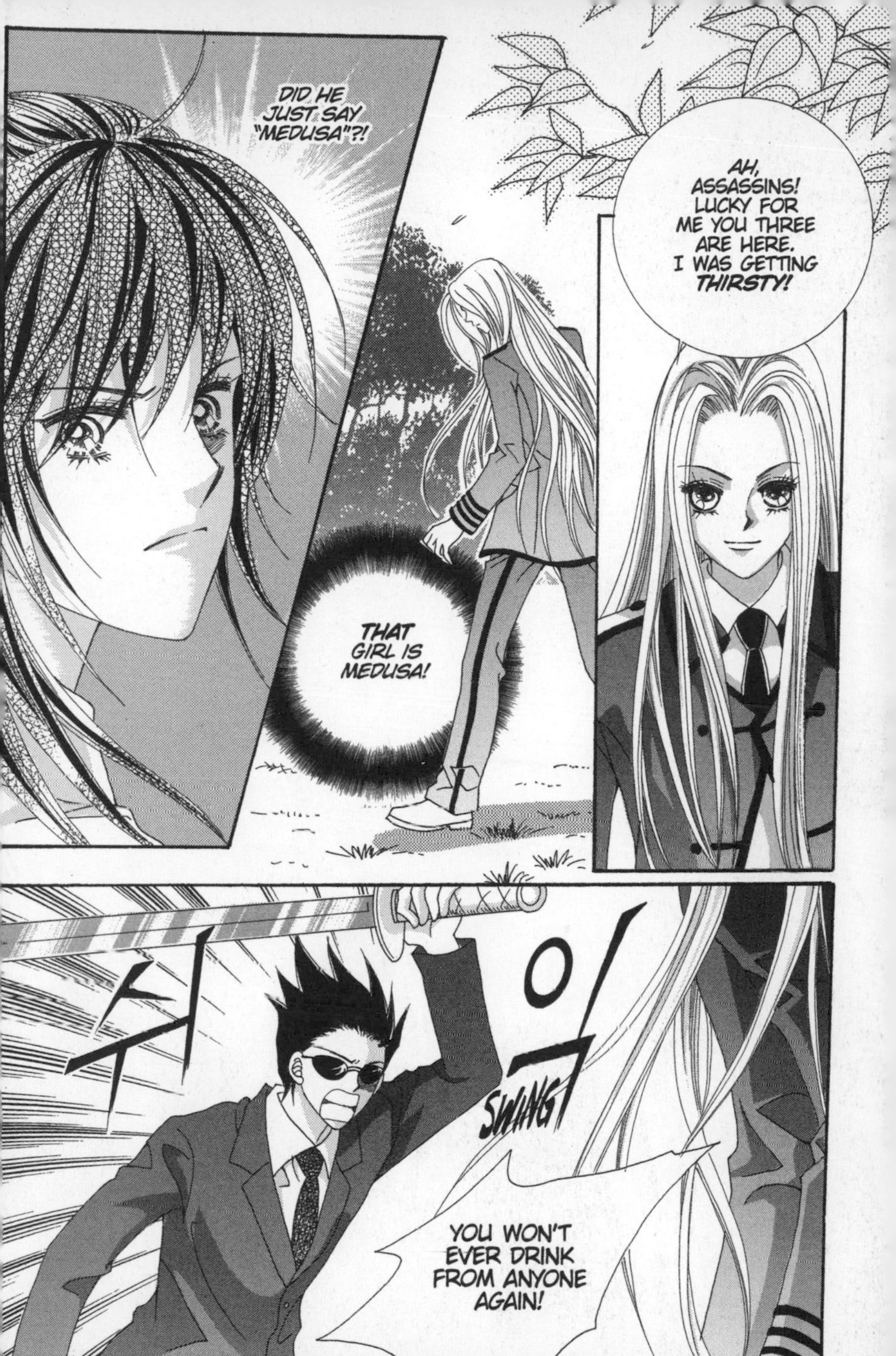
DID HE JUST SAY "MEDUSA"?!
THAT GIRL IS MEDUSA!
AH, ASSASSINS! LUCKY FOR ME YOU THREE ARE HERE. I WAS GETTING THIRSTY!
SWING
YOU WON'T EVER DRINK FROM ANYONE AGAIN!

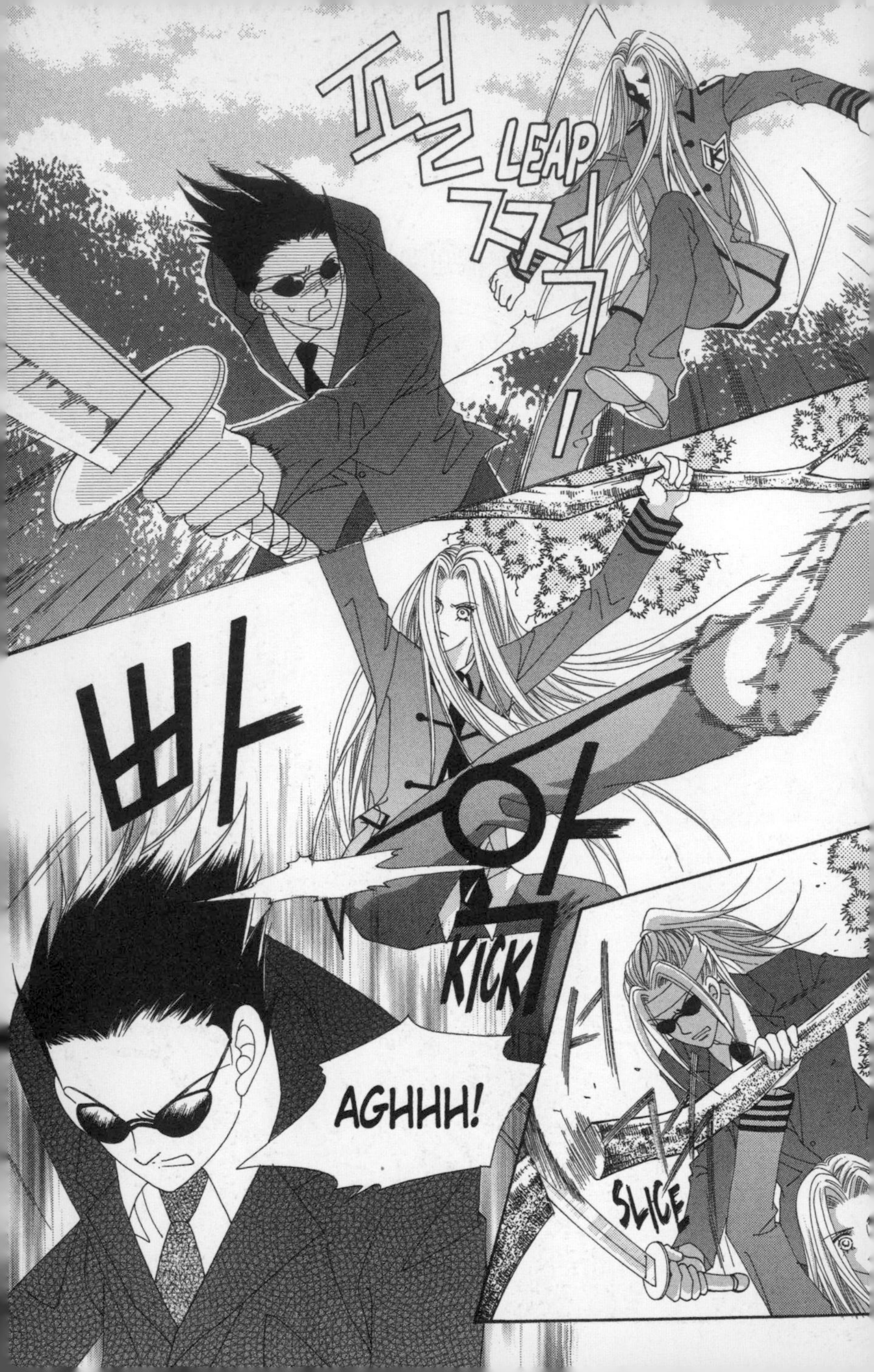
펄쩍
LEAP
빠악
KICK
AGHHH!
SLICE

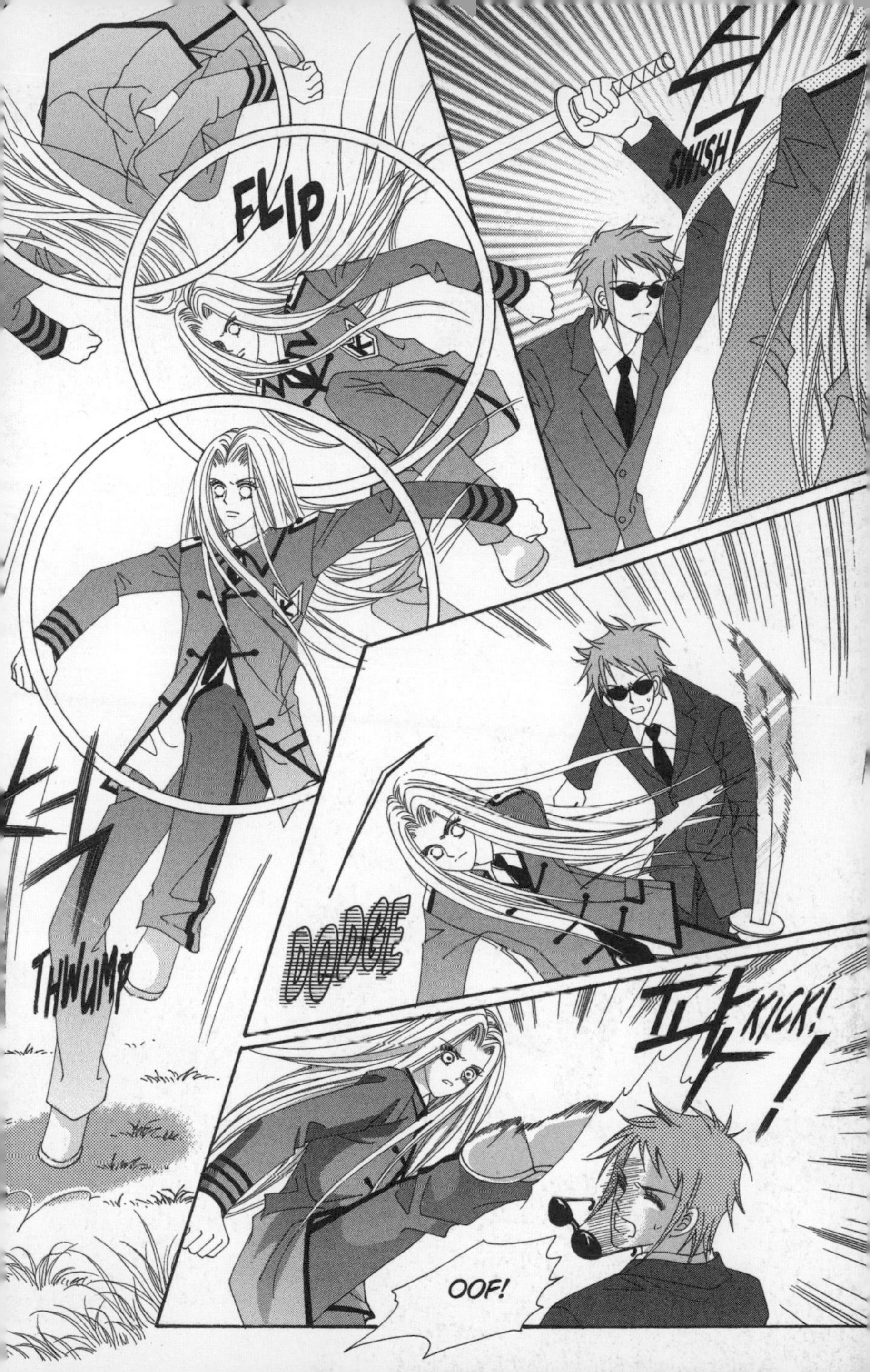
FLIP
THWUMP
SWISH
DODGE
KICK!
OOF!

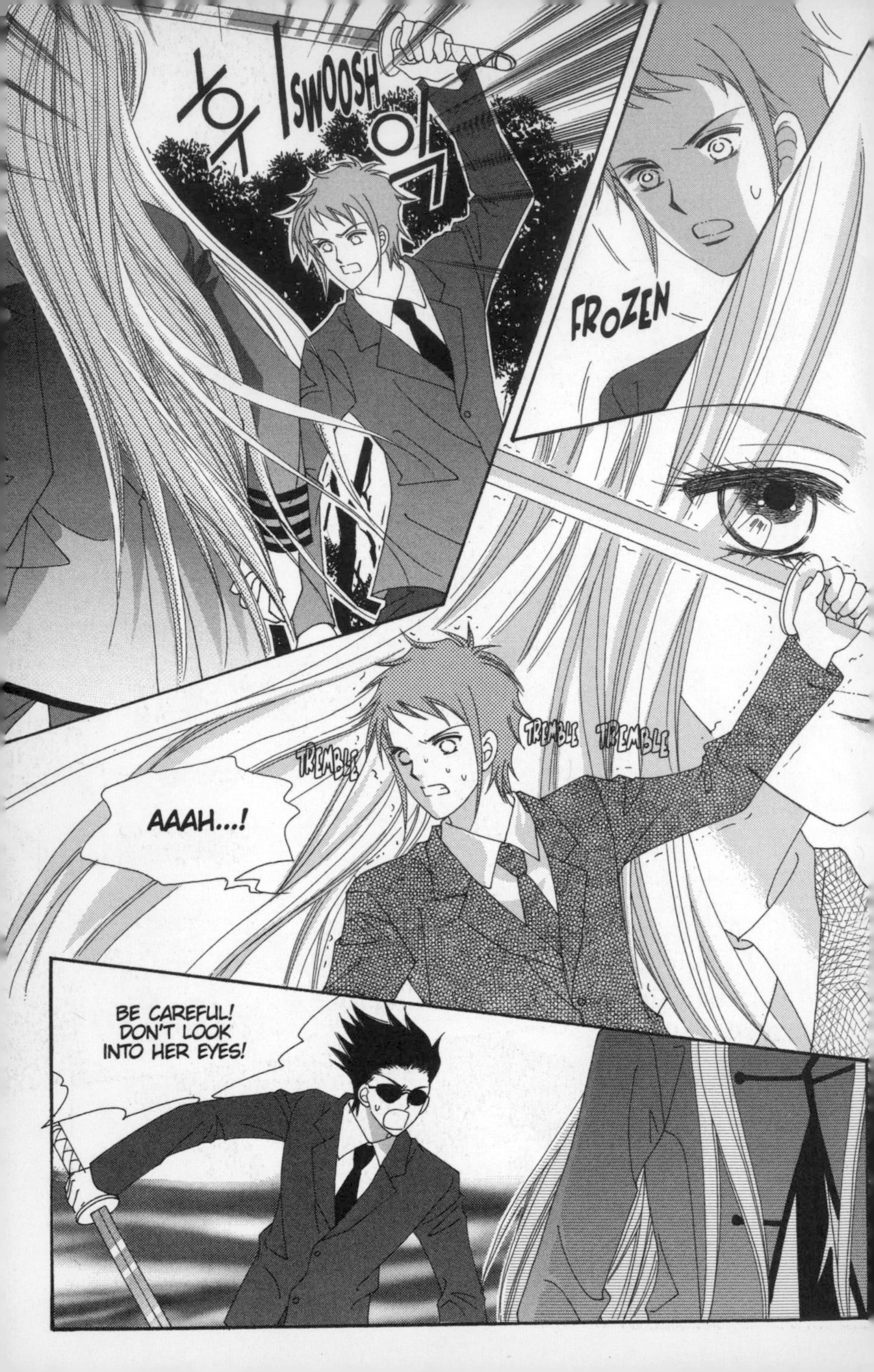
SWOOSH
FROZEN
TREMBLE
TREMBLE
TREMBLE
AAAH...!
BE CAREFUL! DON'T LOOK INTO HER EYES!

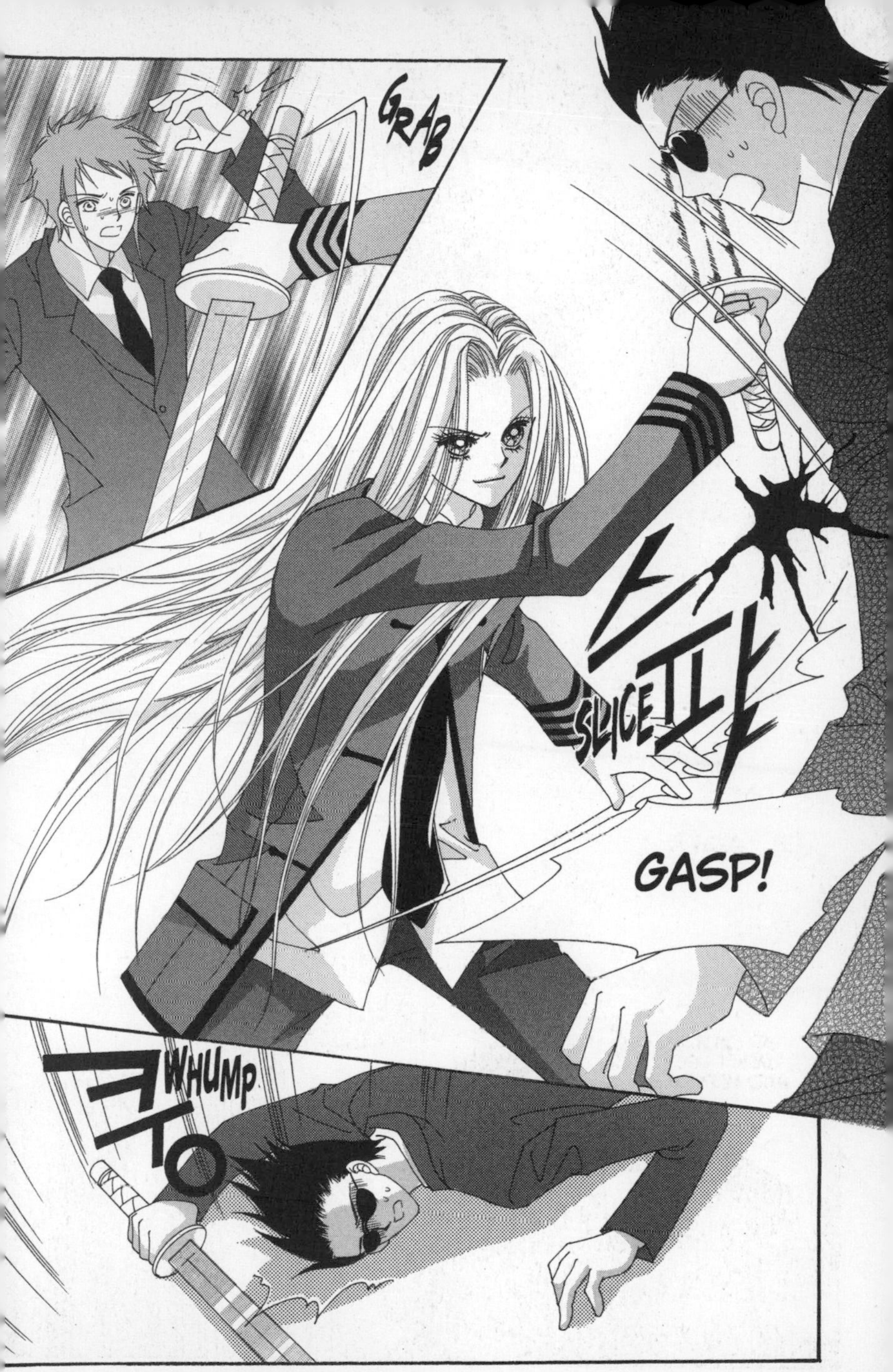
GRAB
SLICE
GASP!
WHUMP

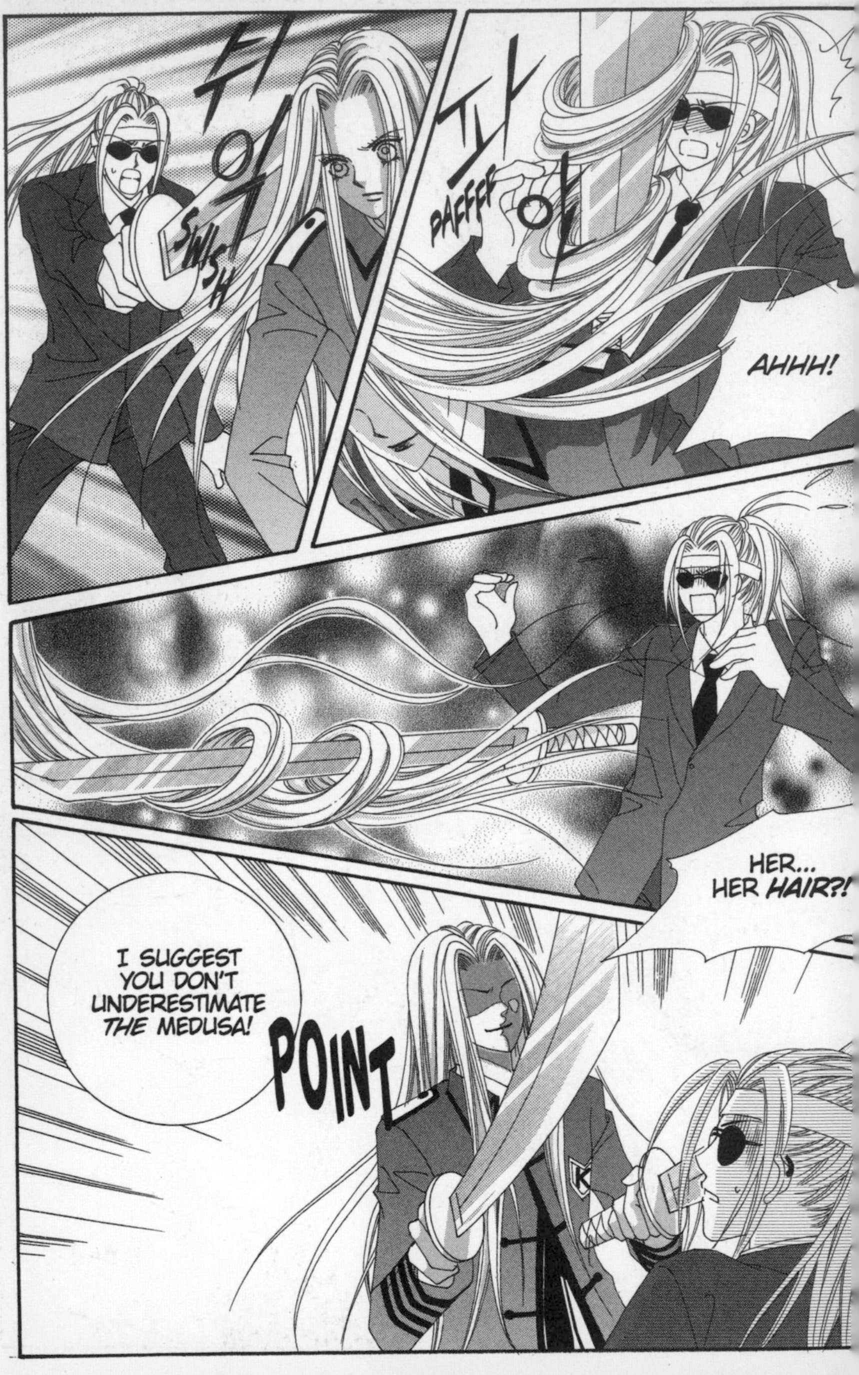
SWISH
PAFFFF
AHHH!
HER...
HER HAIR?!
I SUGGEST YOU DON'T UNDERESTIMATE THE MEDUSA!
POINT

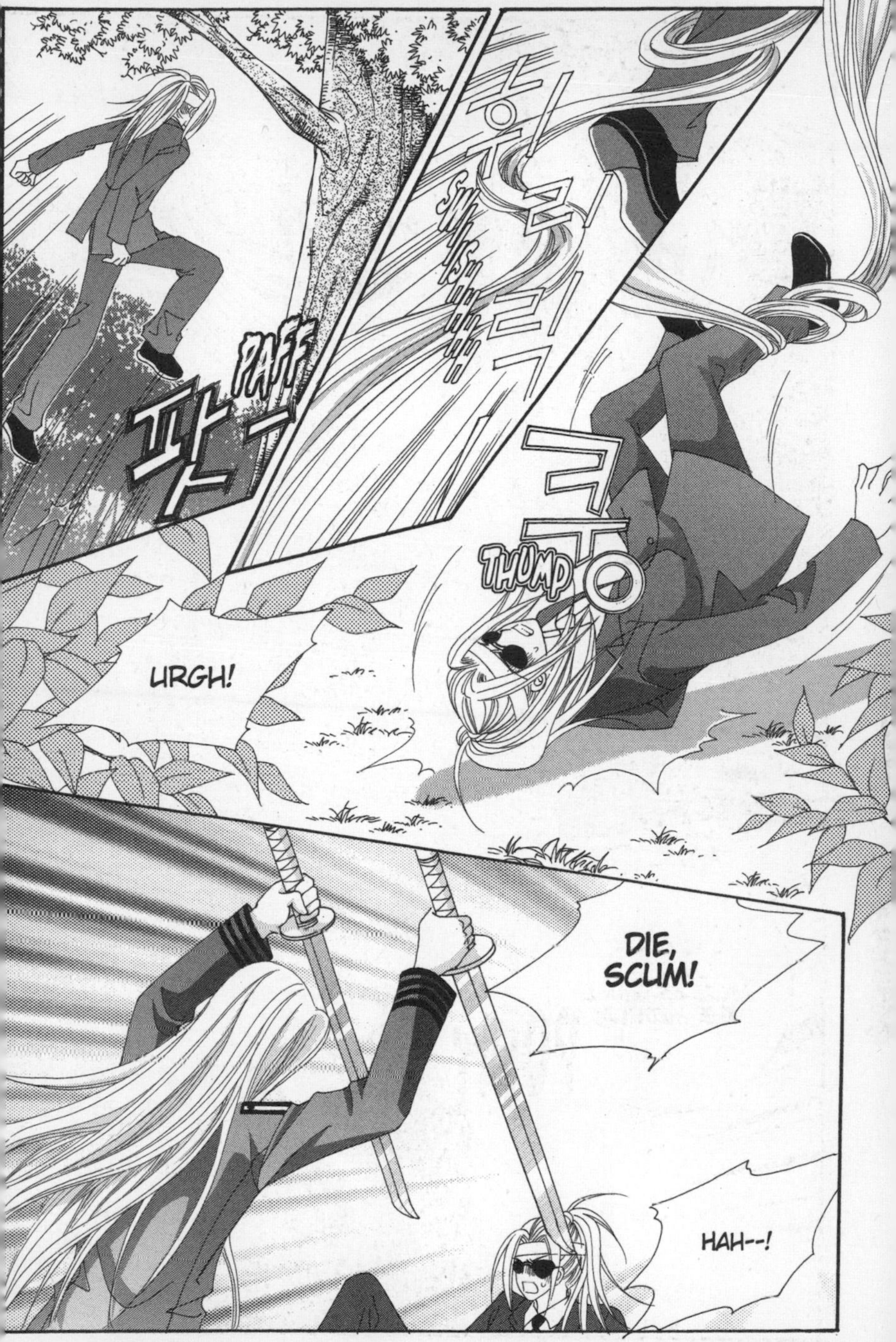
PAFF
SWISHHH!!
THUMP
URGH!
DIE, SCUM!
HAH--!

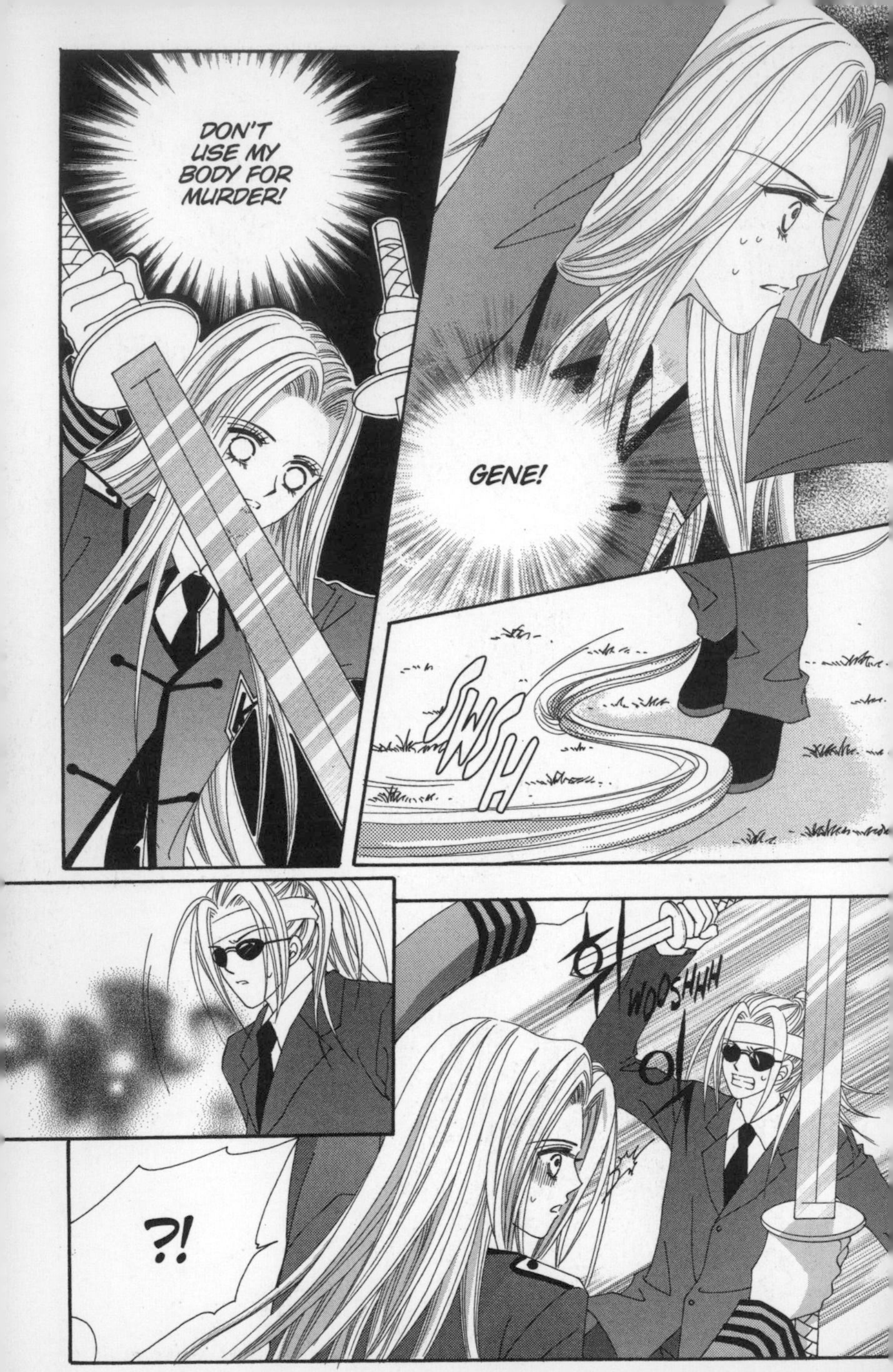
DON'T USE MY BODY FOR MURDER!
GENE!
SWSH
?!
WOOSHHH

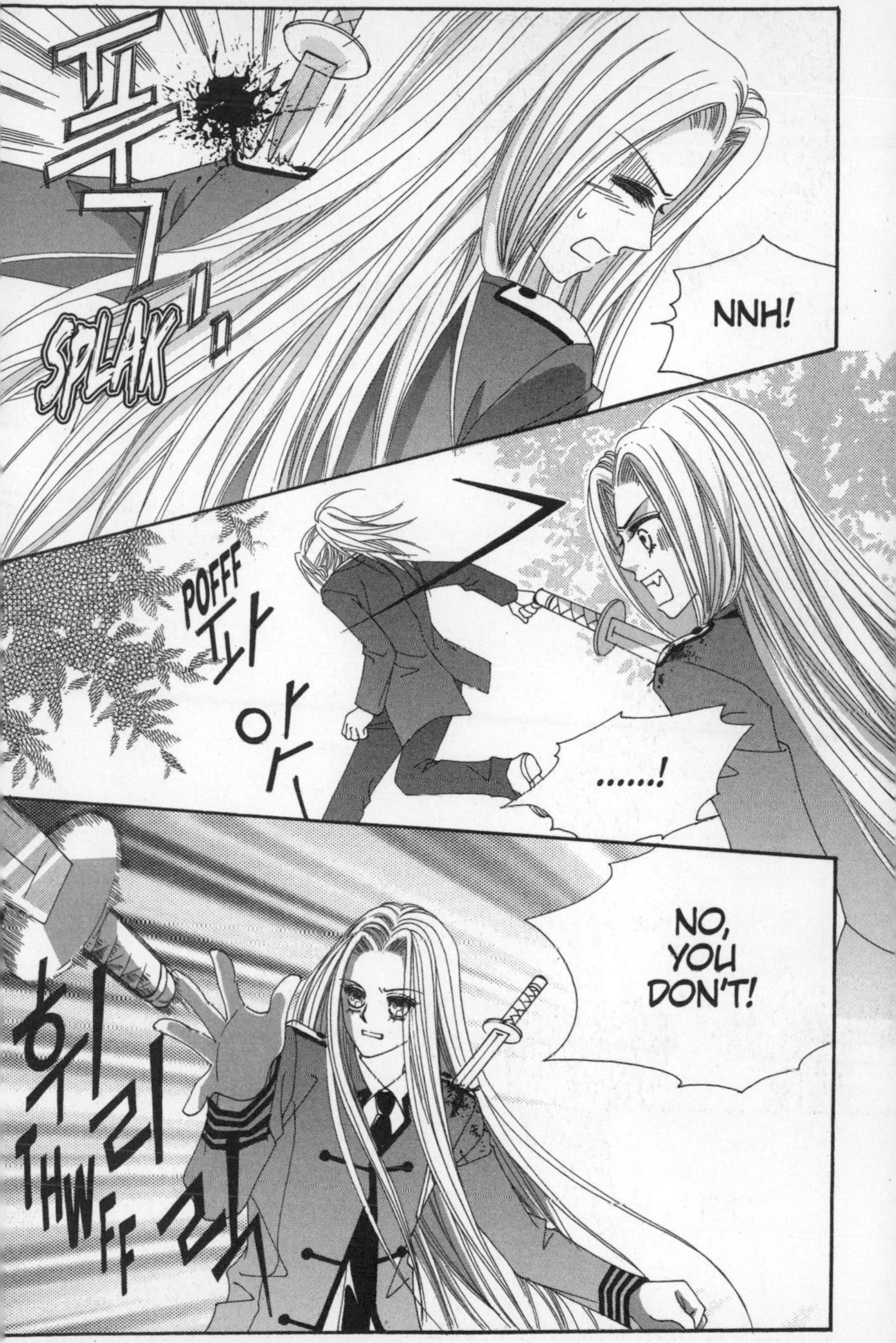
SPLAK
NNH!
POFFF
......!
NO, YOU DON'T!
THWFF

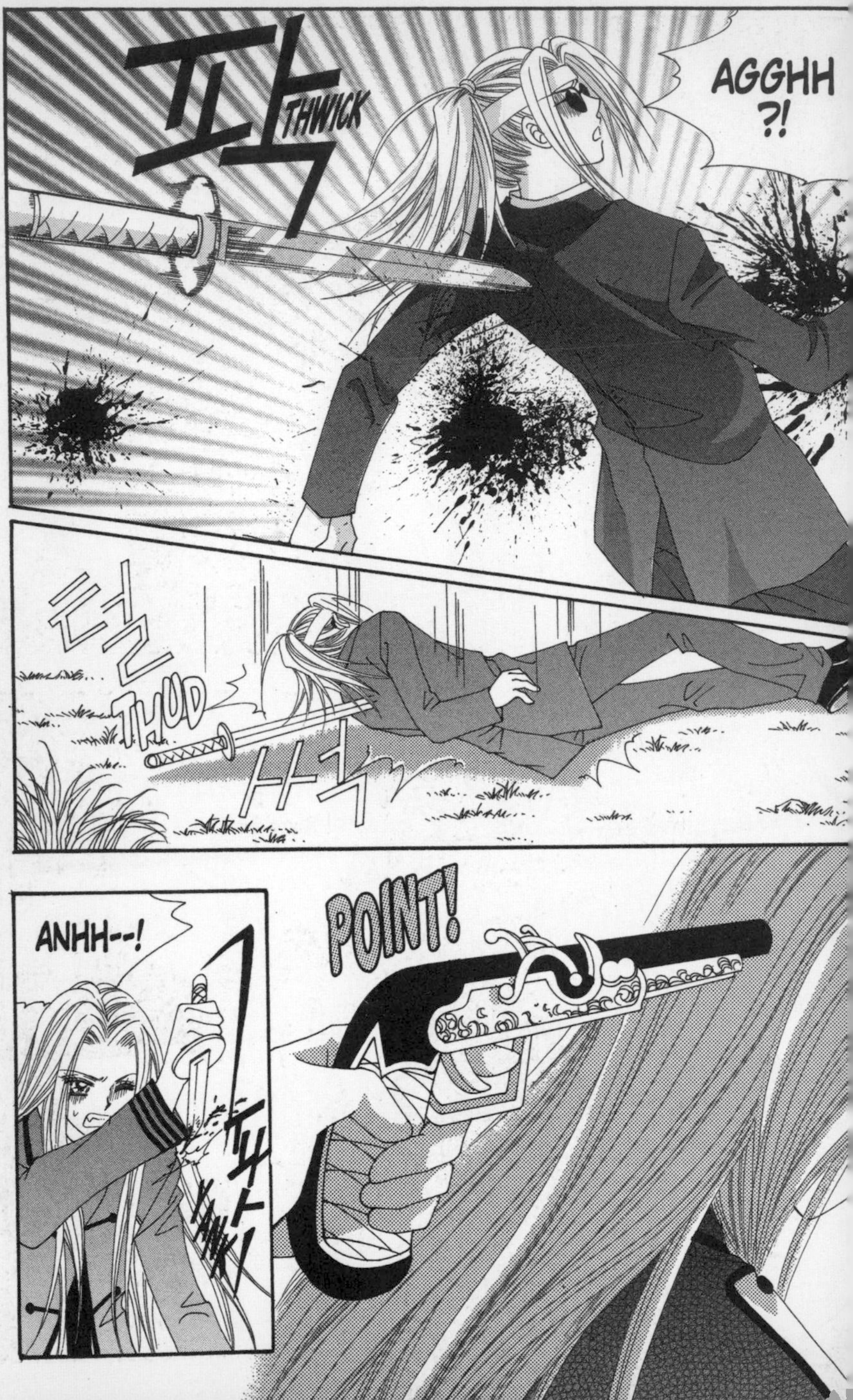
THWICK
AGGHH ?!
THUD
ANHH--!
YANK!
POINT!

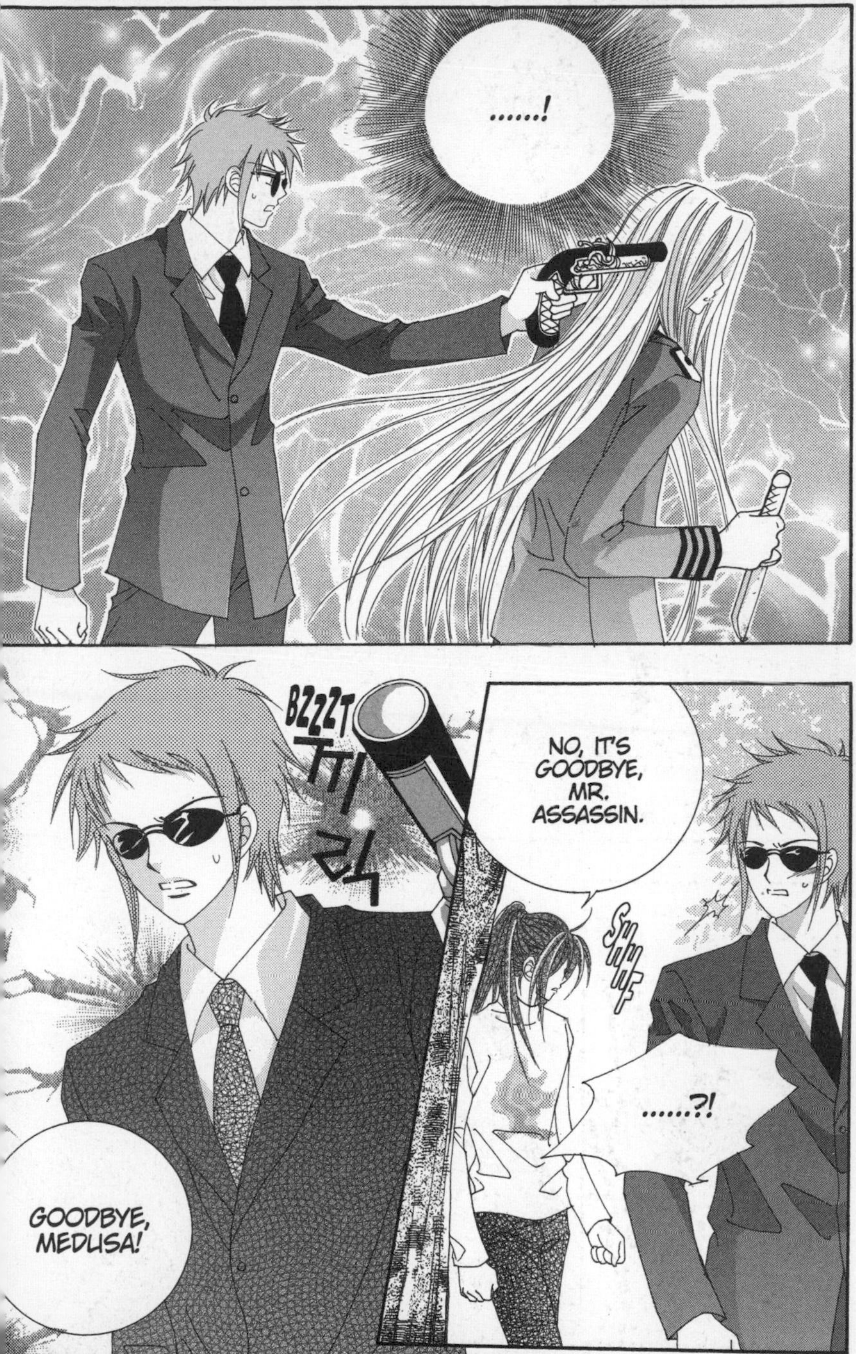
......!
BZZZT
GOODBYE, MEDUSA!
NO, IT'S GOODBYE, MR. ASSASSIN.
......?!

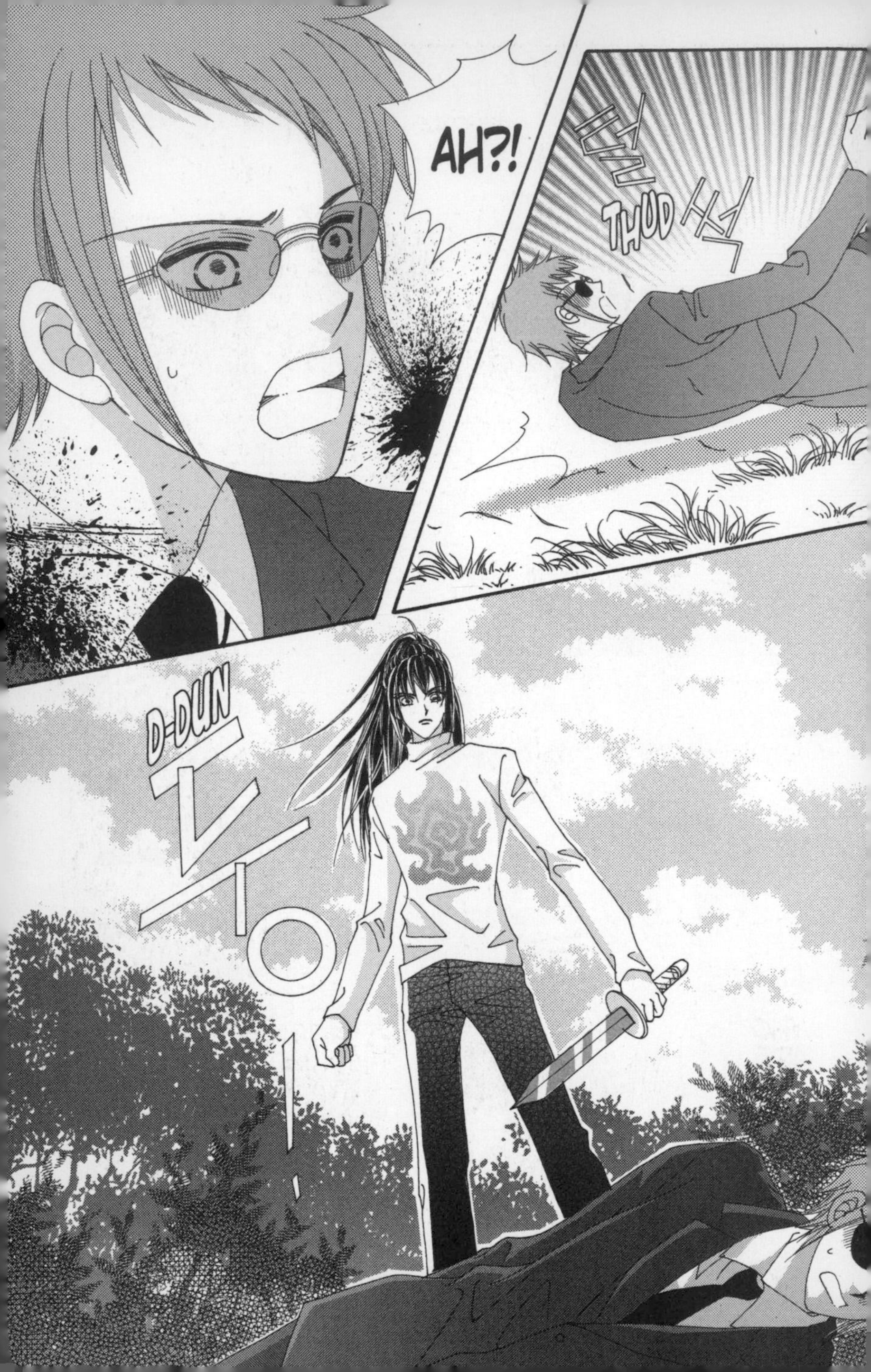
AH?!
THUD
D-DUN

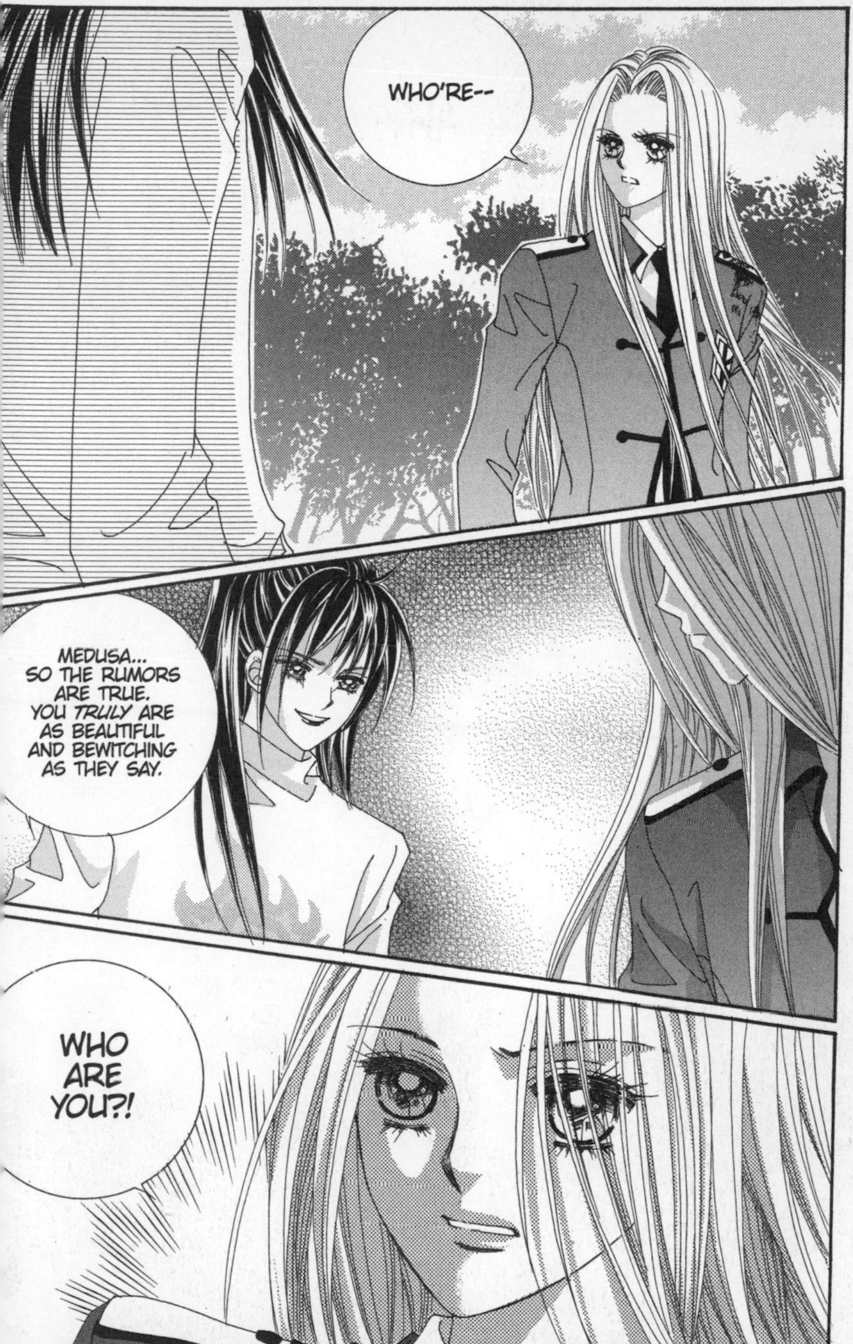
WHO'RE--
MEDUSA... SO THE RUMORS ARE TRUE. YOU TRULY ARE AS BEAUTIFUL AND BEWITCHING AS THEY SAY.
WHO ARE YOU?!

☆To be continued...☆

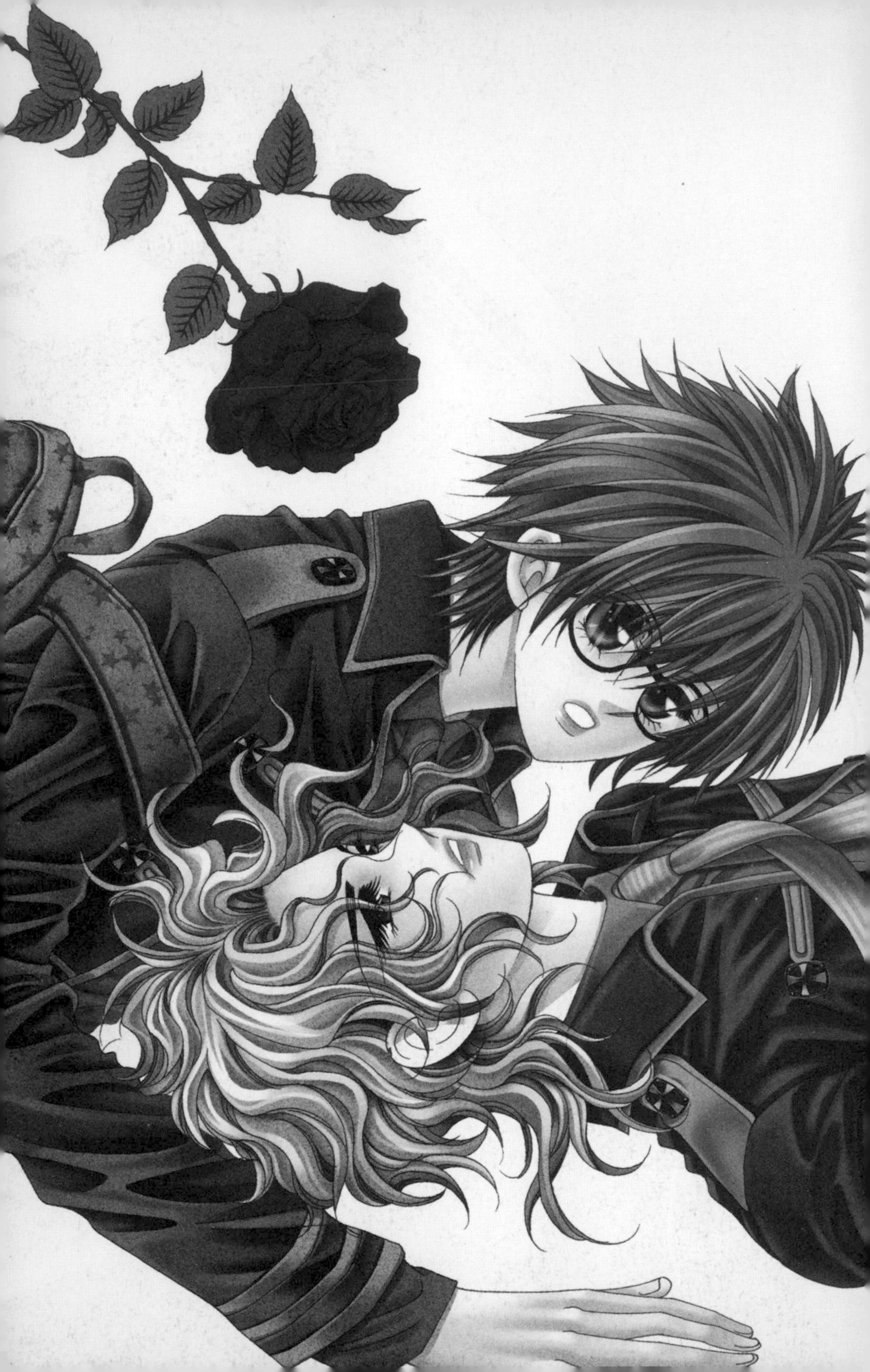

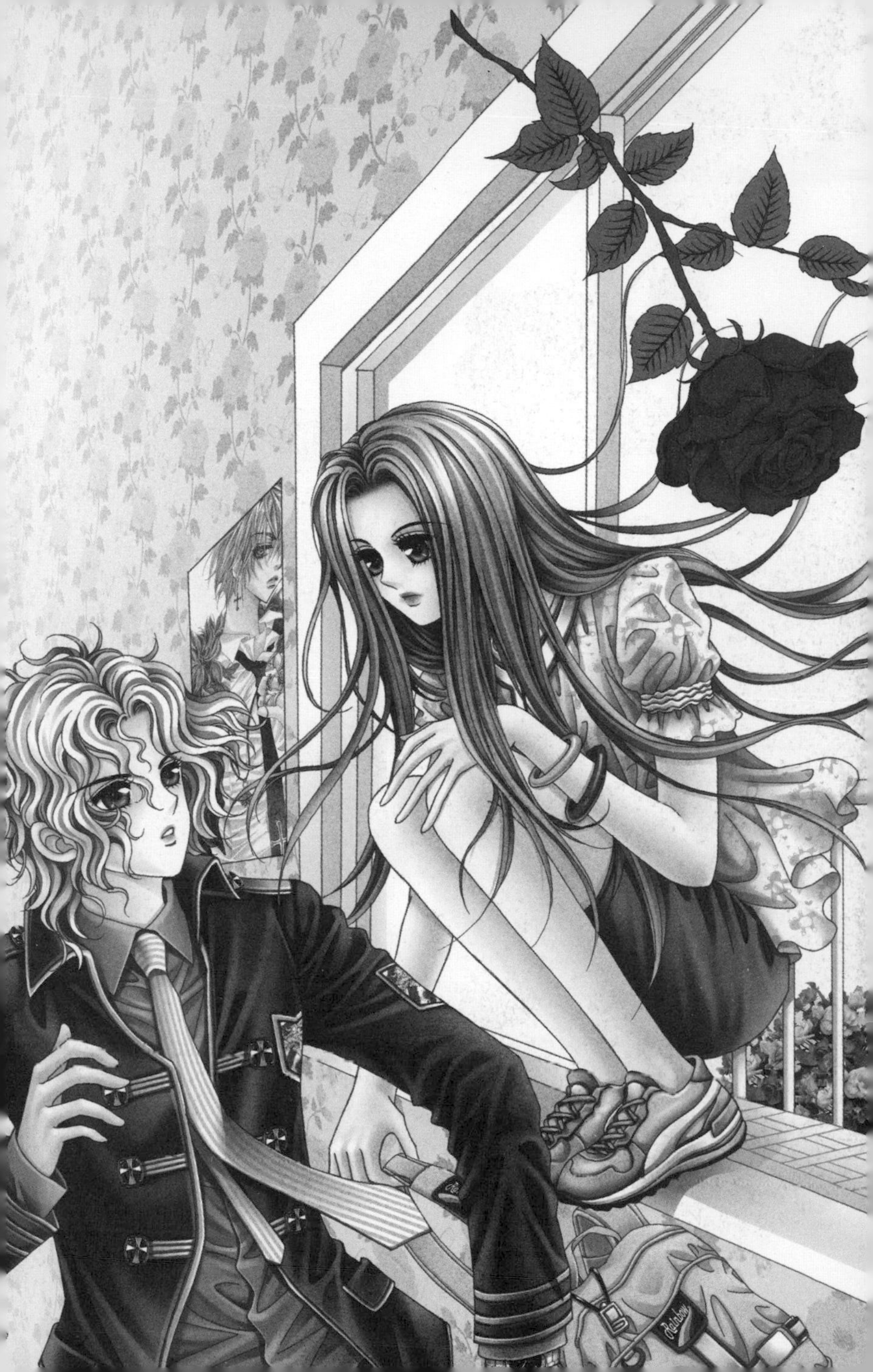

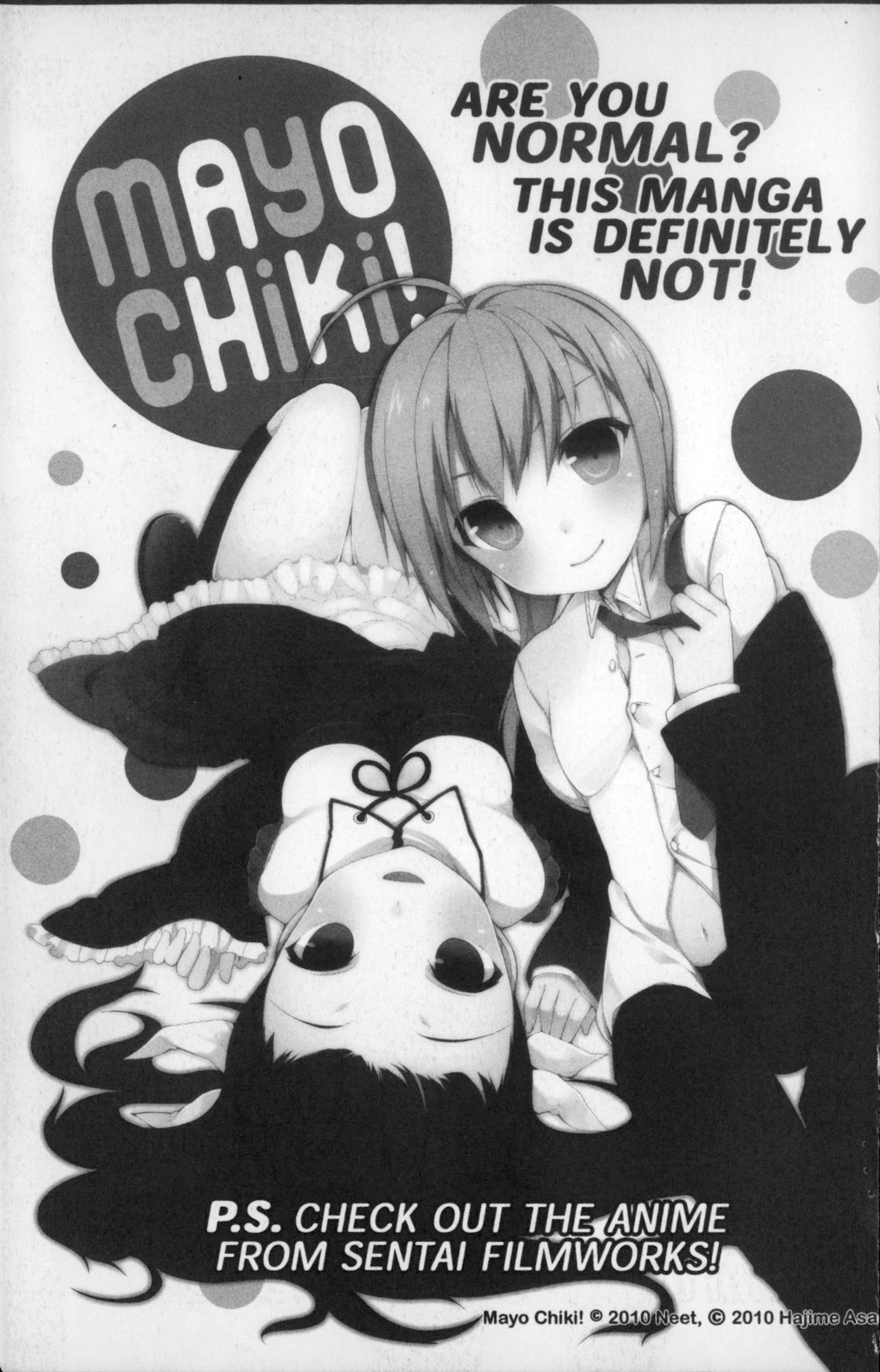
MAYO CHiKi!
ARE YOU NORMAL? THIS MANGA IS DEFINITELY NOT!
P.S. CHECK OUT THE ANIME FROM SENTAI FILMWORKS!
Mayo Chiki! © 2010 Neet, © 2010 Hajime Asa

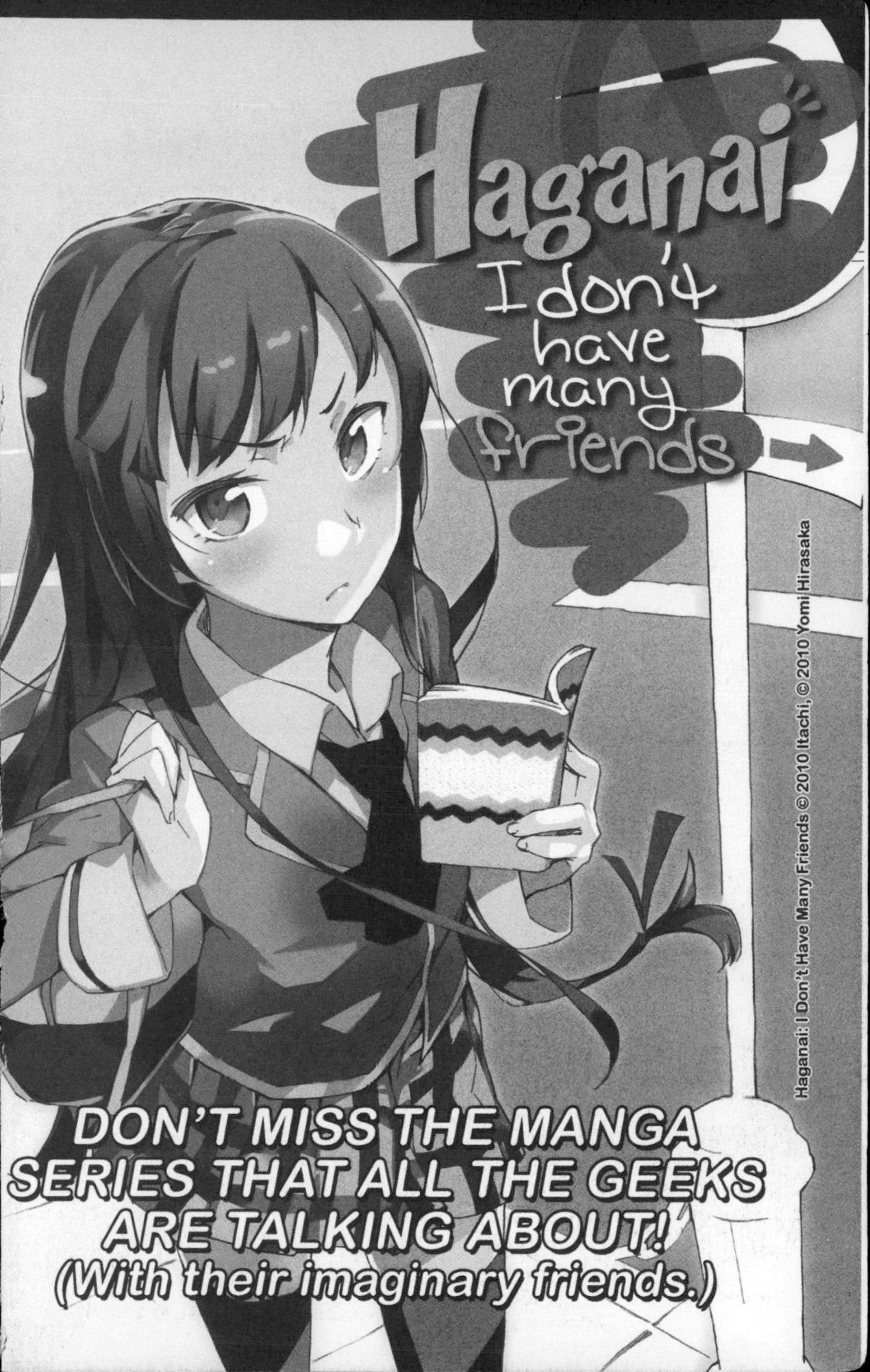
Haganai
I don't have many friends
DON'T MISS THE MANGA SERIES THAT ALL THE GEEKS ARE TALKING ABOUT!
(With their imaginary friends.)
Haganai: I Don't Have Many Friends © 2010 Itachi, © 2010 Yomi Hirasaka

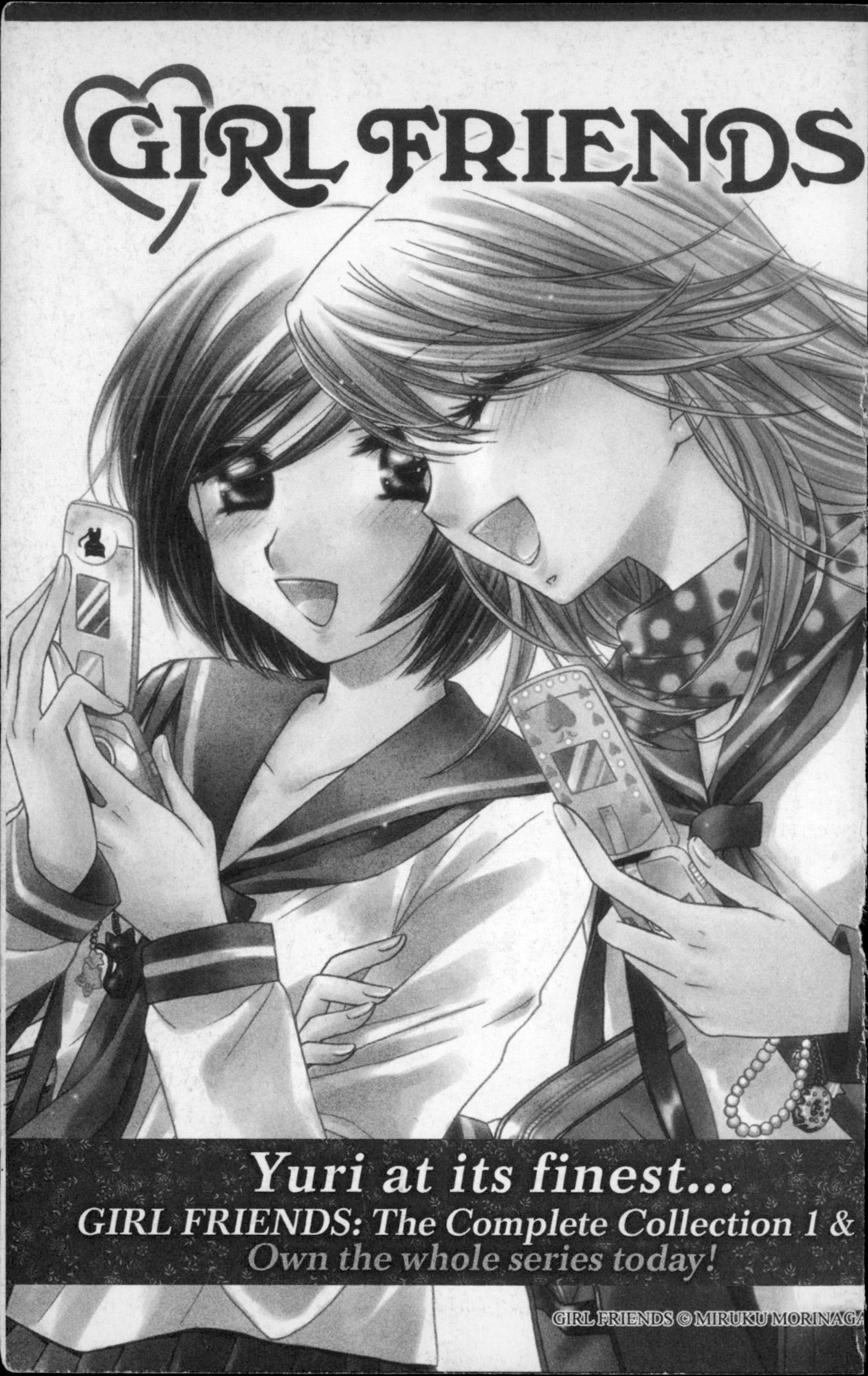
GIRL FRIENDS
Yuri at its finest...
GIRL FRIENDS: The Complete Collection 1 &
Own the whole series today!
GIRL FRIENDS © MIRUKU MORINAGA

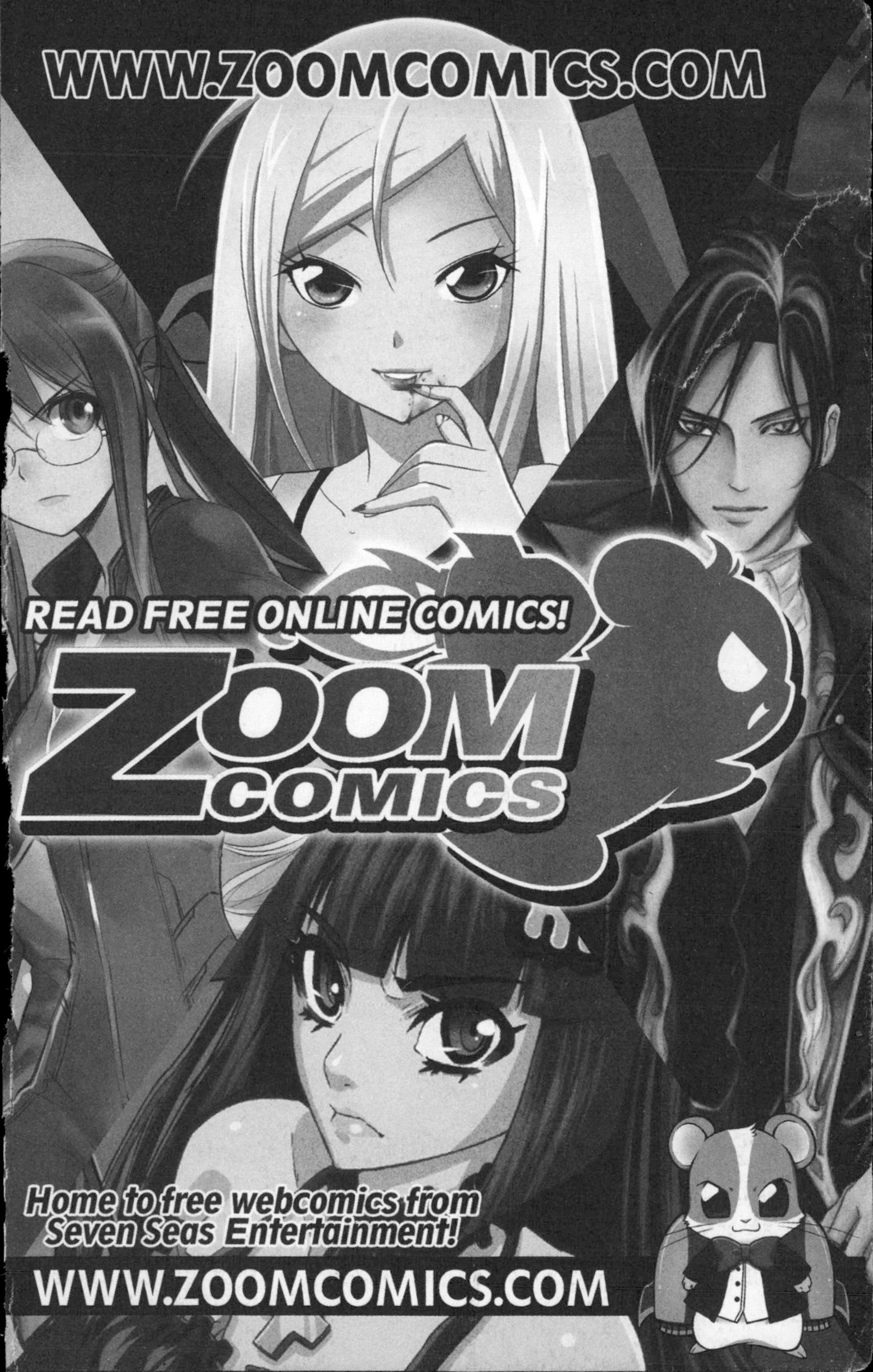

WWW.ZOOMCOMICS.COM
READ FREE ONLINE COMICS!
ZOOM COMICS
Home to free webcomics from Seven Seas Entertainment!
WWW.ZOOMCOMICS.COM

## Experience all that *SEVEN SEAS* has to offer!

Amazing Agent Luna
8
DelFilippis & Weir • Shiei
4-6
Dance in the Vampire Bund
Story & Art by NOZOMU TAMAKI
07
A Certain Scientific Railgun
Story by KAZUMA KAMACHI
Art by MOTOI FUYUKAWA
Alice
Clover
CHESHIRE CAT WALTZ
4
QuinRose
Mamenosuke Fujimaru
Haganai
I don't have many friends
2
art by ITACHI
Story by YOMI HIRASAKA
My Boyfriend is a VAMPIRE
7-8
Yu-Rang Han
MAYO CHIKI!
Story by HAJIME ASANO
Art by NEET
2
JACK THE RIPPER
Hell Blade
JE-TAE YOO
4
GIRL FRIENDS
The Complete Collection 2
Story & Art by yuri icon MILK MORINAGA

## Visit us Online and follow us on Twitter!

***WWW.GOMANGA.COM***

***WWW.TWITTER.COM/GOMANGA***

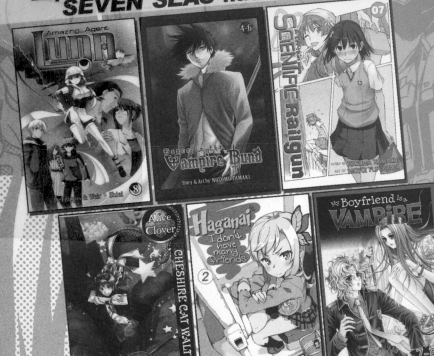

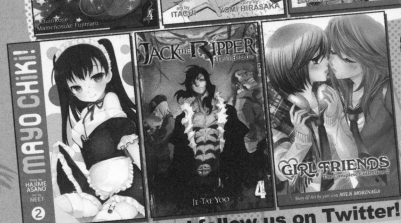